COMPUTER COMMUNICATION NETWORKS

NATO ADVANCED STUDY INSTITUTES SERIES

Proceedings of the Advanced Study Institute Programme, which aims at the dissemination of advanced knowledge and the formation of contacts among scientists from different countries.

The series is published by an international board of publishers in conjunction with NATO Scientific Affairs Division

A	Life Sciences	Plenum Publishing Corporation
B	Physics	London and New York
C	Mathematical and Physical Sciences	D. Reidel Publishing Company Dordrecht and Boston
D	Behavioural and Social Sciences	Sijthoff International Publishing Company Leiden
E	Applied Sciences	Noordhoff International Publishing Leiden

Series E: Applied Sciences
Volume 4 – Computer Communication Networks

COMPUTER COMMUNICATION NETWORKS

edited by

R. L. GRIMSDALE

Professor of Electrical Engineering
University of Sussex, U.K.

and

F. F. KUO

Professor of Electrical Engineering
University of Hawaii

NOORDHOFF – LEYDEN – 1975

Proceedings of the NATO Advanced Study Institute
on Computer Communication Networks
Sussex, United Kingdom

September 9-15, 1973

ISBN-13: 978-94-011-7582-1   e-ISBN-13: 978-94-011-7580-7
DOI: 10.1007/978-94-011-7580-7

© 1975 Noordhoff International Publishing, a division of A. W. Sijthoff International
Publishing Company B.V.
Softcover reprint of the hardcover 1st edition 1975

PREFACE

In 1968 the Advanced Research Projects Agency (ARPA) of the U.S. Department of Defense began implementation of a computer-communication network which permits the interconnection of heterogeneous computers at geographically distributed centres throughout the United States. This network has come to be known as the ARPANET and has grown from the initial four node configuration in 1969 to almost forty nodes (including satellite nodes in Hawaii, Norway, and London) in late 1973. The major goal of ARPANET is to achieve resource sharing among the network users. The resources to be shared include not only programs, but also unique facilities such as the powerful ILLIAC IV computer and large global weather data bases that are economically feasible when widely shared.

The ARPANET employs a distributed store-and-forward packet-switching approach that is much better suited for computer-communications networks than the more conventional circuit-switching approach. Reasons favouring packet switching include lower cost, higher capacity, greater reliability and minimal delay. All of these factors are discussed in these Proceedings.

Since the initial ARPA experiment and success, a number of packet-switched networks have been planned and designed and some are well on their way towards fully operational status. These networks include: COST-11 being developed by a multinational European effort, which when completed in 1975, would link together major computer science centres in England, France, Switzerland, and Italy; CYCLADES, a French network linking centres in Paris, Rennes, Toulouse and Grenoble, planned for initial operation in early 1974; the Experimental Packet Switching System (EPSS) of the British Post Office which has reached the advanced design stage, and which when completed will represent the first major packet-switched service offered by a common carrier; and SITA, a fully operational, special purpose network for European airlines, developed and operated by Societe Internationale de Telecommunications Aeronautique.

With so many diverse networks being designed, we, the organizers of the Institute, felt that it was important to bring together most of the networks groups for the purpose of learning each other's design approaches and philosophies and to evaluate each other's methods to determine their advantages and drawbacks. Thus the programme of the Institute focussed upon the major problem areas in the design and operation of these networks. Topics included: Software and Hardware Design, Analytical Techniques, Network Design, Satellite Transmission, Economic Considerations, and Descriptions of Existing and Planned Networks.

About 200 people attended the Institute, representing 22 nations. From the many enthusiastic comments we have received from the participants, and the press, the Institute seems to have been a great success. We hope that the following set of papers will be equally useful.

We express our gratitude to the NATO Scientific Research Division and the U.S. Army Research Office, Europe for their generous financial support of the Institute. Dr. T. Kester of NATO and Lt. Col. I.G. Kinnie of ARO deserve particular thanks for their help and support. We are most grateful to Messrs. Trevor Beeforth, David Woollons and the Staff of the Applied Sciences Laboratory of the University of Sussex for their efforts on behalf of the Institute. Finally we should like to thank the lecturers of the Institute whose cooperation and support made the Institute an enjoyable undertaking.

R.L. Grimsdale

F.F. Kuo.

TABLE OF CONTENTS

A REVIEW OF COMPUTER COMMUNICATION TECHNOLOGY

Donald W. Davies

National Physical Laboratory, UK

Computers and communications go together naturally, not just because their technologies have obviously converged but mainly because they are both concerned with information handling, processing it and transporting it.   When the present explosive growth of data communication is over, it will seem that the majority of information handling is teleprocessing – in other words the majority of data needs transport as well as storage and processing.   It is very rare that data to be processed originates and reaches its end user at one computer-site.   From this future viewpoint the way that computers were used before the mid sixties will seem extremely restricted and unnatural.

Teleprocessing systems tend now to be custom built, difficult to develop and therefore expensive.   Part of the trouble lies in the absence of an effective public data communication service. The proliferation of private networks and leased lines, though it may give some profit to the communication authorities, points to the failure of all of us to get a real understanding of the nature of data communication.   Those who operate the present public networks cannot be blamed very much for a lack of understanding which affects us all.   Personally, I expect our conception of the data communication task to become clearer and simpler in the next few years.   This must happen if we are to interconnect many different national networks.

The world's telecommunication network is basically a telephone network.   Until about 1950 the majority of information processing was done by people so the telephone system could immediately be used for 'teleprocessing'.

The telephone network is closely fitted to the special requirements of human conversation. All its design features, from the terminal equipment through to the switching and transmission, are determined by human speech and conversational requirements. The advent of computer communication requires a complete rethinking of what the network should provide. Obviously, the telephone network with the addition of modems was the first method to be used for data communication and it will perhaps always be convenient to use this method in some cases. For some years there was a danger that the telephone network with all its limitations would be accepted as the answer to all communication problems. This phase has passed and we are now able to move into an era where telephone and data communications can exist side by side.

COMMONALITY BETWEEN TELEPHONE AND DATA NETWORKS

It is hardly necessary, at this stage, to argue the necessity for a specialised data communication network. A tremendous development effort has been applied to the transmission of data over the 4 KHz bandwidth of the analogue telephone channel. But, by comparison with what can be achieved, the result is very limited in bandwidth, subject to noise and slow in its switching. Alternatively, leased lines overcome some of the difficulties for the big user but hardly provide a universal solution. Once it is accepted that a data network will split away, functionally, from the telephone system then a whole range of new technologies is possible and the ARPA network, about which we shall hear a great deal in the following week, is a good practical demonstration that the newer systems work.

Nevertheless, transmission of data and speech are not essentially separate problems. With the wider use of digital transmission technology, speech channels will increasingly be carried economically in digital form at 56 Kbit/s and the consequence for data transmission is to make these higher speeds economic. By itself, data could never justify the investment necessary to provide a widespread data communication service at the lowest price. Therefore, future transmission plant will tend to carry digital streams whose use for data and speech can be adjusted as data increases in volume (with the certainty that data communication will never take a large proportion of total channel capacity). Though transmission plant is conveniently and economically used in common, the switching requirements of data and speech are so different that they need separate systems.

Figure 1 shows the way in which new technology, based on larger and larger channel capacities, increases the economy of transmission. Digital transmission is taking over from analogue in all the newer transmission methods, certainly for waveguides, satellite relay, optical and the higher end of the microwave spectrum. Digit rates of 500 Mbit/s will be used in the Post Office Corporation's waveguide trials. The reason for this present digital revolution is the same as that which revolutionised

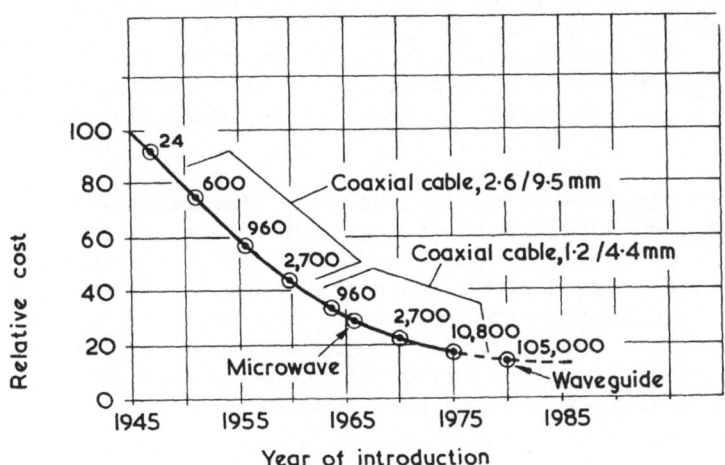

RELATIVE ANNUAL COST OF TRUNK CIRCUITS
(LINE EQUIPMENT ONLY)

Figure 1

computing 25 years ago - the value of frequent regeneration which eliminates the effect of noise and distortion. This trend will very soon make the long distance transmission costs in data communication extremely small, leaving the local distribution networks as the most expensive part of the whole system. The telephone local distribution network could be greatly improved by the use of high bandwidth cables and digital transmission, but these changes will be very slow because of the immense capital cost. The local transmission network must at least be designed to carry all the data services in a completely inter-compatible way. This has great significance for the standards now being formulated for new data networks.

It would in theory be possible to modify the telephone network gradually to meet the new requirements of data in a unified manner. We often hear predictions of a "unified communication network" which will serve all purposes. There are great problems in this approach. Telephone traffic is so much greater than data traffic, measured in whatever way you please, and the revenue from telephone traffic is so much greater that a combined network must necessarily be optimised in design for its telephone role.   Also, the amortisation period of telephone equipment is very long, about thirty years, and the requirements for the building up of data services are extremely urgent.   There is a definite limit to the amount of tinkering which is possible in the telephone network and the only practical course is to attach to it a functionally separate data network with all the properties that data communication demands.   This additional network or "overlay" will be functionally separate but use large parts of the existing network such as the transmission plant and some of the local distribution system.

The way in which the telephone companies are regulated in USA and Canada produces a different pattern of development in which specialist carriers build separate networks.   In the long run, this approach loses the economies that are possible with very large-capacity transmission channels and we are now seeing the entrance into the field of a third kind of company which rents transmission capacity from the telephone companies and sells a specialised communication service to the user.

TYPES OF DATA COMMUNICATION

It is a characteristic of data communication that at one end of the line is a computer.   According to whether the other end has a computer or a terminal, we have two types of communication situation, terminal-to-computer or computer-to-computer.   Let us consider some examples of communication situations, beginning with the terminal-to-computer cases.

(a)   Stereotyped transactions between a terminal and a central computer can take place with simple terminals such as a cash register or credit validation device.   A predetermined exchange of short messages takes place.   For example, the terminal sends a message identifying the user and the computer replies with an acknowledgement or reply.   There may be between 2-4 messages in this kind of transaction, and their format and procedure is entirely fixed.   There are no buffer allocation problems because the message lengths are known in advance, and they are small.

(b)   A less stereotyped transaction can take place with a small keyboard and display, as for example in the passenger check-in routine at an airport.   Here, the procedure may allow a number of alternatives but the whole transaction is still very brief. The messages are sufficiently short that there are no buffer or flow control problems and, from a communication point of view, it is little different from the previous case.

(c) Longer transactions, generally called "conversations", can take place with a general purpose keyboard display. Considered as information processing, some of these may take a very simple form, such as the simulated 'conversation' that takes place in computer-aided instruction or medical interviewing. Others, as in time-sharing systems, are much more variable in their content and structure. But from the communication point of view, their characteristics are similar. The messages from man to

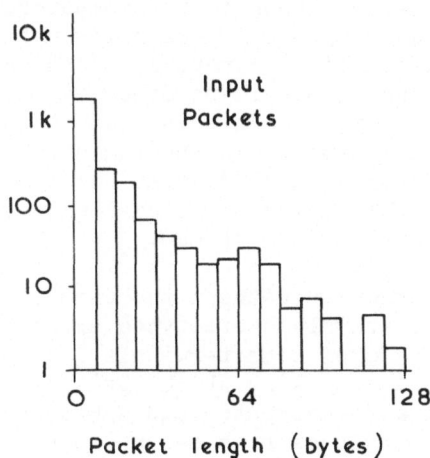

Packet length (bytes)

Input	Output
29,500 bytes _ _ _ _ _ _ _ _ _ _ 1,100,000 bytes	
2,700 packets _ _ _ _ _ _ _ _ _ _ 2,200 messages	
	└ 500 short messages

89 % of responses less than 1 second

SCRAPBOOK TRAFFIC, $\frac{1}{2}$ DAY

Figure 2

machine are typically short and the outputs to the display rather longer. Figure 2 shows an example of this kind of traffic in an information storage and retrieval service. The conversation may last for many minutes and during this time a kind of conceptual connection or "liaison" takes place between the terminal and a particular "port" of the computer service. Control messages may also be needed, for example to halt output when the operation of the 'liaison' is constrained to be half duplex.

(d) Another terminal-to-computer interaction is the remote job entry terminal in which the blocks of data comprising a "message" are typically much longer and there is consequently a need for a protocol to deal with problems of flow and error control. Flow control is needed because the terminal may be able to provide data faster than the computer can accept it while dealing with other demands. In the other direction, though the terminal's rate of acceptance may be known to the computer, the flow of data must be controlled because the terminal's rate is not constant and it might have to halt for manual attention. Error control is important because there is no other way of checking the accuracy of transmission. In this kind of communication the block length is usually in the region of 1000 to 10,000 bits, and there are also acknowledgement and control messages of a few bits only. The choice of block length for transmitting long messages shows a broad optimum.

(e) Moving on to the interaction between two computers, it is possible to have the same relatively stereotyped exchange of messages that we found in the case of some terminals. For example, we can imagine an airline booking which begins as an interaction between a terminal and a computer and subsequently involves passing on a request for space to a second computer. The request and the reply can be in the form of pre-formated messages. This kind of computer-to-computer transaction is not yet common but could very well become significant.

(f) A more open-ended type of computer-to-computer inter-action takes place where one machine is employing the file store of another. (Such a system is provided in the NPL local network). Here, the transaction involves preliminary negotiations such as fixing buffer sizes. The completion of the transaction is by large messages carried by block transmission, rather like the case of the RJE terminal.

(g) In the most general case of resource sharing, processes in different computers interact like interacting processes in one machine. It is important that a communication network should allow this to take place efficiently. Perhaps the best informa-tion we have about the traffic generated by these 'close' inter-actions is given by the higher level protocols of the ARPA network.

If we consider these examples, the first obvious character-istic is that messages from the two ends alternate. This is actually a definition of the idea of "message" rather than a real observation, but it does illustrate the "half-duplex" nature of the interactions which is usually preserved as far as possible.

In each example, short messages are an essential part of the procedures. In the simple cases they form the whole conversation and in longer data transfers they are the acknowledgements which maintain flow and error control. Very long messages are broken into convenient units for the purpose of conserving buffer space as well as correcting errors more economically. In the more complex interactions (f) and (g), short messages are used to 'negotiate' the conditions for longer transfers. In cases (c), (d), (f) and (g) there seems to be a need for short 'control' messages which bypass the normal protocol.

At the beginning of modern data communication developments, the study of time sharing had led to a prediction that messages would be short. The result of later experience has been to confirm the predominance of short messages. The message sizes range from the few bits used in acknowledgements through to medium-sized blocks used to transmit long messages. A compromise must be decided for a public network. Opinion is settling in the region 1000-2000 bits for the basic unit or 'packet' handled by the network.

COMMUNICATION REQUIREMENTS

At this point we are faced with the controversial question - where should the partition of the network system be made dividing it into a communication network and the set of computers and terminals which it serves? The conventional view of a communication network is that it provides circuits between the subscribers, the circuit having a defined channel capacity. This puts all the requirements of defining messages and carrying out flow and error control firmly on the users. But since the communication procedures are best described in terms of messages, and predominantly short messages, an alternative view is that the function of the communication subsystem should be the carriage of messages. Then the communication circuits, though they still exist, are buried within the message communication subsystem. The way in which this works out can be seen in practice both in the ARPA network and the experimental local network at my own laboratory. There need be no difference in the appearance of the network to the users because a message-carrying structure would necessarily be imposed on any circuit-switched network. We have found that, for a country the size of UK, the cost of the two kinds of communication network is identical, being dominated by the local distribution system. Therefore, if the message approach is helpful to the users it can be obtained at no additional expense.

The term "packet switching" has been adopted for a message handling system where the transmission unit is fixed and relatively small. The user's messages, if they are longer than a packet,

must be broken up into packets for transmission. This contrasts
with the "message switching" as practised in the telegraph network
where the user's messages are accepted in their entirety. The
use of packets reduces the delay arising from repeated storing
and forwarding of packets and reduces the amount of storage needed
for transit.

Packet switching requires the network to provide its own
error control and therefore gives very low error rates. Because
each channel has, in effect, a variable bandwidth depending on
the rate at which packets are sent, there is a new problem of
flow control in the network very like the problem of traffic
control in a road network.

We said earlier that packet and circuit switching differed
in where they placed the boundary between communications and
computers. This is a rather critical decision, and enables us
to classify networks further. The following four examples show
how the responsibility for different communication functions can
be placed either in the subnet or with the users.

	Circuit switched	Packet switched		
		Cyclades	ARPA	EPSS
transmission circuit	SN	SN	SN	SN
packet transport	C	SN	SN	SN
message transport	C	C	SN	SN
virtual circuit	*	C	C	SN
higher level protocol	C	C	C	C

SN — communication subnetwork is responsible

C — implemented only by attached computers

* — not usually relevant, but it is possible
to multiplex several virtual circuits on
one real one

Which of these packet-switched schemes should we recommend?
By allowing as much as possible to be implemented in users'
computers, Cyclades provides an ideal experimental tool, in which
several ways to perform each function can be tested and compared.
In the long run, for ease of communication with a multitude of
distant and unknown subscribers there will have to be network
standards that are rarely departed from.   At this stage, it
will be an advantage to perform most of these functions in the
network, thus ensuring that they are completely standardised
and the user's behaviour is fully checked.   A gradual progression
from the Cyclades division of functions to that of EPSS is
indicated.   But perhaps the need to agree standards is so urgent
that an EPSS-like definition must be attempted at once.

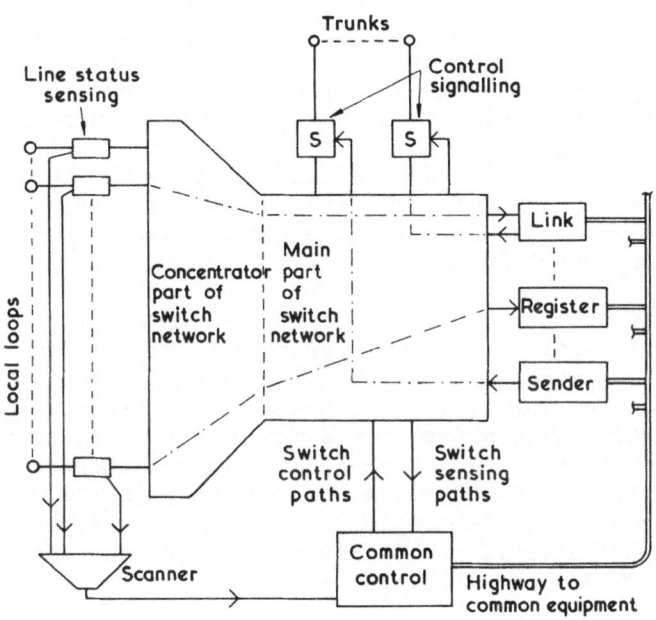

ELEMENTS OF A CIRCUIT SWITCH

Figure 3

CIRCUIT AND PACKET SWITCHING

Figure 3 shows schematically the elements of a circuit switch, based in this case on the telephone network. The system can be divided into the switching network and the controller. The switching network may employ time division, space division or a combination of these, but in any event its technology is rather different from that of the control system, which is typically based on stored program computers. The control system has its sensory organs and its effectors and, most important, it has links to the control systems of neighbouring switches. These comprise the "signalling system" which is a most important part of the circuit switched network.

The setting up of a call through the network begins with dialling information being passed between the subscriber and the first switch. This is digital information, different in nature from the voice information which normally passes between the telephone and the network. There is a corresponding requirement (dealt with differently) in data networks. As the path finding process progresses through the network to its destination, short messages must be passed between the switching centres to carry forward the routing information such as the number required and the destination exchange. In modern systems, these short messages pass over special links to avoid equipping all the telephone channels for control signalling. Thus we have a control signalling system which is, in effect, a packet switching network adapted to the very short messages used in telephone routing.

The telephone network can economically set up a circuit because the circuit will be used on average for 2-3 minutes. The overhead of processing and control signalling involved in setting it up and clearing it down becomes progressively more uneconomic for short calls where only a few messages are exchanged in the whole interaction. For these, the packet switching approach is clearly more appropriate. From one point of view, the packet switched system is simpler in concept because it uses only one kind of technology. The control messages use the same transport mechanism as the customers data.

Long conversations also take place in data communication and, where these employ a packet switch, we need to establish a "liaison" between the two ends of the call so that the various procedures take place over what is, in effect, a two-way circuit. This appears at first sight to spoil the apparent simplicity of packet switching, but then this "virtual circuit" is not used in all kinds of calls and, when it is used, it is constructed out of the primitive process of packet delivery which is provided by the overall network.

Figure 4 attempts to sum up the technology used in the two kinds of network.

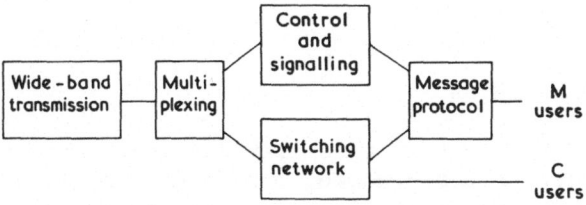

CIRCUIT-SWITCHING TECHNOLOGY DIAGRAM

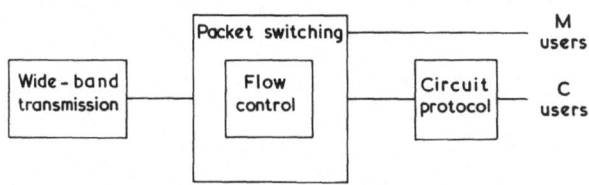

PACKET-SWITCHING TECHNOLOGY DIAGRAM

Figure 4

Packet switching has proved to be a very simple method of handling data communication and has been implemented without difficulty, for example, in the ARPA Network and the NPL Local Network. Other implementations such as the SITA high-level network are completely effective but a little more complicated because they combine some of the features of telegraph message switching with its responsibility for long messages and the requirement for back up storage in the switching centres and duplicate computers on hot standby.

Packet switching brings two new problems into the foreground, those of routing and flow control. In fact, these are present in a different form in any switched communication network.

Consider routing first. A circuit switch has to find a route for the circuit between a pair of subscribers and it does this by routing tables with some degree of alternate routing to cover breakdowns and congestion. Packet switching has such a convenient mechanism for control information that designers have decided to provide very rapid adaption to failures or changes in traffic. There is perhaps a greater need for this in data systems because heavy data users can occupy 1000 times the channel capacity of a small user, whereas telephone conversations are all

the same.   Nevertheless, the degree of adaption attempted in
recent packet switching networks may be unnecessarily elaborate.
The SITA high-level network shows how a rather simpler method can
be made to operate.

OPTIMISATION OF NETWORK DESIGN

    Routing is one of the factors which the designer can change
in order to improve network performance, others are the location
of nodes, topology of the node-node links, capacity of links and
so forth.   The criteria for optimisation are usually cost,
throughput and delay - all interdependent.   Several papers to be
presented to the Institute describe optimisation methods.   In an
endeavour to clarify the factors involved, the following scheme
might be considered.

        Node location and traffic matrix
        Topology of links
        Capacity of links
        Routing
        Other network design, flow control etc.

    In attempting to optimise any one of these, it is usually
necessary to assume the factors higher in the list are given.
But deciding the optima for these higher factors may need detailed
calculations (usually by simulation) of all the lower ones.   So,
in principle, node location, if it is a design variable, is the
most difficult to optimise.   Fortunately, practical problems
usually fix some of these variables.

    In one respect, packet switching has not yet developed very
far - in the hierarchical network structure.   Telephone networks
have been forced into a hierarchy of switching centres and transmission paths.   This has been necessary in order to concentrate
the large blocks of traffic needed for economical long distance
lines.   It has also been necessary to simplify the control of
routing.   In the existing telephone network there is another,
even more pressing reason for the hierarchy, the noise and
distortion introduced by switching and transmission.   This last
factor does not apply directly to data networks, but there is a
corresponding limitation in a store and forward network, namely
the delay introduced by switching centres.   For all these reasons,
any networks of 100 or more switching centres will have to be
organised on a hierarchical basis, and the experience of the
telephone network will be very useful.

FLOW CONTROL

The telephone network provides a constant bandwidth channel, which is open throughout the call, and in this context flow control has little meaning. Wherever data is transmitted between asynchronous devices, flow control becomes important because the speed of the receiving device may be unknown to the sender, or even variable. Then the receiver must have some control over the speed of the sender. Buffers can be used to average out the rapid variations and to cover the time-lag in the flow control system, but if the buffers are not to be very large, rapid feedback from the destination to the source is still necessary. This kind of feedback in its simplest form can be seen in the "handshaking" which is applied over simple interfaces. (For example, in the ARPA Host-IMP interface, single bits are acknowledged, whereas in the British Standard 4421 interface the unit for acknowledgment is the 8 bit byte).

End-to-end flow control is therefore essential and, to some extent, this protects the network against being left with a large backlog of undelivered material. In the event that the users fail to operate their own flow control properly, the network can be excused for losing the undeliverable data. But we would like to minimise such events. When a destination is, for a short while, unable to take incoming data, it would be useful to stop transmission automatically and resume without having lost data in the stream. Therefore, in most advanced networks, the network itself is involved with the end-to-end flow control.

Unfortunately, end-to-end flow control cannot protect the network entirely from possible congestion. A large amount of data can converge on one place and overload a switch without disobeying the end-to-end flow control rules. In general it appears that the whole network might become overloaded at a much lower level than the end-to-end flow control would allow. This is principally due to the low storage capacity of switching nodes. The low storage capacity is a design requirement in order to keep 'store and forward' delays to a minimum. Overcoming congestion by simply increasing storage would increase the delays proportionately.

Basically, congestion must be avoided by building a network with enough carrying capacity, nevertheless, momentary overloads should not be allowed to cause local congestion which then spreads, nor should there be logical lockups (deadly embraces) which tend to appear at high levels of loading. The ARPA Network's history shows examples of the discovery of logical lockups and their resolution. We have devised a form of overall flow control called 'isarithmic' which looks after the health of the network as a whole. There is also evidence that, if the

details of network design such as the protocol for transmission
between switches (Imp-Imp protocol) and priorities in switching
are designed correctly, overall congestion will be prevented
without such a superimposed mechanism.   Such control can only
function by refusing to take new traffic beyond a certain level.
It is usually better to refuse traffic at the point of entry to
the network rather than increase the network's capacity and fill
it up with data which will experience greater and greater delays.

This close attention to flow control and congestion avoidance
should not be seen as something peculiar to packet switching.
A circuit switch reacts to congestion by refusing new calls
entirely but a packet switch can, if desired, ration the available
bandwidth.   By cutting down some of the high bandwidth calls a
little, capacity can be provided for a great number of average
users.   Thus flow and congestion control techniques for packet
switching actually enable designers to chose from a wider range
of network behaviour.

PROTOCOLS

A computer network is constructed from a communications subsystem and a set of computers and terminals which employ this
subsystem.   In the development of the ARPA Network, the
communications subsystem was completed and made operational very
quickly, though it employed some principles which were then very
new.   Building this into a computer network took much longer.
Part of the reason was the number and complexity of protocols
which were needed.

This apparent preoccupation with protocols may seem strange,
but there are analogies both in existing telecommunications
networks and in computer systems generally.   The use of the
telephone involves protocols which have become so customary that
we hardly notice them any more.   We use a well defined protocol
to make a telephone call and when the call is answered a short
conversational protocol between the two subscribers begins the
call.   Within the telephone network the seizing or release of
links between telephone exchanges also employs protocols.   What
is different in the packet switching case is that almost all the
protocols can be expressed in terms of the exchange of messages
whereas in the telephone network a great variety of signals such
as voltage levels, ringing current, audio signals, loop discon-
nection etc is used.   In the packet switching network the convenience of message exchange enables us to invent new protocols
and to build hierarchies of protocols.   We may, perhaps, tend to
become unnecessarily complex.   Certainly there are some doubts
about the efficiency of having many levels in the hierarchy of
protocols.

The analogy with computer systems is possibly even stronger. Here, the communication subsystem is rather like the computer hardware which is instructed in a machine code. On top of this, programmers build assembly languages, high level languages and application software. In a similar way, the primitive operations of packet transport which are provided by the communication subsystem are transformed, by the lower level protocols, into more convenient operations which already have several safeguards against various kinds of failure, both by the system and by its users. It is very important in this situation that the higher levels do not complicate the way simple things are done. There will be many important network applications which can, with great simplicity and efficiency, utilise the simplest facilities of packet transfer which the communications subsystem can give.

Protocols are like languages but in one respect more complicated because they concern dialogues rather than monologues. Protocols must be designed not to lock up, or demand increasing amounts of store, even in the presence of occasional hardware

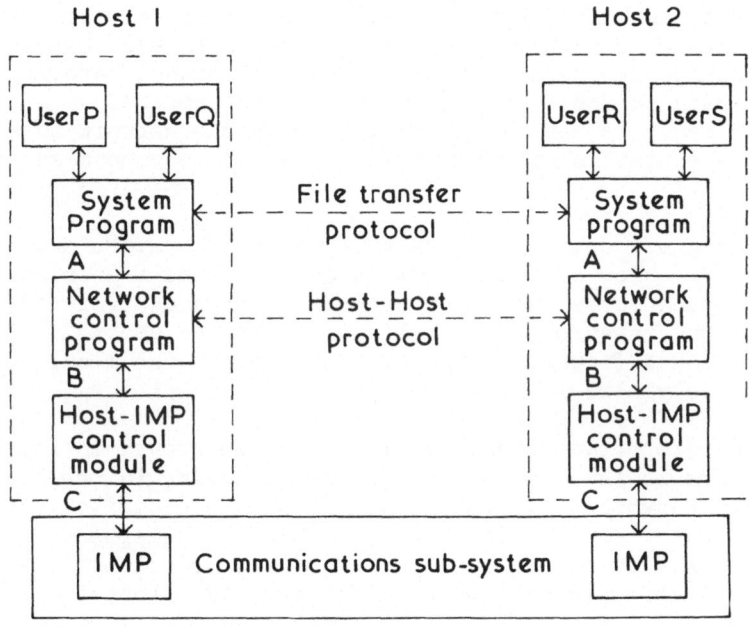

EXAMPLES OF PROTOCOLS AND INTERFACES

Figure 5

errors.   Defining a protocol accurately is difficult enough,
exploring all the possibilities of its use and misuse is extremely
difficult.   Attempts to formalise protocols are just beginning
and some will be described later in the meeting.

Protocols are closely related to interfaces.   At an interface, the signals do not usually suffer much distortion or delay
so the design of procedures across the interface is relatively
simple.   Protocols can be thought of as "interfaces at a
distance" and Figure 5 shows how this works out in a typical
computer network.   The connections at A and B are interfaces.
At C we may have an interface together with a local protocol.
The broken lines show typical network protocols.

FUTURE TRENDS IN COMPUTER COMMUNICATIONS

The trends in computer communications technology will be
determined by the growth of large public networks serving an
increasing population of terminals and processors.

One effect will be that traffic is concentrated on to main
routes operating at higher data rates.   We have seen that this
allows economies of transmission, though the channel capacity
needed for data is small, megabits per second compared with
hundreds of megabits per second in the telephone network as a
whole.   Concentration of traffic also gives some economies in
switching.

These higher capacity trunks will reduce the store and
forward delay.   For a 3000 mile wide country, the transmission
delay by surface route begins to swamp the store and forward
delays at trunk rates of about half a megabit per second.   The
largest store and forward delays will then be in the local network
where relatively slow links are used.

The most important economic effect of the growth in the number
of subscribers is the opportunity for multiplexing in the local
distribution network.   Ultimately, this will use digital transmission to the subscriber for both the data and telephone
services.   This is a long term prospect because of the capital
invested in multi-pair cables but it is very important to explore
possible solutions early, so that solutions adopted for the
telephone network do not exclude data.   It will prove to be very
fortunate that the PCM sample of 8 bits coincides with the widely
adopted data byte (accommodating the ISO 7 bit code).   But we
need to add the signalling or qualifying bit which distinguishes
between signals and customers' information.   This feature should
be properly worked out for the telephone network before the
Procrustean solution of a 6 bit byte in an 8 bit PCM slot proceeds
too far.

We have already mentioned the problems of flow control, routing and network optimisation. Adequate methods already exist, though they will be refined. The development of computer communications does not depend on new discoveries in this area.

On the other hand, the development of a resource sharing network out of a collection of computers and terminals with its communication subsystem still demands new ideas and much more experience. It will develop into practical engineering by the adoption of international standards, for the terminals and for the protocols which build up the network functions from the communication primitives. A very important factor will be the formalisation of protocols so that they can be described with precision and implemented reliably.

When we look at the rate of development in transmission technology, in switching technology and in terminal design, we can see very few limitations in the engineering of computer communication networks. This rapid advance in the engineering technology will quickly expose the real limitations in our knowledge which is how to organise a community of computers and their users, how to ensure that these systems are used in a socially acceptable manner and how to design the interaction itself so that the average person, without special training, can employ all these new possibilities.

THE ARPA NETWORK

F.E. Heart

Bolt Beranek and Newman Inc.
Cambridge, Massachusetts

The technology involved in the ARPA Network has become a major theme in the information processing literature of the early 70's. Many papers have been written about various aspects of that technology and many individual portions of that technology are covered in detail by other papers in this collection. The present note is intended to provide a very short technical overview of the ARPANET as a whole, describing its current status and emphasizing a few selected areas that we believe are of particular interest.

A geographical map of the net as of mid-1973 is shown in Figure 1. At this time, the first satellite

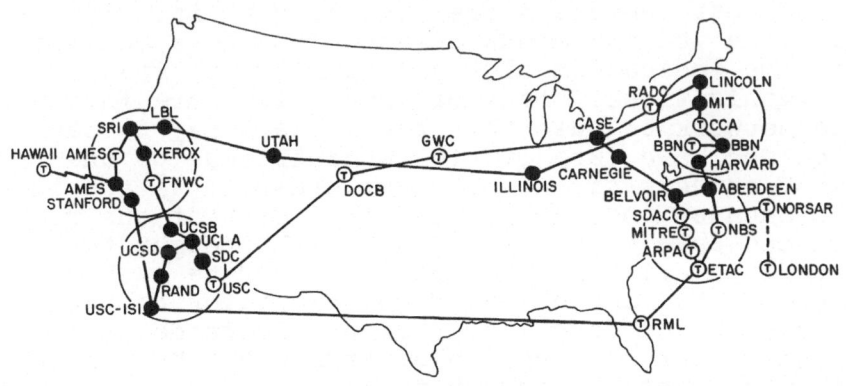

Figure 1   The ARPA Network, Geographic Map, August 1973

20

link to Europe has been put in operation and the connection to London is in process. Figure 2 is a
logical map of the same net, showing the subnetwork
of Interface Message Processors (IMPs) and Terminal
IMPs (TIPs) along with the actual Host computers at
each appropriate site.

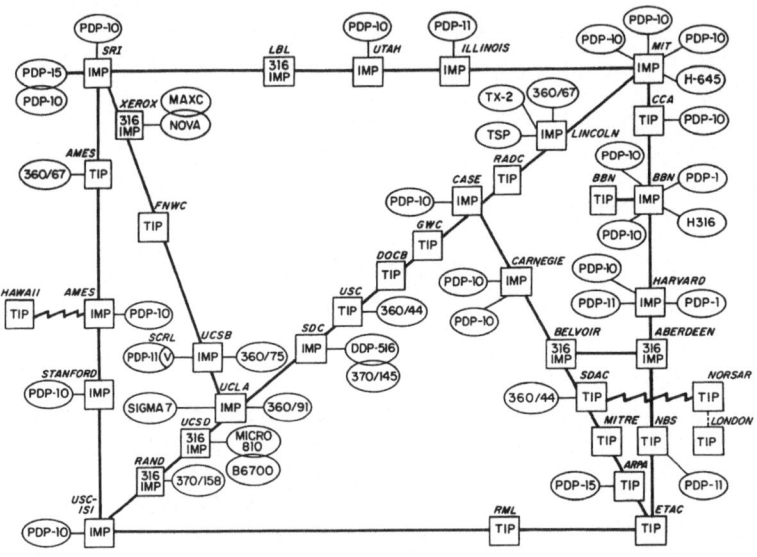

Figure 2   The ARPA Network, Logical Map, August 1973

      The network is somewhat unusual in that it in-
volves a number of different types of organizations
and it is certainly unusual in that many different
kinds of Host computers are connected to it. Figure
3 lists the various kinds of Host computers and also
gives some indication of the disparity of types of
Host organizations. Many of these sites are involved
in the network because they really want day-to-day
service and have very little to contribute to the
research aspects of the network; other sites are involved because they are an integral part of the research and development activity which brought the
network into existence. Trying to operate such a
network in the face of the requirement for complex
new research and development right alongside the
requirement for very reliable service has been a
fascinating exercise in arbitration.

COMPUTER TYPE ● NUMBER

B6700	● 1	360/91	● 1	PDP-10	● 16
H316	● 1	370/145	● 1	PDP-11	● 4
H-645	● 1	370/158	● 1	PDP-15	● 1
360/44	● 2	MAXC	● 1	SIGMA 7	● 1
360/67	● 2	PDP-1	● 2	TSP	● 1
360/75	● 1			TX-2	● 1

ORGANIZATION TYPE ● NUMBER

UNIVERSITY/ NON PROFIT ● 18
GOVERNMENT ● 15
PROFIT-SEEKING ● 6

Figure 3   Host/Site Characteristics

To give some reality to the equipment, Figures
4, 5, and 6 show respectively the original 516 IMP
(with a cabinet holding four 50-kilobit modems), the
newer 316 IMP, and the terminal-handling version
known as the TIP. As a convenient scale factor,

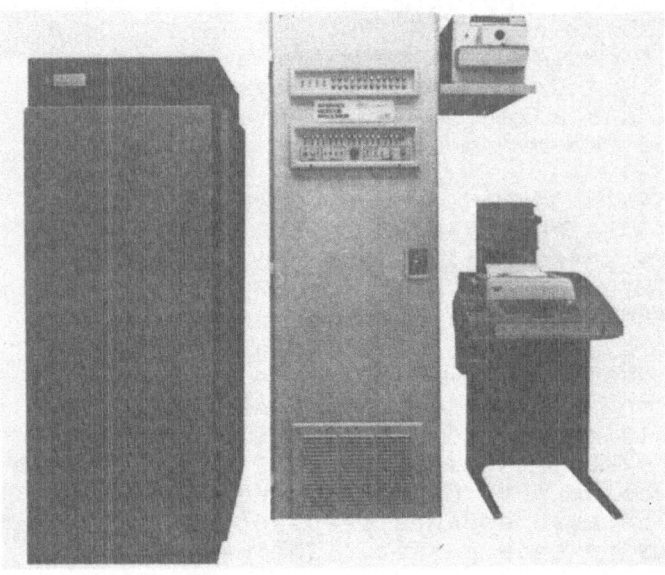

Figure 4   Model 516 IMP, Modem Cabinet, and Teletype

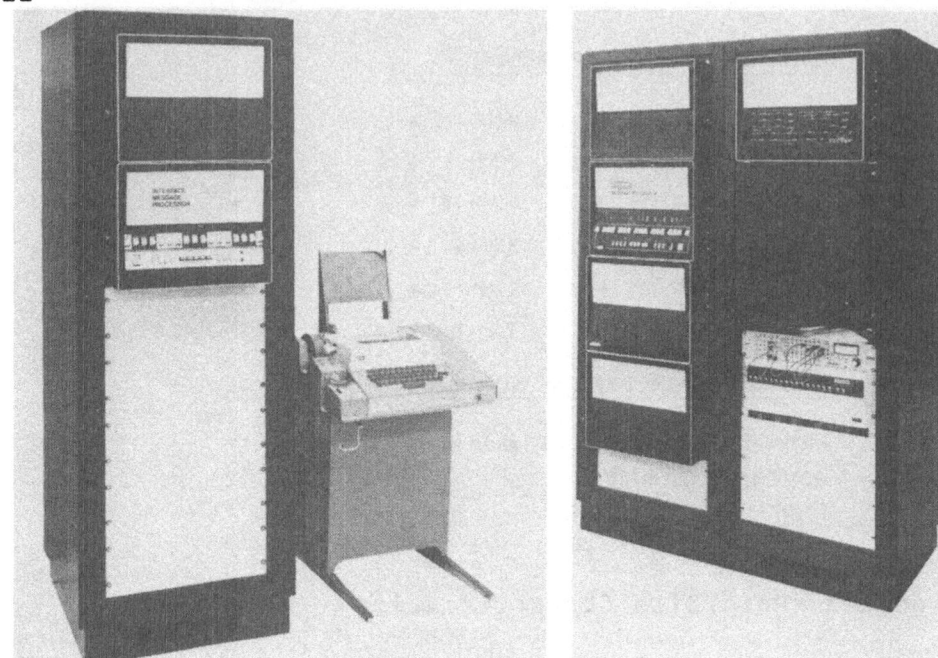

Figures 5,6   Model 316 IMP and Teletype; Terminal IMP

the original 516 IMP costs approximately $100,000, the newer 316 IMP costs approximately $50,000, and the TIP costs approximately $100,000. Each of these machines can be connected to a total of seven communication circuits and/or Hosts in varying combinations. A typical installation would have two or three circuits and two or three Hosts.

Turning to basic design, Figure 7 shows the main goals and some of the key aspects of the design of the network. From these basic ideas flowed the notion of small IMPs located next to large Hosts and acting as switching nodes in a message-switched system. For economy, the net is not "fully-connected," but the design assumed multiple connectivity for reliability, and most sites in the ARPA Network are at least doubly connected. A superficial view of the transmission system is depicted in Figure 8. Each IMP breaks messages up into packets, appends headers to each packet, and also appends feedback shift register checksums to each packet. The next IMP then receives such packets and acknowledges them. The preceding IMP tenaciously holds the packets until they have been acknowledged. In addition, the end-to-end

GOALS	KEY ASPECTS
● RESOURCE SHARING	● 50 KB CIRCUITS
	● < 1/2-SECOND TRAVEL TIME
● CHEAPER, MORE RELIABLE DIGITAL COMMUNICATION	● ESSENTIALLY ERROR-FREE TRANSMISSION
	● USE OF IMPS AS SWITCHING NODES

Figure 7   Goals and Key Aspects of Design

acknowledgment system called "ready for next message"
or RFNM indicates to the source IMP that the destination IMP has received the entire message, and the
RFNM flow is also acknowledged from IMP to IMP. The
actual details of this transmission scheme are a bit
more complicated: for example, several acknowledgments at a time are transmitted back as single bits
in returning packets. Figure 9 shows the actual
packet format on the IMP-to-IMP circuits. Most network IMP-to-IMP circuits operate at 50 kilobits/sec,
but IMPs are able to operate with circuit rates from
about 7 kilobits/sec to over 230 kilobits/sec without
any internal changes.

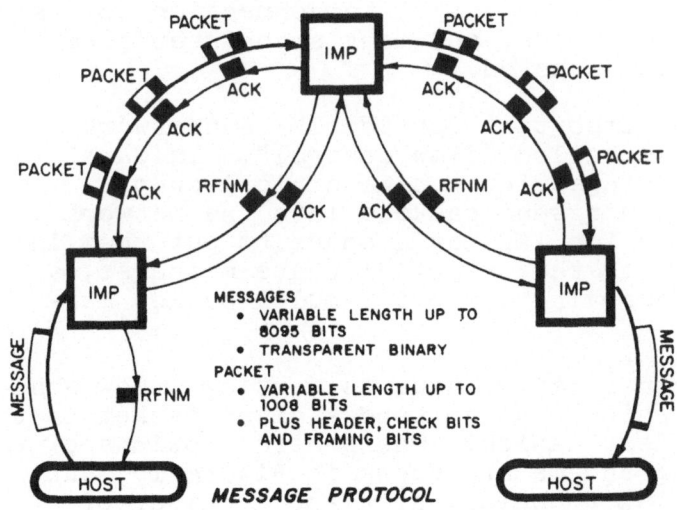

Figure 8   Message Protocol

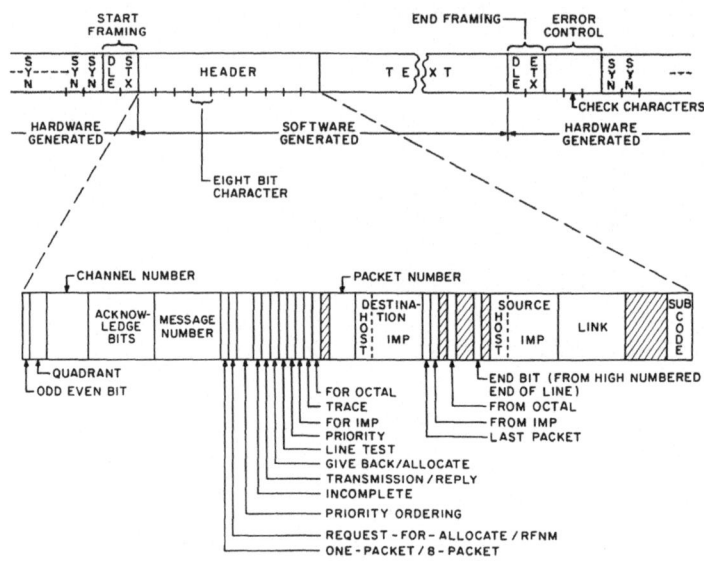

Figure 9   Format of Packet on Phone Line

Hosts are connected to IMPs over bit serial interfaces of standardized types; versions are available
for local connection, distant connections (up to 2000
feet), and very distant (error-controlled) interfaces
that employ modems. The Host interface specifications
were designed to permit easy interconnection to Hosts
of many different types, and many such interfaces
have now been constructed.

It is very important for the IMP subnetwork to
maintain what is called "flow control". In particular, to avoid congestion and possible lockup, a
source IMP must not send packets into the network
unless a destination IMP has a space to put them in.
This is handled by the use of allocate messages, a
technique of reserving space for multi-packet messages.

Still another major issue is routing: how shall
an IMP decide which line to send a given packet on to
reach a given destination? The general notions of the
present routing scheme are shown in Figure 10, but
this is a complex technical area and a number of
improvements are currently in process; at the bottom
of Figure 10 some of the areas of current work are
indicated. Figure 11 gives a somewhat more detailed
view of the flow of data through the IMP program.

- Distributed Computation
- Minimum Delay and Identify Dead/Unreachable IMPs
- Each Pair of IMPs Exchanges a Routing Message Every $2/3$ Second; Message Contains Delay Estimate and Hop Count to Each IMP in Net
- Roughly, Each IMP Uses Minimum of Delay Estimates to Choose Appropriate Path to Any Destination
- Unreasonably High Hop Count Implies an Unreachable IMP

Better Load Splitting for High Throughput

Satellite Broadcast Routing

Area Routing

Figure 10   Routing

As a general remark, it has been intended that each IMP in the network be extremely autonomous; a (trivial) example of this autonomy is that each IMP is equipped with power-fail recovery devices which allow it to come back onto the network automatically after a local power failure.   Serious attempts were also made in the network design to simplify debugging and troubleshooting.   For example, each IMP under program control can, by "crosspatching" output lines back into inputs, attempt to determine whether errors or troubles lie in the IMP itself, in the modems, or in the circuits.

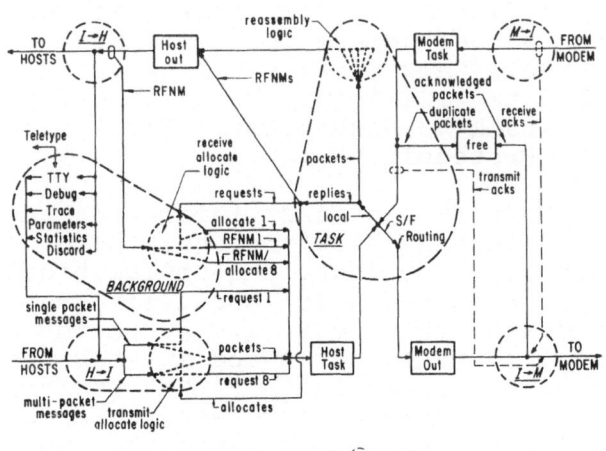

Figure 11   Packet Flow and Processing

Before leaving the area of design, it is appropriate to comment on the actual performance of an IMP
in terms of its throughput. Figure 12 gives some
indication of this throughput as a function of the
number of packets in a message; it is possible to
obtain higher bandwidth by using multi-packet messages, since the message processing overhead is
amortized over many more bits. Speaking rather
roughly an IMP can handle about 3/4 of a megabit
of traffic.

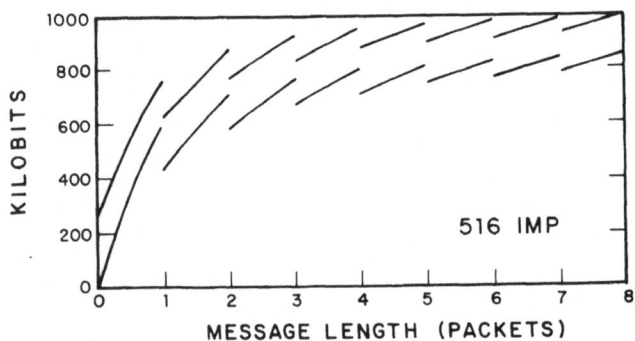

Figure 12   IMP Throughput vs. Message Length

The IMPs and circuits thus form a communication
system, but one that leaves a major issue still to
be resolved. With the best communication system
in the world, if people talk different languages,
very little useful data will flow. The Hosts must
now agree on how to talk to each other. This general
area is called Host Protocol.

When the ARPA Network was first initiated, the
difficulties in implementing Host protocols were
somewhat underestimated. In fact, the implementation
of Host protocols represented a serious delay in the
early utilization of the ARPA Network. Furthermore,
the area is technically complicated and at this time
the protocols that are used on the ARPA Network are
far from perfect. This represents a research area
about which much will be learned in years to come.
Figure 13 gives some indication of the kinds of
programs which must or may reside inside a given
Host on the ARPA Network. At the very center is

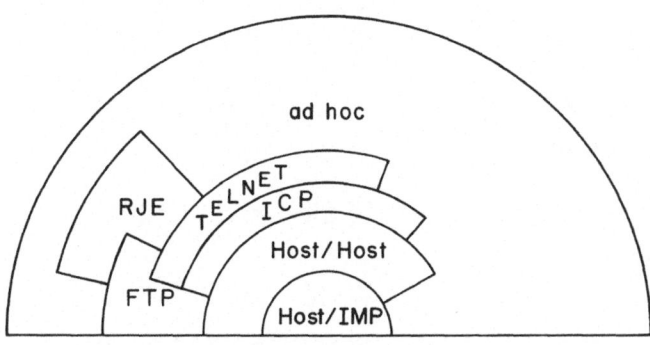

Figure 13   Layers of Protocol

the lowest level protocol, for the communication
which must take place between the Host and its
local IMP.   Then there is the basic protocol
between two Hosts.   On top of that is the initial
connection protocol (ICP), for making initial login
connections, and then the protocol for TELNET (which
is for communicating between a "virtual" terminal
and a Host).   Other protocols shown are Remote Job
Entry (RJE), and File Transfer Protocol (FTP).   In
addition to all the protocols which have been more
or less standardized by the ARPA Network community,
a number of pairs of Hosts have chosen to communicate
with one another in some non-standard way.   Since
the IMPs send a message only to the specified
destination, there is no reason why any given pair
or group of Hosts cannot decide to implement an ad
hoc kind of protocol for their personal intercommunication.   In fact, such specialized protocols
may become quite common when and if networks of this
kind spread, become very large, and serve many different populations of users.   Figure 14 gives an
idea of the actual status of protocols in the ARPA
Network as of the middle of 1973.

The initial network was intended to serve Host-
to-Host communication.   The early part of this note
dealt with the basic design of the net and then
mentioned the Host protocols for attempting to use
the net.   We will now turn to the development of
the terminal-handling node, the TIP.   Once the net
began to thrive, people who did not have a terminal-
oriented time-sharing Host wished to obtain access
to the resource pool that was coming into existence.

Name	Status	Documents	General Role
· Host-to-IMP	Official and widely implemented	BBN #1822 RFC #381 RFC #394	Basic electrical and logical connection from a Host to an IMP
· Host/Host Protocol	Official and widely implemented	NIC #8246	Establishes logical "lines" between Hosts and controls flow
· Initial Connection	Official and widely implemented	NIC #7101 RFC #202 NIC #7103	Provides a dispatching method for new "LOGINS"
· TELNET	Official and widely implemented	RFC #318 RFC #495	Establishes a Network Virtual Terminal; reduces mapping from M^2 to M
· File Transfer	Official and widely implemented	RFC #354 RFC #385 RFC #542	Rules for file and data transfer
· Remote Job Entry	Official — a few implementations	RFC #407	Rules for Remote Job Entry
· Level Ø Graphics	Under study	RFC #336 RFC #178 RFC #493 RFC #553	Establishes a simple-minded Network Virtual Graphic Display
· Mail	Under study	RFC #524	Rules for handling network mail distribution
· Various Ad Hoc Protocols			

Figure 14   ARPA Network Protocols

The TIP was designed as an add-on to a basic IMP and permits up to 63 low and medium speed devices to access the network directly. Now, almost everybody wants to obtain Terminal IMPs rather than ordinary IMPs, even if they already have terminal-oriented time-sharing systems; it turns out that the TIP is a very reasonable front end and often represents an attractive way to attach terminals to the local machine as well as the appropriate way to attach terminals to the net.

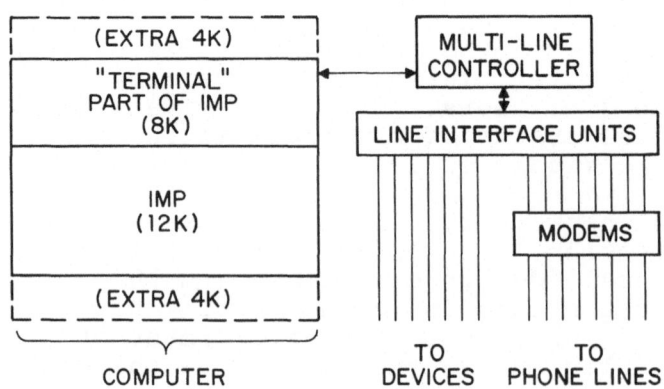

Figure 15   Terminal IMP System

A general block diagram of the Terminal IMP is shown in Figure 15. The TIP program must really be a mini-Host since it must communicate with Hosts and, of course, it must also have terminal-handling hardware and software. On the terminal side, a choice was made to handle character-oriented terminals over a wide range; Figure 16 shows the data rates supported by the TIP. In some cases modifications to the TIP code are required in order to handle particular terminal types. Figures 17 and 18 give some

EXTERNAL CLOCK	INTERNAL CLOCK (Nominal Rates, bits/sec)	
ANY RATE UP TO AND INCLUDING 19.2 kilobits/sec*	75	1200
	110	1800
	134.5	2400
	150	4800
	300	9600 } OUTPUT ONLY**
	600	19,200

*Output above 3300 Baud not Presently Supported by Software

**Not Presently Supported by Software

Figure 16   Data Rates Supported by Hardware

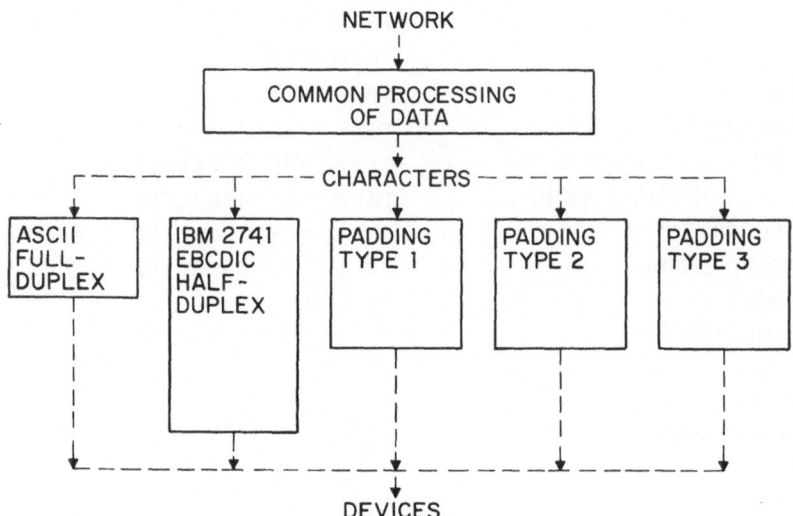

Figure 17   Terminal Variety

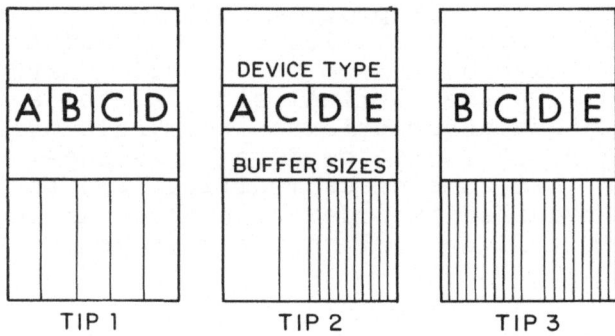

Figure 18   Site Tailoring

idea of what kinds of tailoring might be available
to handle different kinds of terminals.   Figure 19
shows a list of terminals that we know have been
tried with reasonable success at one TIP or another.

A.B. DICK VIDEOJET LINE PRINTER	ODEC 132 LINE PRINTER
ANDERSON-JACOBSON	SUGARMAN
ARDS	TECTRAN CASSETTE
CALCOMP 565 PLOTTER	TEKTRONICS
DATA 100	TELETERM
DATAPOINT	TELETYPE INKTRONICS
DELTADATA TELTERM 2	TELETYPE MODEL 33
DIGITAL EQUIPMENT CORP.	TELETYPE MODEL 35
EXECUPORT	TELETYPE MODEL 37
HAZELTINE 2000	TELETYPE MODEL 38
IBM 2741	TERMINET 300
INFOTON VISTA I	TI SILENT 700
IMLAC	TYCOM
LINOLEX	TRENDATA
MEMOREX 1240	UNIVAC DCT 2000
	VIDEO SYSTEMS

Figure 19   Terminals Used with the TIP

The development of the Terminal IMP has been accomplished within a rather "public" environment,
and a number of issues have been somewhat controversial. Should the machine be large or small?
Should it permit users to write their own code for
doing special jobs at a given site? Should the
machine handle block-type protocols such as arise
from Remote Job Entry terminals? Should the TIP be
two machines or should it be built directly into
the IMP? What should be the echoing behavior of
the TIP relative to a distant site? Should it be
allowed that computers connect into the Multi-Line
Controller or not?

While there certainly are many pressures for
economy, it has been difficult to satisfy people
with the terminal-handling performance of a small
machine. What people really wanted was for it to
be economical and, at the same time, to act like
the best large time-sharing system that they have
ever encountered. This conflict, in fact, was sufficiently severe to lead to competing developments
(you may have heard about the ANTS development at
the University of Illinois). As a result of living
through these difficulties, however, a very important
new concept was born, the notion of using a large
Host somewhere in the network to help the TIPs appear as if they were far more potent than they really
were. In this matter we cooperated with the Tenex
development group at BBN and attempted to use the
"resource sharing executive". Now, when someone
enters the network via a TIP, he can obtain a variety
of services from the "nearest" (most responsive)
Tenex system, and this will soon occur without his
even being aware of it. The TIP simply appears to
be a much more powerful computer. We believe this
approach will allow us to continue the use of relatively inexpensive terminal-handling machines in the
network and still have those machines appear to provide great power to users.

An important aspect of the net is how it is kept
working and how it is possible both to develop it
and to change it continuously while it is working.
For these purposes we operate a Network Control
Center. That name is somewhat of a misnomer; no
control is required for the network in normal use.
The control is needed when we wish to change the
network or repair it.

Figure 20 gives an overview of the Network Control Center's operations. Every few seconds each IMP in the network sends a message to the Network Control Center indicating how it feels and what is happening at that node. From these reports the Network Control Center can use computer programs to generate statistics about performance and statistics about traffic, and also to provide the operators in the control center with information on which to base immediate maintenance activities. From the Network Control Center it is possible to look remotely into the operating program of any IMP in the net and to change the program of any IMP in the net. This ability to debug IMPs in the field remotely is invaluable in keeping a distributed network of this kind up and running. In addition, it is possible to completely reload portions of the program, or the whole program, of any operating IMP or TIP in the network from the Cambridge center. It is further possible to tailor the TIP programs in the field, from the Network Control Center, by sending special pieces of code (over the network) to particular sites. Again, this is simply a clear necessity if one is to avoid an astronomical number of airplane trips. The Network Control Center also provides a central place to obtain information, and a place to complain to; special steps have in fact been taken to make complaining easy, including 24 hour manning of a central phone number, and a "gripe" Teletype on the net itself.

- Diagnose Difficulties; Coordinate Honeywell, Carrier and BBN Field Maintenance Activities
- Release New Software Systems, Tailor Software in Field
- Prepare Reports on Traffic and Performance

- Manned 24 Hours / Day; Supervisor + 5 Operators + "On-Call" Staff
- Uses Three Hosts on the BBN IMP:
  H-316   Receives Reports from Each IMP Every Minute and Drives Buzzers, Lights and Printouts

  PDP-1   Maintains System Software, Used for Tailoring Software in Field, Used for Software Verification

  TENEX PDP-10   Limited Use to Make Traffic Statistics Available via Network

Figure 20   Network Control Center

Figure 21 shows a summary of recent network reliability performance and recent traffic measurements in the network. It is worth noting that really large growth in network traffic began to occur once the Host protocols had been implemented in a reasonable number of network sites and that traffic has been steadily and rapidly growing ever since that time as more users and resources have joined the network.

| | | | IMP DOWN | | | | AVERAGE HOST TRAFFIC | |
| | Line | All | Hardware/Software | | | # of | packets/day | |
Month	Outage	Causes	Percent	MTBF	MTTR	nodes	Internode	Intranode
June '72	1.27%	.97%	.48	325	1:34	29	807,164	199,873
July	2.69%	5.56%	2.34	320	7:29	29	501,896	460,844
August	.66%	1.79%	.66	434	2:51	29	682,502	287,953
September	1.17%	1.44%	.64	684	4:23	30	828,917	252,988
October	1.44%	1.92	1.14	491	5:35	32	1,357,048	452,972
November	1.81%	1.68%	1.06	444	4:43	32	1,187,062	241,884
December	2.63%	3.40%	3.12	422	13:11	34	1,139,590	173,573
January '73	1.28%	2.55%	1.77	.335	5:55	36	1,455,325	337,308
February	2.08%	2.27%	1.95	300	5:51	35	1,603,569	328,594
March	1.24%	3.61%	2.12	232	4:58	36	1,945,023	691,212
April	.54%	1.75%	1.38	646	8:54	36	2,387,259	657,253
May	1.31%	1.74%	.99	441	4:21	36	2,324,373	760,884
June	1.08%	1.87%	.85	323	2:45	36	2,341,516	953,659
July	1.72%	2.27%	1.76	310	5:27	37	2,693,523	1,877,767

Figure 21   Network Summary

The ARPA Network today is still a major research and development project. Significant effort is going into the addition of satellite links and the related development of a broadcast satellite technology whereby many users multiplex in a complex way over a single satellite frequency. Other efforts are underway to study radio versions of packet-switching systems. Other specialized machines currently being designed include a mini-Host to allow Remote Job Entry terminals to directly access the network, and a "private line interface" (PLI) which will permit transmission over the network of data streams which must be kept private or even secure. The existence of the net is encouraging the development of many novel and important Host services; an example is "sendmessage" where communities of users can very easily send and receive messages, around the clock, in a powerful and reliable way. Finally, and perhaps most important, a complete new design for IMPs and TIPs is in progress; that new design is discussed in my companion paper in this collection.

BASIC ANALYTICAL TECHNIQUES AND ROUTING PROCEDURES

by

Luigi Fratta

Politecnico di Milano,
Milano,
Italy.

The aim of this paper is twofold: first derive some of the basic analysis equations which define the performance parameters utilized in the analysis and synthesis of computer communication networks and second present an overview of the existing routing procedures with some evaluations of their performances.

1. INTRODUCTION

The different communication networks which can be utilized for connecting computers may be grouped in the two following classes:

(1) circuit switching networks

(2) message switching (or store-and-forward) networks.

In the networks of the first class the nodes perform only a switching operation between the input lines and the output lines according to the distribution of the messages. This kind of operation requires that before initiating a communication between two nodes of the network a physical path has to be set up and maintained for the duration of the transaction.

On the contrary, in the message switching networks the messages between two nodes are stored in queue at any intermediate node and sent forward to the next node on the route only when the output channel is free. More precisely the behaviour of a node (Interface Message Processor) is the following: when a message is received, it is stored and checked for errors via an error detecting code. If correct, then a positive acknowledgment is sent back to the preceeding node. When an IMP receives a positive acknowledgment it destroys its copy of the message, otherwise it retransmits the message. If the message is not destinated to its local computer (HOST) the IMP determines, by means of a specified routing procedure and utilizing the destination address given in the header preceding the message text, the next node the message will traverse on the path to its destination HOST and put it on the queue of the output channel connecting to the next node.

Which is the most convenient kind of communication network to be utilized in connecting computers is a hard question to be answered and will be probably a subject of discussion for many years.

We will not go into details discussing advantages and disadvantages of both solutions but we would only state that the decision to use either method will depend upon the type of traffic and services it will be used for. Currently circuit switching requires connect time and ties up transmission capacity for long periods while message switching makes more efficient use of lines by time sharing them and provides quick connect time.

In the ARPA network the second solution has been preferred because a cost analysis (1, 2) indicated that the use of message switching would lead to more economical communications, greater flexibility, higher reliability and better availability and utilization of resources than other methods.

A recent study (3) has shown that, from the delay point of view, neither system presents a clear advantage which would justify preference of one or the other switching method.

Fig. 1 shows the behaviour of the link utilization α for two different link capacities as function of the message lengths with an assigned message delay. It follows that message switching is more convenient than circuit switching only for frequent calls with very short duration (4). This is the case for messages exchanged in a computer network.

In the next section we will develop the analytical methods utilized in the analysis of message switching networks.

2. NETWORK ANALYTIC MODELS

Queueing models have been developed (5), in order to evaluate the message switching network performances expressed in terms of average time delay suffered by a message as it passes through the communication network. Applying these models good delay predictions have been obtained in stochastic communication networks the results being fairly close to those obtained by simulation in real systems as ARPANET (6, 7).

The results obtained by analytic models are useful not only in the analysis of a network but also in the synthesis where for instance the optimum channel capacity assignment has to be computed in order to minimize the delay.

From the brief description of the operation of a store-and-forward network given in the previous section it appears that at each node we have queues and finding an analytic expression for the message delay requires the solution of a system of queues which is a very difficult problem in its most general formulation.

As many tools from queueing theory will be utilized let us first recall the solution of a very simple system in which messages place demands for transmission (service) upon a single communication channel (single server).

Further simplifications are obtained by assuming that the distribution of interarrival times between messages, $A(\tau)$, and the distribution of service times $B(t)$, are both exponential (i.e. Poisson arrival and exponential service time) and statistically independent. With such hypothesis and transmitting messages on a first-come-first-served basis, the average time T spent in a system with infinite queue is

$$T = \frac{\overline{t}}{1 - \rho} \tag{1}$$

where $\overline{t}$ = average service time (sec/messg)
$\rho = \lambda \overline{t}$ = utilization factor of the channel
λ = average arrival rate of messages (messg/sec).

Equation (1) can be rewritten as follows

$$\overline{T} = \frac{1}{\mu C - \lambda} \tag{2}$$

where: C = channel capacity (bits/sec)

$\frac{1}{\mu}$ = average message length (bits/messg).

The behaviour of T as function of $\rho = \lambda/\mu C$, depicted in Fig. 2, shows that even for $\rho < 1$ (i.e. table system) the average delay can be very very large as $\rho \to 1$.

When only $A(\tau)$ is exponential the expression of T becomes slightly more complicated because it depends on the second moment, $\overline{t^2}$, of $B(t)$ anc can be written as follows

$$T = \frac{1}{\mu C} + \frac{\lambda \overline{t^2}}{2(1 - \rho)} \tag{3}$$

which is simply derived by the Pollaczek-Khinchin formula.

The solution to a single server system becomes complex when both $A(\tau)$ and $B(t)$ are arbitrary distributions and no exact expression is available for T (8).

This is what concerns a single queue but as we already pointed out we are interested in networks of queues. The basic approach to solve such a problem is to decompose it into solvable single-server problems taking into account the original network structure and the traffic flow. This decomposition is possible with Poisson arrival process and exponential service time statistically independent at different nodes (9). Unfortunately this is not our case because the length of a message remain constant and the duration of service at different nodes is the same for the same message.

Kleinrock (5) has shown that, although the independence assumption does not correspond to the actual situation in any message switching network, the message delay behaviour obtained by simulation in many real networks agrees with the analytic prediction computed assuming the message length as an independent random variable from node to node. Furthermore as the size and connectivity of the network increase, the independence assumption becomes more realistic due to the fact that at each node messages arrive from many different sources increasing the randomness of the service process.

We will therefore consider all channels in the network separately. The average time T_i, a message spends waiting for and using the i-th channel is given by equation 2 where C_i is its capacity and λ_i the average message traffic it carries.

Let $\Gamma = [\gamma_{jk}]$ be the requirement traffic matrix whose entry γ_{jk} represents the average message traffic entering the network at node j with node K as destination and $\gamma = \sum_{j,K} \gamma_{jK}$ be the total thruput in the network.

<u>The total average delay, T*,</u> suffered by a message is defined as follows (5):

$$T* = \sum_{j,K} \frac{\gamma_{jK} \, T_{jK}}{\gamma}$$

where: T_{jK} = average message delay from node j to node K.

A very straightforward computation of T* is obtained using Little's result (24) and its analytic expression is

$$T* = \sum_{i} \frac{\lambda_i}{\gamma} \, T_i \tag{4}$$

Eq. 4 shows that the problem has been decomposed into a set of simple single-channel problems whose solutions yield the values T_i.

Let us note that λ_i is easily computed when both matrix Γ and the routing procedure are assigned.

If we go into details in the operation of a store-and-forward network we realize that eq. 4 can be refined in order to achieve a more realistic model. In fact a propagation delay, p_i, exists on the i-th channel and the nodal processing time, K, is not negligible. Assuming the latter constant at each node and taking into account that an equal delay time is introduced by the final destination network control unit (IMP) in delivering the message to its HOST, eq. 4 becomes

$$T* = K + \sum_{i} \frac{\lambda_i}{\gamma} \left[T_i + p_i + K \right] \tag{5}$$

The delay T_i suffered by a message is due to different effects: service (or transmission) and queueing.

The first depends on the average length, $\frac{1}{\mu'}$, of the Host messages and is given by $\frac{1}{\mu' C_i}$ which represents the average time to transmit a message. The second depends on the average length, $\frac{1}{\mu}$, of all messages including Host messages as well as acknowledgments, headers, requests for next messages and parity checks and is given by $\frac{\lambda_i/\mu C_i}{\mu C_i - \lambda_i}$ which represents the average time spent by a message in queue waiting for a free channel.

From previous considerations eq. 5 can be rewritten as follows

$$T^* = K + \sum_i \frac{\lambda_i}{\gamma} \left[\frac{1}{\mu' C_i} + \frac{\lambda_i/\mu C_i}{\mu C_i - \lambda_i} + p_i + K \right] \quad (6)$$

T* as in the previous formulation is largely used as parameter to evaluate the efficiency of a communication network and most of the optimization techniques (10-13) minimize eq. 6 subject to some cost constraints.

The total average delay will assume reasonable small values until the flow in one channel approaches capacity and its own delay goes to infinite.

However it might happen that even if the delay in one channel is very high its effect is not relevant for T* because the flow on it is very small. This would imply that some messages are delayed too much with consequent troubles for some of the customers. To avoid this effect some authors (14, 15) suggested to utilize

$$T^{*(K)} = \left[\sum_i \frac{\lambda_i}{\gamma} (T_i)^K \right]^{\frac{1}{K}} \quad (7)$$

as performance evaluation.

Analysis and synthesis of store-and forward networks utilizing equations 6 and 7 will be discussed in details later on in some other lectures.

Notice that when the network's nodes are supposed to have finite storage capacity, as it is in practice, the arrival processes at nodes are no longer Poisson distributed (16) and the decomposition previously carried out is not applicable. Only if the node blocking probability is very small the evaluation of the average message delay can still be performed by Eq. 5 where channel capacities are suitably reduced (10). When this probability is not small it is interesting to study the blocking phenomenon and the behaviour of its probability as function of the traffic rate and of the storage capacity size.

Some efforts have been made in this topic (17, 18) but only a few weak results have been obtained. In (18) a synchronous network model, where the length of messages (packets) has been assumed constant, is presented.

By this assumption upper and lower bounds (Fig. 3) to the blocking probability are easily computed in the case of a loop network.

The analysis of such a network can be exhaustively carried out and the previous bounds may be utilized during the network synthesis phase to choose the storage size of each IMP.

3. ROUTING PROCEDURES

The topology of a message-switched computer net-work generally provides, for reliability reasons, two or more alternate routes between each pair of nodes. Therefore a routing problem has to be solved in order to route the external message traffic and achieve the best network performance in terms of message delay.

The determination of efficient routing procedures is important for both design and operation of a net-work.

In the following as <u>routing procedure</u> we will mean a set of rules following which and according to the message destination each IMP selects the output channel for message forwarding.

The requirements of a message routing procedure for which a grade of service has been specified can be stated as follows:

(i)   it should adapt to changes in the network topology due to node and link failures

(ii) it should adapt to variations of source-destination traffic loads in order to maintain small message delay

(iii) it should route the messages around nodes that are heavily congested or blocked due to a full storage.

The most commonly used procedures can be divided into two main classes: <u>deterministic</u> and <u>adaptive</u>.

The deterministic procedures compute the message routing according to a time invariant network status information (topology and traffic load) and are generally used for network design as they are easy to compute analytically. On the other hand adaptive procedures, which can adjust to traffic fluctuations and node and channel failures, are implemented for the real network operation and this performance can be evaluated only by means of computer simulations.

In the following we will briefly outline the existing routing procedures in order to gain insight into their structure, complexity and performance.

DETERMINISTIC PROCEDURES

Flooding

Each node of the network when receiving a message transmits a copy of it over the set of the outgoing links or over a subset of them. This transmission occurs only after two obvious conditions are satisfied: a- the node is not the destination node of the message, b- the message has not been previously transmitted (19).

This technique is highly inefficient in the sense that it increases the traffic rate in each link. Its use is tolerable if one has only a few messages to deliver and a high reliability is required as for instance in military applications. Furthermore the implementation of this technique requires that at each node a mechanism exists to recognize previously trans- mitted messages.

Fixed Routing

Fixed routing techniques specify a unique path for any couple of nodes (source and destination).

This means that the path followed by a message depends only upon the node at which the message is located in the network and its destination node.

To accomplish such a technique, an N-1 dimensional routing vector has to be specified at each node where N is the number of nodes in the network. The index of the vector corresponds to the destination node and the entry specifies the next unique node in the message path. These techniques have been utilized to obtain analytical computation of the average delay in message switching networks (6, 7).

The performances of fixed routing are complementary to those of flooding in the sense that it allows to route efficiently high volume of traffic but is highly vulnerable: in fact it is enough a node or link failure to destroy the communications between all nodes whose paths are interrupted by the failure.

Variations to the above fixed routing are obtained by applying split traffic routing procedures which allow traffic to flow on more than one path between a given source-destination node pair.

In such a case the routing at node i is defined by an N-1 x L_i matrix RM_i where L_i is the number of output lines for node i. The entry RM_i (j,ℓ) represents the fraction of incoming traffic at node i destinated to j which is transmitted through line ℓ.

This bifurcation (or splitting) of traffic yields a better balance of traffic throughout the network with a consequent smaller average message delay.

The deterministic policies minimize the average delay T* (computed either by Eq. 6 or 7) for assigned external traffic requirements. This minimization corresponds to the solution of a convex multicommodity flow problem and very efficient algorithms for both optimal (23) and suboptimal (10, 12) solutions are available.

A very important property of those procedures is that they do not allow loops: i.e., a message on its way to the destination will never traverse the same node.

In spite of the fact that these techniques are easily computed and implemented by means of routing vectors they are not used for real operation because of the unrealistic assumptions of a network perfectly reliable and invariant external flow requirements.

ADAPTIVE PROCEDURES

The major goal of any adaptive routing procedure is to recognize changes in the traffic distribution and network topology through message time delay estimates and then route messages such that the high congestion nodes in the network are avoided. In this way the average message delay can be reduced (20, 21).

Isolated and Distributed Routing Procedures

All isolated and distributed routing algorithms

operate in a similar manner and fundamental for their
operation is the construction of a <u>node delay table</u>
(Fig. 4) at each node. The entry $T_i(j, \ell)$ is the
estimate delay for a message leaving the node i to
reach the destination node j using line ℓ. The method
by which the estimate $T_i(...)$ are formed and updated
and how often the delay tables are interrogated for
route selection depends upon the specific structure of
the routing algorithm.

As an example of routing selection, suppose that
the route selection algorithm is based upon selecting
the line out of a node whose estimated delay is minimum.
Then a <u>routing vector</u> can be formed at each node from
the node delay table as follows: For the j-th row the
output line corresponding to the minimum value on the
delay table is chosen as the j-th entry R(j) of the
routing vector. Mathematically

$$R(j) = m$$

such that

$$T_i(j, m) = \min_{\ell = 1, 2, ..., L_i} (T_i(j, \ell)) \tag{8}$$

Performing this operation for all rows the
routing vector is easily obtained and it is used for
message routing until a new updating is computed.

In the adaptive routing procedures there are
basically two mechanisms which cause the delay table
estimates to change value. The first is common to both
the isolated and distributed routing algorithms: as
messages are placed on (or taken off) an output channel
queue, all entries in the corresponding column are
increased (or decreased) to reflect the change in the
expected delay for the channel.

The second mechanism, which characterizes the
distributed techniques, makes changes in the delay
table utilizing information from neighbour nodes delay
tables.

The simplest algorithm of the class of the isolated routing is the "shortest queue". This essentially applies the "Hot Potato" routing concept as it routes the message placing it in the shortest output channel queue with no regard to its destination node. In this case the delay table reduces to a row whose entries are the channel queue lengths.

As a second example of isolated routing let us consider the "local delay estimate" algorithm (19) which chooses the message route via equation 8. The delay table i is also up-dated when a message enters the node i by using its time spent in the network traveling from source j to node i. Mathematically it can be expressed as follows

$$T_i(j, \ell)_{new} = K_1 \, T_i(j, \ell)_{old} + K_2 \cdot TIN(j,i)$$

where $TIN(j,i)$ = Time spent in the network traveling from j to i, and K_1 and K_2 are constants.

As an example of distributed routing procedure, suppose a decision at node i has been made to inform its neighbour nodes 1, 2 and 3, see Fig. 5 of its current minimum estimated delays to reach all nodes within the network. Node i then forms a minimum delay vector $V_i = (T_i(1), T_i(2), ...)$ where j^{th} component is

$$T_i(j) = \min \{ T_1(j, \ell) \} \qquad \text{for } j \neq i$$

$$\ell = 1, 2, ..., L_i$$

$$T_i(j) = 0 \qquad \text{for } j = i$$

and transmits it on the form of a delay table updating message.

Upon receipt of a minimum delay vector, a node (say node 3) adds its current output queueing time (line 2 in our example) plus transmission and propagation times to all entries of the vector V_i and replaces the corresponding column (2) in its delay table with these new values.

Mathematically the updating operation for an arbitrary node k adjacent to i is given by

$$T_k(j, \ell) = T_i(j) + Q_k(\ell) + T_T + T_p(k, \ell)$$

where $Q_k(\ell)$ = output queueing time for channel ℓ at node k

T_T = average time to transmit a message

$T_p(k, \ell)$ = propagation time for channel ℓ .

There are at least three methods which may be employed to cause the transmission of the updated vectors V_i:

(1) at a single node when a line failure has been recognised

(2) periodic updating at all nodes

(3) asynchronous updating: a node transmits V_i when a change greater than a specified amount has occurred.

The third method allows the vectors V_i to percolate through the network in a short time period and adjust rapidly the routing to changes in traffic distribution.

The distributed routing algorithms use different updating techniques and it is apparent that the transmission of vectors V_i increases the effective channel traffic. Thus, generally, the more sophisticated the updating technique is the larger is the required increase of traffic.

Furthermore, as disconnected nodes can not be detected rapidly enough from delay vectors, additional information is exchanged by nodes. For instance a vector representing the minimum number of intermediate nodes to reach all destinations is periodically transmitted to the neighbours. When an entry of such a vector becomes larger than N-1 the corresponding destination is considered disconnected.

Notice that, between subsequent updates, the previous adaptive procedure uses only one route per destination and this in some traffic distributions leads to an unbalanced routing with a consequent high message delay.

Network Routing Control Center (NRCC)

The NRCC, which is a node of the network, collects performance informations about the network operation, computes routing vectors and transmits them to each node of the network. Thus a node performs a fixed routing on the basis of the received routing vector which is time to time updated.

Such a technique combines the ability to adjust to load fluctuations and failures of the previous adaptive procedure, and the simultaneous use of alternate routes, proper to deterministic procedures.

This policy seems to be better than those above examined; nevertheless some drawbacks exist as for instance the synchronous updating of all routing vectors, the additional transmission costs and the fast variations in the network state.

In (22) a possible implementation of such a procedure is sketched out and comparisons with other techniques are reported.

Ideal Observer Routing

When a new message enters a node from the external source (HOST), its route is computed based upon the present information about the messages in the network and their already known routes. The ideal observer could also utilize for route computation any information about the future events.

This technique, which provides the minimum average delay compared to all other routing algorithms, has only a theoretical interest as its implementation is unfeasible for an operational network.

4. CONCLUSIONS

In order to evaluate the performances of a routing procedure the behaviour of the average message delay T* versus the effective data rate RE in the network is very significant. For any RE it will exist an optimum deterministic routing that minimizes T* for the given value RE. Fig. 6 shows the performances of some optimized procedures. Curve 1 is obtained by routing the traffic along the shortest path between all pairs of nodes. This is the optimal routing when RE goes to zero, that is when the queueing delay is much smaller than the transmission delay. T_{sp} represents the minimum average message delay achievable in a network for any value of RE; i.e., no routing algorithm, neithe deterministic nor stochastic, can achieve an average message delay smaller than T_{sp}.

The dotted curve in Fig. 6 represents a lower bound on the achievable message delay for fixed routing schemes.

Fig. 7 shows the performance of the optimum bifurcated traffic routing algorithm. RE_{sat} determines the network saturation level above which no additional traffic can be supported by the network.

The optimum bifurcated routing curve represents an upper bound on the performance of the ideal observer routing algorithm since the ideal observer has the ability to route the traffic based upon future messages that will enter the network and reduce the additional queueing delays due to statistical variations in the traffic.

The comparison between deterministic and adaptive procedures has been carried out (50, 20, 21) for different network configurations and generally a very good agreement between the respective delays was found. As an example in Fig. 8 the delay of an adaptive algorithm obtained by simulation is compared for different values of data rate with the delay of a nearly optimum deterministic procedure. The difference between the two curves, which refer to a 19 node ARPA Network, is less than 10% .

Finally we can say that at steady state and with reasonably uniform traffic requirements the two procedures, deterministic and adaptive, offer almost the same performances in terms of average message delay and total thruput in the network. It is therefore justified the use of deterministic procedures for network analysis and design; and the use of adaptive procedures for the real network operation.

52

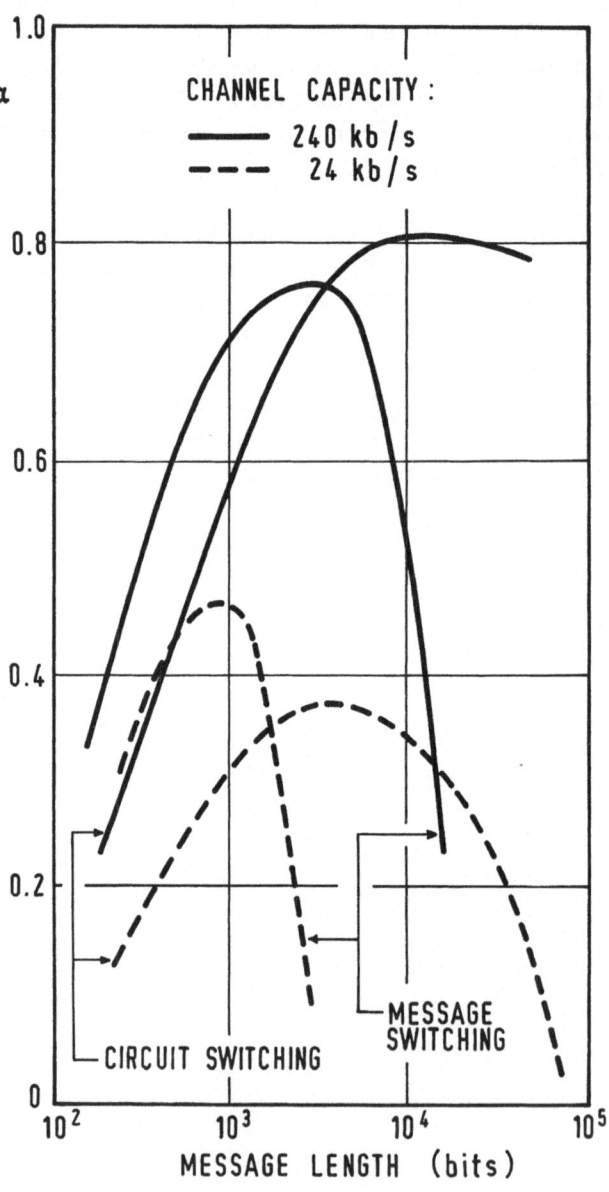

FIG. 1

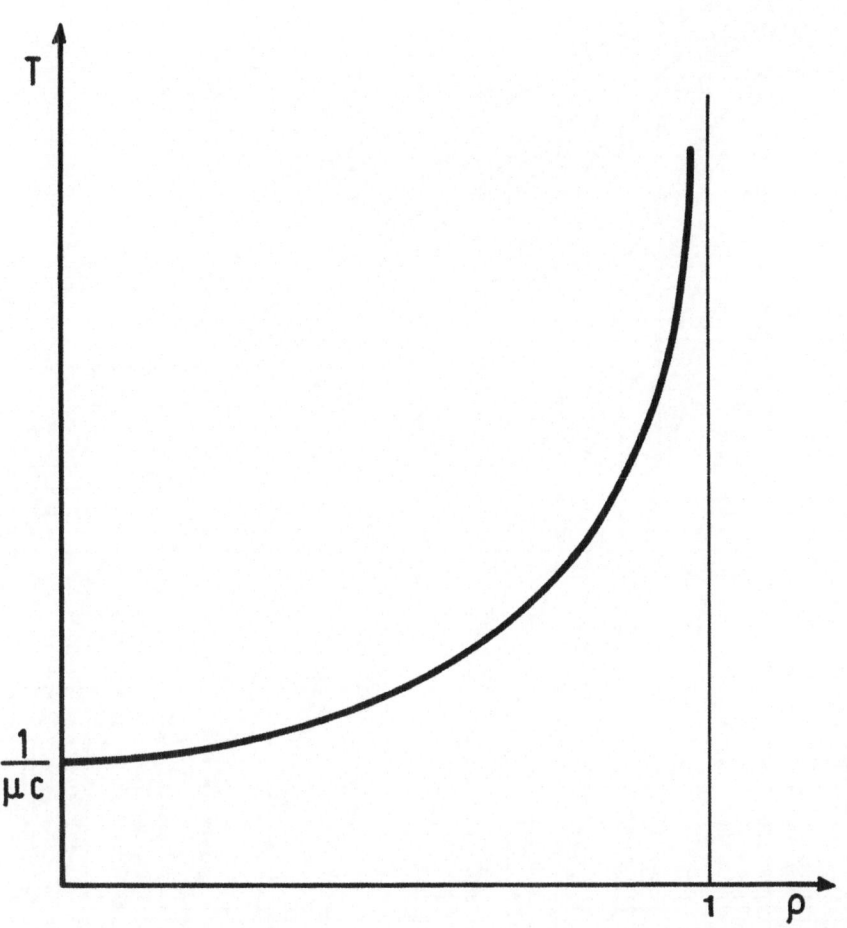

FIG. 2

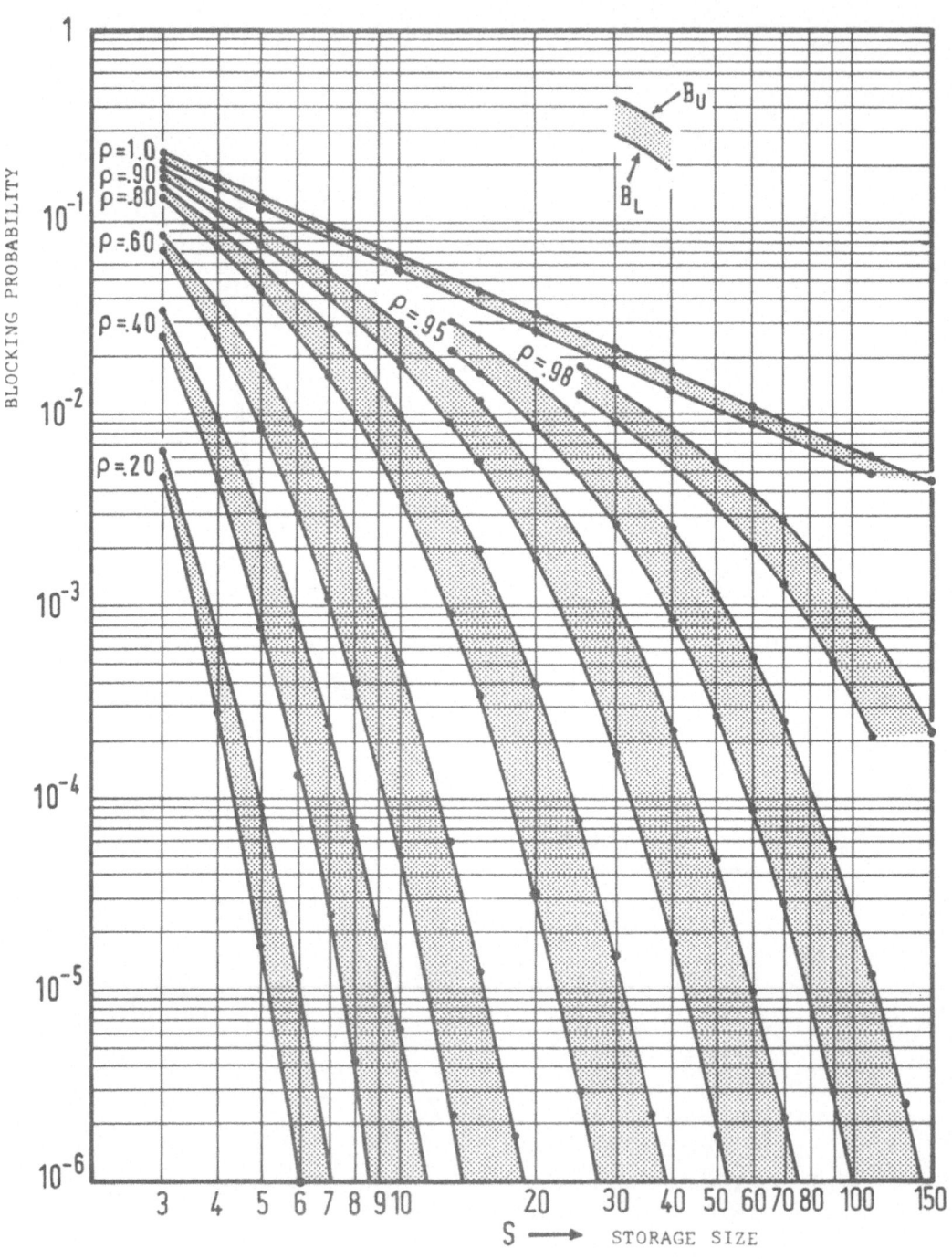

FIG. 3

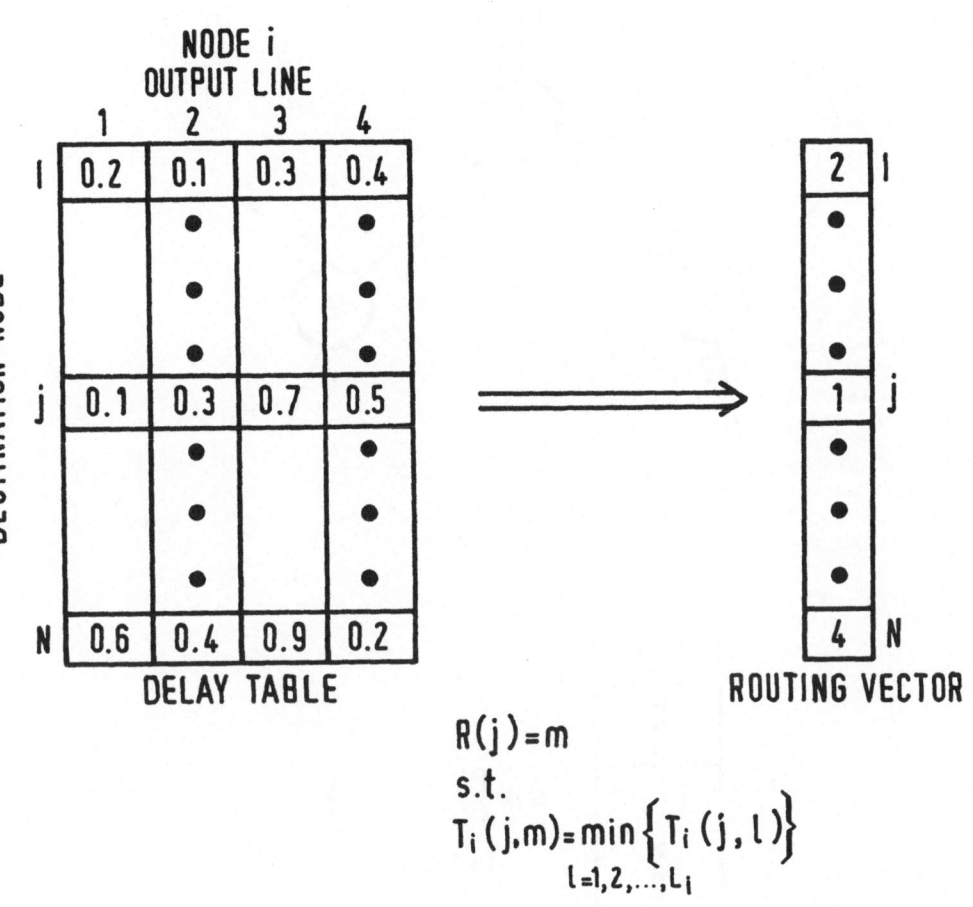

FIG. 4

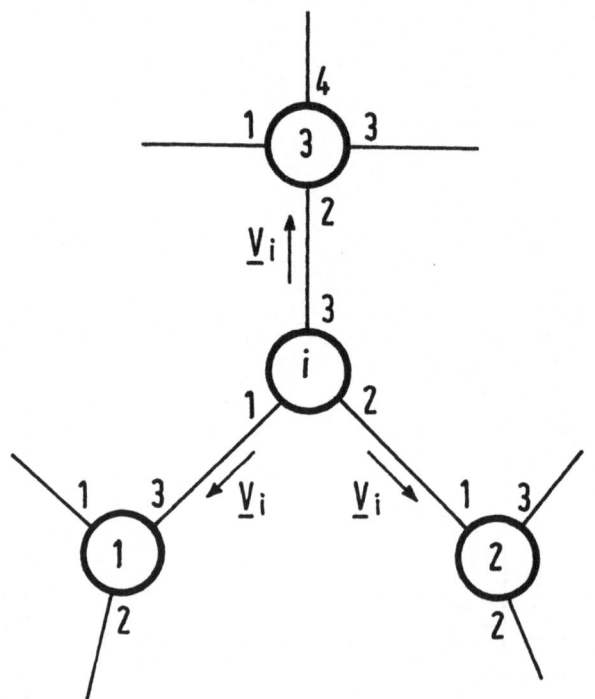

$$T(j) = \text{MIN}\left\{T_i(j,l)\right\}$$
$$l = 1,2,3$$

VECTOR $\underline{V}_i$

FIG. 5

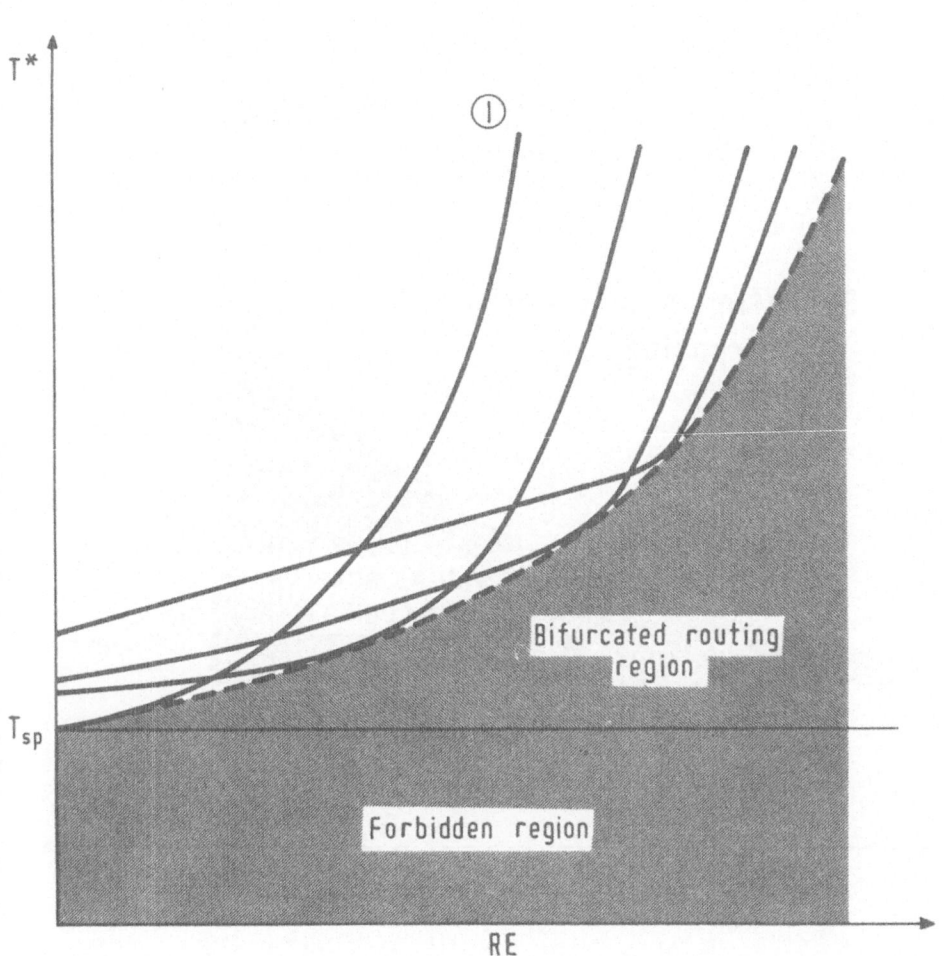

FIG. 6

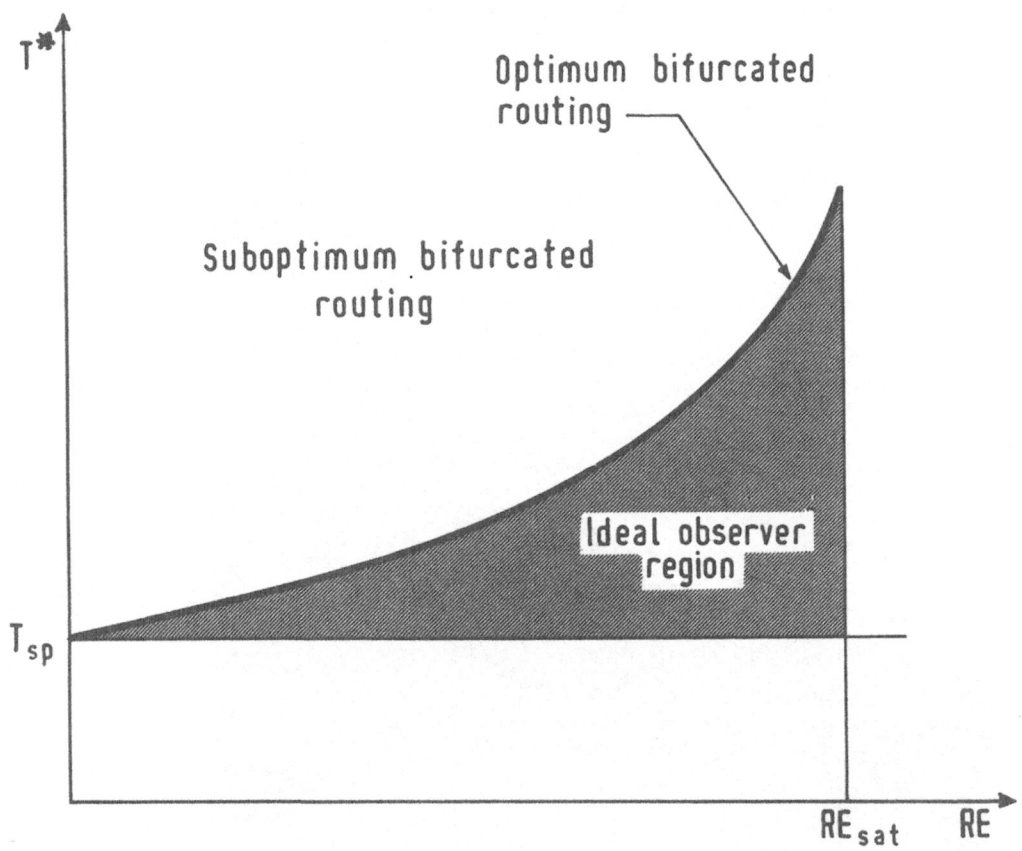

FIG. 7

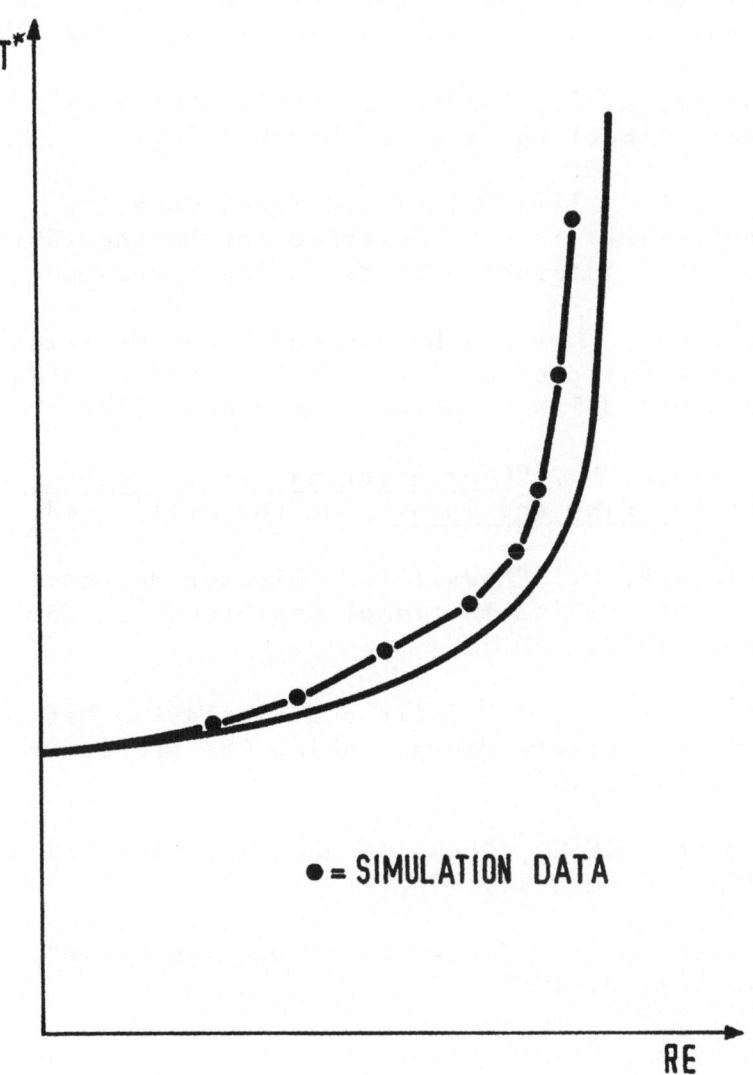

FIG. 8

60

REFERENCES

(1)   Roberts; L. G., "Multiple Computer Networks and Inter-Computer Communications", ACM Symposium on Operating Systems, Gatlinburg, Tenn., 1967.

(2)   Roberts, L. G., "Resource Sharing Networks", IEEE International Conference, March, 1969.

(3)   Closs, F., "Time Delays and Trunk Capacity Requirements in Line-Switched and Message-Switched Networks" International Switching Symposium, 1972.

(4)   Closs, F., "Message Delays and Trunk Utilization in Line-Switched and Message-Switched Data Networks First USA-JAPAN Computer Conference, 1972.

(5)   Kleinrock, L., "Communication Nets: Stochastic Message, Flow and Delay", McGraw-Hill, 1964.

(6)   Kleinrock, L., "Models for Computer Networks", Proc. of The International Conference on Communications, 1969.

(7)   Kleinrock, L., "Analytic and Simulation Methods in Computer Network Design" AFIPS Conference Proceedings, SJCC, 1970.

(8)   Kingman, J.F.C., "Some Inequalities for the Queue GI/G/1" Biometria, 1962.

(9)   Jackson, J. R., "Networks of Waiting Lines", Op. Res. Vol. 5, 1957.

(10) Frank, H., Frisch, I.T., and Chou, W., Topological Considerations in the Design of the ARPA Computer Network", AFIPS Conference Proceedings, SJCC, 1970.

(11) Frank, H., Kahn, R.E., and Kleinrock, L., "Computer-Communication Network Design-Experience with Theory and Practice", AFIPS Conference Proceedings, SJCC 1972.

(12)   Fratta, L., Gerla, M. and Kleinrock, L., "The
        Flow Deviation Method: An Approach to Store-and-
        Forward Communication Network Design", Networks,
        Vol. 2, No. 2, 1973.

(13)   "Analysis and Optimization of Store-and-Forward
        Computer Networks", N.A.C. Second Semiannual
        Technical Report for the Project, Defence
        Documentation Center, December 1970.

(14)   Meister, B., Muller, H., and Rudin, Jr., H.
        "Optimization of a New Model for Message-Switching
        Networks", Proceedings of the International
        Conference on Communications, 1971.

(15)   Meister, B., Muller, H., and Rudin, Jr., H.,
        "New Optimization Criteria for Message-Switching
        Networks", IEEE Transactions on Communication
        Technology, Com-19 June 1971.

(16)   Burke, P., "The Output of a Queueing System",
        Operation Research, 1956.

(17)   Ziegler, J. F., "Nodal Blocking in Large Networks",
        Ph.D. Dissertation, Computer Science Dept., Univ.
        of California at Los Angeles, UCLA-ENG-7167, 1971.

(18)   Borgonovo, F., and Fratta, L.: "A Model for
        Finite Storage Message Switching Networks" 5th
        IFIP Conference on Optimization Techniques, Rome,
        1973.

(19)   Boehm, B.W., and Mobley, R.L., "Adaptive Routing
        Techniques for Distributed Communication System",
        Rand Corp. Memorandum RM-4781-PR, 1966.

(20)   Fultz, G.L., "Adaptive Routing Techniques for
        Store-and-Forward Message-Switching Computer-
        Communication Networks" Ph.D. Dissertation,
        Computer Science Dept., Univ. of California at
        Los Angeles, UCLA-ENG-7252, 1972.

(21) Fultz, G. L. and Kleinrock, L. "Adaptive Routing
      Techniques for Store-and-Forward Computer
      Communication Network" Proceedings of Internation-
      al Conference on Communications, 1971.

(22) Gerla, M., "Deterministic and Adaptive Routing
      Policies in Packet-Switched Computer Networks"
      ACM Conference and Data Communication, Nov. 1973.

(23) Gerla, M., "The Design of Store-and-Forward
      Networks for Computer Communications" Ph.D.
      Dissertation, Computer Science Dept., Univ. of
      California at Los Angeles, UCLA-ENG-7319, 1973.

(24) Kleinrock, L., "Queueing Systems: Theory and
      Applications" to be published by Wiley Inter-
      science, New York, 1973.

PERFORMANCE MODELS AND MEASUREMENTS OF THE ARPA COMPUTER NETWORK*

Leonard Kleinrock**

Computer Science Department, University of California,
Los Angeles.

1 Introduction

The purpose of this paper is to describe some of the analytical modeling procedures which have been found useful in predicting the performance of the ARPA Computer Network and to relate these predictions to simulation and measurement results for that network. This material is presented mainly as a survey with ample reference to the published literature for further details.

In 1967 Roberts (1) proposed an experimental computer network which was later to become the ARPA Net. In September 1969 the network came to life when the first Interface Message Processor (IMP)*** was connected to the UCLA Sigma-7 computer. Thus began the interconnection of many main processors (referred to as HOSTs) at various university, industrial and government research centers across the United States. The message switching service itself consists of the IMPs and high-speed (50 kilobit per second) lines linking them. In 1970, a series of five papers was presented at the Spring Joint Computer Conference in Atlantic City which summarized what was known about the network at that time (2-6). The evolution of that network from a small four-node net in 1969 to the proposed 34-node net later this year in Fig.1. At this year's

* This research was supported by the Advanced Research Projects
  Agency of the Dept. of Defense under Contract No. DAHC-15-69-C-0285.

** Guggenheim Fellow, 1971-72.

*** The message switching computer used in the ARPA Network.

This paper was first published in the Proceedings of the ON-LINE 72
International Conference and is reprinted by kind permission of
On-Line Computer Systems Ltd.

Spring Joint Computer Conference an additional five papers were
given which summarized our experiences with this network (7-11).

2 Network Considerations

Let us discuss a few of the salient features of the ARPA Network and also list some of its design goals. The HOST computers
generate messages (whose maximum size is approximately 8000 bits)
which are delivered to their local IMPs; the IMPs further partition these messages into packets (whose maximum size is approximately 1000 bits) and these packets make their way through the
network independently in a store-and-forward fashion. Upon arrival
at the "destination IMP", these packets are then reassembled into
the original messages and delivered to the destination HOSTs. The
message service generated by this collection of IMPs and 50 kilobit lines was originally specified to have the following properties

. A communications cost of less than 30 cents per thousand
  packets (approximately a megabit)

. Average packet delays under 0.2 seconds through the net.

. Capacity for expansion to 64 IMPs without major hardware
  or software redesign.

. Average total throughput capability of 10-15 kilobits/
  second for all HOSTs at an IMP.

. Peak throughput capability of 85 kilobits/second per pair
  of IMPs in an otherwise unloaded network.

. Transparent communications with error rates of one bit in 10^{12}
  or less.

. Approximately 90% availability of any IMP and close to 100%
  availability of all operating IMPs from any operable IMP.

We do not discuss the IMP design in this paper, nor do we
discuss the HOST-HOST protocol for establishing connections and
transmissions at that level. Rather, we are interested in the
delay messages experience, in the routing procedures that handle
the messages as they flow through the network, and in the throughput that the network delivers. The topology of the network has
been sub-optimized by means of specially designed heuristic programs which achieve low cost and reasonably high throughput. The
50 kilobit lines provide rapid transmission for the short messages
as well as high throughput for the long ones. Network reliability
is enhanced by providing two independent paths between each pair
of IMPs. The basic optimization method was described in Ref.(5).
The choice of the particular heuristic used for exchanging conn-

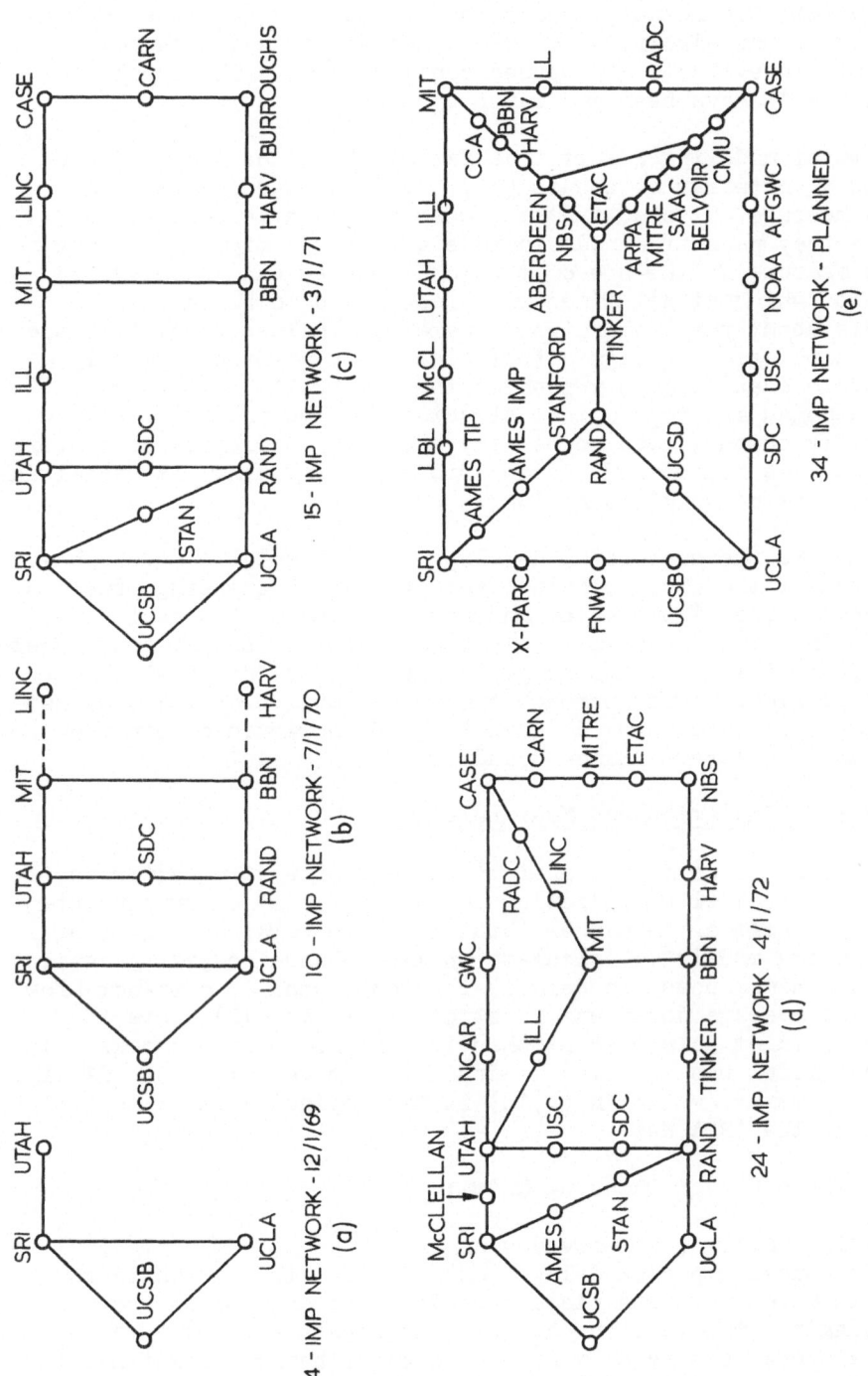

Fig. 1 Evolution of the ARPA Network.

ections within the network appears not to be critical; the important aspect of the algorithm for the topological design is how rapidly it can evaluate a proposed configuration. The topologies shown in Fig.1. have been generated by this procedure.

The major modeling effort thus far has been the study of the behaviour of networks of queues (12). This emphasis is logical since in message switched systems, messages experience queueing delays as they pass from node to node and thus a significant performance measure is the speed at which messages can be delivered. The models, which at all times were recognized to be idealized statements about the real network, were nonetheless crucial to the ARPA Net topological design effort since they afforded the only known way to quantitatively predict the properties of different routing schemes and topological structures. The models have been subsequently demonstrated to be very accurate predictors of network throughput (see below) and indispensible in providing analytical insight into the network's behaviour.

The key to the successful development of tractable models has been to factor the problem into a set of simpler queueing problems; if one specializes the problem and removes some of the real constraints, then theory and analysis become useful in providing understanding, intuition and design guidelines for the original constrained problem. This approach uncovers global properties of network behaviour, which provide keys to good heuristic design procedures and ideal performance bounds.

3 Analysis, Simulation and Measurement

The effort to determine analytic models of system performance has been involved with predicting the average time delay encountered by a message as it passes through the network, and in using these queueing models to calculate optimum channel capacity assignments for minimum possible delay. The model used as a standard for the average message delay was first described in (12) where it served to predict delays in stochastic communication networks. In (13), this model was modified to describe the behaviour of ARPA-like computer networks, while in (4,15) it was refined further to apply directly to the ARPA Net.

3.1 The Single Server Queueing Model:

Queueing theory (16) provides an effective set of analytical tools for studying packet delay. Much of this theory considers systems in which messages place demands for transmission (service) upon a single communication channel (the single server). These systems are characterized by $A(\tau)$, the distribution of interarrival times between demands and $B(t)$, the distribution of service times. When the average demand for service is less than the capacity of the channel, the system is said to be stable.

Whe $A(\tau)$ is exponential (i.e. Poisson arrivals), and packets are transmitted on a first-come-first-served basis, the average time T in the stable system is

$$T = \frac{\lambda \overline{t^2}}{2(1 - \rho)} + \overline{t} \tag{1}$$

where λ is the average arrival rate of messages, $\overline{t}$ and $\overline{t^2}$ are the first and second moments of $B(t)$, respectively, and $\rho = \lambda \overline{t} < 1$. If the service time is also exponential, then

$$T = \frac{\overline{t}}{1 - \rho} \tag{2}$$

When $A(\tau)$ and $B(t)$ are arbitrary distributions, the situation becomes complex and only weak results are available. For example, no expression is available for T; however, the following upper bound yields an excellent approximation (17) as $\rho \to 1$.

$$T \leq \frac{\lambda(\sigma_a^2 + \sigma_b^2)}{2(1 - \rho)} + \overline{t} \tag{3}$$

where σ_a^2 and σ_b^2 are the variance of the interarrival time and service time distribution, respectively.*

3.2 Networks of Queues:

Multiple channels in a network environment give rise to queueing problems that are far more difficult to solve than single server systems. For example, the variability in the choice of source and destination for a message is a network phenomenon which contributes to delay. A principal analytical difficulty results from the fact that flows throughout the network are correlated. The basic approach to solving these stochastic network problems is to decompose them into analyzable single-server problems which reflect the original network structure and traffic flow.

* Approximation techniques are currently being developed which permit one to estimate system behaviour in the overloaded (unstable) case $(\rho \geq 1)$.

Early studies of queueing networks indicated that such a decomposition was possible (18,19); however, those results do not carry over to message switched computer networks due to the correlation of traffic flows. In (12) it was shown for a wide variety of communication nets that this correlation could be removed by considering the length of a given packet to be an independent random variable as it passes from node to node. Although this "independence" assumption is not physically realistic, it results in a mathematically tractable model which does not seem to affect the accuracy of the predicted time delays. As the size and connectivity of the network increases, the assumption becomes increasingly more realistic. With this assumption, a successful decomposition is possible which permits the following channel-by-channel analysis.

The packet delay is defined as the time which a packet spends in the network from its entry until it reaches its destination. The average packet delay is denoted as T. Let Z_{jk} be the average delay for those packets whose origin is IMP j and whose destination is IMP k.

We assume a Poisson arrival process for such packets with an average of γ_{jk} packets per second and an exponential distribution of packet lengths with an average of $1/\mu$ bits per packet. With these definitions, if γ is the sum of the quantities γ_{jk}, then

$$T = \sum_{j,k} \frac{\gamma_{jk}}{\gamma} Z_{jk} \tag{4}$$

Let us now reformulate Eq.(4) in terms of single channel delays. We first define the following quantities for the ith channel: C_i as its capacity (bits/second); λ_i as the average packet traffic it carries (packets/second): and T_i as the average time a packet spends waiting for and using the ith channel. By relating the $\{\lambda_i\}$ to the $\{\gamma_{jk}\}$ via the paths selected by the routing algorithm, it is easy to see that (12)

$$T = \sum_i \frac{\lambda_i}{\gamma} T_i \tag{5}$$

With the assumption of Poisson traffic and exponential service times, the quantities T_i are given by Eq. (2). For an average packet length of $1/\mu$ bits, we have $\bar{t} = 1/\mu C_i$ seconds, and so

$$T_i = \frac{1}{\mu C_i - \lambda_i} \tag{6}$$

Thus we have successfully decomposed the analysis problem into a set of simple single-channel problems as given by these last two equations.

A refinement of the decomposition permits a non-exponential packet length distribution and uses Eq.(1) rather than Eq.(2) to calculate T_i; as an approximation, the Markovian character of the traffic is assumed to be preserved. Furthermore, for computer networks we include the effect of propagation time and overhead traffic to obtain the following equation for average packet delay (4,13).

$$T = K + \sum_i \frac{\lambda_i}{\gamma} \left[\frac{1}{\mu' C_i} + \frac{\lambda_i/\mu C_i}{\mu' C_i - \lambda_i} + P_i + K \right] \tag{7}$$

Here, $1/\mu'$ represents the average length of a HOST packet, and $1/\mu$ represents the average length of all packets(including acknowledgments), headers, requests for next messages, parity checks, etc.)within the network. The expression $1/\mu'C_i + [(\lambda_i/\mu C_i)(\mu C_i - \lambda_i)] + P_i$ represents the average packet delay on the ith channel. The term $(\lambda_i/\mu C_i)/(\mu C_i - \lambda_i)$ is the average time a packet spends waiting at the IMP for the ith channel to become available. Since the packet must compete with acknowledgments and other overhead traffic, the overall average packet length $1/\mu$ appears in the expression. The term $1/\mu'C_i$ is the time required to transmit a packet of average length μ'. Finally; K is the nodal processing time, assumed constant, and for the ARPA IMP approximately equal to 0.35 ms; P is the propagation time on the ith channel (about 20 ms for a 3000 mile channel).

Assuming a relatively homogeneous set of C_i and P_i, no individual term in the expression for delay will dominate the summation until the flow λ_i/μ in one channel (say channel i_0) approaches the capacity C_{i_0}; at that point, the term T_{i_0}, and hence T will grow rapidly. The expression for delay is then dominated by one term and exhibits a threshold behaviour. Prior to this threshold, T remains relatively constant.

This time delay model was demonstrated on a 19-node network (15) originally proposed (but never implemented) for ARPA and produced the results shown in Figs.2. and 3. In Fig.2 we see the single-packet message delay as a function of the load on the network (RE)*; Eq. (7) is plotted as a solid line and the simulation data is shown by dots. The agreement is remarkable. Moreover,we begin to see the threshold effect in which the packet delay rises much more rapidly in the network than would be predicted for a single node (as in Eq. (1)). Fig.3 is concerned with multi-packets as well as single packets; recall that messages are decomposed into packets as they pass through the network, and a message consisting of more than one packet is referred to as a multi-packet message. For this simulation, it was assumed that single-packet messages had priority over multi-packet messages when competing for a channel. In Fig.3 we plot message delay as a function of the percentage of traffic which is single-packet while maintaining the constant average bit rate into the network; when V = 1.0, we have all single-packets, whereas V = 0 corresponds to all multi-packets. A multi-packet model similar to Eq.(7) (20), provides the solid theoretical curves in this figure and again the dots represent simulation results. From these two figures it is clear that we have generated a suitable model for predicting average message delay.

For the ten-node ARPA Net derived from Fig.1(c) by deleting the five rightmost IMPs, and using equal traffic between all node pairs, the channel flows λ_i were found using a simple routing algorithm,and the delay curves shown in Fig.4 were calculated. Curve A was obtained with fixed 1000 bit packets,**while curve B was generated for exponentially distributed variable length packets with average size of 500 bits. Note that the delay remains small until a total throughput slightly greater than 400 kilobits/second is reached. The delay then increases rapidly. Curves C and D, respectively, represent the same situations when the overhead of 136 bits per packet and per RFNM (see below) and 152 bits per acknowledgment are included. Notice that the total throughput per IMP is reduced to 250 kilobits/second in case C and to approximately 200 kilobits/second in case D. In the same figure, we have illustrated with X 's the results of a simulation performed with a realistic routing and metering strategy. The simulation assumed fixed lengths of 1000 bits for all packets. It is notable that the delay estimates from the simulation (which used a dynamic routing strategy) and the computation (which used a static routing strategy and the message delay equation) are in close agreement.

*RE = 1.0 corresponds to a total throughput (γ) of 225 kilobits/ second using a non-uniform traffic matrix (see (13)).
** In case A, the application of Eq.(1) allows for constant packet lengths (i.e., zero variance).

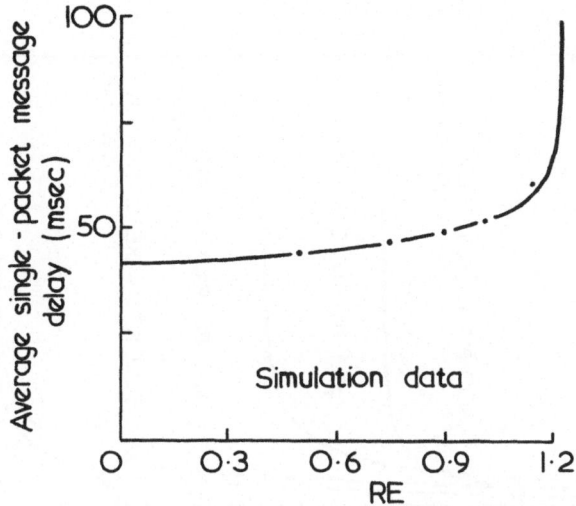

Fig. 2 Single - packet message delay
as a function of network load.

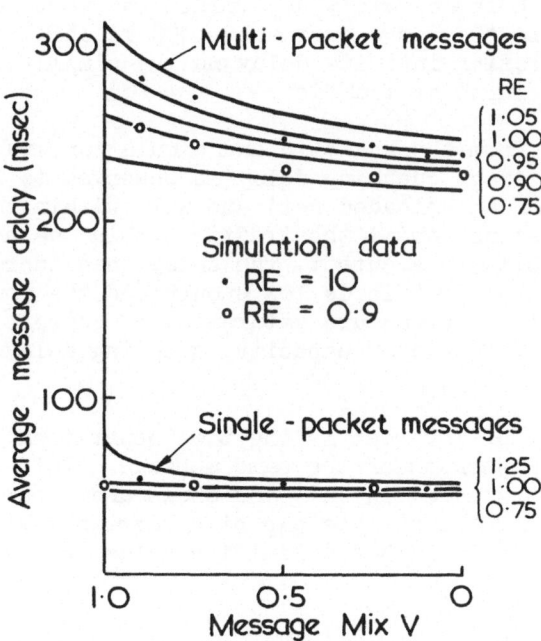

Fig. 3 Message delay for the 19 - node
net versus message mix.

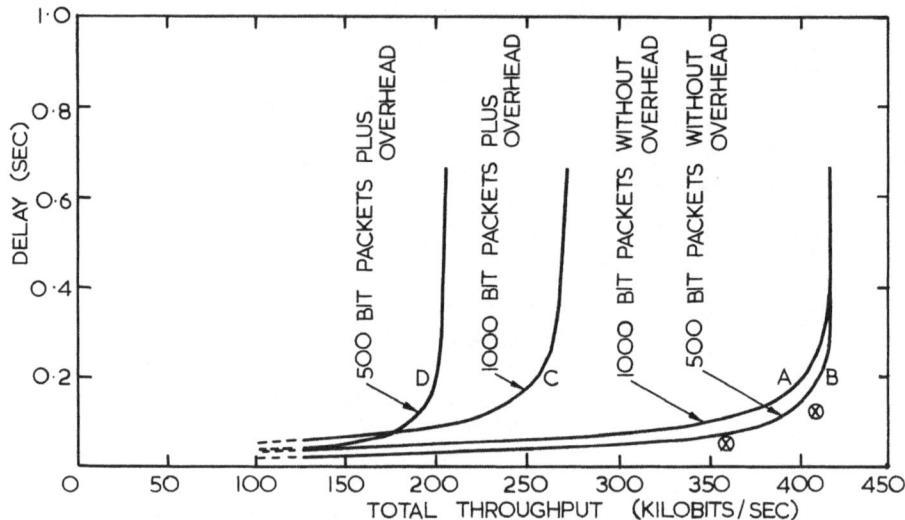

Fig. 4   Delay as a function of throughput   (network load).

In particular, they both accurately determined the vertical rise
of the delay curve in the range just above 400 kilobits/second,
the formula by predicting infinite delay and the simulation by rejecting the further input of traffic.

In practice and from the analytic and simulation studies of
the ARPA Net, the average queueing delay is observed to remain
small (almost that of an unloaded net) and well within the design
constraint of 0.2 seconds until the traffic within the network
approaches the capacity of a cutset. The delay then increases rapidly.   Thus, as long as traffic is low enough and the routing adap
tive enough to avoid the premature saturation of cutsets by guidin
traffic along paths with excess capacity, queueing delays are not
significant.

Another quantity of interest is the time separation at the des
tination IMP between packets of the same message.   This inter-
packet time has been studied in (21) and shows under certain simpl
fying assumptions that the average gap size increases with the
message path length, but reaches a limiting value as a function of
path length.

3.3 Routing Procedures:

An efficient message routing procedure is an essential ingredient for the successful operation of a computer network.   The

function of a routing procedure is to direct the message traffic
along paths within the network in a fashion which avoids congestion. In conjunction with a routing procedure one must provide
methods for controlling the flow of traffic entering the network
which would otherwise congest the system. It is not difficult to
conceive of "good" routing procedures, and even of "fair" flow
control procedures; however, at this time there are virtually no
optimum procedures known. In what follows we describe some simulation and measurement experiments which have been performed for
the ARPA Network as it currently functions. Some alternative algorithms have been described in (22) and are to be implemented shortly
as the operating procedure for the network; we have little experience with these new procedures and therefore defer commenting on
their effectiveness until the appropriate measurements have been
made.

The basic requirements for a good routing procedure are as
follows:

. It should insure rapid delivery of messages.

. It should adapt to changes in the network topology
  resulting from nodal and channel failures.

. It should adapt to varying source-destination traffic
  loads.

. It should route packets away from temporarily congested
  nodes within the network.

In (15,20) a number of routing algorithms have been defined
and classified. It has been possible to generate approximate
lower bounds on the message delay as a function of load for various
of these algorithms, and in Fig.5 this lower envelope is shown.
This figure corresponds to the 19-node network mentioned earlier.
Shown also is the performance of a routing procedure similar to the
one currently used in the ARPA Network, namely a periodic update
algorithm (PUA1). We see that its performance deteriorates as the
network load grows. Procedures using an asynchronous update algorithm (AUA) or the shortest queue plus bias algorithm (SQ+BA)
are seen to be superior, although they are more costly in terms
of the processing load they place upon the IMP. A good candidate
for a routing algorithm is the shortest queue plus bias plus periodic update algorithm (SQ+B+PUA) which is reasonably simple to implement and not too costly in processing load.

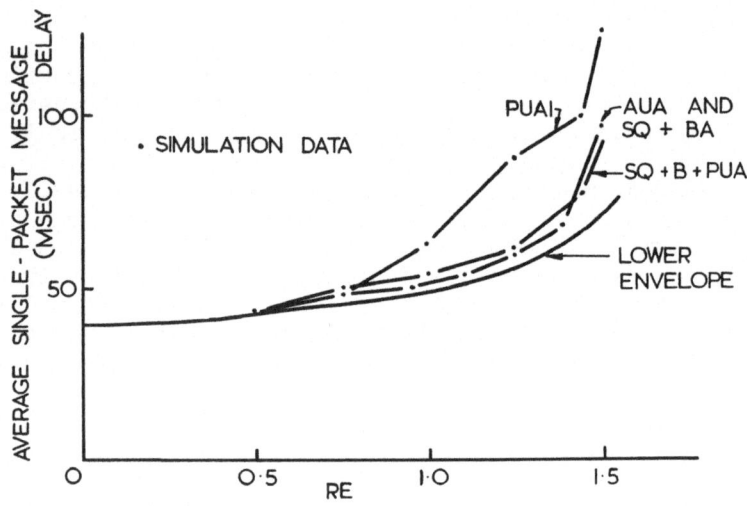

Fig. 5 Comparison of routing algorithm performance as a function of network load.

3.4 Network Measurements:

Measurement of network activity is of major importance in the ARPA Net. These measurements provide information regarding the traffic on the network, provide means for testing the limits of its traffic-carrying capacity, provide a method for validating and improving the theoretical models, as discussed herein, and lastly, may eventually provide an on-line mechanism for controlling network traffic and routing. Measurements of round trip message delay and throughput have been conducted at UCLA, and we wish now to compare these measurement results with some of the theoretical and simulation results we have so far discussed. In (21) it is shown that a simple calculation for the expected round trip delay between two nodes in the network (SRI-Utah) may be calculated to give 20 + 0.48L milliseconds where L is the length of the message (in IMP words) travelling this round trip; this equation assumes no other traffic exists in the network and therefore provides a strict lower bound on such delays. In Fig.6. we give the measured results for this round trip delay, along with the theoretical equation just described; the calculations are shown to be accurate, and the delays above the minimum are due to interfering traffic within the network. A throughput measurement made for the network of Fig.1(c) is shown in Fig.7. Here we see the flow of traffic from UCLA to UCSB. This test was made using an artificial traffic generator at UCLA which has the capability of creating more than one "conversation" between a pair of sites. The current network

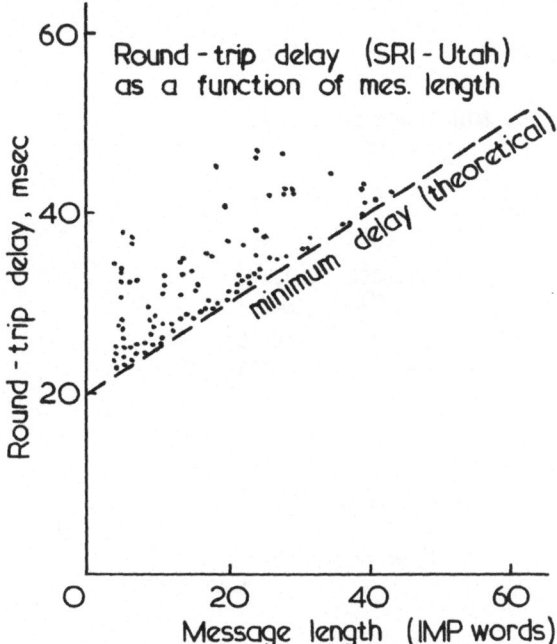

Fig. 6 Round - trip delay measurements of the SRI - Utah traffic.

network flow control procedure constrains each conversation to have at most one message in the network at any time; only when that message is delivered may the next message be generated in this conversation. That is, when a message reaches its destination, the flow control procedure sends a message (known as a RFNM, a "request for next message") from the destination IMP back to the source IMP which signals its readiness to accept a new message into the network. In Fig.7. we see the effect of this control procedure. The lower curve corresponds to single packet messages, and we see the growth in throughput as the number of generators (conversations) increases, reaching a plateau when two or more generators are in operation; this plateau occurs at approximately 40 kilobits/second, which corresponds to the effective data rate permissible on a single 50 kilobit line when overhead considerations are accounted for. This level of traffic is not obtainable with a single message generator due to delays created by the RFNM. Note that the routing procedure permits alternate routing to take place when more than six generators are active; at this point a large enough queue is formed at UCLA to trigger the introduction of alternate routing. The upper curve in Fig.7 corresponds to full length messages composed of eight packets each. Here, we do not expect

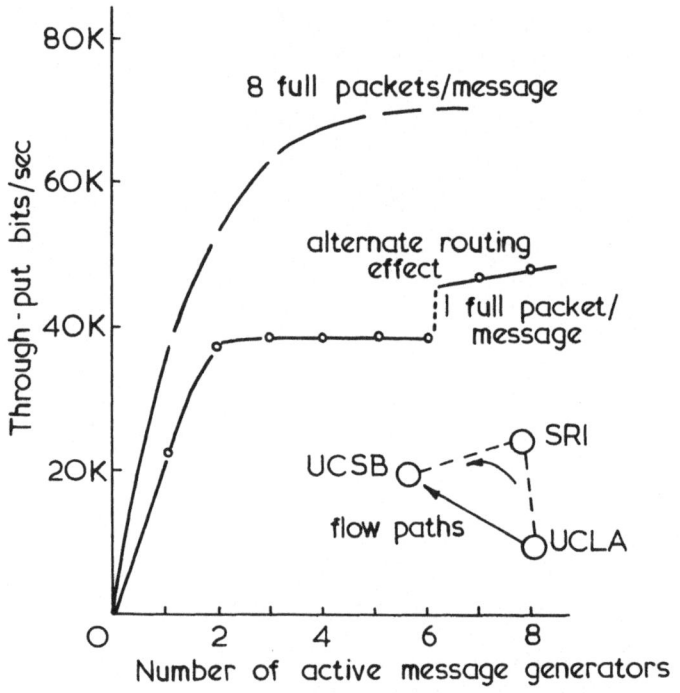

Fig. 7 Throughput measurements between
UCLA and the neighbouring UCSB IMP.

the RFNM to constrain the throughput in a significant way since it comes only once in every eight packets now, and we note that a single message generator immediately achieves the "plateau" value of throughput seen earlier. In this multi-packet mode we observe that its plateau is reached at about 70 kilobits/second; this is below the expected 80 kilobit/second for the two paths in use since the finite storage capacity of the IMP was saturated at this point.

This last throughput measurement was carried out in the presence of no interfering traffic from other sources. A more interesting experiment is to observe the mutual interference among competing conversations within the network. This was done for a network similar* to that in Fig. 1(d) in which UCLA was attempting to

* The measured network differed from that in Fig.1(d) as follows: NCAR and GWC were not yet connected, and so there was a direct link from Utah to Case; furthermore in series with the MIT-BBN link there was placed an additional node (BBNTIP).

send message traffic to RAND. Measurements were taken at UCLA
(which is the Network Measurement Center) as, one by one, additional nodes were instructed to send interfering traffic to RAND (each
IMP has the capability for generating artificial traffic of a
simple type for such purposes). The order in which new IMPs entered this sequence is as follows:

Number of Senders	Next Additional IMP
1	UCLA
2	BBN
3	SDC
4	Stanford
5	Harvard
6	Utah
7	Ames
8	MIT
9	Illinois
10	BBNTIP
11	Case
12	Linc
13	Carnegie

In Fig.8 we show the way in which the average round trip
delay (from UCLA to RAND and back) varies with the number of interfering users. Three curves are shown, each for different message
lengths; these are the lengths used for all messages generated
within the network for this experiment. We note for the single
packet messages that essentially no interference occurred as the
number of users increased;* however, with four,and in particular
eight, packets per message, the interference caused significant
round trip delays to the message traffic. A large part of this
delay was due to the competition for reassembly storage space at
the RAND IMP. In Fig.9. we see a similar plot for the throughput
per user. Again, the single-packet messages maintain an essentially constant data rate. When we go to four packets per message,
and then to eight packets per message, we observe that the data
rate increases so long as the number of senders is less than four.
This increase in throughput is due to the large penalty paid by
smaller messages for the flow control procedure and its use of RFNM's.
The delay due to a RFNM comes once per packet for single-packet
messages, but only once per eight packets for eight-packet messages,

*This result is conditional on the fact that UCLA is directly con-
 nected to RAND. Experiments with longer paths and with paths
 through "congested" nodes are currently being conducted.

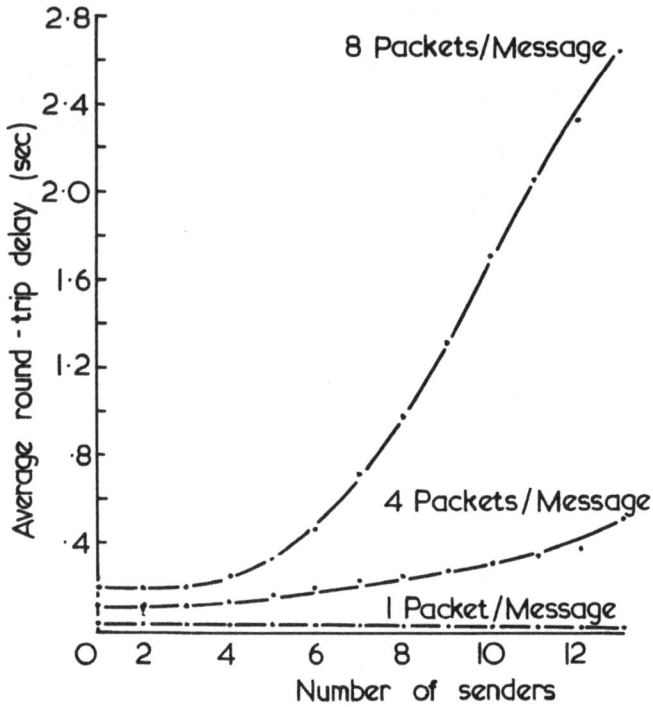

Fig. 8   Measured round – trip times.

and this accounts for the increased throughput for a small number
of interfering users. The reason that the multi-packet message
throughput begins to deteriorate seriously when four or more
senders are active is due to the finite storage capacity at each
IMP which is set aside for the reassembly of multi-packet messages; at present, this storage is sufficient to hold approximately
three eight-packet messages. From Figs. 8 and 9 we see the effect
of this interference on the increase in delay and the decrease in
throughput. However, one may argue that the total throughput in
the network is increasing as the number of conversations increase.
In Fig.9 we displayed the throughput per user as a function of
number of users. We may approximate the total throughput as a
function of number of users by taking each measured point in Fig.
9 and multiplying by the number of users to which that point corresponds; this, of course, is a fiction, since the measured points
from Fig.9 correspond to the throughput seen in the UCLA-RAND trans
mission only. However, this derived curve will provide some insight as to what is happening with regard to total throughput, and
this we show in Fig.10. We see that the single packet per message case yields a linearly increasing total throughput which is

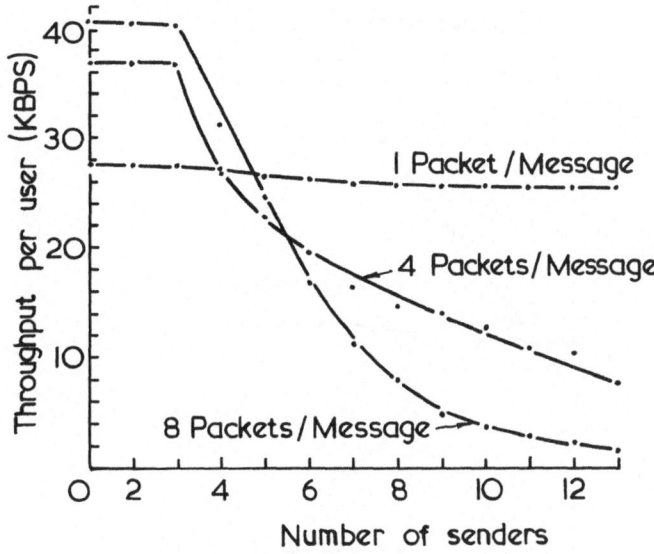

Fig. 9 Measured throughput per user.

part of the fiction since, clearly, this function can rise only
until it reaches the maximum throughput capability of the IMP itself. In the case of four packets per message, we see that the
throughput saturates when three or more senders are active, and
this saturation level occurs somewhat above 100 kilobits/second.
The more interesting (albeit unfortunate) case is for eight packets per message in which the total throughput peaks at around four
users and then begins to fall off in a disasterous fashion* as the
network goes into what is known as reassembly lockup (22). This
again is the effect of the flow control procedure choking off the
input traffic as messages take longer and longer to reassemble;
in the limit, reassembly lockup occurs when partially reassembled
messages cannot be completely reassembled since the congested network prevents their remaining packets from reaching their destination.

*This is similar to the fundamental diagram of road traffic (14)
 for which strong analogies may be drawn.

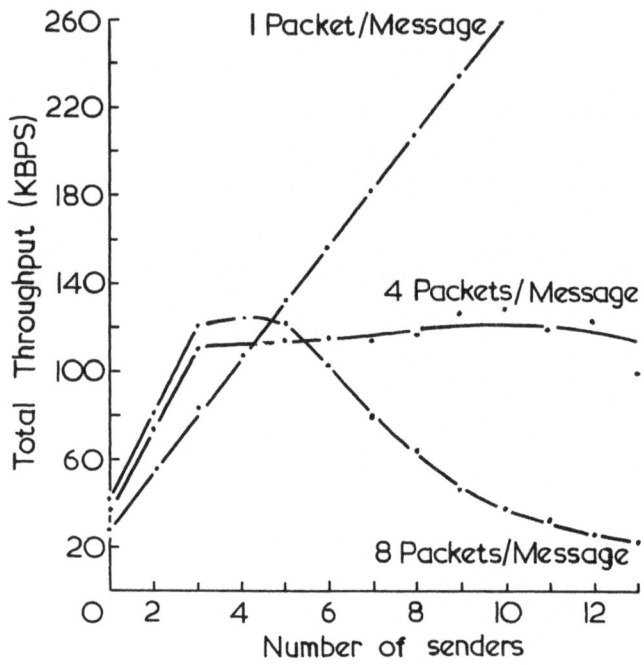

Fig. 10   Measured   total   throughput.

3.5 Network Optimization:

One of the more difficult design problems is the optimal selection of capacities from a <u>finite</u> set of options. Although there
are many heuristic approaches to this problem, analytic results
are relatively scarce. (For the specialized case of centralized
networks, an algorithm yielding optimal results is available (23))
While it is possible to find an economical assignment of discrete
capacities for up to, say, a 200 IMP network, very little is known
about the relationships among such capacity assignments, the message delay, and cost.

To obtain theoretical properties of optimal capacity assignments, we first ignore the constraint that capacities are obtainable only in discrete sizes. In (12) the problem was posed where
the network topology and average traffic flow were assumed to be
known and fixed and an optimal match of capacities to traffic flov
was found. Also, the traffic was assumed to be Markovian (Poissor
arrivals and exponential packet lengths) and the independence assumption and decomposition method were applied. For each channel
the capacity C_i was found which minimized the average message de-

lay T. Since λ_i/μ is the average bit rate on the ith channel, the solution to any optimal assignment problem must provide more than this minimal capacity to each channel. This is clear since both Eqs. (6) and (7) indicate that T_i will become arbitrarily large with less than (or equal to) this amount of capacity. It is not critical exactly how the <u>excess</u> capacity is assigned, as long as $C_i > \lambda_i/\mu$. The optimization further assumed that a total of D dollars was available to provide the channel capacities and that the cost of the ith channel was linear at a rate of d_i dollars per unit of channel capacity; that is, $D = \Sigma d_i C_i$. The simpler form for T_i in Eq.(6) is used in this formulation and T is as given in Eq. (5). The solution to this problem assigns a capacity to the ith channel in an amount equal to λ_i/μ plus some excess capacity proportional to the square root of that traffic. With T evaluated for this assignment,

$$T = \frac{\bar{n}}{\mu D_e} \left(\sum_i \sqrt{d_i(\lambda_i/\lambda)} \right)^2 \qquad (8)$$

Here $\lambda = \Sigma \lambda_i$ represents the total rate at which packets flow within the net and D_e is the difference between D and the amount which must be spent to provide each channel with capacity λ_i/μ, namely

$$D_e = D - \sum_i \frac{\lambda_i d_i}{\mu} \qquad (9)$$

Moreover, $\bar{n} = \lambda/\gamma$ is easily shown to represent the average path length for a packet.

If $d_i = 1$ for all channels, $D = \Sigma_i C_i = C$ where C represents the total capacity within the network.* In this case,

---

*The assumption $d_i = 1$ is of practical importance in the case of satellite channels (24).

$$T = \frac{\bar{n}}{\mu C(1 - \bar{n}\rho)} \left(\sum_i \sqrt{\lambda_i/\lambda} \right)^2 \tag{10}$$

Here $\rho = \gamma/\mu C$ is the ratio of the rate γ/μ at which bits enter the network to the rate C at which the net can handle bits. The quantity ρ represents a dimensionless form of network "load". As the load ρ approaches $1/\bar{n}$, the delay T grows very quickly, and the point $\rho = 1/n$ represents the maximum load which the network can support. If capacities are assigned optimally, all channels saturate simultaneously at this point. In this formulation $\bar{n}$ is a design parameter which depends upon the topology and the routing procedure, while ρ is a given parameter, which depends upon the input rate and the total capacity of the network. Equation (10) provides insight into topological structure and routing procedures (12).

In a recent paper (25), it was observed that, in minimizing T, a wide variation was possible among the line delays T_i. As a result, the problem of finding the sets of channel capacities which minimize $T^{(k)}$ was considered, where

$$T^{(k)} = \left[\sum_i \frac{\lambda_i}{\gamma} (T_i)^k \right]^{1/k} \tag{11}$$

The solution for the optimal channel capacity assignment with a given value k, denoted by $C_i^{(k)}$ is

$$C_i^{(k)} = \frac{\lambda_i}{\mu} + \left(\frac{D_e}{d_i} \right) \frac{(\lambda_i d_i^k)^{1/k+1}}{\sum_j (\lambda_j d_j^k)^{1/k+1}} \tag{12}$$

With this capacity assignment,

$$T^{(k)} = \left(\frac{\bar{n}}{\mu D_e} \right) \left(\sum_i (\lambda_i d_i^k/\lambda)^{1/1+k} \right)^{1/k} \tag{13}$$

Note that the assignment $C_i^{(1)}$ is the previously mentioned assignment which minimizes T, and $T^{(1)}$ is the previous value for T in Eq. (8). As k increases, the variation in the T_i decreases and as $k \to \infty$

$$\lim_{k \to \infty} C_i^{(k)} = \frac{\lambda_i}{\mu} + \frac{D_e}{\sum_j d_j} \tag{14}$$

In this limit, the channel capacity is assigned to give each channel its minimum required amount λ_i/μ plus a <u>constant</u> additional amount; all the T_i are equal, and so

$$T = \frac{\bar{n}}{\mu D_e} \sum_j d_j \tag{15}$$

On the other hand, setting k = 0 yields

$$C_i^{(0)} = \frac{\lambda_i}{\mu} + \frac{\lambda_i D_e}{\bar{n} \gamma d_i} \tag{16}$$

For this assignment, the value of T is identical to the value it achieves in Eq. (15) for $k \to \infty$, although different channel capacity assignments typically occur at these extremes (26). If all $d_i = 1$ a channel capacity is assigned in proportion to the traffic carried by that channel (commonly known as the proportional capacity assignment). Although the value of T is minimized for the capacity assignment which results when k = 1, T increases rather slowly as k varies from unity, and moreover, the variance of packet delay is minimized when k = 2.

In studying the ARPA Network (4) a closer representation of the actual tariffs for high speed telephone data channels used in that network was provided by setting $D = \Sigma_i d_i C_i^\alpha$ where $0 \leq \alpha \leq 1$.* This approach requires the solution of a non-linear equation by numerical techniques. On solving the equation, it can be shown that the packet delay T varies insignificantly with α for $.3 \leq \alpha \leq 1$. This indicates that the closed form solution discussed earlier with $\alpha = 1$ is a reasonable approximation to the more difficult non-linear problem.

*Of course the tariffs reflect the discrete nature of available channels. The use of the exponent α provides a continuous fit to the discrete cost function. For the ARPA Net, $\alpha \cong .8$.

In practice, the selection of channel capacities must be made from a small finite set and not from a continuum as assumed above. Although some theoretical work has been done in this case by approximating the discrete cost-capacity functions by continuous ones, much remains to be done (27-29). Because of the discrete capacities and the time varying nature of network traffic, it is not generally possible to match channel capacities to the anticipated flows within the channels. If this were possible, all channels would saturate at the same externally applied load. Instead, capacities are assigned on the basis of reasonable estimates of average of peak traffic flows. It is the responsibility of the routing procedure to allow the traffic to adapt to the available capacity (15). Often two IMP sites will engage in heavy communication and thus saturate one or more critical network cutsets. In such cases, the routing will not be able to send additional flow across these cuts. The network will therefore experience "premature" saturation in one or a small set of channels leading to the threshold behaviour described earlier.

4. Conclusions

In this paper we have surveyed some of the modeling techniques which have been found useful in the study of the ARPA Network. We have also reviewed some of the simulation and measurement results which, by and large, lend validity to the mathematical models we have used. We see that message switching networks of the ARPA type may be implemented in a rather straightforward fashion and provide an economical message service compared to other current techniques. We observe the heavy reliance in this paper on approximate methods, simulation and actual network measurement, which together permit us to understand some aspects of network behaviour. Heuristics are also necessary in this process for the selection of good topologies and traffic flow assignments. The study of really large networks (hundreds of nodes) will undoubtedly require the development of new tools; it is clear that some clever decomposition or partitioning of the network into supernodes and regions (perhaps in a hierarchical structure) will be necessary.

Among the more difficult design problems which remain are: the specification of routing and flow control procedures; the design of optimal topologies; the optimal assignment of capacities with nonlinear discrete cost functions; the consideration of large message-switching nodes judiciously placed in the network; and many other related questions. Considerable work is being expended in these directions, and we hope that some of these questions will be answered in the near future.

Acknowledgments

The author takes great pleasure in acknowledging the assistance rendered by Gary L. Fultz in the simulation experiments and by Gerald D. Cole, Willam E. Naylor, and Vinton G. Cerf in the measurement experiments.

References

1. Roberts, L.G., "Multiple Computer Networks and Inter-Computer Communications, " Proc. of the ACM Symposium on Operating Systems, Gatlinburg, Tenn., 1967.

2. Roberts, L.G., and Wessler, B., "Computer Network Development to Achieve Resource Sharing," AFIPS Conference Proceedings, Spring Joint Computer Conference 1970, 36:543-549.

3. Heart, F., R. Kahn, S. Ornstein, W. Crowther and D. Walden, "The Interface Message Processor for the ARPA Computer Network," AFIPS Conference Proceedings, Spring Joint Computer Conference 1970, 36:551-567.

4. Kleinrock, L., "Analysis and Simulation Methods in Computer Network Design," AFIPS Conference Proceedings, Spring Joint Computer Conference 1970, 36:569-579.

5. Frank, H., I.T. Frisch, and W. Chou, "Topological Considerations in the Design of the ARPA Computer Network," AFIPS Conference Proceedings, Spring Joint Computer Conference 1970, 36:581-587.

6. Carr, S., S. Crocker, and V. Cerf, "Host-Host Communication Protocol in the ARPA Network," AFIPS Conference Proceedings, Spring Joint Computer Conference 1970, 36:589-597.

7. Crocker, S.D., J.F. Heafner, R.M. Metcalfe, and J.J. Postel, "Function-Oriented Protocols for the ARPA Computer Networks," AFIPS Conference Proceedings, Spring Joint Computer Conference 1972, 40: 271-279.

8. Frank, H., R. Kahn, and L. Kleinrock, "Computer-Communication Network Design - Experience with Theory and Practice," AFIPS Conference Proceedings, Spring Joint Computer Conference 1972, 40:255-270.

9. Ornstein, S.M., F.E. Heart, W.R. Crowther, H.K. Rising, S.B. Russell, and S. Michel, "The Terminal IMP for the ARPA Computer Network," AFIPS Conference Proceedings, Spring Joint Computer conference 1972, 40: 243-254.

10. Thomas, R.H., and D.A. Henderson, "McRoss – A Multi-Computer Programming System," <u>AFIPS Conference Proceedings</u>, Spring Joint Computer Conference 1972, 40:281–293.

11. Roberts,L.G., "Extensions of Packet Communication Technology to a Hand-Held Personal Terminal," <u>AFIPS Conference Proceedings</u>, Spring Joint Computer Conference 1972, 40:295–298.

12. Kleinrock, L., <u>Communication Nets: Stochastic Message Flow and Delay</u>, McGraw-Hill, 1964.

13 Kleinrock,L., "Models for Computer Networks," <u>Proc. of the International Conference on Communications</u>, 1969, pp.21-9 to 21-16.

14. Haight, F.A., <u>Mathematical Theories of Traffic Flow</u> (New York: Academic Press), 1963.

15. Fultz, G., and L. Kleinrock, "Adaptive Routing Techniques for Store-and-Forward Computer-Communication Networks," <u>Proc. of the International Conference on Communications</u>, 1971, pp.39-1 to 39-8.

16. Kleinrock, L., <u>Queueing Systems: Theory and Application</u>, to be published by Wiley Interscience,1973.

17. Kingman, J.F.C., "Some Inequalities for the Queue GI/G/1," <u>Biometrica</u>, 1962, pp.315-324.

18. Burke, P., "The Output of a Queueing System," <u>Operations Research</u>, 1956, 4: 699-704.

19. Jackson, J.R., "Networks of Waiting Lines," <u>Operations Research</u>, 1957, 5: 518-521.

20. Fultz,G., "Adaptive Routing Techniques for Message Switching Computer-Communication Networks," Ph.D. Dissertation, Compute Science Department, School of Engineering and Applied Science, University of California, Los Angeles, Calif. June 1972.

21. Cole, G.D., "Computer Network Measurements: Techniques and Experiments," Ph.D. Dissertation, Computer Science Department, School of Engineering and Applied Science, University of California, Los Angeles, 1971, UCLA Engineering Report UCLA-ENG-7165.

22. Kahn, R.E., and W.R. Crowther, "A Study of the ARPA Network Design and Performance", BBn Report No. 2161, August 1971.

23. Frank, H., I.T. Frisch, W. Chou, and R. Van Slyke, "Optimal Design of Centralized Computer Networks", _Networks_, John Wiley, 1971, 1:43-57.

24. Raymond, H.G., "A Queueing Theory Approach to Communication Satellite Network Design," _Proc. of the International Conference on Communication_, 1971, pp.42-26 to 42-31.

25. Meister, B., H. Muller and H. Rudin, "New Optimization Criteria for Message-Switching Networks," _IEEE Transactions on Communication Technology_, Com-19, June 1971, pp.256-260.

26. Kleinrock, L., "Scheduling, Queueing and Delays in Time-Sharing Systems and Computer Networks", in _Computer Communication Networks_, Abramson, N., and F. Kuo (eds.), Prentice-Hall, Englewood Cliffs, N.J. 1972.

27. Fratta, L., M. Gerla, and L. Kleinrock, "The Flow Deviation Method: An Approach to Store-and-Forward Network Design," to be published in _Netwo rks_.

28. Meister,B., H. Muller and H. Rudin, "Optimization of a New Model for Message-Switching Networks," _Proc. of the International Conference on Communications_, 1971, pp.39-16 to 39-21

29. Cantor,D.G., and M. Gerla, "The Optimal Routing of Messages in a Computer Network via Mathematical Programming," to be presented at the IEEE Computer Science Conference, San Francisco, Calif., September 12-14, 1972.

COORDINATED INFORMATION SERVICES FOR A DISCIPLINE- OR MISSION-
ORIENTED COMMUNITY

Douglas C. Engelbart

Augmentation Research Center
Stanford Research Institute

INTRODUCTION

Generally, adoption of a multi-access computer network is
promoted on the basis of increased accessibility and economy of
computational and data-bank resources for a distributed
community of users. But visualize this resource-sharing
computer network as a general-purpose digital-packet
transportation system linking resources, processors, vendors,
brokers, customers, etc.; then consider that the existence of
such a transportation system will inevitably stimulate growth of
an information market involving many processes, products, and
services. A distributed community availing itself of such a
transportation system should rightfully count on such market
development for much of its payoff from its early investment.

In particular, the "Knowledge Workshop" services described
below will grow to become very important to network-coupled
communities that are involved with a common discipline or
mission -- my judgement is that this use of computer networks
will come to dominate over the purely computational use in scale
and generally perceived social worth, with today's type of
computer services being seen as but a special subset of the
tools integrated into a coherent knowledge workshop.

THE KNOWLEDGE WORKSHOP

In using the term "knowledge workshop", I build directly
upon terms "knowledge work" and "knowledge worker", whose special
use I first came across in reading Peter Drucker.[1] He develops

a much larger theme about these concepts in Reference 2, adding terms such as "knowledge technologies", "knowledge economy", and "knowledge society", and pointing out that the growing level and importance of knowledge-work activity in our society will produce a discontinuity in our cultural evolution of a scale commensurate with that of the industrial revolution.

The knowledge workshop is the specially provided environment in which knowledge workers do their knowledge work. We can talk about a small knowledge workshop for an individual, or a large knowledge workshop for an organization. Knowledge workshops have existed for centuries, but here we consider maximizing their effectiveness by systematically evolving tools, methods, etc., with heavy dependence upon the new technologies of computer time sharing and networking. (In the text below, read "knowledge workshop" for "Workshop".)

Basic Workshop functions must serve the daily handling of the users' working information -- of their notes, things-to-do lists, memos, letters, designs, plans, budgets, announcements, commentary, proposals, reports, programs, documentation, item-control catalogs, etc. And before it can sensibly be of much value, we believe that a Workshop has to provide for the grubby cut-and-try detail involved in the minute-by-minute, day-after-day worker's handling of this information: in its composition, studying, commenting upon, arguing about, modifying, communicating, publishing, presenting, etc. There are many exciting, elegant tools in the offing -- superlative graphics, artificial-intelligence services, etc. -- but their serious application will only be sensible within an integrated Workshop, and in a manner whose associated conceptual and procedural skills are consistent with those of tools and techniques that support the basic Workshop functions.

For the past ten years in the Augmentation Research Center (ARC), at Stanford Research Institute, we have concentrated in succession on exploring the computer augmentation of knowledge workshops, first for an individual, then as extended for a project team, and then for a network-coupled, distributed community (see Reference 3). Over the past three years we have developed a beginning set of prototype "community-Workshop" services on the ARPANET, as associated with our serving as the Network Information Center (NIC).*

* The following agencies have contributed components of direct support to this ten-year development: The Information Processing Techniques Office (ARPA), Langley Research Center (NASA), Rome Air Development Center (USAF), and the Information Systems Branch (ONR).

Our focus all along has been toward supporting R&D workers, and we have followed the empirical, bootstrapping approach of doing as much of our own work as possible in our Workshop, continuously building, using, and evolving it. Our Workshop services are supplied by a large software system that we call NLS, running under TENEX on a PDP-10. It provides a large repertoire of functions to display terminals (DNLS), online typewriter terminals (TNLS), or via deferred-execution of commands and text from offline typewriters as accumulated on ·assettes or other intermediate storage (DEX). Hardcopy output is available on typewriters, online printers, or through an offline phototypesetting device providing publication-grade quality for multi-font text, computer-directed graphic constructs, or scan-stored diagrams.

Besides giving constant, pragmatic attention to the needs and possibilities for evolution of support functions and working methods, we have had to struggle with what is a soul-wrenching burden for people whose orientation is toward exploratory development -- trying to meet the absolutely necessary requirements of organizing, documenting, maintaining, and operating the hardware/software and clerical services towards being responsive and reliable, minute after minute and day after day.

Technology has reached a state warranting much more activity explicitly applied toward the evolution both of better workshops, and of a coherent discipline associated with Workshop-system development; for this to happen, it is obvious that more people must take on the challenge of becoming "Workshop architects", and that more pilot-plant Workshops need to be set up for exploratory support of real knowledge-work activities. There are (will be many) approaches to be tried besides ours, of course; but to do our bit toward accelerating this process, we intend to share and extend our developments and knowledge by making our Workshop tools available for exploratory application in distributed, modular, pilot-Workshop sites, and by offering close collaboration with the pilot-Workshop architects. (Note below that an important Workshop feature being offered is designed to facilitate such "distributed collaboration".)

PROTOTYPE COMMUNITY-WORKSHOP SUPPORT

We aren't ignoring exploratory use within localized organizations, but we are committing a substantial portion of our energy toward the early, exploratory use of knowledge-workshop services to support distributed, network-coupled communities. There are two special reasons for this commitment:

The first reason concerns relative payoff: if a service
facilitates hobnobbing via terminals, there is extra value
when this supplants air fare and a two-day trip in contrast
with supplanting a walk down the hall; there is more payoff
from relatively costly augmentation services when they
facilitate collaboration among participants who are
distributed rather than among those who are already
clustered.

The second reason concerns a wider awareness of the
possibilities for augmenting knowledge workshops, and a
wider interest and involvement in their accelerated
evolution -- things we hope to enhance by facilitating
community-Workshop exploration. We find that toward
significant Workshop innovations a user needs a sort of
warming-up process before gracefully giving something a new
try. Thereafter, in the right environment, he will
"naturally" adopt successive stages of significant new
Workshop techniques. This process is noticeably facilitated
by steady exposure to the products and conventions of
Workshop services; and it helps considerably to have a
variety of opportunities and materials to stimulate and
support the "giving it a try" -- for instance, to try a
little online dialogue with a distant, more-advanced
colleague, dealing with materials already in the community
data base. Also, if a new stage of service is available in
this "community way", a large number of people will benefit
from the lower threshold of investment and determination
needed to give it a try.

Following is a brief description of community-workshop
applications that special communities can consider exploring.
The sequence represents an explicit progression, beginning with
tested techniques whose "cultural shock" and financial investment
are relatively low, and offering paced, open-ended evolution
with time, experience, and perceived payoff. We are arranging
for computer support of these services by a commercial-quality
"utility" service connected to the ARPANET. We will provide
this Workshop support (at cost) over the Network to selected
subscribers for setting up and exploring prototype, augmented-
Workshop applications. We expect the Workshop toolkit to be
continually expanding and improving, and plan for much of the
evolutionary energy and direction to come from the subscribers.

COLLABORATIVE DIALOGUE

We offer computer aids for the composition of messages and
for their subsequent reviewing, cross-referencing, modification,
transmission, storage, indexing, and full-text retrieving. A

"message" may be one word in length, or a hundred printed pages. In any message there may be formalized citations pointing to specific passages in prior messages, so that a group of related messages becomes a network of recorded-dialogue contributions. There is also: automatic delivery of messages; full cataloging and indexing; online accessibility both to message notification and to the full text of all messages; and open-ended storage of the dialogue records. These services enable a community of people who are distributed in space and time to maintain recorded, collaborative dialogue at a new degree of effectiveness.

Then to support "real-time" remote dialogue (teleconferencing), we have the following facility: Any two DNLS users can "link up" at any time, so that each party sees a common display view, including both his and the other person's cursor; either party is able to point or control, and they mutually have access to the full range of Workshop functions, over any of the online information. The responsiveness and bandwidth of the ARPANET provide remarkable good support of our highly interactive DNLS service to remote display users, so that when used to supplement a telephone conversation, the speed and flexibility of this shared, "augmented blackboard" brings a new quality to teleconferencing that is really quite dramatic.

DOCUMENT DEVELOPMENT, PRODUCTION, AND CONTROL

We offer a rich set of computer aids for the composition, study, and modification of document drafts, and for automatically generating high-quality photocomposition output with flexible controls for font-designation and formatting, to enable the production of publication-grade hardcopy (printing masters, or microform masters). There are processes for collaboration between several writers, and with an editor, in the process of evolving a final draft. Included among such helpers can be experienced production people to help in laying out a finished document, in inserting proper designations for specifying font, size, and density of different character strings, and for manaiing footnotes, cross-references, tables of contents, indices, etc. There are also aids for the people who must keep control of changes, new-version distributions, etc., and provide the indexing to complex documents or sets of documents. Planned improvements include facility for handling complex graphic portrayals and extensive special symbols.

RESEARCH INTELLIGENCE

The provisions within the Dialogue Support System for cataloguing and indexing internally generated items also support the management of externally generated items -- bibliography, contact reports, clippings, notes, etc. With these centrally supplied (therefore uniformly available) services, a community can maintain a dynamic and highly useful "intelligence" data base to help it keep up to date on external happenings that particularly affect it. Microform distribution can provide for mass replication of this data base at remote sites, and computer-generated indexes of on-line retrieval can facilitate access. Citations of external items from within the internally-generated dialogue base -- in the form of annotations, miscellaneous commentary, or supportive references -- offer computer-sensible interlinking of the external information with the internal, and considerably facilitate browsing, retrieval, back-citation searching, etc.

The Community could choose to operate a special Information Analysis and Integration Center as a nucleus to this activity, but the notes and private-collection records of individual users, integrated into the "recorded dialogue", could well add the more value. (Reference 4 describes some developments and possibilities for support of research intelligence.)

COMMUNITY HANDBOOK DEVELOPMENT

We are extending the above services toward the coordinated handling of a very large and complex body of documentation and its associated external references. I use the term "superdocument" to refer to such material when integrated into a monolithic whole. There are a number of important applications for a system that facilitates the responsive development and evolution of a super-document by many (distributed) individuals. In particular, for either a discipline- or project-oriented community, one very important application of a centrally available "superdocumentation" service would be to maintain "The Community Handbook" -- i.e., a uniform, complete, consistent, up-to-date integration of the special knowledge representing the current status of the Community.

The Handbook would include: principles, working hypotheses, practices, special-term glossaries, standards, goals, goal status, supportive arguments, techniques, observations, how-to-do-it items, etc. An active community would be constantly involved in dialogue bearing upon the contents of the last formal version of its Handbook -- comments, errata, suggestions, challenges, counter examples, altered designs, improved arguments, new experimental techniques and data, etc. Constant updating would provide a "certified, community position structure" about which the real evolutionary work would swarm; flexible aids for online "navigation and view generation" would be very important, as would the facility for automatic publication (especially into microform editions).

COMPUTER-BASED INSTRUCTION

If relatively widespread applicability of Computer-Based Instruction (CBI) were suitable for the Community, then there would likely be advantage gained from pooling resources and utilizing a community-coordinated instructional service. For a community also utilizing other centrally managed Workshop services of the scope and power described here, there would be considerable overlap between them and their CBI processes and activities.

Even though CBI has more visibility and momentum as a discipline than does CBKW (Computer- Based Knowledge Workshop), it seems inevitable that the former will end up as being but a special, integrated component of the latter. One should expect CBI service anyway in his Workshop, and he won't expect to go to a different terminal or to learn a different set of interactive concepts and skills to get that service; and also, that service will often bear directly upon concepts and matters deeply embedded in the workaday domain of his Workshop system.

It is also very probable (to my mind) that communities will ultimately integrate their Handbook and CBI techniques so that their monolithic, superdocument Handbook would contain the special tags, links and etc. required by the CBI computer processes so that a significant portion of the instructional services would be generated directly from the primary knowledge source, the Community Handbook.

MEETINGS AND CONFERENCES

This refers to assemblies of people, which occurrences aren't likely for a long time yet to be supplanted in total effect by technological aids. In supporting our own ARC meetings, demonstrations, etc., we use TV-projector equipment that projects our regular work-terminal display images onto a movie screen, easily readable in a meeting room having enough ambient light for comfortably reading notes and seeing each other. Images from live TV-cameras or from video recorders can also be projected. We make use of commercial devices for controlling these various video signals -- switching, mixing, and frame-splitting. We can mix two signals to get image superposition, or split the video frame to get a computer-display picture on one part of the screen and a camera image on the other (for example, simultaneously showing the camera view of the user's controlling actions right along with the display responses from the computer).

With this projector setup, we use our regular Workshop techniques in meetings to present and explain material from the on-line data base. It is easy to review and change the agenda and the meeting notes; some meetings operate very profitably in a mode of "collaborative position-statement development", with a facility that for many purposes is far superior to using a blackboard -- it is as though the blackboard now is very easily stretched to make room for new notes, edited, scrolled, folded, reorganized, or etc., and any available online material may be copied onto it for integration into the study, re-organization, re-wording, development process. A skilled Workshop user can operate this "blackboard" with enough speed and flexibility that these processes often don't seem to be what limits group progress (in the midst of questions, deliberations, etc.).

Any workshop user at the gathering can call on part of his own online notes, or use his familiarity with certain material, to bring special information before the assembly. Or, the whole assembly can see the display being controlled by another individual (or assembly) at a remote site, in shared-display dialogue. There are many further technical and procedural innovations to explore in improving the effectiveness of meetings -- e.g. computer-processed bio-feedback, radical changes in the "rules of order", and giving each participant independent use of a private display terminal.

COMMUNITY MANAGEMENT AND ORGANIZATION

Where the Community has conventional, project-management operations, their Workshop can include computer aids for such as PERT and CPM, plus the enriching services of dialogue support, document development, and a "Handbook" system. An extension of the Handbook could contain plans, commitments, schedules, specifications, current-state records of work in progress, etc., with special Workshop tools to support management analysis and control.

But also, with the probable increase in the amount and intensity of distributed collaboration within the Community, "committee work" would become more widespread, dynamic, and important. Thus there would be greater dependence upon better techniques for intercommunication and management within the committee-like structures by which a Community goes about its composite business. Harnessing these new techniques will lead to very different ways in which distributed communities can be organized and in which they can go about their business -- and the possibility of considerable improvement here, stemming from relatively modest innovative investments, is an important part of our motivation toward facilitating Community Workshop exploration.

SPECIAL KNOWLEDGE WORK BY INDIVIDUALS AND TEAMS

Assumedly, Community members could avail themselves of the
above types of Workshop service in support of their own daily
work -- i.e., for other than their participating in community-
oriented activities. There are obvious benefits to almost any
knowledge worker from use of general Workshop facilities such as
listed above; and for a team (or any close-working organizational
unit) of augmented knowledge workers, there is yet another level
of benefit to be gained by adopting new organizational structure
and collaborative methods that harness better the new capabilities
existing within the Workshop (as extended by a few special team-
support tools).

Then further, the particular set of disciplines and pursuits
which characterize the Community will generally have special
computer-based processes and data that are important in its work
-- i.e. unique functions and forms in its analytical programs,
statistical processes, numerical data, conceptual/analytic models,
graphic portrayals of subject matter, etc. Assuming that they are
available within the same computer network that distributes the
Community's Workshop-support services, then access to these
special computer-based resources can be provided to a worker
"through" the coordinated Workshop in which he does his other
work -- and to a distinct advantage.

In any of this special work, there is basic advantage in
having a flexible, powerful facility for managing mixed text and
graphics -- composing, studying, modifying, integrating new
material into working notes and reports, publishing, doing collaborative dialogue, giving presentations, etc. When doing tasks
of this sort in association with his special computer-based
operations, it is an important advantage to the worker to do so
within a familiar and consistent working environment. Our Workshop flexibly provides for special translation of information
passing back and forth to any such "external" computer service,
so that for access to a wide variety of such services the Workshop can provide users with consistent conventions and methods
in whose use his other Workshop tools would be of maximum support.

CONCLUSION

The full sense of what computer networks offer in the way of
"resource sharing" contains some special twists of significance
here: for one thing, a truly complete Workshop will contain a
very large repertoire of service functions, and the evolution,
operation, and maintainance of these functions (and their support
software) will require highly trained specialists. Any sort of
widespread exploration of augmented-Workshop techniques will be

very much facilitated by the network's capability for sharing the
expertise of such specialists -- by enabling central computational
resources that they develop and maintain to service distributed
users. Note that specialists working from their home workshop
will be able to reach through the network to install and maintain
software in remote hardware installations, which will be important, too; but note also that many already-present local computers
and operating systems are inappropriate for supporting all of the
important Workshop functions.

For another thing, the vocabulary and procedural skill
required to harness these functions effectively and smoothly into
one's worklife will become very extensive and sophisticated (the
pidgin-English approach won't provide the power, and full-state-
ment natural language isn't fast enough), and again special expertise will be necessary to help people through the learning
stages as their Workshop matures. Therefore, although the network
can very much facilitate bringing into user reach these powerful
Workshop tools, it requires the additional network-supported
(Workshop) facilities such as teleconferencing to enable a limited
number of Workshop specialists to give close support to these
learning processes, without which the computer services would have
much less value.

If exploration of Workshop use were to occur only where there
exists both an appropriate local computer system and trained
specialists to maintain the software and train the users, there
would be a very much slower evolution toward the increased
effectiveness possibilities offered by computer augmentation.

Finally, the "digital-packet transportation system" aspect of
a computer network seems quite essential to the practical, effective support of an augmented Community Knowledge Workshop --
which in turn seems to offer a really important and unique means
for sharing among a community of humans the distributed nuclei of
human resources represented by individuals with special knowledge,
judgement, intuition, imagination, conceptual skills, etc. This
human-resource sharing has explosive potential -- I look to it witl
a biological metaphor as providing a new evolutionary stage for
the nervous system of social organisms, from which much more highly developed institutional forms may evolve that are much improved
in: awareness of self and environment, situational cognizance and
response, visualization of the future, problem-solving capability,
etc. (See Reference 5 for expansion of this theme.)

REFERENCES

1. Drucker, Peter F., The Effective Executive, Harper and Row,
    New York, 1966. (XDOC --   3074,)

2. Drucker, Peter F., Age of Discontinuity: Guidelines to Our
    Changing Society, Harper and Row, New York, 1969. (XDOC --
    4247,)

3. Engelbart, D.C. and English, W.K., A Research Center for
    Augmenting Human Intellect, AFIPS Proceedings, Fall Joint
    Computer Conference, 1968, 33, 1, p. 395, 1968. (XDOC --
    3954,)

4. Engelbart; D. C., Experimental Development of a Small Computer-
    Augmented Information System, Annual Report to Office of
    Naval Research, covering period 15 April 1971 through 15
    April 1972, SRI-ARC 1972. (Journal -- 10045,)

5. Engelbart, D.C., Intellectual Implications of multi-access
    Computer Networks, Paper presented at the Interdisiplinary
    Conference on Multi-access Computer Networks, Austin, Texas,
    April 1970. To be published. (Journal -- 5255,)

6. Engelbart, D. C. , Coordinated Information Services for a
    Discipline- or Mission- Oriented Community, Proceedings of
    the Second Annual Computer Communications Conference at
    California, State University, San Jose, California,
    January 24-25, 1973, p.2.1 (Journal -- 12445,).

7. Engelbart, D. C., Watson, R. W. and Norton, J. C., The Aug-
    mented Knowledge Workshop, AFIPS Proceedings, National Com-
    puter Conference, June 1973, New York, p.9 (Journal -- 14724,)

8. Engelbart, D. C., Design Considerations for Knowledge Workshop
    Terminals, AFIPS Proceedings, National Computer Conference,
    June, 1973, New York, (Journal -- 14851,).

Topological Design Considerations in Computer Communication Networks

V. G. Cerf   D. D. Cowan   R. C. Mullin

Stanford   University of   University of
University   Waterloo   Waterloo

and

R. G. Stanton

University of
Manitoba

INTRODUCTION

In designing a computer-communication network, a large number of constraints must be considered so as to produce a reasonable network topology. Time delays, throughputs, cost, and reliability are some of the major factors connected with producing an optimum design. Each of these factors encompasses a large amount of detailed analysis which must be completed in order to check a network design.

Since network design is such a complex task, it is important to provide the designer with simple criteria for evaluation. Such criteria permit the network designer to develop an intuitive feeling for his designs, and to be aware of the effects of modifications on its parameters.

This paper uses a linear graph model of computer-communications networks to establish a lower bound on delay and vulnerability[1] for such networks. The networks which are analyzed have the property that their graphs are regular. The lower bound on delay is characterized by measuring the average minimum path length in these regular graphs. The vulnerability of these same networks is shown to be equal to the valence of one of the vertices for the trivalent graphs, and it is conjectured that this is true for higher valences.

Both these criteria would appear to be useful in that designers may measure their network against these so-called "ideal" networks. This paper will only describe the bounds. Subsequent papers will provide algorithms for construction of graphs which satisfy these bounds and proofs of the vulnerability criteria.

BACKGROUND

Many factors can influence the design of computer-communication networks. Constraints such as acceptable upper bounds on cost and delay and lower bounds on throughput and reliability can strongly influence the final design. In packet-switched store-and-forward networks[2,3], topology can play a major role in satisfying the delay and reliability constraints.

Packets leaving a source node are routed to intermediate nodes until they finally arrive at their destination node. At each node, a packet undergoes several forms of delay. These include processing delay, queueing delay (if other packets are also routed over the same channel), transmission delay, and propagation delay on the channel. Typically, a packet carries a checksum with it; thus, a packet arriving at a node cannot be forwarded until the last bit of the packet has arrived and the checksum has been verified. It seems apparent that minimizing the average number of nodes and communication lines a packet has to pass through to reach its destination can reduce delay; of course, an alternative routing strategy which is sensitive to local congestion may not always route the packet along the shortest path[4].

Reliability of networks can be characterized in several different ways depending upon the degree of refinement one requires in an analysis. Once a network has been designed, there are a variety of computational approaches to analyzing reliability which are neatly summarized in Frank and Chou[2]. According to Frank and Chou, present analytical approaches are computationally intractable for large networks and a combination of analysis and simulation is required to obtain estimates of parameters which characterize the reliability of a network and its components. Very little is known, a priori, about the reliability of networks except that duplication of components and selected over-connection seem to improve it.

There are several possible strategies for reducing delay and increasing reliability of a network, but in this paper we

concentrate on the effects of topology. Specifically, we examine
the relationship between average path length and the number of
nodes connected directly to a node (valence of the node).

This paper presents a study of networks which are represented
as linear graphs, and it is assumed the reader is familiar with
elementary notions of graph theory[5]. The analysis will be
directed to packet-switching networks, but most of the work
presented should be applicable to networks which use other
mechanisms for routing and switching data. The nodes or vertices
of the graph will be the packet-switching computers, and the
edges or links will represent the transmission lines.

It is possible for networks of arbitrary size to maintain a
maximum and average path length of either one or two. If every
node in an N-node network is connected to every other node, then
we have a network where each node has valence N-1 and the shortest
and average shortest path lengths are one. Figure 1 shows an
example for N=6. The reliability of this network is very high,
since every node is connected to every other node; however, the
number of edges is $\frac{N(N-1)}{2}$, and thus the cost of transmission lines
would increase with the square of the number of nodes. Such a
scheme is completely impractical for even moderate values of N.

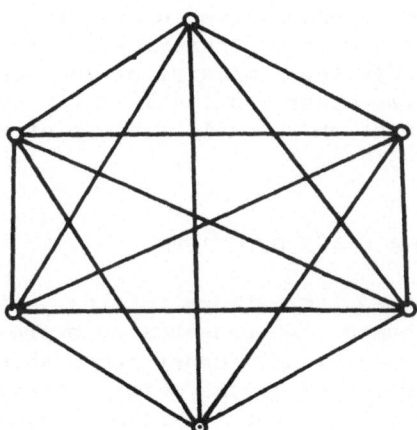

Fully connected 6 node graph

Figure 1

To keep the maximal shortest path length constant at two, one
can join all nodes through a central node as shown in the star
network of Figure 2. Here transmission line costs increase
linearly with N, but reliability and capacity of the central node

pose serious problems.

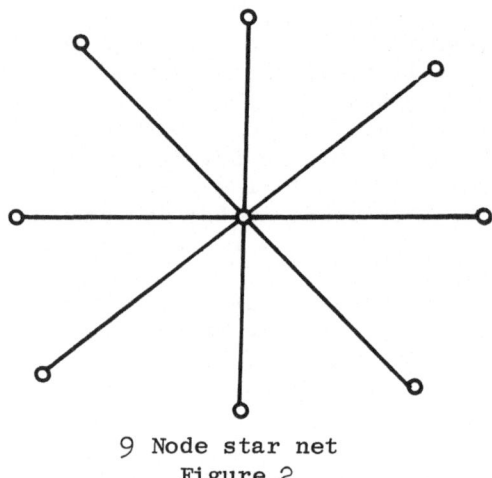

9 Node star net
Figure 2

Such extreme cases are impractical, and hence intermediate schemes with average valence between 2 and N-1 are of prime interest. The next portion of this paper examines the relationship between valence, average path length, and reliability. This relationship will allow an examination of the trade-off between average path length and number of transmission lines in the network; thus, we will develop a measure of the cost of a network as a function of its size under a suitable delay constraint. Some comments will also be made on the relationship of reliability and valence.

AVERAGE PATH LENGTH IN A CLASS OF GRAPHS

This section examines the network topology which produces minimum average path length, and presents an expression which is a lower bound on average path length under reasonable constraints. There is a short discussion of graphs which satisfy this lower bound, but the actual construction techniques are discussed in another paper[6].

The analysis is started by considering a tree with

$$1 + V \sum_{j=0}^{m-1} (V-1)^j \tag{1}$$

nodes in which each node has either valence V or valence 1. A

tree with 10 nodes and V=3 is illustrated in Figure 3. One node
is chosen as the root node and is labelled R in Figure 3. The
root node R is considered to be at distance zero from itself in
the tree, the V nodes adjacent to R are at distance one from R,
the $V(V-1)$ nodes adjacent to those at distance one are at distance
2, etc. For ease of expression nodes at distance m from R will be
referred to as "nodes at level m". The levels are shown on the
right side of Figure 3. A tree such as the one just described is
called a complete tree since new nodes can only be added by
starting a new level. In order to find the average path length
from R to all nodes in the tree, it is necessary to sum all paths
and then divide by N-1. Since there are V paths of length 1,
$V(V-1)$ paths of length 2, $V(V-1)^2$ paths of length 3, etc., the
average path length of a complete tree with m levels is

$$\frac{1}{N-1} \left[V \sum_{j=0}^{m-1} (V-1)^j (j+1) \right] . \tag{2}$$

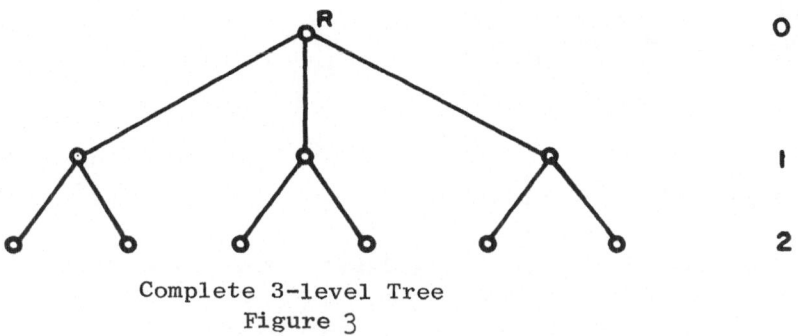

Complete 3-level Tree
Figure 3

By removing monovalent nodes at the highest numbered level
and their associated edges in the complete tree it is possible to
arrive at a formula for average path length in a more general tree
of this type. If the number of vertices in this tree is N, then
the number of vertices removed is

$$1 + V \sum_{j=0}^{m-1} (V-1)^j - N. \tag{3}$$

Then the average path length $P(N,V)$ in this "pruned" tree is

$$P(N,V) = \frac{1}{N-1} \left[V \sum_{j=0}^{m-1} (V-1)^j (j+1) \right.$$

$$\left. - \left(1 + V \sum_{j=0}^{m-1} (V-1)^j - N \right) m \right], \tag{4}$$

which can be written as

$$P(N,V) = \frac{1}{N-1} \left[V \sum_{j=0}^{m-1} (V-1)^j (j+1-m) + (N-1)m \right]. \tag{5}$$

One might note that

$$1 + V \sum_{j=0}^{m-1} (V-1)^j - N \geq 0. \tag{6}$$

and that m is the smallest integer which satisfies this inequality. Since

$$\sum_{j=0}^{m-1} (V-1)^j = \frac{(V-1)^m - 1}{V-2} \tag{7}$$

then

$$1 + \frac{V}{V-2} \left[(V-1)^m - 1 \right] - N \geq 0. \tag{8}$$

Also, if we use $\{y\}$ to denote the least integer $\geq y$, then

$$m = \left\{ \log_{V-1} \frac{N(V-2) + 2}{V} \right\}, \text{ for } V > 2. \tag{9}$$

If we substitute for m, it is possible to obtain a more explicit relation between the average path length $P(N,V)$, the number of nodes N, and the valence V.
It can easily be seen that

$$V \sum_{j=0}^{m-1} (V-1)^j (j+1) = \frac{V}{(V-2)^2} \left[m(V-1)^{m+1} \right.$$

$$\left. - (m+1)(V-1)^m + 1 \right] \tag{10}$$

and, using (7) and (10), the average path length can be written as

$$P(N,V) = \frac{1}{N-1}\left[V\left(\frac{m(V-1)^{m+1} - (m+1)(V-1)^m + 1}{(V-2)^2} \right) \right.$$

$$\left. - mV\left(\frac{(V-1)^m - 1}{V-2} \right) + (N-1)m \right]$$

$$= V\left[\frac{1 - (V-1)^m + m(V-2)}{(V-2)^2(N-1)} \right] + m$$

$$= \frac{V}{N-1}\left[\frac{1 - (V-1)^m + m(V-2)}{(V-2)^2} \right] + m \qquad (11)$$

Expression (11) can be rewritten, using (9), as

$$P(N,V) = \left\{ \log_{V-1} \frac{N(V-2) + 2}{V} \right\}$$

$$+ \frac{V}{(N-1)(V-2)^2}\left[1 - (V-1)\left\{ \log_{V-1} \frac{N(V-2) + 2}{V} \right\} \right.$$

$$\left. + (V-2)\left\{ \log_{V-1} \frac{N(V-2) + 2}{V} \right\} \right] \qquad (12)$$

This expression is dominated, for reasonably large N, by the leading logarithmic term. Therefore, the average path length from R to all nodes of the tree in Figure 3 is primarily logarithmic in N except for the case V=2 in which it is linear. Curves for P(N,V) for $2 < V < 6$ and $V+1 < N < 1000$ are shown in Figure 4, and these graphically illustrate the logarithmic nature of the average path length (and hence the delay) as a function of the number of nodes in the network. Table I presents a few values of average path length for different N and V. The reader should note the drastic reduction in average path length between the cases V=2 and V=3. But an increase to V=6 for N=900 only reduces the average path length by a factor of approximately 2, while it increases the number of edges in the graph from 1350 for V=3 to 2700 for V=6.

This analysis presents a derivation of the average path length for trees similar to the tree of Figure 3. It is certainly the minimum for a tree joining N nodes, since any method of connecting the nodes would either produce the same configuration or would violate the valence constraint. An important related question is whether it is possible to construct a graph which has valence V and for which expression (12) is also the minimum average

108

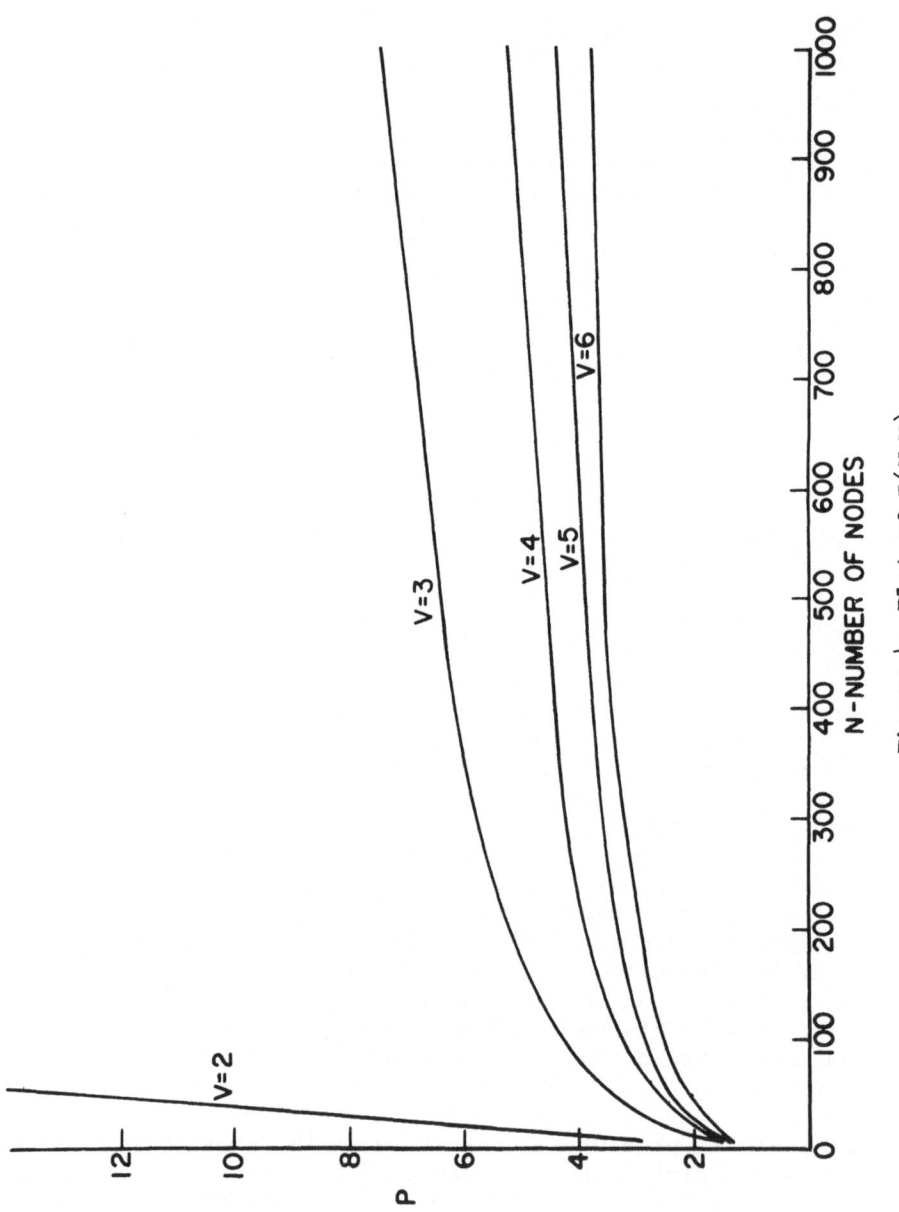

Figure 4 Plot of $P(N,V)$

path length. Such a graph could possibly be constructed if the nodes of valence unity of a tree such as the one in Figure 3 could be joined to make a V-valent graph such that, by choosing every node in turn as the root node, we could redraw the graph as a tree having a complete set of nodes at each of levels 0,1,2,...,m-1. Since all distance sets would be identical for each root node, the minimum average path length from each node would be the same, and therefore the minimum average path length for the entire graph would be expression (12). The maximum path length in such graphs is just m; so equation (9) shows that this quantity also grows logarithmically. Even if graphs with this property cannot be constructed for particular N and V, expression (12) still represents a desirable lower bound on average path length, and thus presents information about the behaviour of average path length, and hence delay, as a function of valence.

		V				
		2	3	4	5	6
	8	2.29	1.57	1.43	1.29	1.14
	20	5.26	2.37	1.95	1.74	1.68
N	50	12.76	3.41	2.59	2.39	2.14
	100	25.25	4.27	3.27	2.70	2.58
	250	62.75	5.55	4.07	3.45	3.08
	500	125.25	6.52	4.57	3.88	3.54
	900	225.25	7.32	5.20	4.38	3.75

Table I
Some Typical Values of $P(N,V)$

Fortunately, we are able to construct graphs which attain this lower bound for many values of N and V. The analysis of this problem in graph construction and the complete enumeration of many of the cases is discussed in another paper[6]. So far, graphs are known for V=3, and N=4, 6, 8, 10, 12, 14, 16, 18, 20, 24, 26, 28, 30, 34. It is also known that graphs do not exist for certain values of N[6]. An example of such a minimum average path length graph is shown in Figure 5. This is the graph for V=3 and N=10, and is the well known Petersen graph.

RELIABILITY OF NETWORKS

This section describes some preliminary results on the reliability of networks with minimum average path length. In particular, vulnerability of these networks is examined.

A basic measure of vulnerability[1] is usually defined to be the number of nodes and/or edges which must be removed from a network or connected graph in order to separate it into two disconnected components. An algorithm has been devised[1] which will compute the vulnerability of a given network, but there are no known results to describe the behaviour of a class of networks. The availability of knowledge of the behaviour of such a class would provide the network designer with an intuitive feeling for what could be achieved.

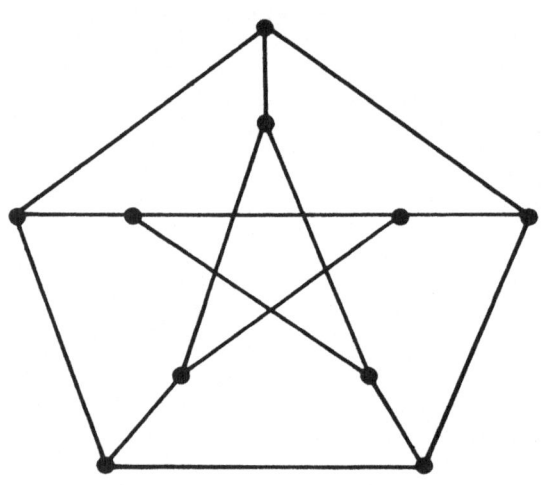

Figure 5
A Minimum Average Path Length Graph
for $N = 10$, $V = 3$, $P(N,V) = 5/3$

The class of graphs with minimum average path length has many properties which make it amenable to vulnerability analysis.

It has been shown[7] that the class of cubic or trivalent graphs satisfying the minimum average path length constraint are 3 - connected. This means that at least 3 nodes must be removed from the network before two disconnected components can be realized.

If we define connectivity or node-connectivity $K = K(G)$ as the minimum number of nodes in a graph G whose removal results in a trivial graph or a graph of two or more components, define line-connectivity $\lambda = \lambda(G)$ in an analogous fashion, and define $\delta = \delta(G)$ as the minimum valence in a graph, then these three quantities are related by an inequality due to Whitney [5,8], namely,

$$K(G) \leq \lambda(G) \leq \delta(G).$$

This inequality implies that, if each node of a graph has uniform valence V and if K=V, then λ=V also. For the case V=3, then λ=3.

We conjecture that graphs with minimum average path length and valence V are V-connected for V > 3. This conjecture seems reasonable, since graphs which satisfy the path length condition would have vertices "closely coupled" by edges.

The question of separating a graph into components by removing a mixed set of points and lines has been studied[5,9]. The separation of a graph G is characterized by a connectivity pair (a,b) which is an ordered pair of non-negative integers such that there is a set of a nodes and b edges whose removal disconnects the graph, and there is no set of a-1 nodes and b edges or a nodes and b-1 edges with this property.

For graphs which are V-connected, it has been shown[7] that there is a unique sequence of connectivity pairs which completely characterizes the vulnerability of the graph. The general expression for this sequence is

$$(V=0), \ (V-1,1), \ (V-2,2) \ ... \ (2,V-2), \ (1,V-1), \ (0,V).$$

The sum of the two entries in each pair is a constant V, and this means that a combination of nodes and edges whose sum is V will completely disconnect the graph or reduce it to the trivial graph.

CONCLUSIONS

This paper has studied certain properties of linear graphs representing computer-communication networks. In particular, an expression has been derived which provides a lower bound on the average path length of a graph with N nodes and constant valence V for each node. Graphs which satisfy this lower bound have been constructed for many values of N with particular emphasis on the value V=3. These graphs with minimum average path length have other properties which make them useful models for networks. Since they have nodes of constant valence, they also provide a convenient model for reliability analysis. In particular, for V=3, it has been shown that the graphs are 3-connected and that their complete connectivity, and hence vulnerability, can be specified. It is conjectured that such graphs with higher valence V are V-connected. If this is the case, their vulnerability can also be completely specified.

This analysis describes an achievable lower bound on both path length and vulnerability for constant valence graphs, and provides a convenient norm against which the network designer can compare his designs.

ACKNOWLEGEMENTS

The authors would like to acknowledge the support of the Joint Services Electronics Program under contract number N-0014-67-A-0112-0044.

REFERENCES

1. Frisch, I. T., Analysis of the vulnerability of communication nets, Proceedings of the First Annual Princeton Conference on Systems Science, 1967, 188.

2. Frank, H. and Chou, W., Topological optimization of computer networks, IEEE Proceedings, 60, Nov 1972.

3. Gerla, M., The Design of Store-and-Forward (S/F) Networks for Computer Communications, School of Engineering and Applied Science, University of California, Los Angeles, 1973 (UCLA-ENG-7319).

4. Fultz, G. L., Adaptive Routing Techniques for Message Switching Computer-Communication Networks, School of Engineering and Applied Science, University of California, Los Angeles, 1972, (UCLA-ENG-7252).

5. Harary, F., Graph Theory, Addison-Wesley Publishing Co., New York, 1969.

6. Cerf, V. G., Cowan, D. D., Mullin, R. C. and Stanton, R. G., The Generalized Moore Graph, to appear.

7. Cowan, D. D., Some Results on the Connectivity of Trivalent Generalized Moore Graphs, Computer Communications Network Group, Department of Computer Science, University of Waterloo, Waterloo, 1973.

8. Whitney, H., Congruent graphs and the connectivity of graphs, American Journal of Mathematics, 54, 150, 1932.

9. Beineke, L. W. and Harary, F., The connectivity function of a graph, Mathematika, 14, 197, 1967.

DESIGN APPROACH TO A COST EFFECTIVE ENVIRONMENTAL PROTECTION
DATA BASE SYSTEM

D.N. Berg

Stanford Research Institute, Menlo Park, California USA

INTRODUCTION

This paper is based upon experiences obtained during the
development of a concept definition of the U.S. Navy Environmental
Protection Data Base (NEPDB) System.[1] This concept definition was
done by SRI for the Navy Civil Engineering Laboratory at Port
Hueneme, California, in 1972 as the first phase in a design and
development effort for a Navy system for the accumulation and
organization of environmental data to allow the Navy to meet its
environmental protection responsibilities.

The impetus for the design of such a system came from a
series of Presidential Orders, Department of Defense Directives
and Navy Instructions that detailed the responsibilities of Navy
operating elements to meet environmental laws and standards
promulgated at all governmental levels. In order to meet these
environmental protection responsibilities, the Navy had to have a
mechanism by which they would know what effect each Navy facility
was having on the environment. This mechanism took the form of a
system that would collect data on Navy activities as they pertain
to the environment and provide an information service for all Navy
elements that sought data to help these elements meet their
environmental protection responsibilities. The goal of the NEPDB
conceptual design effort was to develop a system that would provide
maximum utility to its users and that, within the available
resources and technology, would be the most cost effective.

The challenge in this project was strengthened by various uncertainties that exist within the environmental area. Environmental technology is developing swiftly and changing rapidly. A great deal is not known at this time of environmental effects and of the interactions between various pollutants. Additionally, the Navy has unique user requirements as well as the need to have a system that would have an early operating capability plus the ability to respond to ever-changing environmental protection standards and regulations over a long period of time.

METHOD OF APPROACH

The basis for this design was the development of the NEPDB system user's requirements the type of data needed, the form desired and the response time demands envisaged. From this the data base contents and organization were defined and the services that the system would provide to the users were determined.

Several specific analyses were required at this point. The first was to obtain a desirable mix of automatic and manual operating capabilities. The second was to examine the issues of centralization or decentralization of the location of operational facilities which would form a part of the data base system. The third was to define the functions that the system was to perform and the alternatives for performing these various functions.

Based upon the foregoing analyses, alternatives could be developed that postulated the establishment of a small relatively manual capability with some computer aids phased over a time period that would allow the incorporation of subsequent sophisticated data processing hardware and software.

Evaluation of the various alternatives to verify cost effectiveness results that were postulated was undertaken. Estimates of development and operating staff were made for the initial operating period. Additionally, a set of possible trouble areas were specified and a set of possible approaches were suggested to ensure that the design would follow a set of procedure leading to a cost effective approach.

USER REQUIREMENTS STUDY

Because the desired outcome of this study by the Navy was maximum system usefulness yet a cost effective system structure, this design effort emphasized the analysis of the needs of potential system users. A system's acceptance by its intended users has been dependent in the past upon the ease by which it can be used, the system's ability to provide either an answer directly or at least to point toward the location of an answer and by the form and context in which an answer is given. To be able to provide the above listed capabilities, an extensive analysis of the present responsibilities for and the activities in relation to environment protection in the Navy were required.

Thus, the first step in this study was an extensive analysis of the environmental orders, directives and instructions that were issued from the President, Department of Defense and top level Navy authorities. Each authority has outlined what is required within its purview, but each authority addresses a different level of management. Thus, these pronouncements specify policy, responsibility or requirements, depending on the level at which they apply. Each of these levels had to be examined to determine the environmental information required to support the activity.

This latter effort required an understanding of the Navy's complex organizational structure and the location of organizational entities that had responsibilities for each type of environmental protection activity. This examination indicated that the information required should be aggregated and summarized at the higher authority levels and become definitive and detailed as the information was required at the lower levels of authority.

Another portion of this user requirements analysis addressed the question of which Navy elements should be direct participants in NEPDB system either as a contributor of environmental data or as a user of environmental information. It is evident that this system requires the cooperation of Navy agencies in providing data that the system needs to hold and manage. Furthermore, it was recognized that in order for the system to function properly that certain selected Navy entities be formally made a part of the NEPDB system. This latter step would ensure that collected environmental data be put into the system on a regular basis and that a means for involving potential users in systems be developed.

ENVIRONMENTAL DATA BASE

The environmental data base to be used in this system was
developed based upon two different approaches: (1) analysis of
the environmental events framework within which the Navy operates
and interacts with the environment, and (2) analysis of user
requirements and expected queries of the NEPDB. Each of these
approaches taken separately and carried out in sufficient detail
for a long enough time would produce the desired information as to
what data should be kept in the data base. As there was insufficient time and resources available to pursue these courses, a
combination of the two approaches was taken in an attempt to produc
a similar result in the alloted time.

The Environmental Effects Framework (EEF) is basically a
model which provides a way to relate each of the actions within
an operation to its effect on the environment. This model uses
those actions that produce effects on their surroundings and show
each step in this process occurs. As the EEF is quite generalized,
it was necessary to develop specific interactions between Navy
operations and the environment in which such operations were
performed. In this way certain types of data could be identified
as necessary components of the data base.

The other approach allowed a categorization of environmental
data based upon the user requirements analysis. This approach
required an examination of the basic operations of Navy organizational elements with regard to the environmental impacts they
produced. Following this data categorization effort, specific
types of data within each category that were required to satisfy
user's needs were determined.

NEPDB SYSTEM FUNCTIONS

The basic operations required of the NEPDB system had been
specified by the client at the beginning of the study. That is,
the system must have the capability to answer user's questions
and produce periodic status reports on the system operation.
Except for these basic functions, the designer was given wide
leeway in the selection of the remaining functions, as long as
they could be justified. Therefore, SRI specified a set of
basic functions comprising the following: referral to obtain the
location of a source of information; retrieval of information

located in existing NEPDB accessible data bases; periodic inspection
and analysis of measurement data produced by Navy monitoring
stations to determine if standards were being met; and various
system support functions necessary to update, maintain and modify
system operation.

These functions were explicitly defined and their operations
and interactions shown in a series of flow charts. Detailed flow
charts were not produced, except as an example of two or three
special functions to show what level of detail would have to be
eventually done in the next design stage.

SYSTEM OPERATION

In addition to the basic design constraints of system usefulness and cost effectiveness, the client specified that the system
must obtain an initial operating capability in less than a year
following the completion of the preliminary deiign. This latter
requirement meant that a detailed system design and initial system
implementation had to be completed in a much shorter time than
was usual for a system of this size and complexity. The only way
that such an accelerated result could be obtained was to specify
an appropriately limited initial operating capability and provide
for a moderate and well planned growth capability. This approach
would ensure that the system was able to provide a set of
satisfactory services for a limited number of topics and, in some
cases, provide results with a relatively slow response time.

Given these constraints, an examination was made of how the
specified NEPDB functions would be performed. It was evident that
a number of functions could be performed by or supported by a
computer, but the development of the software and overall system
to support such automatic operations could not be completed and
checked out by the time of initial operating capability.

Therefore, the initial system would have to be largely
manually operated with some limited amount of computer support.
A preliminary manually operated system was consistent with our
basic design concept--that an implementation of a complete system
capable of responding to all inquiries in an environmental field
frought with rapidly changing technology and incomplete understanding of environmental effects should not be completed in one
effort; rather, the system implementation should be carried out in

a series of steps with the progress from one step to the next being made possible by the learning process obtained from the previous stage's operating experience.

Among the various possibilities for computer support to perform system functions, the automation of indices that provide information locations was the most promising. The most often performed function is that of searching for an information source or for expert opinion on a given topic. If, for example, a question is raised about the environmental impact of constructing a new paint removing facility, then several pieces of information are required. The environmental standards regarding establishing a new facility and operating a paint removing process that are specified by the federal, state, city and local governments must be examined. These standards may be stored in a file drawer, in documents in a library, in microfilm or microfiche form, etc. These standards may be located in one building, in dispersed repositories throughout the country or a combination of these two possibilities. The form in which standards can be kept are also varied; i.e., the standards can be kept in their entirety or abstracts of the standards can be held, etc. No matter which of these possibilities occur, the person seeking standards information must have an index or directory that will provide information as to their location, how they can be accessed and, possibly, the form in which the information is kept.

Thus an index or directory is a vital part of such a system and compelling reasons exist for developing it on a computer. First, the computer is well suited for holding large quantities of data that must be quickly and easily accessed. Cross referencing of items requires two way links between pieces of data that are related and, by use of "pointers", computers can handle such operations efficiently. The strongest reason for using a computer for the indexing is that the updating of the index is much faster, simpler, efficient and less error prone than a manual updating process. For a properly designed index the computer programs are written to allow insertion, deletion, modification and all updating to employ the full capability of the computer to do the drudgery and bookkeeping ordinarily done by a clerk. The computer also allows a self checking and validation process to be employed and this significantly reduces the possibility for errors.

Another type of automation that could aid the system operation is that of a microfilm document handling capability. Documents or pages of data can be indexed on microfilm in several ways. The location of a particular material can be specified by a microfiche number and frame or the first frame of microfiche used as the index to the remaining frames on that fiche. The present state of microfilm handling technology is rapidly changing and costs are becoming quite competitive. However, there are a few technical problems to be solved when large amounts of data are to be stored on microfilm. Additionally, there has been a general reluctance for people to use microfilm on a regular working basis due to previous cumbersome equipment and accessing methods. This latter problem is serious in that a system can fail to be used if complex or tedious processes discourage potential system users.

SYSTEM CONFIGURATION AND ORGANIZATION

The user requirements analysis established that the participation of personnel, that were presently involved in the system or that were projected to be responsible for collecting environmental data throughout the U.S., was necessary for the NEPDB system. These personnel were to be alloted official duties in support of the NEPDB system to ensure that the system was not just an information center dependent on the voluntary support from outside sources. Specific guidelines for the interaction between participating Navy agencies were outlined within the design study.

A major design activity was the analysis to determine the extent of centralization or decentralization of the NEPDB computing resources. A small NEPDB information center had already been established with very limited personnel and computing resources. This effort focused mainly on the gathering of some reference material on environmental protection and one or two experimental computer programs. This information center could be expanded and could obtain more computing capability if that was recommended by the design. The Navy has the possibility of accessing several computers throughout the U.S. that are presently being partially used for other purposes. Another alternative would allow this Navy sponsor to buy or rent, as appropriate, computers to support the NEPDB activities.

Each of these computing alternatives were feasible as long as
their use was justified. In order to decide which alternative
was the most suitable, several other factors had to be investigated.
For example, it had to be decided if environmental data collected
at Navy facilities would be transmitted as raw data or if it would
be computer processed first before being transmitted. The method
of transmitting data via mail, telecopier, special messenger or
computer network had also to be considered.

Furthermore, the question of how a user that wished to put a
question to the NEPDB system would access it--via telephone, mail,
computer network, etc.--had to be decided. Inherent in this last
question is the role that would be performed by NEPDB system
members (members can be located at various Navy facilities across
the U.S. or at the NEPDB information center). If the widely
distributed NEPDB members were either to answer questions directly
or following a referral from the center, then some communication
means would have to be considered that would provide easy access to
these decentralized contacts by a questioner. In this case
communication by telephone would likely be the easiest method that
would provide relatively fast response. Communication via a
computer network would be at least as fast as by telephone and
could provide additional valuable capabilities that could not be
obtained otherwise; however, the cost would be higher.

The advantages provided by a computer network, such as the
ARPANET, are quite impressive for the use by the NEPDB system. The
ability to communicate with another person via a computer terminal
enhances the mutual exchange and understanding between two people
sharing similar concerns. For example, information can be efficientl
obtained, reports or data files can be rapidly transferred, news of
current events can be quickly disseminated, common information
files can be updated in a much easier and efficient manner, etc.
Networks can also allow a person to access other computers and
programs that otherwise could not be feasibly used--a wealth
of resources become available through a computer network. In the
case of the NEPDB system, the use of networks appears to be most
valuable when the system has grown enough to have settled on the
services it would find most useful to offer and when the system
growth has stabilized. The cost of providing network capabilities
is still quite high, but, as seen from the ARPANET experience, these
costs are becoming lower all the time and appear that they will be
competitive before too long.

COST EFFECTIVENESS CONSIDERATIONS

Almost each of the areas of the study discussed up to this point have already considered many different concepts in terms of their cost effectiveness. The most constraining requirement has been the necessity for an initial operating capability in less than a year. This latter requirement eliminated many possible alternatives for the initial system as there would be no assurance of the system's effectiveness under the constraint of insufficient time to develop capabilities and test them out.

Other considerations that affected the system effectiveness that could be obtained were those involving the agencies that would be used as a part of the system and those procedures that were acceptable to other Navy elements as users of the system. That is, realistically, the NEPDB system had to operate within an internal political milieu that exists in the Navy and, thus, could not expect to implement operating conditions that were unacceptable to other Navy elements.

Cost factors turned out to be less of a constraint than the above, due to the early system operation deadline. However, the centralization of computing resources was more attractive from a cost viewpoint that decentralization via computer networks or otherwise due to the availability of computers in this particular situation in the initial NEPDB stage. Further stages of the NEPDB system growth would have to reassess the cost questions when more capability would be added and more computer support would be used.

STUDY CONCLUSIONS AND RECOMMENDATIONS

The NEPDB design study reached several conclusions for the initial NEPDB system that were based upon the very short deadline for an initial operating capability and that were developed to meet the system usefulness and cost effectiveness criteria. These conclusions are:

(1)   The NEPDB System must employ representatives from Navy facilities that produce measurements and collected environmental data.

(2)   The initial NEPDB system will be mostly manually operated, with computer support increasing as the system grows.

(3) The NEPDB system will employ extensively computer
     generated indices to locations of standards, pollution
     control authorities, Naval elements, facilities
     inventories, environmental data sets, etc.

(4) Microfilm will be initially used for archive data, but
     consideration will be given to the use of microform
     equipment for retrieval and storage of data or documents.

(5) The NEPDB system will be decentralized in terms of
     supporting agencies and personnel, but centralized in
     its computing resources at least initially.

(6) The assumptions and decisions upon which this design
     effort has been based must be validated by actual
     experience with the initial system operation.

(7) The growth and direction for expansion of the NEPDB
     system must be based upon a learning process obtained
     from each stage of the system's augmentation.

REFERENCES

1. Berg, D.N., Concept Definition of the Navy Environmental
    Protection Data Base (NEPDB) System, Stanford Research
    Institute Final Report for U.S. Naval Civil Engineering
    Laboratory, June 1972

SIMULATION STUDIES

by

T. H. Beeforth and D. J. Woollons

University of Sussex
Falmer, Brighton,
Sussex.

This paper is in two sections and deals with some of the work on data communications which has been conducted at the University of Sussex. Firstly there is a general description of the packet switching system which has been studied, together with some performance characteristics obtained by simulation. Secondly there is a discussion of research which has been conducted into routing strategies for data communication networks in general. The aim of the latter work is to give optimum traffic distribution over the network and high acceptance of new calls under heavily loaded conditions.

First the Sussex proposals. These relate to a packet switched system as mentioned above and assume that a partly connected high level network is to be used. In this network messages are transmitted between exchanges as a series of discrete packets of information, each of which is a self-contained entity containing the data needed to govern its route through the system. Packets can be stored temporarily within the exchanges comprising the network, thus allowing the effects of heavy short-term loading of the network to be alleviated.

ROUTING

In such a data communication network, operating upon store-and-forward principles three approaches may be considered for establishing routes between source and destination exchanges.

(a)   Fully predetermined routing in which every message between any pair of exchanges always follows the same route.

(b)   Adaptive packet routing in which individual packets of any message are free to travel different routes from source to destination; that is routing is a dynamic process determined for each packet from considerations of system loadings, delay times, etc.

(c)   Adaptive message routing in which all packets of a particular message follow the same route, but other messages between the same pair of exchanges are free to travel along different routes.

This last alternative is the one which has been adopted. When a call is to be set up a single route search packet is passed through the network from source to intended destination and reserves link capacity appropriate for the subsequent message proper. The route search packet is forwarded progressively from exchange to exchange within the network, each one deciding the most suitable forwarding link.

If a route is established all subsequent message packets are then constrained to follow it. This procedure confers several advantages.

(1)   It forms a convenient method for limiting the total input traffic into the network to below the desired maximum level.

(2)   By the use of a route-reply message which is returned from destination to source the source

terminal is advised, <u>before</u> commencing to send
the actual message, of the availability of both
a route through the network and of the destination
terminal.

(3) As has been mentioned, sophisticated route search
techniques can be employed to distribute traffic
more evenly over the network.

(4) The routing and control information required in
each message packet can be reduced since each one
need contain only abbreviated routing data to
allow it to follow the previously determined path.
It is not necessary, for example, for each packet
to hold the complete destination address.

(5) Finally, a consequence of the route search is the
possibility of the inclusion of facilities such
as the provision of different priority classes for
use during busy periods.

It should be emphasised that any routes established
involve only that proportion of the available link
capacities which are required to cater for the mean
expected information rate of the message packets following their corresponding route searches. Instantaneous,
or short-term overloading of the inter-exchange links,
which is inevitable if messages having uneven data rates
are traversing the network, is automatically accommodated by the storage facilities of the node exchanges.

The flow of packets in the network is controlled
by an acknowledgement and signalling system. All
packets are checked for possible transmission errors
between each pair of exchanges, and a positive acknowledgement is returned for each packet correctly received
by an exchange. In addition, the progress of message
data packets is controlled by a number of flags at
every exchange, one allocated to each message passing
through that exchange.

This is illustrated in Figure 1. Initially a data packet enters exchange P, on the left. This is forwarded to Q and the flag, which is shown symbolically above the exchange at P, is set (put down). The packet reaches Q, and an acknowledgement is returned to P. This packet is then forwarded from Q to R, setting the flag at Q. When it reaches R an acknowledgement is sent to Q and thence is returned as a signalling packet to P resetting the flag there. This allows a further message packet to enter exchange P - an action which can only occur when the flag at that exchange is reset.

This system ensures that:-

(1) Packets of a message can only enter an exchange when the previous packet has been successfully received by the exchange next but one along the route. Or, to put it another way, they can only enter an exchange when a packet has been successfully <u>forwarded</u> from the <u>next</u> exchange along the route.

(2) The number of data packets of a particular message that can reside in any exchange at a given time can be readily controlled. For a given packet length this limits the peak storage necessary in individual exchanges. At present it is proposed to have one packet per message stored per exchange. Even so it is still possible to have a large number of different messages using each inter-exchange link simultaneously, and thus it would be uneconomic to provide buffer storage sufficient for one packet of each of them at every exchange. Hence less storage than this is provided at the exchange and an additional count system, operating in parallel with the flag and signalling system is used to restrict the number of packets which may reside in an exchange at any time.

(3) The control and signalling system ensures that data packets are passed along the route in the correct sequence, eliminating ordering problems at the destination.

(4)   Transmission errors arising in the network can be
      corrected by retransmission thus reducing the
      number of such errors which need to be referred
      to the subscriber.

(5)   In the event of a serious fault developing within
      an exchange, or within a transmission link, the
      absence of acknowledgement and signalling packets
      ensures that the flags at previous exchanges along
      the route become progressively set. In other words,
      message packets accumulate, one per exchange for
      each message, back to the source. This may be
      used to notify the subscriber that unanticipated
      delays are occurring and to advise him to cease
      transmission.

(6)   On the debit side the acknowledgement procedure
      limits the rate at which packets can be passed
      along a link. Because a message cannot be for-
      warded from an exchange until the previous one has
      been successfully received by the next exchange
      but one, the shortest interval between transmission
      of successive packets of any message is equal to
      the sum of the delays incurred by a message packet
      in traversing two successive exchanges along the
      route plus the time taken for the subsequent ack-
      nowledgement and signalling procedure. This
      determines the effective maximum rate at which a
      message can be transmitted through the network.

      Figure 2 shows the packets involved in a complete
message. Firstly the route-search and route-reply and
their acknowledgements. Secondly two data packets, one
in each direction, and their acknowledgement and
signalling packets. Finally the message shut down
procedure using a clear packet.

EXCHANGE ORGANISATION

      The packet switching exchange performs three
main functions, namely reception of message packets,
processing of message packets and transmission of

message packets. Hence it consists of input link terminal units, output link terminal units, a control processor, and blocks of store which are used both for holding message packets being handled by the exchange and for containing the exchange control program.

Each packet, whether control or data, received by an exchange is stored in a sequential block of store starting at a specified block pointer address. All subsequent reference to the packet information by control programs is then made with respect to this block pointer address. After a packet has been correctly received and stored the input link terminal unit transfers the packet block pointer address to the tail of an input queue. There is a common input queue for all input links.

When the block pointer address reaches the head of the input queue the packet is processed and the block pointer address is either transferred to the tail of an output queue if forward transmission is required, or if no further transmission of the packet is necessary, is placed in the list of available block pointer addresses. Each outgoing link has its own output queue.

The output link terminal unit reads entries from the head of its output queue, transmits the message packet referenced by these entries and places the block pointer addresses of these packets at the tail of an associated repeat queue to await erasure by subsequent acknowledgement of correct receipt from the following exchange, or to be retransmitted if such acknowledgement is not received.

Each input and output link terminal unit consists of a small processor operating independently of the main control computer. Communication between these units and the central control is via shared buffer stores, removing the necessity for interrupting the control processor, and as a consequence, eliminating the time overheads which would be incurred in servicing such interrupts.

EXCHANGE PERFORMANCE

The exchange computer has been simulated using a double processor Modular One system. One processor acts as the control machine whilst the other simulates the external world generating and receiving messages and acting as input and output link terminal units. The control programs necessary to implement the system philosophy just described have been written and the run times of these, together with the associated context changing overheads have been used to estimate the exchange performance.

As has been seen, for each message an exchange must process a route search, route reply and clear packet plus associated acknowledgement and signalling packets, in addition to the message data packets. The number of data packets to be processed, and hence of acknowledgement and signalling packets, is dependent on the ultimate message length and packet size. In general, a link fully loaded with short packets requires more computation than a link with all long packets.

This is summarized in figure 3 and shows the maximum throughput to subscribers data which the exchange can accommodate, for a maximum packet length of 1024 bits, as a function of message length. The corresponding link traffic is also shown and this includes all the previously mentioned overheads together with those incurred by the necessity to transmit error check and packet framing digits.

EXCHANGE DELAYS

Figure 3 shows the performance which could be expected from an isolated exchange. In order to predict the response time of the proposed system a simulation has been performed to estimate the effect of varying system parameters upon exchange delays within the network. The delay encountered by a packet travelling along a route involving several exchanges can then be deduced from the individual stage delays.

Individual stage delays may be defined as <u>the time interval between the last bit of a packet arriving at an exchange and its subsequent arrival at the following exchange</u>. They are made up of a number of terms.

(1)   The delay waiting in the input queue after arrival at an exchange. This is a function of processor loading.

(2)   The processing time. In our case this is approximately constant and independent of loading.

(3)   The delay whilst the processed packet waits in the output queue ready for onward transmission. This delay depends on the output link loading and link rate.

(4)   The time taken to send the packet on the output link. When the packet reaches the head of the output queue it is transmitted. This takes a time governed by the packet length (L bits) and the link rate (R bits/sec).

(5)   Finally there is the link transmission delay. The effect of system loading variations upon these delays has been investigated both by simulation and by the application of queueing theory and closely corresponding results have been obtained.

The simulation has been performed for an exchange serving 3 full-duplex links. It incorporates the run times of the individual control programs and the acknowledgement generation procedure of the proposed network. Four types of packet are considered: data packets, data packet acknowledgements, signalling packets and signalling packet acknowledgements. A rectangular distribution is used to determine the type of packet entering the exchange and a similar distribution is used to determine the input and output link to be employed. Data packet acknowledgements are converted to signalling packets and routed through the exchange but signalling packet acknowledgements terminate at the exchange. This corresponds to the actual operation of an exchange within the proposed network. For packets being routed through the exchange a test is made to ensure that the input and output links are different. The exact time of arrival of a packet on a link is adjusted so as to produce the particular desired loading of that link. The input and output processes are arranged to work autonomously with the main process.

Results of the simulation are shown in Figure 4. These were obtained for an exchange serving three 48 k tered by a sample of 300 data packets traversing the exchange.
exchange.

At low output link loadings the waiting time in the output queue is low compared to the actual time (L/R) taken to place the packet on a link. As the mean loading of the link increases, however, due to the increased probability of packets simultaneously requiring it, the output queue delay becomes more dominant.

Figure 5 shows the effect of varying link rates and packet lengths. Mean delays are reduced by increasing the link rate since the output time (and hence output queue service time) of a packet is decreased as the link rate rises. Moreover reducing the packet size also decreases the output queue service time and hence decreases the stage delay. However it should be pointed out that, for a given message length, reducing the packet size increases the load upon the control processor and reduces the link efficiency. This effect is seen in curves D and C. In curve C the control processor can cope with three input and output links operating at 480 k bit/s and a packet length of 1024 bits. But when the packet size is reduced to 512 bits (curve D) the processor maximum loading is exceeded.

As has been mentioned earlier the acknowledgement and signalling procedure used in the proposed system imposes a limit on the maximum rate at which packets of the same message can flow through the network. The delay between the time when the first packet of a message is placed in any exchange output queue to the time when the next packet of the same message can commence queueing is determined by the delay which the first packet incurs in passing to the next-but-one exchange plus the delay which the acknowledgement and signalling packets incur in returning from that exchange. The individual stage delays just described have been used to obtain estimates of the maximum message rates which are attainable in the system.

All links are assumed to have the same loading, in other words the network traffic is assumed to be evenly distributed. The results are shown in the lower curve of figure 6.

At low network loadings, and using 48 kbit/s links a maximum rate of 22 kbit/s can be obtained. Messages with rates below the values upon this curve may be sent through the network without the control procedure introducing any additional delays. And, of course, a number of messages at these rates can be accommodated simultaneously upon each link.

Alternative packet-handling philosophy

As the system has been described, and indeed in switching systems in general, it is usual to store each message packet in its entirety at each exchange along a route. At each exchange packets commence queueing for service by the exchange control processor only after the complete packet has been received within the exchange. Hence even if the exchange loading is light there is still a significant delay due to the waiting necessary whilst the packet is received from the link (this takes 22 ms for a 1048 bit packet at 48 kbit/s.

For message packets, however, it is strictly only necessary to have received the packet heading information before forward transmission can start. Hence there is a possible advantage to be gained if queueing for the control processor starts immediately after the header is received.

Under lightly loaded conditions this policy results in packets being stored simultaneously at the exchanges along a route, rather than sequentially as is normal, since actual output of a packet may be started before the complete packet has been received. As the network becomes more loaded however this probability decreases.

The effect of this procedure upon maximum message rate is also shown in figure 6, this time by the upper curve.

The procedure necessitates more processing by the exchange than did the original system. For example

(1) The exchange must distinguish between message data packets and network control packets.

(2) Each packet must contain two checks - one for the header and one for the data.

(3) The processing needed to determine when an acknowledgement should be returned must test that both the header and data checks are correct.

However, as can be seen from the figure, a worthwhile increase in maximum message rate can be achieved, especially at low network loadings.

SIMULATION OF NETWORK ROUTING METHODS

In the first part of this paper, the overall Sussex system, and the individual data switching exchanges have been described. Obviously, the characteristics of the exchange are of great importance in

determining the characteristics of the complete network,
but of equal importance is the effectiveness with which
the high-level network can be matched to actual traffic
demand.

This matching is determined to a large extent by the
particular method chosen to route traffic through the
network. The object of this second part of the paper
is to compare the effectiveness of different strategies,
and to explain the desirability of using some form of
adaptive routing.

Figure 7 shows the Sussex high-level network. A
very simple routing method would be to ascribe in
advance a particular route to each possible source-
destination combination, which will always be used when
the corresponding route request arises. If the route
is not available when required because of an overload,
or breakdown somewhere along it, the route search will
be terminated as a failure; no alternatives will be
considered.

In setting up these predetermined routes, an
arbitrary choice is made, once and for always, where
there is more than one equivalent direct route.

The resultant performance of the network operated
with this very simple routing method is shown in figure
8. At zero system loading, any request for a route will
be met, and the traffic acceptance rate is 100%. At
higher loadings congestion develops until at only 43%
overall loading the system saturates. Some of the
links are now full to capacity and routes that should
be using those links are rejected, and the acceptance
rate falls abruptly below 100%.

The abrupt fall in acceptance rate seems to be a
typical characteristic of the different routing methods
studied, although the system loading at which it occurs
is found to vary considerably from one method to
another. In practice, the break point may well indicate
the limit above which the acceptance rate would no

longer be acceptable to the subscriber.

It is to be noted that this saturation occurs at a system loading well before the average message delay time has risen appreciably above its minimum, zero-loading value, e.g. figure 5, but saturation neverthe-less has important repercussions on the overall subscriber-to-subscriber delay, since an additional, external delay arises, before subscribers are accepted by the system.

For a given network, then, it is important both that individual exchange delays be minimised, and that the routing strategy be chosen to raise the onset of saturation to as high system loading as possible.

At Sussex University there is no real-life system. The individual exchange study is carried out by emulat-ing a complete exchange on a Modular One computer, and similarly, the network of figure 7 exists only as data fed to a simulation program.

It is therefore, a simple matter to modify the system. The topology of the high-level network, the individual exchange and link capacities, the traffic demand pattern, and the routing method may all be altered comparatively quickly and at little cost. By using an interactive light pen facility networks may be drawn manually, and the corresponding network perform-ance displayed within a few seconds.

The value of simulation results is often questioned, in view of the fact that high-level simulations gloss over many of the low level, but nevertheless essential, practical operating details, and indeed the 43% saturation point of figure 8 may be considerably different from the value that would be observed if such a system were actually built. The value of the simula-tions here, as will be seen later, is in the comparative nature of the results rather than in their individual absolute values.

The simulation proceeds by generating source-destination pairs of exchanges at random, and using the particular routing method being studied, attempts to establish a route between each source and destination. If the route-search is a success, network loadings are correspondingly augmented so that the overall system loading gradually increases up to, and beyond, saturation.

Saturation can be due to either maximum link or exchange processor capacities being reached. Each packet passing through a network is subject essentially to a series of two alternating queueing delays, either for an exchange processor, or for an appropriate output link. In a link limited situation, queueing for an output link introduces the most significant delay, and figure 8 referred to such a situation. Later figures will refer to the exchange limited system.

Clearly at 43% saturation, much of the network is still very lightly loaded. It would therefore appear desirable, in preventing the localised congestion that results in saturation, to spread the network load more evenly, and the objective of the remaining routing methods is basically just that.

When selecting predetermined direct routes for the simple routing method described above, the choice between alternative possibilities should be decided not arbitrarily, but in such a way as to even out the expected link usage.

For example, the route between exchanges 8 and 20 may be expressed

$$R_{8 \to 20}: \quad L_{8 \to 14} + C_n(L_{14 \to 19} + L_{19 \to 20}) +$$
$$(1 - C_n)(L_{14 \to 15} + L_{15 \to 20})$$

where the value of C_n is constrained to be either unity, indicating the route $8 \to 14 \to 19 \to 20$, or zero, indicating the route $8 \to 14 \to 15 \to 20$.

Six hundred such expressions are written, one for each source-destination combination, and then summed to give each link usage in the form:

$$L_{14 \to 19}: 39 + C_a + C_d - C_j + C_n \text{ ---}$$

Linear programming may then be used to find values of the various C such that the spread in values of L is minimised.

Figure 9 shows the improvement in system performance resulting from such an approach. The saturation break point has been raised from about 43% to about 68%.

Since the simulation is at a comparatively high level, the precise values of the saturation figures of 43 and 68% above, may each be individually suspect, but there is little doubt about the real conclusion, namely, that the mark 2 predetermined, direct routing is very significantly better than the original version.

At this stage the obvious development is to let the choice between alternative direct routes be made at the time of the actual route-search. To find a route from exchange 8 to exchange 20 , the route search packet would be forwarded first to exchange 14 since any other link must involve a longer than the shortest, direct route. At exchange 14, the choice between forwarding to either exchange 19 or 15 is made as a result of considering local conditions at exchange 14. The final link in the route is fixed, being the direct link between either exchange 19 or 15 and the destination, 20.

Figure 10 shows network performance when an adaptive, progressive, direct routing method as above is employed. Route selection as at exchange 14 in the example, is simply by taking the least loaded of the possible forwarding links. The saturation breakpoint at 72% loading appears marginally better than the 68% of the mark 2 predetermined method but the difference is probably not very significant.

For interest rather than with any likelihood of practical implementation, figure 11 shows the result of a centralised routing control. Routes are decided only after reference to the state of the entire system and are not necessarily constrained to the most direct route. This difference between actual and shortest rout lengths gives rise to a corresponding difference between the actual system loading and the effective or useful load that the system is carrying. It is difficult to envisage routing strategies that could prove more effective than the centralised control method, and the 92% break point shows the efficient manner in which the network capacity is being used. However, the overheads associated with the method, in maintaining complete up-to-date information about the system, and in transmitting routing information, and also the vulnerability of the system if only a few control exchanges are used, suggest that alternative routing methods may be preferable provided they lead to comparable results with minimum complexity.

Figure 12 compares the improved predetermined, and the simple progressive adaptive routing methods compared where the limiting system factor is exchange processor capacity. Selection between alternative forwarding links is again by the loadings of those links rather than of the exchanges to which they go, despite the exchanges being the limiting factor. This is clearly simpler to implement in practice, and the high break-point justifies the decision.

While a system is operating under fairly constant, known, conditions it is matching a known demand to a known load, and it is not too surprising that a predetermined routing method can be devised that works more-or-less as well as the adaptive method. However the inherent inflexibility of a predetermined method suggests a weakness in coping with a changing demand pattern, or a changing network.

Figure 13 shows the system upset quite considerably by the total failure of exchange 8, and simultaneously link 14-18. That is to say one exchange and seven links out of action. Figure 14 shows the performances of the predetermined and adaptive routing methods in the link limited situation. Figure 15 shows the same thing for the exchange limited situation. Clearly neither method is able to cope with the changed network.

However, more subtle adaptive methods can be readily devised without introducing much more complexity, whereas nothing can be done about the non-adaptive, predetermined method. Figure 16 shows the result of a progressive adaptive method in which all links from the intermediate exchanges are considered, suitably weighted, before a route selection is made. It should be noted that the maximum acceptance rate with one source, destination exchange out of action is 92%. (The acceptance rate in figure 16 is plotted against remaining-system loading). Again, since indirect routes are allowed, a distinction has to be made between actual and useful system loading, and in the practical implementation some means of preventing excessive deviation of routes, circling etc. must be included. This is discussed in more detail elsewhere.

Finally, here, it is necessary to check whether once more a routing method has been devised that will only match the traffic demand to the reduced network of figure 13, and might not be satisfactory with the different, original network of figure 7. The result of applying the improved adaptive routing method to the original network is shown in figure 17, where it can be seen that the saturation breakpoint (90%) is almost equal to that of 'ideal' central control.

By not having a real system, we have a very flexible research tool. It is a simple matter to modify network topology, link and exchange capacities, traffic demands, and operating philosophies, as desired, and it is basically easy to compare system performance under variations in any of the above parameters, both quickly and cheaply.

The object of the latter part of the paper was to exemplify the use of this tool by comparing the effectiveness of some different routing strategies, under different network conditions. It should not be assumed that figure 17 necessarily represents the best that can be done with progressive adaptive routing methods, where in view of the capital cost of providing the network even a few percent improvement in the breakpoint should not be overlooked.

The authors gratefully acknowledge the assistance of Professor R. L. Grimsdale, and the contributions of Messrs. M. C. Daniels, C. Hall, and F. Halsall to the work described in this paper.

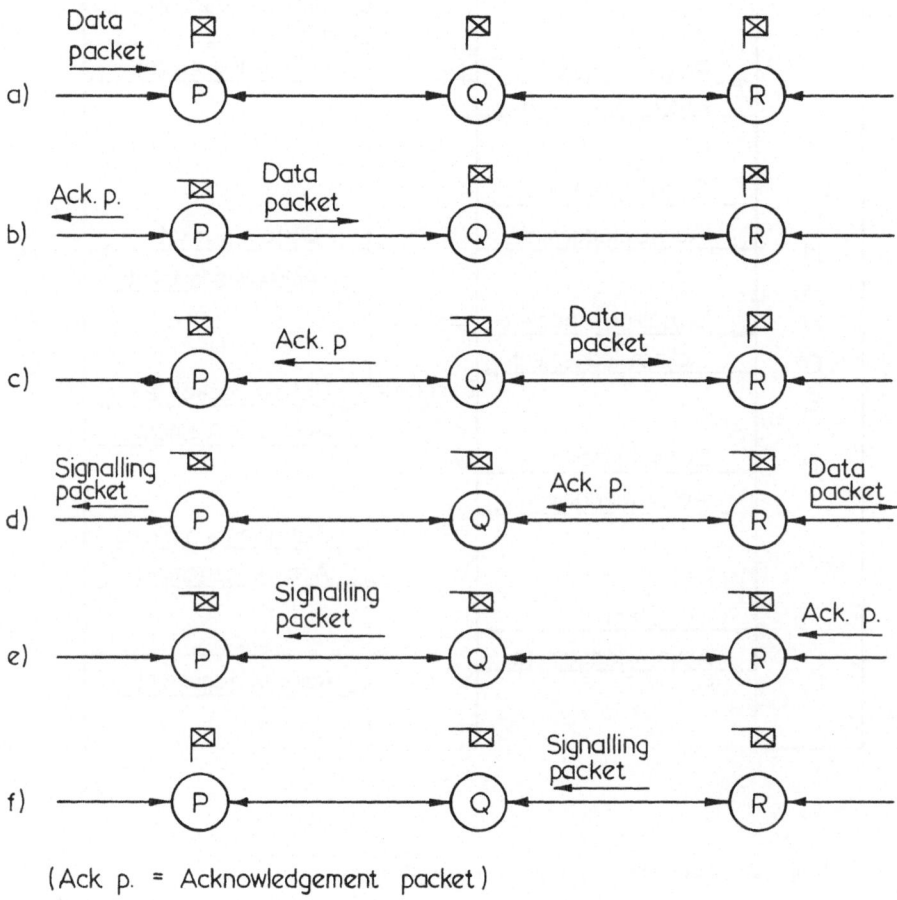

a) Data packet

b) Ack. p.   Data packet

c) Ack. p   Data packet

d) Signalling packet   Ack. p.   Data packet

e) Signalling packet   Ack. p.

f) Signalling packet

(Ack. p. = Acknowledgement packet)

Fig. 1   Acknowledgement and Signalling Procedure

142

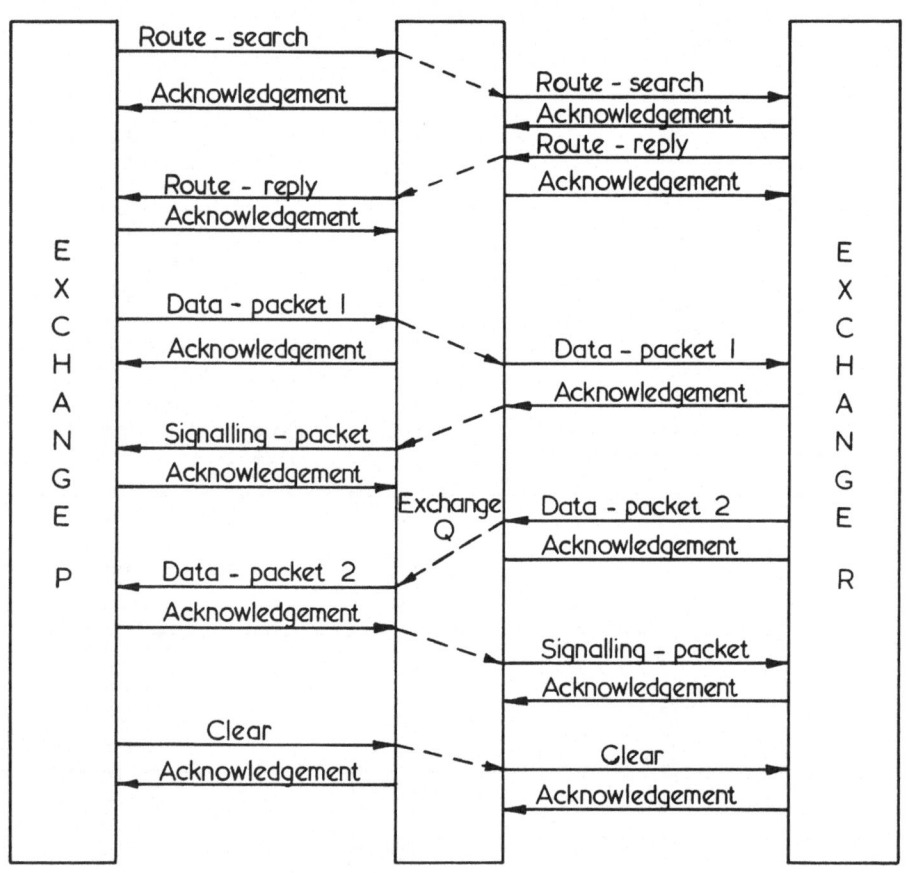

Fig. 2 Packets in a Complete Message

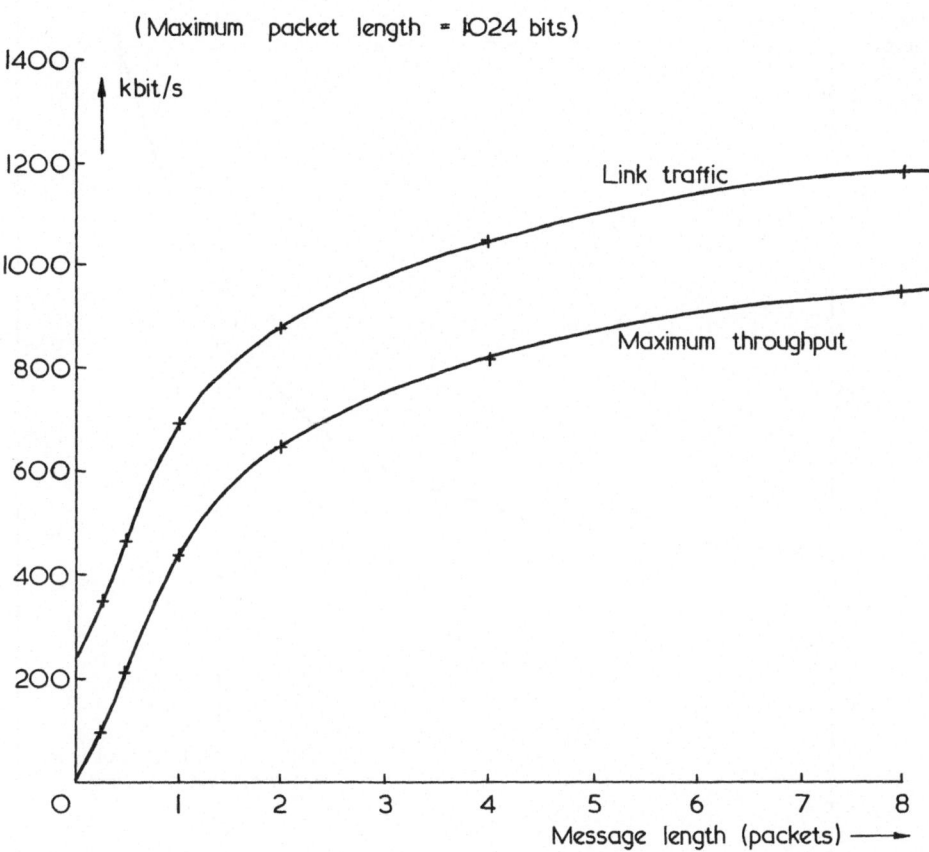

Fig. 3   Throughput and Corresponding Link Traffic for Various
Message Lengths

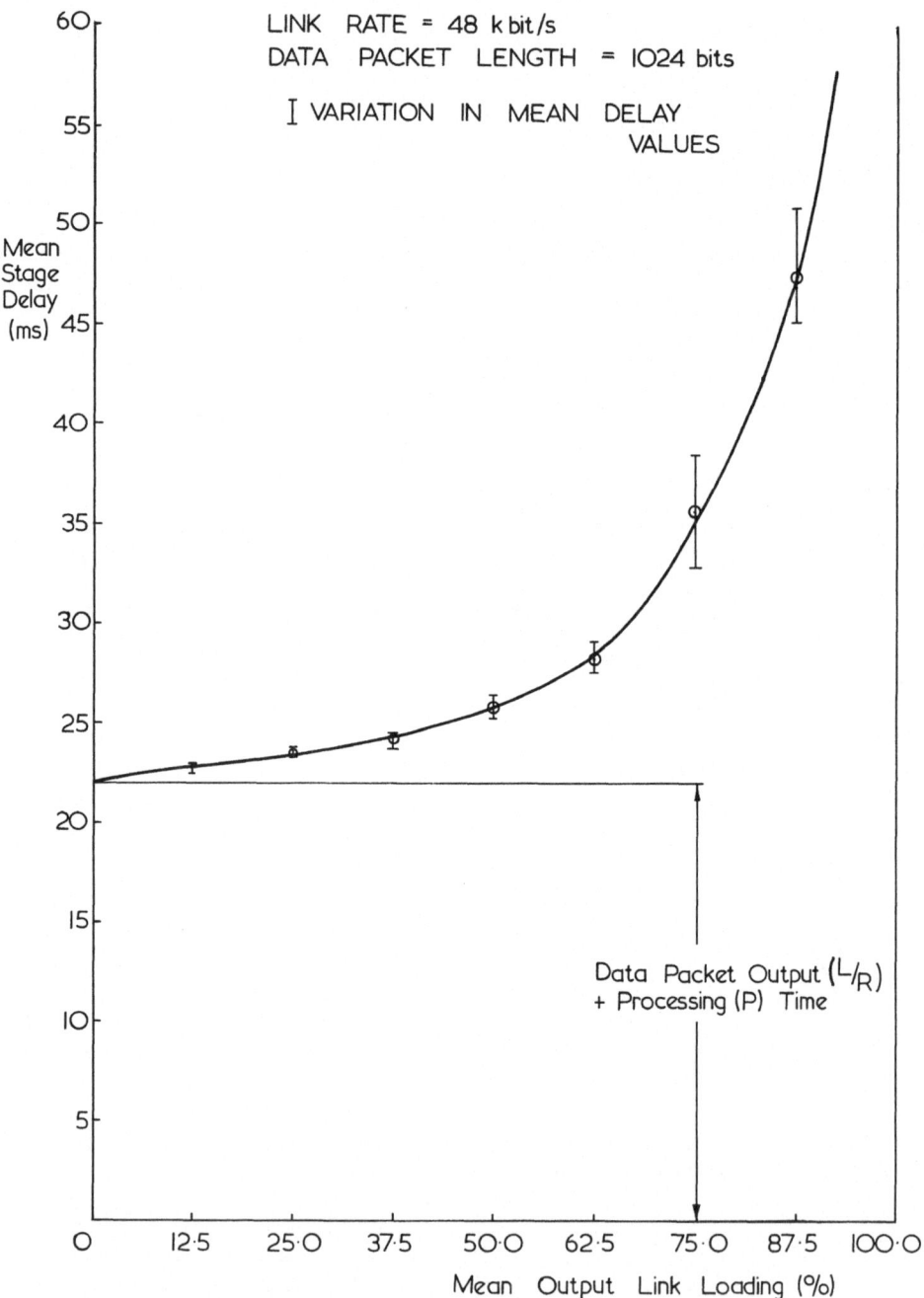

Fig. 4   The Effect of Output Link Loading on Stage Delay

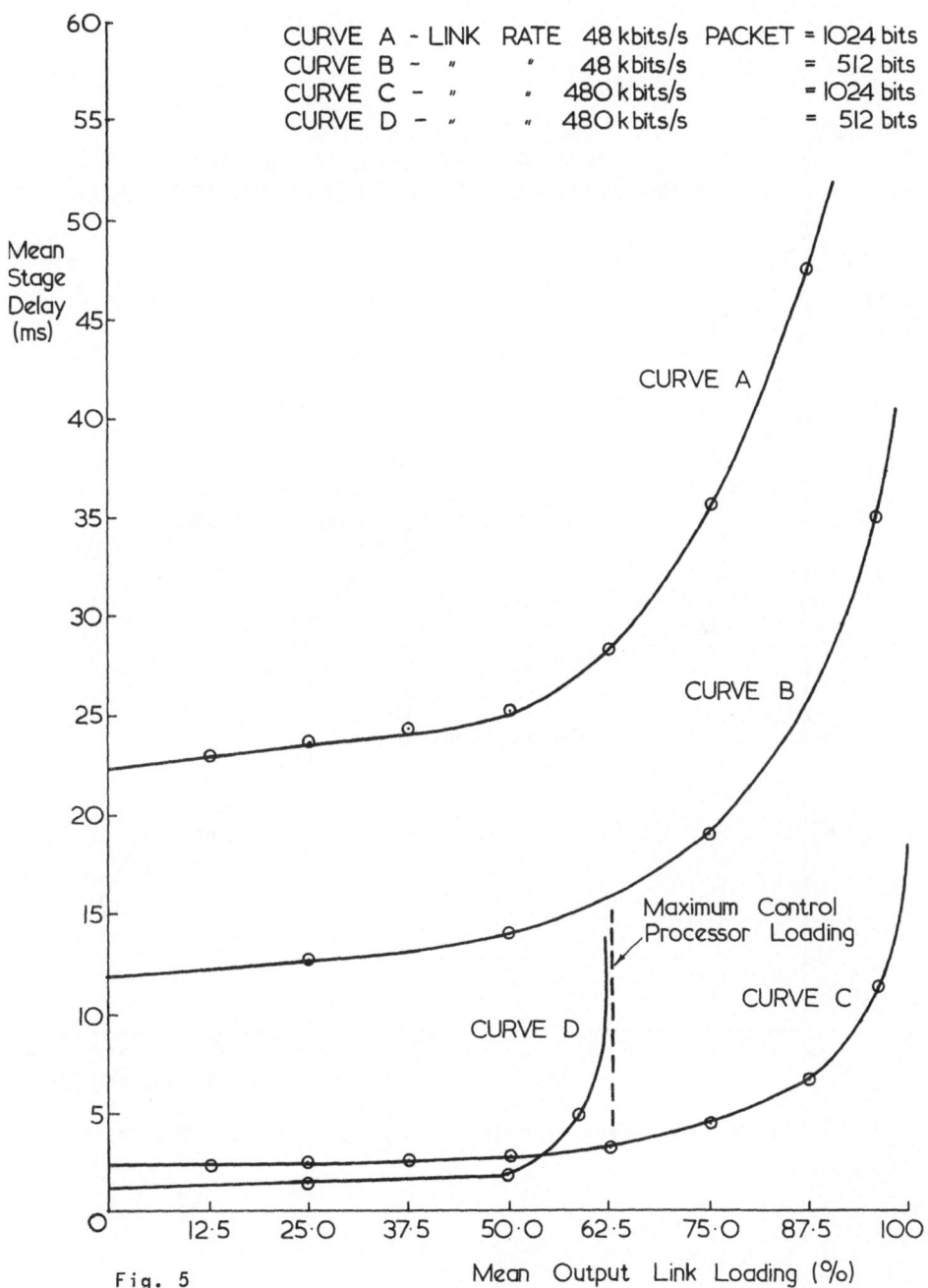

CURVE A – LINK RATE 48 kbits/s PACKET = 1024 bits
CURVE B – " " 48 kbits/s = 512 bits
CURVE C – " · 480 kbits/s = 1024 bits
CURVE D – " " 480 kbits/s = 512 bits

Mean Stage Delay (ms)

CURVE A

CURVE B

Maximum Control Processor Loading

CURVE C

CURVE D

Mean Output Link Loading (%)

Fig. 5

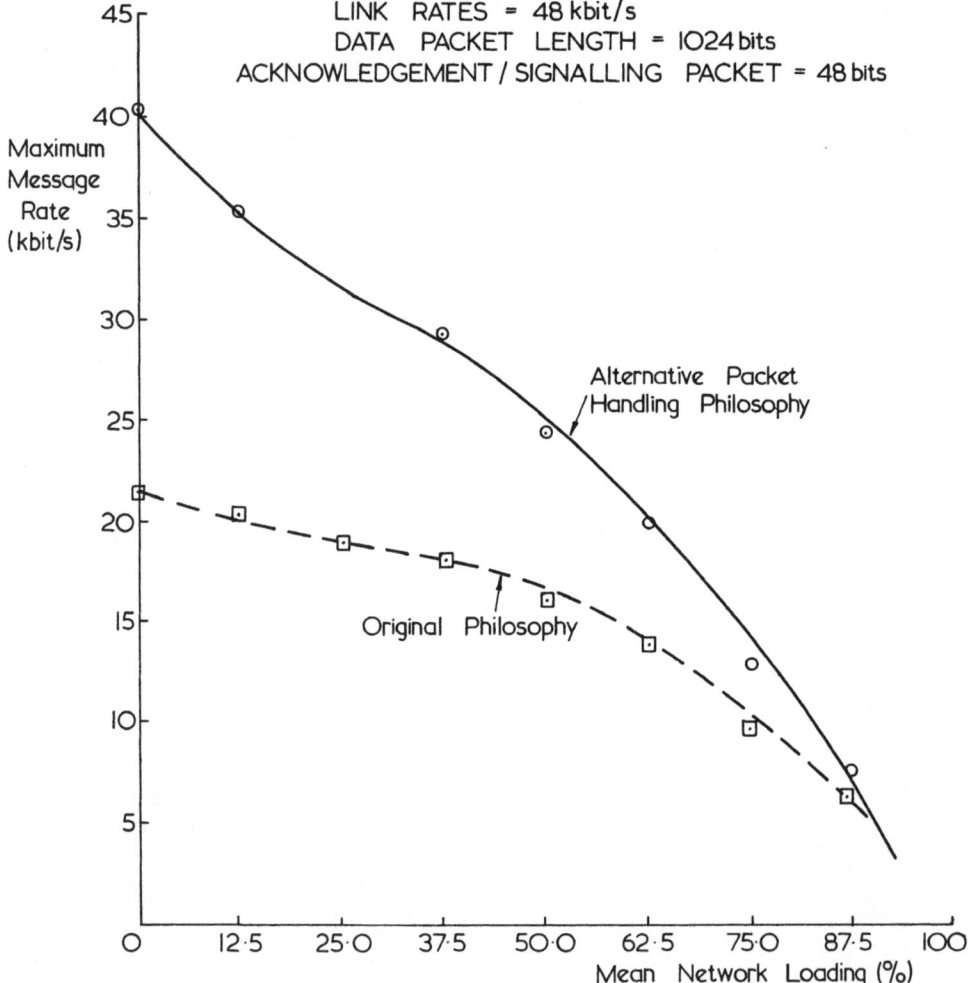

Fig. 6   The Effect of Network Loading on Maximum Message Rate

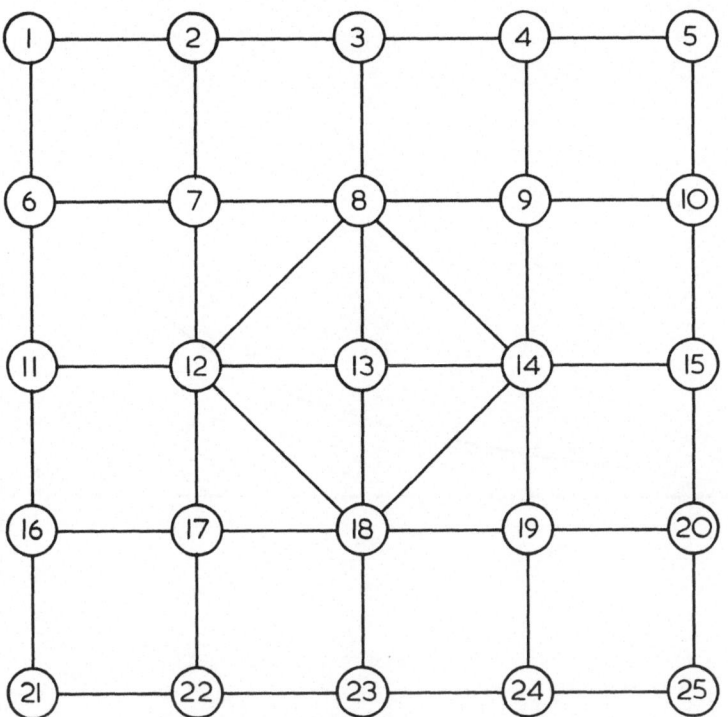

Fig. 7   The Sussex High-level Network

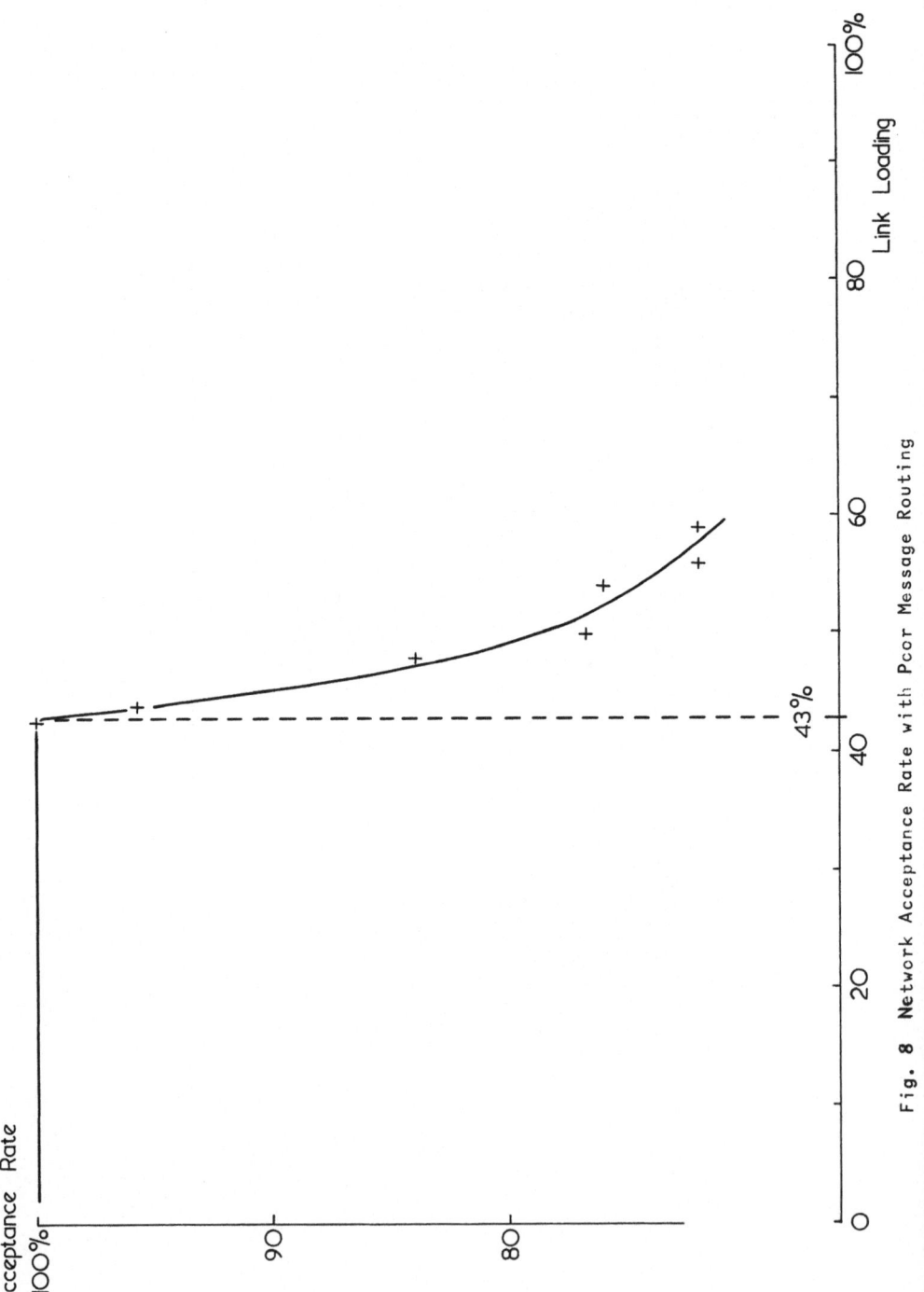

Fig. 8   Network Acceptance Rate with Pcor Message Routing

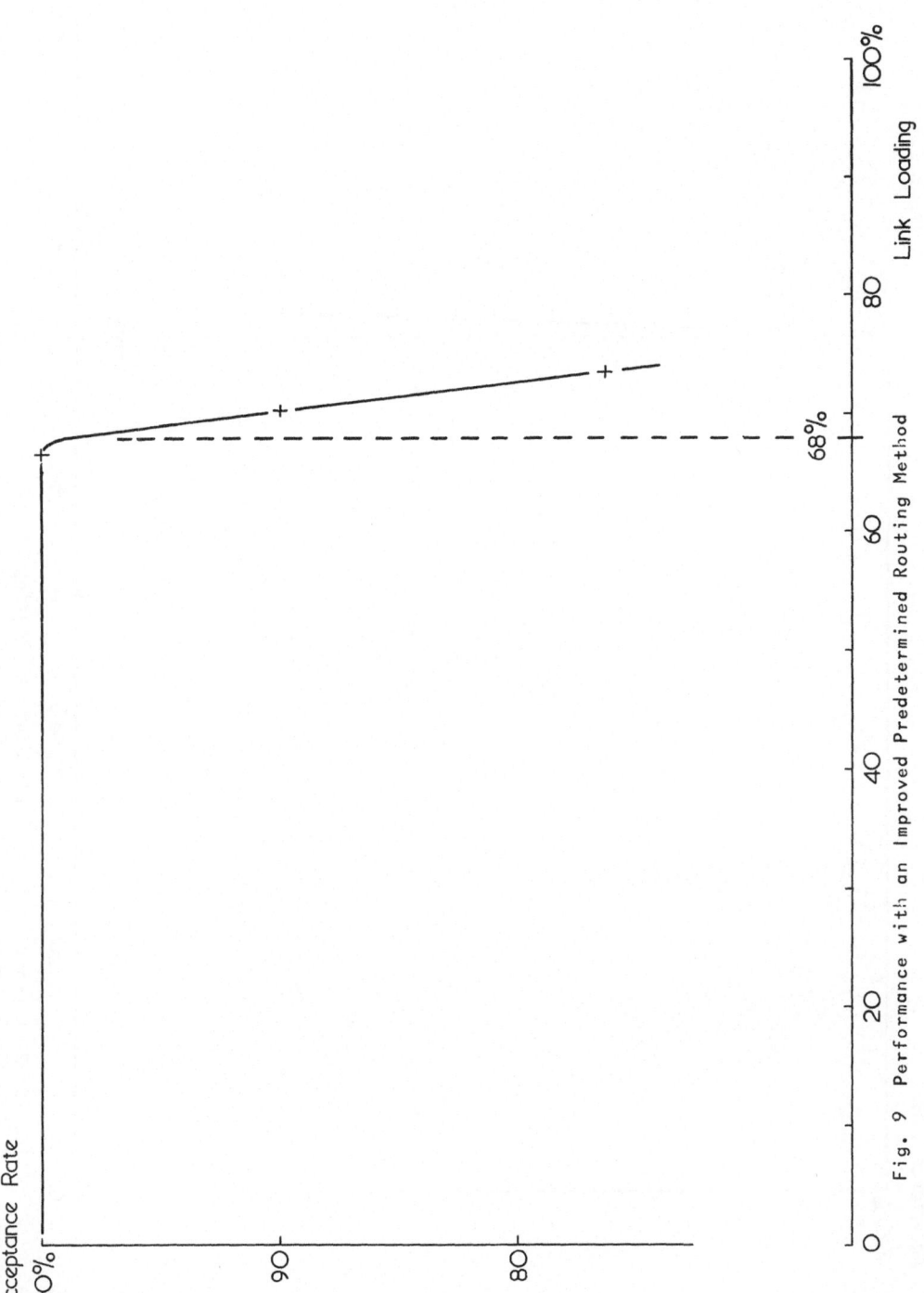

Fig. 9 Performance with an Improved Predetermined Routing Method

150

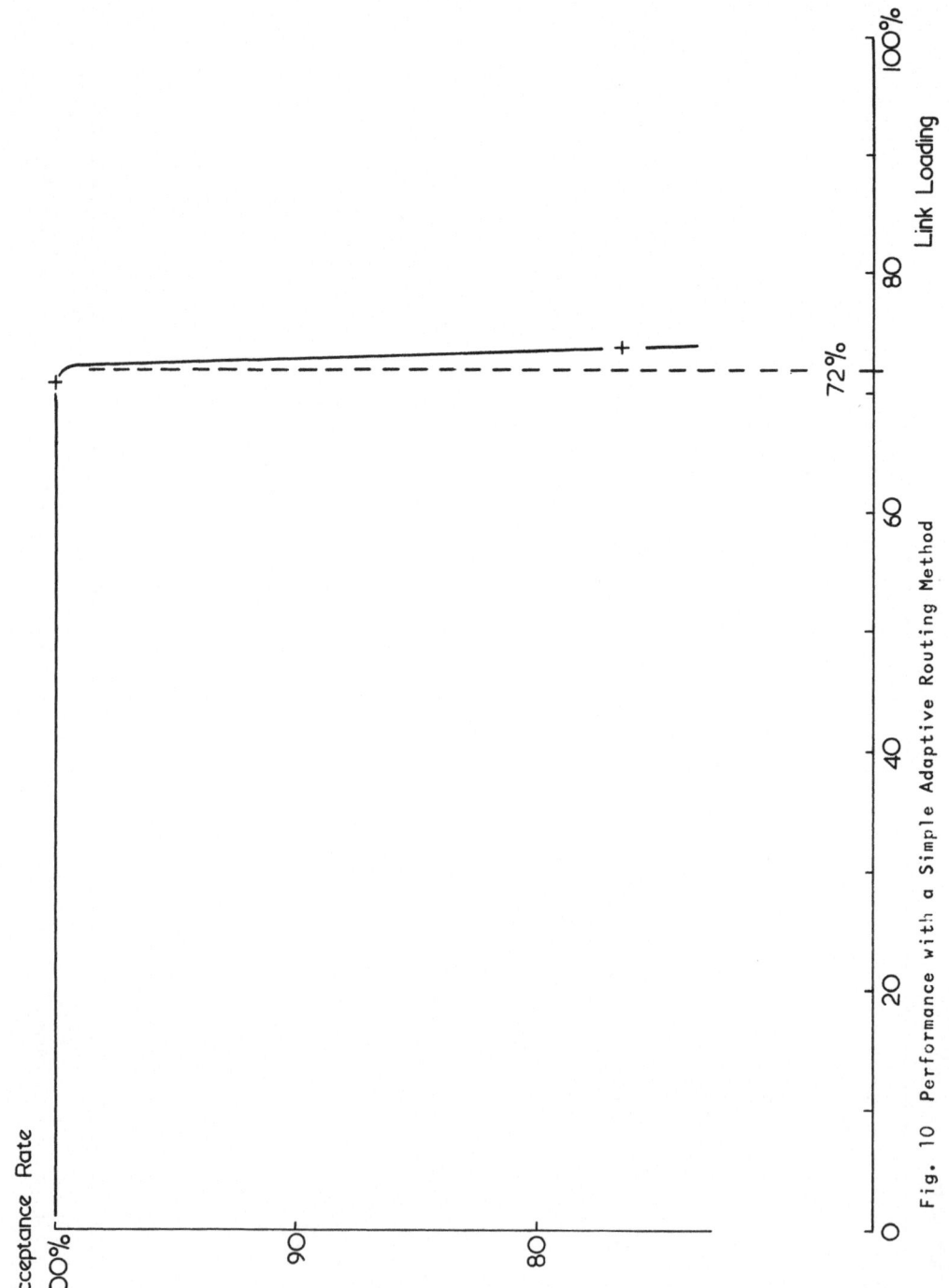

Fig. 10 Performance with a Simple Adaptive Routing Method

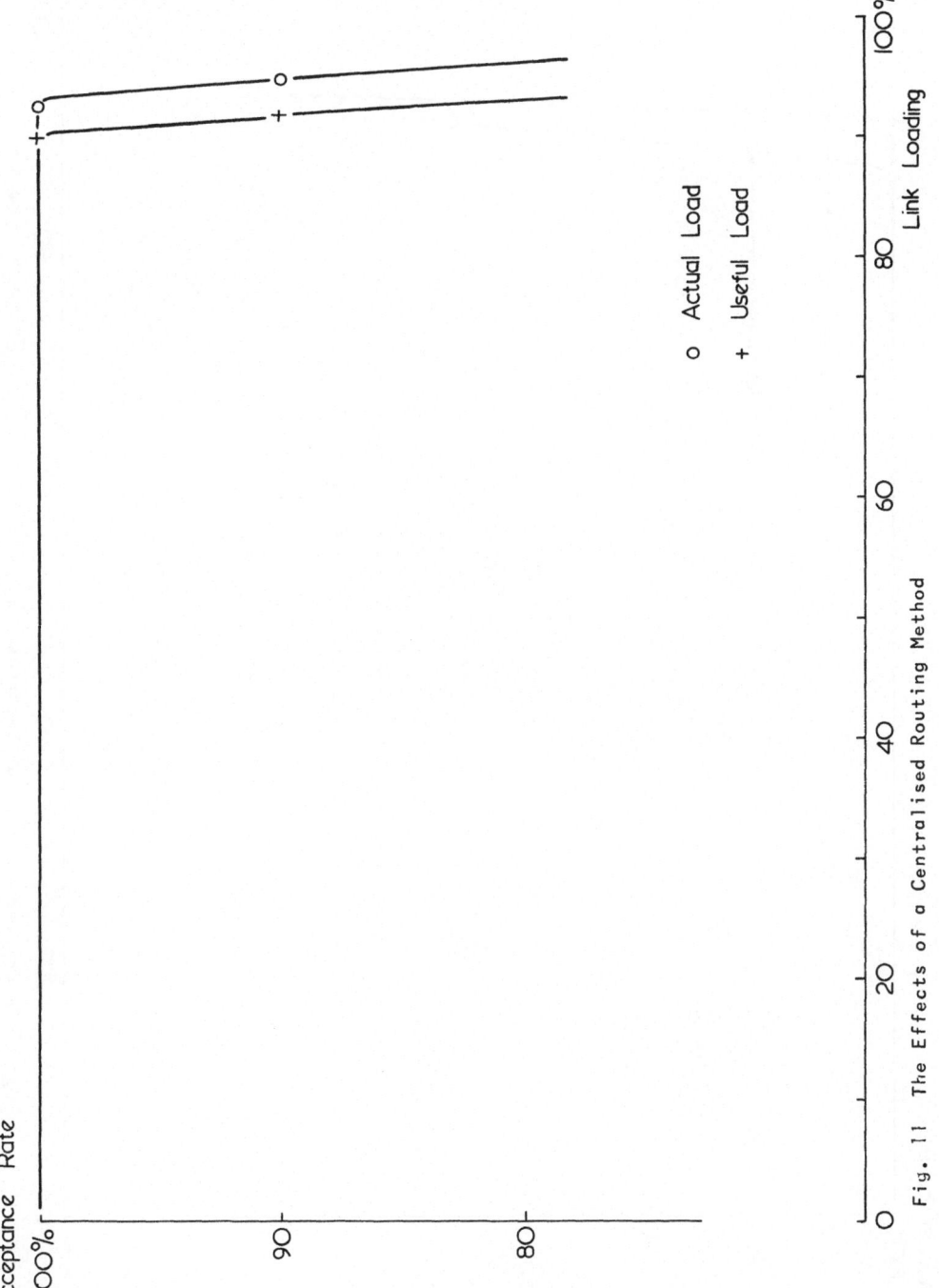

Fig. 11 The Effects of a Centralised Routing Method

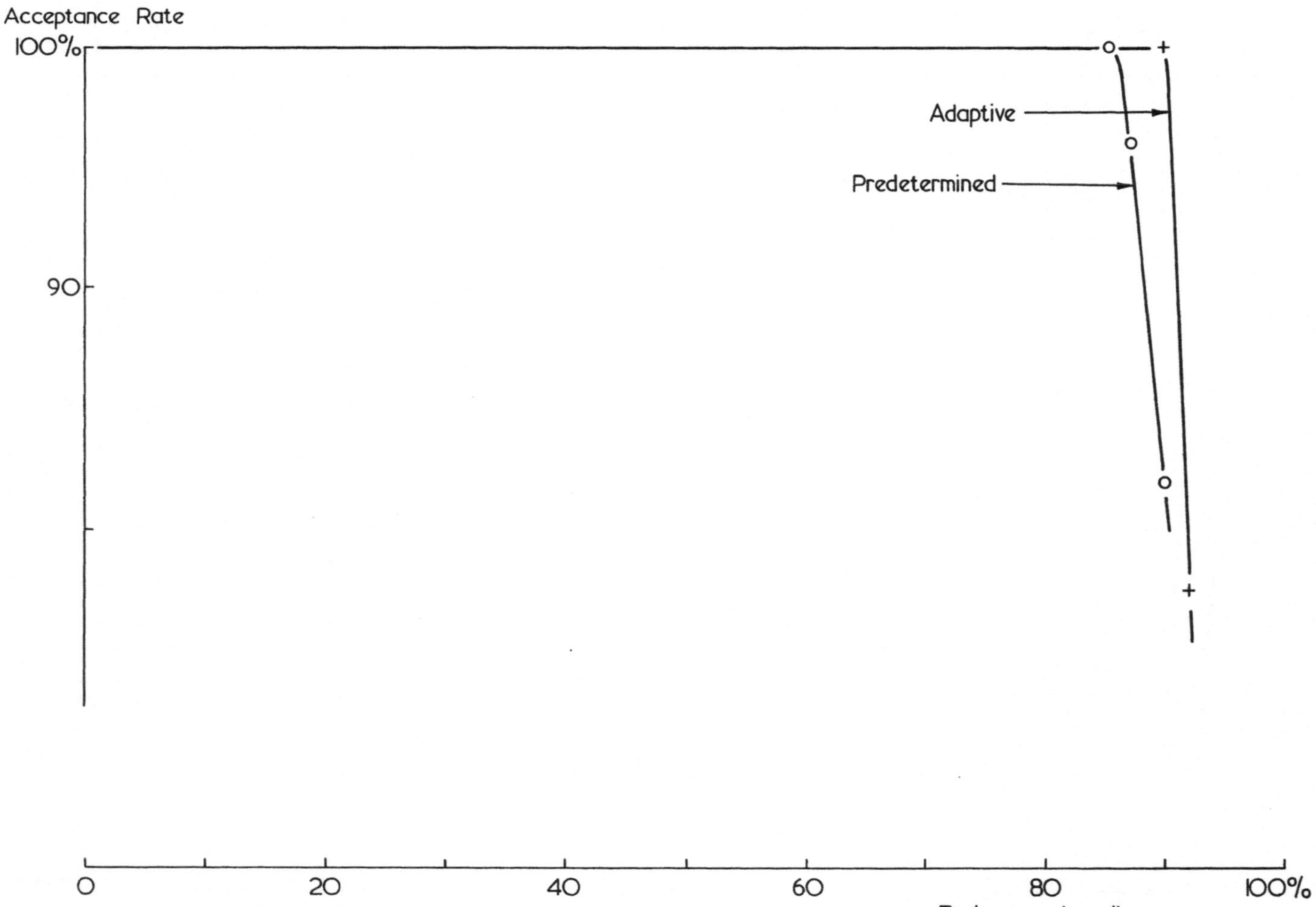

152

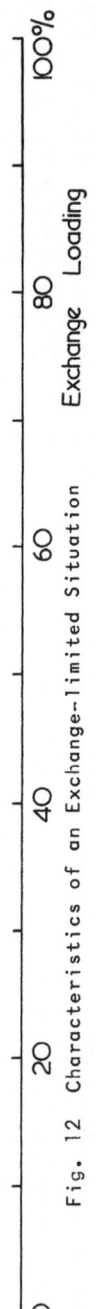

Acceptance Rate

100%

90

Adaptive

Predetermined

0   20   40   60   80   100%

Exchange Loading

Fig. 12 Characteristics of an Exchange-limited Situation

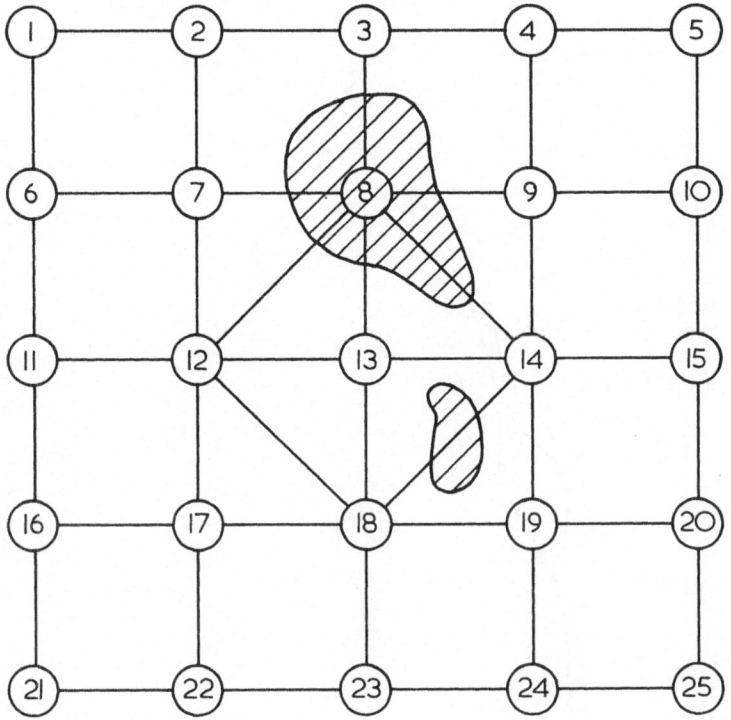

Fig. 13 The Sussex Network in Modified (Failure) Conditions

154

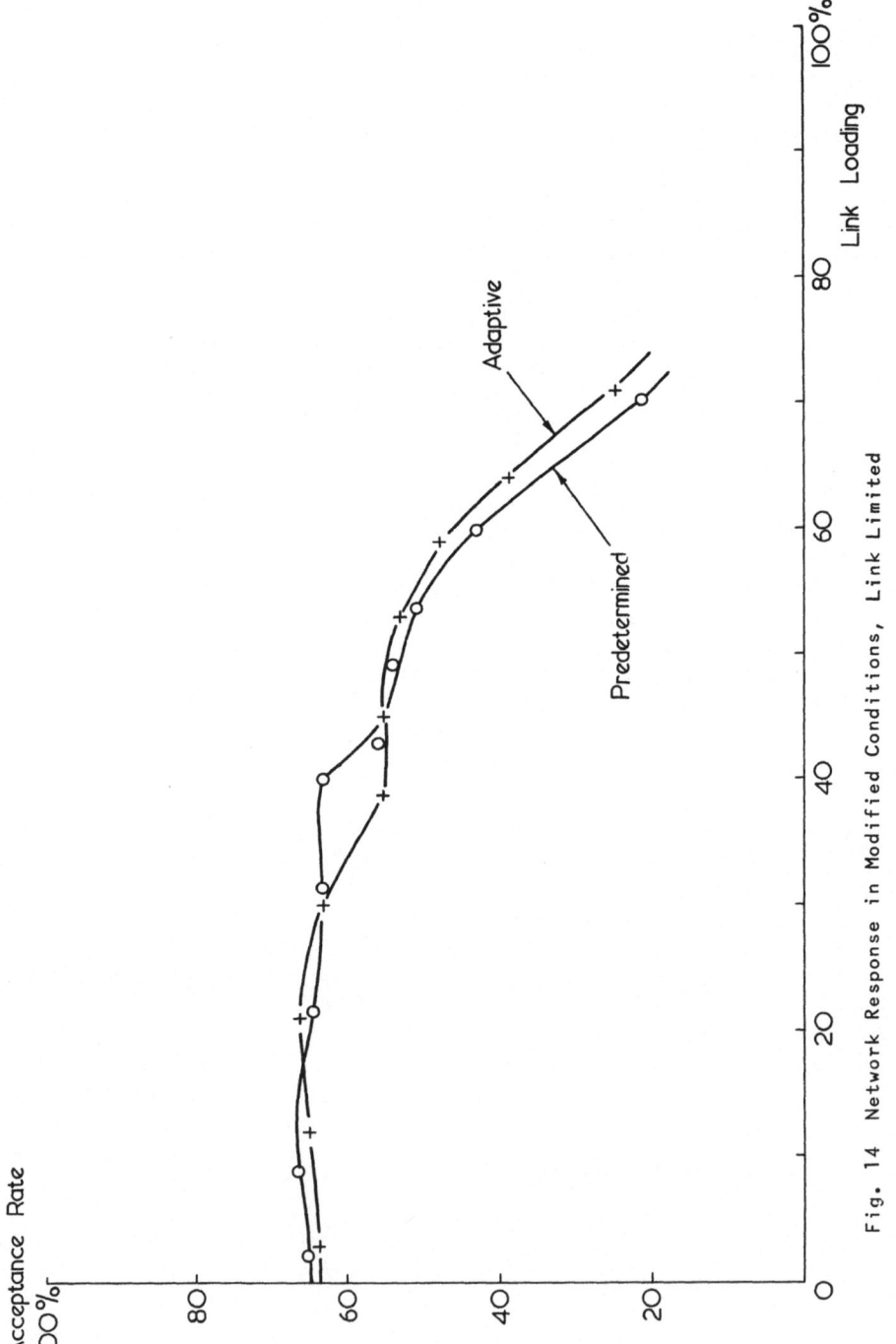

Fig. 14 Network Response in Modified Conditions, Link Limited

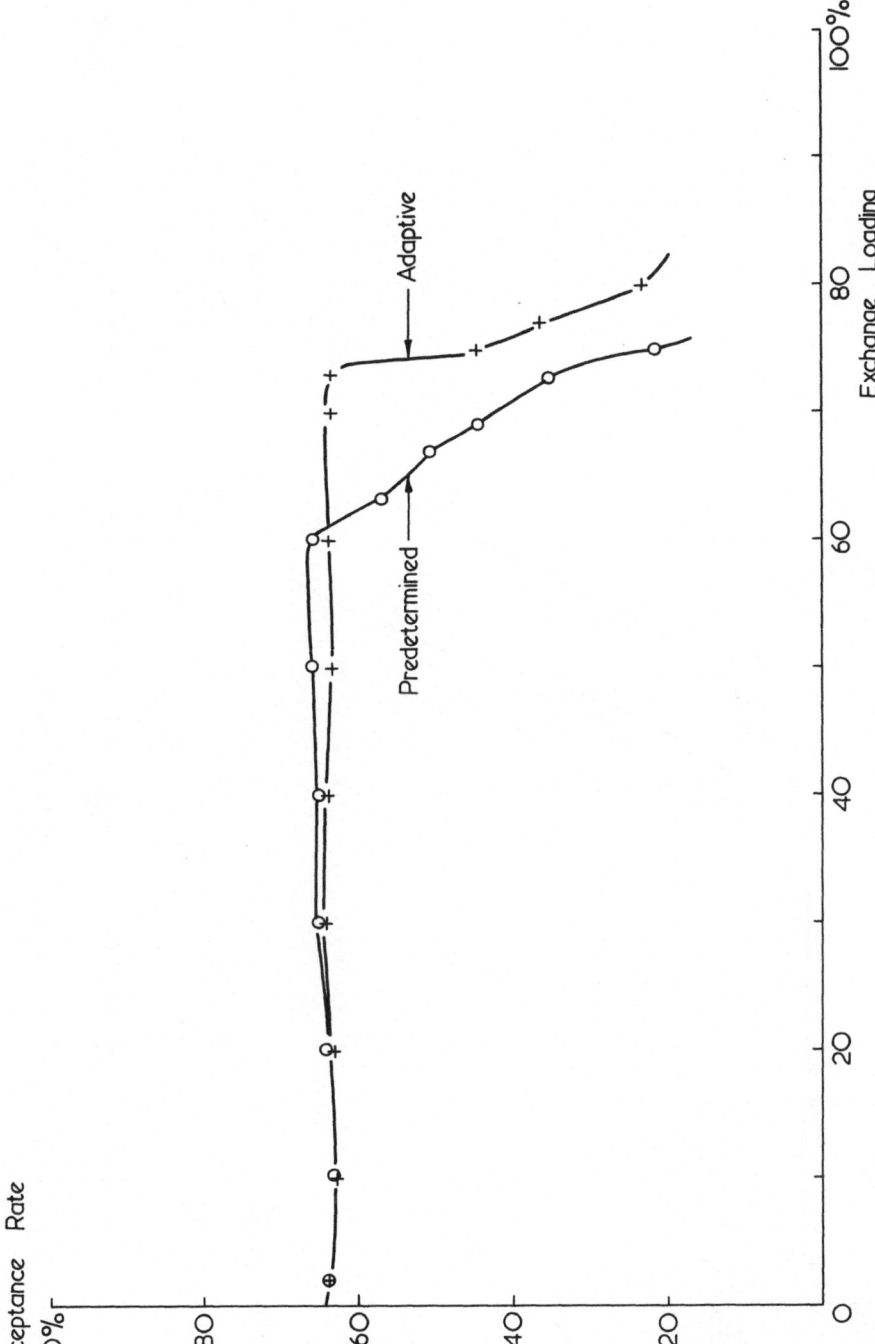

Fig. 15 Network Response in Modified Conditions, Exchange Limited

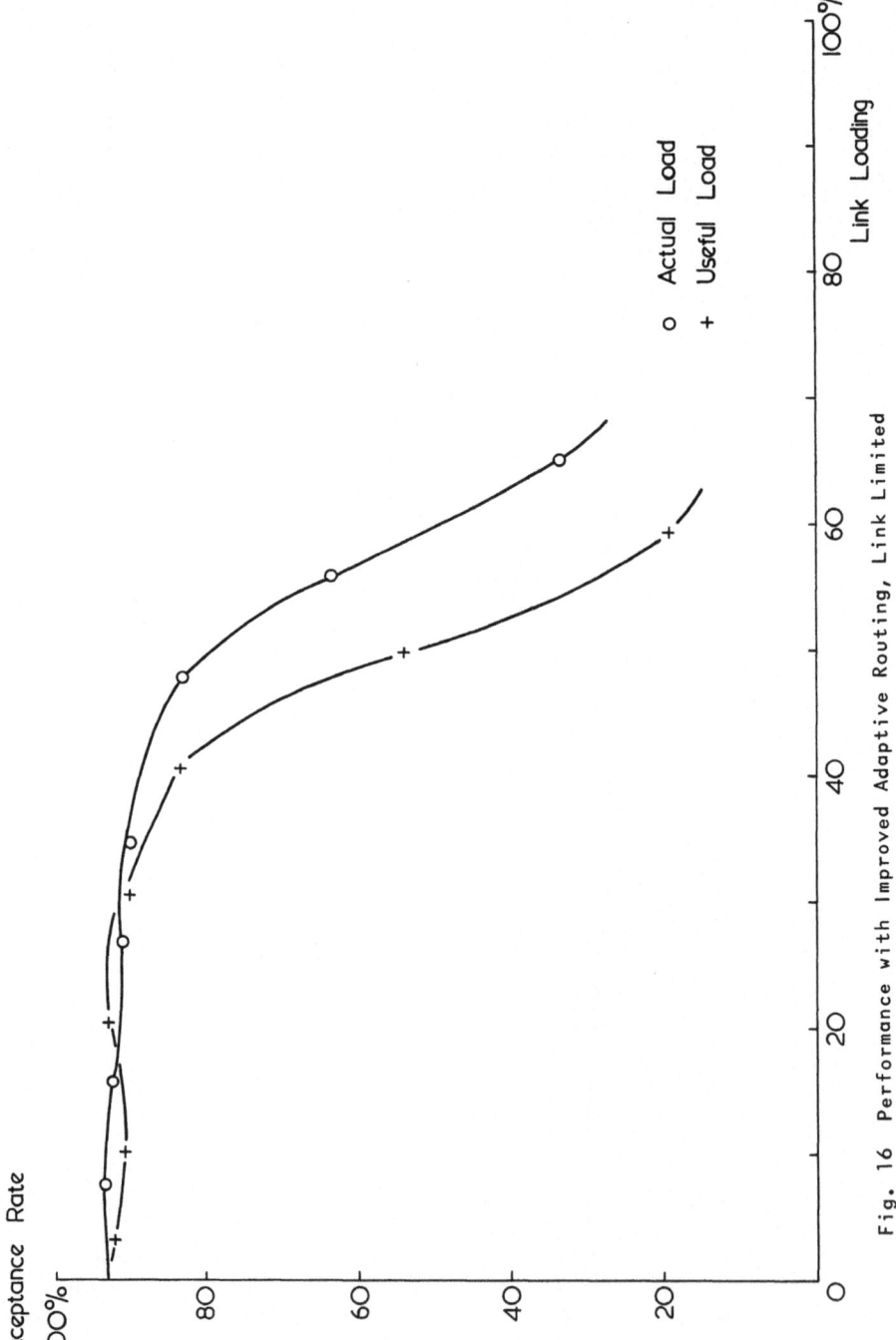

Fig. 16 Performance with Improved Adaptive Routing, Link Limited

157

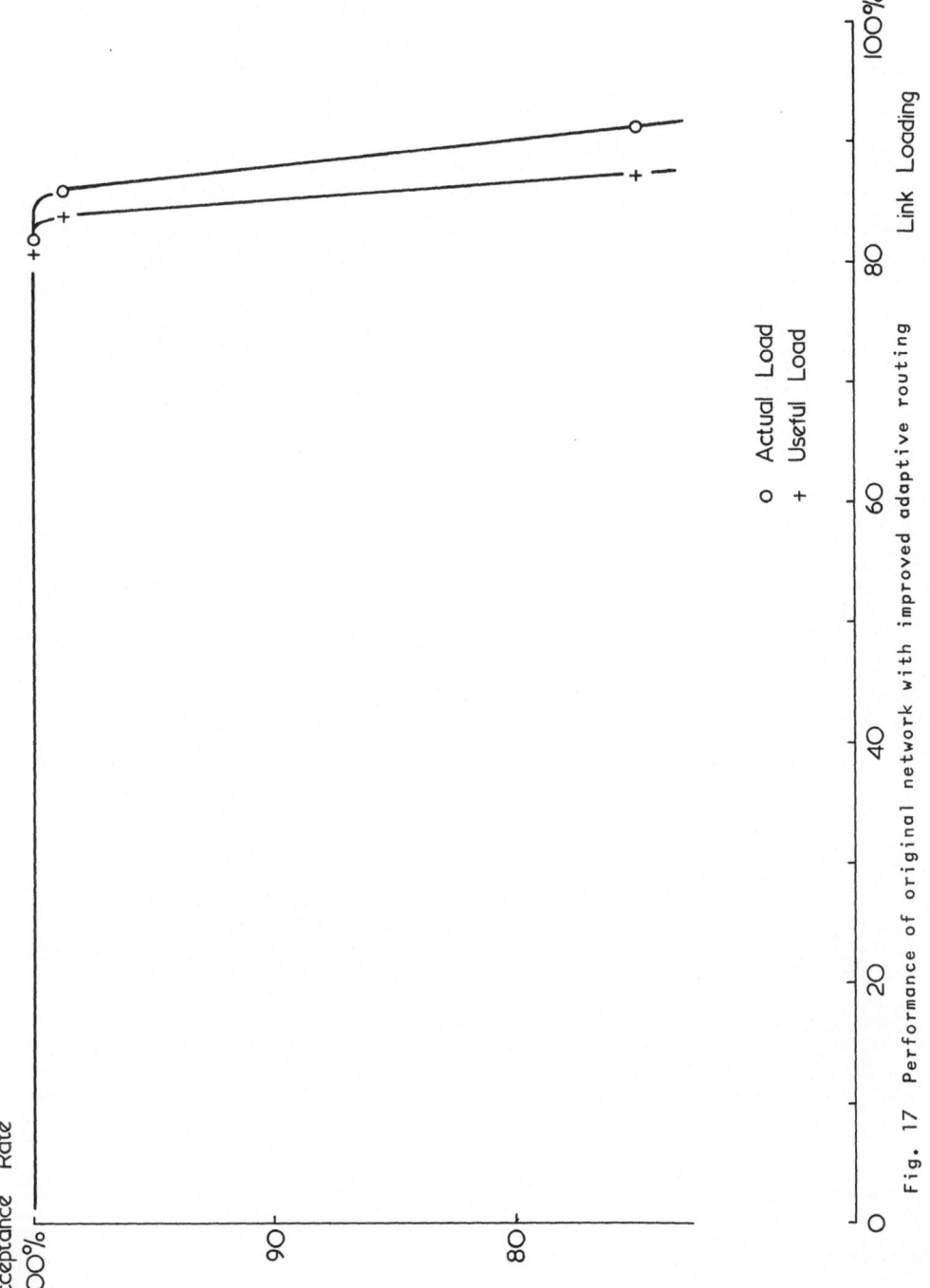

Fig. 17 Performance of original network with improved adaptive routing

o Actual Load
+ Useful Load

Acceptance Rate

A NEW MINICOMPUTER/MULTIPROCESSOR FOR THE ARPA NETWORK*

F.E. Heart, S.M. Ornstein, W.R. Crowther, and W.B.Barker.

Bolt Beranek and Newman Inc. Cambridge, Massachusetts.

Introduction

Since the early years of the digital computer era, there has been a continuing attempt to gain processing power by organizing hardware processors so as to achieve some form of parallel operation.[1,2] One important thread has been the use of an array of processors to allow a single control stream to operate simultaneously on a multiplicity of data streams; the most ambitious effort in this direction has been the ILLIAC IV project.[3,4] Another important thread has been the partitioning of problems so that several control streams can operate in parallel. Often functions have been unloaded from a central processor onto various specialized processors; examples include data channels, display processors, front-end communication processors, on-line data preprocessors - in fact, I/O processors of all sorts. Similarly, dual processor systems have been used to provide load sharing and increased reliability. Still another thread has been the construction of pipeline systems in which sub-pieces of a single (generally large) processor work in parallel on successive phases of a problem.[5] In some of these pipeline approaches the parallelism is "hidden" and the user considers only a single control stream.

In recent years, as minicomputers have proliferated, groups of identical small machines have been connected together and jobs

*This work was sponsored by the Advanced Research Projects Agency under contracts DAHC15-69-C-0179 and F08606-73-6-0027.

This paper has been reprinted from NCC Proceedings, June 1973, with kind permission of the publishers.

partitioned quite grossly among them.   Most recently, our group
and several others have been investigating this avenue further,
attempting to reduce the specialization of the processors in order
to employ independent processors with independent control streams
in a co-operative and "equal" fashion.[6,7,8]

This paper describes a new minicomputer/multiprocessor architecture for which a fourteen-processor prototype is now (February
1973) being constructed. The hardware design and the software
organization include many novel features, and the system many offer
significant advantages in modularity and cost/performance.   The
system contains an expandable number of identical processors, each
with some "private" memory; an expandable amount of "shared" memory to which all processors have equal access; and an expandable
amount of I/O interface equipment, controllable by any processor.
The system achieves unusual modularity and reliability by making
all processors equivalent, so that any processor may perform any
system task;   thus systems can be easily configured to meet the
throughput requirements of a particular job.   The scheme for interconnecting processors, memories, and I/O is also modular, permitting interconnection cost to vary smoothly with system size.
There is no "executive" and each processor determines its own
task allocation.

A key issue throughout most of the attempts at parallel organization has been the difficulty of partitioning problems in
such a way that the resulting computer program(s) can really take
advantage of the parallel organization. This issue is raised in
its most serious form when the parallel machine is expected to
work well on a great diversity of problems as, for example, in a
time-sharing system. Our machine design has been developed under
the highly favourable circumstances that (1) the initial application, and a prior software implementation in a standard machine,
was well understood; (2) the initial application lent itself to
fragmentation into parallel structures; and (3) the design would
be deemed successful if it handled only that one application in a
meritorious fashion. However, we now believe that the design is
advantageous for many other important applications as well and
that it may herald a broadly useful new way to achieve increased
performance and reliability.

The machine has been designed to serve initially as a modular
switching node for the ARPA Network[9] and, in the following section,
we briefly describe the ARPA Network application and the requirements that the network imposed upon the machine design.   In subsequent sections we discuss our choice of minicomputer, describe
our system design in some detail, discuss certain of the more
interesting characteristics of multiprocessor behaviour, and
summarize our present status and plans for the near future.

ARPA Network Requirements

The ARPA Network, a nationwide interconnection of computers and high bandwidth (50 Kb) communication circuits, has grown during the past four years to include over 35 sites, with more than one computer at many sites. The computers at each site, called Hosts, obtain access to the net via a small communications processor known as an Interface Message Processor or IMP.[10] In order to permit groups without their own computer facility to access this powerful set of computer resources, a version of the IMP called a Terminal IMP allows, in addition attachment of up to 63 local or remote terminals of a wide range of types.[11]

As a considerable simplification, the job to be handled by an IMP is that of a communications processor. Arriving messages must pass through an error control algorithm, be inspected to some degree (e.g. for destination), and generally be directed out onto some other line. Some incoming messages (e.g. routing control messages) must be constructed or digested directly by the IMP. The IMP must also concern itself with flow control, message assembly and sequencing, performance and flow monitoring. Host status, line and interface testing, and many other housekeeping functions. To perform these functions an IMP requires memory both for program and for message buffers, processing power for executing the program, and I/O units of various sorts for connecting to a variety of lines and devices. The original IMP, built around a Honeywell 516 processor with a 1 μs cycle time, could handle approximately three-quarters of a megabit per second of full duplex communication traffic. A later, smaller and cheaper (Honeywell 316) version handles about two-thirds as much traffic.

As the network has grown and as usage has increased, a number of demands for improvement have led to the need for a new 'line' of IMP machines. Our intent is to provide a modular arrangement of flexible hardware from which it will be possible to construct both smaller and less expensive IMPs as well as far more powerful IMPs. An important specific objective is to obtain an IMP whose communications bandwidth could be at least an order of magnitude greater than the 516 IMP; such a high speed IMP would permit the direct connection of satellite circuits or land T-carrier circuits operating at approximately 1.3 megabits/second.

It is also desirable to improve the present IMP design in a number of other areas, as follows:

. Expandability of I/O: the present IMPs permit connection to a total of only seven high-speed circuits and/or Host computers. We would like to permit a much greater fan-out so that an IMP might be connected to as many as 20 or more Host computers or to hundreds of terminals. This means that the number of interface units should be expandable over a wide range.

. Modularity: A number of groups have wished to make a network
  connection from a single Host at a considerable distance (miles)
  from the nearest IMP. We feel that such Hosts should be locally
  connected to a very small IMP in order to preserve consistency
  and standardization throughout the network. Therefore, a goal
  of this new hardware effort is the provision of a small and inexpensive but compatible IMP which could serve to connect a
  single, distant spur Host.

. Expandability of Memory: The new line of equipment is required
  for use in connection with satellite links (or longer faster
  links in general) and must therefore be able to expand its memory easily to provide the much greater buffer storage requirements of such links.

. Reliability: The new line of processors should be more reliable
  than the existing IMPs and ought to permit better self-diagnosis
  and simple isolation and replacement of failing units.

Of the requirements posed by the ARPA Network application, the
most central was to obtain an order-of-magnitude traffic bandwidth
improvement. We first considered meeting this requirement with
highly specialized hardware, but the need to allow evolution of
the communications algorithms, as well as the "bookkeeping" nature
of much of the IMP task, militate against hardwired approaches and
require the flexibility of a stored program computer. Thus we
need a machine with an effective cycle time of 100 nanoseconds, a
factor of ten faster than the present 1 μs IMP. Realizing that a
single very fast and powerful machine would be difficult to build
and would not give us compatible machines with a wide spectrum of
performance, we began to consider the possibility of a minicom-
puter/multiprocessor in order to achieve the flexibility, reliability and effective bandwidth required.

With the idea of a multiprocessor in mind we considered the
IMP algorithm to determine which parts were inherently serial in
nature and which could proceed in parallel. It seemed difficult
to process a single message in a parallel fashion: the job was
already relatively short and intimately coupled to I/O interfaces.
However, there was much less serial coupling between the processing of separate messages from the same phone line and no coupling
at all between messages from different phone lines. We thus envisage many processors, each at work on a separate message, with
the number of processors carefully matched to the number of messages we expect to encounter in the time it takes one processor to
deal with one message. With this simple image there seems to be
no inherent limit to the parallelism we can achieve - the ultimate
limit would be set by the size of the multiprocessor we can build.

Choice of the Processor

In designing a multiprocessor for the IMP application, we found ourselves iteratively exploring two related but distinct issues. First, assuming that the problem of interconnection could be solved, what minicomputer would be a sensible choice from the price/performance and physical points of view? Second, and much harder: for any specific machine, how did the CPU talk to memory, how would multiple CPUs, memories, and I/O be interconnected to form a system, and how would the program be organized?

Since the program for the existing IMPs was well understood, it was possible to identify key sections of that program which consumed the majority of the processing bandwidth. Then, for each sensible minicomputer choice, we could ask how many CPUs of this type would be needed to provide an effective 100 nanosecond cycle time; and given a price list, physical data, and a modest amount of design effort, we could define the physical structure and the price of the resulting multiprocessor. With this general approach, we examined the internal design of about a dozen machines, and actually wrote the key code in many cases. Using the fastest available minicomputers it was possible to arrive at configurations with only three or four processors; using the slowest choices, systems with 20 CPUs or more were required.

If we defer the interconnection and contention problems for a moment, it is interesting to note that "slow and cheap" may win over "fast and expensive" in this kind of multiprocessor competition to achieve a stated processing bandwidth. This is an especially happy situation if, as in our case, a spectrum of configurations is needed, including a very tiny cheap version.

In considering which minicomputer might be most easily adaptable to a multiprocessor structure, the internal communication between the processor and its memory was of primary concern. Several years ago machines were introduced which combined memory and I/O busses into a single bus. As part of this step, registers within the devices (pointers, status and control registers, and the like) were made to look like memory cells so that they and the memory could be referenced in a homogeneous manner. This structure forms a very clean and attractive architecture in which any unit can bid to become master of the bus in order to communicate with any other desired unit. One of the important features of this structure is that it made memory accessing "public"; the interface to the memory had to become asynchronous, cleanly isolable electrically and mechanically, and well documented and stable. A characteristic of this architecture is that all references between units are time multiplexed onto a single bus. Conflicts for bus usage therefore establish an ultimate upper bound on overall performance, and attempts to speed up the bus eventually run into serious problems in arbitration.[12]

In 1972 a new processor - the Lockheed SUE[13] - was introduced which follows the single bus philosophy but carries it an important step further by removing the bus arbitration logic to a module separate from the processor. This step permits one to consider configurations embodying multiple processors and multiple memories as well as I/O on a single bus. The SUE CPU is a compac relatively inexpensive (approximately $600 in quantity), quite slow processor with a microcoded inner structure. This slowness can be compensated for by simply doubling or trebling the number of processors on the bus; performance is limited largely by the speed of the bus. With the bus architecture it becomes attractive to visualize multi-bus systems with a "bus coupling" mechanis to allow devices on one bus to access devices on other busses.

Similar approaches can be implemented with varying degrees of difficulty in systems with other bus structures, and we examined several approaches in some detail for those processors whose cost performance was attractive. Rather fortuitously, the minicompute which exhibited the most attractive bus architecture also was extremely attractive in terms of cost/performance and physical characteristics. This machine, the Lockheed SUE, would require fourteen processors to achieve the effective 100 nanosecond cycle time, and we embarked on the detailed design of our multiprocesso on that basis.

System Design

Although our design permits systems of widely varying size ar performance, in the interest of clarity we will describe that des ign in terms of the particular prototype now under construction. Our overall design is represented in Figure 1. We require four-teen SUE processors to obtain the necessary processing bandwidth, and we estimate that 32K words of memory will be required for a complete copy of the operational program and the necessary commu-nication buffer storage. The I/O arrangements must allow easy connection of all the communications interfaces appropriate to tl IMP job (modem interfaces, Host interfaces, terminal interfaces) as well as standard peripherals and any special devices appropri to the multiprocessor nature of the system.

Some of the basic SUE characteristics are listed in Table 1.

TABLE 1

SUE Characteristics

16-bit word
8 General Registers
  3.7 µs add or load time
Microcoded
Two words/instruction typical
8-1/2" x 19" x 18" chassis
64K bytes addressable by a single instruction
~$3K for: 1 CPU + 4K Memory + Power,Rack,etc.
200 ns minimum bus cycle time
850 ns memory cycle time
425 ns memory access time

From a physical point of view, the SUE chassis represents the
basic construction unit; it incorporates a printed circuit back
plane which forms the bus into which 24 cards may be plugged.
From a logical point of view this bus simply provides a common
connection between all units plugged into the chassis. We are
using these chassis for the entire system: processor, memory,
and I/O. All specially designed cards as well as all Lockheed-
provided modules plug into these bus chassis. With this hardware,
the terms "bus" and "chassis" are used somewhat interchangeably,
but we will commonly call this standard building unit a "bus".
Each bus requires one card which performs arbitration. A bus
can be logically extended (via a bus extender unit) to a second
bus if additional card space is required; in such a case, a
single bus arbiter controls access to the entire extended bus.

We can build a small multiprocessor just by plugging several
processors and memories (and I/O) into a single bus. For larger
systems we quickly exceed the bandwidth capability of a single
bus and we are forced to multi-bus architecture. Then, from a
construction viewpoint, our multiprocessor design involves assign-
ing processors, memories and I/O units to busses in a sensible
manner and designing a switching arrangement to permit interconnection of all the busses. Of course, the superficial simplicity
of this construction viewpoint completely hides the many difficult
problems of multiprocessor system design; we will try to deal
with some of those issues in the following sections.

Resources:

A central notion in a parallel system is the idea of a "Resource," which we define to mean a part of the system needed by
more than one of the parallel users and therefore a possible
source of contention. The three basic hardware resources are
the memories, the I/O, and the processors. It is useful to

consider the memories, furthermore, as a collection of resources
of quite different character: a program, queues and variables of
a global nature, local variables, and large areas of buffer storage.

The basic idea of a multiprocessor is to provide multiple
copies of the vital resources in the hope that the algorithm can
run faster by using them in parallel. The number of copies of
the resource which are required to allow concurrent operation is
determined by the speed of the resource and the frequency with
which it is used. An additional advantage of multiple copies is
reliability; if a system contains a few spare copies of all resources, it can continue to operate when one copy breaks.

It may seem peculiar to think of a processor as a resource,
but in fact in our system the parallel parts of the algorithm compete with each other for a processor on which to run. We take
the view that all processors shall be identical and equal, and we
go to some trouble to insure that this is in fact so. As a consequence no single processor is of vital importance, and we can
change the number of processors at will. A later section will
describe how the processors co-ordinate to get the job done without a master of some sort.

Processor Busses:

A SUE bus can physically and logically support up to four
processors. As more processors are added to a bus, the contention for the bus increases, and the performance increment per processor drops; but the effective cost per processor also drops,
since the cost for the chassis, power supply, bus arbitration, etc.
is amortized over the number of processors.

Roughly speaking, using two processors per bus loses almost
nothing in processor performance, using three processors per bus
loses significant efficiency, and adding a fourth processor gains
less than half an "effective processor". After careful examination of the logical, economic and physical aspects of this choice,
we decided to use two processors per processor bus, and we thus
require seven processor busses in our initial multiprocessor
system.

The next question was how the processors should access the
program. In our application, some parts of the program are run
very frequently and other parts are run far less frequently. This
fact allows a significant advantage to be gained by the use of
private memory. When a processor makes access to shared memory
via the switching arrangement, that access will incur delays due
to contention and delays introduced by the intervening switch. We
therefore decided to use a 4K local memory with each processor on

its bus to allow faster local access to the frequently run code; these local memories all typically contain the same code. With this configuration and in our application, the ratio of accesses to local versus shared memory is better than three to one. This not only reduces contention delays for access to the shared memory but also cuts the number of accesses which suffer the delays.

The final configuration of a processor bus is shown in Figure 2(a). The units marked "Bus Coupler" have to do with our multiprocessor switching arrangement, which will be discussed below.

Shared Memory Busses*:

The shared memory of our multiprocessor is intended to contain a copy of the program as well as considerable storage space for message buffering, global variables, etc. Application-dependent considerations led us to select a 32K memory, but it is possible to configure this memory on a single bus or to divide the memory onto several busses. We first concluded that four logical memory units would be appropriate in order to reduce processor contention to an acceptable level. Then, since the bus is considerably faster than the memories, it is feasible to place two logical memory elements on a single bus with almost no interference. Thus, we are planning two memory busses in the initial multiprocessor; the configuration of a common memory bus is shown in Figure 2(b).

I/O Busses:

The I/O system of the multiprocessor employs standard SUE busses with standard bus arbitration units on those busses. Into the bus will be plugged cards for each of the various types of I/O interfaces that are required, including interfaces for modems, terminals, Host computers, etc., as well as interfaces for standard peripherals. Our initial system has a single I/O bus and Figure 2(c) shows its configuration; the specialized units shown (a "Clock" and "Pseudo Interrupt Device") are system-wide resources that are used to control the operation of the multiprocessor. The I/O bus will also be the access route for the multiprocessor console; we plan to use a standard alphanumeric display terminal which can be driven by code in any processor, and no conventional consoles will be used.

*The terms "I/O bus" and "memory bus" as used here and henceforth are not the same as conventional I/O and memory busses.

Interconnection System:

Our prototype multiprocessor is now seen to contain seven
processor busses, two shared memory busses and an I/O bus. To
adhere to our requirement that all processors must be equal and
able to perform any system task, these busses must be connected
so that all processors can access all shared memory, so that I/O
can be fed to and from shared memory, and so that any of the processors may control the operation and sense the status of any
I/O unit.

A distributed inter-communication scheme was chosen in the
interest of expandability, reliability, and design simplicity.
The atom of this scheme is called a Bus Coupler, and consists of
two cards and an interconnecting cable. In making connections
between processors and shared memory, one card plugs into a shared
memory bus, where it will request cycles of the memory; the other
card plugs into a processor's bus, where it looks like memory.
When the processor requests a cycle within the address range
which the Bus Coupler recognizes, a request is sent down the
cable to the memory end, which then starts contending for the
shared memory bus. When selected, it requests the desired cycle
of the shared memory. The memory returns the desired information to the Bus Coupler, which then provides it to the requesting
processor, which, except for an additional delay, does not know
that the memory was not on its own bus. Note that the memory
access arbitration inherent in any memory switching arrangement
is handled by the SUE Bus Arbiter controlling the shared memory
bus, while the Bus Coupler itself is conceptually straightforward.

One additional feature of the Bus Coupler is that it does
address mapping. Since a processor can address only 64K bytes
(16 bit address), and since we wished to permit multiprocessor
configurations with up to 1024K bytes (20 bit address) of shared
memory, a mechanism for address expansion is required. The Bus
Coupler provides four independent 8K byte windows into shared
memory. The processor can load registers in the Bus Coupler
which provide the high-order bits of the shared memory address
for each of the four windows.

Given a Bus Coupler connecting each processor bus to each
shared-memory bus, all processors can access all shared memory.
I/O devices which do direct memory transfers must also access
these shared memories. These I/O devices are plugged into as many
I/O busses as are required to handle the bandwidth involved, and
bus couplers then connect each I/O bus to each memory bus. Similarly, I/O devices also need to respond to processor requests
for action or information; in this regard, the I/O devices act
like memories and Bus Couplers are again used to connect each
processor busses and I/O busses is also used in a more sophisti-

cated fashion to allow processors to examine and control other processors; this subject is described in a later section.

The resulting system is shown in Figure 3. One is struck by the number of bus couplers: P*I+I*M+P*M bus couplers are required for a system with P processor busses, I I/O busses, and M memory busses. In the case of our initial multiprocessor, 23 are needed.

This modular interconnection approach clearly permits great flexibility in the number of configuration of busses, and allows interconnection cost to vary smoothly with system size. We believe that this modular interconnection scheme also permits a complex hierarchical arrangement of busses. Actually the system exhibits a pronounced heirarchical structure already. A processor accesses the local memory when it needs instructions or local variables. Two such processor-memory combinations form a dual processor, which can be regarded as a unit and which needs access to shared resources, such as global variables, free buffers, and I/O interfaces. When one copy of a resource can only support a limited number of users, it seems sensible to provide only the corresponding limited number of connections. If a multiprocessor of this type were to grow larger, the physical number of bus couplers as well as increasing contention problems might not permit the connection of each processor to all of common memory, but might instead require a multi-level structure where groups of processors were connected to an intermediate level bus which was in turn connected to a centralized common memory. We have not explored this domain but feel it is an interesting area for future work.

Multiprocessor Behaviour

Until the processors interact, a multiprocessor is a number of independent single processor systems: it is the interaction which poses the conceptual as well as the practical problems. If the various processors spend their time waiting for each other, the system degrades to a single processor equivalent; if they can usefully run concurrently, the processing power is multiplied by the number of processors. If the failure of a single processor takes the system down, the system reliability is only the probability of all processors being up; if working processors can diagnose and heal or amputate faulty processors and proceed with the job, the system reliability approaches the probability of any processor being up. We now consider how to keep the system running in the case of module failure.

The first problem in making the machines run independently is the allocation of runnable tasks to processors, so that the full requisite power can be quickly brought to bear on high priority tasks. Our scheme for doing this rests on four key ideas: 1) We break the job up into a set of tiny tasks. 2) Our processors are all identical, asynchronous, and capable of doing any task. 3) We keep a queue of pending tasks, ordered by priority, from which each processor at its convenience gets its next task. 4) For speed and efficiency, we use a hardware device to help manage the queue.

By breaking the job up into smaller and smaller tasks until each one runs in under 300 µs, we effectively determine the responsiveness of our system. Once started, a task must run to completion, but there will be a reconsideration of priorities at the beginning of each new task. We have chosen 300 microseconds as the maximum task execution time because this compromise between efficiency and responsiveness is well matched to the execution time of key IMP functions.

By making the processors identical, we can use the same program in systems of widely varying size and throughput capability. Any processor can be added to or removed from a running system with only a slight change in throughput. The power of all processors quickly shifts to that part of the algorithm where it is most needed.

By queuing pending tasks, we keep track of which must be done while focusing on the most important tasks. By using a passive queue in which the processors check for a new task when they are ready, we avoid some nasty timing problems. Tasks may be entered into the queue at any time, either by a processor or by the hardware I/O devices. This approach is an extremely important departure which avoids the use of conventional interrupts and the associated costs of saving and restoring machine state. Further, this approach neatly sidesteps the problem of routing interrupts to the proper processor.

We could not afford a software queue both because it was slow to use and because processors would have been waiting for each other to get access to the queue. Instead we use a special hardware device called a Pseudo Interrupt Device (PID), which keeps in hardware a list of what to do next. A number can be written to the PID at any time and it will be remembered. When read the PID returns (and deletes) the highest number it has stored. By coding the numbers to represent tasks, and keeping the parameters of the tasks in memory, a processor can access the PID at the end of each task and determine very rapidly what it should do next.

Contention:

Clearly, the PID must give any task to exactly one processor. This is guaranteed because the PID is on a bus that can be accessed by only one processor at a time and because the PID completes each transaction in a single access. This is an example of the

more general problem that whenever two users want access to a
single resource there must be an interlock to let them take turns.
This is true at many levels, from contention for a bus to processor contention for shared software resources such as a free list.
When all the appropriate interlocks have been provided, the performance of the multiprocessor will depend rather critically on
the time wasted waiting at these interlocks for a resource to become free. As discussed above, whenever conflicts become a serious
problem one provides another copy of the resource. We studied our
system behaviour carefully, noting areas of conflict, in order to
know how many additional copies of heavily accessed resources to
provide. Table II provides examples of delays due to various conflicts. Practically speaking, the curve of delay vs. number of
resouces has a rather sharp knee, so that it is meaningful to
make such statements as "a memory bus supports eight processors"
or "a free list supports eight processors". Of course, these
statements are application related and depend on the frequency and
duration of accesses required.

Table II

Expected System Slowdown due to Contention Delays

Slowdown	Cause
5.5%	Contention for a Processor Bus
3%	Contention for the Shared Memory Busses
5%	Contention for the Shared Memories
10%	Contention for a single system-wide software resource, assuming each processor wants the resource for 6 instructions out of every 120 instructions executed.
1.7%	Contention for one of two copies of a system-wide software resource, as above.
0.15%	Contention for the parameters of a single 1.3 megabit phone line, assuming the parameters will be used for 160 microseconds every 800 microseconds.

With interlocks, deadlocks become possible (in both hardware
and software). For example, a deadlock occurs when each of two
processors has claimed one of two resources needed by both. Each
waits indefinitely for the other's resource to become available.[14]
Unless there is a careful systematic approach to interlocks, deadlocks become almost a certainty. One technique is to assign a
unique number to each resource for which there is an interlock,
and require that a processor never compete for a resource when it
already owns a higher numbered resource. It is not always practical

or possible to do this, although we expect to be able to do so
with the IMP algorithms.

An interesting example of a deadlock occurs in our bus coupling. To permit processors to access one another, for mutual
turn on, turn off, testing, etc., the path connecting each processor bus with the I/O bus is made bi-directional. Thus processors access one another via the I/O bus. In a bi-directional
coupler, a deadlock arises when units obtain control of their
busses at each end and then request access via the coupler to the
bus on the other end. Because the backward path is infrequently
used, we simply detect such deadlocks, abort the backward request
and try again.

Reliability:

We have taken a rather ambitious stand on reliability. We
plan to detect a failing module automatically, amputate it, and
keep the system running without human intervention if at all possible. Critical to our approach is the fact that there are several
processors each with private memory and thus each able to retreat
to local operation in the face of system problems. To reduce our
vulnerability further, power and cooling are provided on a modular
basis so that loss of a single unit does not jeopardize system
operation. We are only mildly concerned with the damage done at
the time of a failure, because the IMP system includes many checks
and recovery procedures throughout the network.

The first sign of a failure may be a single bit wrong somewhere
in shared memory, with all units apparently functioning properly.
Alternatively, the failure may strike catastrophically, with
shared memory in shambles and the processors running protectively
in their local memories. Against this spectrum we can not hope
for a systematic defense; instead we have chosen a few defensive
strategies.

So long as a module is failing, recovery is meaningless. We
must run diagnostics to identify the bad module, or see if cutting
a module out at random helps things. We feel that identifying suc
a solid failure will be relatively easy. Since a processor without couplers is completely harmless, once we identify a malfunctioning processor, we amputate it by turning off its bus couplers.
We considered the possibility of a runaway processor turning good
processors off. This is unlikely to begin with but we decided to
make it even less likely by requiring a particular 16-bit password to be used in turning off a coupler. A runaway processor
storing throughout shared memory would need this password in its
accumulator to accidentally amputate. Similarly we require a pass
word for one processor to get at another's local memory.

Against intermittents we use a strategy of dynamic reinitiali-
zation. Every data structure is periodically checked; every waiting state is timed out; the code is periodically checksummed;
memory transfers are hardware parity checked; memory is periodically tested; processors are periodically given standard tests.
Whenever anything is found wrong, the offending structure is in-
itialized. Using this scheme we may not know what caused a failure, but its effects will not persist. In the most extreme cases
we will need to reload all the program in main memory. Fortune-
ately we have a communications network handy to load from. This
technique of reloading has worked remarkably well in the current
ARPA Network. Each processor has a copy of the reload program in
its local memory, thus making loss of reload capability unlikely.

We might seem to be vulnerable to memory or I/O failures,
particularly those involving the PID and the clock. If these
modules fail it does indeed hurt us more, but only because we have
fewer modules of these types in our system. If we provide redundant modules, the system can reconfigure itself to substitute a
spare module for a failed one. Our design allows muliple I/O busses with multiple PIDs and clocks, and we could even have separate
backup interfaces to vital communication lines on separate busses.

To summarize, the mainstay of our reliability scheme is a system continually aware of the state of things and quickly responding to unpleasant changes. The second line of defense consists of
drastic actions like amputation and reloading. Assuming we can
make all this work, we will have quite a reliable system, perhaps
even one in which maintenance consists of periodic replacement of
those parts which the system itself has rejected.

Status and Near Future

In February 1973, as this paper is submitted, we are very much
in the middle of our multiprocessor development. Much progress
has been made and we are increasingly confident of the design,
but much work remains to be done.

The broad design is complete; all Lockheed-provided units
(CPUs, memories, busses, etc.) have been delivered; prototype
wire-wrapped versions of the crucial special modules have been
completed, including the Bus Couplers, Pseudo Interrupt Device,
clock, and modem interfaces; and a multi-bus, multi-processor-
per-bus assembly has been successfully tried with a test program.
A substantial program design effort has been in progress and
coding of the first operational program has been started. We are
still doing detailed design of some hardware, and we are still
learning about detailed organizational issues as the software
effort proceeds. An example of such an area is: exactly how it
is best for processors to watch each other for signs of failure?

We currently anticipate the parts cost of the prototype fourteen-processor system, without communication interfaces, to be under $100K.

Hopefully, by the time this paper is presented in June 1973, we will be able to report an operational prototype multiprocessor system. Beyond that, our schedule calls for the installation of a machine in the ARPA Network by about the end of 1973. We also plan to construct many variant systems out of this kit of building blocks, and to experiment with systems of varying sizes. As part of this work, we plan to concentrate on the very smallest version that may be sensible, in order to provide a minimum cost IMP for spur applications in the ARPA Network.

As the design has proceeded, our attraction to the general approach has increased (perhaps a common malady), and we now believe that the approach is applicable to many other classes of problems. We expect to explore such other applications as time permits, with initial attention to two areas: (1) certain specialized multi-user systems, and (2) high bandwidth signal processing.

With our presently planned building blocks, although we do not yet know what will limit system size, we do not now see any intrinsic problem in constructing systems with fifty or a hundred processors. As improvements in integrated circuit technology occur, and processors and memories become smaller and cheaper, organization and connection become the paramount questions in multiprocessor design. We expect to see many attempts at multiprocessors, and are hopeful that the ideas embodied in this design will help to steer that technology. Perhaps minicomputer/multiprocessors will soon represent real competition for the various brontosaurus machines that now abound.

Acknowledgements

Our new machine design is a product of many minds. We gratefully acknowledge the specific design contributions of M.Kraley, A. Michel, M. Thrope, and R. Bressler. Helpful criticisms and an important idea about the Pseudo Interrupt Device were contributed by D. Walden. Assistance in planning and in the choice of buildin blocks was contributed by H. Rising. Helpful ideas and criticism were provided by J. McQuillan, B. Cosell, and A. McKenzie. Assistance with support software was provided by J. Levin.

We also wish to express appreciation for the support and encouragement provided by Dr. L. Roberts of the Advanced Research Projects Agency.

Heart
A new mini / multi

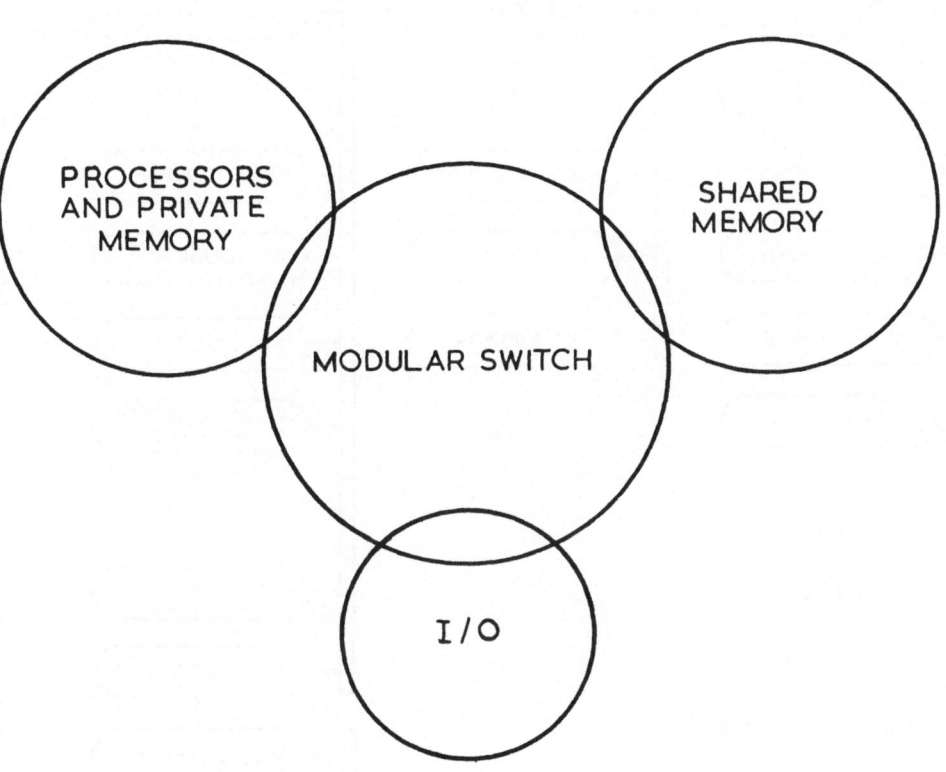

Figure 1   System structure

176

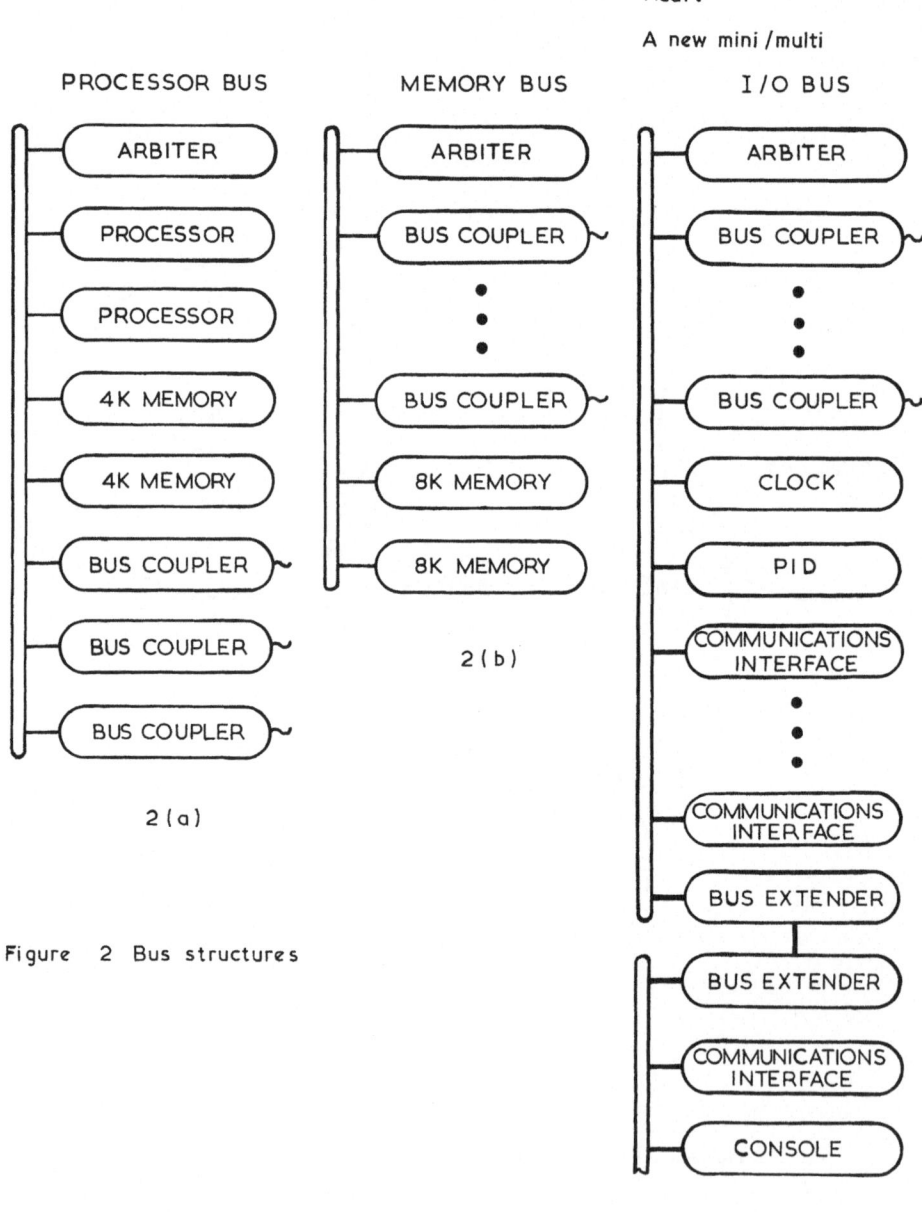

PROCESSOR BUS   MEMORY BUS   I/O BUS

2(a)   2(b)   2(c)

Figure 2 Bus structures

177

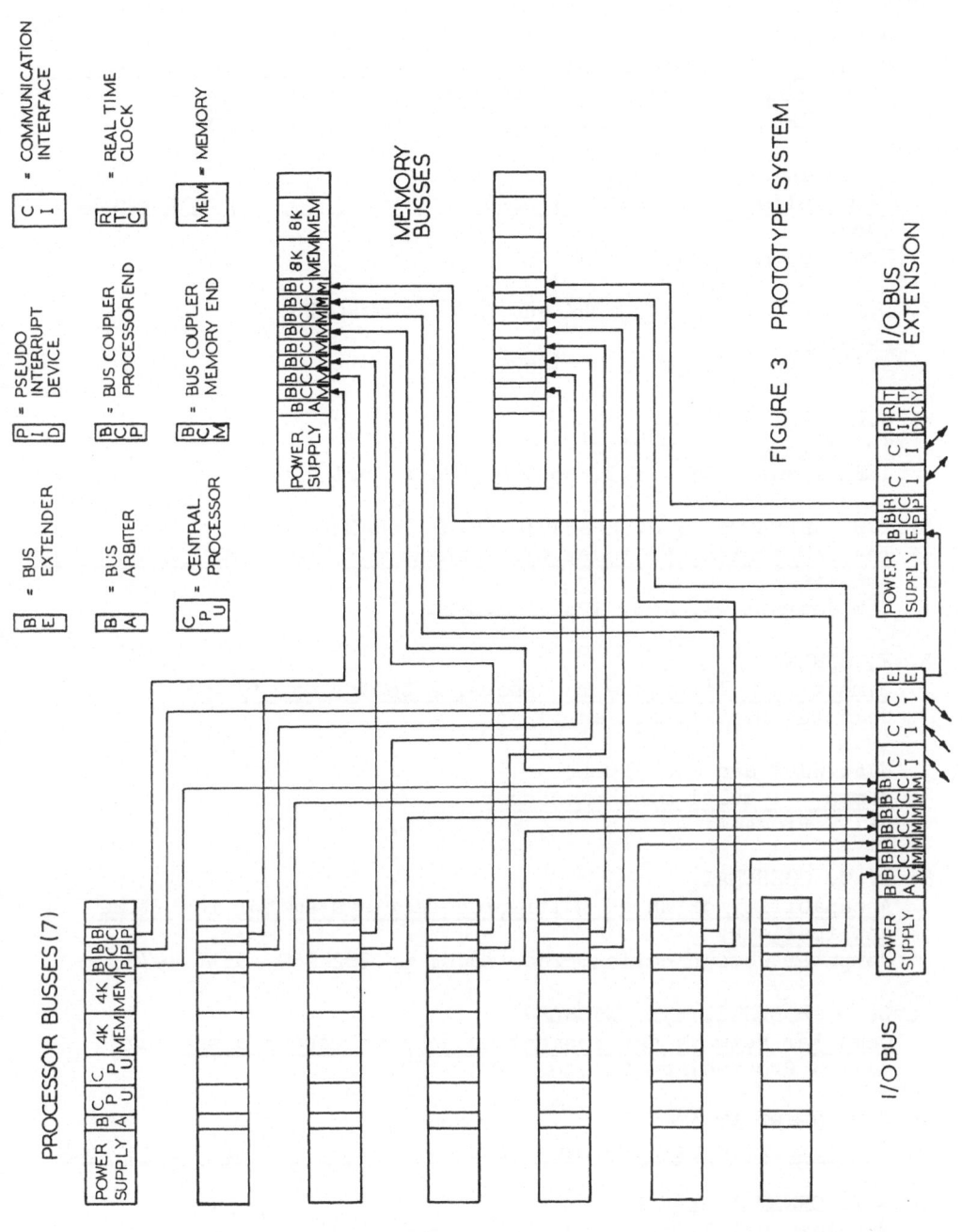

FIGURE 3 PROTOTYPE SYSTEM

References:

1. M. LEHMAN
A survey of problems and preliminary results concerning parallel processing and parallel processors.
Proc. IEEE, Vol.54, No.12, pp.1889-1901, Dec. 1966.

2. H. LORIN
Parallelism in hardware & software: real and apparent concurrency.
Prentice-Hall 1971.

3. D.L. SLOTNICK, W.C. BORK and R.C. McREYNOLDS.
Solomon
AFIPS Proceedings FJCC, 1962.

4. G.H. BARNES ET AL.
The Illiac IV computer
IEEE Trans C-17 Vol.8. pp.746-757, August 1968.

5. D.W. ANDERSON, F.J. SPARACIO, R.M. TOMASULO,
The IBM system/360 model 91: machine philosophy and instruction handling.
IBM Journal 11, Jan. 1967. pp.8-24.

6. E. COHEN.
Symmetric multi-mini-processors, a better way to go?
Computer Decisions, Jan. 1973.

7. W.A. WULF and C.G. BELL,
C.mmp - a multi-mini processor
AFIPS Proceedings, Vol.41, FJCC 1972.

8. D. C. COSSERAT,
A capability oriented multi-processor system for real-time applications.
Computer Communication, Proc. ICCC, pp.282-289, Oct. 1972.

9. L. G. ROBERTS, B.D. WESSLER
Computer network development to achieve resource sharing
AFIPS Proceedings Vol.36, SJCC 1970.

10. F.E. HEART ET AL
The interface message processor for the ARPA computer network

11. S.M. ORNSTEIN ET AL
The terminal IMP for the ARPA computer network
AFIPS Proceedings, Vol.40, SJCC 1972.

179

12. T. CHANEY, S. ORNSTEIN & W. LITTLEFIELD
    Beware the synchronizer
    Proc. COMPCON Conf 1972.

13. LOCKHEED ELECTRONICS COMPANY
    SUE Computer handbook
    Los Angeles 1972

14. R.C. HOLT
    Some deadlock properties of computer systems
    ACM Computing Surveys Vol.4, No.3. pp.179-196, Sept. 1972.

Supplementary Bibliography:

G.M. AMDAHL
Engineering aspects of large high-speed computer design:
part II logical organisation
IBM Tech. Report TROO.1227, Dec. 1964.

H.B. BASKIN ET AL
A modular computer sharing system
CACM Vol.12. No.10, Oct, 1969, p.551

BELL & NEWELL
Computer Structures
McGraw-Hill 1971

G. BELL ET AL
C.mmp the CMU multiminiprocessor computer
Dept. of Computer Science, Carnegie Mellon Univ. Aug. 1971.

G.J. BURNETT,ET AL
A distributed processing system for general purpose computing
AFIPS Proceedings, Vol.31, FJCC 1967

E.W. DIJKSTRA
Cooperating sequential processes
In: Programming Languages
Edited by F. Gennys,Academic Press pp.43-110, 1968.

M.J. FLYNN
Some computer organizations and their effectiveness
IEEE Transactions on Computers Vol.C-21, No.9, Sept. 1972.

M.J. FLYNN
Very high-speed computing systems
Proc. IEEE Vol.54, No.12 pp.1901-1909, Dec. 1966.

J.H. HOLLAND
A universal computer capable of executing an arbitrary number of
sub-programs simultaneously
1959, Proc. EJCC pp.108-113

J.M. MCQUILLAN ET AL
Improvements in the design and performance of the ARPA network
AFIPS Proceedings, Vol.41, FJCC 1972.

S.M. ORNSTEIN, M.J. STUCKI AND W.A. CLARK
A functional description of macromodules
AFIPS Proceedings Vol.30, SJCC 1967

M. PIRTLE
Intercommunication of processors & memory
AFIPS Proceedings, Vol.31, FJCC 1967

B. RANDELL
Operating systems: the problems of performance and reliability
IFIP Congress 71, Ljubljana, North Holland Pub.Co. 1972, pp281-290.

A description of the advanced scientific computer system
Texas Instruments Inc. 1972.

J.E. THORNTON
Parallel operation in the control data 6600
AFIPS Proceedings Vol.26, FJCC 1964.

W. WULF ET AL
Hydra- a kernel operating system for C.mmp
Dept. of Computer Science,Carnegie Mellon Univ. 1971.

A PARALLEL PROCESSING APPROACH
TO COMPUTER COMMUNICATION

Dan Cohen and Edward Taft

Center for Research in Computing Technology
Harvard University
Cambridge, Massachusetts

1. Abstract

This paper presents a model of bidirectional asynchronous computer communication. Parallel processing representation is used for the model, in a manner which allows mathematical computation of the duration of all the elements involved in the communication process, and the duration of the associated waiting periods which are caused by the self-synchronization of the entire system. The idea of multiple messages (multiple threads) is discussed in the context of band network-provided storage.

2. A Simple Model of Computer Communication

When two computers communicate, there is ordinarily a bidirectional exchange of information. In some applications, one computer provides data for a second, with the second simply signalling when it is ready for more information; in other applications, each computer periodically needs information from the other in order to proceed. The case in which we have strictly one-way communication is relatively uninteresting and will not be considered here.

Dr. Cohen is currently at the University of Southern California, Information Sciences Institute, Los Angeles, California. Mr. Taft is currently at the Xerox Palo Alto Research Center, Palo Alto, California.

In our first model of computer communication (Figure 1), communication is both synchronized and sequential. The vertical lines represent the flow of control for each of the two processors during real time, while the arrows leading from the output

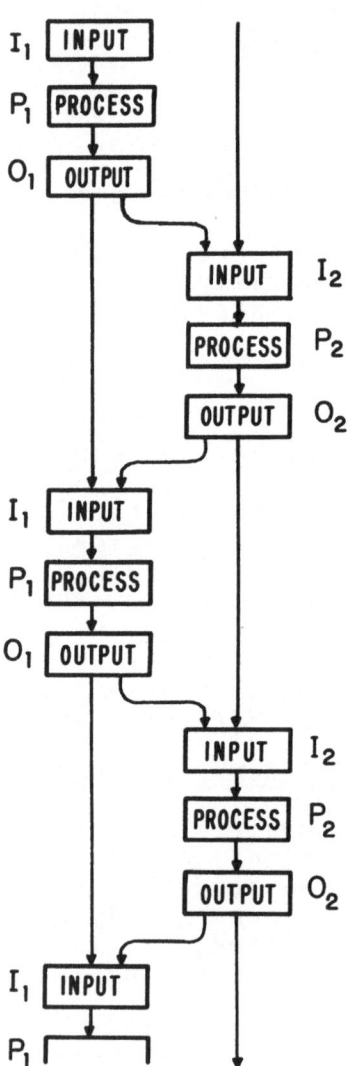

FIGURE 1

operations of one processor to the input operations of
the other represent the transfer of information (data
or control). The important feature in this model is
that each computer operates in a strictly
input-process-output sequence and is waiting while the
other computer is performing its operations.

The same model may be presented in a more compact
fashion by folding each processor's flow of control
into a loop, as shown in Figure 2. In this
illustration, the boxes labeled 'input', 'process', and
'output' now represent complete processes rather than
single instances of processes at particular moments.

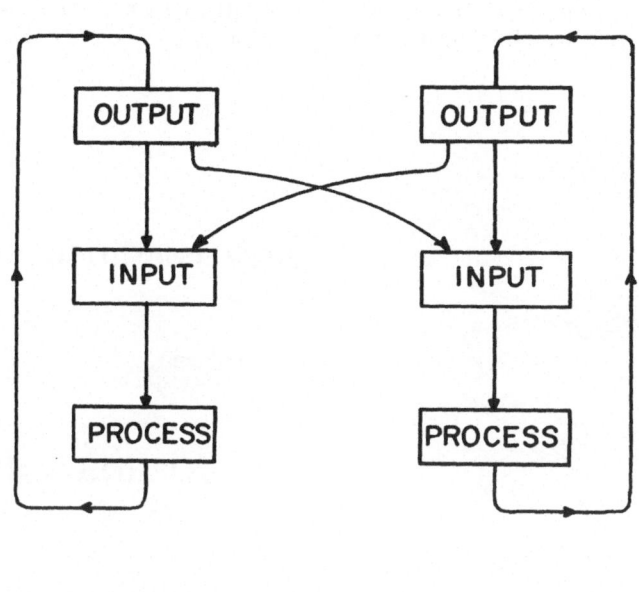

PROCESS 1   PROCESS 2

FIGURE 2

3. Processes and Tokens

A process is an entity with a positive duration
from the time it starts until it completes. The
process starts when all its preconditions are
satisfied. The completion of a process may in turn be
a precondition for the starting of another process.

In our model, processes will be represented by large, filled-in arrows, and the preconditions by tokens whose paths are indicated by thin arrows, as shown in figure 3. If the completion of process A is a precondition for the starting of process B, a path is defined to exist from the head of process A to the tail of process B. At any moment, a token may be either inside a process (thick arrow), indicating that the process is currently active, or waiting at the head of the thick arrow, indicating that the process has been completed and the respective precondition satisfied for the next process. When a process is active, it holds as many tokens as the process has preconditions; when the process terminates, all these tokens are released. The number of paths leading to a process is equal to the number of paths emanating from it.

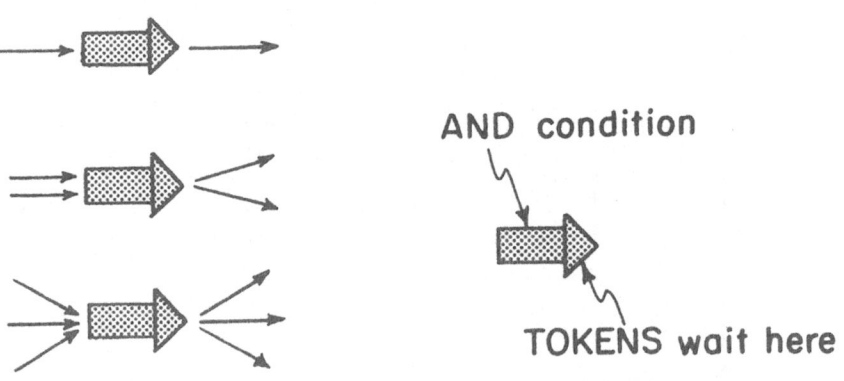

AND condition

TOKENS wait here

FIGURE 3

The processes are connected by paths to form loops, as shown in Figures 4 and 5. A loop is a chain (minimal set) of processes such that the completion of each process is a precondition for another process in the chain; together, the processes form a closed loop. Each token belongs to one and only one loop and always traverses that loop. Every path is a segment of exactly one loop. The position of a token in a given loop represents the state of that loop.

Figure 4 illustrates two possible control structures involving the same set of processes, in a pipeline configuration. The upper example contains only one loop and represents a strictly sequential flow of control. In other words, only one process may be active (containing a token) at a given moment. In contrast, the lower example contains five loops and hence has potential for some degree of parallelism.

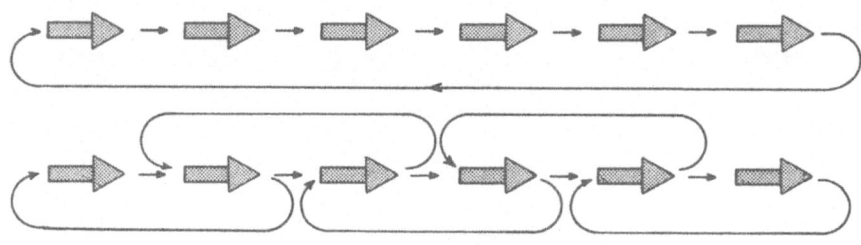

FIGURE 4

It can be shown that in a closed, connected system of processes, all loops are traversed by their respective tokens at the same rate [1]. Therefore, the entire system cannot be faster than the slowest loop. To improve the throughput of the system, one should attempt to shorten the longest loop.

Figure 5 illustrates this principle. The figures over the processes indicate the amount of time the processes require for completion. In the upper system, the longest loop, consisting of processes D and E, has a cycle time of 15; hence, the cycle time of the entire system is 15. In the lower system, the throughput of the system is improved by decreasing the cycle time of the longest loop to 9+ε, where ε is the time required by a newly-introduced process F, whose operation may be likened to that of a buffer. It should be noted that the loop containing processes A and B in the upper system has been lengthened by the addition of process C in the lower system. However, this has no effect on system throughput because the length of the loop in question, 6, is still less than that of the longest loop in the system.

----

[1] if averaged over a suitably long time. Within any given time interval, the number of traversals of all loops by their tokens would not differ by more than a constant whose upper bound is the number of loops.

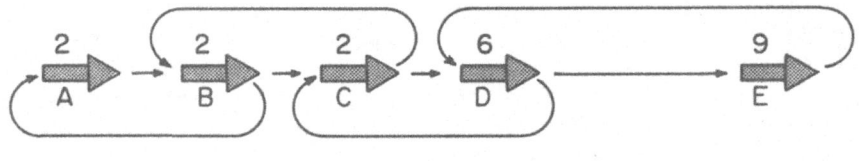

THRUPUT = 9 + 6 = 15

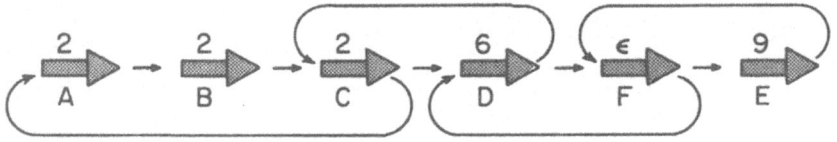

THRUPUT = 9 + ϵ

FIGURE 5

4. Processes and Computer Communication

The system in Figure 2 can be redrawn to conform
to the model just presented, as shown in Figure 6.
This system contains three loops and three tokens, two
of which represent the states of the two processors and
the third the state of the communication between the
processors. The labels over the processes indicate
both the names of the processes and the time required
for completion.

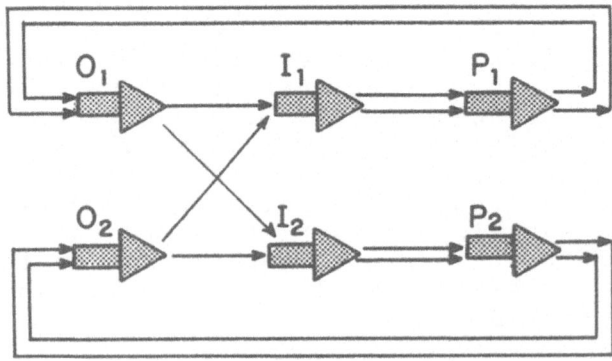

FIGURE 6

The lengths of the three loops are:

```
L1 = O1 + I1 + P1
L2 = O2 + I2 + P2
Lc = O1 + I2 + P2 + O2 + I1 + P1
```

Since Lc=L1+L2, Lc is obviously the longest loop. Also, since all the processes in the system are on this loop, only one process can be active at a time and the system is strictly sequential.

In order to improve the throughput of the system, we shorten the longest loop by eliminating the processing (P1 and P2) from the communication loop, as shown in Figure 7, hence introducing parallelism. This restructuring of the system implies that on each cycle, processing (P1, P2) is performed using data provided during the input phase (I1, I2) of the previous cycle. As a result, some buffering scheme is required and initialization of the system becomes slightly more complicated, but the significantly improved system performance is well worth this added complication.

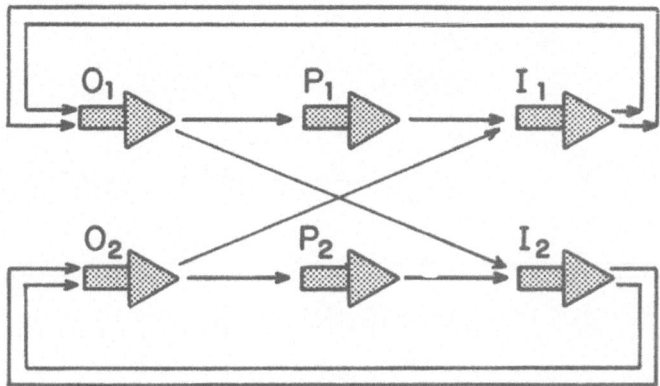

FIGURE 7

To facilitate analysis of this system, we present in Figure 8 a more detailed diagram in which the delays are represented explicitly as processes. X1 and X2 are the data transmission times between the processors, A1 and A2 are the times during which transmitted data waits in input buffers before being used, and W1 and W2 are the times during which the processors are waiting for input. While the Xi can be considered legitimate

188

processes, the Ai and Wi are not really processes in the sense that they perform useful operations whose duration depends on the work to be done. Rather, they represent the times during which only one of the necessary two preconditions are present for starting the Ii processes. Further, the Ai and Wi are interdependent in that only one member of an Ai-Wi pair can be nonzero during any given system cycle.

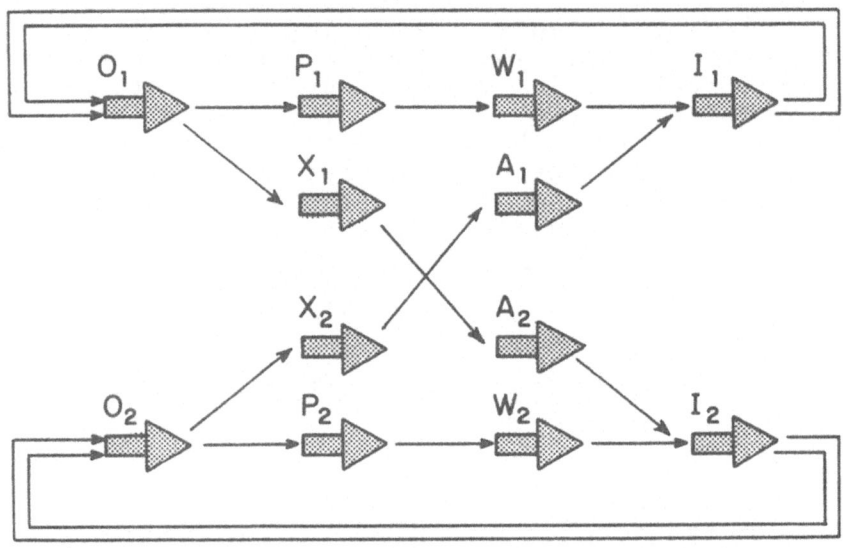

FIGURE 8

5. Analysis

There are three basic cycles, with a token associated with each of them:

```
Processor 1:      C1 = O1+P1+W1+I1
Processor 2:      C2 = O2+P2+W2+I2
Communication:    Cc = X1+X2+A1+A2+O1+I1+O2+I2
```

For ease of notation we define:

$$Ti = Oi + Ii \qquad \text{combined output/input operation}$$
$$RT = X1 + X2 \qquad \text{hardware round trip time}$$
$$B = A1 + A2 \qquad \text{buffering by the network.}$$

Rewrite the cycles:

$$C1 = W1 + T1 + P1$$
$$C2 = W2 + T2 + P2$$
$$Cc = B + RT + T1 + T2$$

Note that we have three equations in six unknowns: C1, C2, Cc, W1, W2, and B. However, since the duration of all these cycles must be the same, we have:

$$C = C1 = C2 = Cc$$

Now we have three equations in four unknowns: W1, W2, B, and C.

Define:

$$C1' = T1 + P1$$
$$C2' = T2 + P2$$
$$Cc' = RT + T1 + T2$$

These are the minimum cycle times for the three loops, that is, under the condition of no waiting times. Further, it can be shown that

$$C = MAX(C1', C2', Cc')$$

With no loss of generality, we can assume that processor 1 is not slower than processor 2; this implies that, $C1' \leq C2'$.

There are two important cases:

(a) $Cc' \geq C2' \geq C1'$ communication bound
(b) $Cc' < C2' \geq C1'$ processing bound.

In case (a), clearly B=0, and C=Cc', hence

$$W1 = C-T1-P1 = RT+T1+T2-T1-P1 = RT+T2-P1$$
$$W2 = C-T2-P2 = RT+T1+T2-T2-P2 = RT+T1-P2$$

In case (b), clearly W2=0, and C=C2', hence

$$W1 = C-T1-P1 = T2+P2-T1-P1 = (RT+T2-P1)-(RT+T1-P2)$$
$$B = C-RT-T1-T2 = T2+P2-RT-T1-T2 = -(RT+T1-P2)$$

Define $Di=RT+Tj-Pi$, where $j \neq i$. Using this notation, we get:

for case (a):
$$W1 = D1$$
$$W2 = D2$$
$$B = 0 \quad (i.e. \; A1 = A2 = 0)$$

and for case (b):
$$W1 = D1 - D2$$
$$W2 = 0$$
$$B = -D2$$

Since Ai and Wi cannot both be positive (nonzero) for the same i, if $D1 \neq D2$ then $A1=0$ and $A2=-D2$. If $D1=D2$ then $W1=W2=0$, and $B=-D2$. In this case, the value of B can be divided in any way between A1 and A2 without affecting anything but the phase difference between the processors.

The ease in which Di is used suggests that it has a meaning. If we rewrite it as

$$Di = (RT + Tj) - Pi$$

we see that Di measures the difference between the time required for communication $(RT+Tj)$ and the time used meanwhile for processing (Pi). Hence, $Di \geq 0$ implies $Wi \geq 0$ (communication bound), and $Di < 0$ implies $Ai > 0$ (processing bound).

It follows from processor 1 being not slower than processor 2 $(C1' \leq C2')$ that $D1 \geq D2$.

Case (a) is $\quad Cc' \geq C2' \geq C1'$
which implies $\quad D1 \geq D2 \geq 0$

and case (b) is $\quad Cc' < C2' \geq C1'$
which implies $\quad D1 \geq D2 < 0 \quad$ (where D1 can be negative or positive)

These conditions guarantee that in case (a)

$$W1 = D1 \geq 0 \qquad A1 = 0$$
$$W2 = D2 \geq 0 \qquad A2 = 0$$

and in case (b)

$$W1 = D1-D2 \geq 0 \qquad A1 = 0$$
$$W2 = 0 \qquad A2 = -D2 > 0$$

6. Multiple Threads

Figure 9 illustrates the communication system discussed above. The sequence T1-P1-X1-T2-P2-X2-T1... is called a 'thread'.

In practice, it is often the case that the processor idle time (Wi) is significantly greater than the useful processing (Ti+Pi). In such cases, it is possible to introduce an additional 'thread' of communication, as shown in Figure 10. If there is sufficient idle processor time, more threads may be added, without causing unnecessary delays to the system.

It should be noted that the introduction of additional threads implies a different initialization strategy for processor 1 (in this example) but no change to the operation of processor 2, which operates as before by responding as fast as it can to all its incoming messages.

An important feature of the operation with N threads is that the received response to a specific inquiry by either of the processors is delayed by N-1 messages.

7. Analysis of Multiple Threads

Suppose that N tokens are assigned to the communication loop. This is possible since the Ai are processes whose nature allows them to contain more than one token at a time (remember that the Ai are not real processes, but simply represent the availability of information). The manner in which packet-switching networks operate allows the Xi to contain more than one token at a time as well.

By having N communication tokens, one could reduce the average minimal communication loop (Cc) to one Nth of its original length (duration). However, it cannot be reduced to less than the length of its sequential components; hence

$$Cc' = MAX(T1, T2, (RT+T1+T2)/N)$$

It is clear that by increasing N (the number of threads) Cc' can be reduced to as little as the maximum

192

of T1 and T2, hence being smaller than C2'. When this
is the case, the system becomes processing bound, which
is the best that can be expected from the communication
system.

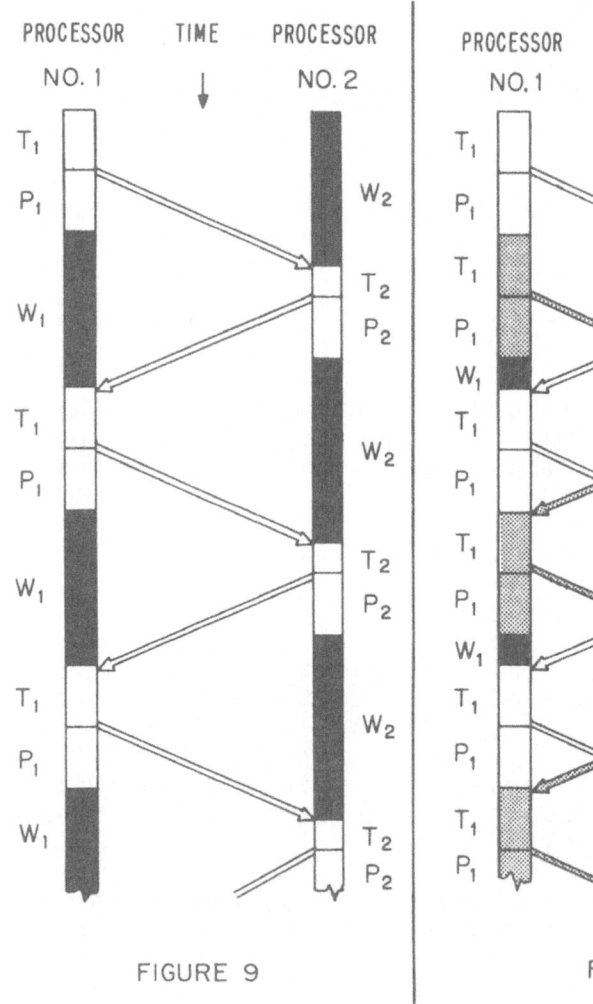

FIGURE 9

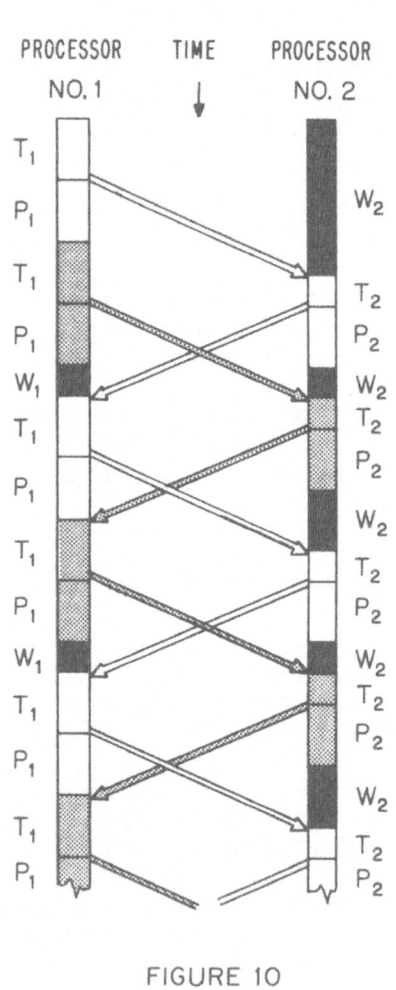

FIGURE 10

8. Practical Considerations

Let 'delay' be defined as the time from sending information to the other processor until the corresponding response arrives. It is desirable to minimize the delay, which has a lower limit due to the finite signal propagation speed and to network delays.

It is also desirable to maximize the bandwidth between the processors. This bandwidth has an upper limit, due to the finite capacity of the communication lines in use.

In Figure 11, delays (Y axis) are plotted versus bandwidth (X axis). The ideal operating point is at the intersection of the minimum possible delay and the maximum possible bandwidth. In practice, communication probably takes place somewhere on the line of minimum delay, but with less than maximum bandwidth. By adding more threads, the communication characteristics move first to the right, improving the bandwidth, keeping the delay at minimum, but as soon as the maximum bandwidth is reached (saturation) the communication characteristics move up, keeping the same full bandwidth but generating bigger delays.

By constant monitoring of the network performance, systems could dynamically change the number of threads, to keep the communication as close as possible to the ideal bandwidth/delay combination.

It is important to understand that in the ideal situation, from the user's point of view, some messages are always stored inside the network. When the user's program in one of the computers needs data, it is more efficient if this data is already available (and waiting) to be used than if a message has to be sent across the network to request transmission of the information. To carry this further, more pieces of information should already be in transit when the user program takes its input. This is very efficient for the user but may impose storage problems on a network, which is not designed to provide this storing capability.

194

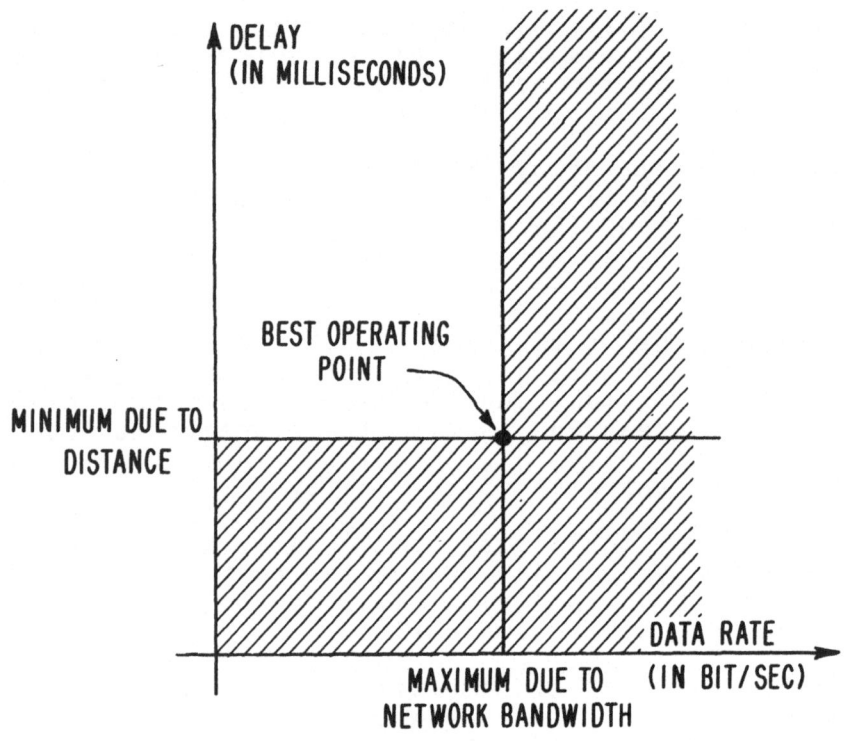

FIGURE 11

COLLOQUIES IN COMPUTER NETWORKS

G. Le Moli

Instituto di Elettronica ed Elettrotecnica, Politecnico
di Milano.

1 Introduction

In the last few years a great deal of interest has arisen in
communication problems in the field of data processing. Starting
from communications between computers and terminals, this technique
has quickly developed to more sophisticated applications in the
form of computer networks. A common background for all the above-
mentioned applications is the existence of a kind of "colloquy"
between remote entities at the ends of a physical communication
path, very often a telephonic line.

Although colloquies are often needed to support sequential information transmission on a single line (half/full duplex), they
are intrinsically necessary whenever co-operation among different
devices is to be achieved, even if it is difficult to identify the
communication path, as in the case of the interaction among the
various modules (both hardware and software) composing a single
computer.

We can find the most interesting cases of colloquies in the
computer networks field: there exist for example, colloquies between the communication computers (IMP's in ARPA terminology (1)),
between IMP's and HOST's, between operating systems of different
HOST's and finally between processes and between processes and

* Sections 1 to 6 and 10 have been reproduced respectively from
  (12) and (11) by kind permission of "Alta Frequenza".

users (2).   All these different colloquies are nested in such a
way that they can be thought of as organised in layers of different levels (2)(10).   The same problems arise in other computer
networks and are quite general.

Colloquies similar to those found in computer networks can be
found in other fields.   An example is given by the colloquy between
two telephonic centers, in order to provide a calling user connected to one of them with the facility of directly dialling a user
connected to the second one.   A quite different example is constituted by the contract bridge game, in which the final contract
is reached by means of a colloquy.

Colloquies arise from interactions among two or more entities
and therefore they can be studied from this point of view. Nevertheless, the colloquy is a very peculiar case of interaction and,
taking into account its current widely diffused applications, it
is worthy to be the subject of a special study.   One of the main
purposes of such a study is to construct a general theory suitable
to treat colloquies and related problems.   This can be done defining colloquies and entities which take part in them, and stating
methods to describe them in an easy to handle way.

Let us consider the colloquy between a computer and its terminal.   Hand-books describing such colloquies usually give a word
description of them; it is well known that a word description is
not suitable to contain all the information in an effective way.
It is a common experience indeed, that the simulation of a terminal requires a lot of information that cannot be extracted from the
often painful reading of hand-books.   Such approaches have been
followed which give a formal description of colloquies: in (3),
(4) and (5) a colloquy is described by means of automata[1]; in (6)
another colloquy is described by means of a grammar.   In (7)
they are described by means of graphs.   Nevertheless no general
treatment has been done for the whole subject in a unified way.
This paper and another to follow are an attempt to treat in a
unified way some problems about the theory of colloquies.   A
first approach to this theory has been given in (8).

In this paper some definitions are given about interlocutors
and colloquies to provide a terminology and to introduce some concepts about colloquies; then a way for formally describing colloquy
procedures is exposed.

---

[1]In (5) the behaviour of a couple of speakers is modeled as a couple
of automata in order to study the dialogue rhythms.

2 Preliminary Example

In this Section we shall refer as a working example to the colloquy between a batch terminal and the computer to which it is connected. Let us suppose this terminal is supplied with a card-reader, a printer, an operator console with some switches and some console lights. This terminal can be considered as a device with three inputs and three outputs (see fig.1). Inputs are labelled with greek lower-case letters, outputs with latin lower-case letters.

Output m consists of the messages the terminal sends to the computer; input μ consists of the messages the terminal receives from the computer: these messages travel on two logically different channels, irrespective of the fact that usually they are carried by the same telephonic line connecting the terminal to the computer.

Input τ consists of the information the user wishes to send to the computer by means of the terminal. This input is represented, in our example, by the punched cards to be transmitted.

Output t consists of information the user receives from the computer: in our example this output is represented by the received printed lines.

Let us now suppose that in the course of a colloquy the operator at the terminal wants to change the operation being performed; let us suppose, for example, he wants to abort the work being printed, or he wants to start the transmission of a deck of cards. He gives such an instruction to the terminal by means of the console switches which therefore represents input η .

Output c consists of the information to the operator concerning the operation being performed. In our case it is represented by the console lights.

The device outlined above and shown in fig.1, is called <u>interlocutor</u>: a formal definition of it will be given later on.

Now let us consider those hardware and software modules of the remote computer that carry on the colloquy with the terminal. It is easy to recognise that these modules of the computer communicate with the remaining parts of it by means of six logical ports analogous to those of the above considered terminal. While inputs τ, η, and outputs t,c are physically evident in the terminal, they are not always clearly identifiable inside the computer. Nevertheless such ports always exist, at least logically. In other words, another interlocutor exists inside the computer.

The connection between the interlocutor inside the computer and the one inside the terminal is drawn in fig.2, which represents the schema of this colloquy (9). In fig.3. the general schema of the colloquy between two interlocutors A and B is shown.

3 Interlocutors, messages and colloquies

In this Section we shall give a set of definitions.

a) Definitions concerning the interlocutor:

Let us label all the input-output ports as in fig.1. The interlocutor can now be defined as follows:

Def.1. - Interlocutor: a device with 3 inputs, 3 outputs, a set of internal states, such that:

- new internal state depends on the old one and on inputs μ and η;

- output m depends on the internal state and on inputs μ, η;

- input τ is completely inserted in output m;

- output t is completely extracted from input μ;

- output c depends on the internal state and on inputs μ and η.

Def.2. - Message: a piece of information received from input μ or sent on output m.

Def.3. - Text-in: information that is given the interlocutor by means of input τ: it is to be inserted unchanged in messages on output m;

Def.4. - Text-out: information extracted by the interlocutor from messages on input μ and transferred unchanged to output t;

Def.5. - Input commands: the commands received by the interlocutor on input η.

Def.6. - Output commands: the commands given by the interlocutor at output c.

b) Definitions concerning the messages:

Let us consider an output message at output m: this message contains two different kinds of information: the first one is (a piece of) text information entered in the interlocutor through input τ (text-in); the second one is all the remaining information, that can be called control information, entered in the interlocutor by means of inputs μ or η. Let us consider now an input message at input μ. It contains two kinds of information: (a piece of) text-out and control information. The latter will possibly produce information at output c and will be taken into account in determining the output message that will be given as answer. Two parts of the message can therefore be distinguished according to the following definitions:

Def.7. - "<u>Text</u>": it is as the piece of text-out contained in an input message as the piece of text-in inserted in an output message.

Def.8. - "<u>Envelope</u>": it is that part of the message that is not text.

Therefore in the output message given as answer to an input message, the output envelope depends on the input envelope, on the internal state, and on the input command, while the output text is simply a piece of the text-in. It must be noted that some messages do not contain text: this is the case of control messages. These message consist only of the envelope.

Here are two other definitions:

Def.9. - "<u>Output dictionary</u>": the list of all the envelopes the interlocutor can send.

For input messages, an interlocutor is built for acknowledging a finite set of input envelopes; any other envelope,(or a message containing a parity error) is considered a wrong envelope.[2]

Def.10. - "<u>Input dictionary</u>": the list of all the input envelopes. Among them one (or more) special envelope is considered: the wrong envelope.

c) Definitions concerning the colloquy:

To have a "colloquy", two interlocutors, A and B must be connected in such a way (see fig.3) that output messages of A are given as input messages to B and vice versa. This implies that a communication path exists between A and B.

[2] An interlocutor can be made in such a way as to treat different kinds of errors in different ways: in this case different kinds of wrong envelopes can be introduced. Also output dictionary can contain some "wrong" envelopes: see Sec.3 c).

Since the error rate of the communication path can be non-zero, it may happen that an interlocutor, say B, receives a message different from the one sent from the other one (A): we shall suppose that this message is always identified from the receiving interlocutor B as a wrong message. In this case B usually asks the message to be repeated until it is correctly received.

If A and B have been built to perform a particular colloquy, then the input dictionary of A will contain the output dictionary of B plus some wrong envelopes, and vice versa. If to the contrary, the output dictionary of, say, A, contains envelopes that are not in the input dictionary of B, then those envelopes will be considered by B as wrong envelopes. However, this wrong message has really been sent by A. This case is therefore different from the preceding one: in fact B will not acknowledge this message, and will ask for it to be repeated: If A really repeats it, then an endless loop arises.

Without loss of generality we can therefore say that both the input and output dictionary of both interlocutors contain wrong envelopes, and that the non-wrong subset of the output dictionary of each interlocutor is equal to the non-wrong subset of the input dictionary of the other one.

Now let us suppose that two interlocutors are connected, as in fig.3: let us suppose that they start to send each other messages and continue for a finite time. Now some definitions concerning more specifically the message can be given:

Def.11 - <u>Session</u>: a finite period of time during which two interlocutors A and B connected as in fig.3. send each other messages.

Def.12 - <u>Script between A and B</u>: the ordered set of messages sent by both the interlocutors during a session.

Def.13 - <u>Colloquy between A and B</u>: a set of scripts between A and B.

Def.14 - <u>Procedure</u>: the set of rules that an interlocutor follows to produce its output messages in the colloquy, depending on input commands and on internal state.

Def.15 - <u>Protocol of the colloquy between A and B</u>: the set of the procedures of A and of B.

Such a definition of colloquy corresponds in the theory of languages to the definition of a language by means of all the well-formed strings by which it is constituted. Then the protocol of the colloquy corresponds to the grammar generating that language.

In fact a colloquy can be described as a language and a protocol
as a grammar (6). Also graphs used in (7) describe the protocol
while in (3), (4) and (5) automata are used to describe procedures and the protocol arising from their interaction. In (12)
procedures are described by means of logical matrices.

4 Interlocutors and colloquies in computer communications:

The definitions given above are quite general: in fact nothing
has been said about the nature or format of the information involved, or about synchronization. At this point some hypotheses
will be introduced in order to allow a theoretical treatment for
interlocutors most commonly used in computer communications.

a) The Interlocutor:

Most of the interlocutors used in computer communications act
as follows: When the interlocutor is given a message at input μ,
it starts to work and produces a new internal state, a message
at output m, and commands at output c.[3] If the input message
contains text, this text is presented at output t; if the output
message contains text, this text is taken from input τ. Therefore
suitable buffers must be inserted between the interlocutor and
external devices connected to t and τ ports in order to allow them
to be asynchronous with respect of the interlocutor itself.[4]

Concerning input commands, they are usually in binary form.
Two kinds of commands can be distinguished:

i) State commands η_s: these commands have no immediate effect:
they are buffered and will be taken into account next time the
interlocutor will operate. Thus they can be considered as
causing some internal state variables to assume assigned values[5]:
if such variables are binary variables, the state commands have
the meaning of set/reset inputs. For example: abort, or wait
commands for printed lines or printed cards, and so on.

ii) Operate commands η_o: they too cause some internal state variables to assume assigned values;[5] moreover, they have an immediate effect and act as a trigger causing the interlocutor to
send an output message. This message depends on the given com-

[3] For some interlocutors, however, there exist input messages or
states such that they do not produce any output message.

[4] Otherwise such external devices should be directly driven by
the interlocutor itself.

[5] In other words input commands cause the interlocutor to assume
a new internal state.

mand, the internal state and possibly on the last input message received. Some examples: the command to start a colloquy, time-out command from an external clock, etc.

Therefore, the interlocutor is asynchronous with respect to the external devices connected to input state commands. The inter locutor is triggered only by messages on input μ and by operate commands.

b) The message:

Problems concerning messages are very well known and will be only recalled here. Texts and envelopes can be both a series of bits or a series of characters as well. Let us now consider the case in which both envelopes and text are characters: it is then convenient that some characters be reserved for envelope: text is not allowed to contain such control characters. In this way an easier treatment of control information is possible and some char-acters can be detected and handled by hardware devices at the I/O interface level.

When text consists of bits and an envelope of characters, pro-vision must be made in order to avoid the possibility that control characters contained in text are considered as pieces of envelope (transmission in transparent mode).

Text (or pieces of text) are often embedded between a "start of text" and an "end of text" character. Also messages are often embedded between a "start of message" and an "end of message" character. Messages are usually preceded by a series of "Synch-ronization characters" and followed by at least one parity check character. In some colloquies, messages with text are allowed to have text of any length from zero to a fixed maximum; in other colloquies, messages with text must have text of a fixed length. Furthermore, in some colloquies text is subdivided in several pieces embedded between pieces of envelope.

c) The colloquy:

Now let us connect two interlocutors as in fig.3: the communi cation path between A and B can be a telephonic line, a bus inside a computer connecting two different devices, or a logical connect-ion between two software modules (e.g. of an operating system), et

As we said above, an interlocutor sends a message when it receives a message or when an operate input command is given. Ther fore interlocutors will start to perform the colloquy if, and only if, a suitable operate command is given to one of the interlocutor They will continue to perform the colloquy until one of them does not reply any more to the other one. This happens usually when a

suitable input command is given. However, some procedures are
such as to give no answer when a particular input message is
received or when a particular internal state is reach (see
footnote (3)).

5 A Model of the Interlocutor:

In this section a model of the interlocutor is proposed. In
fig.4. some functionally autonomous parts are proposed and will
now be discussed (10).

a) Input unit: This element receives the input μ, checks the
message, splits it into its two components, the text and the envelope, delivers it, if any, text to the t-buffer and the envelope to the procedure unit. The envelope is possibly coded in some
way by the input unit.

b) Procedure unit: this element receives the (possibly coded) envelope of the input message and produces the (possibly coded) envelope of the output message depending on input envelope and its
own internal state (and thus on the input commands). The procedure unit is a sequential device with two inputs and two outputs.
Different ways of formalizing an interlocutor are based on different ways of formalizing the behaviour of the procedure unit.

c) Output unit: this element receives the output (possibly
coded) envelope from procedure unit, takes, if needed, a piece of
text-in from τ-buffer, produces the output message and finally
delivers it to output m.

d) t-buffer and τ-buffer: these buffers allow t and τ channels
to be asynchronous. In fact t-buffer acts as temporary storage
device between the instant at which a received text is available
to the external device and the instant at which this text is actually used by the device. The function of τ-buffer is analogous.
Both these buffers can be of different types. Let us consider for
example, the case of the τ-buffer. Usually, in any message, a
piece of text-in with a maximum fixed length can be included.
Therefore text-in must be divided in sub-texts of suitable length.
If this partition is made by the external device, the τ-buffer is
composed of a certain number of τ-sub-buffers, each of them being
filled by the external device with a sub-text. The output unit
inserts one sub-text in every message, in the same order in which
they have been introduced. If on the other hand the partition is
made by the interlocutor itself, the external device fills τ-
buffer continuously, while the output unit extracts from the
τ-buffer that amount of text every time it is required.[6]

e) η-buffer and c-buffer: these buffers allow η input commands
and c output commands to be asynchronous. It must be noted that
if, as usual, both input η and internal state are coded in binary
form, then η-buffer can be conceived of as a part of the state
buffer that contains the internal state variables in the procedure unit: the main difference is that values of the variables in
η buffer can be set/reset also from the external world.

6 Some Examples of Multiple Interlocutors

The interlocutor which we have discussed so far is the simplest
one: it performs a colloquy with only one partner, accepts and delivers text from and to only one external device. This is due to
the fact that it has only one port of each type (μ, η, m, c, t).

In computer networks there exist applications in which interlocutors with more than one port for each type are needed. We
shall refer to them as multiple interlocutors. In this Section
we shall treat two examples of multiple interlocutors.

A very interesting case of an interlocutor for computer networks is shown in fig.5, in which output t and input τ are split
into several (sub)-outputs t_1, t_2, t_3, . . . and (sub)-inputs,
τ_1, τ_2, τ_3, . . . [7] . This is the case, for example, of a terminal that has both a printer and a card punch: text-out must be
divided into two parts, one to be printed, the other one to be
punched.

Generally speaking interlocutors of this kind can be connected
to make a colloquy with the aim of transferring information presented at the input τ_{Ai} of interlocutor A into output t_{Bj} of interlocutor B. In other words, (fig.6) the colloquy between A and B
maps τ_{Ai} inputs onto t_{Bj} outputs and vice versa: a common physical
communication path (on which m and μ messages travel) is shared
among several logical links connecting inputs τ_{Ai} to outputs t_{Bj}

---

[6] The τ-buffer is also related to another problem: when a sub-
text has been inserted in an output message, it cannot be can-
celled until a good acknowledgment message has arrived from the
other interlocutor: therefore only the procedure unit can give
the external device the permission to fill sub-buffers. This
permission is given by means of an output command. Analogously,
external devices which use text-out must give the procedure unique information about free t-buffers; this information is given
by means of input commands. The procedure unit must therefore
give information about the availability of t and τ-buffers
respectively to input and output units.

[7] For the sake of simplicity, commands have been omitted in fig.5,6,7

and vice versa.   Therefore we have the following definition:
Def.16 - <u>Link</u>: the virtual communication path between a τ-input
　　　　　of an interlocutor and a t-output of the other one.

Information about links must be inserted in any message with
text.   In fact besides text (to be delivered to t-buffer) and
envelope (to be delivered to procedure unit) the input message
must contain information (directed to the input unit) concerning
the t-output the text is addressed to, and possibly the τ-input
of the other interlocutor the text is coming from.   This third
part of the message is now defined:

Def.17 - <u>Link address</u>:   that part of the message that contains
　　　　　information concerning the links.

Each input τ_i and output t_j is assigned a buffer; therefore a
link connecting a couple (t_i, t_j) is identified by the addresses of
the two buffers that it connects: this is generally the information contained in the "link address" part of a message.

Two different kinds of links can be considered; depending on
the way they are handled:

i)　Internal links: Any τ-buffer of A is always connected to the
　　same t-buffer of B and vice versa.   In this case any input τ_i
　　of A is always connected to the same output t_j of B.   External
　　devices that use such inputs and outputs are therefore pro-
　　vided with a sort of line switching service.

ii)　External links: any τ-buffer of A is filled by external de-
　　vices with the text to be transmitted and with the address of
　　the t-buffer of B to which this text must be delivered.   In
　　this case each input τ_i of A is allowed to state, for every
　　text, which output t_j of B the text must be delivered to.
　　External devices that use such inputs and outputs are there-
　　fore provided with a sort of message switching service.

We shall now describe a model for these interlocutors that
can be built by means of elements only slightly different from
the ones of the proceding Section.

a) Input unit: This element operates as before and delivers the
received text, if any, to the t-buffer addressed by link address,
b) Procedure unit: This element gives the output envelope to the
output unit: interlocutors exist in which this unit also gives
the link address, that is the τ-buffer to be transmitted.   In this
case, τ-buffers are transmitted with a strategy depending on the
colloquy being developed.

c) Output unit: this element inserts into the message, text from
   the proper τ-buffer; it also inserts the link address, when
   this is not done by the procedure unit.

d) t and τ-buffers: there is one buffer for each input τ_i and one
   for each output t_j. Each buffer is identified by an address.

Another important type of multiple interlocutor used in computer networks is given in fig.7 in which an interlocutor with
several μ_i inputs and m_j outputs is drawn. This interlocutor can
be triggered by an operate input command or by a message in any
input port μ_i. When triggered the interlocutor sends an output
message on one or more output ports m_j: the message produced and
the output port depend on the input message, on the input port, on
internal states and on input commands.

7 The Communication Device (CD)

Now let us consider a couple of interlocutors, A and B, connected as in fig.3: we shall hereafter say that they are MM-connected. Let us consider the ensemble of them as a new device with
four I/O text ports and four I/O command ports: if it happens
that text-out of B is the text-in of A, and vice versa, then the
device will be called a "Communication Device".

Let us assume some conventions:

T_A is the set of t_A, τ_A;

M_A is the set of m_A, μ_A;

H_A is the set of C_A, η_A;

$T_A = T_B$ means that t_A result to be always equal to τ_B, and t_B
result to be always equal to τ_A.

Now, a general definition of a communication device can be
given:

Def.18 – Communication device (CD): a device with two groups of I/
   ports, which has just the task to perform a colloquy. A
   common example is the colloquy between a user and its
   process. Input data constitute the messages from the
   user to the process, output data consitute the messages
   from the process to the user. Another example is the
   colloquy between two processes.[9]

---

[9] Another example is the contract phase in contract bridge game.

These interlocutors will be referred to as terminal interlocutors; they do not constitute a CD.

8 Other connections of two Interlocutors

In this Section we discuss other ways in which output ports of an interlocutor can be connected to input ports of another interlocutor[10]. Since the ports of an interlocutor are not equal to each other, different interactions arise depending on which ports are connected; moreover, only the following connections are meaningful:

T ports to T ports
T ports to M ports
M ports to M ports
H ports to H ports

Let us now consider the device in fig.9, in which M ports of A are connected to T ports of B: we shall say that they are MT-connected. In this case the interaction between the two interlocutors is imposed only by A since, by definition, B does not relate t_B to τ_B. The device of fig.9 is a new interlocutor, C the I/O ports of which are related to the ones of A and B as shown in the figure. Some commands are also exchanged between A and B: some others can be exchanged with the external of the composite interlocutor C.

Two interlocutors A and B can also be connected as in fig.10 in order to constitute a new device: this device may be called, as a whole, "procedure adaptor" because its effect is to extract from input messages of A a text and commands and insert them into output messages of B, and vice versa (commands could also be exchanged with the external of the procedure adaptor). We shall say that they are TT-connected.

Let us suppose for example that we wish to transmit texts and commands between an interlocutor A' (say a terminal) and another interlocutor B' (say a computer of a different manufacturer) and procedures P_A and P_B, do not match in such a protocol to allow a correct transmission. In this case a procedure adaptor can be inserted between A' and B' (fig.11) implemented with the proper partner A of A' and the proper partner B of B', A and B being TT-connected.

[10]The case in which output ports of an interlocutor are connected to input ports of the same interlocutor is not of interest.

Obviously an output command of A can be fed as input command of B only if the protocol between B and B' allows such a command; for example, if the last protocol has not the "kill print" command, it will not be possible to prevent B' from ending the transmission of printed lines.

9 Chains of Interlocutors

Let us consider a CD (fig.8): it can be used as a connection device (fig.13) between two interlocutors C and D that use it as a message exchange path. Both C and D exchange commands with their side H ports of the CD. Note that the protocol of the colloquy between C and D is not affected by the CD: the presence of the CD is important only as a possible source of commands[11]. If the ensemble of C.A.B.D is another CD, and this connects two other interlocutors, and so on, several times, a chain of interlocutors is built.

Let us now start from another point of view, that in a certain sense can be considered the opposite one. Let us consider two assigned interlocutors I_1, I_n (n even) which perform a colloquy. They might have been designed to be directly MM-connected, but they might not; in fact, no matter which way messages are to go through, a colloquy can be performed provided that there is a path from one interlocutor to the other one, such as to enable message exchange. However some properties of such a pth have been assumed especially for what concerns commands for controlling the path. Therefore a suitable CD has been supposed to be the message exchange path between the considered interlocutors I_1, I_n: their messages are seen as a text by this CD and transferred unchanged from I_1 to I_n and vice versa. But, as it was seen, the CD is, in its turn, a couple of interlocutors, say I_2 and I_{n-1} performing their colloquy: therefore, there are two nested colloquies (as in fig.12). Now let us introduce another CD between I_2 and I_{n-1}, constituted by the interlocutors I_3 and I_{n-2}, and so on to the couple $I_{n/2}$ and $I_{n/2+1}$ (fig.13)[11]. We say that interlocutors $I_1, I_2, \ldots I_{n-1}, I_n$ constitute a chain.

Here is the definition of a chain:

Def.19 - Interlocutor Chain: an ordered set of interlocutors I_1, I_2 $\ldots I_n$ such that any $I_i, 2 < i < n-1$ is MM or MT or TT connected with both I_{i-1} and I_{i+1}. Moreover I_i can have H connections with I_{i+1} and/or I_{i+1}.

[11] In order to simplify the figures, commands are hereafter omitted.

Now some properties of an interlocutor chain will be examined. First of all, a chain will result in a CD, a procedure adaptor, or a composite interlocutor if its ports at both ends are respectively TT [12], MM, TM(MT).

The way in which the chain in fig.13 has been built shows that the internal interlocutors have been introduced in order to provide a message path for the external ones. In a certain sense, the more external the interlocutor is, the more important it is. Now let us assign to each interlocutor I_i an integer number l_i as level, such that

1) $l_i = l_j$ if interlocutors I_i and I_j are MM-connected by a CD, or if they are directly MM-connected; (in all other cases $l_i \neq l_j$);

2) $l_i > l_j$ if I_i is on the T side and I_j on the M side of a composite interlocutor, or if they are TM-connected (I_i on T side);

For the sake of simplicity, it is convenient to add two other conditions:

3) $\left| l_i - l_j \right|$ be minimum for any i and j;

4) $\min_i l_i = 1$

For the chain in fig.13, the above rules bring to the following assignment: starting from I_1 the level decreases by 1 at each interlocutor, until the couple directly MM-connected ($I_{n/2}$ and $I_{n/2+1}$) is encountered: they perform the innermost (lowest level) colloquy and may be considered the logical medium point of the chain: therefore, $l_{n/2} = l_{n/2+1} = 1$. The interlocutors of the second half have increasing levels, until I_n, for which $l_n = l_1 = n/2$. Such a chain may be considered as constituted of nested levels (or layers (2)), until the medium point: each interlocutor has as partner the interlocutor at the same level in the other half of the chain.

Let us now suppose that a new chain is obtained from the one in fig.13, by substituting I_2 and I_3 with a composite interlocutor: we get the new chain of fig.15, in which CDs involved are

---

[12] To be a CD it is however necessary also to have condition $T_1 = T_n$. Fig.14 shows an example of a chain with TT ends that is not a CD. ($l_1 > l_3$).

indicated. It is easy to see that in giving the levels to interlocutors of this chain, it is necessary to state [13]

$$l_1 = l_2 + 2$$

A situation as in fig.15 can arise because sometimes inter-
locutors(and levels) do not correspond to well defined physical
devices but rather they are to be obtained by a decomposition of
a complex system: this must be done suitably. From the definition
of levels, the statement directly follows:

- each couple of interlocutors directly MM-connected is at a
relative minimum of level;

- each couple of interlocutors directly TT-connected is at a
relative maximum of level.

Let us say that an interlocutor i is right-oriented if its
M ports are connected to interlocutor i + 1, and that it is left-
oriented if its M ports are connected to interlocutor i - 1.
Two interlocutors are counter-oriented if one of them is right-
oriented and the other one is left-oriented. Now we shall give
this definition of a chain:

Def.20 - Regular interlocutor chain: a chain which is a CD and
moreover for every interlocutor in such a chain there
is a counter-oriented interlocutor in the same chain
such that they are MM-connected by a CD or are directly
MM-connected.

Now the following theorem will be proved:

Th.1: A regular chain is constituted of an even number of interlocutors.

A regular chain is a group of interlocutors that constitute
a CD. In its turn a CD can be constituted by 2 interlocutors
directly MM-connected, or by some CD in cascade. Therefore, the
total number of interlocutors is even.

Now we state the following:

Th.2. In a regular chain, $l_1 = l_n \geq l_i$ for i = 1, . . . n

[13]Interlocutor $I_6(l_6 = 3)$ in fig.15 does not have its partner; it
is therefore to be expected that the other level 3 interlocutor
does not exist.

Let us suppose that there is an i for which $l_3 > l_1$; let us consider the interlocutor I_i with i minimum for which $l_i > l_1$: this interlocutor would be left-oriented because $l_{i-1} < l_i$; therefore it would not have its counter-oriented interlocutor: this is not possible because the chain is supposed to be regular: therefore, $l_i \leqslant l_1$, i = 1, . . . n. Analogously it can be shown that $l_i \leqslant l_n$, i = 1, . . . n. It follows that $l_1 = l_n > l_i$.

From this theorem the following properties follow. Let I_j, j < n be the first interlocutor from the left for which $l_j = l_1$; then:

$$I_j \text{ is left-oriented}$$

$$I_{j+1} \text{ is right-oriented}$$

$$l_{j+1} = l_j = l_1 = l_n$$

the chain breaks into two CDs in cascade.

Th. 3: If in a regular chain a group of interlocutors, I_i, I_{i+1},... I_j, constitute a CD then $l_i = l_j$.

The theorem is a consequence of the definition of levels: in fact $l_{i+1} = l_{j+1}$, and therefore $l_i = l_j = l_{i-1} - 1$.

Let us state that the level l_α of a CD, say d, is the level of its end interlocutors; then

- two counter-oriented interlocutors I_i and I_j connected by α can be assigned levels $l_i = l_j = l_{\alpha+1}$.

- if two CDs α and β, are connected in cascade, then they constitute a new CD, say γ, such that $l_\gamma = l_\alpha = l_\beta$.

Here is the last theorem:

Th.4: A chain is regular if, and only if, for any i < n, $\left| l_i - l_{i+1} \right|$
       = 1, and moreover $l_1 = l_n \geqslant l_i$.

The 'if' part of the theorem is a consequence of the definition of levels: in fact, let us start from a relative minimum of level (a direct MM-connection): these two interlocutors constitute a CD that connects two other interlocutors: if they are MM-connected by this CD, they constitute a new CD with level increased by 1; if this new CD in its turn MM-connects two other interlocutors, a new CD with level increased by 1 is obtained; this procedure continues until a relative maximum of level is reached, that is, until a CD that does not MM-connect two interlocutors is found. In this case the CD is connected in cascade with another CD: let us start again from another minimum and so on until all relative minima have been used. Now, some CDs in cascade exist, and constitute a new CD. The procedure continues until the ends are reached: this is guaranteed by the fact that $l_i < l_1 = l_n$. The "only if" part of the theorem is proved by showing that it is not possible to assign in an irregular chain levels such that

$$\left| l_1 - l_{i+1} \right| = 1, \text{ and } l_i \leqslant l_1 = l_n.$$ In fact, in an irregular chain, there is an interlocutor, say I_i, that is not MM-connected to a counter-oriented interlocutor by means of a CD. If this is due to a situation such as the one in fig.15, then the condition

$$\left| l_i - l_{i+1} \right| = 1$$ cannot be satisfied. Otherwise, interlocutor I_i is oriented with its M ports to one end of the chain and is at a higher level than the end: in this case the condition $l_1 = l_n \geqslant l_i$

is not satisfied.

Connections of interlocutors provide a useful tool in computer network modelling: in this Section we have only treated some sampl problems in this field. A general treatment of interconnected interlocutors will be given in a further paper.

10. A Computer Network model by means of protocols

In this Section we shall give, as an example of the use of the concepts exposed in the preceding Sections, a model of the protocols involved in a computer network. Let us consider two computers 1 and 2 directly connected and two processes P_1 and P_2 in each computer that exchange messages (fig.16). Messages M_{P1} and M_{P2} are text for operating systems OS_1 and OS_2; their messages M_{OS1} and M_{OS2}, are text for the couple of interlocutors X_1 and X_2, implementing the protocol between computers 1 and 2[14].

Let us now consider n processes P_{11}, P_{12} ... P_{1n} in computer 1, each of them connected by means of a link with one of n processes P_{21} ... P_{2n} in computer 2. In fig.17 it is shown that the pair of operating systems act as the interlocutors in fig.5 and 6.

---

[14] It must be noted that interlocutors X are acutally a module of the operating system: however, it is convenient here to emphasize their presence.

Let us now consider the same two computers of fig.17, connected by means of three nodal centres (fig.18). Two new protocols must be introduced: the protocol of interlocutors Y, i.e. the protocol between hosts and nodal centres[15], and the protocol ZZ between nodal centres. As it can be seen in fig.18, YY protocol has been used between C1 and NC1, and between C2 and NC3, while protocol ZZ has been used between NC1 and NC2, Nc2 and NC3.

In fig.19 a tentative model of a nodal centre operating in a complex network is drawn: some more protocols have been introduced to this purpose.

In order to illustrate the role of the various protocols in a network, let us suppose that the maximum text length is 8 k bits between hosts and nodal centres, and 1 k bit between centres (1.1 k bit "packet": such lengths are those used in the ARPANET, and have been chosen in relation to transmission error rates also (1)). Let us also consider an operating system sending messages to other operating systems in the network. These messages are fed as text to interlocutor X which sends them to its partner in the receiving host. For flexibility reasons, it is convenient to assume that I/O messages of user processes and I/O messages of operating systems will have any length. I/O messages of X at M ports will be of 8 k bit.

Transmission between the above-mentioned interlocutors and their partners in the recieving host is achieved by means of a chain of groups of interlocutors. The first group is the pair YY (host to IMP protocol) that has text of 8 kbit. The second group consists of interlocutors W W' W". They will direct the O.S. messages to the destination, distinguishing first the O.S. messages directed to other local hosts or local terminals from O.S. messages directed to other nodal centres. The first ones are given as text to interlocutor Y connected to the addressed local host or to interlocutors J connected to local terminals (interlocutor W' represents the local fictitious host for terminals directly connected to nodal centres and interlocutors J's implement the protocols for such terminal connections). Messages directed to other nodal centres enter another group of interlocutors. This group

---

[15] This protocol must be introduced because host and nodal centre are possibly two remote machines, nearly always very different from each other; therefore a protocol is needed at least to avoid transmission errors and to allow them to be asynchronous.

consists of C parts of all the nodes.[16]   These messages are
given as text to interlocutor K, that splits 8k bit text into
eight pieces, inserts or extracts them into or from 1.1k bit
packets. Finally interlocutor Z implements node to node protocol.

Now we shall use the above model to make some considerations
about links in the network. Let us call "Transmission subsystem"
the collection of all the parts C in every nodal centre, and of al
the communication lines. Hereafter we shall indicate simply as C
the part C of a central node. The transmission subsystem has this
unique feature: if a text (hereafter called t-text) is given to a
C, together with the name of another C, the t-text will be delivered to the addressed C within a fixed maximum delay, together
with the name of the sending C.

The maximum length (e.g. 1.1 kbit) of t-messages (or packets)
that two nodal centres can exchange depends on the transmission
lines used and on error probability; the length of t-text to be
transmitted is unrelated to the length of the t-messages and depends upon factors such as buffer storage limitations. Therefore,
the sending C (that is interlocutor K) must divide the t-text into
a proper number of pieces of t-text (t-sub-text), and include each
of them in a t-message. The receiving C(interlocutor K)will need
some information for reassembling the received t-sub-texts in t-
text. For this reason the sending C is required, when transmitting a t-text, to give the t-text an identification symbol α , and
send t-messages containing its name, the name of the addressed C,
the symbol α, a t-sub-text and the ordering number of it in the
original t-text; in this way the symbol α is a sort of logical
link (t-link) for the C's, and is a generalization of the "link
address". Note that when the t-text has completely arrived to the
final nodal centre, then the symbol α of the t-link is free and
can be used again. The main point to be emphasized is that these
t-links have not to impose any constraints on the entities that
use the communication subsystem and must be unknown to them.

Other links are needed in a complete network: t-link is the
lower level of link.

---

[16]Each nodal centre is considered constituted by the parts A,B,
and C (fig.19). Part A takes care of the connection with the
local host, part B takes care of the local directly-connected
terminals (and constitutes the fictitious host), and part C
takes care of the connections with other nodal centres.

In the nodal centre, interlocutors Y are in principle not essential to the communication subsystem; in fact, they act only as interfaces between the hosts and the communication subsystem; also interlocutors J act as interfaces between the communication subsystem and direct terminals. In fact, text port of interlocutor W or W' is the actual entry point to the communication subsystem. Let us now call "proper communication subsystem" the collection of all nodel centres after taking off all interlocutors Y and J, and all lines connecting nodal centres: the difference between the proper communication subsystem and the transmission subsystem is that the first one has only one host or direct terminal at each port, while the seond one has at each port several hosts, one of them possibly the fictitious one. The proper communication subsystem is analogous to the transmission subsystem: therefore the same considerations can be repeated and c-text defined analogously to t-text.

Let us consider two operating systems (interlocutor X now considered into the O.S) of two different hosts, exchanging information. The information to be transmitted is originated outside the O.S's, e.g. by processes, and is delivered to the O.S's as s-text to be transmitted; the transmission is accomplished by means of s-messages, some of those s-messages carrying s-sub-texts. We have therefore the same situation as before, and in particular we will define s-links. Since the direct connection of two operating systems is not feasible, a proper communication system must be inserted between them: therefore s-messages are given as c-texts for the proper communication system.

The final step is to remember that s-text of the O.S8s is actually constituted by p-messages exchanged between remote processes.

It is now clear that the protocol between nodel centres (t-protocol), the protocol between O.S's (s-protocol) and the protocol between processes (p-protocol) can be made largely independent from each other. If this is not done, and the user must himself handle c-links and s-links, then the use of the network becomes very difficult: c-links and s-links must therefore be operated by the network operating system.

Let us now show by means of a working example, how the above concepts could be used in defining messages for the network in fig.19.

Let us suppose that a sub-process PS in a computer wishes to send a p-message of 61·kbit to a receiving sub-process PR in a remote computer. Establishing the protocol of the colloquy between the sub-processes is the task of the user: however, p-messages must be such as to be processed by the operating system: let us suppose, for the sake of simplicity, that in this network every

216

sub-process is given a name that is addressable from every other process in the network (we are not here concerned with how such names are given), and that a p-message is constituted by the name of PS, the name of PR, and a text. Therefore, PS will deliver the following p-message:

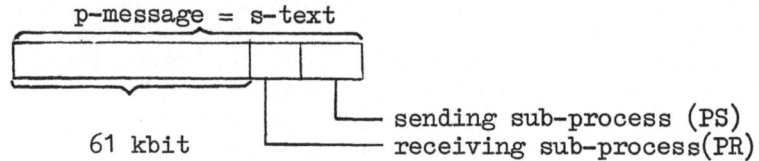

p-message = s-text

61 kbit

— sending sub-process (PS)
— receiving sub-process(PR)

This p-message will be considered as s-text by the operating system. Then, the OS will subdivde the s-text into 7 pieces of 8 kbit each and one piece of 5 kbit. Each one of these eight s-sub-texts will be inserted in an s-message together with the name of the sending OS, of the receiving OS, and the s-link; moreover the ording number of the s-sub-text, and e.g. a bit indicating the last one are needed[17].

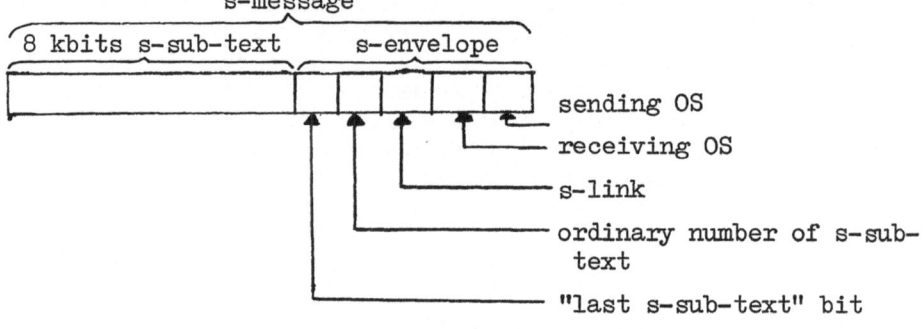

s-message

8 kbits s-sub-text   s-envelope

— sending OS
— receiving OS
— s-link
— ordinary number of s-sub-text
— "last s-sub-text" bit

<hr/>

[17] In this case it has been supposed, for the sake of simplicity, that the s-envelope (and later on the t-envelope also) contains only the names of the sender, of the receiver, and the link, besides the ordering number of the "last sub-text" bit.

The first s-message will contain as s-sub-text the first piece of the p-message:

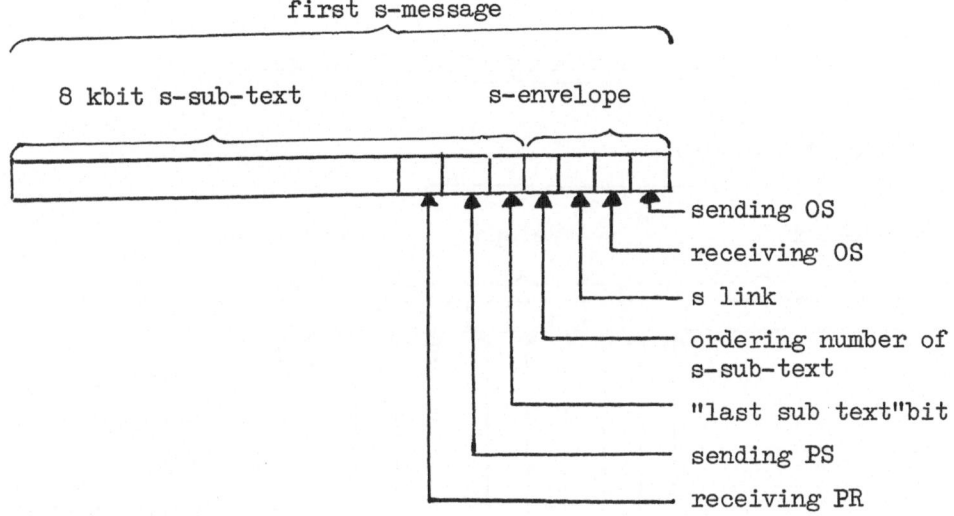

These eight s-messages will be given as c-texts to the communication device (T ports of interlocutor W): the ones directed to hosts connected to the same NS (possibly the fictitious one) are delivered to the corresponding W (or W') interlocutor. The ones directed to other nodal centres are given to the transmission system (interlocutors W'' and K) as t-text. Interlocutor K divides this t-text into eight pieces of 1 kbit (the last one into five pieces), and inserts each of them in a t-message:

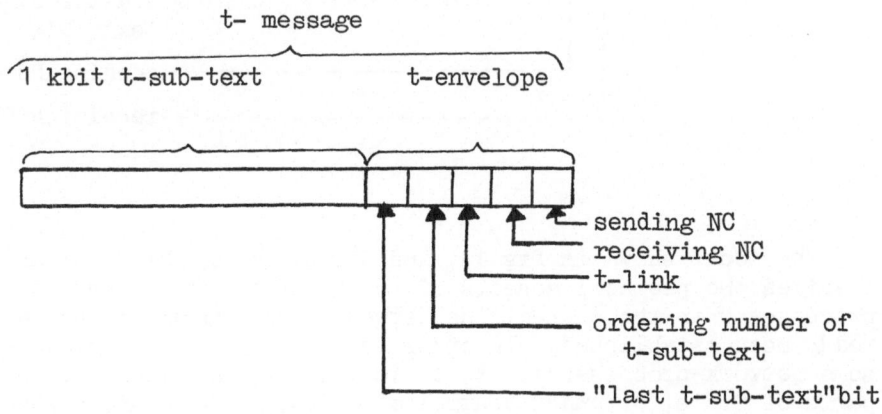

The original p-message of 61 kbits has given rise to seven groups of eight t-messages each and a last group of five t-message the shape of the first t-message of the first group is the following one:

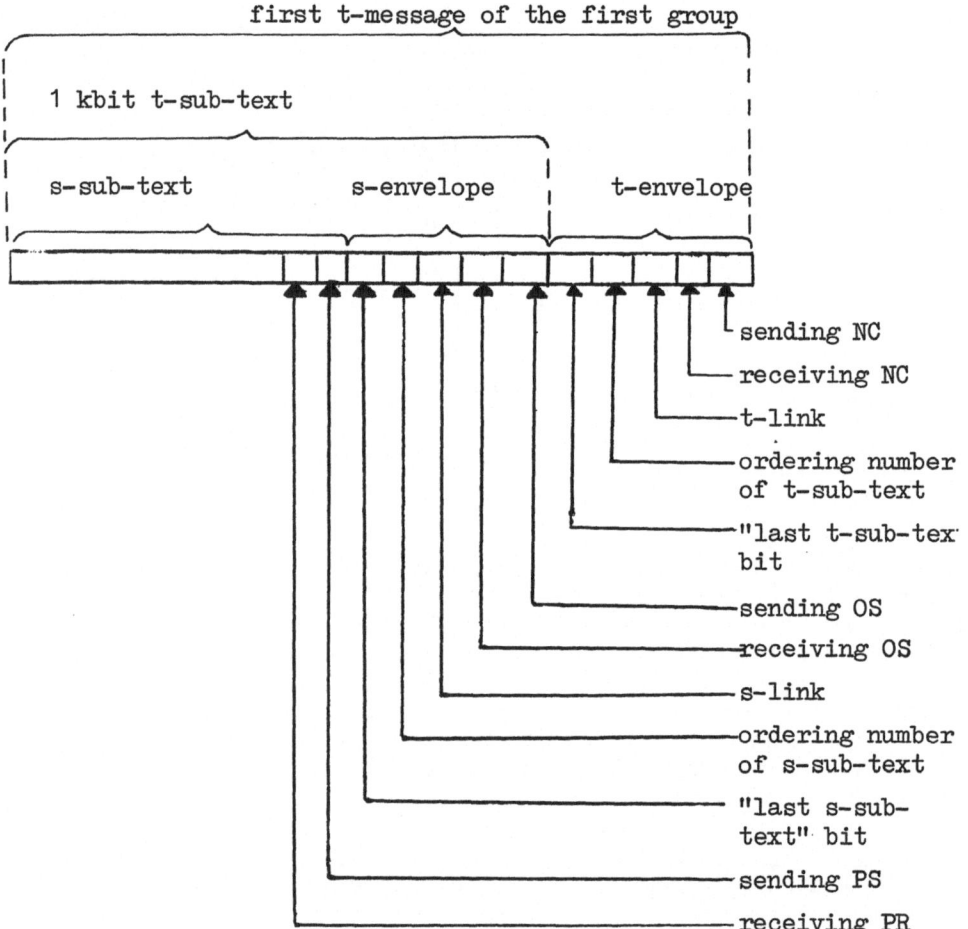

first t-message of the first group

1 kbit t-sub-text

s-sub-text   s-envelope   t-envelope

- sending NC
- receiving NC
- t-link
- ordering number of t-sub-text
- "last t-sub-text" bit
- sending OS
- receiving OS
- s-link
- ordering number of s-sub-text
- "last s-sub-text" bit
- sending PS
- receiving PR

The model shown in fig.19, and discussed in this Section emphasizes the protocol aspects of the network between user's-processes when the connections between such processes have already been established. In order to implement such protocols some network-processes are to be implemented and included as parts of O.S's, or under control of O.S.,(both in hosts and in nodal centre computers). Particularly important are O.S. sub-processes necessary for establishing and using links.

References

(1) F.E. Heart, R.E. Kahn, S.M. Ornstein, W.R. Crowther, D.C. Walden: "The Interface Message Processor for the ARPA Computer Network". Spring Joint Computer Conference, 1970, 551 - 567.

(2) S.D. Crocker, J.F. Heapner, R.M. Metcalfe, J.B. Postel: "Function oriented protocols for the ARPA Computer Network". Spring Joint Computer Conference, 1972, 271-279.

(3). M. Fracassi: "Simulazione di un 1004" - Centro di Calcolo del Politecnico di Milano, Internal Report, Jan. 1971.

(4). L. Alleva, S. Boiti: "CORE: COllegamento REmoto tra gli elaboratori 1108 UNIVAC e 1800 IBM" - CISE, Segrate (Milano), Internal Report, N. 131, Oct. 1969.

(5) J. Jaffe: "Linked Probabilistic Finite Automata: A Model for the Temporal Interaction of Speakers" - Mathematical Biosciences, 7, (1970), 191 - 204.

(6) H.J. Hoffman: "On Linguistic Aspects of Communication Line Control Procedures", IBM Research, Internal Resport RZ 345, February 2, 1970.

(7). B.W. Stuzman: "Data Communication Control Procedures" - Computer Surveys, Vol.4, No.4, Dec.72, 197-220.

(8) G. Le Moli: "Introduction to Theory of Colloquies" - Istituto di Elettrotecnica ed Elettronica, Politecnico di Milano, Internal Report, 72/1, 1972.

(9) L. Dadda: "Computer Networks" - Ettore Maiorana International School of Theory and applications of computers" - 1972.

(10) G. Le Moli, L. Mezzalira: "Some Considerations on Interlocutor Behaviour and their Interactions" - Istituto di Elettrotecnica ed Elettronica, Politecnico di Milano, Internal Resport 72/7, 1972.

(11) L. Dadda, G. Le Moli: "An Introduction to Computer Networks", European Seminar on Computer Networks" - Arles, April 24/ May 4, 1973: to be published in "Alta Frequenza".

(12) G. Le Moli: "A Theory of Colloquies" - European Seminar on Computer Networks, Arles, April 24/May 4, 1973, to be published in "Alta Frequenza".

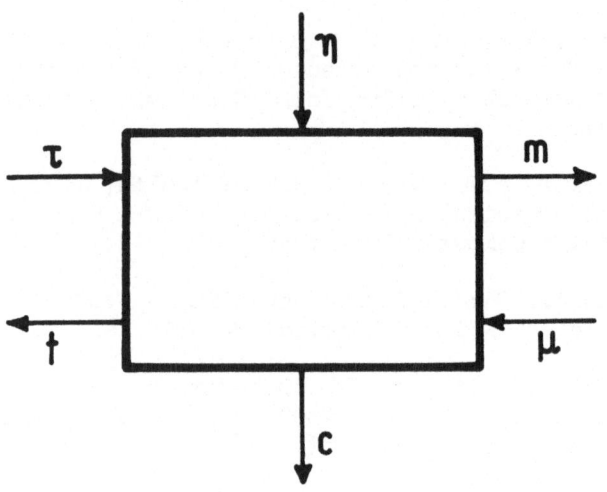

Figure 1

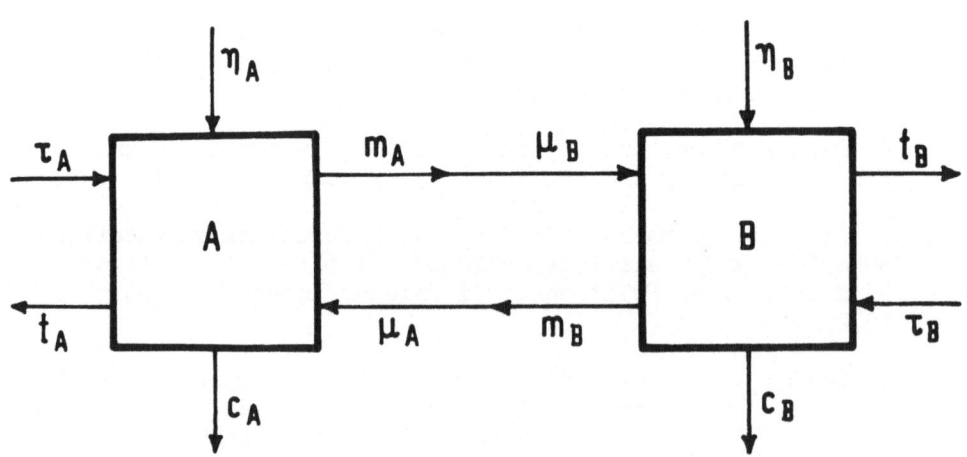

Figure 3

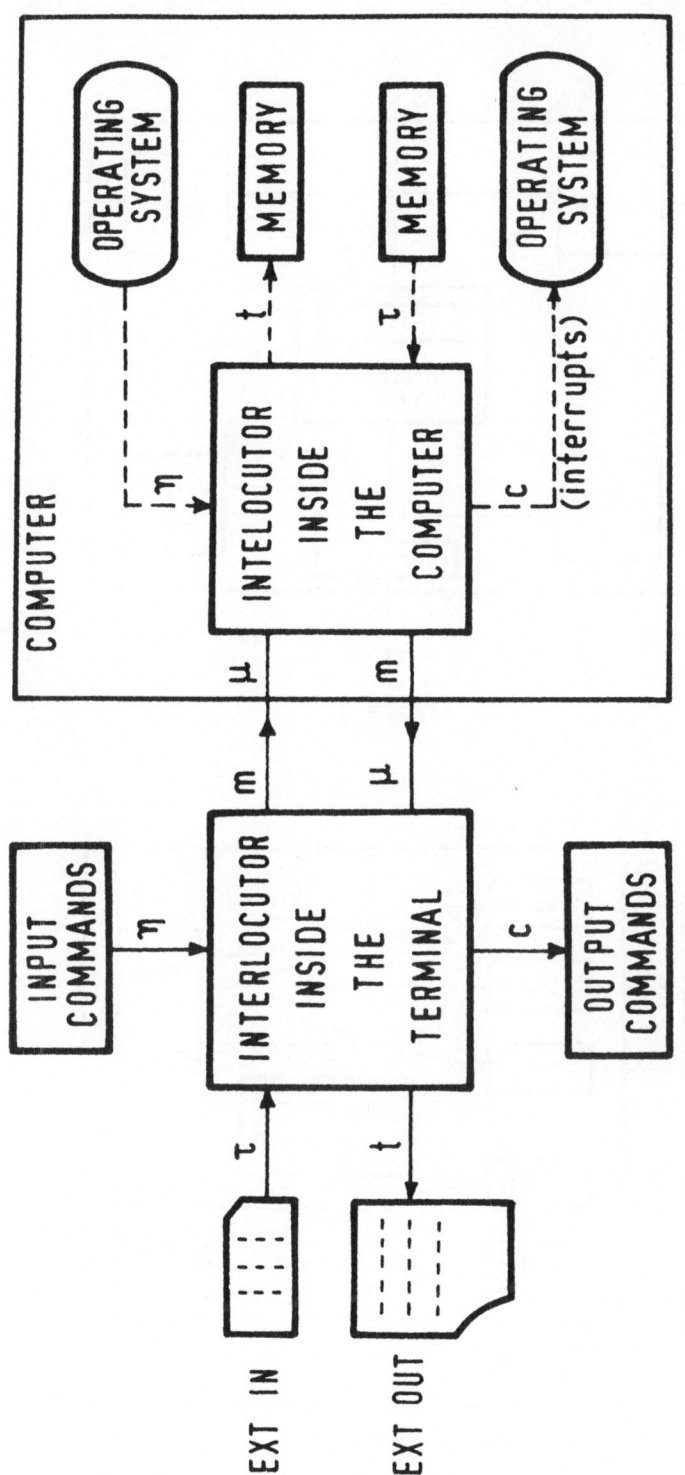

Figure 2

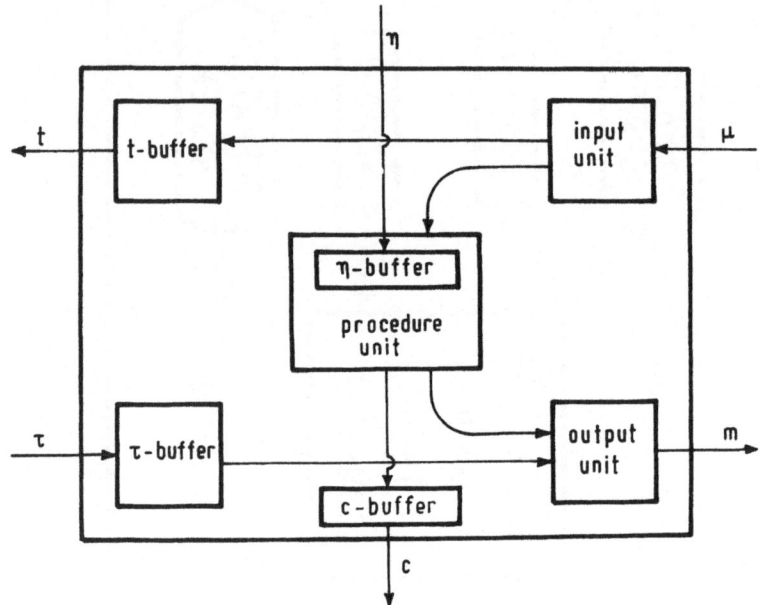

Figure 4

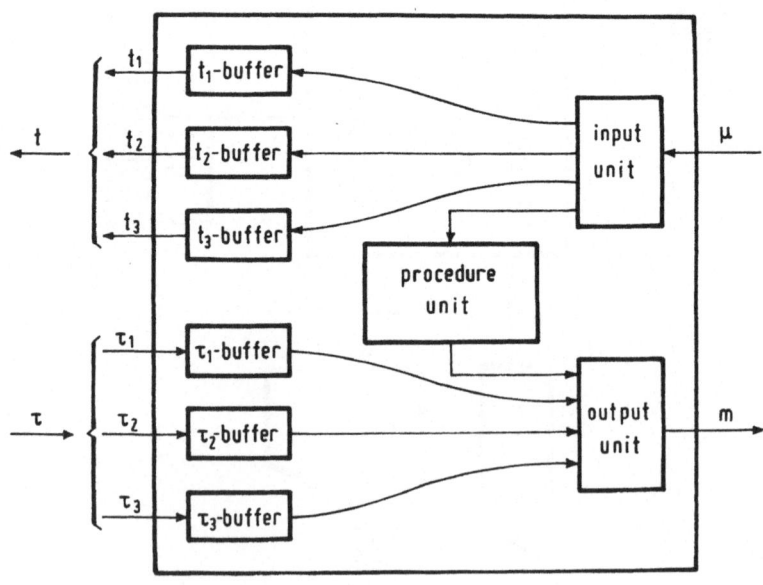

Figure 5

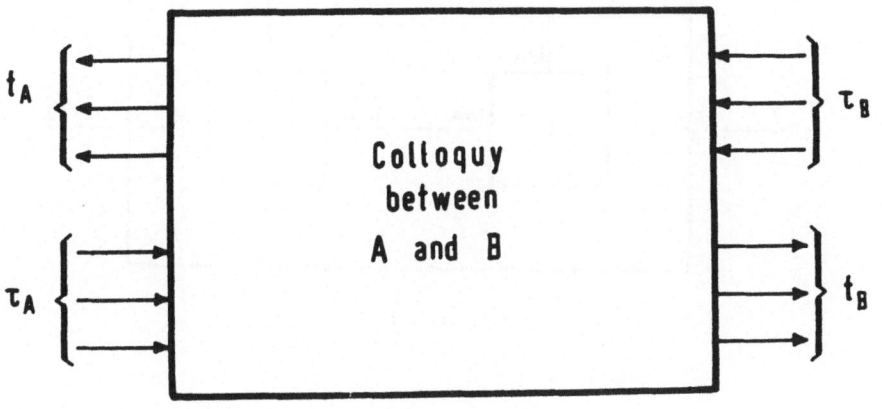

Figure 6

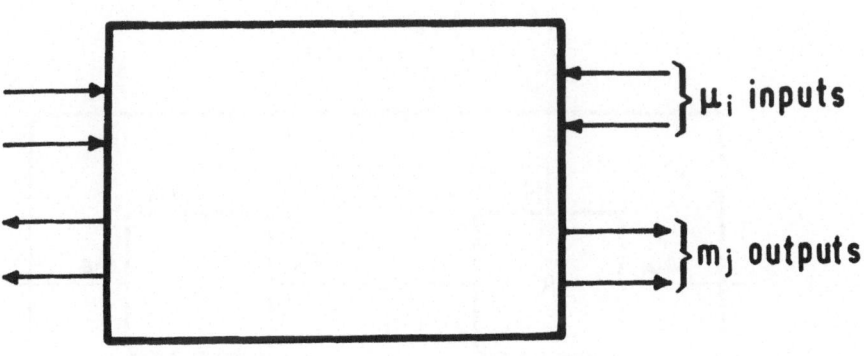

Figure 7

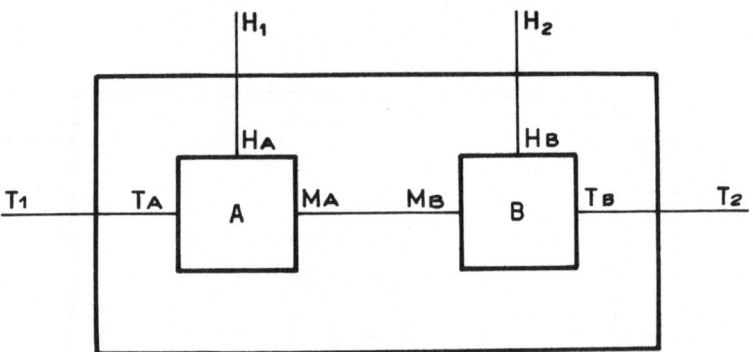

Figure 8

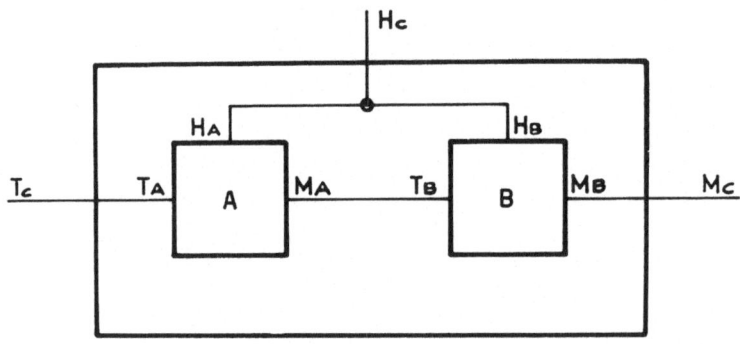

Figure 9

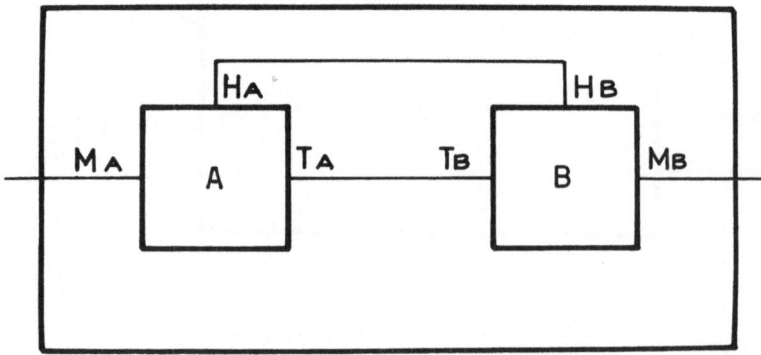

Figure 10

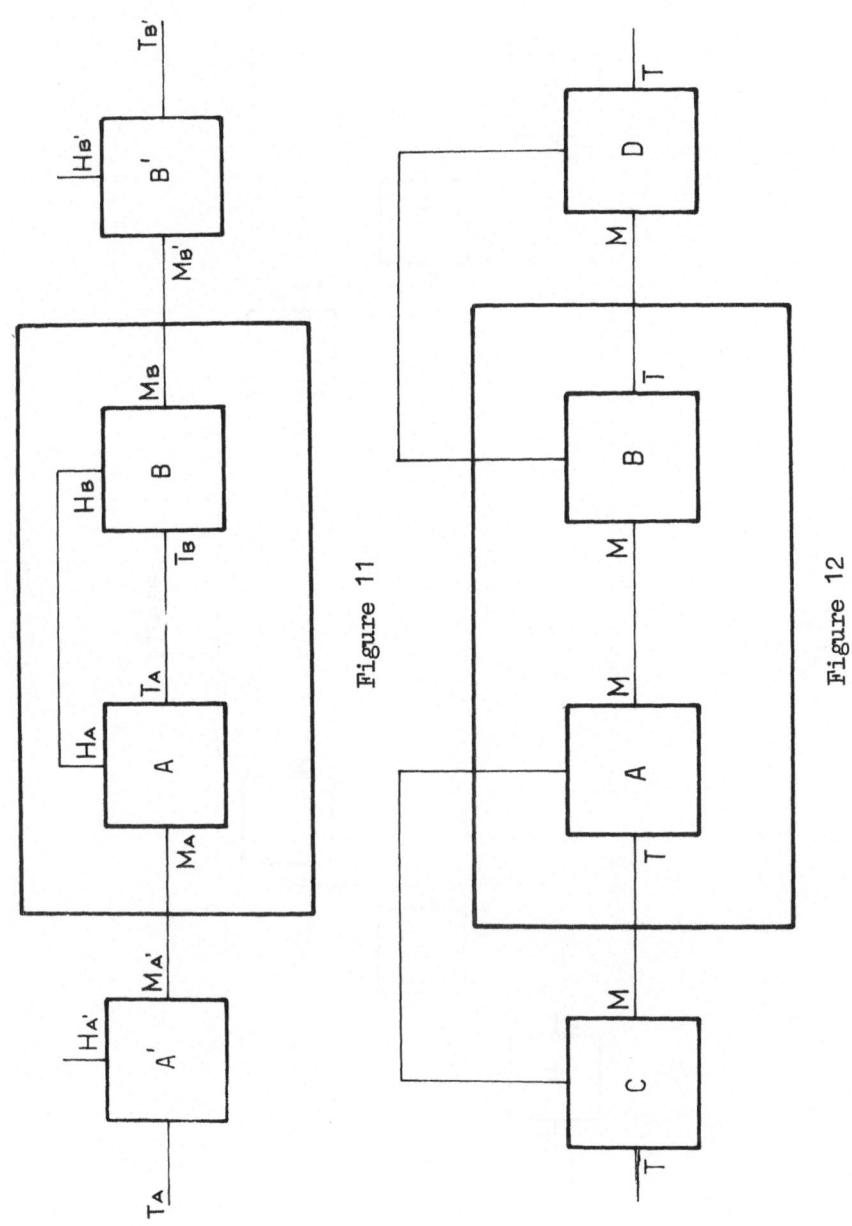

Figure 11

Figure 12

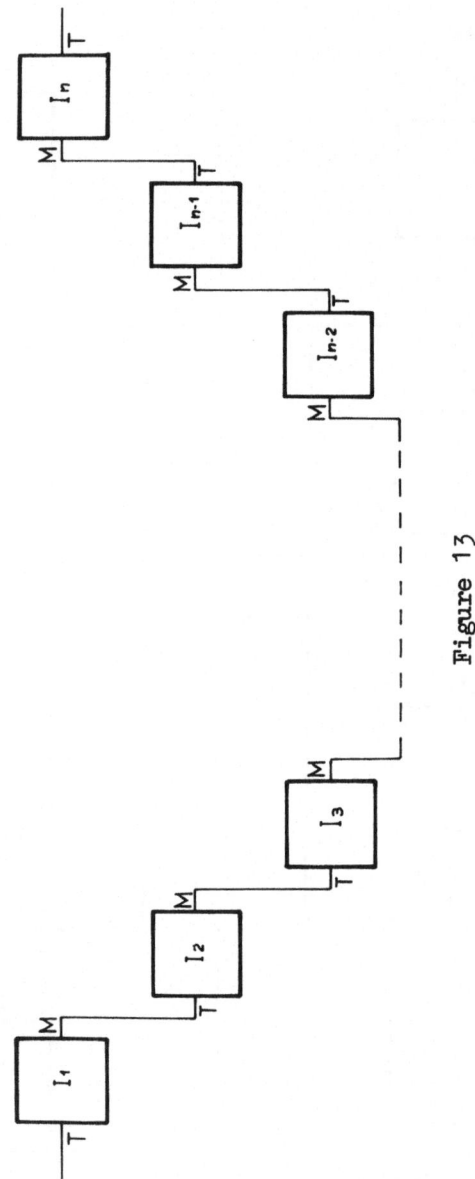

Figure 13

227

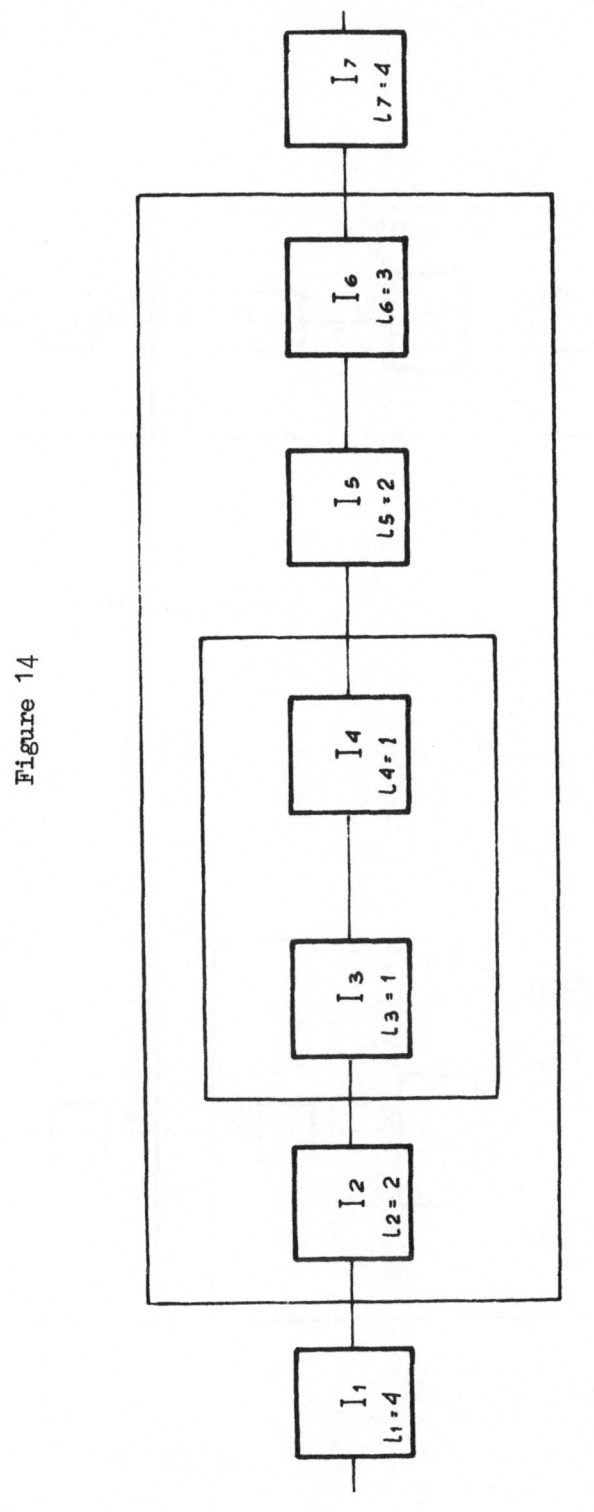

Figure 14

Figure 15

228

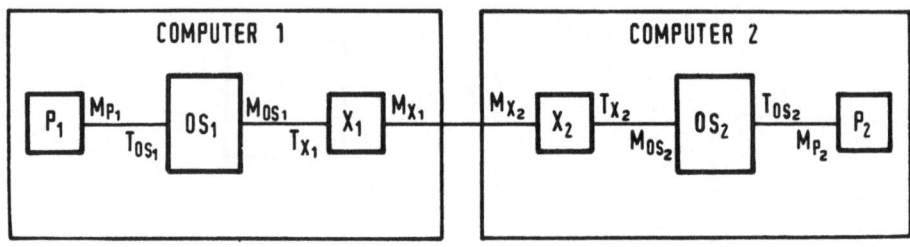

Figure 16

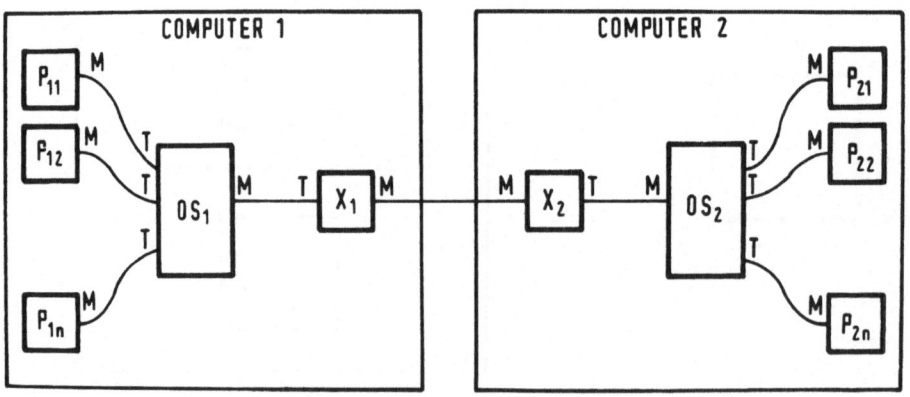

Figure 17

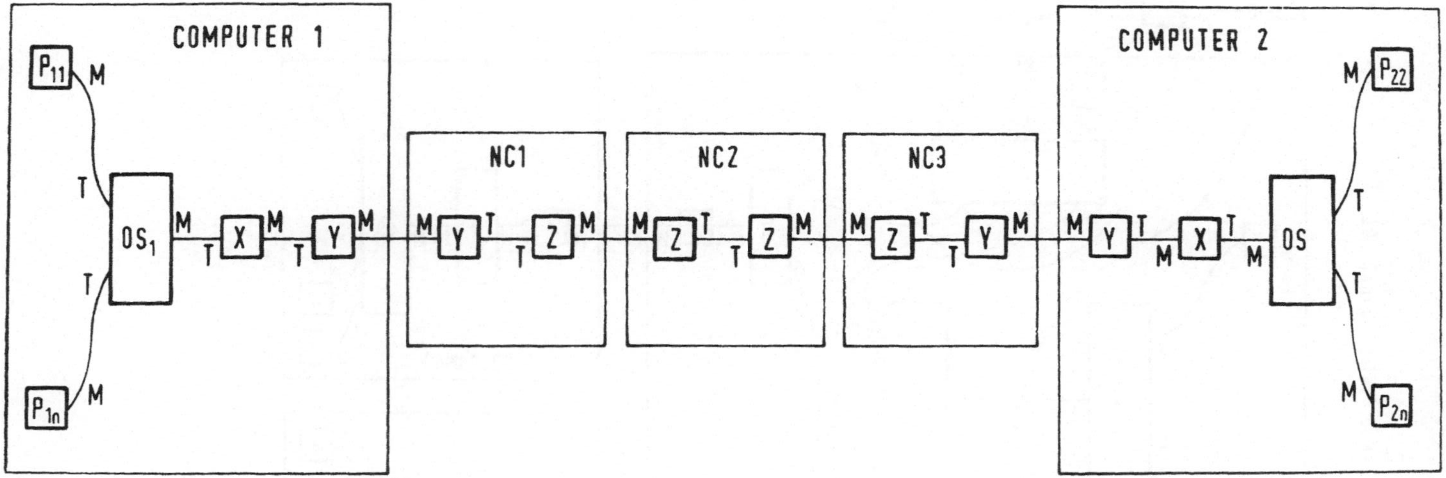

Figure 18

230

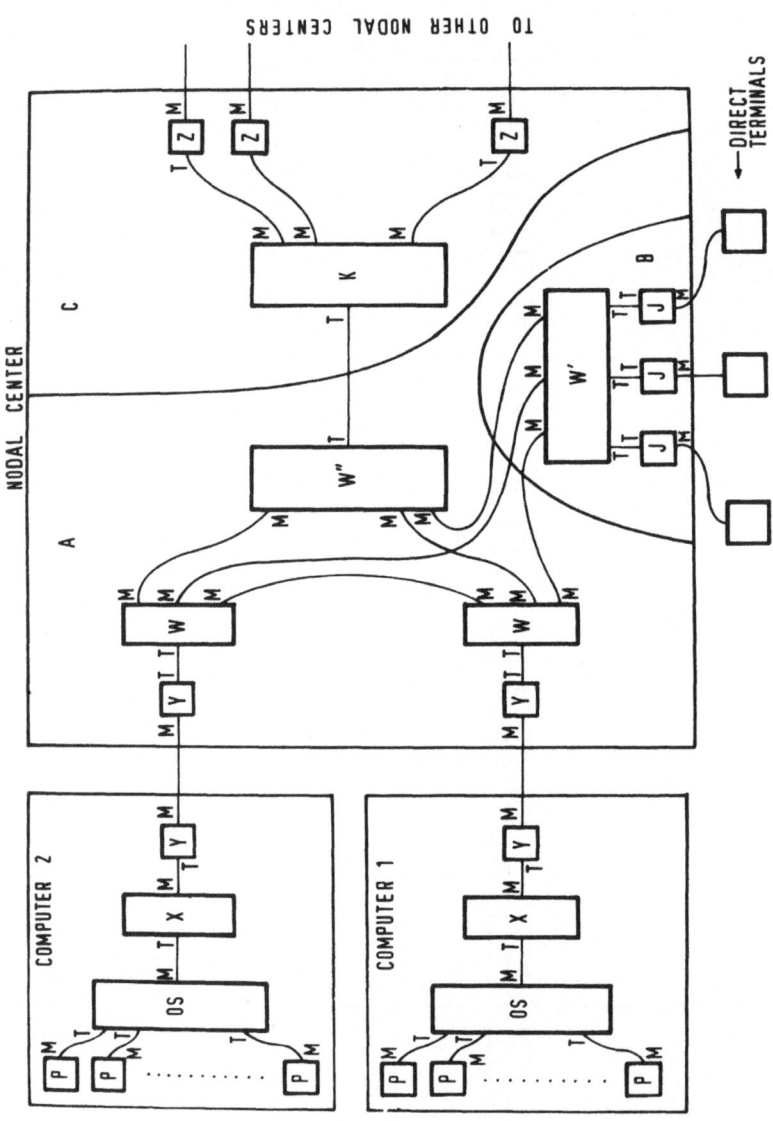

TO OTHER NODAL CENTERS

Figure 19

NETWORK PROTOCOLS

Louis POUZIN

Institut de Recherche d'Informatique et d'Automatique (IRIA)

Rocquencourt, France

SUMMARY

Various data transfer capabilities are required for user traffic.
The set of rules governing exchanges is called a protocol, which
is a variety of language. Protocols use communications tools on
which assumptions must be made. In particular they are not error
free.
Protocol implementations are distributed machines whose components
must be synchronized. Error detection and back-tracking are necessary functions, and require internal communication for control
information.

At the lowest level one needs a basic message transfer capability
insuring reliable communications over an unsafe medium. This can
be achieved with named messages and acknowledgements, and a few
other limited assumptions. Varieties of communication procedures
are actually based on this simple scheme. Options arise in managing the message name space. A window technique reduces overhead
while allowing non sequential transfers.

User protocols implement various tools tailored to common requirements. There are discussions about the proper localization of functions in the system hierarchy. Server protocols are typical cases
of distributed machines requiring a specialized user language, and
an internal communication machinery. The Arpanet file transfer
protocol is discussed.

Host protocols are a mixture of functions which can be put to work
independently. They should be stripped down so as to provide just
a basic communications layer allowing arbitrary extensions. Other
approaches are possible.

I. USER REQUIREMENTS

Programming a computer has a variety of acceptations. E.g. :

. Write a program in assembly language to develop a tape handler
. Use an access method to update an index-sequential file
. Write a COBOL program
. Sort a file using a library processor
. Submit a job from a remote card reader
. Login and type commands to a time-sharing system, then work with
  a conversational text-editor.

All these activities require using some kind of language, typically several, depending on which component or which level of system
is to be dealt with. Each language is supposedly well defined,
supported by a gamut of tools : manuals, compilers, interpreters,
debugging aids. In many cases components can be implemented in
one language, handled with another, and used as a building block
(macro, sub-routine, processor) in the context of yet another
language. All that makes up the traditional resource environment
of a computer system.

Computer networks have brought about an additional set of user
needs, owing to the geographical dispersion and the heterogeneity
of their resources. Furthermore, the practical implementation of
appropriate user tools has to cope with specific problems resulting from present communications technologies. Investigations
pursued so far generally reveal the following main problem areas :

a) Physical I-O ports between a computer (host) and a communications network must be limited to a small number (1 to 3). A
   multiplexing machinery is needed to funnel all host-to-host
   messages through a few I-O lines.

b) In order to exchange messages, host processes need some network-
   wide name space for addressing each other.

c) The communications network imposes a maximum message length.
   Longer items must be fragmented and reassembled.

d) Some messages may not reach their destination. Hence error
   control.

e) Unchecked message traffic may flood the receiving host. Hence
   flow control.

f) I-O streams should extend over the network. Hence the need for
   virtual links between processes.

g) File transfer between different hosts.

h) Job submission to a distant host.

j) Communications between various servers and terminals.

k) Data conversion and reformating.

1) Distributed data base management.

m) User identification, accounting.

n) Information centers, and how to get help.

... etc...

There is no doubt that users would find overly cumbersome and inefficient to use for similar functions as many different languages as hosts. This is yet quite awkward to have a Babel on a single computer. Consequently network standards must be defined for the more popular functions, so that they use the same language on every host.

On a single computer instructions of a program are fed into a processor. In a network several processors may be involved simultaneously on different hosts. Conceptually they interact with one another as if in direct contact. However, some mechanisms are required to bridge the physical distance. Therefore additional network standards must be defined to reckon with inter-processor exchanges. They have been called "protocols", but they are also languages as we shall see.

In Arpanet protocols tend to be limited to the definition of an inter-processor language for a particular network usage. In Cyclades protocols tend to include also the definition of a user language network-wide.

II. COMMUNICATIONS PRINCIPLES

System structures :

When analyzing the functions of system components, it is customary to refer to predefined underlying mechanisms called the "lower level", with which one assumes a set of well defined relations. Similarly, each component is supposed to implement a set of functions to be invoked by a "higher level" in a well defined manner. This layered approach is now classical and needs no further comment in this context.

Confusion may arise when "high" and "low" are taken from a different realm, such as history, efficiency, sophistication, priority. E.g. the SITA High Level Network is actually a lower level structure to a message carrier service. Particularly, in dealing with message transmission, one frequently introduces another (outer) level of envelope, which only reflects another (inner) level of system. These obvious remarks intend to dispel any persistent misunderstanding which sometimes degenerates into a religion war.

In purely hierarchical systems, any level sees only its next lower neighbor as being a simplified model of whatever happens to be built underneath, (Fig. 1). A frequent terminology refers to the higher level as the user, and the lower levels as the system, while the set of rules governing the mutual relationship is an interface. Communications between both levels is often straightforward, when they share a common store, and this function is not even identified as a relevant subject.

It may happen that "the system" is so constructed that it cannot be reached by "the user" without resorting to non-trivial mechanisms. Communications become a problem per se, and results in a more intricate structure. This is the case when physical components are geographically separate, but it also appears in multiprocessor computers (1). A communication level slips in between "user" and "system", (Fig. 2). Is it higher or lower than what ?

As emphasized previously, high and low levels are just conventional visions of structural relationship. They do not have to carry any connotation of physical or time dependencies. There cannot be any formal proof leading to a proper layered structure. In a subjective sense, a good one should simplify and help to understand, while conserving flexibility, autonomy, and efficiency in implementation. It comes as no surprise that interpretations vary widely about the fulfillment of such objectives. As for beauty or virtue it relates to personal background.

Having to deal with a communications level may be a technical necessity, but that should not blur the fact that the fundamental objective is to interface two levels, as simply as if there were no communications problem at all. In other words, our simple 2-level structure should not be defaced by an accidental component though its presence must be recognized. This concern results in a 3-component structure, where "user" and "system" maintain their relationship through a virtual interface, which the communications component endeavors to make look real. As long as "user" and "system" are concerned, they only need to know in a well defined manner how to invoke functions of the communications component, in order to simulate their mutual direct interaction. In the same sense as we have introduced the relationship "user-system", the communications component is a sub-system to both. It does not have to make any assumption about the relative levels of the two others, as this is only a convention in our mind. If we take the viewpoint of the communications component, the structure rotates 90° to the right, (Fig. 4). "User" and "system" become equal : they are only parties engaged in communications.

Recap : communications are a lower level transparent to higher levels dependencies. Hence they are <u>symmetrical</u>.

<u>Protocols</u> :

Since higher level relative dependencies are immaterial at communications level, we use the term "correspondent" to mean either one of the two levels engaged in communications. They interfere over a virtual interface, but have no direct exchange except through the communications component. The set of rules governing the exchange between the two correspondents has come to be called a "protocol". It is invisible at communications level (2).

Since we are dealing with computers, information exchanged between correspondents are <u>messages</u>. According to the protocol, they may contain ASCII text, <u>control</u> fields, floating point numbers, relocatable binary programs, or whatever. At communications level all messages appear as bit strings. Each message composed by the sender and interpreted by the receiver must conform to the protocol. Consequently there must be some mechanisms in charge of enforcing rules, and rejecting inacceptable messages. These can be viewed as opposite automata, one is the <u>generator</u> of productions of a <u>language</u>, the other is the <u>recognizer</u>. Productions are either accepted or rejected. In the latter, error recovery must be performed. Clearly the sender automaton needs some feedback when it has to stop generating messages and go to error recovery. This means that communications are always <u>bi-directional</u>, and that sender and receiver automata exchange also <u>control</u> information in addition to correspondent messages. This is equivalent to status codes returned to the caller when using a direct interface.

Assuming a reliable communications component, messages are only rejected when they are ill formed, in which case error recovery requires the sender to correct the situation (e.g. when the sender is a person at a console). This should be part of the protocol. But rejection may also be traced to message corruption within the communications component. This is expectable when communications use long distance transmission equipment. Here we have several options :

a) Correcting communications errors may be included as a normal function of the protocol. This means that there is to be some departure from the way correspondents would dialogue, should they interface directly. On the other hand error control encompasses every possible failure <u>end-to-end</u>.

b) A lower level communications protocol may be contrived, to govern exchanges between sender and receiver automata, and correct only communications errors. The corresponding logic is split into a user protocol, assuming perfect communications, and a communications protocol, nested in the former, (Fig. 5).

c) One may contend that correcting communications errors should logically be put at communications level anyway. Correspondents would only implement a user protocol, assuming perfect communications.

d) But no physical system is perfect. Even though the communications component would correct errors, there would still be unrecoverable or undetected ones. Consequently the user protocol must be designed to make up for rare yet undesirable communications error, lest being occasionally fooled.

e) It may cost the same at user level to detect and correct rare or not quite rare failures. Therefore why put additional mechanisms at communications level ?

f) If communications are extremely reliable, it may be sufficient for users to rely upon deferred control, so reducing the logic embedded in their protocols.

g) The argument can go on and on. Again, there is no possible proof for the best structure, except by experience. Behind all this rationale there is a subjective premise : "I trust my part, not yours". But this is such a common attitude in human life that it should not be discarded as unreasonable in networks. Instead one should identify carefully areas where components are to be legitimately mutually suspicious.

III. DISTRIBUTED MACHINE

A particular network service (e.g. file transfer) is implemented as a set of processors available to users in every host, and defined by a set of rules, (e.g. the file transfer protocol). While a protocol can be viewed as a language, by extrapolation it can also be taken to mean a machine executing programs in that language. Users of that protocol are higher levels in the system hierarchy. Within the network at large they interface the same service with the same language. Conceptually this set of processors make up a single homogeneous machine, whose components happen to be geographically located in various hosts (3). We call such a construction a "distributed machine".

As every abstract view the concept of distributed machine does not change anything in the internal structure, which is a set of autonomous distant processors. But it helps to present a simpler model at user level, by screening out all considerations not relevant to user processing, such as internal message exchange between components. The description of a distributed machine can be reduced to an instruction set, and corresponding actions on internal states and input-output (4).

In order to execute an instruction the components of a distributed machine must cooperate. Aside from transferring operands (data), they must keep a consistent set of internal states which constitutes the execution context directing actions to be performed. Thus, part of the communications established between components is devoted to carrying control information for action reports and context updating.

Communications failures are not unlikely, and components may occasionally exhibit erratic behavior without necessarily go dead. In a network environment resorting to manual intervention on several hosts may turn out an impossible task. Consequently, error recovery should be automated as often as possible. This means that execution mechanisms must include back-tracking and retry, somewhat like a few present day computers.

As can be inferred intuitively the critical area in a distributed machine is communications. Not because it is intrisically less reliable or more costly than other functions, but because we are not yet trained to use it as a basic ingredient of computer system architecture.

IV. BASIC COMMUNICATIONS

The one-message case :

A component (S) wants to transmit with certainty a message to another component (R) . No assumptions are made about communications reliability : the message can be delivered correctly within some undefined delay, altered, lost, delivered in several copies, etc... The R-state is unknown to S, since any information received by S about R relates only to some past point in time.

In normal conditions the following sequence of events might take place :

    S sends message M1 to R
    R receives message M2
    R sends M2 back to S
    S receives M3
    S compares M3 with M1 and finds them equal

At this point can S hold certain that R has received one good copy of M1 ? Not quite, unless we introduce some assumptions :

- M3 really comes from R
- there cannot be an alteration which would turn a bad M2 back into a good M3.

A first conclusion is that messages must contain two addresses. M1 contains R, but also S so that R can send back M2. And M2 contains S and R, so that S can check that M3 comes from R. But this is only valid to the extent that no other receiver can put the R address when sending M2 back to S. Consequently either of the following assumptions must be made :

- the originating address is put in messages off sender's reach
- senders can be trusted for originating addresses.

The previous scheme has the obvious drawback of transmitting the same message twice. We can reduce the loss of bandwidth in having R send back a short checksum of M2, which S can verify for correctness. Then certainty give way to high probability, actually as high as desirable with a proper checksumming algorithm.

But we save even more if S sends the checksum along with M1, and if R checks M2 correctness. Then a simple empty message (ACKnowledgement) from R to S can be taken to mean correct reception. But more assumptions must be made :

- a receiver can be trusted for checksumming
- incorrect messages are not acknowledged.

We introduce now abnormal conditions. Messages may be lost or delivered after a very long time. At some point S must decide not to wait any longer for ACK. Hence the need for a time-out mechanism. After a number of unsuccessful attempts, S should give up. But what conclusions can be inferred ? Any of the following causes may have been present :

- S to R communications down
- R to S communications down
- R down
- unusual delays

One cannot conclude that R did not receive the message. Actually it may have received all attempts. S ends up with uncertainty.

If R is expecting only one message, all additional copies do no harm. But if it executes a specific action whenever it receives a message, it may not be S intent to have several executions. However there is no way to insure that only one copy will be delivered to R. Even if S never repeats sending, the communications machinery may create duplicates. Consequently R needs some information to be able to inhibit actions for redundant messages. This can be provided in the form of a name attached to the message. All messages bearing the same name will be considered as a single copy, as far as actions are concerned. But each one is acknowledged, since repetitions may be due to the loss of ACK's.

Once received a message name is kept within the R context. In other words, R creates a name space of received messages in which names must be unique. Before entering a new name it is checked against present ones, and if found the message is a duplicate.

Message set :

When S transmits successive messages to R, and receives ACK's, it has no way to correlate them, if it uses the previous scheme. Counting the number of ACK's and messages is unreliable, due to duplicates and losses. Since R can cope with duplicates, S must insure that every message in the set has been received, therefore acknowledged, at least once. This requires that S keep track of unacknowledged messages and R send back named ACK's.

With this additional feature, message control is performed on each message independently from the others. We only need a simple one-message protocol along with a name space in S and R. A summary of mechanisms introduced so far appears in (Fig. 6).

An obvious weakness of this scheme is the necessity for R to retain every distinct received message name in its own space. Aside from storage and look up overhead, names cannot be indefinitely unique, or they would grow continuously. Duplicates would appear when the name space is exhausted. Consequently a mechanism must be introduced to release dead names and refill the not yet received message name space. Of course both S and R must agree on a common scheme, or else messages would be accepted or discarded untimely.

No matter how S and R draw up their name trade, the communications system might throw in an old message bearing a new name. As this would have an undesirable effect, one relies upon another assumption :

- the communications system can be trusted for delivering messages within well defined limits in time, or not at all.

Let T.min and T.max be the minimum and maximum delay that a message may take to travel from S to R. Then, a message name may be reused after a minimum delay : T.max - T.min, unless repetitions are necessary.

This is a major characteristic of the communications system, since it has a direct impact on the amount of information which makes up the context of S and R. Indeed, knowing the maximum message traffic, a delay corresponds to a certain number of messages.

Let M be the maximum number of messages per unit of time.
Assuming S keeps sending messages it must hold for possible
repetition copies of unacknowledged ones, viz :

$$2M \; T.max$$

R must hold for possible duplicates the names of last received
messages, viz :

$$M \; (T.max - T.min)$$

As can be inferred, the value and the first moment of transit
delay in the communications system are to be taken into account
in S and R design parameters such as buffer length and time-out.
This is an example of cross-level interference within the system
structure. In order to meet the time deviation requirement, the
communications system may contain a built-in mechanism to exter-
minate outdated messages. Nevertheless, there is always some
marginal probability that a stranded message be delivered out of
the regular time span.

At this point it is clear that the reliability of basic communicati
relies upon statistics. No control mechanism is 100 % safe, it
only reduces the undetected error rate to a lower figure. The
basic scheme outlined so far makes some assumptions about the
good behavior of the correspondents. It also assumes a somewhat
predictable transit time in the communications system, but nothing
else. Eventually error detection is based on the proper management
of a message name space, without eradicating completely failure
possibilities. Therefore some room is left for more stringent
control depending on the actual environment.

All basic communications protocols stem from the above scheme,
which is primarily a simple send-receive-acknowledge sequence
for each individual message. Their differences are in the way they
manage their message name space. In the following we illustrate a
few typical communications protocols.

ISO basic mode :

It is termed : basic mode control procedures for data communications systems (5). As customary, protocols controlling exchanges
over a transmission line are called procedures. This protocol is
intended for data exchange between a master station (computer) and
slave stations (terminals) through multi-drop lines. Using wires
allows additional assumptions about the communications system :

- there is no duplicate message
- messages are delivered in the same order as sent.

Every message is acknowledged, and there is only one message in
transit at any moment (alternate). But in many cases acknowled-

gements are in the form of special messages, carrying other
meanings, (NAK, EOT, ENQ). This is a typical exemple of mixing
two levels of protocols, one for message control, the other for
syntax correctness in data and device control.

Since there is never more than one outstanding message, they have
no name. However acknowledgements may have two different names,
alternately, to allow checking for not loosing any. This means
that message names (0, 1) are implied by the sender. As long as
no two successive ACK's are lost, it allows the sender to diffe-
rentiate between an ACK or message loss. But not so for the
receiver. Therefore, error recovery belongs to the high level of
the procedure.

ISO HDLC :

This is again an attempt to mix a message transfer protocol and
a component operation protocol (6). Several messages may be sent
and acknowledgements deferred. This means that the communications
system may have a storage capacity of several messages, as store
and forward networks do. But without stating it explicitly, the
draft standard assumes sequential communications, i.e. message
names are sequence numbers and must be received in order.

The message name space is typically numbers 0 - 15. It is reused
in a circular fashion, by releasing names of acknowledged messages.
These are only accepted in the correct sequence, therefore any
acknowledgment stands for all previously numbered ones. As in our
basic scheme, the number they carry relates to the message being
acknowledged.

BBN ARPANET :

This one is used for inter-IMP exchange over telephone circuits
(7). Thus, only the sender may create duplicates. The message
name space is 16. It is managed in 8 pairs. For each pair both
names are used alternately. Conceptually this is equivalent to 8
autonomous parallel channels controlled by a 2-name alternate
procedure. Since only one message can be in transit on each
channel, two names are enough to tell duplicates (8). Acknowledgements are control bits tacked on reverse messages. They carry
the acknowledged message name (odd-even bit), and can be sent
redundantly, the same way as regular messages.

Message name management :

Like any other space the message name space may be managed using
well known techniques depending on environment constraints. E.g.
circular space with IN and OUT pointers (HDLC), individual table
entries (BBN), dynamic allocation of chunks, degenerate 1-name
case (ISO basic mode). It all depends on the size of the space,

i.e. of the storage capacity between sender and receiver, and
assumptions made about the communications system (duplicates,
losses, sequencing). As a result, designing a protocol is a
matter of good balance between reliability and efficiency. There
is no ultimate solution. E.g. for packet communications over
transmission lines, it seems that a BBN-like procedure is the
most efficient (9).

In end-to-end protocols encompassing intricate and obscure inner
levels, users may want to take every reasonable precaution to
avail themselves with reliable communications, no matter what
happens out of their area of control. As we have seen, the basic
scheme provides for safe communications, but may require a large
name space to cater both for delays and duplicates. A way around
this overhead problem consists in "clipping" out the name space
to reduce the active area to a narrow window, which can be twitched
on at some intervals of time. Since transit delays are not
randomly distributed (they are more like Poisson), the window can
be set to focus on the main cluster of messages in transit. Thus
duplicates are either recognized or rejected as irrelevant. Some
proportion of regular messages are also rejected, because they
fall off the window, but they are retransmitted. A good balance
must be found between space and transmission overhead. One more
remark : no message sequencing is required. Sequencing is a
particular case when the window of acceptable names is reduced
to one.

Error recovery :

A basic communications protocol is nonetheless an instance of a
distributed machine, to which general principles apply. Once a
correspondent has got out of hand, due to unanticipated failure
of critical parts, or a protocol flaw, exchanges are meaningless
until a common state of agreement is reinstated. Consequently
mechanisms are necessary to direct both automata to a recovery
procedure.

One of the correspondents may discover an error condition and
decide for itself, but it must insure that the other will follow
on. Therefore control messages unrelated to the regular message
traffic should be included in the protocol. In case the other
component cannot be made to go to recovery state, the healthy
correspondent should report an error to its next higher level and
reset its state. In any case, recovery may be requested by the
higher level if it detects an inconsistency not visible by basic
communications (syntax error).

Following an error, correspondents can no longer count on their
execution context, which may be inconsistent. But we have seen
that this context (name space) is necessary to detect losses and

duplicates in oncoming messages. Consequently all traffic (except error control messages) arriving after an error is detected should be discarded.

Recovery consists in cleaning out the context in "backspacing" up to a point in past traffic which both parties consider safe. It may be a prior checkpoint, or may result from a negotiation according to a recovery protocol. Once consistent contexts have been reinstalled, regular traffic is resumed. Since both corres- pondents possess the same naming scheme, they can usually restart from the earliest unacknowledged message, unless directed other- wise by the higher level.

Checksumming :

In some cases parity codes are used, but their efficiency is limited in serial transmission. More efficient techniques are based on cyclical redundancy codes (CRC), which can yield an undetected error rate less than 1 bit in 10^{10} with 1000-bit messages and 16-bit CRC.

Due to the substantial time which would be required for software checksumming, this operation is usually done by the I-O hardware. However, in store and forward systems, checksums are stripped off on input, and recomputed on output. In the meantime messages may be damaged when they lay unprotected. This is a present weakness, which could be eliminated with an end-to-end checksum.

V.   USER-TO-USER PROTOCOLS

Basic level :

When two user programs running in different hosts want to start communicating the least they should be able to do is to exchange simple messages, since any more sophisticated tool requires an initial set up based on messages. This allows bootstrapping whatever protocol they might want to use for private or experimen- tal purpose. Furthermore many simple tasks can be implemented quickly with a few communication primitives, particularly when they are limited to a straightforward dialogue. However, what can they send messages to ?

Subscribers :

It would be unpractical to address messages with names as used locally in each host, because formats would be dependent on particular operating systems. They might also be ambiguous, or unpredictable when a user process is given a name dynamically.

It is much more convenient to create a <u>network-wide name space</u>, and assign subscriber numbers in a structured manner, in the same vein as P.O. Box 62492, Zip 53017.

For convenience in routing messages part of the subscriber name can be a <u>geographical locator</u>, like region, city, host. Without being a compelling feature, it certainly saves time and overhead not to have to look up a general network directory to find out a subscriber location. However "floating" subscribers are perfectly acceptable as long as someone pays for the associated cost.

It is also more convenient to assign <u>permanently</u> subscriber names to correspondents such as human user, terminal, server process, sub-system. As the total number of subscribers is likely to be much larger than the number of simultaneous active correspondents, it may be contended that using too large a name space carries transmission and storage overhead. But if there were a dynamic allocation of subscriber names, some other permanent names would have to be used anyway for correspondents to get in touch initially. On the other hand this problem is already well known in areas such as file systems. Overhead can be reduced by building tables of "active " subscribers, while others reside on secondary storage.

<u>Ports - Links</u> :

Most existing software use the concept of ports to defer till execution time the <u>binding</u> of data streams and I-O devices, or files. Conventional inter-process communications are also modeled after I-O streams. Distributed activities, distant site peripherals or files require cross-network binding. From communications standpoint, it is somewhat similar to connecting two subscribers in the telephone system. Software <u>links</u> should be established between corresponding ports. Again, we have the same problem as in addressing processes. Since port names are local, they are not suited for network naming.

A first solution is to use <u>global</u> network names as a substitute in exactly the same fashion as we have introduced subscriber names. This is the Arpanet way (10). It requires dynamic allocation of global names as anchoring points for port-to-port links. Since these names (sockets) are managed at host level, they require allocation to users either on a permanent or dynamic basis. When it is dynamic, some preliminary protocol must take place to exchange socket names before setting up a link.

Another solution is to use network names having a well defined format, but <u>local</u> to a subscriber. This is the Cyclades way (11). No allocation is necessary, as names are given by users. Furthermore they are only paired at link set up, which does not require prior knowledge of the opposite name. Thus, they are transient names, because links and ports exist only during execution of a process.

Since a data stream requires some error and flow control, it always has to be matched by a reverse stream. Thus one has the choice to use uni-directional links and set up two for every stream, (Arpanet), or to use bi-directional links (Cyclades).

Sequencing :

This concept applies only to a link. It means that messages are delivered to a port in the same order as they have been sent. This is so obvious in wired communications that not everyone questions the very necessity of that property. In data streams, sequencing is intrisic. But one may think of other types of data transfer for which sequencing is immaterial, as long as no data are altered. E.g. transferring an index-sequential, or direct access file ; or funneling independent transactions toward a common processor ; or collecting statistics ; or transferring a sequential file to a SORT processor, etc...

The alternative is : should all communications be sequential because it is often required, or should that be left up to the user ? Indeed, a multi-node packet switching network is not intrisically sequential, and it takes overhead and restrictions to make it look that way. There is no definite answer yet, as we do not know enough about economics and user experience.

Events :

Like I-O streams, links are subjected to unexpected conditions : accidental closure, message loss ; or they have to relay conditions noticed by a connected process. In other words, in addition to data lines a link should have interrupt lines, so that a signal can jump ahead of the data still in transit. This can be obtained with higher priority messages over a link, or by having a dedicated link for events. In case of erratic behavior of a correspondent, "escape" events should be picked up by the addressee controlling environment. But this can be a dedicated event link.

Fragmentation :

At some point in the communications path there is a maximum message length. The packet switching principle is based on short messages, typically a maximum of 500 to 2000 bits. This is perfectly satisfactory for conversational traffic with short terminals, short transactions, or control messages. This is much too short for data processing, with 500 to 2000-character records, or device handling using blocking factors. Not to mention file transfer. Therefore logical user messages must be broken down into fragments and later on reassembled in the proper order, when they are too long.

Whether this operation should be performed only once per message, or at several levels, is purely a matter of economics or technological constraints. A typical packet switching network using mini-computers cannot store very long messages. Furthermore, they would block I-O ports and delay other messages. Therefore only sub-fragmentation can be performed within the communications network. Another level is required anyhow. Then what is the benefit of having fragmentation within packet switching, vs. the resulting constraints ? This is an open question.

A common answer is that it saves on host overhead, notably I-O. But if we look at the way many an operating system handles communications I-O, overhead can be traced back to poor design. Transmission line I-O should be an independent system, possibly wired-in or micro-programmed, instead of a nightmarish kludge of interrupts, clock routines, scheduling, argument checking, register saving, ... except I-O.

If users want to send or receive long messages, they have to provide some corresponding buffers. It may be an appropriate place to fragment and reassemble. Or is it ?

Error control :

If one assumes that lower mechanisms are error free, then error control should be of no concern at user level. But everyone is entitled to his own suspicion. If user protocols do not provide for end-to-end control, at least as an option, likely some users will want to put their own. Bit pattern control may usually be entrusted to lower levels, where it is done quite efficiently. But message naming and acknowledgement may well be organized at user level, because it allows a variety of techniques depending on the type of traffic.

E.g. in a conversational application, control may be based on message syntax and contents ; in a D.P. application, it may be done by matching a master file, checksumming a record, adding up fields ; in a program library, there are often specific redundancies which may be taken advantage of.

There may be some inconvenience to handle time-outs as interrupts at user level, because operating systems do not always offer adequate user services in this area. On the other hand system primitives such as SEND, RECEIVE, WAIT, may be equipped with a built-in time-out and an appropriate return status when the user process is awakened.

Likely some error detection and recovery are exercised at lower levels. This might appear redundant, since it usually applies only to some sections of the communications path. But it is not

useless, because it allows quicker detection and reporting of
component failures, and recovery at inner levels costs less
overhead. Nevertheless, there are always anomalies which cannot
be detected or corrected at lower levels, hence an error recovery
procedure is always necessary at user level. It may be tailored
to the failure rate reported at this level.

However it can be argued whether it is desirable to put error
control entirely in user's hands, since he may not be trusted
to always do the right thing, and unjustified complaints can
deteriorate the network image. Probably a standard error control
mechanism should be offered as an alternative, so that casual
users have not to make any effort in working one out. This can be
a simple acknowledgement of named messages.

Flow control :

For reasons similar to error control, one may contend that users
are in the best position to know how much storage they will have
available and expected rates of data transfer. Since throughput
and overhead are closely tied with flow control, it may be the
best (or the worse) choice to leave it up to the user. Flexibility
goes with some risks of inappropriate tuning. But it is certainly
easier to correct particular user situations than to redesign and
phase in a network standard flow control.

It is clear that buffering at lower levels cannot go without its
own flow control. The same is true for a communications network.
Then one might wonder whether all these layers of control are
really useful or whether they result from mutual suspicion and
inadequacy. Although the latter may be true, it does not seem to
be the fundamental motivation. Flow control is intrisically a
resource sharing exercise between different flows and different
users. There is nowhere in a system an ideal observation point
from which all resources could be apportionned. Depending on level,
one sees different flows and resources. E.g. if a user interleaves
a diagnostics output stream and a file inquiry onto the same link,
he is the only one in a position to control each flow independently and to divide up the link bandwith. This means that flow
control, like resource management, is a layered and distributed
set of functions. Thus some of it belongs to user level.

VI. SERVER - PROTOCOLS

Server level :

Customarily a server is a non-trivial user system to which commands
are adressed directly in some form of high level lingo. It is an
abstract machine which converts the traditional user interface
into a more sophisticated and spezialized one. Servers are accessed
by "users". In this chapter the term user shall mean user of a
server.

A file transfer protocol :

We shall take an example with the Arpanet file transfer protocol
(12), just to show typical communications aspects of the server
level, (Fig. 7). Transferring a file requires the cooperation of
two machines, a "reader-sender" (RS) and a "receiver-writer" (RW).
But these machines cannot get to work without being fed a program
specifying all parameters pertaining to the files being worked on,
and the operations to be performed. This program is conveyed into
both RS and RW in a conventional command format through TELNET
links, a lower level protocol for character string transfer. Since
RS and RW do not "understand" character strings, they are assisted
with "front-end" (SFE) processors translating commands into an
executable form. This is the well known structure of a language
interpreter. SFE's are syntax analyzers ; RS and RW are semantic
actions.

Commands are sent from a user front-end (UFE) in charge of interfacing with the external user (typically a conversational
terminal), and producing commands for SFE's. UFE can be in a third
host. After execution commands are acknowledged with status reports
flowing back to UFE via the TELNET links.

The file transfer protocol specifies in every detail the relations
between UFE and SFE's. It does not specify an external user language, although commands are represented with character strings
which could well be a direct console input. Similarly status
reports are made up of a (specified) printable code, plus an
(unspecified) comment. Here follows a sampling of commands :

class A	class B	class C	
USER	BYTE	RETRIEVE	LIST
PASSWORD	MODE	STORE	ALLOCATE
ACCOUNT	SOCKET	APPEND	RESTART
REINIT	STRUCTURE	DELETE	ABORT
BYE	TYPE	RENAME	

N.B. Spelling is occasionally a short form of the above words.

Class A commands set up a user context. Class B commands set up
a file context. Both make up the execution context of the server
machine. Class C commands are instructions.

The set of components on (Fig. 7) is nothing but a distributed
machine, with its internal communication machinery for synchro-
nizing its processors.

From this observation one might draw some thoughts. Since internal
server communications are machine language, is there any subtle
advantage to make it look like high level ? Wouldn't it be more
efficient to have straight forward communication tools tailored
to exchanging contexts, instructions, and operands in a compact
form ? On the other hand wouldn't it be rational to have a well
defined external user language network-wide ? But that's
sociology.

VII. HOST-TO-HOST PROTOCOLS

Host properties :

If one looks for the use made of a host entity within network
mechanisms, one finds that it only serves as a geographical pointer.
It cannot be allocated, copied, or updated ; it has no attribute ;
it is just a name. From communications standpoint, it can be up
or down : it is a device. Within hosts there are subscribers,
users, servers, files, etc... Hosts are resource containers.
Resources are accessible individually from local activities.
They can also be accessed remotely from distant activities distributed throughout the network. A communications path is established
through a carrier network, and a single device comprising modems,
transmission lines, and I-O adapters. For reliability we may want
to have two, but that is a separate issue.

Hosts are organized so that parallel activities can execute
independently, or in cooperation. Each activity may communicate
with other network activities and to that effect calls for communications mechanisms. As seen previously, these are a subscriber
name space and a gamut of user protocols. They all must share
common physical devices to communicate. Therefore we need a tool
to control that multiplexing. Furthermore they do not want to get
involved in the details of communications technology. Therefore
we need a basic communications facility providing straight forward
message transfer.

These are the three basic requirements for a host kit :

- I-O multiplexing
- subscriber name space
- message transfer

Practically, for various extraneous reasons, other functions are also required, such as : - diagnostics, - operator service, - measurement, etc... But these are additional real life aspects not directly implied in network communications.

Network control pool :

As is instantly visible the three functions listed above are quite independent and need not be intertwined. It is even tempting to introduce a tree structure :

a) One I-O multiplexer, with one or several paths to the communications network,

b) An open-ended set of subscriber name spaces,

c) For each subscriber name space, an open-ended set of basic message transfer protocols.

But this may be somewhat arbitrary. A single level for b and c might be more general, since it allows potentially any combination of subscriber and transfer schemes.

Let us call that set of functions a "network control pool" (NCP). Altogether NCP's are a distributed machine establishing a common lower level interface giving access to any host in any other network, provided that matching subscriber and message conventions are implemented.

Design options :

The network control philosophy just brought about is an approach situated at one end of the spectrum of possibilities. Its rationale is to delineate self-contained functions which can work independently assuming only a minimum set of properties about other components, most of which are actually invisible. Sophisticated services are just a juxtaposition of simple functions. Redundancy in implementation can be reduced by a clever design of shared sub-routines.

Another extreme approach is to bury user protocols deep through lower levels, including the communications network. This is typical of one of a kind systems carefully tailored to the requirements of a particular set of applications.

In between lays probably a cost-effective blending to which
networks will gradually converge after years of experiment and a
few more <u>standards</u>. Presumably communications tools will become
basic building blocks in systems architecture, hardware and
software. There won't be any more host problems, since <u>hosts will
be networks</u>.

VIII. <u>ACKNOWLEDGEMENT PROTOCOL</u>

The author is indebted to countless colleagues in the protocol
saga, who made their mind, writings, and time available for
scrutiny and discussions. This paper reflects views shared at
some degree by many a "networker". In somes cases controversy
may develop. Thanks to it, communications will keep on.

IX. REFERENCES

1 - POUZIN L. - Multi-processor problems and tools for process coordination. NATO Internat. summer school, Copenhagen (Aug. 1970), 30 p.

2 - ELIE M., ZIMMERMANN H. - Vers une approche systématique des protocoles sur un réseau d'ordinateurs, application au Réseau Cyclades. Congrès AFCET (Nov. 1973), 19 p.

3 - THOMAS R.H., HENDERSON D.A. - MC ROSS, a multi-computer programming system. SJCC, (May 1972), 281-293.

4 - POUZIN L. - Network architectures and components. 1st European workshop on computer networks, Arles (Apr. 1973), 35 p.

5 - ISO - Basic mode procedures for data communication systems. Doc. 1745.

6 - ISO - High-level data link control procedures. TC 97/SC6, Doc. 794, (Jun. 1973), 33 p.

7 - MC QUILLAN J.M. et al. - Improvements in the design and performance of the Arpa network. FJCC, (Nov. 1972), 741-754.

8 - BARTLETT K., SCANTLEBURY R., WILKINSON P. - A note on reliable full-duplex transmission over half-duplex links. CACM 12, 5, (May 1969), 260-261.

9 - POUZIN L. - Efficiency of full-duplex synchronous data link procedures. Réseau Cyclades, TRA 510, (Jun. 1973), 9 p.

Also available as doc. IFIP/TC6/INWG, Arpa NIC 18255.

10 - CARR C.S., CROCKER S.D., CERF V.G. - Host-host communication protocol in the Arpa network. SJCC (May 1970), 589-597.

11 - POUZIN L. - Presentation and major design aspects of the Cyclades computer network, 3rd data comm. symp., Tampa, (Nov. 1973), 8 p.

12 - NEIGUS N. et al. - File transfer protocol. Arpa network information center, NIC 17759, (Jul. 1973), 50 p.

253

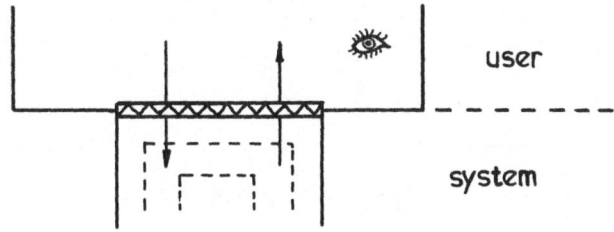

Fig. 1   Interface

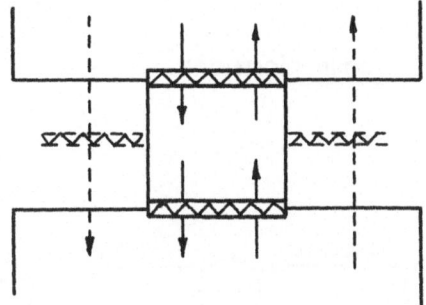

Fig. 2   Communications   interface

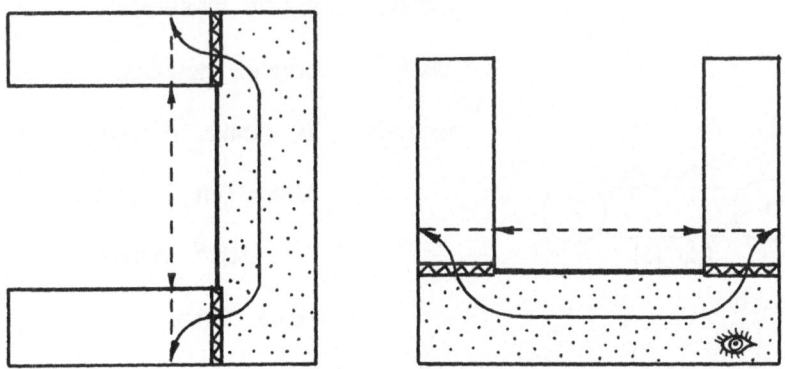

Fig. 3   Communications   sub - system   Fig. 4

254

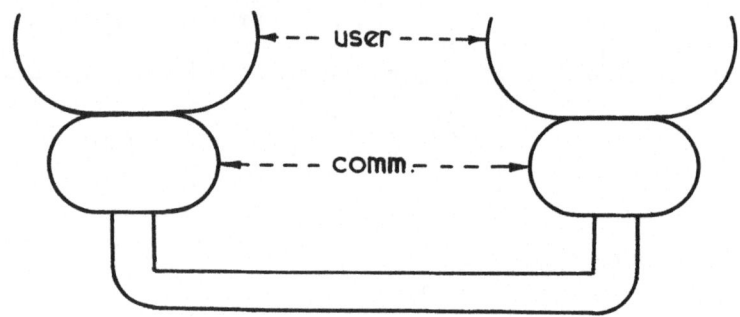

Fig. 5   Communications

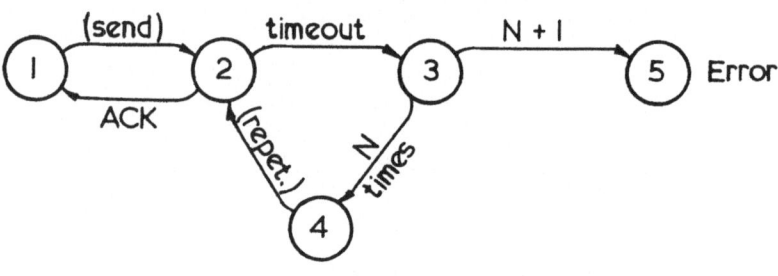

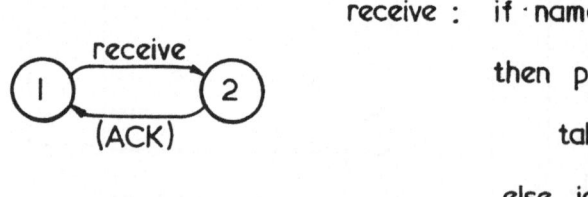

(send) : store message

ACK : cancel message

receive : if · name · ≠ store

then put in store

take action

else ignore

Fig. 6   Basic scheme

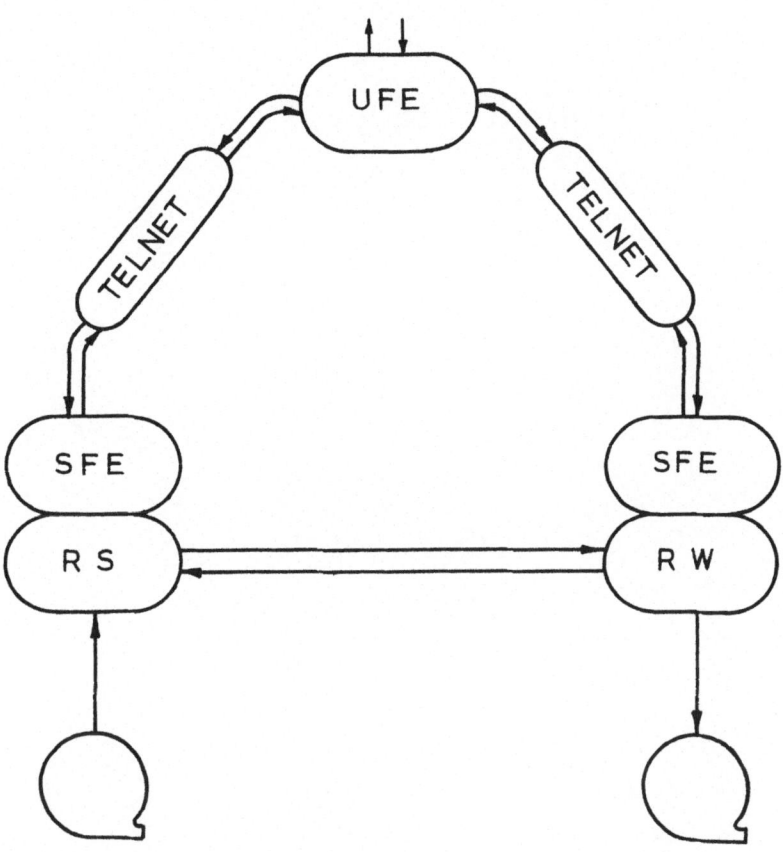

Fig. 7   File transfer protocol

A SURVEY OF PRESENT AND PLANNED GENERAL PURPOSE EUROPEAN DATA AND COMPUTER NETWORKS

Peter T. Kirstein

University of London

1. INTRODUCTION

In this paper we give a brief overview of the special data networks which have been announced in Europe. First two special line switched networks are discussed (§2), which are already operational. The first, the French Caducee, uses modems; the second, the German EDS, so far is handling only experimental telex traffic, but will soon go on line at higher speeds. The present generation of data networks is being developed slowly on only an experimental scale, because it is universally realised that synchronous networks with digital transmission are the way to go in the future. Because of the need to interwork internationally, careful attention is being paid to common standards on such networks. So far the most of the telecommunications authorities have only been convinced to provide line-switched services, and some of the plans in this area are described in §3. Two European countries, Spain and the UK, are definitely providing packet switched services - at least on an experimental scale. These activities are discussed in §4.

So far the discussion has been restricted to data networks - irrespective of the terminals or computers to be attached to them. A few distributed computer networks have started to be developed amongst similar machines. Two of these, one French and one British, are discussed in §5. These networks have started to address the problems which arise when one tries to use computers in the network environment.

Many restricted use data networks have been set up to widen the catchment area for particular large hosts - the banks have many

examples of this type of network. Comparatively few of these
networks use packet switching, or are designed to link a heterogenous set of computers and terminals. Two networks which have
these properties, one for airlines and one for banks, are considered briefly in §6. The European heterogeneous general use
networks are only being designed at this time. Two such networks,
one French and one European,are mentioned in §7. Fuller details
of these networks are given in other papers at this symposium, but
they are mentioned here to round off the picture.

On the whole this paper has dealt with European developments.
There are many papers here on different aspects of ARPANET. However no mention is made of other highly reliable commercial networks in the US. Because a comparison of the technologies of
these networks with other described here is important, two commercial US time-sharing networks are discussed in §8.

Finally, an attempt is made in §9 to draw some conclusions
from this rather patchy overview of the European scene. It is
clear that for some time to come the development of data networks
and <u>ad hoc</u> computer networks will develop in parallel. To what
extent the data networks being developed by the PTTs will meet
the network needs of users is of considerable interest to all at
this symposium.

2. PRESENT LINE SWITCHED DATA NETWORKS

Two countries, France and W. Germany, have started introducing
special line-switched data networks.

The French have introduced the Caducee system, sketched in
Fig.1. This system is based on an Erikson CP 410 crossbar
switch. It is a circuit switched system for the speed range 2400-
72K bps using analogue transmission. The system is based on 2000
line exchanges as sketched below:

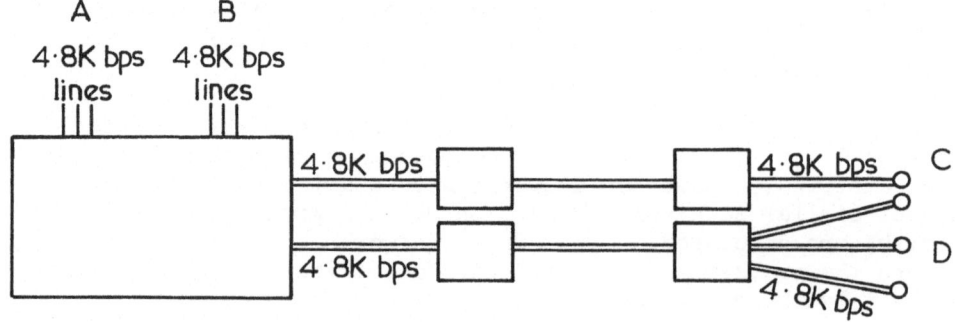

Fig. 1   Schematic of French CADUCEE

There are four classes of subscribers:

A. Those within 30 km of an exchange using ordinary modems

B. Those within 30 km of an exchange using a base-band modem

C. Those at larger distances from an exchange with heavy traffic using ordinary modems.

D. Those at larger distances from an exchange with less traffic, connected to it through a concentrator, again via ordinary modems.

Although any modems can be connected, the French PTT will supply modems at 2.4K bps and later 4.8K bps for Classes A, C and D, and a modem at 19.2K bps for B. Later they hope to provide higher speed modems. The same quality of four-wire lines will be used as for leased telephone service. Call set-up time is six seconds, and there is out-of-band signalling via a touch-tone telephone. A typical configuration is shown in Fig.2.

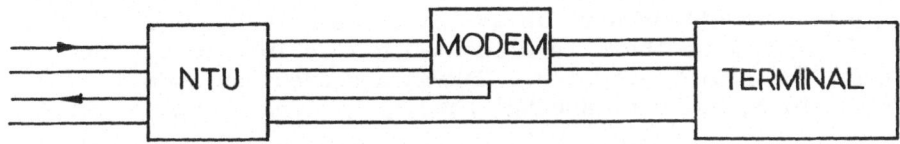

Fig.2   Schematic of Caducee Network
Terminal Unit Attachment

The NTU has a telephone, twelve push buttons for signalling, and six lights (intervention, out of order, busy, indication to dial, transmission in progress, and free), and eight buttons (make busy, manual call, manual intervention, automatic call, free line, register intervention, clear intervention register).

Each Caducee exchange can handle about 2K duplex circuits; 1600 are ordinary lines, 240 lines with remote concentrators for calling in, 240 with remote concentrators for calling out. The concentrators concentrate forty channels onto twenty lines, and are envisaged for circuits with 0.2 erlang traffic or less. Initially there is one exchange, but as needs grow additional exchanges will be installed initially in remote towns. Added stations will increase the area over which high speed traffic is possible. The first Caducee exchange became operational in early 1972.

A far more ambitious system, the EDS system is being developed

by Siemens for the German Post Office. A fairly complete description in English is now available[1],[2].

The system has been discussed in the references, so will not
be described in detail here. The important point is that the
system is essentially asynchronous. Schematically it is shown in
Fig. 3.

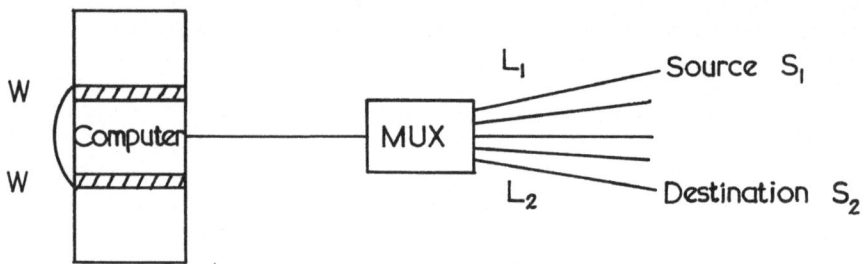

Fig. 3.   Schematic of EDS exchange

A computer is attached to up to 13K lines by a special multiplexor. To each line there is allocated a word in core W. Any
data input from L will affect W. Making a connection from a
terminal S_1 to S_2 would be accomplished by setting a pointer in W_1
to W_2 and vice versa. Once a connection has been made, the MUX
will detect any change in state of the bistable line L_1. If a
number of lines change state simultaneously, since the computer
can service only one line at a time, there will be a delay in some
of the changes being passed on; this delay will show up as distortion in the transmitted signal. Provided this distortion is
not too serious there will be almost complete transparency in
data speed or format with this network. I say almost complete
transparency, because signalling to make a connection will be at
a specific speed with LSO Alphabet No. 5.   While the connect time
is designed to be 100 ms, the time to terminate a call may take
250 ms, or 300 ms if remote concentrators are used.

The main purpose of this system was initially to take over the
50 bps telex and the 200 bps telex (the DATEX system). Typical
numbers of lines active on a 13K line exchange envisioned by
Siemens in early studies are shown in Table 1:

Class	Speed K bps	Signalling Rate K bps	No. of Active Connections	% of Machine Cycles
1	<.85	.05	4300	13
2	.050<S<.2	.2	375	5
3	.2<S<2.4	2.4	275	39
4	2.4<S<9.6	2.4	75	43

Table 1: Speeds and Signalling Speeds
of Different Classes

Clearly a small proportion of higher speed traffic would saturate this system. The Germany PTT has stated that for the time being it will only use this system asynchronously for classes 1 and 2 up to 200 bps. Above that speed Siemens is now developing synchronous units. It seems clear that the growth of the EDS system[3] will be in accordance with the other networks of $3.

Siemens claim that when the EDS exchange is working synchronously, its throughput is much higher than indicated in Table 1. When it is equipped with a 200 ns memory and a single set of buffers it can handle the following traffic:

Speed (K bps)	0.6	2.4	9.6	48
No. of full duplex connections	25K	6.24K	1.56K	312

Table 2: Capacity of EDS exchange for
Synchronous traffic

However the time to set up calls is comparatively long - 20ms. Thus at most 50 calls/sec could be set up. This implies that the EDS system is not ideal for short transactions. For comparison, in the packet switching ARPANET IMP[4] it would be possible to generate an order of magnitude more short messages to different sites.

In the EDS system there will also be a remote controlled concentrator, with 10 lines to the exchange and 100 to subscribers. It will have facilities for abbreviated dialling, multi-address messages, calling station identification and closed user groups. Facilities for packet switching, hot-line and delayed delivery have been announced on the EDS exchange by Siemens, but the German PTT have not said that they will provide these facilities. A prototype exchange is being operated in Munich, and the first real exchange is scheduled for 1974. Some ten exchanges are scheduled by 1976.

3. SYNCHRONOUS DATA NETWORKS

Many of the wide spread computer networks have implemented a
communication subsystem, which operates over the analogue telephone network.   Some of these subsystems are described briefly in
this paper.   For some years the international body called "Committee Consultative Internationale de Telegraphe et Telephone"
(CCITT) has studied the requirements for specialised data networks
in their working party on New Data Networks (NRD).   The CCITT is
a consultative committee to the International Telecommunications
Union, and its recommendations are usually followed by the national telecommunications administrations (PTTs).

The NRD has concluded that it is the declared intention by
a number of PTTs to provide data services over synchronous networks[5].   At the moment the only facilities which will be provided
by most such countries are for circuit-switched connections, in
which a single channel is provided between two terminals.   On the
present analogue public switched telephone network, full duplex
facilities are usually provided only up to 200 or 300 bps, with
half-duplex facilities up to 1200 or 2000 bps.   The New Networks
will use pcm digital transmission, and plan to provide a number
of user classes with full duplex capability as indicated in Table
3.   The new networks are planned for introduction between 1975
(US) and 1985, with many starting about 1980.   For this reason
it is felt that a little information about these networks is of
some importance.   Further details are given elsewhere[6,7].

Class	User data class of	Address Selection and Service Signals (Alphabet No. 5)
1	200 bps, 11 units/char start/stop	200 bps
2	50-200 bps, 7.5-12 units/char start/stop	200 bps
3	600 bps synchronous	600 bps
4	2400 bps synchronous	2400 bps
5	9600 bps synchronous	9600 bps
6	48000 bps synchronous	48000 bps

Table 3:   Classes of User Services Recommended

Certain specific recommendations have been made on class 2, so
that the combinations of speed and units/character match present
terminals.

It is proposed that these new data networks have a public switched capability of making a call "reasonably fast"; however the present set of recommendations do not seem to guarantee such a call being set up in less than 10 secs, or shut down in less than 1 sec. It is supposed to be symmetrically duplex, bit sequence independent, with automatic calling and answering. It is recommended that direct call, abbreviated address and closed user groups be provided. Remote terminal identification, multi-address, and delayed delivery for class 1 service may be provided.

The actual transmission between exchanges will be at a multiple of 64K bps (usually 2.048 M bps in Europe which uses 32 64K bps channels). It will usually share the same long distance transmission as the telephone system, but use different exchanges. It will use different terminating units to subscribers' premises from the present modems. In many countries the new network is intended to carry the telex traffic, and possibly also facsimile.

There are a number of consequences of the need for interworking between countries, together with facilities for complete bit transparency[5]. Several countries (particularly ATT and Canada) have opted for wishing to have a frame consisting of some synchronising or control bytes followed by data bytes:

SYN data data data ... SYN data data data SYN

Others have preferred to have each bytes carry information on whether it is control or data e.g.:

Bit	1	2-7	8
Content	Frame	Information	Status

Table 4: Frame Format for synchronous Data

Here for one value of status the information is data, for another control. Denmark, Finland, W. Germany, Norway, Sweden and the UK have opted for this system; France and Italy have said they would use both methods. The two systems will be kept capable of interworking, because it has been agreed to use a 32 bit frame consisting of four 8 bit bytes. In the first scheme there will be one control byte followed by three data bytes/frame; in the second each frame will have four bytes of which again up to 24 bits are data.

Since the control and framing information is put in by the switching exchanges, the relative transmission rates in the classes are shown below:

Class	1	2	3	4	5	6
Rate bps	266	266	800	3,200	12,800	64,000
Repetition in 64K bps stream	240	240	80	20	5	1

Table 5: Signalling speeds and number of bytes in 64K bps channel for data for a signal user class

The typical schematic of a system of this sort is indicated below:

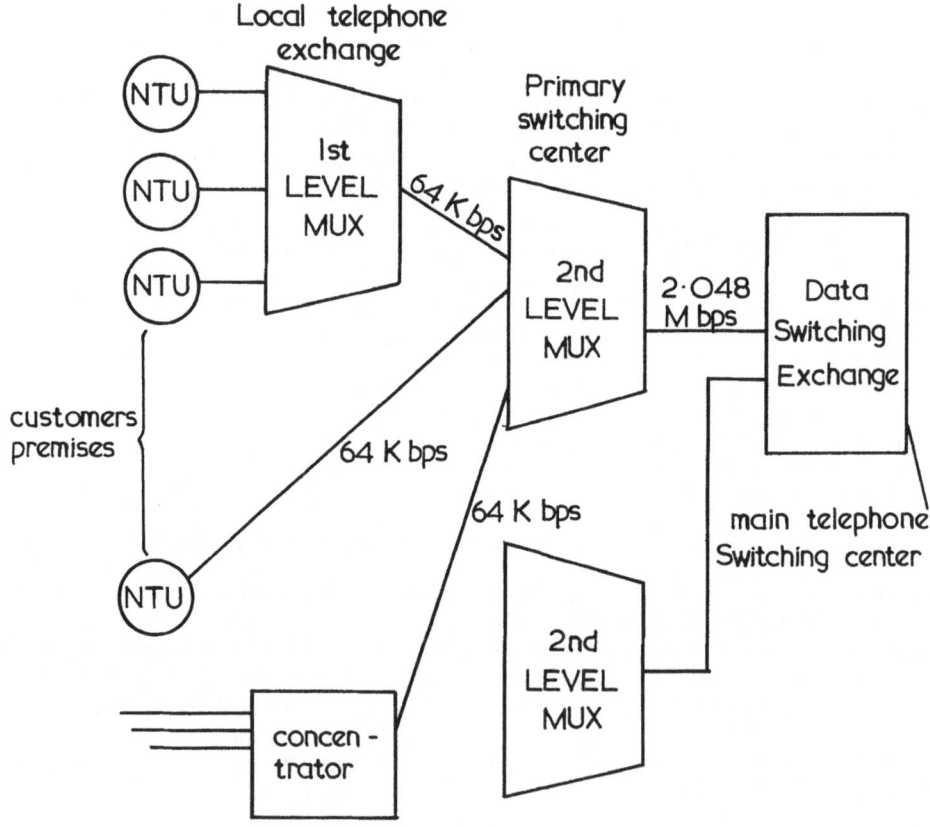

Fig.4: Schematic of Data Network Multiplexing

It would be possible to add packet switching to such a system, but the NRD has not made any recommendations on this point.

The UK BPO[7] claimed that while most of the traffic in a network can be best handled by circuit switched techniques, others can be handled better by breaking up the data into packets; these are then sent by fairly standard store and forward techniques. They claimed that a DSE built to handle packets would be only 15% more than one without, and the DSE costs is only 25% of the network. At that time (1971) they aimed at an installed capital cost of switch of $600/line. A schematic of the DSE for mixed packet and circuit switching is shown in Fig.5.

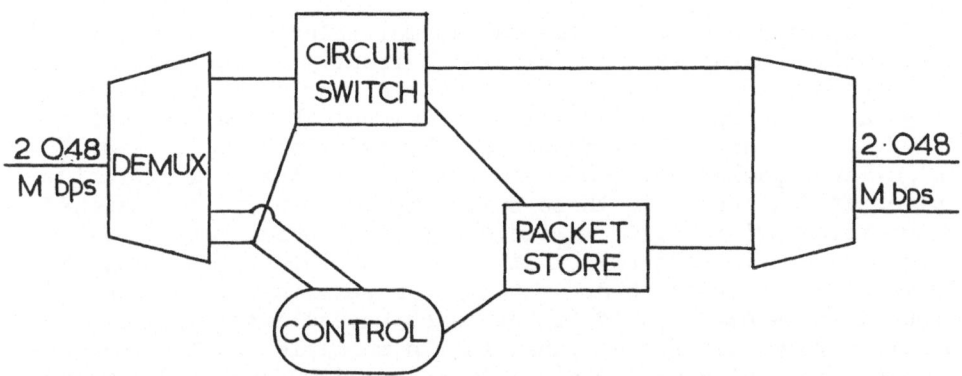

Fig.5: Schematic of Packet and Circuit Switched Operation in the Data Switching Exchange (DSE)

The above is an example of how packet switching could be added to synchronous line-switched networks. No European PTT has committed themselves to provide such a service, however.

The PTTs of a number of countries have announced definite plans to introduce trial networks of this kind (without packet working). Amongst these are Norway[8] and Sweden[6]. Both of these two will have three nodes. The Norwegian one will have initially 72K bps transmission between nodes at Oslo, Trondheim and Bergen. At each city there will be a 512 port multiplexor to subscribers' equipment, and between the subscriber and the multiplexor analogue transmission via modems will be used. There will be initially only leased line service in 1974, and switching may be added later.

The Swedish system (also to commence in 1974) is somewhat more ambitious. It will have a switching exchange in Stockholm,attached by 42K bps lines to concentrators in Stockholm, Malmo, and Gothenberg. It will have limited capacity, initially for only 100 terminals of different types. Transmission speeds of 2.4K bps will be offered initially, with 9.6K bps and 600 bps following later; the customer interface will be as for synchronous modems. This system will use something like the CCIT envelope scheme, and have a call set-up time of 100-200 ms. France and the UK[7] are studying larger networks (the UK with capacity for 50K terminals), and W.Germany[9] is looking at transforming its EDS network into a synchronous one.

4. PUBLIC PACKET SWITCHED NETWORKS

Only the Spanish PTT has declared itself for packet switched working[10]. However both the UK[11] and France[12] decided to intro-duce experimental services. All these networks use (or will use) analogue transmission via modems at this time.

The Spanish system is directed at multiplexing terminal traffic to real-time computers. It is based currently on duplexed Univac 418 computers as switches (DSE) at Madrid, Barcelona and Seville, though a fourth will be installed at Valencia before the summer of 1974. The configuration planned by 1978 is shown in Fig. 6. A high-level packet-switched network connects the main switching centres at 48K bps. To these switching centres can be attached customers computers (TA), multiplexors (M), concentrators (C), or customers terminals (T). At the moment three computers, with 150 terminals are attached. The system permits both virtual circuits to be set-up, and to have each packet containing its own header. Terminals are attached to the multiplexors M or concen-trators C initially at 200 bps, 600 bps or 1200 bps. The M and C are themselves attached to the DSE initially at 4.8K bps; I presume the computers are attached to the DSE currently at the same speeds. Already the Spanish experience with their switches has caused them to modify their line handling hardware and soft-ware.

The British experimental service is being described in consid-erable detail at this symposium. It is again initially based on three DSEs at London, Manchester and Glasgow – connected to each other by several 48K bps lines. Packet-based connection to the DSEs is at 2.4 or 48K bps; start-stop access from terminals is at up to 300 bps. The DSEs are capable of handling up to 24 pac-ket type of terminals each. The first node is scheduled for op-eration in early 1975, with the other two following within the following six months.

The French plans are more modest. They again will have three DSEs (PDP 11/20s), sited at Paris, rennes and Lyons. These are scheduled to be working internally by the end of 1973 with a public service in 1974. The connection between the DSEs will be only at 2.4K bps, but the total instantaneous rate of traffic to a DSE can attain tens of K bps on up to 200 lines. One of the aims

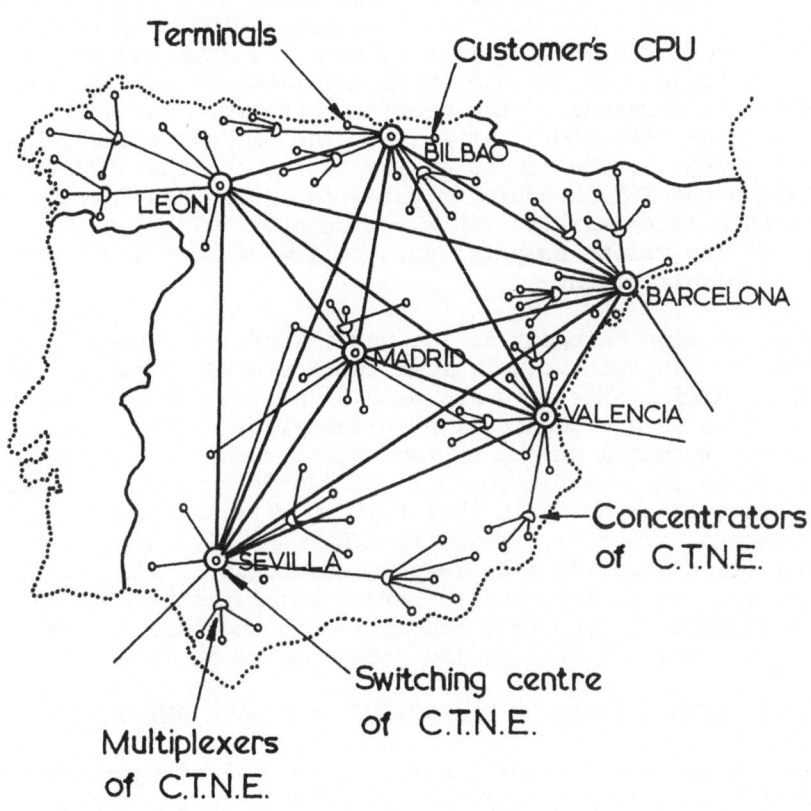

Terminals

Customer's CPU

BILBAO

LEON

BARCELONA

MADRID

VALENCIA

SEVILLA

Concentrators
of C.T.N.E.

Switching centre
of C.T.N.E.

Multiplexers
of C.T.N.E.

Fig.6: Schematic of Spanish CTNE packet switched Network

of the system is to investigate what occurs when the DSE becomes over-loaded. The terminal access can be at up to 9.6K bps in a burst mode, but clearly such rates could not be sustained.

All the three services mentioned above are essentially packet-switched data networks. They are designed to handle the idiosyncracies of certain types of terminals - but it is not clear how far the PTTs will go even in that regard. The PTTs certainly do not regard the procedures for handling computer-computer connections to be part of their brief.

5. HOMOGENEOUS PACKET SWITCHED COMPUTER NETWORKS

Two packet switched computer networks based on homogeneous computers deserve mention. In one, a number of IBM computers in France are linked by 4.8K bps lines without a communication sub-network[13]. Although all the computers involved are IBM 360s, they do run different versions of the operating system. The computers in the network are the 360/91 at Saclay, the 360/75 at CRNS, the 360/67 at Grenoble U, the 360/50 at IBM Paris, and the 360/40 at Ecole de Mines and IBM Grenoble. Beside the store and forward operation, facilities existed, by the middle of 1972, for inter-active use of the remote computer and the transfer of whole files, and remote job initiation.

In much the same category is the network of the UK South West Universities[14]. In this network four ICL System 4 computers (at Bristol U, Cardiff U, Exeter U and Bath U) are attached to a CDC 1700, which acts as a communication switched, by 48K bps lines. Here again any terminal on one system computer can have inter-active access to programs in another, and it is possible to transfer files and submit jobs. In this network virtual circuits, rather than packets, are sent. There is a Network File System, and the communication computer also keeps a catalogue of all the files in the network. It is intended to permit automatic off-loading of restricted classes of jobs from one system to another. At the moment this is only possible if its jobs require no files.

6. RESTRICTED USER CLASSES OF PACKET-SWITCHED DATA NETWORKS

Two packet switched networks are in a special category. They are international data networks but intended for a particular user community.

The SITA network is a store and forward message switching network for airlines with DSEs in London, Amsterdam, Brussels, Frankfurt, Rome Madrid, Paris and New York. It is over-connected, and consists of Univac 418 and Philips DS 714 computers. There are remote concentrators (mainly Raytheon 706) attached to the DSEs; many of the airlines connect their terminals to the DSEs via the

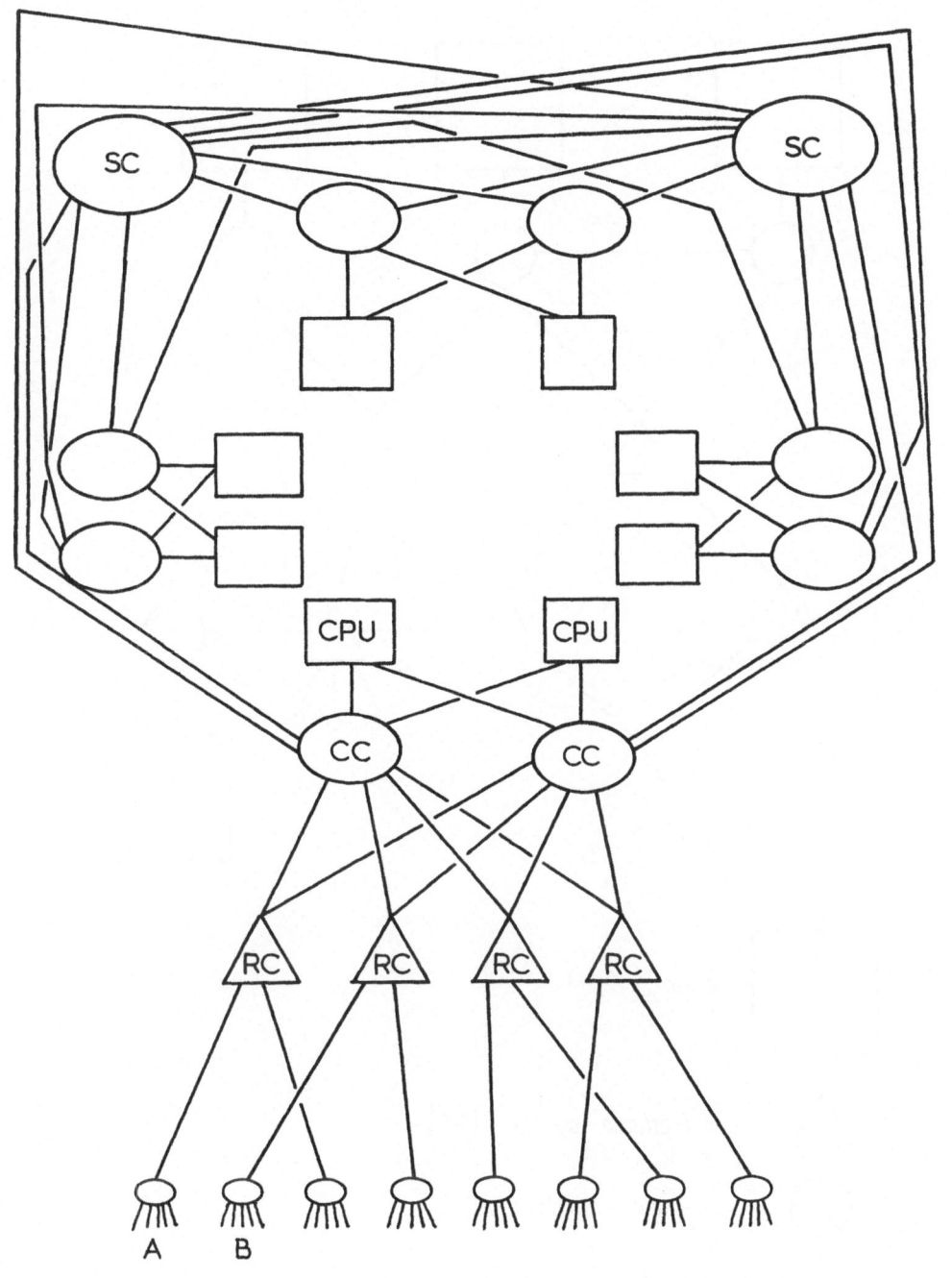

Fig. 7 Schematic of GE Data Network

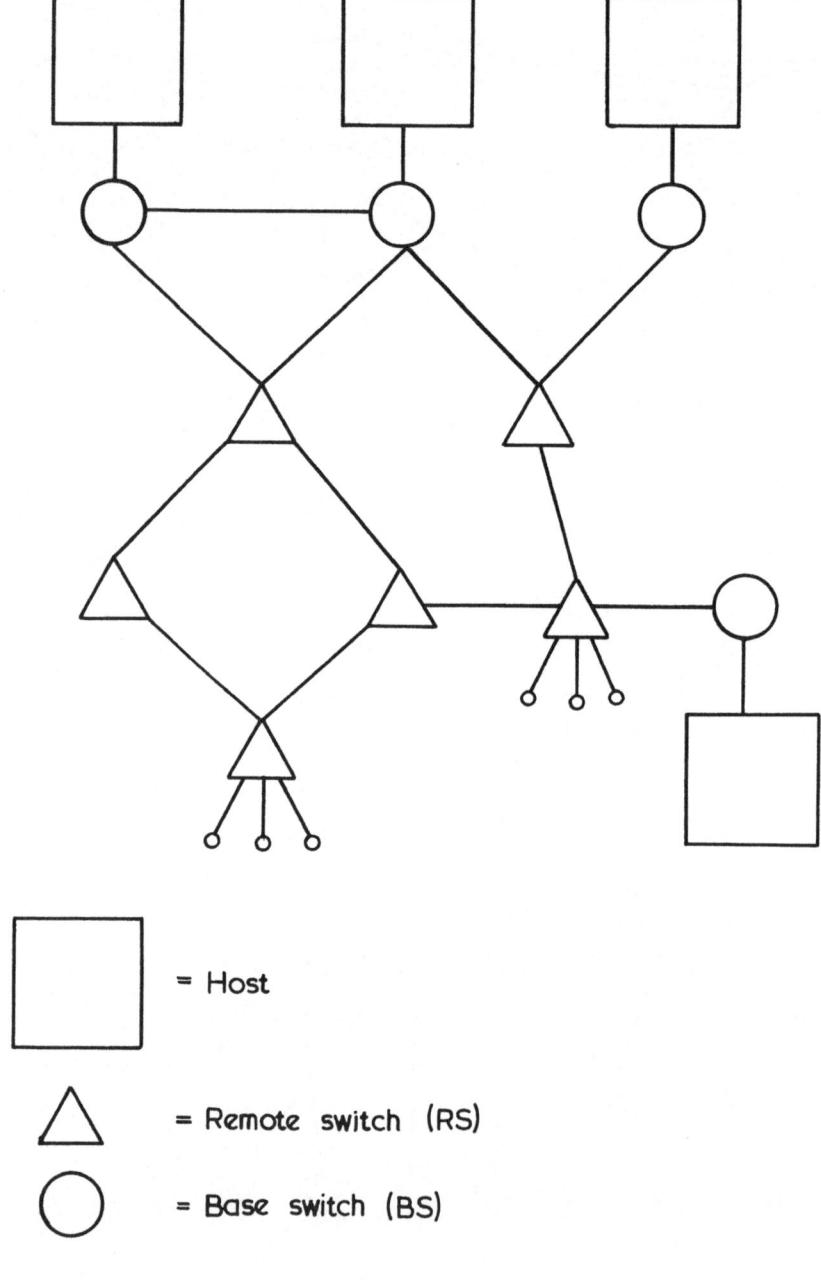

Fig. 8   Schematic of TYMNET topology

remote concentrators. Most of the traffic on the network is terminal based message traffic, but several airlines have tied their computers directly to the DSEs with medium speed lines. Typical responses to messages in the network are 6 secs; the message length has been carefully chosen to meet the average message length of 180 chars.

The Banks are setting up the SWIFT message switching system for inter-bank transfers. This system will have initially the switching centres in Brussels and Amsterdam, and concentrators in eleven countries. It will handle a number of terminals including keyboard terminals, magnetic tape units, minicomputers controlling clusters of terminals, and the front-end computers of the Banking System computers. Few details have been released yet, but it is expected to start operation in 1975. Opposition from the US record carriers, who have a monopoly at this time of US-international data traffic, has so far prevented approval for the SWIFT system to be extended to the US.

7. GENERAL USE HETEROGENEOUS COMPUTER NETWORKS

The only European packet-switched system actually operational is the one internal to the National Physical Laboratory[15]. This system was conceived about the same time as ARPANET, and uses already digital transmission. It connects a number of host computers and terminals through a single packet switching exchange, and is therefore like one node of a system like the EPSS.

Two heterogeneous computer networks of different types are being developed. The aim of both systems is to access data bases on computers attached to one DSE from terminals attached to computers on another DSE. Both are discussed in details at this conference, and so will only be mentioned briefly here.

In CYCLADES[16], the French are developing the first general purpose heterogeneous computer network in Europe. At the moment its DSEs, which are MITRA 15 computers, are stated to have connections only to Host computers. It is planned to have five DSEs, in Grenoble, Paris, Rocquencourt, Rennes and Toulouse. The DSEs will be connected by 48 or 4.8K bps lines; some 16 hosts will be connected to the DSEs with lines at speeds varying between 4.8 and 48K bps. The communication between the DSEs and between the DSEs and Hosts are packet based. The network is being developed by computer specialists, so that the higher level protocols between the operating systems of the Hosts are of considerable concern.

This is also one of the first networks in which the problem of connecting different networks is being considered. The Hosts planned for attachment include CDC 6000, IBM 360, CII 10040, IRIS 80 and Philips P1100 computers, so that the network will be truly heterogeneous. The first DSE is now operational, and the first Hosts will be attached in 1974. The system is expected to be operational in 1975.

The second similar network being designed is the inter-European COST 11 one.[17] Here DSEs will be sited at London, Paris, Zurich, Ispra and Milan. The specifications have just been completed for the DSEs, so that one may expect the communication subsystem complete in 1975, with Hosts attached by 1976. The applications to be made of, and Hosts to be attached to, this network are still not settled.

The US ARPANET chose to attach some DSEs which handled terminals as well as Host computers[18]. The main reason that such a development is not currently envisaged on CYCLADES and COST 11, is that terminal traffic is really the prerogative of the PTTs, who are developing their own networks. The development of these computer networks is proceeding in collaboration with the PTTs; one may expect either that DSEs with terminal handling facilities will be developed for these networks, or that the National data networks will be attached in due course.

8. THE PROPERTIES OF TWO COMMERCIAL DATA NETWORKS

Two commercial US data networks are of interest in the context of ARPANET and the other networks which have been discussed in this paper. The first is the GE Time-sharing network, and the second Tymeshares' TYMNET.

The GE Time-sharing network, routes terminal traffic to a number of computer systems, which are currently located at one site. Previously the computer systems were at several sites, and the network design is not affected by the single location. A schematic of the GE Network is shown in Fig.7. Here the central computers (CPU) are attached in pairs to the Central Concentrators (CC). These are themselves attached to a number of remote concentrators (RC), to each of which are attached a number of low speed terminal channels by a TDM or FDM multiplexed line. By arranging that, for example, the multiplexor terminals A and B in Fig.7 are in the same town, routes to a specific CPU may be found even if one RC, one CC and several lines were all faulty. It is possible to arrange that the rerouting of traffic is dynamic if equipment failures occur beyond the RC; if they occur between the RC and the subscriber, only a new local call need be made. In order to access other Hosts in the complex, all the CCs are connected to two switching computers. It is possible therefore to route traffic to any of the other computers in the network.

This type of topology has many similarities but many differences from ARPANET. It uses packet transmission from the RC upstream, so that it makes the most of the long-line saving possible. It has a high reliability, and can be made to have high capacity. It uses virtual line switching to set up calls, and is therefore not very appropriate to short message traffic - but excellent for bursty time-sharing usage for which it was designed. Provided the traffic is largely regional, so that only a small percentage passes through the switching computers SC, the capacity of the network is good. It is considerably more expensive, however, than the store and forward type of the ARPANET, which can use a smaller number of high speed line.

TYMSHARE uses a quite different technology of distributed control. Their system is more like ARPANET in some ways. A schematic of their topology is shown in Fig.8. Now each Host is fronted by a base switch (BS). There is also a store-and-forward network of remote switches (RS), which forward traffic from other BS or RS, and also concentrate terminal traffic. There are several different types of Hosts, and the TYMNET also acts as a data network to Hosts belonging to other organisations, who connect their host into a BS. Between the RS and RS or RS and BS data is sent in a block format. However in each block are sent a number of messages prefixed by two bytes - message length and channel number. When a terminal is logged on, a virtual circuit is established through the Network between the terminal and the Host. The RS nearest the terminal affixes the channel number. Each block sent can include a number of such messages. The RS (or BS) will then break up the blocks it receives and make up new ones related to the connections attached to it. This type of network requires one or more supervisors to set up the virtual circuits - i.e. assign the channel numbers. Usually only one supervisor is active, with others in a waiting state. If, however, the network becomes cut, from a number of faults or insufficient line redundancy, several hosts may act as supervisors.

Both the GE and TYMNET networks have local echoing at the nearest RS or BS. They also have techniques in each switch to limit the data flow which can be accepted from the terminals. Such techniques are necessary when faults occur in the store and forward network, or when the potential input from terminals becomes greater than the network can guarantee to accept. Both networks have much lower capacity lines, and therefore less capacity for high speed file-oriented traffic, than ARPANET. However both networks have a higher degree of over-connection, and greater reliability, than the present ARPANET.

There are some significant differences between the two networks. The GE one is clearly hierarchical, with powerful switches capable of taking a substantial number (several dozen) inputs and at least two outputs. The TYMNET is pretty homogeneous (with the exception of the BS). TYMNET is very distributed; the GE network has all intersystem traffic going through one of two special switches. Both have had to modify their switches for file transfer, and are catering for this by using large block sizes and faster switches with less ports.

9. CONCLUSIONS

In this survey we have described a variety of current European developments. Here we will summarise some of the trends which are emerging. The PTTs are developing synchronous line-switched digital data networks which shall be able to interwork internationally. These should make 4.8K bps available economically by 1980 in many countries. Most PTTs are not yet convinced on the need for packet switched systems, though some are starting experimental services. The results of these early services will clearly affect the rate at which packet switching is introduced. Internationally packet-based broadcast satellite transmission is interesting. Some PTTs are interested enough for them to wish to try experiments with it. Unlike the US, the monopoly position of the European PTTs make it difficult to get packet-switched services started in Europe until the PTTs are convinced about their desirability. For telex-like services they are already convinced, for data networks less so.

Some interesting information is coming from several homogeneous computer networks. Usually the homogeneity leads to the network procedures relying heavily on the properties of the existing operating systems. Some of the heterogeneous computer networks being implemented now attempt to avoid this pitfall. Most still are being developed without a clear need for them. A new generation of these networks is being planned because the need exists. These new computer networks may well be built around the generalised switched data networks developed - particularly in the UK, France and Germany.

Some of the commercial time-sharing networks have some lessons for the future computer networks. These networks while much simplet in concept than ARPANET have a better reliability and availability. This is due to careful engineering of the redundancy and duplication at all stages of the system. ARPANET has alternate routing only between IMPs; each Host is simply connected, for example, and few hosts are themselves duplicated with common file access. Some commercial time-sharing networks are duplicated right through the system.

It seems clear that there will still be many developments in reliability and simplicity in the networks. The new generations are starting to consider also the functions which should be carried out in the communication sub-network. This is leading to some significant deviations from the complext set of ARPANET protocols. We can be sure that the next decade will still be interesting in this field.

REFERENCES

1. Gabler, H.: The German EDS network, Proc 2nd Symposium on the Optimization of computer networks, 80, 1972.

2. Goslau, R.et al: EDS - A new electronic data switching system for data communications, Nachrichtentechn Z.,22,444, 1969.

3. Fick, H. et al: Multiplexing and switching of data in synchronous networks and the realisation in the EDS-system, Proc. Int. Zurich Seminar on integrated sys. for speech, video and data communication, C5, 1972.

4. Heart, F. et al: The Interface Message Processor for the ARPA Computer network, Proc SJCC, 36, 551, 1970.

5. CCIT: Preliminary Report on the work of joint working party on "New Data Networks", GM/NRD No.98, Geneva, 1972.

6. Larsson, T.: Data Communication in Sweden - and some aspects of the situation in Europe, Proc Conf on Computer Communications, Washington, 17, 1972.

7. Dell, F.R.E.: Features of a proposed synchronous data network, Proc 2nd symposium on the optimization of data networks, 50,1972.

8. Bothner-By, H.: System Forslag et prevendatanett, Telektronikk, 1-2, 34, 1973.

9. Bocker, P. et al: Der aufbau von datennetzen mit dem elektronischen datenvermittlungssystem EDS, Narchrichtentechn Z, 26, 297, 1973.

10. - : General Description of the special network for data transmission and switching of C.T.N.E., C.T.N.E., 1971.

11. - : Experimental Packet Switched Services, Specification, BPO, 1973.

12. Depres, R.: La Commutation de pacquets dans un nouveau resea de transmission de donnees, Proc. Int. Zurich seminar on integrated syst. for speech, video and data communication, 1972.

13. Girardi, S.: SOC Project; an experimental computer network, <u>Proc. 2nd ACM Computing Symposium, Venice</u>, 210, 1972.

14. Howell, R.H.: The integrated computer network system, <u>Proc Conf. on Computer Communications, Washington</u>, 214, 1972.

15. Barber, D.L.A. et al: Operating experience with the NPL Network, <u>Proc ACM Symposium on Computer Networks, IRIA</u>, 145, 1972.

16. Pouzin, L.: Presentation and major design aspects of the Cyclades computer network, to be presented at the Third Data <u>Communications Symposium</u>, 1973.

17. Barber, D.L.A.: The European Computer Network Project, <u>Proc. Conf. on Computer Communications, Washington</u>, 192, 1972.

18. Ornstein, S.M. et al: The Terminal IMP for the ARPA network, <u>SJCC</u>, 40, 243, 1972.

19. Tymnes, L.R.: TYMNET - A terminal oriented communications network, <u>SJCC</u>, 34, 211, 1971.

LOCAL DATA NETWORKS

D. L. A. Barber

National Physical Laboratory, U.K.

There are a number of standard topological forms for a group
of subscribers to be connected together in a network. These
topologies, of course, take no account of the distance between
subscribers, but this is a dominating factor in deciding the
practical form of any network. The extent to which subscribers
are clustered together determines whether a hierarchy comprising
a trunk network with local areas is sensible. In the early stages
of a new network the local areas will cover wide areas and costs
will be high, because the communications resources will be in-
efficiently used. Figure 1 shows a group of subscribers connected
in two clusters around switching centres A and B and also connected by a ring of circuits, shown dotted. The total circuit
mileage required is 3,500 for full connection (not shown), 181 for
a ring connection and 171 for two clusters. Clearly, in a particular network, an optimum arrangement of circuits may be computed
for the tariffs obtaining when the network is designed.

In any kind of network, road, rail or telecommunications, resources must be shared between as many users as possible in order
to keep the cost per user low. Starting from the subscriber in a
telecommunications network, the first resource that can be shared
is the communication channel. Multiplexing is a method of sharing
a channel between several subscribers. There are two basic ways
to do this; the first gives each subscriber a portion of the available bandwidth, and is called frequency division multiplexing;
the second gives each subscriber the whole bandwidth for a portion
of the available time, this is called time division multiplexing.
In multiplexing, the capacity of the channel which all the subscribers share must be equal to the sum of the peak requirements
of each subscriber. This ensures that adequate capacity is avail-

ailable for any subscriber whenever he requires it.

In practice, not all subscribers to a network are active at the same time and multiplexing is not the most efficient way of using communications resources. Efficiency is improved when switching is introduced. Switching is, effectively, a technique for moving resources to meet the requirements of subscribers as and when they arise. The introduction of switching into a network enables resources to be shared between the active subscribers rather than all the subscribers, but it becomes necessary for subscribers to contend for the available resources and, if more subscribers become active than the network was designed for, congestion will occur and late-comers will be unsuccessful.

The use of switching allows traffic to be concentrated on to a network's communication channels. The savings arising from the better utilisation of links has to be balanced against the cost of the switching. The balance changes with technological developments so, networks may be expected to evolve.

Figure 2 shows some possible ways of connecting subscribers. At the top, four subscribers are fully connected, and no switching is required. In the middle of the diagram, four subscribers are shown connected in a star with a central switch, and three subscribers are shown arranged in the form of a tree joined by a switch, while a ring arrangement of four switches is shown at the bottom.

The introduction of storage into a communication network adds a new freedom. It becomes possible to store information from a subscriber until the network resources are available to handle it. Sometimes the necessary delay is small and the subscriber is not conscious of it; for example in a time division multiplex telephone exchange a delay of one frame, i.e. 125 microseconds, is undetectable by subscribers, but allows tandem PCM exchanges to be constructed. On the other hand, for some subscribers there may be no urgency about certain messages. So, in a message switching system, with the agreement of the subscriber, information may be delayed for hours to avoid periods of peak activity. Figure 3 shows how storage may be used to interleave three signals A,B and C. Each signal is delayed by storage until the line is able to accpet it. Switches at the sending and receiving ends of the line are used to collect and distribute signals as appropriate. This principle applies equally to a wide range of communication systems.

It is difficult to define what constitutes a local area. One definition might be, "the set of subscribers that may intercommunicate through a single switch". If this is accepted as the definition, our first concern will be the possibilities of sharing the communications channels between subscribers and the switch. Most channels have plenty of capacity and the bandwidth and time available for communication may be subdivided by FDM, TDM and (if storage is used) by asynchronous TDM techniques. With FDM and TDM the channels, or time slots, assigned to inactive subscribers are wasted. Also, when active subscribers fall temporarily idle, further time slots or channel time will be lost. With ATDM some of the bandwidth must be given over to identifying the time slot but idle time slots occur only when none of the subscribers is active. ATDM provides a form of concentration akin to that given by switching, and also leads to contention by subscribers for the available time slots. Figure 4 illustrates how the product of band-width and time for a communication channel may be divided up in various ways. With FDM, a narrow band width is available for a long time, while with TDM a wide band width is available for a short time. Note that with FDM the connect-disconnect-connect time is a waste of resource, as is an idle slot in a TDM system. With a synchronous time division multiplexing part of the available band width must be given over to an address, but there need be no other waste of resource while enough users are contending for the channel.

The basic network forms of star and ring are closely related. In each case, there is a network termination unit to which subscribers are connected. This is connected to a demand sorter, forming part of a multiplexer or concentrator, which has a channel connecting it with the rest of the network. With a star network, the demand sorters responsible for allotting channel space to active subscribers are located inside the multiplexer; with a ring network the demand sorters are distributed around the loop. But their function in each case is similar. Figure 6 shows the similarity of the basic forms of network. In practice, the delay in the transmission between component parts of the different configurations require particular engineering solutions to be adopted.

If computing power is associated with the storage in a network, it becomes more difficult to decide what constitutes the local area. For example, the multipoint circuit arrangements common in private networks contain concentrators which are often small processors. If these concentrators permit local communication between terminals connected to them, the set of terminals could be regarded as a local area data network according to the definition given above. In such networks, the terminals and concentrators share a common circuit. The way in which they share the circuit is controlled by polling. Two basic types of polling are common. Figure 6 shows 'roll-call' polling under the direct control of the processor; figure 7 shows 'hub-polling' which is useful when lines are very long as delays are minimised by arranging for terminals to poll each other in turn.

When information to be carried in a network is time dependent, or the source of the information handled is almost continuously active, the use of digital techniques in a local area can lead to an efficient sharing of communication resources by time division multiplexing, particularly if all parts of the network can be synchronised together. This kind of network is proposed for PCM telephone networks, and, possibly, for future data networks. A possible local area synchronous public network handling bytes has been described by the British Post Office.

When information is time independant, or when terminal usage is low, the use of storage with asynchronous multiplexing and concentration is more efficient than synchronous multiplexing. The NPL local network is a good example of an asynchronous local area network, where the information is handled as bytes. The NPL network which has been well described in the literature, comprises three main building blocks. The peripheral control unit (or network termination unit), the line terminal communication subsystem, and the multiplexer. The multiplexer has 8 inputs (with parallel byte interfaces) which contend for one output channel. The line terminals allow the parallel interfaces to be recreated at a distance; they exchange serial characters over 1 Mbit/s links using coaxial cables. The peripheral control unit presents British Standard 4421 interfaces to the subscriber, and, by interacting with the central switch software, effects the necessary control signalling in the network. The NPL Network is illustrated by Figures 8 and 9. The first shows the possible arrangement of multiplexers and links, the second outlines the use of push buttons and lamps for control signalling between a user and the network.

It is always attractive to reduce the cost of one service by sharing resources with another. Resource sharing even makes possible the provision of a service where it would otherwise be economically viable. This is why data continues to be carried on the telephone network despite the problems that arise, and why the use of a domestic television set by an adapter may be the only acceptable solution for a home data terminal. The common antennae television (CATV) system using cables for the local distribution of television programmes may help to bring the data terminal into the home. Present CATV schemes allow the distribution of a wide bandwidth for many television channels. It is, of course, very much easier to provide broadcast facilities, than to engineer individual links which permit many independent interactions between subscribers over a common cable. However, the wide bandwidth available and the regulation imposed by the US Federal Communications Commission that all systems from 1975 should permit two way communication is noteworthy.

The question of the terminals that will be used is often ignored when planning a public data network; it is considered suf-

ficient to provide a standard interface of some description.
In the long term this is not acceptable. A public network should
have available a standard terminal for subscribers to rent. This
would go a long way towards solving the terminal handling problems
in a network. The availability of a standard terminal must not
prevent subscribers using any terminal they wish, but if the handling of such terminals had to be done in a non-standard way, any
extra costs should be borne by the particular subscriber. A
distinction must be made between varieties of terminals of the
same kind, such as VDU's, and the new terminals we might see in
the future, such as a portable, radio-coupled, personal terminal.
If a special local area was required for such terminals, the
demand for them would have to be considerable. It is perhaps
worth noting that a personal portable telephone would be relatively easy to engineer, but there seems no sign of this happening at
the moment. An entirely different case for radio coupling may be
made for an expensive terminal, where easy transportability is
required, and where high bandwidth cable links are not readily
available.

Let us now turn our attention to problems of using a local
area, rather than those of its design. First there is that of
communicating with the local area switch in order to obtain the
connections and services required. The way this is done in the
NPL local network is probably typical of what will be required in
a public network. Figure 10 shows a simplified list of control
signals that are likely to be needed in such networks. Essentially,
protocols or procedures must be devised to cover the interactions
between the component parts of the network and between the network
and the subscribers' equipment. Protocols may conveniently be organised in hierarchies, and are of two basic kinds. Those that
cover communication between equivalent levels in a network, and
those that govern communication between adjacent levels.

Protocols have to be agreed before effective communication can
occur. Varieties of protocols have been devised for all the large
private networks, but it is much more difficult to agree protocols
for use with a public network. Within a local network no special
technical difficulties arise in devising protocols, but this may
not be the case for communication between local areas separated by
a trunk network. An example of the problems that can arise is
the difficulty of implementing an echoing type of interaction over
a satellite link.

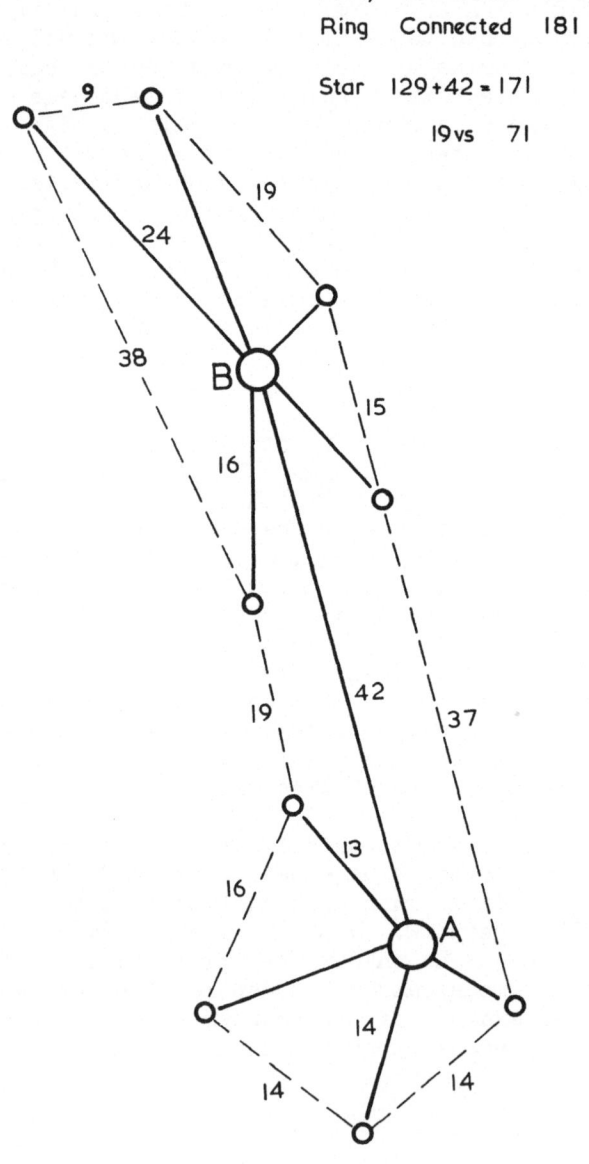

Fully Connected 3500
Ring Connected 181

Star 129+42 = 171

19 vs 71

Figure 1   Clustering

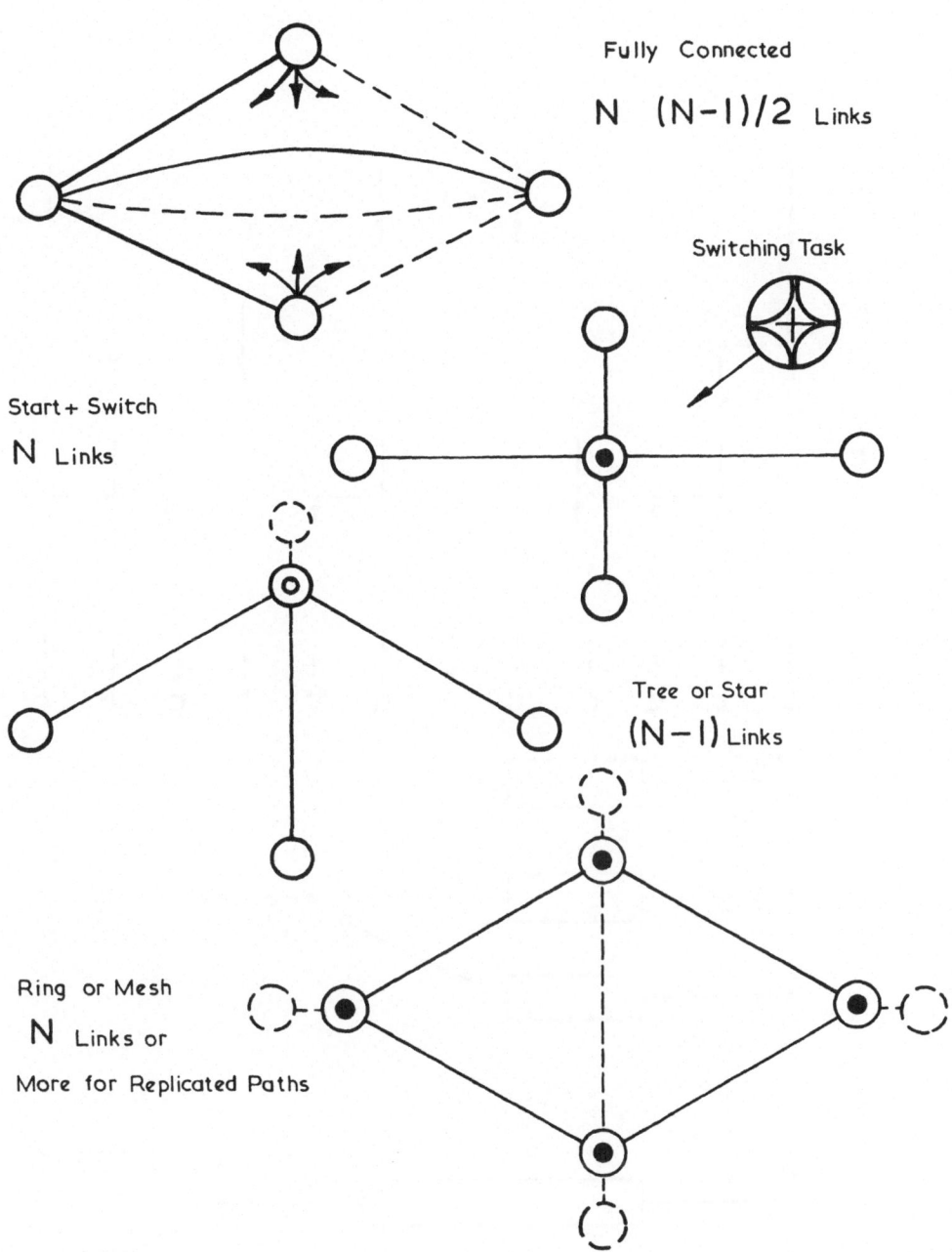

Fully Connected

N (N−1)/2 Links

Switching Task

Start + Switch

N Links

Tree or Star

(N−1) Links

Ring or Mesh

N Links or

More for Replicated Paths

Figure 2   Topology

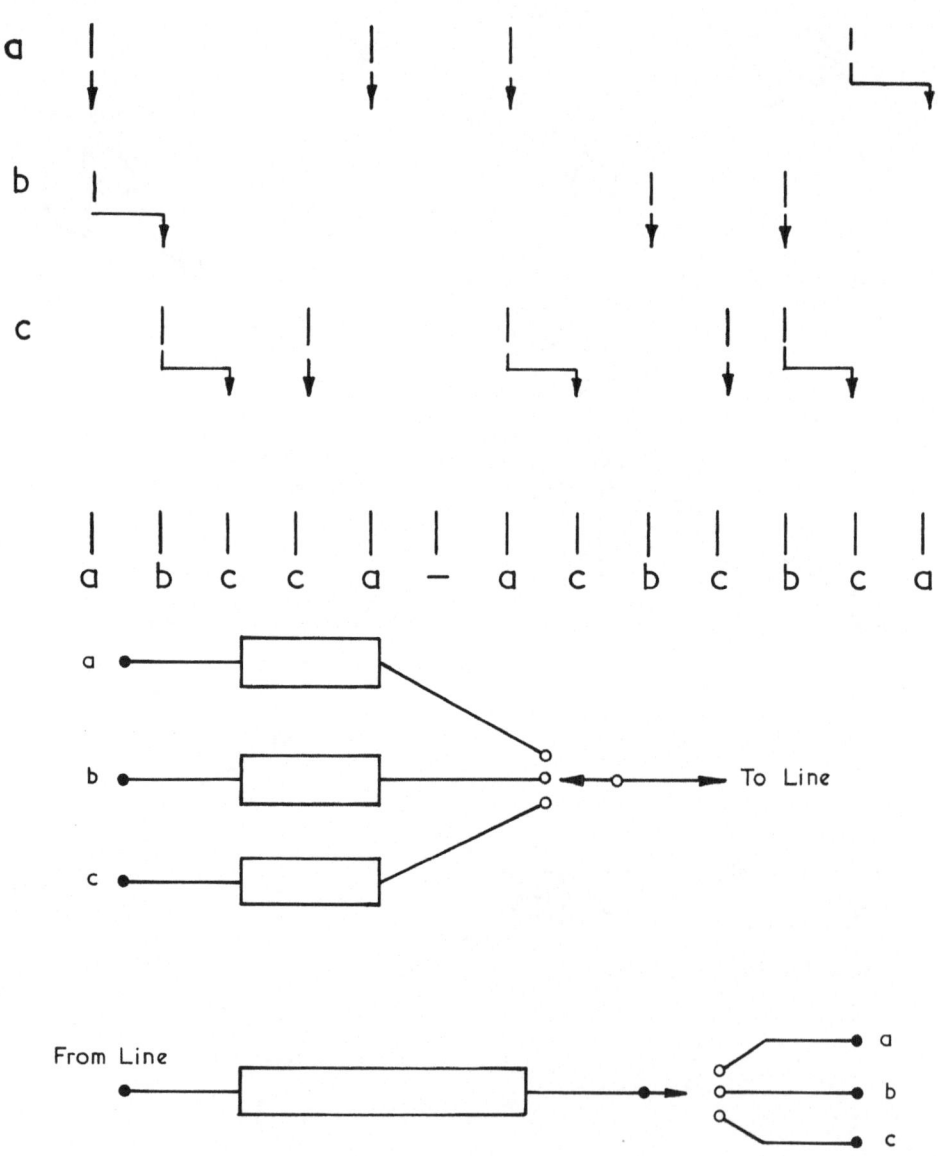

Figure 3 Use of Storage

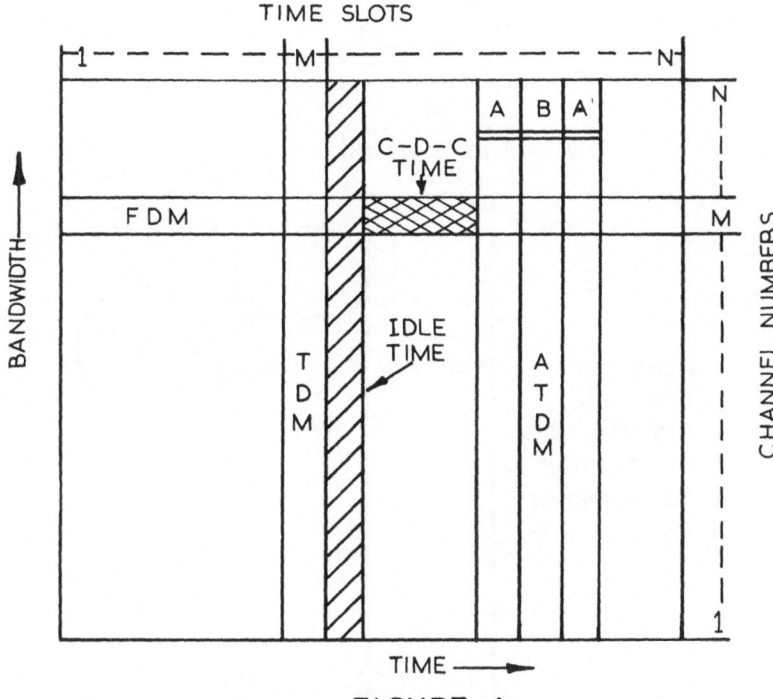

FIGURE 4
Resource Usage

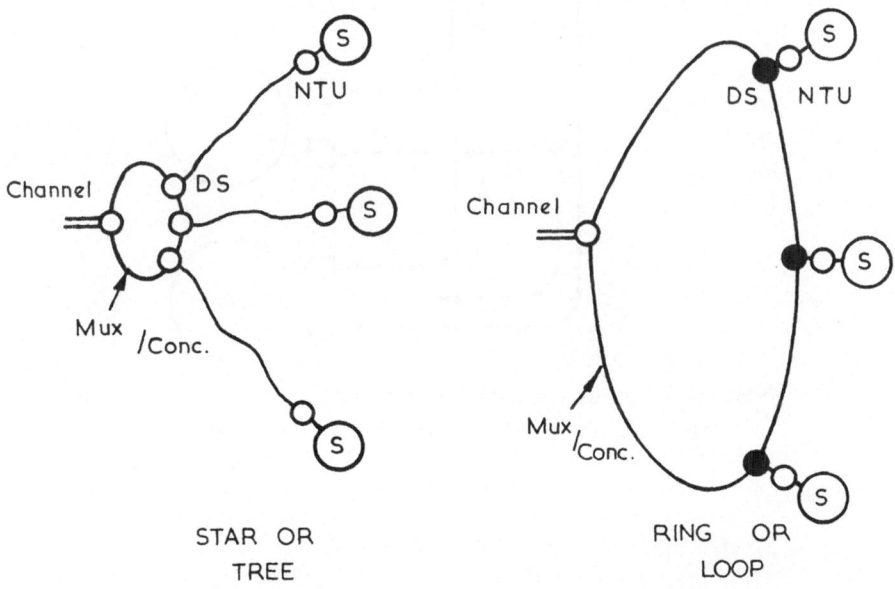

STAR OR
TREE

RING OR
LOOP

FIGURE 5   Star-Ring Systems

286

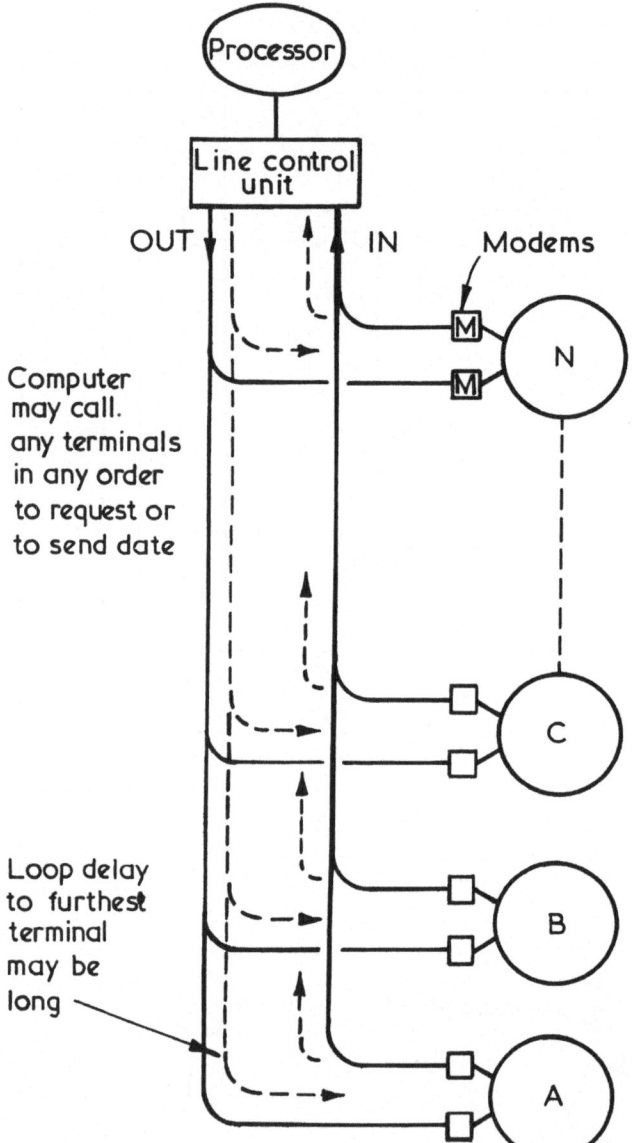

Processor

Line control unit

OUT   IN   Modems

M

M   N

Computer may call. any terminals in any order to request or to send date

C

Loop delay to furthest terminal may be long

B

A

NB: Reply message may be data or a negative acknowledgement

Fig 6 Roll call polling

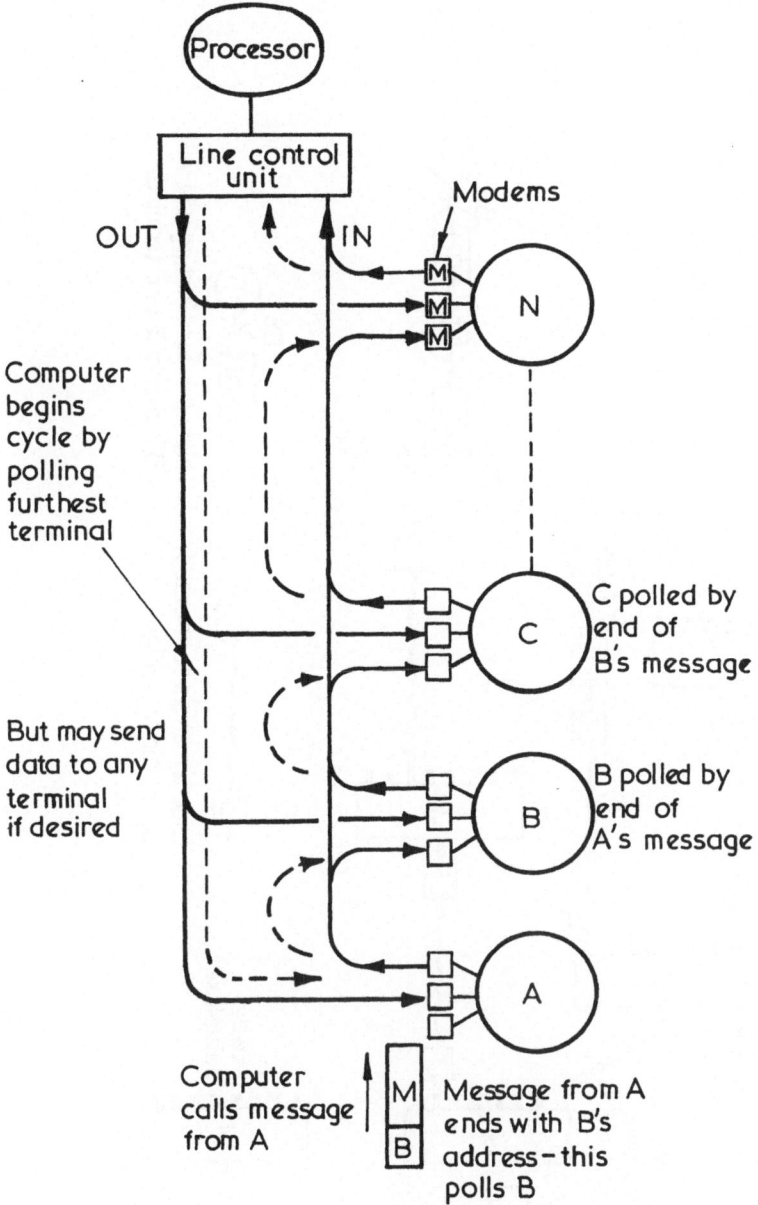

Fig. 7 Hub Polling

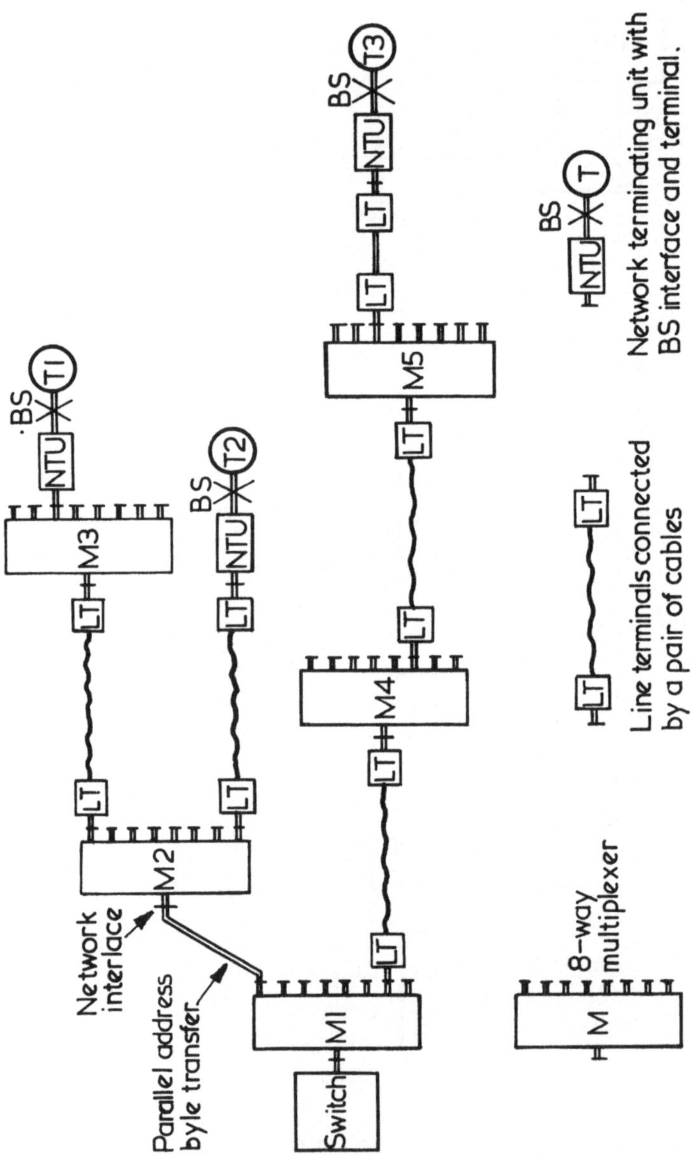

Fig. 8 NPL Multiplex Scheme.

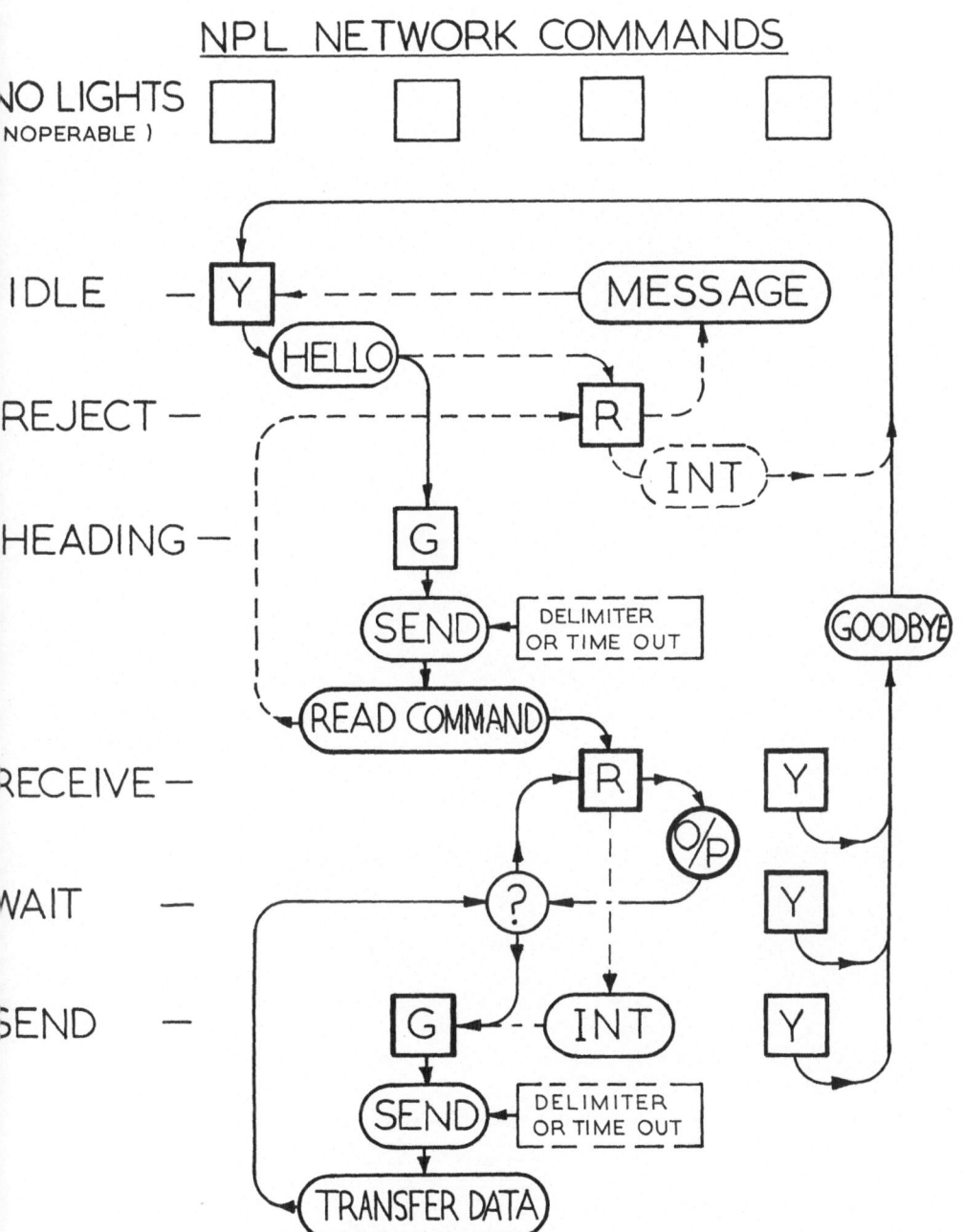

289

NPL NETWORK COMMANDS

NO LIGHTS
(NOPERABLE)

IDLE

REJECT

HEADING

RECEIVE

WAIT

SEND

MESSAGE
HELLO
R
INT
G
SEND — DELIMITER OR TIME OUT
READ COMMAND
R — %
?
Y
Y
Y
G — INT
SEND — DELIMITER OR TIME OUT
TRANSFER DATA
GOODBYE

Fig. 9 NPL NETWORK COMMANDS.

PACKET SWITCHING WITH SATELLITES*

Norman Abramson

University of Hawaii

INTRODUCTION

History

The first computer-communication networks put into operation were designed around the communications provided by the existing worldwide telephone network. Lucky has given a convincing rationale for that decision.[1]

> "The voice telephone network is perhaps the most remarkable information processing system yet constructed by man. In 1970 it served 100,000,000 telephones in the United States. The number of possible interconnections is clearly enormous. The worth of this plant is approximately 50 billion dollars. Over one million people are employed by AT&T alone in the care and feeding of this huge network. Virtually every statistic associated with the telephone network can be phrased in some extraordinary manner. Its ready accessibility and virtual ubiquity make it the obvious first contender for handling data traffic."

* THE ALOHA SYSTEM is a research project at the University of Hawaii, supported by the Advanced Research Projects Agency under NASA Contract No. NAS2-6700 and by the National Science Foundation under NSF Grant No. GJ-33220. Part of the work reported in this paper was supported by Systems Research Corporation, Honolulu, under ONR Contract N00014-70-C-0414.
- This paper is reprinted from the Proceedings of the National Computer Conference, New York, 1973, pp. 695-702.

As the limitations of this system for data communications became apparent, a number of methods were introduced to overcome the limitations of dial-up telephone and leased line systems. Data concentrators are used to increase the utilization of expensive long distance lines. High speed, wideband facilities are used to handle those situations where the burst data rate requirement of the network is larger than can be transmitted in a single voice channel. A few large systems use leased line data channels in a network with multiple paths between nodes for increased reliability All of the systems built before 1970 however based the organization of their data communication channels on the circuit switching methods developed for voice signals during the latter part of the 19th century.

As the need for more powerful and more flexible computer-communication networks, distributed over large geographical areas, increased the basic limitations imposed by the organization of circuit switched systems was questioned.[2,3,4] By 1970 the ARPA Network,[5] the first computer-communication system to employ packet switching techniques suited to the peculiar statistics of digital data had gone into operation. The network is described in Reference 6:

> "The ARPA Network is a new kind of digital communication system employing wideband leased lines and message switching, wherein a path is not established in advance and instead each message carries an address. Messages normally traverse several nodes in going from source to destination, and the network is a store-and-forward system wherein, at each node, a copy of the message is stored until it is safely received at the following node. At each node a small processor (an *Interface Message Processor*, or *IMP*) acts as a nodal switching unit and also interconnects the research computer centers, or *Hosts*, with the high bandwidth leased lines."

By January 1973 the use of packet switching techniques in the ARPA Network had made possible a resource sharing computer network among more than 30 large machines; these machines represent an investment of more than $80,000,000, span a geographical region from Hawaii to Massachusetts and the network is still expanding at a rapid rate. At this time packet switched techniques are under consideration for other computer-communication networks in the USA, Canada, Japan and Western Europe.[7,8] But no common carrier has yet announced plans for a packet switched data service for the general user of data communications.

Although the basic packet switched method of organizing communication channels in the ARPA Network represents a significant

step forward from the circuit switched methods of the voice oriented common carriers the communications medium of the ARPA Network
(with the exception of a special satellite link to the University
of Hawaii) is still the point-to-point wire (or microwave) channel.

The medium is the multiplexor

In June 1971 the first remote terminal in THE ALOHA SYSTEM, an
experimental UHF radio, packet switched network was put into operation at the University of Hawaii.[9] THE ALOHA SYSTEM is a packet
switched computer communication network using many of the design
concepts of the ARPA Network. The design of THE ALOHA SYSTEM de-
parts from that of the ARPA Network in two major respects however.
The first is in the use of a new form of burst random access method of employing a data communication channel. That method is
particularly attractive for use with a broadcast radio channel such
as in THE ALOHA SYSTEM; the characteristics of the ALOHA burst random access communication method are described in the next section.

The other respect in which the design of THE ALOHA SYSTEM de-
parts from that of the ARPA Network, and indeed from the design of
all other computer networks, is in the form of multiplexing which
occurs in THE ALOHA SYSTEM. The network uses two 24,000 bits/second
channels for all remote units -- one of these channels is used by
all remote units for data into a central machine (an IBM 360/65)
and the other channel is used for data out of the central machine.
Since data packets from all remote users access the same 24,000
bits/second radio channel in 30 millisecond bursts, each user automatically multiplexes their data onto that single channel at the
time it transmits its packet. Thus the multiplexing is accomplished between the transmitting antenna at each user station and the
receiving antenna at the central station. Steven Crocker of ARPA
has characterized this effect by noting that in THE ALOHA SYSTEM,
"the medium is the multiplexor".

A final point should be brought out about the lack of need for
multiplexing equipment in THE ALOHA SYSTEM. The cost of communications for a network of terminals connected to a central time sharing
system is often thought of as being composed of the line charges
(lease cost or dial-up charges), the modem charges at either end of
the link plus perhaps some portion of the cost of the communications
processor. For long distance connections to a machine the line
charges will usually dominate the cost of communications. Even for
local connections however the real costs of simply connecting a
terminal to a machine by common carrier communication facilities
are hard to come by. A good portion of these costs can often be
attributed to the front end communications processor and multiplexor.
The need to sample telephone input lines on a frequent basis and to
assemble characters, limits the number of input lines which can be

handled by a single processor and the data rates at which these lines can operate. Some indication of the magnitude of the cost of performing these functions can be obtained from a survey of nationa time sharing services published in November, 1971.[10] The typical charge for connect time to one of these services (that is, the cost necessary for simply tying up communications resources, not CPU time) was about $10/hour.

Since multiplexing in THE ALOHA SYSTEM is accomplished automatically the channel now used in the system is capable of handling over 500 active terminals[9] each transmitting packets at a *burst* data rate of 24,000 bits/second. (Of course the *average* data rate of each user must be well below 24,000 bits/second.)

The ALOHA channel

Consider a number of widely separated users each wanting to transmit data packets over a single high speed communication channel Assume that the rate at which the users generate packets is such that the average time between packets from a single user is much greater than the time needed to transmit a single packet. (In THE ALOHA SYSTEM the ratio of these times is about 2,000 to 1.)

Conventional time or frequency multiplexing methods or some kind of polling scheme could be employed to share the channel among the users. Some of the disadvantages of these methods are discusse by Roberts in a related paper in this session.[14] The method used b THE ALOHA SYSTEM is suggested by the statistical characteristics of the packets generated by remote users. Since each user will generate packets infrequently[11] and each packet can be transmitted in a time interval much less than the average time between packets the following scheme seems natural.

Each user station has a buffer which it uses to store one line of text. When the line is complete a header containing address, control and parity information for a cyclic error detecting code is appended to the text to form a packet and the packet is transmitted to the central station. Each user at a console transmits packets to the central station over the same high data rate channel in a completely unsynchronized (from one user to another) manner. If an only if a packet is received without error it is acknowledged by th central station. After transmitting a packet the transmitting station waits a given amount of time for an acknowledgment; if none is received the packet is automatically retransmitted. This process is repeated until a successful transmission and acknowledgment occurs or until some fixed number of unsuccessful transmissions has been attempted.

A transmitted packet can be received incorrectly because of tw different types of errors; (1) random noise errors and (2) errors

caused by interference with a packet transmitted by another console. The first type of error has not been a serious problem on
the UHF channels employed. The second type of error, that caused
by interference, will be of importance only when a large number of
users are trying to use the channel at the same time. Interference
errors will limit the number of users and the amount of data which
can be transmitted over this ALOHA random access channel as more
remote stations are added to THE ALOHA SYSTEM.

Capacity of ALOHA channels

In order to describe these limits we assume that the start
times of message packets in our channel comprise a Poisson point
process with parameter λ packets/second. If each packet lasts τ
seconds we can define $S=\lambda\tau$, where

$$S = \text{normalized channel message rate} \tag{1}$$

S is called the normalized channel message rate since a value
of S equal to one would correspond to a channel with packets synchronized perfectly so that the start of one packet always coincid-
ed with the end of the previous packet. (Of course this will not
occur because of our Poisson assumption.) Note that S takes into
account only message packets, not retransmission packets.

In addition we assume that the start times of the message packets plus packet retransmissions comprise another Poisson point process. (This assumption will hold only if the packet retransmission
delays are large. See Reference 9.) Then we can define a quantity
G, analogous to the normalized channel message rate, which takes
into account the message packets plus the retransmission packets.

$$G = \text{normalized channel traffic rate} \tag{2}$$

In general we know that

$$G \geq S \tag{3}$$

In Reference 9 we showed that

$$S = Ge^{-2G} \tag{4}$$

and this relationship is plotted in Figure 1.

Note from Figure 1 that the message rate reaches a maximum
value of $\frac{1}{2}e=0.184$. For this value of S the channel traffic is equal
to 0.5. The traffic on the channel becomes unstable at $S=\frac{1}{2}e$ and
the average number of retransmissions becomes unbounded. Thus we
may speak of this value of the message rate as the *capacity* of this

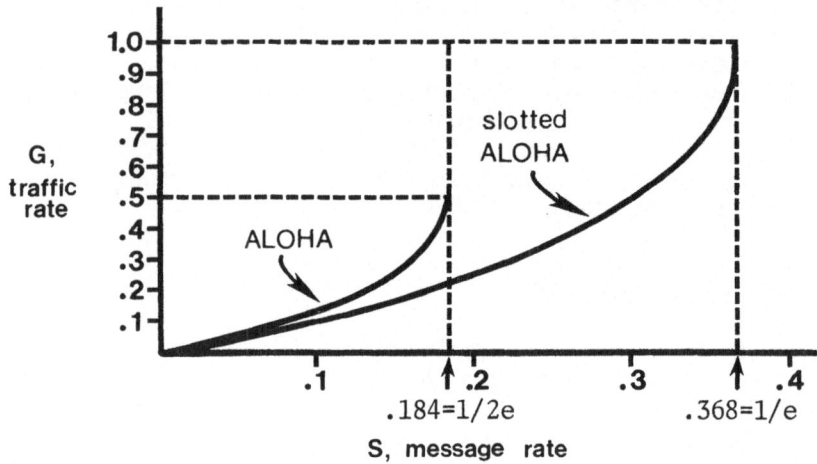

Figure **1** – Traffic rate versus message rate for a pure
ALOHA channel and a slotted ALOHA channel

random access data channel. Because of the random access feature
the channel capacity is reduced to roughly one sixth of its value
if we were able to fill the channel with a continuous stream of uninterrupted data.

The form of channel analyzed above corresponds to THE ALOHA
SYSTEM channel now in operation.

It is possible to modify the completely unsynchronized use of
the ALOHA channel described in order to increase the capacity of
the channel. In the pure ALOHA channel each user simply transmits
a packet when ready without any attempt to coordinate his transmission with those of other users. While this strategy has a certain elegance it does lead to somewhat inefficient channel utilization. If we can establish a time base and require each user to
start his packets only at certain fixed instants it is possible to
increase the channel capacity. In this kind of channel, called a
slotted ALOHA channel, a central clock establishes a time base for
a sequence of "slots" of the same duration as a packet transmission.
Then when a user has a packet to transmit he synchronizes the start
of his transmission to the start of a slot. In this fashion, if two
messages conflict they will overlap completely, rather than partially.

To analyze the slotted ALOHA channel define S_i as the probability that the i'th user will send a packet in some slot. Assume
that each user operates independently of all other users and that
whether a user sends a message in a given slot does not depend upon

the state of any previous slot. If we have n users we can define
$S=\sum_{i=1}^{n} S_i$, where

$$S = \text{normalized channel message rate} \qquad (5)$$

As before we can also consider the rate at which a user sends
message packets plus packet retransmissions. Define the probability
that the i'th user will send a message packet or a packet retransmission as G_i. Then, for n identical users we define $G=\sum_{i=1}^{n} G_i$,
where

$$G = \text{normalized channel traffic rate} \qquad (6)$$

and, as in the pure ALOHA channel

$$G \geq S \qquad (7)$$

We note here that although S, the sum of the S_i, is the probability that some user will send a message packet in a given slot,
the analogous statement is not true for G. The sum of the G_i is
not the probability that some user will send a message or repetition packet in a given slot. In fact even though G is the sum of
the probabilities G_i, G is not itself a probability and G may be
greater than 1.

For the slotted ALOHA channel with n independent users, the
probability that a packet from the i'th user will not experience an
interference from one of the other users is

$$\prod_{j=1, j\neq i}^{n} (1-G_j)$$

Therefore we may write the following relationship between the message rate and the traffic rate of the i'th user.

$$S_i = G_i \prod_{j=1, j\neq i}^{n} (1-G_j) \qquad (8)$$

If all users are identical we have

$$S_i = \frac{S}{n} \qquad (9)$$

and

$$G_i = \frac{G}{n} \qquad (10)$$

so that (8) can be written

$$S = G\left(1 - \frac{G}{n}\right)^{n-1} \tag{11}$$

and in the limit as $n \to \infty$, we have

$$S = Ge^{-G} \tag{12}$$

Equation (12) is plotted in Figure 1 (curve labeled Slotted ALOHA). Note that the message rate of the Slotted ALOHA channel reaches a maximum value of $1/e = 0.37$, twice the capacity of the pure ALOHA channel.

This result for Slotted ALOHA channels was first derived by Roberts[12] using a different method.

PROPERTIES OF SATELLITE CHANNELS

The cable in the sky

In the worldwide telephone system satellites are used more or less interchangeably with cables for transmission of voice signals. Because of this desirable feature, it is not surprising that the common carriers and even satellite designers have tended not to emphasize the differences between cable and satellite channels.

A communications satellite however is not just a big cable in the sky. There are several significant differences between the communication channel properties of a cable or microwave link and the communication channel properties of a satellite transponder.

In the next three sections we shall explain some of these differences and how they can affect the operation of a packet switched system using a satellite. But first we should mention one property of a satellite channel which the common carriers have emphasized. A satellite transponder in geosynchronous orbit is stationed 36,000 kilometers above the equator. A signal transmitted using the satellite will therefore experience a delay of about a quarter second, corresponding to the round trip propagation time up to the satellite and down again. This delay can decrease the effective data rate of certain error control schemes requiring positive acknowledgments sent from the receiver back to the transmitter. Such schemes should not ordinarily be used over satellite channels.

There are three properties of communication satellites which we want to discuss here, in terms of their significance to packet switched communications. These are:

(a)   data rates
(b)   bilateral broadcasting
(c)   perfect information feedback

Data rates

The first property of satellite channels is not a fundamental
property of the satellite itself, but rather a property of how the
satellite is used. A single voice channel on INTELSAT IV uses a
bandwidth of 45 Khz. and provides the capability of transmitting
data at 56 kilobits on a single voice channel. This mode of operation is in fact employed in the SPADE demand assignment system now
used in the Atlantic satellite; it is employed in the single-channel-
per-carrier digital voice link installed in the Paumalu earth station in Hawaii and the Jamesburg earth station in California. Since
December 1972, THE ALOHA SYSTEM has been linked to the ARPANET using
a single leased satellite voice channel to transmit data at 50 kilobits to NASA Ames Research Center in California.

Bilateral broadcasting

In the conventional use of communication channels the term
"broadcasting" refers to the fact that many receivers may obtain the
transmission from a single transmitter. Perhaps the most striking
feature of a satellite channel is its broadcast nature as opposed
to the point-to-point nature of wire channels. The reception of
broadcast signals for satellite communication channels used with
conventional circuit switched methods is a natural idea. But when
a satellite channel is used in a packet switched mode it is possible
to consider broadcasting use of the channel by transmitters as well
as receivers. This capability we have called *bilateral broadcasting*.

Since a number of transmitting ground stations operating in a
packet switched mode may all access the same channel in an unsynchronized (from ground station to ground station) fashion the analysis of an earlier section applies to bilateral broadcasting without
any change. Each of the twenty or more ground stations accessing a
given INTELSAT IV channel can transmit packets at will up to the
ALOHA random access capacity of that single channel.

There is no technological reason why such a system could not
be employed now to extend the capabilities of the existing worldwide
satellite communication network in data communications. There is
an existing regulatory restriction on such an unconventional use of
INTELSAT IV however and discussions are under way with several agencies to remove these regulatory barriers in either the INTELSAT system or one of the several domestic satellite systems to be installed
(or already installed in two countries).

Except for the not inconsiderable constraints imposed by regulatory considerations the same 50 kilobit leased satellite channel linking THE ALOHA SYSTEM to the ARPANET could be used to link machines in Alaska, Japan, Australia and any of the other sixteen earth stations which access the Pacific satellite. While these regulatory problems are being worked out however THE ALOHA SYSTEM has established a limited burst random access satellite network using the packet switching techniques described. In a joint experiment with NASA Ames Research Center in California and the University of Alaska we are operating such a link by means of the NASA ATS-1 satellite. The satellite transponder is operated as an unslotted ALOHA channel between earth stations in Hawaii, Alaska and California, and although usage of that channel is now restricted to two hours per day or less and the data rate of the channel is only 20,000 bits/second, the experiment is providing valuable information on this new communications technique.

Perfect information feedback

In the use of satellites for packet switching yet another property of little value in circuit switching assumes importance. In a packet switched system each ground station has the capability of transmitting packets up to the satellite addressed to any other ground station (or to all other ground stations). Each packet is then received by all ground stations, *including the ground station which transmitted the packet*, approximately one quarter second late Therefore each ground station can initiate transmission of a packet at will as in THE ALOHA SYSTEM. However, whereas in THE ALOHA SYSTEM, it is necessary to provide information on packet interference to the sender in the form of positive acknowledgments, such information is not necessary in the system we are describing. Since each sender can listen to his own packet retransmitted from the satellite each sender can be considered to have the same information on packet interference available to the receiver earth station. (I information theory terms, these channels are modeled as channels with perfect information feedback.)

Unfortunately in the real world, nothing is perfect and there will undoubtedly be circumstances when the transmitter and the receiver do not detect the same bit string from the satellite. The fact remains however that positive acknowledgments to combat packet interference are not required, and the more efficient use of a nega tive acknowledgment scheme in conjunction with packet numbering is feasible for this system.

EXCESS CAPACITY OF AN ALOHA CHANNEL

The idea

The type of packet switched satellite data channel we have described so far (either pure ALOHA or slotted ALOHA) has a certain elegant simplicity to it. The user of the channel simply transmits a burst of data when he wants at a data rate equal to that of the entire channel. Nevertheless there is a price to be paid for this simplicity in terms of channel capacity and in terms of delay. The question of delay is dealt with by Kleinrock[13] and Roberts[14] in the other two papers of this session. Roberts also discusses an effective method of employing the channel at rates significantly higher than the 37 percent capacity indicated by Figure 1. In the next section we provide some results which show that a slotted ALOHA channel can be used at rates well above 37 percent of capacity, if all users of the channel do not have identical message rates.

The idea of excess capacity in an ALOHA channel was first suggested by Roberts who derived a result for the case of several small users and a single large user of a slotted ALOHA channel. Roberts' proof was published along with a number of other interesting analytic results by Kleinrock and Lam.[15] The approach we shall take was suggested by Rettberg,[16] who also treated the case of a single large user and was able to obtain numerical results for that case. In the next section we provide a complete analytic and numerical solution to the use of slotted ALOHA channels by any number of users, each operating at an arbitrary rate.

The theory

From equation (8) we have a set of n equations relating the message rates and traffic rates of the n users

$$S_i = G_i \prod_{j=1, j \neq i}^{n} (1-G_j) \qquad i=1,2,\dots,n \qquad (13)$$

Define

$$\alpha = \prod_{j=1}^{n} (1-G_j) \qquad (14)$$

then (13) can be written

$$S_i = \frac{G_i}{1-G_i}\alpha \qquad i=1,2,\dots,n \qquad (15)$$

For any set of n acceptable traffic rates G_1, G_2,...,G_n these n equations define a set of message rates S_1, S_2,...,S_n, or a region in an n-dimensional space whose coordinates are the S_i. In order to find the boundary of this region we calculate the Jacobian,

$$J\left(\frac{S_1,S_2,\ldots,S_n}{G_1,G_2,\ldots,G_n}\right).$$

Since

$$\frac{\partial S_j}{\partial G_k} = \begin{cases} \prod_{i\neq j} (1-G_i) & j=k \\ -G_j \prod_{i\neq j,k} (1-G_i) & j\neq k \end{cases} \tag{16}$$

after some algebra we may write the Jacobian as

$$J\left(\frac{S_1,S_2,\ldots,S_n}{G_1,G_2,\ldots,G_n}\right) = \alpha^{n-2} \begin{vmatrix} (1-G_1) & -G_1 & -G_1 \\ -G_2 & (1-G_2) & -G_2 & \cdots \\ -G_3 & -G_3 & (1-G_3) \\ & \vdots & \end{vmatrix}$$

$$= \alpha^{n-2}[1-G_1-G_2-\cdots-G_n] \tag{17}$$

Thus the condition for maximum message rates is

$$\sum_i G_i = 1 \tag{18}$$

This condition can then be used to define a boundary to the n dimensional region of allowable message rates, $S_1, S_2, \ldots, S_n$.

The results

Consider the special case of two classes of users with n_1 users in class 1 and n_2 users in class 2.

$$n_1 + n_2 = n \tag{19}$$

Let S_1 and G_1 be the message and traffic rates for users in class one, and S_2 and G_2 be the message and traffic rates for users in class 2. Then the n equations (13) can be written as the two equations

$$S_1 = G_1(1-G_1)^{n_1-1}(1-G_2)^{n_2} \tag{20a}$$

$$S_2 = G_2(1-G_2)^{n_2-1}(1-G_1)^{n_1} \tag{20b}$$

For any pair of acceptable traffic rates G_1 and G_2 these two equations define a pair of message rates, S_1 and S_2, or a region in the S_1, S_2 plane.

From (18) we know that the boundary of this region is defined by the condition

$$n_1 G_1 + n_2 G_2 = 1 \tag{21}$$

We can use (21) to substitute for G_1 in equation (20) and obtain two equations for S_1 and S_2 in terms of a single parameter G_2. Then as G_2 varies from 0 to 1 the resulting S_1, S_2 pairs define the boundary of the region we seek. A FORTRAN program to calculate the

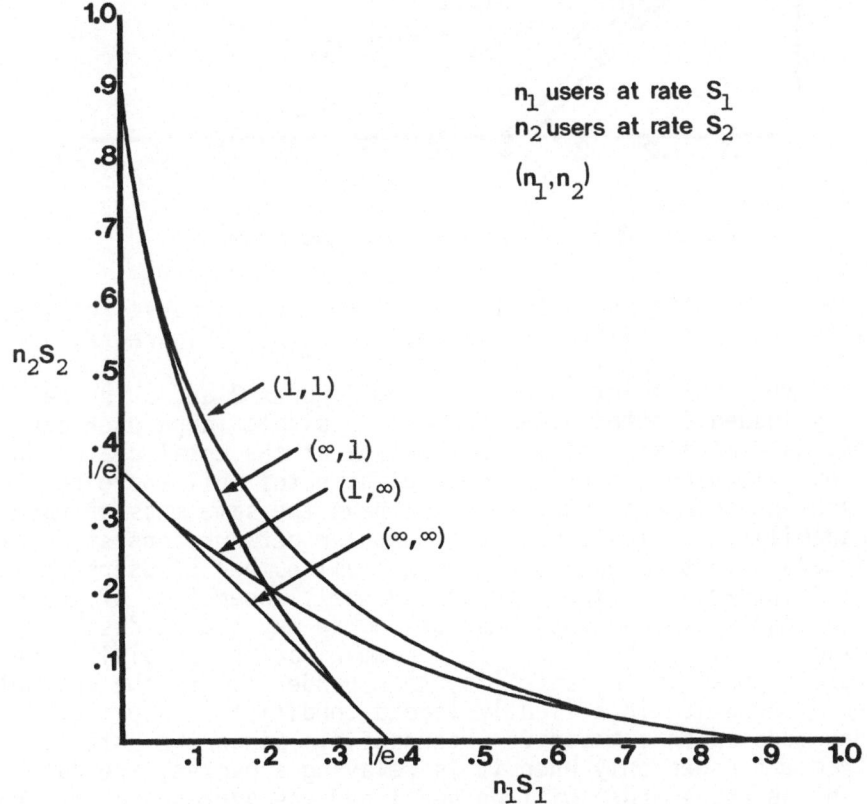

Figure **2** — Allowable message rates

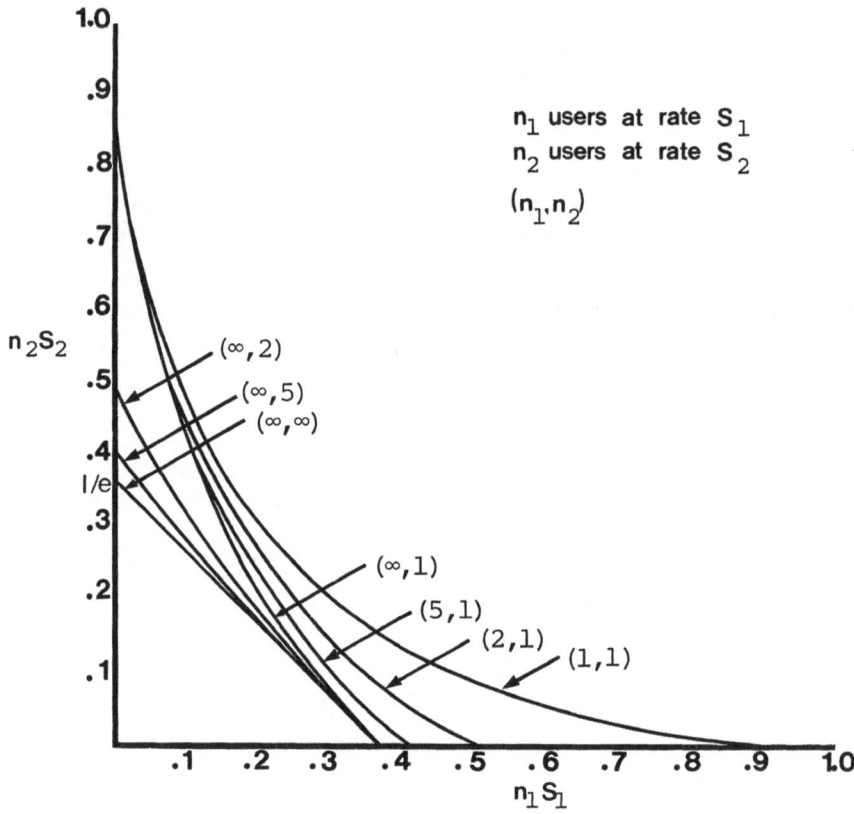

Figure 3 — Allowable message rates

boundary was written and used to calculate several curves of the
allowable region for different values of (n_1, n_2) (Figures 2,3).

The important point to notice from Figures 2 and 3 is that in
a lightly loaded Slotted ALOHA channel, a single large user can
transmit data at a significant percentage of the total channel data
rate, thus allowing use of the channel at rates well above the limi
of 37 percent obtained when all users have the same message rate.
This capability is important for a computer network consisting of
many interactive terminal users and a small number of users who se
large but infrequent files over the channel. Operation of the cha
nel in a lightly loaded condition of course may not be desirable i
a bandwidth limited channel. For a communications satellite where
the average power in the satellite transponder limits the channel
however[19] operation in a lightly loaded condition in a packet
switched mode is an attractive alternative. Since the satellite
will transmit power only when it is relaying a packet, the duty
cycle in the transponder will be small and the average power used
will be low.

Finally we note it is possible to deal with certain limiting cases in more detail, to obtain equations for the boundary of the allowable S_1, S_2 region.

(a)   for $n_1=n_2=1$
      Upon using (21) and (20) we obtain

$$S_1 = G_1^2 \tag{22a}$$

$$S_2 = (1-G_1)^2 \tag{22b}$$

(b)   for $n_2 \to \infty$

$$S_1 = G_1(1-G_1)^{n_1-1} \cdot \exp[-(1-n_1 G_1)] \tag{23a}$$

$$S_2 = (1-n_1 G_1)(1-G_1)^{n_1-1} \cdot \exp[-(1-n_1 G_1)] \tag{23b}$$

(c)   for $n_1=n_2 \to \infty$

$$S_1 = \frac{G_1}{e}$$

$$S_2 = \frac{1-G_1}{e}$$

Additional details dealing with excess capacity and the delay experienced with this kind of use of a slotted ALOHA channel may be found in References 17 and 18.

PACKET SWITCHING IN DOMSAT

Background

The 50 kilobit INTELSAT channel now being used to link THE ALOHA SYSTEM to the ARPA Network could employ the techniques we have described to link additional nodes in the ARPANET at each of the 16 earth stations with access to the Pacific satellite. These same techniques could also be employed by a common carrier to offer packet switched data communications of a quality to which we would all like to become accustomed.

As this is being written, there are in operation two domestic satellite systems (Molniya in the USSR and Anik in Canada) in addition to the worldwide INTELSAT system. Seven US domestic systems (DOMSAT) are under consideration and one has entered the construction phase with a first launch planned for 1974. Japan has announced plans for its domestic communications satellite and several other national systems are expected in the late 1970's. Most of the DOM-SAT proposals plan a system of less expensive and therefore more numerous earth stations than the standard 97 foot earth station antennas now used in the INTELSAT system. Thus the advantage of using a lightly loaded packet switched channel in a power limited situation[19] assumes added importance.

A proposal

Consider the use of a single transponder in a US domestic satellite system to provide a public packet switched data communication service. INTELSAT IV employs 12 transponders each with 36 Mhz. bandwidth. Only one of these transponders devoted completely to a public packet switched service in a US domestic satellite system could easily provide data at a rate of 10 million bits/second into a small earth station. The public packet switched service in the US could provide burst data rates between small communication controllers at each earth station of 10 megabits. Assuming 100 earth stations over the US, and assuming the system is operated at a message rate S=0.15, the average data rate into and out of each station would be about 15 kilobits although the variance about this average (both from earth station to earth station and at different times at the same earth station) would be large. A packet switched system would function without difficulty in the face of large variations of this type.

The capacity of such a system measured in terms of interactive users of alphanumeric terminals would be about 100,000 such active users at any one time on the system. Of course the system would be used by other devices generating larger amounts of traffic than a single terminal and the number of active users would have to be decreased accordingly. The point is that in a public packet switched service using a US domestic satellite the user of data communications could be charged by the packet, since the user would consume resources in the system proportional to the number of packets sent and received.

The preceding three sections and the accompanying papers by Kleinrock and Roberts explain many of the technological advantages of such a system. We need only add some short observations concerning the operational advantages of a public packet switched service. The system would possess a flexibility of operation simply not attainable with circuit switched systems. Although the *average* data rate into each of 100 earth stations would be 15 kilobits, the *burst* data rate into any given terminal could be close to 10 megabits. This capability for remote job entry and file transfer leads to the same potential for resource sharing shown to be so valuable in the ARPANET.

Another kind of flexibility is the flexibility in being able
to start such a system with a small number of communication controllers at a few earth stations. The system would become operational
with only two stations and would yield data on packet interference
patterns and delay with only three stations. Since the computer-
communication network brought into being by such a service is completely connected (topologically) there is no need for routing algorithms at each earth station (such as used in the ARPANET IMPs
and TIPs) and to add a new earth station into the network it is only
necessary to activate the identification number of that station.
Peak load averaging of such a system would operate to increase its
total capacity since the system is peak load limited only at the
satellite and not at the separate ground stations. (This particular
advantage could be especially important for a Pacific packet switched service where the international dateline would serve to average
peak loads over different days as well as different hours.)

Finally we note that the economics of such a system are consistent with the economics of existing computer communication systems. The ARPANET in its present configuration provides a factor
of ten or more in cost advantage over conventional circuit switched
systems.[5] During the month of January 1973, approximately 45,000,000
packets were transmitted by the ARPANET. The capacity of the ARPA-
NET based on an eight hour day was about 300 million packets per
month at that time. A public packet switching service using a single transponder of a domestic satellite system, operating at a normalized message rate of 0.15 would have a capacity of about 1,500
million packets per month, again based on an eight hour day. Furthermore, at such a low message rate the system would easily accommodate intermittent users with large files at a megabit data rate
and still draw average power from the satellite corresponding to a
transponder duty cycle of less than 16 percent. The 50 kilobit
lines now used in the ARPANET cost about $1,200,000 per year in
January 1973 and this figure was growing rapidly. The ARPANET is
but one possible customer of a public packet switched service. The
projected average annual revenue of a single transponder in the
several proposed US domestic satellite systems ranges from less than
$1,000,000 to about $3,000,000 per year.[20]

REFERENCES

1. Lucky, Robert W., "Common carrier data communication," in *Computer-Communication Networks*, Abramson, Norman and Kuo, Franklin,
   Eds., Prentice-Hall, New Jersey, 1973.
2. Baran, Paul, "On distributed communications: V. History, alternative approaches, and comparisons," *Memorandum RM-3097-PR, The
   Rand Corporation*, August 1964.
3. Baran, Paul, "On distributed communications: XI. Summary overview," *Memorandum RM-3767-PR, The Rand Corporation*, August 1964.

4. Davies, D.W., Bartlett, K.A., Scantlebury, R.A. and Wilkinson, P.T., "A digital communication network for computers giving rapid response at remote terminals," *ACM Symposium on Operating System Principles*, Gatlinburg, Tennessee, October 1-4, 1967.

5. Roberts, Lawrence G., "The ARPA network," in *Computer-Communication Networks*, Abramson, Norman and Kuo, Franklin, Eds., Prentice-Hall, New Jersey, 1973.

6. Ornstein, S.M., Heart, F.E., Crowther, W.R., Rising, H.K., Russell, S.B. and Michel, A., "The terminal IMP for the ARPA computer network," *AFIPS Conference Proceedings, Spring Joint Computer Conference*, 1972, 243.

7. deMercado, J., Guindon, R., DaSilva, J. and Kadoch, M. "The Canadian universities computer network topological considerations," *Computer Communication: Impacts and Implications, Proceedings of the First International Conference on Computer Communication*, Washington, D.C., October 1972, 220.

8. Barber, D.L.A., "The European computer network project," *Computer Communication: Impacts and Implications, Proceedings of the First International Conference on Computer Communication*, Washington, D.C., October 1972, 192.

9. Abramson, Norman, "THE ALOHA SYSTEM," in *Computer-Communication Networks*, Abramson, Norman and Kuo, Franklin, Eds., Prentice-Hall, New Jersey, 1973.

10. Trifari, J.C., "Rating national timesharing services," *Computer Decisions*, 28, November 1971.

11. Jackson, P.E. and Stubbs, C.D., "A study of multi-access computer communications," *AFIPS Conference Proceedings, Spring Joint Computer Conference*, 1969, 491.

12. Roberts, Lawrence G., "ALOHA packet system with and without slots and capture," *ARPANET Satellite System Note 8, NIC Document No. 11290*, Stanford Research Institute, June 1972.

13. Kleinrock, L. and Lam, S.S., "Packet switching in a slotted satellite channel," *Proceedings of the National Computer Conference*, June 1973.

14. Roberts, Lawrence G., "Dynamic allocation of satellite capacity through packet reservation," *Proceedings of the National Computer Conference*, June 1973.

15. Kleinrock, L. and Lam, S.S., "Analytic results with the addition of one large user," *ARPANET Satellite System Note 27, NIC Document No. 12736*, Stanford Research Institute, October 1972.

16. Rettberg, R., "Random ALOHA with slots-excess capacity," *ARPANET Satellite System Note 18, NIC Document No. 11865*, Stanford Research Institute, October 1972.

17. Abramson, Norman, "Excess capacity of a slotted ALOHA channel," *ARPANET Satellite System Note 26, NIC Document No. 12735*, Stanford Research Institute, November 1972.

18. Abramson, Norman, "Excess capacity of a slotted ALOHA channel (continued)," *ARPANET Satellite System Note 30, NIC Document No. 13044*, Stanford Research Institute, December 1972.

19. Cacciamani, E.R., Jr., "The Spade system as applied to data communications and small earth station operation," *COMSAT Technical Review*, Vol. 1, No. 1, Fall 1971.
20. McDonald, J., "Getting our communication satellite off the ground," *Fortune*, July 1972.

SYNCHRONIZATION AND CODING IN DATA COMMUNICATIONS SATELLITE NETWORKS

E. R. Cacciamani, Jr.

American Satellite Corporation

ROLE OF SATELLITES IN DATA TRANSMISSION

Historical Background

Satellite communications has promoted the development of high data rate transmission systems that are necessary to provide efficient data transfer for computer to computer communications as well as many other high speed data applications. Two most important characteristics of satellites in serving this role are the relatively unencumbered bandwidth constraints, as differentiated from long haul terrestrial facilities, as well as multi-access, multi-destination use capability which enables simultaneous transmission and reception to all points in the satellite network. A single satellite channel, for example, can be used to simultaneously access multiple receive terminals.

Satellite Communications During 1965-1972 Era

During the first seven years of commercial satellite communications, 1965-1972, most of the satellite data circuits were restricted to voice bandwidth data rates (typically teletypewriter rates up to 9600 bps) with a few wideband data circuits operating over 48 KHz analog bandwidths. During this time period frequency modulation (FM) was used exclusively. One or more FM carriers were transmitted from each earth station, which accessed the satellite trans-

312

ponder in a frequency division multiple access (FDMA) mode as shown in Figure 1. Almost all of INTELSAT's traffic today is transmitted in this manner.

Data transmission over these channels has been historically limited to the data rates previously mentioned, i.e., data rates accommodated over a 4 KHz bandwidth voice channel as well as a few wideband data circuits operating over a 48 KHz bandwidth. The derivation of the latter service (such as 50 Kbps data) has been at the equivalent service of twelve 4 KHz voice channels, thus making this service nominally twelve times the cost of a single analog voice channel. Extrapolating further, the provision of 1.544 mbps data service via FM/FDMA communications will require the equivalent of 300 or more analog voice channels, thus making this service offering prohibitively expensive when using analog transmission facilities.

PREASSIGNED MULTIDESTINATION FDM/FM CARRIERS

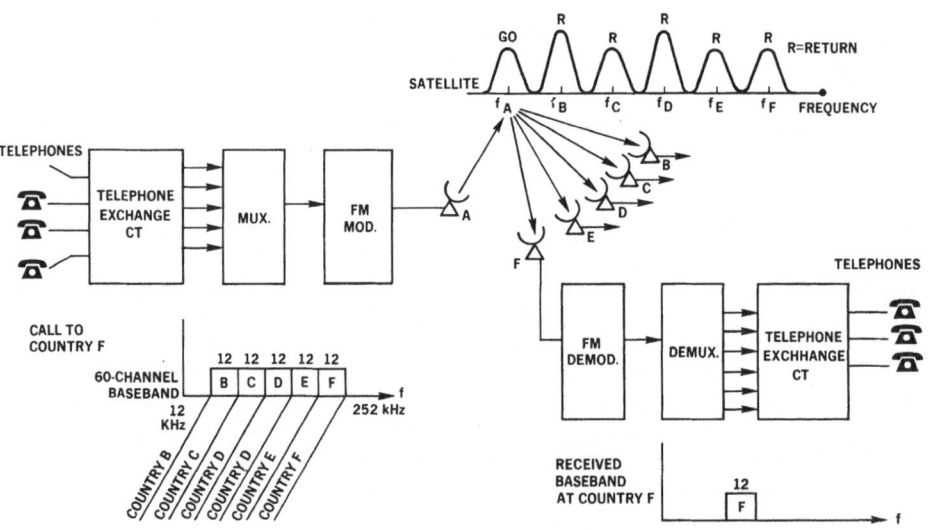

Figure 1

Advent of Digital Communication Techniques in the Commercial
Satellite System

Concurrent with the 1965-1972 time period several digital
communication systems were developed and field tested proving the
technical feasibility of using such systems to provide greater
efficiencies and flexibilities in multiple access satellite communications. The MATE [1] system was the first TDMA system developed
for satellite communications. The system was successfully field
tested in 1966 and verified that synchronization, with guard times
of less than 200 nanoseconds, can be maintained when operating over
a synchronous orbiting satellite. In 1970 the MAT-1 TDMA system [2]
was successfully field tested operating at 50 mbps rate. This system was capable of maintaining adjacent earth station transmission
bursts to accuracies within 100 nanoseconds. Subsequent developments in TDMA systems indicate that data rates up to at least one
gigabit per second will be feasible. Experimental TDMA modems
have been developed today which operate at these rates.

Simultaneously, with the development of the MATE and MAT-1 TDMA
systems was the development of the SPADE system. SPADE [3] is a frequency division multiple access system which utilizes single-chan-
nel-per-voice-carrier PCM/PSK transmissions. Since SPADE is a
digital transmission system, it has also been shown [4,5] that it
inherently lends itself more efficiently to digital data transmissions as opposed to the analog modulation methods. Data rates up
to 10 mbps and higher can be easily handled using the SPADE/single-
channel-per-carrier (SCPC) technology. SCPC equipment, providing
50 kbps service between California and Hawaii, has been operational
since December 1972 and the SPADE system has been in operation since
the early part of 1973. Proposed domestic service, using 1.544 mbps
SCPC circuits, will be operating by the end of 1974. In addition
current domestic satellite plans are that high data rate (60 mbps
and higher) TDMA systems will be operating by 1975.

GENERAL DATA USER PROBLEMS OF TODAY

Background

Today's typical data user is restricted, because of economic
and service availability reasons, to voice band data rates. The
number of wideband data users have been increasing, as these services have been made available, but economic considerations still
have a significant restrictive effect.

To date, most of the error detection and correcion techniques that
have been developed for data services have been designed to operate

314

over terrestrial circuits. The majority of the techniques employed
have included repeat transmission techniques (ARQ), which have
depended on either (1) an acknowledgement after the receipt of each
transmission (whether or not the data block was in error, in which
case the block is retransmitted) or (2) a request for retransmissio
only when a block is in error.

Block-by-Block Acknowledgement ARQ

The efficiency (throuput) of the continuous acknowledgement ARQ
is dependent on propagation delay independently of channel error
conditions. The efficiency (over a noiseless channel) can be characterized by Equation (1)

$$n_i = \frac{B}{B + TR} \tag{1}$$

where B is the block length in bits
      T is the total round-trip delay, and
      R is the input data rate (bits per second)

The effeciency of this system approaches 100% under ideal noiseles
channel conditions when the block length, B, is made large relative
to the path delay – data rate (TR) product. However, under channel
error conditions, the block length must be adjusted to compensate

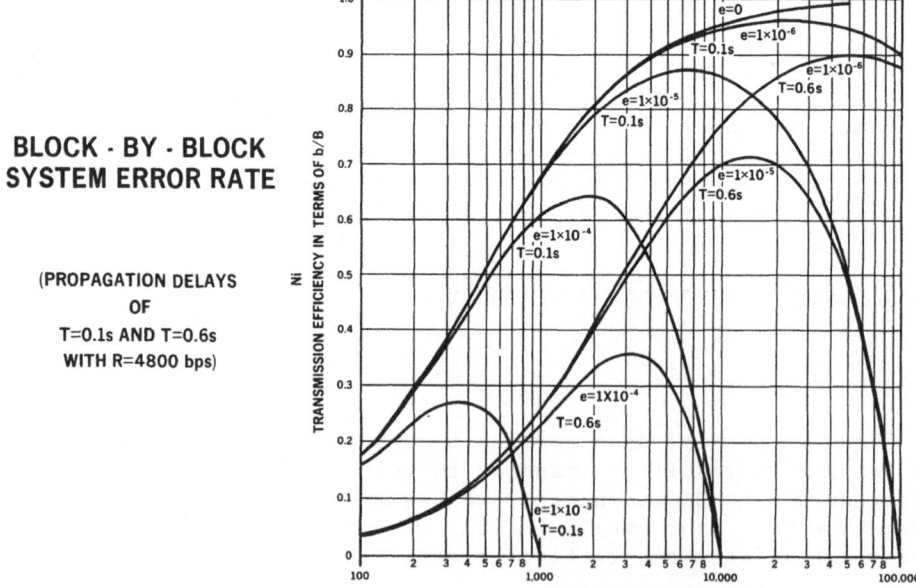

**BLOCK · BY · BLOCK
SYSTEM ERROR RATE**

(PROPAGATION DELAYS
OF
T=0.1s AND T=0.6s
WITH R=4800 bps)

Figure 2

for error rate conditions, since, for a given error rate, a maximum
length will be reached, beyond which the system will experience
errors in every transmitted block. Figure 2 (from Cohen and Germano[7]), shows the tradeoffs described for 4800 bps data links that
have round trip propagation delays of 0.1 and 0.6 seconds (0.6
seconds represents a nominal propagation delay over a satellite
link). As one would expect from Equation (1) the maximum attainable efficiency decreases as the propagation delay is increased
from 0.1 to 0.6 seconds. Another problem with a block-by-block
acknowledgement system is that large block sizes are required to
achieve reasonable throughput efficiencies which in turn dictate
large storage requirements at the transmitter.

Continuous Block Transmission (Go back-N)

These systems require a feedback request only for retransmission of
a block received in error. As described by Cohen and Germano[7] the
method of repeat transmission leads to a number of techniques:

1) Those systems that report an errored block at the end of such
   block;

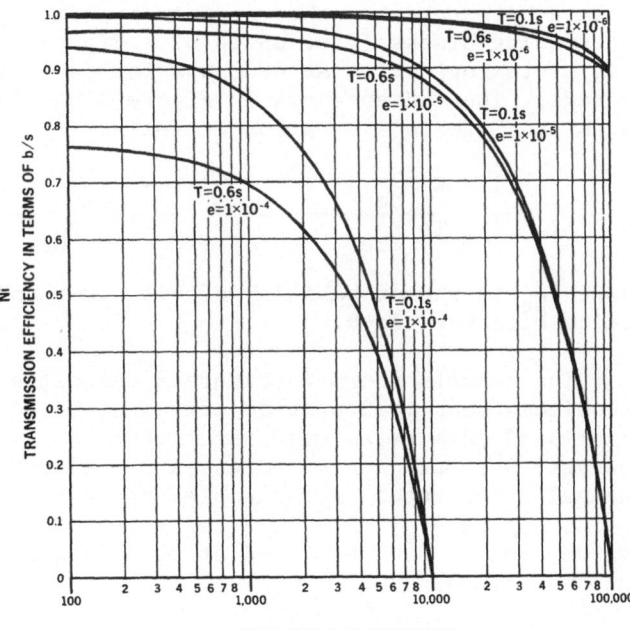

Figure 3

2) Those systems that check and report errors on a character-by-character basis;

3) Those systems that retransmit the errored block and all blocks (or partial blocks) following the errored block;

4) Those systems that retransmit the errored block;

5) Those systems that retransmit from the errored character within a block.

The storage requirement of the transmitting terminal in these systems is a function of the propagation delay and the length and number of blocks (or characters) stored for possible retransmission

The most efficient of the preceding systems are the "selective block or character repeat retransmission where only the elements in error are retransmitted. Recent selective block retransmission experiments have been conducted which demonstrate efficiencies of better than 90% achieved at end-to-end link probability of bit error (P_{be}) = 1 x 10^{-5}, independent of bit rate and propagation delay. Actual satellite tests have been made at 50 kbps that have attained efficiencies better than 90%. Systems available today, however, include those that retransmit the errored block and all blocks following. This technique defines a minimum retransmission of data bits equal to the round trip path delay plus the number of intervening blocks (i.e. up to n). Figure 3 shows the results for this system operating at 4800 bps for path delays of 0.1 and 0.6 seconds. The curves shown in Figure 3 can be characterized by Cohen and Germano's equation as follows:

$$n_i = \frac{1 - B\,P_{be}}{1 + TR\,P_{be}} - \frac{C}{B}\,\frac{1 - P_{be}}{1 + TR\,P_{be}} \tag{2}$$

where P_{be} is the probability of bit error and C is the number of parity bits per block.

The results shown in Figure 3 demonstrate that the go-back-N techniques described provide efficient throughput operation for voice-band data rates over satellite. As the bit rate increases, however, the efficiency decreases non linearly relative to the channel error rate. For example, at 9600 bits per second, the efficiency at P_{be} = 1 x 10^{-5} for a path delay of 0.6 seconds is 94% vs. 96% at 4800 bps, and at P_{be} = 1 x 10^{-4}, it is 62% at 9600 bps, vs. 77% at 4800 bps.

To maintain similar transmission efficiencies at higher data rates implies operating channels where the end-to-end P_{be} is at least 1 x 10^{-6}. Although this performance has not been difficult to achieve over satellite channels, the typical performance obtained over most terrestrial circuits has been $P_{be} = 1 \times 10^{-5}$ and worse. The further problem with terrestrial circuits has been the "bursty" nature of errors (due to line switching, local interference conditions, etc.) which have minimized the effective use of forward error correction (FEC) techniques. In general the satellite channel has distributed errors which enhances the use of FEC as has been done in the INTELSAT SCPC system [4,5]. Since the satellite data circuit often includes terrestrial "tail" circuits at the terminal ends, error detection and correction systems must be employed for high data rates which will provide a high throughput over the end-to-end circuit. Several approaches may be used to provide the necessary efficiencies. Selective block or character retransmission systems may be used end-to-end (provided that the terrestrial circuits are operating at reasonable bit error rate performance) or a combination retransmission system, separately at each terrestrial segment, and a FEC system over the satellite channel.

Typical performance of satellite high speed data circuits [5], using FEC, has been nominally at $P_{be} = 1 \times 10^{-8}$.

SPADE BLOCK DIAGRAM

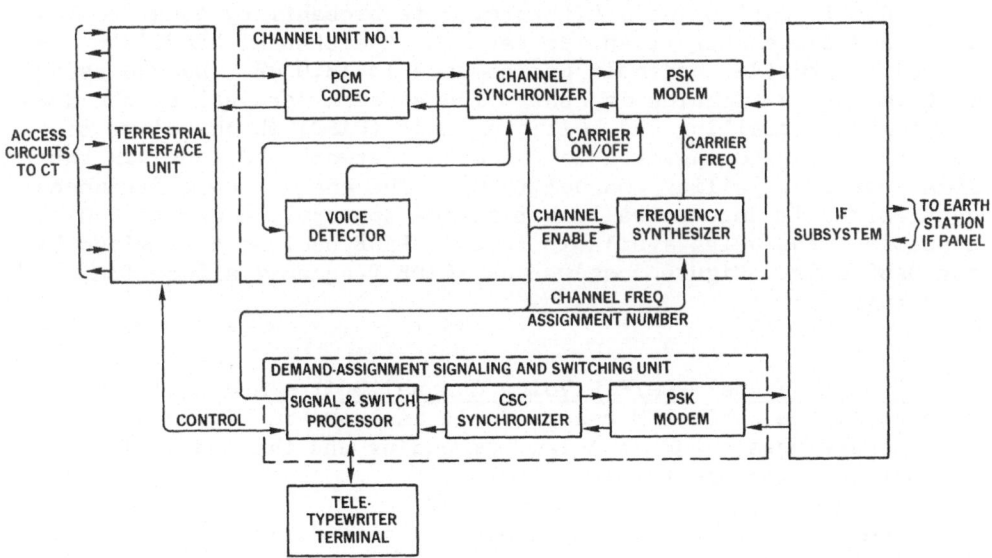

Figure 4

SATELLITE DIGITAL SYSTEMS TECHNOLOGY

Spade

The SPADE/SCPC systems are the first operational digital transmission systems operating over commercial (INTELSAT) satellites.
The SPADE system utilizes single channel per carrier (SCPC) PCM/
PSK transmissions and provides demand-assigned satellite multi-
point-to-multipoint communications. The application of SPADE to
demand-assigned voice traffic has been well documented [3], [8], [9].
Demand-assigned multiple access systems allow satellite circuits
to be shared by a large number of terrestrial users who are in
common view of a satellite. The circuits are assigned on demand,
forming a temporary connection between any two earth stations within the region covered by the satellite. When no longer required,
the circuits are returned to the satellite demand-assignment pool.

Figure 4 is a block diagram of a SPADE terminal as it is configured for PCM voice. The channel unit consists of a pair of
transmit and receiver subunits that provide digital encoding and
decoding of the analog voice, digital synchronization to recover
PCM frame reference and to resolve phase ambiguity of the recovered
four-phase (PSK) carrier, and PSK modulation and demodulation of
the transmitted and received data. Threshold performance of the
PCM codec is defined at a bit-error rate probability equal to 1 x
10^{-4}, and the carrier-to-noise ratio in the channel bandwidth required to provide threshold performance is 13.0 dB. Demand assignment channel allocation is controlled at each terminal by the demand
assignment signalling and switching unit (DASS) which relays signalling and switching data to the other network stations via the
TDMA common signalling channel (CSC). The channel unit frequency
synthesizer is automatically set to the appropriate one of 800
possible frequencies available in the SPADE pool as determined by
the DASS unit. Figure 5 shows the SPADE frequency allocation
spectrum.

Single channel PCM/PSK Voice Channel Unit - A detailed block
diagram of the SPADE PCM channel unit is shown in Figure 6. The
PCM encoder uses standard A-law commanding and the modulation
is four-phase coherent PSK.

The transmit synchronizer consists of a digital voice detector
dual 112-bit memory, a preamble word generator, and associated
input/output timing. The PCM encoded output is at 56 kbps, and the
digital voice detector is used to determine the presence of speech
and provide on-off control of the carrier. If on-off switching of
carrier power is used, the resultant saving in accessed satellite

SPADE MULTICHANNEL FREQUENCY-ALLOCATION SPECTRUM

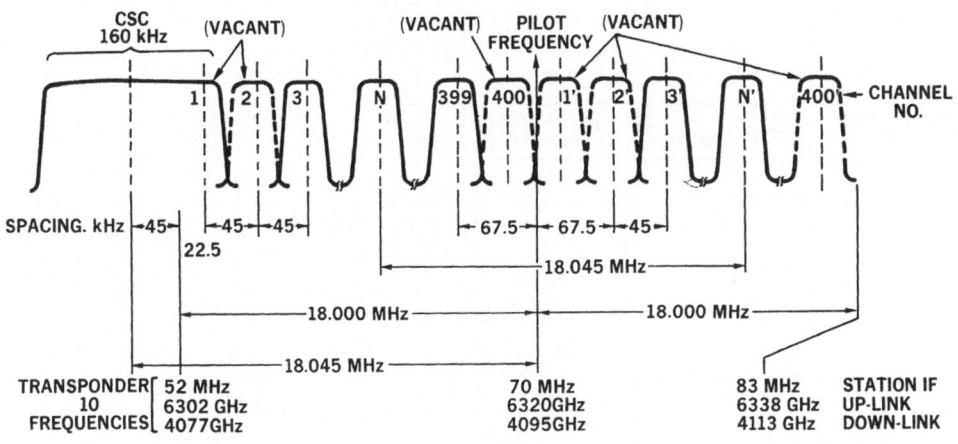

Figure 5

transponder power is approximately 4 dB. The data are stored in memory, and two 16-bit unique words are inserted every 224 data bits. The resultant transmitted bit rate is 64 kbps, and the symbol rate, using four-phase PSK, is 32 kbps.

During the beginning of each voice burst, a preamble word and two unique words are inserted to provide carrier and bit-timing recovery and phase ambiguity resolution at the corresponding receiver. The format is shown in Figure 7. The transmitted carrier and bit timing must be coherently recovered within 1.875 milliseconds at the beginning of each voice burst, and simultanous detection of the two unique words is required to resolve the phase ambiguity of the 4-phase PSK recovered carrier.

In addition to providing resolution of recovered carrier phase ambiguity, unique word detection is used to provide digital frame synchronization. The receive synchronizer observes each unique word detected output and requires two consecutive detections, which are exactly 224 bits apart, at the beginning of each voice burst in order to lock into a closed-aperture mode. During closed-aperture operation, the synchronizer looks for a unique word detection every 224 bits, referenced to the original recovered frame timing. If a detection is absent, the synchronizer inserts a sync signal and continues this procedure until five consecutive miss detections are observed. The synchronizer then drops out of lock and begins again

320

SINGLE-CHANNEL PCM/PSK VOICE CHANNEL UNIT

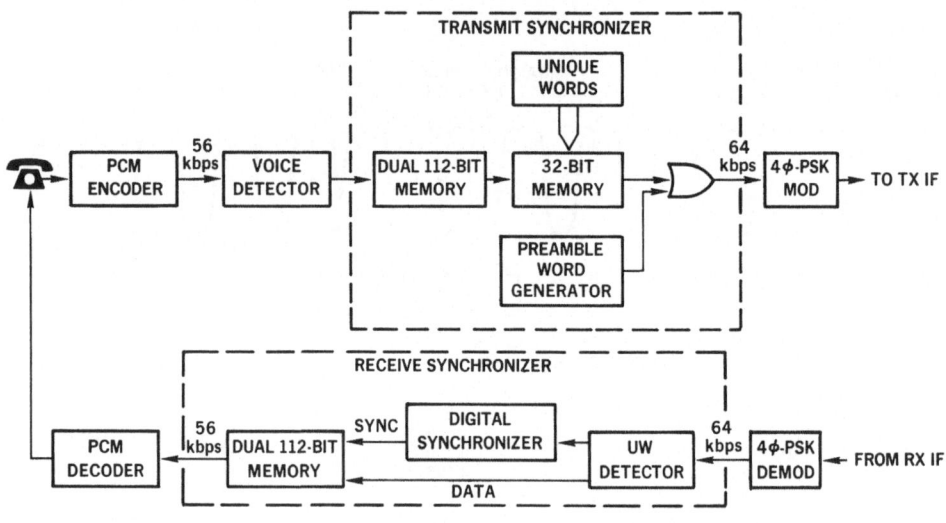

Figure 6

in the open-aperture search mode.

During closed-aperture operation, the occurrence of false unique word detections is ignored; hence, the consideration of false detections is limited to initial acquisition (open-aperture mode) of the digital synchronizer. After the demodulated data have been passed through the synchronizer, they are transmitted to a dual 112-bit memory, where the unique words are removed. The resultant 56-kbps bit stream with associated timing is received by the PCM decoder, where it is reconverted into its original analog waveform.

Single Channel Data Channel Unit - It is apparent from the channel block diagram that other traffic services can be conveniently transmitted. For example, the normal input to the channel unit is a voice band signal contained in a bandwidth of 300-3400 Hz. As a result, the PCM encoder-decoder can faithfully sample and reconstruct the transmitted signal contained in that voice band, whether it is analog voice, telegraphy or data (e.g. 4800 bps, 9600 bps).

An alternate approach is to bypass the PCM codec and transmit the data (or multiplexed data streams) directly. This approach results in a significant improvement in utilization efficiency of the satellite links, enabling data rates up to the channel unit's

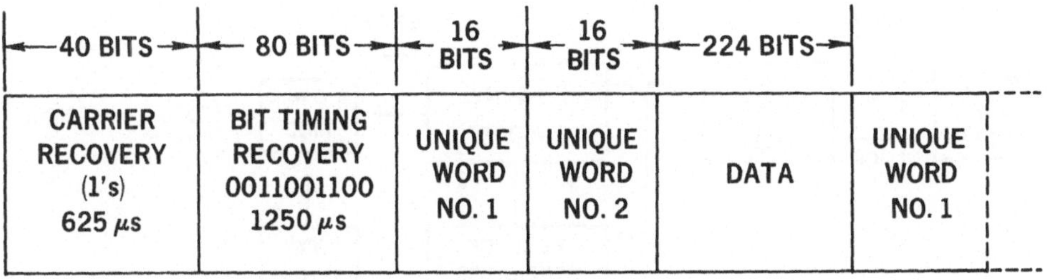

←—40 BITS—→	←— 80 BITS—→	← 16 BITS →	← 16 BITS →	←—224 BITS—→	
CARRIER RECOVERY (1's) 625 μs	BIT TIMING RECOVERY 0011001100 1250 μs	UNIQUE WORD NO. 1	UNIQUE WORD NO. 2	DATA	UNIQUE WORD NO. 1

Figure 7
Preamble and Frame Format

nominal 64 kbps rate. One example has been the transmission of 48-56 kbps wideband data via the SCPC channel unit. Figure 8 is a block diagram of the channel unit implementation to provide service linking the University of Hawaii into the ARPA computer network at Sunnyvale, California. A rate 3/4 convolutional encoder-threshold decoder was used to provide data rate compatibility between the input channel rate (50 kbps) and the channel unit output (66.67 kbps) and, more importantly, to improve the threshold operating performance from $P_{be} = 1 \times 10^{-4}$ required for voice to $P_{be} = 1 \times 10^{-8}$ at the same carrier-to-noise ratio of 13.0 dB. This configuration has thus provided wideband data service at the same satellite power and bandwidth utilized by a PCM voice channel. Figure 9 shows the comparative performance curves of the 50 kbps coded data channel and the 56 kbps uncoded PCM voice channel. The technical operating characteristics of the wideband data channel unit are summarized in Figure 10.

Since the initiation of this first digital transmission circuit in December, 1972 through the first six months of 1973, the reliability performance has been 99.7%, for earth station to earth station operation and 96.63% for end-to-end use. Figure 11 is a photograph of one of the terminals installed in the Jamesburg, California - Paumalu, Hawaii link. The system is wired to accommodate twelve PCM voice/wideband data channel units and is expandable (by adding additional channel unit racks) up to 60 channel units. Figure 12 is a photograph of the rate 3/4 convolutional encoder-threshold decoder synchronizer module which shows the simplicity in number of components required to provide the forward error correction used to derive the necessary improvement in the satellite channel performance.

The synchronization used in the data channel unit differs from the voice channel unit in that it uses the coding structure of the convolutional encoder-decoder (and does not use any additional over-

50-kbps DATA CHANNEL UNIT

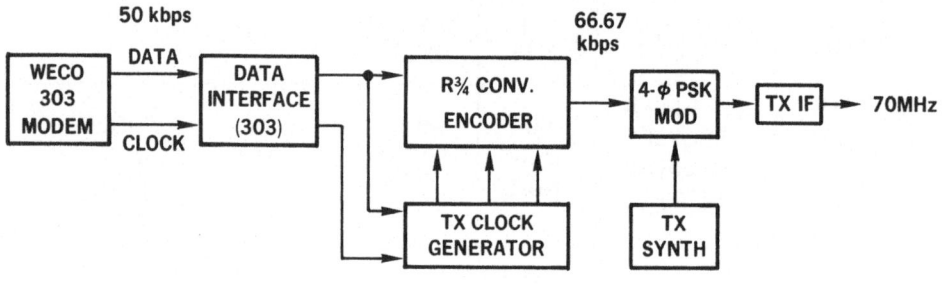

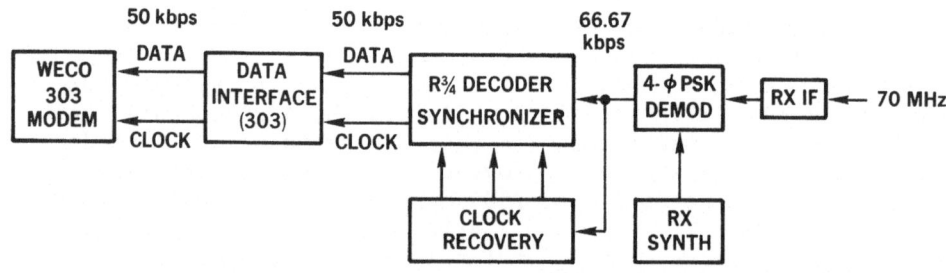

Figure 8

head bits) to derive sync and to resolve carrier phase ambiguity.
The synch process assumes virtual continuous data transmission
since it requires many constraint lengths to establish sync.   To
provide "burst" data transmissions and sync recovery, a hybrid
syncronization scheme utilizing similar techniques developed for
the voice unit and the data unit can be used.

Other data rates that can be transmitted over the SPADE/SCPC
channel unit include multiplexed data (i.e. ten 4800 bps transmission, etc.) and telegraphy (up to 1200 50 baud telegraphy channels) [4], [5].

Although the preceding discussions have emphasized data rates
that can be transmitted via the nominal 64 kbps SPADE/SCPC channel,
higher data rate transmissions can also be considered, utilizing
similar technology.   Experiments [5] have been conducted using simila
transmission techniques to transmit 240 kbps and 1.544 mbps.
American Satellite Corporation (ASC) plans to provide a mixture of
SCPC data rates available at discrete bit rates up to 6.3 mbps per
carrier and higher (depending on requirements).   ASC already is
in the process of installing a specialized satellite communications
network to transmit and receive four separate 1.344 mbps data trans
mission, to begin service in 1974.

PCM/DATA
PERFORMANCE MEASUREMENTS

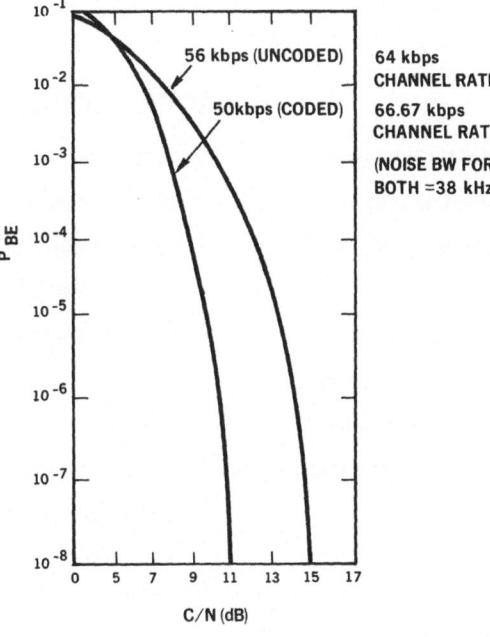

Figure 9

TDMA Systems

As already stated, commercially developed TDMA systems, [1,2] have been successfully tested over satellites and the results of these tests have been used to establish criteria for future operational systems. INTELSAT is currently defining an operational system which will operate nominally at 60 mbps (using four-phase PSK modulation) and will begin field trials within the next several years.

American Satellite Corporation intends to introduce TDMA systems during Phase II of its domestic satellite network, starting in 1975. The systems will use four-phase PSK modulation and will operate nominally at 60 mbps.

Further developments have included an INTELSAT developed eight-phase PSK TDMA modem that will enable up to 108 mbps operation over an INTELSAT IV spot beam transponder.

A more recent INTELSAT development has included the one-gigabit per second four-phase PSK TDMA modem which will have application in future generation satellites.

50 kbps SCPC TECHNICAL SPECIFICATIONS

DATA INPUT RANGE	48 TO 56 bkps
INPUT/OUTPUT INTERFACE	SYNCHRONOUS DATA AND CLOCK WECO 303 OR CCITT V35 TYPE MODEM
ERROR CONTROL	CONVOLUTIONAL CODING - FORWARD ACTING
MODULATION	4 - PHASE PSK
BIT ERROR RATE	1×10^{-7} AT THRESHOLD C/N OF 13 dB
RF CHANNEL SEPARATION	45 kHz
IF NOISE BANDWIDTH	38 kHz
TRANSPONDER CAPACITY (MAX.)	800 DATA CHANNELS
RELIABILITY	REDUNDANT SUBSYSTEMS

Figure 10

CONCLUSIONS

Satellite data communications present a new and expanding medium to provide excellent performing circuits which can satisfy today's proliferating data transmission requirements.

Utilizing forward error correction techniques, satellite communication systems can provide high performance circuits, which operate nominally at $P_{be} = 1 \times 10^{-8}$ and better, at efficient power and bandwidth utilization. High data rate services, 50 kbps to 1.544 mbps, are available today, and recently developed systems, operating at 60 mbps and above, will soon be available in domestic and international satellite communication systems.

ACKNOWLEDGEMENT

Much of the work reported in this paper was developed at COMSAT Laboratories, under Corporate sponsorship and under the sponsorship of the International Telecommunications Satellite Consortium (INTELSAT). The author wishes to acknowledge John G. Puente who has been responsible for inspiring the development of the digital communications systems reported in this paper and the numerous other members who have contributed so much to the systems design, development and implementation.

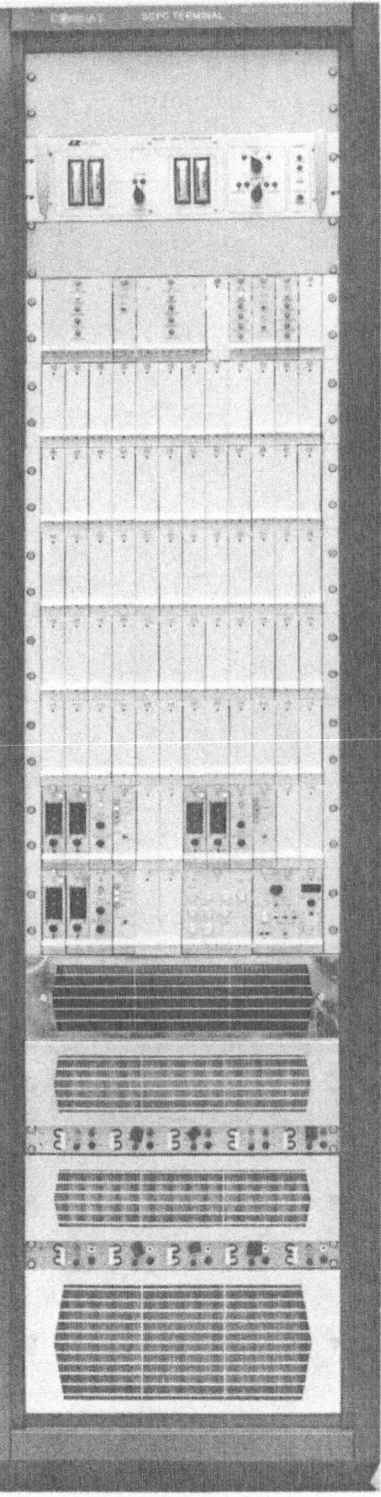

Figure 11
SCPC Equipment

Figure 12
Rate 3/4 Convolutional Encoder - Threshold Decoder

REFERENCES

(1)   T. Sekimoto and J. G. Puente, "A Satellite Time-Division
      Multiple Access Experiment", IEEE Transactions on Communica-
      tions Technology, [Institute of Electrical and Electronic
      Engineers] Vol. COM-16, No. 4, 1968, pp. 581-588.

(2)   W. G. Schmidt, O.G. Gabbard, E. R. Cacciamani, W. G. Maillet,
      and W. W. Wu, "MAT-1: A 700-channel time-division multiple-
      access system with demand assignment features" in IEEE Inf.
      Conf. Communications Conf. Rec., Vol. 5, Boulder, Colo.,
      June 9-11, pp. 15-7 - 15-12.

(3)   J. G. Puente and A. M. Werth, "Demand Assignment Service for
      the INTELSAT Global Network", IEEE Spectrum, Vol. 8, No. 1,
      January 1971, pp. 56-69.

(4)   E. R. Cacciamani, "The SPADE System as Applied to Data
      Communications and Small Earth Station Operation", COMSAT
      Technical Review, Vol. 1, No. 1 Fall 1971, pp. 171-182.

(5)   E. R. Cacciamani, "Satellite Data Transmission Using SPADE",
      presented at the IEEE Eurocon '71 Conference, Lausanne,
      Switzerland, October 1971.

(6)   CCITT Special Study Group A - Contribution No. 120,
      December 1970.

(7)   L. A. Cohen and G. V. Germano, "Gauging the Effect of Propa-
      gation Delay and Error Rate on Data Transmission Systems",
      Telecommunications Journal, Vol. 37-VIII/1970.

(8)   A. M. Werth, "SPADE: A PCM FDMA Demand Assignment System for
      Satellite Communications", IEEE 1970 International Conference
      on Communications, San Francisco, California, June 1970,
      pp. 46-22, 46-32.

(9)   A. M. Werth and E. R. Cacciamani, "Digital Channel Unit
      Technology: A state of the Art Summary", presented at the
      2nd International Conference on Digital Satellite Communica-
      tions, Paris, France, November 28-30, 1972, pp. 84-93.

DYNAMIC ALLOCATION OF SATELLITE CAPACITY THROUGH PACKET RESERVATION

Lawrence G. Roberts

Advanced Research Projects Agency, Arlington, Virginia.

Introduction

If one projects the growth of computer communication networks like the ARPANET (1,2,3,4) to a worldwide situation, satellite communication is attractive for intercommunicating between the widespread geographic areas. For this variable demand, multi-station, data traffic situation, satellites are uniquely qualified in that they are theoretically capable of statistically averaging the load in total at the satellite rather than requiring each station or station-pair to average the traffic independently. However, very little research has been done on techniques which permit direct multi-station demand access to a satellite for data traffic. For voice traffic statistics, COMSAT Laboratories has developed highly efficient techniques; the SPADE (5) system currently installed in the Atlantic permitting the pooled use of 64KB PCM voice channels on a demand basis, and the MAT-1 (6) TDMA (Time Division Multiple-Access) experimental system. Both systems permit flexible demand assignment of the satellite capacity, but on a circuit-switched basis designed to interconnect a full duplex 64KB channel between two stations for minutes rather than deliver small blocks of data here and there. This work forms the technical base for advanced digital satellite communication, and provides a very effective means for moving large quantities of data between two points. However, for short interactive data traffic between many stations, new allocation techniques are desirable.

This paper has been reprinted from NCC Proceedings, June 1973, with kind permission of the publishers.

Traffic Model

In order to evaluate the performance of any new technique for dynamic assignment of satellite capacity and compare it with other techniques, a complete model of the satellite traffic must be postulated. Given the model, each technique can be analyzed and its performance computed for any traffic load or distribution. Although it is difficult to fully represent the complete variation in traffic rates normal in data traffic, the following model describes the basic nature of data traffic which might arrive at each satellite station from local packet network.

There are Poisson arrivals of both single packets (1270 bits including the header) and multi-packet blocks (8 packets) at each station. The overall Poisson arrival rate for both is L with a fraction F of single packets and the remainder multi-packets. For simplicity, the arrival rates at all stations are stationary and equal. This is not completely representative of normal data traffic but for the assignment techniques of interest, non-stationary and unequal arrival rates will produce nearly identical performance to the stationary case. Techniques which subdivide the satellite capacity in a preassigned manner would be seriously hurt by non-stationary traffic rates but the poor performance of these systems will be demonstrated, at least in part, by their inability to handle Poisson packet arrivals effectively. The average station traffic in packets per second is:

$$T = L \left(F + 8(1 - F) \right) \tag{1}$$

The destination of this traffic is equally divided between all of the other stations.

For a truly reliable data communications network, each packet or block should be acknowledged as having been correctly received. Positive error control using acknowledgements and retransmissions is very important for data traffic. Thus, acknowledgment traffic must be added to the station traffic. To achieve rapid recovery from errors there must be one small packet (144 bits) sent for each packet or block sent. This traffic is administrative overhead and will not be counted when computing the channel utilization.

The analytic results presented later in the paper are all for equal arrival rates for single packets and multi-packets (F = 5). Other values of F have been examined as well as cases where the input traffic contains small (144 bit) data packets as well. The detailed effect of these variations is not sufficiently pronounced to consider here, however. For comparing techniques the equal arrival distribution is quite representative.

ARPANET experience indicates that the data traffic one can expect is proportional to the total dollar value of computer service being bought or sold through the network. The total traffic generated by one dollar of computer activity is about 315 packets, half going each way (3). Thus, $200K/year of computer activity within a region produces 2KB of traffic, of which 1KB is leaving the region. Within the next few years it is probable that the computer services exchanged internationally will be between $50K/country and $2M/country which suggests that the traffic levels,T, to consider are from .25KB to 10KB. For domestic satellite usage the dollar flow would be far greater than this if the regions are ones like the east and west coast. However, if small stations become economically attractive, the individual user complexes or computer sites will have traffic levels well within this range. Therefore, several of the analytic results presented are for a station traffic of T = 1KB. This corresponds to one packet or multi-packet arriving every 4.5 seconds, on the average. It is extremely important to note the infrequency of this, considering that the block must be delivered within less than a second. Even at 10KB, with arrivals every .45 seconds, each arrival must be treated independently, not waiting for a queue to build up if rapid response is to be maintained. Only after the individual traffic exceeds 50KB is there significant smoothing and uniformity to the station's traffic flow. Thus, it is quite important to devise techniques which do not depend on this smoothing at each station if stations with under $10M of remote computer activity are to be served economically.

Channelized Satellite Transmission Techniques

FDM - Full Interconnection: The most common technique in use today is for each pair of stations which have traffic to lease a small full duplex data channel directly. If this technique were used for a large net of N stations, it would require N(N-1) half duplex channels, each large enough to provide the desired delay reponse. The total satellite bandwidth required is the sum of the N(N-1) individual requirements plus 2KHz* per channel (minimum) for guardbands. However, since the channels are dedicated, variable packet sizes can be handled and the small acknowledgments fit in efficiently.

* Two KHz is the minimal possible channel separation determined by oscillator stability for current INTELSAT IV equipment based on a private communication with E. Cacciamani, COMSAT Laboratories. Actual guardbands in use are wider.

FDM - Store and Forward Star: Since it is clearly very costly for
full interconnection, store and forward is an obvious alternative.
With short, leased ground lines, the ARPANET very effectively uses
this technique, but since each hop adds at least .27 sec due to
the propagation delay, it is important to minimize the number of
hops. Thus a star design is probably as good an example of this
technique as any. The total number of channels for a star is N-1.
The delay is the two hop total plus any switch delay (herein presumed zero and of infinite capacity).

TDMA

Since all stations could theoretically hear all the transmissions, a store and forward process is really unnecessary if each
packet has an address and its destination can receive it. Further,
the guardbands required for FDM can be eliminated if Time Division
Multiple Access techniques are used. Instead, an 80 bit start up
synchronization leader is required. This increases the small acknowledgment packets to 225 bits and the normal packets to 1350
bits, a 7.6% overhead. For this type of data traffic a strict
alternation of time slot ownership between the stations was evaluated. All slots are the same size, 1350 bits, except for small
acknowledgment packets which are packed in at the necessary intervals. Thus, each station has one Nth of the channel capacity and
can use it freely to send to any station. Each station must examine all packets for those addressed to itself. To adapt to unequal
or non-stationary traffic levels, there are many techniques (6) for
slowly varying the channel split.

ALOHA

Instead of preassigning time slots to stations and often having
them be unused, in the ALOHA system they are all freely utilized
by any station with traffic. When there are many stations this reduces the delay caused in waiting for your own slot, but introduces
a channel utilization limit of 36% to insure that conflicts are not
too frequent. When conflicts do occur the sum check clearly indicates it and both stations retransmit. A very complete treatment
of this technique is presented in the papers by Abramson (7) and
Kleinrock and Lam(8). For the comparison curves presented here,
an approximation to the precise delay calculation was used and the
possibilities of improved performance due to excess capacity were
ignored. Thus, the ALOHA results are slightly conservative.

Reservation System

In order to further improve the efficiency of data traffic distribution via satellite, the following reservation system is proposed. As with TDMA and ALOHA the satellite channel is divided into

V small slots. The small slots are for reservations and acknowledgments, to be used on a contention basis with the ALOHA technique. The remaining M large slots are for RESERVED data packets.
When a data packet or multi-packet block arrives at a station it
transmits a reservation in a randomly selected one of the V small
slots in the next ALOHA group. The reservation is a request for
from one to eight RESERVED slots. Upon seeing such a reservation
each station adds the number of slots requested to a count, J, the
number of slots currently reserved. The originating station has
now blocked out a sequence of RESERVED slots to transmit his packets in. Thus, there is one common queue for all stations and by
broadcasting reservations they can claim space on the queue. It is
not necessary for any station but the originating station to remember which space belongs to whom, since the only requirement is
that no one else uses the slots.

Referring to Figure 1, a reservation for three slots is transmitted at $t = 0$ so as to fall in an ALOHA slot at $t = 5$. If a
conflict occurs, the originating station will determine the sum
check is bad at $5 = 10$ and retransmit the reservation. However,
if it is received correctly at $t = 10$ and assuming the current
queue length is thirteen, the station computes that it can use the
slots at $t = 21$, 22 and 24. It does this by transmitting at
$t = 16$, 17 and 19. By $t = 30$ the entire block of three packets
has been delivered to their destination. If no other reservations
have been received by $t = 19$ the queue goes to zero at this point
and the channel reverts to a pure ALOHA state until the next valid
reservation is received.

Reservations: To maintain coordination between all the stations,
it is necessary and sufficient that each reservation which is
received correctly by any station is received correctly by all the
stations. This can be assured even if the channel error rate is
high by properly encoding the reservation. The simplest strategy
is to use the standard packet sum check hardware, and send three
independently sumchecked copies of the reservation date. A reservation requires 24 bits of information and with the sum check is
48 bits. Three of these together with the 80 bit sync sequence
make a 224 bit packet. Given this size for the small slot and
1350 bits for the large slot, we can pack six reservations in the
large slot space; therefore, $V = 6$. If the channel error rate is
10^{-5} and there are 1000 stations, the probability that one or more
of the stations will have errors in all three sections is approximately $1000 (48 \times 10^{-5})^3$ or 10^{-7}. With a 1.5MB channel this is
one error every three days, a very tolerable rate considering the
only impact is to delay some data momentarily. If the reservation
were not triplicated, however, the probability of an error is .48
sufficient to totally confuse all the stations.

Channel states: There are two states, ALOHA and RESERVED: On start up and every time thereafter when the reservation queue goes to zero, the channel is in the ALOHA state. In this state, all slots are small and the ALOHA mode of transmission is used. Reservations, acknowledgments and even small data packets can be sent using the 224 bit slots. However, the first successful reservation causes the RESERVED state to begin. Let us define Z to be the channel rate in large slots per second and R to be the number of large slots per round trip $(R = .27Z)$. Then, considering time as viewed from the satellite, the data packets associated with the first reservation should be transmitted so as to start $R + 1$ large slots after the reservation. To avoid confusion, M is kept constant for the entirety of each RESERVED state but it is allowed to change each time the state is entered. The initial reservation which starts the state contains a suggested new value for M. This value is used until the state terminates. The determination of M will be considered later.

Channel Utilization: The traffic of small packets (reservations, acknowledgments) is twice the overall arrival rate (NL) since every data block requires a reservation and an acknowledgment. If we assume that the arrival rate of these small packets is independent of the state (a good approximation since they are fully independent at both low and high traffic levels where the average duration of one of the states is short compared to R), then:

Small Slot Channel Utilization in ALOHA State: $S_1 = 2NL/ZV$ (2)

Small Slot Channel Utilization in
RESERVED state: $S_2 = 2NL(M + 1)/ZV$ (3)

The channel utilization for large slots must be computed as if the channel were always in the RESERVED state since the ALOHA state is a result of the non-utilization of the reserved slots, not the cause. Thus:

Large Slot Channel Utilization: $S_3 = BNL (M + 1)/MZ$ (4)

Where, average block size: $B = F + 8 (1 - F)$
$B = 4.5$

For the ALOHA transmissions, the channel utilization is related to the actual transmission rate (G) by the relation (see references 7 and 8):

ALOHA State: • $S_1 = AG_1 e^{-G_1}$

RESERVED State: $S_2 = AG_2 e^{-G_2}$

These relations must be solved for G by iteration since S is the known quantity. The correction constant, A, depends on the retransmission randomization technique and R, but is always between .8 and 1.0. As a result of these relations the maximum useful ALOHA throughput is $S = A/e$. An empirically derived approximation * to A used for this analysis was (K = retransmission randomization period in slots):

$$A = \frac{K - 1}{K} \quad \text{where } K = 2.3\sqrt{R}$$

<u>Small packet Delay</u>: The average fraction of time the system is in the RESERVED state is equal to the large slot channel utilization, S_3, since that is the fraction of time reserved packets are being sent. Thus, if we compute the delay for the small packets in both states a weighted average can be taken, using S_3, to obtain the average daily.

<u>ALOHA State:</u>

Initial queueing delay: $W_1 = \dfrac{G_1/N}{2V(1 - G_1/N)}$

Retransmissions: $H_1 = \dfrac{1 - Ae^{-G_1}}{Ae^{-G_1}}$

Small packet Delay: $D_1 = \dfrac{R + 1.5/V + W_1 + H_1(R+W_1+1/V + K/2V)}{Z}$

<u>RESERVED State:</u>

Initial queueing delay: $W_2 = \dfrac{(M + 1) G_2/N}{2V(1 - G_2/N)}$

Retransmissions: $H_2 = \dfrac{1 - Ae^{-G_2}}{Ae^{-G_2}}$

Small packet Delay: $D_2 = \dfrac{R + 1.5V + M/2 + W_2 + H_2(R+W_2+1/V+\frac{K(M+1)}{2})}{Z}$

* For an accurate and more detailed solution to the effect of a fixed retransmission delay, refer to (8).

Now, the overall average small packet delay can be determined:

Overall Small Packet Delay: $D_s = D_1 (1 - S_3) + D_2 S_3$ （5）

Large Packet and Block Delay: For the reserved packets, the delay has three components; the reservation delay (D_s), the central queueing delay and the transmission-propagation delay of the packet or block. For a block of B packets where the general load is the defined traffic distribution the delay is:

Average Delay for reserved:

$$D_r = \frac{ZD_s + R + B\frac{(M+1)}{M} + \frac{YS_3(M+1)}{2M(1-S_3)}}{Z}$$

(6)

Where: Y = 7.2 packets (second moment of block size/ ave block size)

and: B = 4.5 packets (average block size)

Determination of M: An optimal value for M can now be determined numerically for any given channel and traffic load. However this value is not very critcal at low channel loading factors. It is only when the channel is operating near peak capacity that M affects the delay more than a few percent. Since M cannot be changed rapidly it is desirable to set M to the value which optimizes the channel capacity and thereby minimizes the delay at peak load. For peak capacity, both the small and large slot portions of the channel in the RESERVED state should be fully loaded. This occurs when $S_2 = A/e$ and $S_3 = 1$. Doing this and solving equations (3) and (4) for the arrival rate, L, gives us:

$$L = \frac{Z V A}{2eN(M+1)} = \frac{Z M}{BN(M+1)}$$

Solving for M;

$$M = \frac{AV}{2e}B \quad \text{rounded up to nearest integer}$$

for B = 4.5, V = 6: M = 5.

If this peak capacity value for M is always used the delay is within 10% of optimal and the system is quite stable. As can be seen, the only traffic parameter M depends on is B, the average block size. M can be adjusted by the stations if the channel is monitored and the fractions of each type of packet sent are measured. From these fractions it is easy to determine M.

Performance: Now it is possible to determine the delay given the traffic distribution (F,B), number of stations (N), and input arrival rate (L). One common way to examine performance is by plotting delay versus the channel utilization for a fixed channel. The channel utilization, C, is the ratio of the good data delivered to the new channel speed:

Channel Utilization: $C = NLB/Z$

Figure 2 shows the delay vs. C for the TDMA, ALOHA, and Reservation techniques. The traffic distribution is as previously
defined; half single packets and half blocks of eight.

This type of presentation is not the best for deciding what
technique to use for a specific job, but it does show the general
behaviour of the systems for a fixed channel size, as the traffic
load varies.

In order to really compare the cost of the various techniques
to do a certain job, it is necessary to set the traffic level,
number of stations, and the delay permissible. Then, for each
technique, the channel size required to achieve the delay constraint can be searched for. To make the presentation more meaningful the cost of this channel per megabit of traffic can then be
determined using as a price basis the current tariffed price of
the 50 KB INTELSAT IV channel (45KHZ) used in the ARPANET between
California and Hawaii. It is presumed that any bandwidth could be
purchased for the same price per KHz. Converting the cost to dollars per megabit permits easy comparison with the cost in the current ARPANET where distributed leased line capacity can be achieved
for $.10 per megabit.

Figures 3,4,and 5 show communications cost as a function of the
three variables; delay, traffic and number of stations. Examining
Figure 3 it is clear that if a delay of less than two round trips
(.54 sec) is required, the ALOHA system is superior. However, the
cost for .4 sec service is over 6 times that of .8 sec service (using the reservation technique). It is also clear that delays of
more than .8 sec are not necessary and save very little money.
Figure 4 shows that as the individual station traffic is increased
to 50KB or higher, TDMA becomes almost as good as the reservation
system since there is sufficient local averaging of traffic. Similarly, at this same traffic level FDM - Store and Forward achieves
its maximum efficiency but due to sending each packet twice its
asymptotic cost is twice that of TDMA or Reservation. These traffic
levels for each station are unrealistically high, however, and the
flat performance of ALOHA and the Reservation System is vastly preferable since the cost of data communications to small stations is
the same as for large stations. Finally, Figure 5 shows the effect of adding stations to the net. With FDM the cost grows out of
bounds quickly whereas the reservation technique improves its
efficiency until the total traffic from all stations exceeds 100KB.
Below 5KB total traffic ALOHA is superior, but this is not a very
important case. For large numbers of stations at 1KB traffic per
station and .8 seconds delay, the reservation system is 3 times
cheaper than ALOHA, 6 times cheaper than TDMA, and 56 times cheaper
than FDM Store and Forward.

Conclusions

The reservation technique presented here is one of several techniques which have been developed recently to take full advantage of the multi-access capabilities of satellites for data traffic (9,10). Both the ALOHA technique and the reservation system depend for their efficiency on the total multi-station traffic rather than the individual station traffic as does TDMA and FDM Store and Forward. The performance improvement reflects this with the reservation system being up to 10 times as efficient as TDMA for small station traffic levels. The worst possible technique for data traffic is pure FDM links between each station pair since this is only efficient if all pairs of stations have 50 KB of traffic, driving the cost out of bounds for normal usage. The reservation system is also a factor of 3 more efficient than the ALOHA system and for large (100KB) traffic levels achieves almost perfect utilization of the channels.

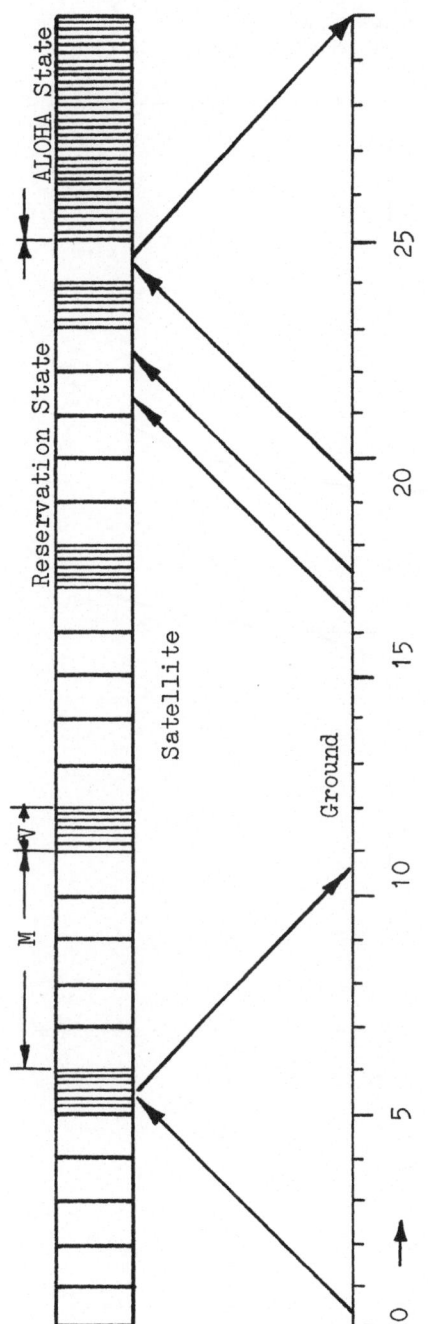

RESERVATION SYSTEM CHANNEL DIVISION

50KB Channel (R = 10 slots per round trip), M = 5, V = 6

Figure 1

340

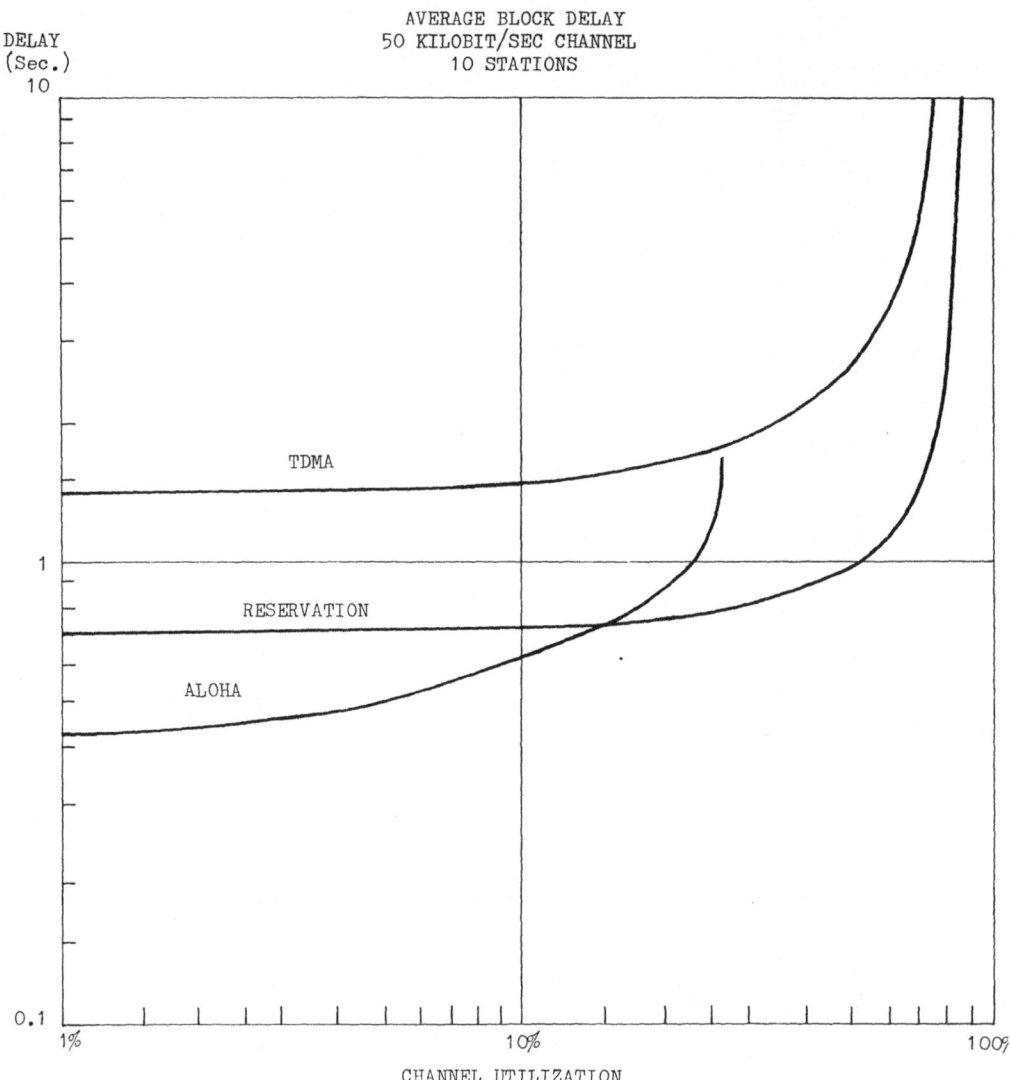

Figure 2

COST
$ per Megabit

RELATION OF COST TO DELAY

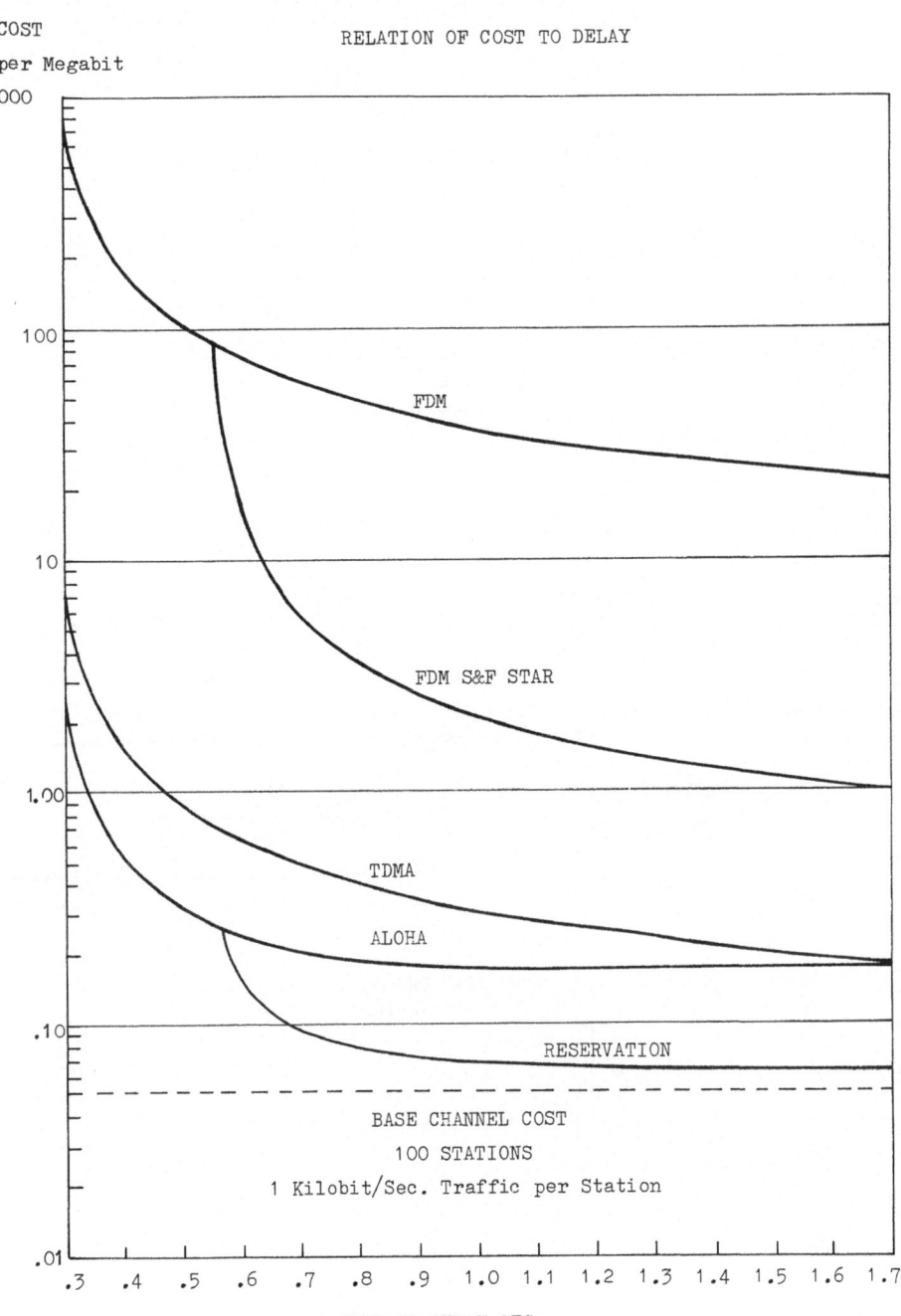

Figure 3

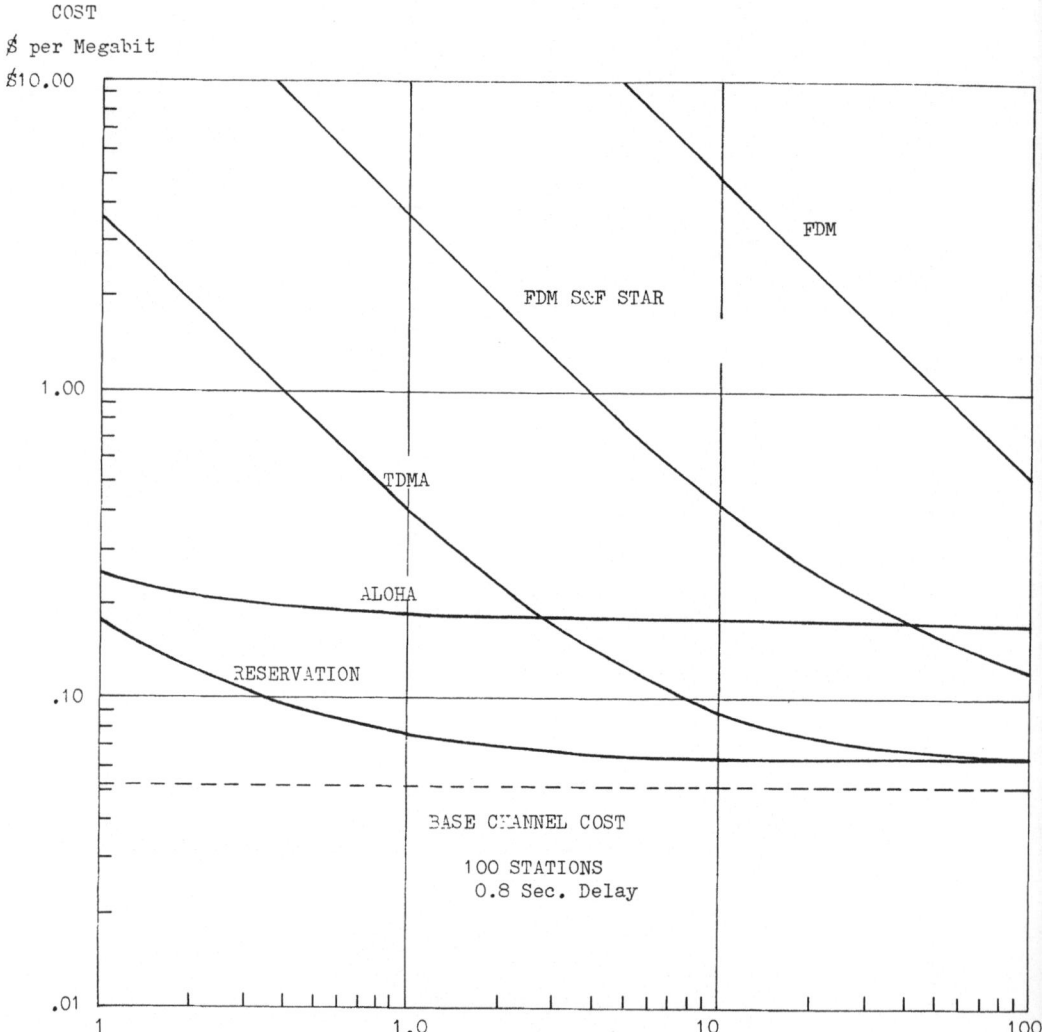

EFFECT OF STATION TRAFFIC ON COST

INDIVIDUAL STATION TRAFFIC IN KILOBITS/SEC.

Figure 4

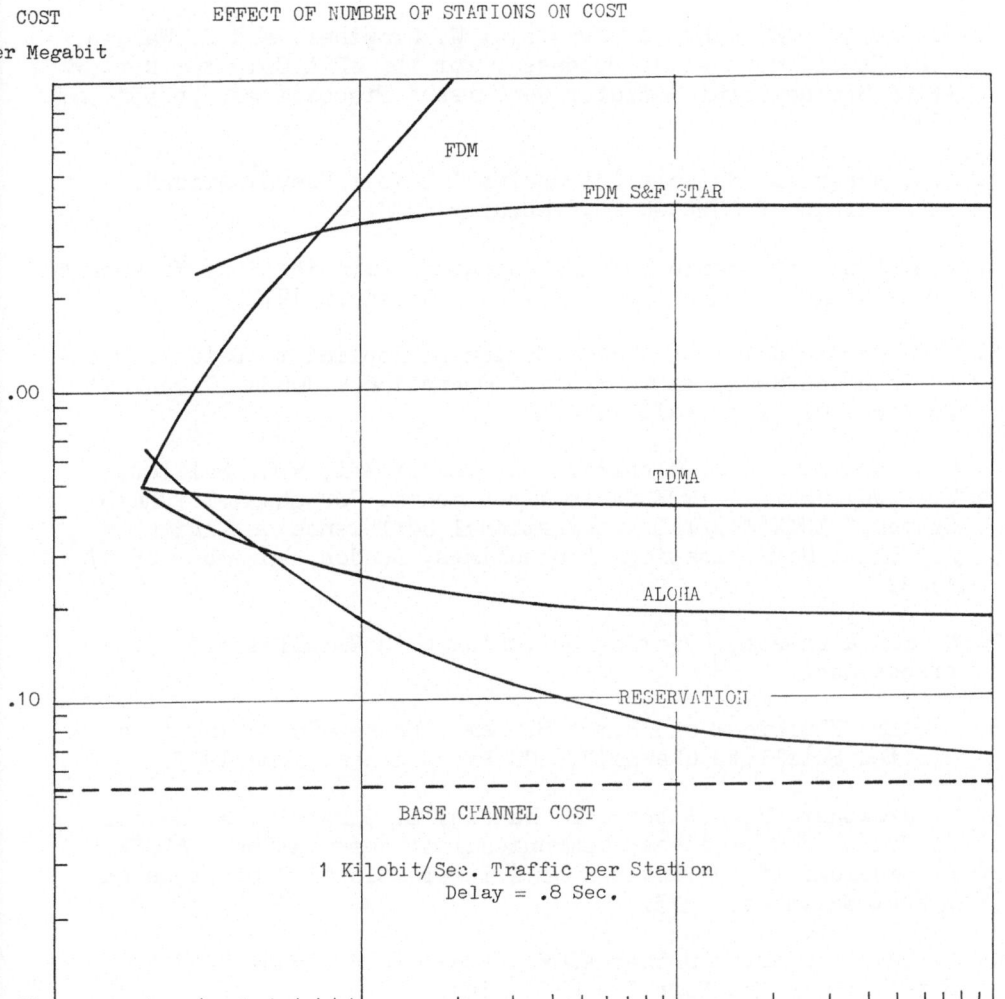

COST per Megabit

EFFECT OF NUMBER OF STATIONS ON COST

FDM

FDM S&F STAR

1.00

TDMA

ALOHA

.10

RESERVATION

BASE CHANNEL COST

1 Kilobit/Sec. Traffic per Station
Delay = .8 Sec.

.01

1   10   100   1000

NUMBER OF STATIONS

Figure 5

References:

1. L.G. Roberts and B. Wessler, "Computer Network Development to Achieve Resource Sharing". AFIPS Spring Joint Computer Conference Proceedings, pp.543-549, 1970.

2. F. Heart, R.E. Kahn, S. Ornstein, W. Crowther, and D. Walden, "The Interface Message Processor for the ARPA Computer Network", AFIPS Spring Joint Computer Conference Proceedings, pp.551-567, 1970.

3. L.G. Roberts, "Network Rationale: A 5-Year Reevaluation", Proceedings of COMPCON 73, February 1973.

4. R.E. Kahn, "Resource-Sharing Computer Communications Networks" Proceedings of IEEE, pp. 1397-1407, November 1972.

5. E.R. Cacciamani, "The Spade System as Applied to Data Communications and Small Earth Station Operation," COMSAT Technical Review, Vol.1, 1, Fall 1971.

6. W.G. Schmidt, O.G. Gabbard, E.R. Cacciamani, W.G. Maillet, W.W. Wu, "MAT-1: INTELSAT's Experimental 700-channel TDMA/DA System," INTELSAT/IEE International Conference on Digital Satellite Communications Proceedings, London, November 25-27, 1969.

7. Norman Abramson, "Packing Switching with Satellites," these proceedings.

8. Leonard Kleinrock and Simon S. Lam, "Packet-Switching in a Slotted Satellite Channel", NCC Proceedings, June 1973.

9. W. Crowther, R. Rettberg, B. Walden, S. Ornstein, F. Heart, "A System for Broadcast Communication: Reservation - ALOHA," Proceedings of the Sixth Hawaii International Conference on System Sciences, 1973.

10.Richard Binder, "Another ALOHA Satellite Protocol," ARPA Satellite System Note 32, NIC 13147.

AUTODIN

L. M. Paoletti

Defense Communications Agency
Washington, D.C.
USA

ABSTRACT

This paper presents a brief history of the development of
AUTODIN, a data communications network of the Department of
Defense of the USA. It covers the general properties of the network, its design characteristics and some of the system statistics acquired from 1963 to the present. A glimpse of what the
future holds for AUTODIN is also presented.

The presentation will address the traffic processing capability of each switching center of the network, the system response
time and the various modes under which the subscriber terminals
can operate through the network. The security aspects and the
reliability features are also addressed. The growth of the network in the past decade, the variety of terminal equipment and
other communications systems that interconnect with AUTODIN are
presented. The major hardware and software components of the
switching nodes together with the general characteristics of the
transmission media and associated error control are discussed.
Finally, a brief presentation is made on the manner in which the
traffic flows through a switching center.

INTRODUCTION

In the mid-50's the Department of the Air Force of the USA
had a manual data communications system for logistics card
traffic, and an automatic teletype communications system for
narrative traffic. The inherent limitations in speed and capacity
and the susceptibility to human error of the manual data system,

combined with the success of the automatic teletype communication system, motivated planning for the purpose of automating the data network. The proposed, automated data communication system, known as the "Combat Logistics Network" (COMLOGNET), would provide for computer controlled data switching centers and automatic data terminals on a nationwide basis. This network was initially planned to be strictly a data oriented system to replace the manual data relay centers then in existence. However, very early in the design phase it was proposed that the system concept be modified so that both narrative and data traffic could be processed in the network. Accordingly, the purpose of the system was broadened and the name changed to "Air Force Data Communications System" (AFDATACOM). The AFDATACOM consisted of five Automatic Electronic Switching Centers (AESC), each of which would provide for both store-and-forward message switching and circuit switching. The program for implementation of these five AESC's lasted from 1958 to 1963.

In 1960 the Defense Communications Agency (DCA) was established with the basic mission of planning, performing system engineering, and maintaining operational control of the Defense Communications System (DCS). The DCS is the communications system needed to meet all long-haul telecommunications requirements, both voice and data, of the Department of Defense (DoD).

Upon activation, test and cutover of the last of the five AFDATACOM centers in the Continental USA (CONUS), the network was made a part of the DCS and it was renamed the "Automatic Digital Network" (AUTODIN). Throughout the 60's AUTODIN underwent significant changes as a network - four AESC's were added in CONUS and eleven new centers, called the "Automatic Digital Message Switching Centers" (ADMSC), were developed and deployed overseas (Europe and Pacific regions). The major difference between an AESC and an ADMSC is that the overseas switches do not have the circuit switching capability. Furthermore, even though the two types of centers are configured with different hardware and operate under somewhat different software, as far as store-and-forward message switching is concerned, they can be considered to be funtionally identical. In CONUS, the network is leased from and maintained by the Western Union Company (WU), but it is operated by DoD personnel; while overseas AUTODIN is owned, maintained and operated by the Government. Finally, from an historical point of view, each center today is called an "AUTODIN Switching Center" (ASC).

NETWORK PROPERTIES

Capacity

The basic function of AUTODIN is to accept, process, store and deliver digital message traffic to and from subscribers located around the world. The relaying of messages by the network is accomplished under the highest possible degree of reliability, speed of service, message security and integrity. The AUTODIN switches employ the store-and-forward concept of transmission in which each message is accumulated and stored in its entirety at an ASC before further transmission along the network is initiated. Accumulation of a complete message at an ASC provides the required message protection since each message is acknowledged and responsibility for it accepted by each node of the network that is involved in the message relay. The routing of messages in the network is accomplished on a deterministic basis. In general, at every node in the network, the destination of a message is assigned a predesignated primary and alternate route which can be modified manually from the supervisory console.

Each ASC has the capability of accepting traffic from, at most, 200 subscriber terminals which can vary in speed from 45 to 4800 bits per second. The average message length is 2,000 characters; the maximum message length is 40,000 characters. The average address multiplicity per message is 1.75. Each ASC can accommodate traffic rates up to the full capacity of all input lines, provided that the subscriber's terminals are distributed, as far as speed is concerned, in such a manner that the switch throughput does not exceed approximately 2×10^5 bits/sec. Message processing by an ASC consists basically in:

> Header Validation - to ensure on both input and output that information such as precedence, security, routing indicators, start of message (SOM) and end of message (EOM) designators are properly contained in the message.

> Journaling - to record pertinent information about a message so that the status of a message at an ASC can be traced as the message is transmitted through the network. This information is recorded on magnetic tape and retained for a period of 30 days.

> Referencing - to record a complete copy of every message for rapid access during a period of 24 hours and for off-line access

during a period of 96 hours immediately
following receipt of message by an ASC.

Security Safeguards – to ensure that both
on input and output and internally within
the ASC the sensitivity of a message is
not compromised.

Traffic Intercept – to provide for temporary storage of traffic destined for
tributary or trunk circuits when the
circuit is known to be out of service
either through scheduled closing of the
tributary or, equipment or circuit
outages.

Retrieval – to provide for either automatic resumption of message processing
after a system malfunction or retransmission of a message by the ASC through
manual intervention of the operator.

Translation – to provide for converting
between ACP-127 and JANAP-128 message
formats and between ASCII and ITA-2 codes.

Responsiveness

Messages are processed and transmitted in AUTODIN on a first-
in-first-out basis in accordance with precedence. Basically, four
precedences are recognized in the network. These are:

Precedence Designation	Precedence Prosign
FLASH	Z
IMMEDIATE	O
PRIORITY	P
ROUTINE	R

On a worldwide basis, the speed of service required for traffic
transmitted over AUTODIN is given below:

Precedence	Communication Handling Time
FLASH	10 minutes
IMMEDIATE	30 minutes
PRIORITY	3 hours
ROUTINE	6 hours

The communication handling times indicate the time elapsed from receipt of a message from the customer at the originating tributary station to receipt of the message at the destination tributary station. The criteria is based upon average message length and upon the receiving tributary station being capable of accepting traffic. It is also based on traffic being distributed by precedence in the following manner:

FLASH	1%
IMMEDIATE	19%
PRIORITY	30%
ROUTINE	50%

To meet the above speed of service requirements, messages with FLASH precedence preempt the transmission of messages of lower precedences on trunks and receive station circuits.

Flexibility

AUTODIN is designed to meet the data and narrative communications needs of subscribers utilizing a large variety of terminal equipment, from teletypewriters to small computers. Furthermore, to preclude rapid obsolescence of the network due to ever changing communications requirements, the system was designed to optimize modular techniques and software rather than hard-wire implementation.

The messages processed by AUTODIN are prepared in either of two formats: ACP-127 or JANAP-128. The basic characteristics of these formats are presented respectively in Figures 1 and 2. The formats are selected based on subscribers communications needs and terminal equipment; and, in general, the JANAP-128 format is used for data communications while the ACP-127 format is used for narrative communications. For transmission purposes, messages in the JANAP-128 format are subdivided in blocks of 84 characters each (80 characters for information and 4 characters for framing). Five operational modes are permissible in AUTODIN for transfer of information between any two elements of the network. These modes provide various levels of sophistication for error detection and correction and message protection. These modes are:

Mode I - defined as duplex synchronous operation allowing for independent and simultaneous two-way communication with automatic error and channel controls. This is accomplished by means of control characters which are used to acknowledge receipt of valid blocks and messages or to return error information.

Mode II - defined as duplex asynchronous operation allowing for independent
and simultaneous two-way communication
normally associated with teletypewriter
equipment. There are no automatic error
or channel controls, and message accountability is maintained through channel
sequence numbers and service message
actions.

Mode III - defined as duplex synchronous operation allowing for only one-way
communication with automatic error and
channel controls. The return path is
used exclusively for error control and
channel coordination. The Mode III
channel is reversible on a message basis.
Control characters are used in the same
manner as in Mode I.

Mode IV - defined as unidirectional
asynchronous operation allowing for one-
way only (send only or receive only)
communication with no error control and
channel coordination. The Mode IV channel
is non-reversible and is equivalent to
one-half of a Mode II channel. Message
accountability is maintained through
channel sequence numbers and service
message actions.

Mode V - defined as duplex asynchronous
operation allowing for independent and
simultaneous two-way communication normally associated with teletypewriter
equipment. Control characters are used
to acknowledge receipt or rejection of
messages. Message accountability is
maintained through the use of channel
sequence numbers and service message
actions.

There are two transmission modes in AUTODIN, synchronous and
asynchronous. Synchronous transmission is used on all channels
which employ the operational Modes I and III and which accomodate
modulation rates of 75×2^m, where m = 0, 1, 2, 3, 4, 5 or 6.
Asynchronous transmission is used on all channels which employ
the operational Modes II, IV and V and which accomodate modulation
rates of 45, 75, 150 and 300 baud. The codes used for transmissio
of information are the American Standard Code for Information

Interchange (ASCII), and the International Teletypewriter Alphabet #2, American Version (ITA-2). ASCII is a 7-level (7 information bits) code, but in AUTODIN a parity bit is added to form an 8-level code. The parity bit is odd for information characters and it is even for control characters. ASCII is always used on synchronous communication channels, and it may be used on asynchronous channels provided that a start bit and a 1 or 2 unit stop bit are added to every character. ITA-2 is a 5-level code and is used only on asynchronous communication channels. A start bit and a 1 to 2 unit stop bit are added when an ITA-2 character is transmitted. No parity bit is utilized with ITA-2.

Speed, message format and code can all be converted by an ASC to permit the variety of subscriber equipments to transfer information to one another.

Security

In military communications the sensitivity of information is identified by a security classification which prescribes the safeguards needed to ensure that the information is not accessible, either intentionally or inadvertently, to unauthorized personnel. Strict measures, both in system design and ASC operation, are taken to ensure that the security safeguards are not compromised. A multiplicity of security checks are performed at an ASC. These include validating on both input and output that the security level of the channel is equal to or higher than that of the message being received/transmitted; attaching the security code on every block of a message which is segmented for internal storage and processing and validating this code for every block at output processing; preventing any single equipment malfunction from causing security checks to be accomplished incorrectly; generating supervisory alarms immediately upon suspicion of a security compromise; and establishing strict procedures for modifications of security safeguards from the supervisory console. Additionally, all channels requiring communications security are encrypted by inserting cryptographic equipment between any information source and sink. The security levels of messages processed in AUTODIN are:

Security Classification	Security Prosign
TOP SECRET	T
SECRET	S
CONFIDENTIAL	C
UNCLASSIFIED EFTO	E
UNCLASSIFIED	U

Categories of traffic with special security are also transmitted through the network.

Reliability

The ASC's are designed to operate on a 24-hours/day, 7-days/week, 52-weeks/year basis. No single failure affects the operational capability of a switching center. Graceful degradation is permissible; however, message security protection and accountability are maintained through all ASC operating states. Isolation of a malfunction, together with recovery and fallback from malfunctions, are automatic. The probability that an ASC loses a message is less than 10^{-8}; while the probability that an ASC is the cause of an error in the relaying of a message is less than 10^{-7}.

NETWORK CONFIGURATION

Topology

The initial configuration of AUTODIN is shown in Figure 3. It consisted in 1963 of five nodal switches, fully interconnected by 2400 bps transmission lines. As communications demands increased in CONUS and developed rapidly overseas the network evolved to the configuration shown in Figure 4. In this stage, the network retained its distributed nature and a large percentage of its full-interconnectivity. The transmission lines tying the nodes together remained at 2400 bps. The AUTODIN configuration of today is shown in Figure 5. The CONUS switches are interconnected by 4800 bps transmission lines; while 2400 bps lines are utilized overseas.

CONUS Nodes

The hardware used to implement a CONUS ASC is shown in block-form in Figure 6. It consists of a Technical Control Unit, a Message Switching Unit (MSU), a Circuit Switching Unit (CSU), a Centralized Control Unit, and a Power Unit.

The Technical Control Unit is used for terminating transmission lines, and for interconnecting transmission lines to the MSU and CSU. It includes the modulating and demodulating (modem) equipment, monitoring and measuring instruments, cryptographic devices, and patching facilities. The modems are used for converting signals carried over transmission lines to a form compatible with digital equipment; while the monitoring and measuring instruments are used for indicating transmission line continuity and signal quality. The cryptographic devices provide traffic security protection on the transmission lines; and the patching facilities provide a flexible means of interconnecting MSU/CSU equipment and transmission equipment in a variety of combinations.

The MSU is the heart of the center. It consists basically of a general purpose computer tailored to perform the store-and-forward message switching function. The MSU is comprised of a front-end and a data processing complex known as the CDP (Communications Data Processor). The front-end consists of buffer elements which perform the basic functions of matching the transmission line speed and signal level to those of the MSU and of translating from bit-by-bit to character-by-character and vice versa. These elements differ in accordance with data transfer rates and transmission mode – synchronous or asynchronous. The accumulation and distribution unit (ADU) is also part of the front-end and it coordinates the transfer of data between the buffer elements and the data processing complex. This unit performs the channel coordination procedures (as described under Transmission), and it converts from ASCII or ITA-2 to Extended Fieldata, the data handling code of the Communication Data Processor. The CDP consists of a central processing unit, a number of high-speed core memory banks, and an I/O complement of disks, magnetic tapes, high-speed paper tape reader and operator's console printer. The CDP, utilizing stored programs, coordinates all message flow and sequencing for both local exchange within itself and other units of the ASC, and external exchange with other ASC's and subscriber terminals. For reliability purposes, the central processing unit and the operator console are duplicated.

The CSU performs direct switching among subscribers connected to the circuit switching units of the network. This unit functions as a space division, common control, multiple register-senders switching system. It provides 4-wire transmission via glass-sealed, dry-reed, relay crosspoints arranged in a non-blocking matrix. The subscribers terminals can operate at speeds from 75 to 4800 bps; however, to transfer information through the CSU, the end terminals must be compatible in speed, format, and code. Both local and tandem calls can be made through the CSU; in tandem calls, the unit will automatically search for alternate routes open to traffic. In-band signalling is used in the CSU. Supervisory signals are either dc levels or 8-bit characters conforming to the modulation rate of 75×2^n where n = 0, 1, 2, 3, 4, 5, 6. The destination address is derived from the message preamble which is used to establish a call and which conforms to the header of a JANAP-128 message format. Both precedence and security checks are performed by the CSU. The Circuit Switch Unit interfaces with the Message Switch Unit on a full-duplex basis; accordingly, any CSU subscriber can obtain store-and-forward service, and any MSU subscriber can transfer messages with any CSU subscriber.

The Central Control Unit consists of a console where central-ized supervision of the major equipments of the switching center is provided by means of controls and status display. Indicators showing the operating condition of the major components of the ASC are located in this unit. Provisions are also made in this console for switching equipment units from stand-by to on-line conditions and for changing programs.

The Power Unit comprises 45 KVA motor-generator sets and regulating and control equipment to supply and distribute voltage-regulated, frequency-regulated and unregulated power in the switching center.

The software that makes the CONUS ASC's perform the store-and-forward message switching functions includes three major routines - the Control Program, the Traffic Handling Program, and the Equipment Handling Program. All programs are written in Assembly Language. The Traffic Handling Program and the Equipment Handling Program are modularly subdivided into functional tasks called units. Basically, a unit is a self-contained portion of coding; it is entered at the beginning and it follows through to the end in performing its assigned task and then exits to the next task via the Control Program. The Control Program, as its name implies, exercises control of the system. It also is divided into functional units; one unit sequences all other program units, while the others control the issuance of instructions to periph-eral devices and the handling of interrupts and abnormal or error conditions. The Traffic Handling Program performs all of the tasks associated with the acceptance of messages into the system, the input and output processing of messages, the storing onto and retrieval of messages from disks, and the delivery of messages to the proper outgoing channel. The Equipment Handling Program pro-vides for the man-machine communication between the system console and the CDP, the handling and servicing of peripheral devices (except for disks), the servicing of ADU requests, and the print-ing-out of information vital to the operation of the system.

Overseas Nodes

The hardware used to implement an overseas ASC is shown in block-form in Figure 7. It consists of the Communications and Technical Control Subsystem, the Automatic Digital Message Switch (ADMS), and the Uninterrupted Power Supply (UPS).

The Communications and Technical Control Subsystem provides facilities for termination of the transmission lines, and for interconnecting transmission lines to the ADMS. As with the

Technical Control Unit of the CONUS nodes, it also includes the modems, monitoring and measuring instruments, cryptographic devices, and patching facilities.

The ADMS performs the store-and-forward message switching function. It also consists of a front-end and a data processing complex. The front-end consists of buffer elements and a Line Traffic Coordination (LTC) unit. The LTC is composed of a Philco Co. 102 processor and 16 K words (32 bits/word) of high speed core memory. The LTC accepts/transmits data from/to the buffer elements on a character basis and transmits/receives data to/from the data processing complex on a block (80 characters/block) basis. It performs also the channel coordination procedures. The data processing complex consists of a message processor (MP, the Philco 102), a number of high-speed core memory units, and an I/O complement of drums, magnetic tapes, high-speed printer, and card reader and punch. A supervisory console to monitor the overall operation and maintenance of the ASC, and a maintenance console to perform specific maintenance functions for the ADMS are also provided.

For reliability purposes, a switching arrangement is provided in the ADMS, whereby a stand-by unit of one type can assume the functions of any on-line unit of the same type (e.g., the stand-by 102 processor can be used for either the LTC or the message processor).

The UPS furnishes continuous regulated power to service the sensitive loads within the switching center. It consists of two dc power supplies, a 240-volt battery, five motor-generator sets, and power control and distribution equipment. The battery consists of 120 two-volt cells connected in series. The battery is connected to the common dc lines in parallel with the output of the dc power supply and is capable of providing power to the motor-generator sets for 15 minutes in the event of primary power source failure.

The software that makes the Overseas ASC's perform the store-and-forward message switching functions includes five major programs - the Executive Control Program, the Line Traffic Coordinator Program, the Message Processor Program, the Supervisory Functions Program, and the Restart and Off-Line Recovery Program. All programs are written in Assembly Language.

The Executive Control Program coordinates and sequences all on-line programs, I/O instructions and LTC/MP operations. It performs magnetic tapes scheduling and drum operations, and monitors overall system performance to assure that any malfunctioning equipment is removed from the system and replaced with operable equipment without impairing system operation.

The LTC Program performs channel coordination on the transmission lines; it allocates dynamically buffer storage in the amount up to 15 data blocks for each input and output line; and it coordinates the exchange of control information pertinent to the transfer of data between the LTC and the MP.

The MP Program performs the data handling functions of the ADMS. It prepares and sequences the I/O instructions to control the message flow; it performs all message processing functions; and it compiles data for statistics about message traffic.

The Supervisory Functions Program provides the means for the operator to issue commands to the system. Through this program reconfiguration of the system devices and supervisory commands such as remove a channel from service, cancel a message, alt-route traffic for a destination, patch a memory location, close history tape, and change routing table are executed.

The Restart and Off-Line Recovery Program provides the means for system initialization, program loading, and automatic recovery from system malfunction and fallback to message processing at the point where the malfunction occurred.

Traffic Flow

To acquaint the reader with a general understanding of how an ASC performs message switching, let us briefly trace a message through the system. Figure 8 illustrates this process. The Overseas ASC will be utilized in this description; the functions performed, however, apply equally well to the CONUS ASC even though they may be executed in a slightly different manner. A series of bits enter an ASC through the transmission lines; these are accepted by the Buffer Elements and are accumulated into characters. Each character is then transferred to the Line Traffic Coordinator where blocks (84 characters) of data are accumulated and each block is assigned a sequence number. Each block is then transferred to the Message Processor where the block framing characters and sequence number are checked and validated to ensure data blocks integrity. When the MP begins to accept blocks of dat from an LTC, it selects an available section of drum where segment (each segment consists of up to 8 blocks) of a message can be stored, and it activates an entry in the drum linking table to control the linking of the segments of a message. Upon reception of the Header block, all of its elements are checked and validated by the MP, a serial number is assigned to the message for referenc purposes during its processing in the ASC, the precedence prosign is checked to determine for each destination where, in the queue, this message should be placed, and the start-of-message-input entry is written on Journal Tape. Once a segment of a message has been written on drum, it is copied onto Reference Tape, and the MP notifies the LTC that the buffer areas for the particular segment can be made available for the reception of additional data. At this point responsibility for the transferred message segment rests with the MP. The transfer of message segments from LTC to MP continues on a periodic basis until a complete message has been received by the message processor. Upon reception of the end of message block, the MP prepares the end-of-message-input entry for the Journal Tape and notifies the LTC of successful acceptance of a message. If, during the transfer of blocks between the LTC and MP, an error or discrepancy is noted, the MP enters into a reject processing routine.

For every message that comes into an ASC, one or more transmission-out must be effected by the ASC, based on the number of destinations contained in the message. Every program cycle, each output line table entry is scanned to determine whether or not a message is being transmitted on that line. If no message transmission is in progress, a check is then made to see if there is a message in queue for the same line. If either a message is being transmitted or a message is available in queue, the MP checks if the LTC can accept data. If such is the case, a read drum list is built by the MP to retrieve data from the drum; and for every block transferred to the LTC, the framing characters, the block count and the security character are validated. For the Header block, routing line segregation is additionally performed, whereby only routing indicators that are pertinent to a destination are retained in the message. Once the header has been validated for transmission, format conversion is performed if necessary, preemption is effected if necessary, a start-of-message-output entry is prepared by MP for Journal Tape, and actual transfer of blocks of data begins between MP and LTC and it continues on a periodic basis until a complete message has been relayed. Basically, the data input process is reversed in that blocks are transferred from MP to LTC, characters are transmitted from LTC to Buffer Elements, and serial bits are placed on the transmission lines by the Buffer Elements. Once all this has been accomplished responsibility for the message passes from the center to the destination, and the drum segments are made available for storage of new messages.

Transmission

The transmission media utilized in AUTODIN include wire lines, LOS microwave, submarine cable, tropospheric scatter and satellite systems. The spectrum utilization on these media, on a channel basis, is basically 4 kHz or a VF channel. For the transfer of information at speeds of 1200, 2400, and 4800 bps, additional requirements with regard to frequency response, envelope delay distortion, idle channel noise, impulse noise, and phase jitter are placed on the VF channel. To achieve operational flexibility and maximum utilization of assigned bandwidth, circuits operating at speeds below 1200 bps are arranged in a frequency division multiplex scheme (FDM) on individual VF channels. The modems utilized to perform the A/D conversion include a low-speed asynchronous unit, which employs a frequency-shift keying (FSK) modulation technique, a low speed synchronous unit which also employs FSK, and a high speed synchronous unit which employs phase-shift keying.

To achieve a BER of 1×10^{-8} or better on synchronous transmission lines, an error control procedure known as ARQ (Automatic Retransmission Request) is employed in AUTODIN. In synchronous operation, the information is segmented into blocks of 84 characters each, and the receiver must verify the accuracy of each block and must acknowledge reception of each error-free block. Character parity, longitudinal parity and character position are employed for block verification. If an error is detected in a block, the receiver sends to the transmitter an "error in block" acknowledgement, and the same block is automatically retransmitted. If necessary, the retransmission of a block is attempted three times, and, if unsuccessful, the ASC supervisor is notified to take remedial action. In asynchronous operation, error control is performed on a message basis. Messages are verified for accuracy at the receiver by the provision of character and control sequency validity checks and start and end of message checks. Messages which are correctly received are acknowledged by the receiver, while messages which are received incomplete or in error result in requests for retransmission.

Terminals

The basic types of subscriber equipment that presently connect to the network are teletypewriters, small-scale computers with either card or magnetic tape capability or both, and optical character readers. Large scale computers can also transfer information through AUTODIN as long as the network procedures are adhered to. Teletype Corporation models 28, 35 and 37 exemplify the type of teletypewriters used to transfer narrative messages. Lately, however, in order to eliminate the rather tedious and time consuming conversion process between page-printed information and information recorded onto paper tape, OCR's are being introduced in the network.

The IBM 360/20/30, the UNIVAC 1004 and DCT 9000, the RCA Spectra 70/45, and Honeywell 200 are representative of computerized terminal facilities used to transfer data recorded on either cards. magnetic tapes, magnetic disks, and paper tape. Other message switching systems are also interconnected with AUTODIN. Some of

these are the Automatic Message Processing System (AMPS), implemented with the Burroughs D825 computer, the Tactical Automatic
Data System (TADS), implemented with the Burrough 3500 computer,
and Local Digital Message Exchanges employing computers such as
UNIVAC 418, IBM 360/40/50, CDC 1700 and RCA Spectra 70/35.

NETWORK STATISTICS

Subscribers

The general categories of terminal equipments accessing
AUTODIN are presented in Figure 9. The teletypewriters can
operate at speeds from 45 to 300 baud and are utilized exclusively
for narrative traffic. The ADP terminals consist of peripheral
devices and controllers (which can be implemented with small
computers such as the IBM 360/20) either as single units, a card
terminal or a magnetic tape terminal, or in combination thereof,
a compound terminal. The latter units can be utilized for both
data and narrative traffic and are identified in Figure 9 as low
speed, below 300 bps, medium speed, from 300 to 600 bps, and high
speed, above 600 and up to 4800 bps.

Traffic Volume

The build-up of traffic in AUTODIN from its initial configuration to present is depicted in Figure 10. The ordinate presents
the total number of originated messages processed in the network
in one year.

Efficiency

Figure 10 shows also how the network has been performing
throughout the years. The network efficiency is the average of
the individual ASC's efficiencies, which are defined as the percentage of time each ASC is operative.

Speed of Service

The average amount of time that has taken to transmit a
message of any precedence through AUTODIN is also given in Figure
10. This time includes manual processes, such as paper tape preparation and message duplication, required at the network origina-
tion and destination points.

THE FUTURE

The modes of communication presently satisfied by AUTODIN, we believe, will continue to exist and even expand in the forseeable future. Improvement programs for the network are continuously being developed to ensure that "customer" service is maintained at a very high degree of efficiency. An area which needs to be improved is terminal facilities. In excess of 90% of the time used to transmit a message in AUTODIN is attributable to such manual operations as paper tape preparation, message logging, message duplication, conversion of destination names to routing codes, and conversion from the page-printed format to either ACP-127 or JANAP-128 formats. We in the defense communications community are constantly striving to find effective means to automate these processes and thus improve the writer-to-reader speed of service. Attractive and feasible solutions to reduce message preparation and handling times are available today in the form of such devices as OCR's, tape cassettes, and facsimile; however, we believe that problems associated with complexity, reliability and cost must be resolved before these equipments can find widespread application in defense communications.

While the 50's and 60's saw the achievement of rapid, reliable and efficient narrative and data communications through AUTODIN, we believe that the 70's and 80's portend the widespread need for other modes of communications for which our present systems were not designed. The types of information transactions that we foresee for these new modes of communications are:

> Interactive - considered to mean the interoperation of a computer with the thought processes of a human through an I/O terminal or the chatter between two humans through I/O terminals. It may be thought of as a rapid series of interrelated questions and responses which converge to the resolution of a complex task. We expect these transactions to be characterized by a nominal length of 600 bits for a question, 6000 bits for a response; and a system response time in the order of seconds.

> Query/Response - considered to be the exchange of one short question followed by a short conclusive answer with no attempt at sustaining continuity of thought within a human or logical continuity within a computer. The characteristics of these exchanges are expected

to be nominally 600 bits for questions,
6000 bits for responses, and system
response time in the order of seconds
to minutes.

Data Base Update - considered to be the
transmission of a short data message to
a computer without expectation of a
response. The transmission is expected
to be typically 600 bits long with a
delivery delay in the order of seconds
to minutes.

Bulk 1 Transfer - considered to be the
transmission of entire files, programs
or processing results. The length of
these transmissions is expected to be in
the order of 10^4 to 10^6 bits with a
delivery delay in the order of tens of
seconds to tens of minutes.

Bulk 2 Transfer - considered to be the
transfer of extremely lengthy information such as an entire data base or
sensor data. The length of these transfers is expected to be greater than 10^6
bits with a delivery delay in the order
of tens of minutes to hours.

To effectively satisfy the present and future communications
needs of the DoD, the Defense Communications Agency is pursuing
analyses of alternative networks ranging from modifications to
AUTODIN, to an interactive ADP systems network, to an integrated
digital DCS permitting global communications between humans in
either voice or record, between men and machines, and between
machines.

ACKNOWLEDGEMENTS

The preparation of this paper has been made possible through
numerous discussions and valuable suggestions of many employees
of the Defense Communications Agency. To my colleagues I am very
much indebted.

		1 to 69 Characters		
Line 1				
Elements	Start of Message Designator	Channel Identification	Message Number	End of Line Designator

More than one of these may be present

	1 to 69	
Line 2		
Elements	Precedence Prosign	Destination(s) Identification(s)	End of Line Designator

	1 to 69		
Line 3			
Elements	End of Destinations Indicator	Originator Identification	Originator Control No.	End of Line Designator

	1 to 69
Line 4	
Elements	Security Designator	End of Line Designator

	1 to 69
Line 5	
Elements	End of Header Designator	End of Line Designator

Header

	1 to 69
Line 6	
Elements	Test Information	End of Line Designator

Text — More than one of these may be present

	1 to 69
Line 8	
Elements	End of Message Sequence

Ending

NOTE: Line numbering is arbitrary

BASIC ELEMENTS OF ACP-127 MESSAGE FORMAT

FIGURE 1

Header	SOM CARD	1 to 80 Characters			
	Elements	Precedence Prosign	Security Designator	Originator Identification	Date & Time	Destination(s) Identification(s)

More than one of these may be present

Text	TEXT CARD(S)	1 to 80 Characters
	Elements	Text Information

Ending	EOM CARD	1 to 80 Characters				
	Elements	Precedence Prosign	Security Designator	Originator Identification	Date & Time	Separators	End of Message Sequence

BASIC ELEMENTS OF JANAP-128 MESSAGE FORMAT

FIGURE 2

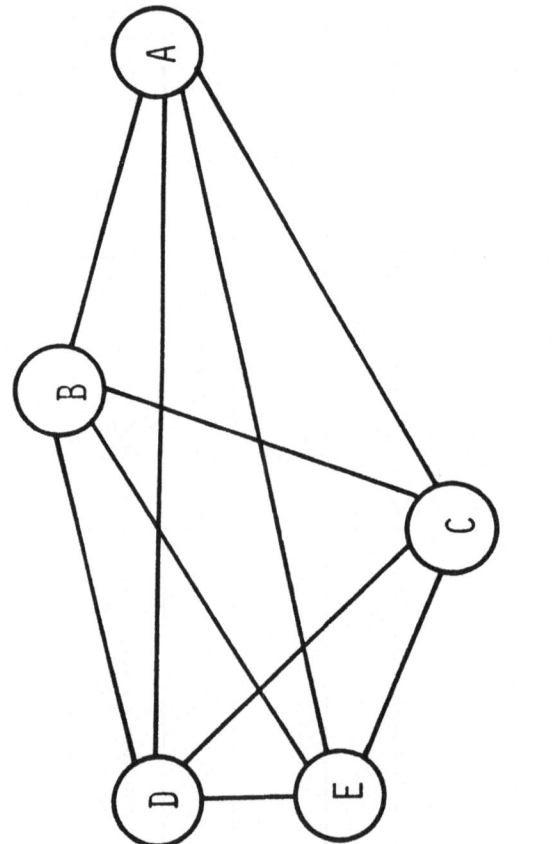

ALL TRUNKS @ 2400 BPS

NETWORK CONFIGURATION 1963

FIGURE 3

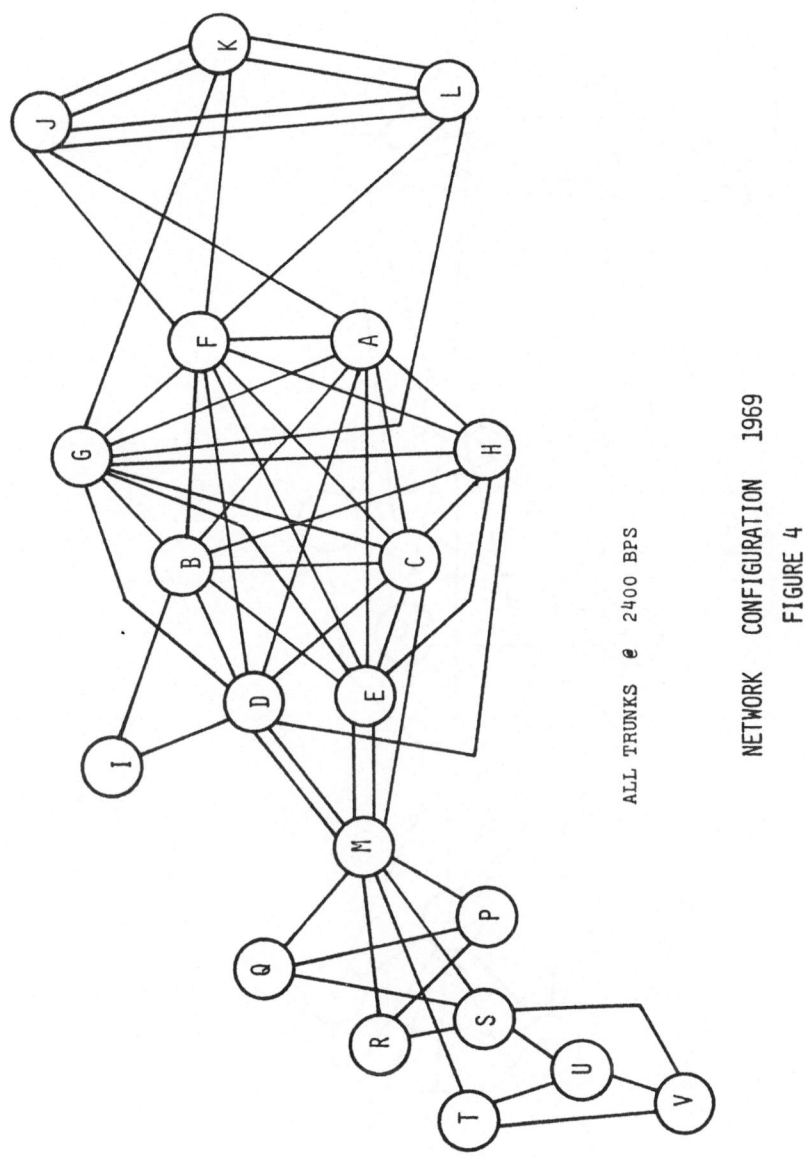

ALL TRUNKS @ 2400 BPS

NETWORK CONFIGURATION 1969
FIGURE 4

366

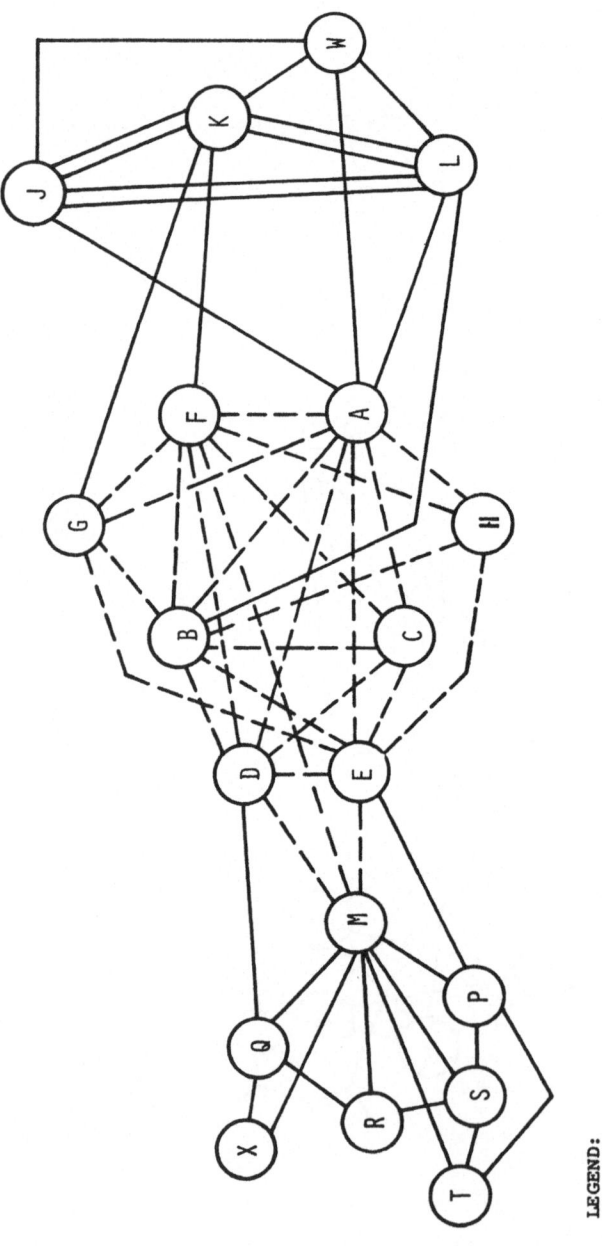

LEGEND:

– – – 4800 BPS

——— 2400 BPS

NETWORK CONFIGURATION 1973

FIGURE 5

367

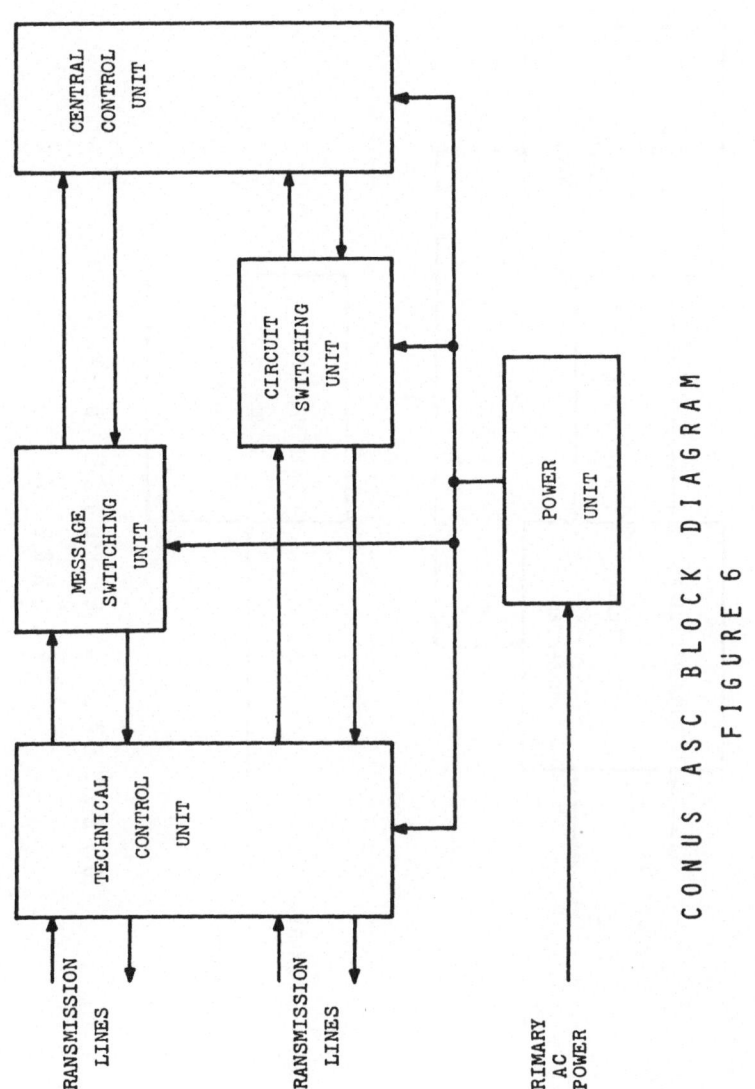

CONUS ASC BLOCK DIAGRAM

FIGURE 6

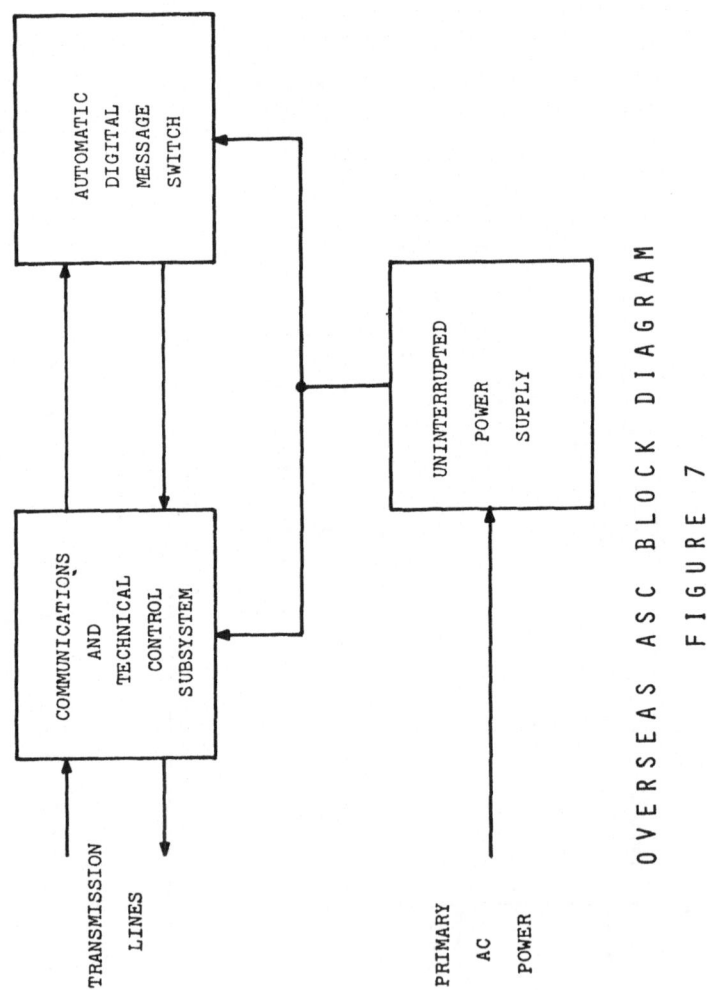

OVERSEAS ASC BLOCK DIAGRAM

FIGURE 7

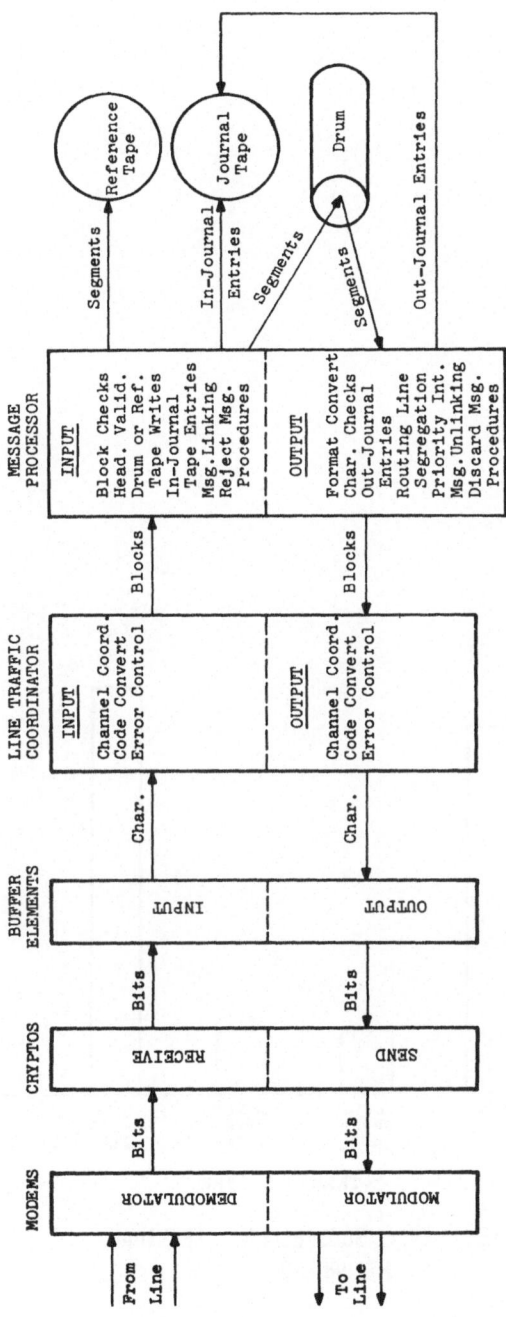

SIMPLIFIED REPRESENTATION OF TRAFFIC FLOW THROUGH THE A S C

FIGURE 8

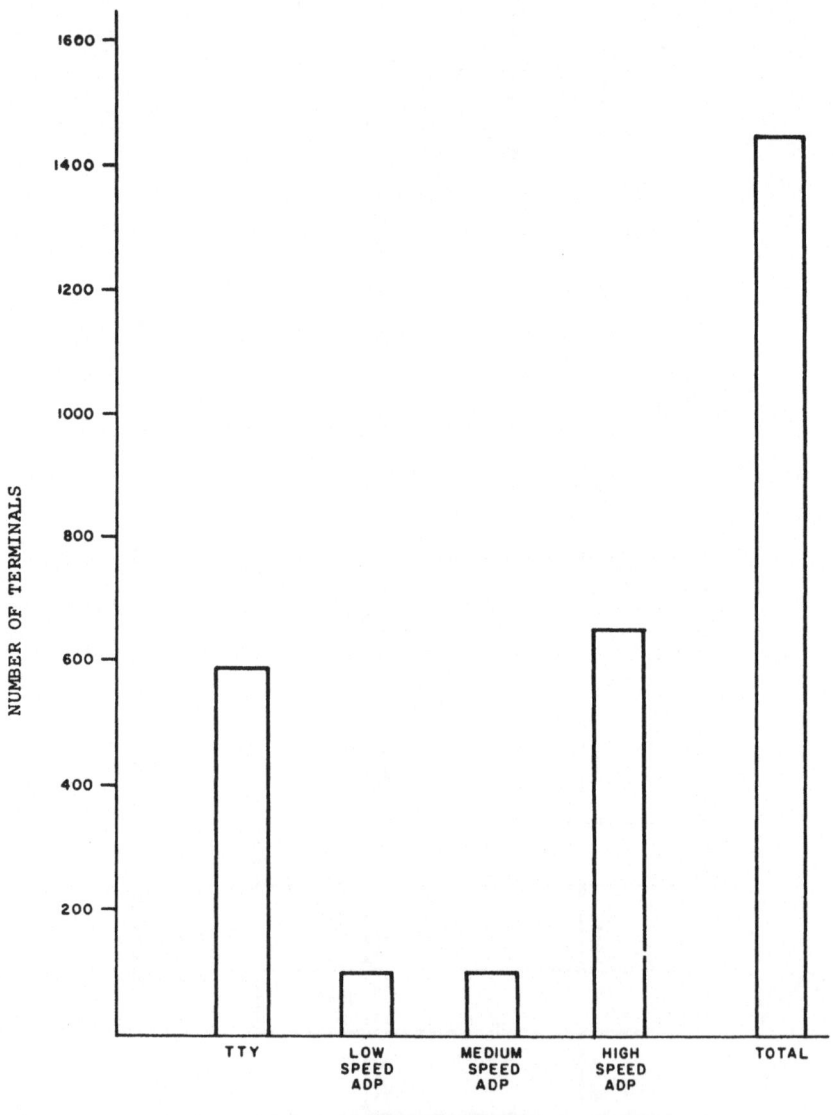

CATEGORIES OF SUBSCRIBER TERMINALS

FIGURE 9

371

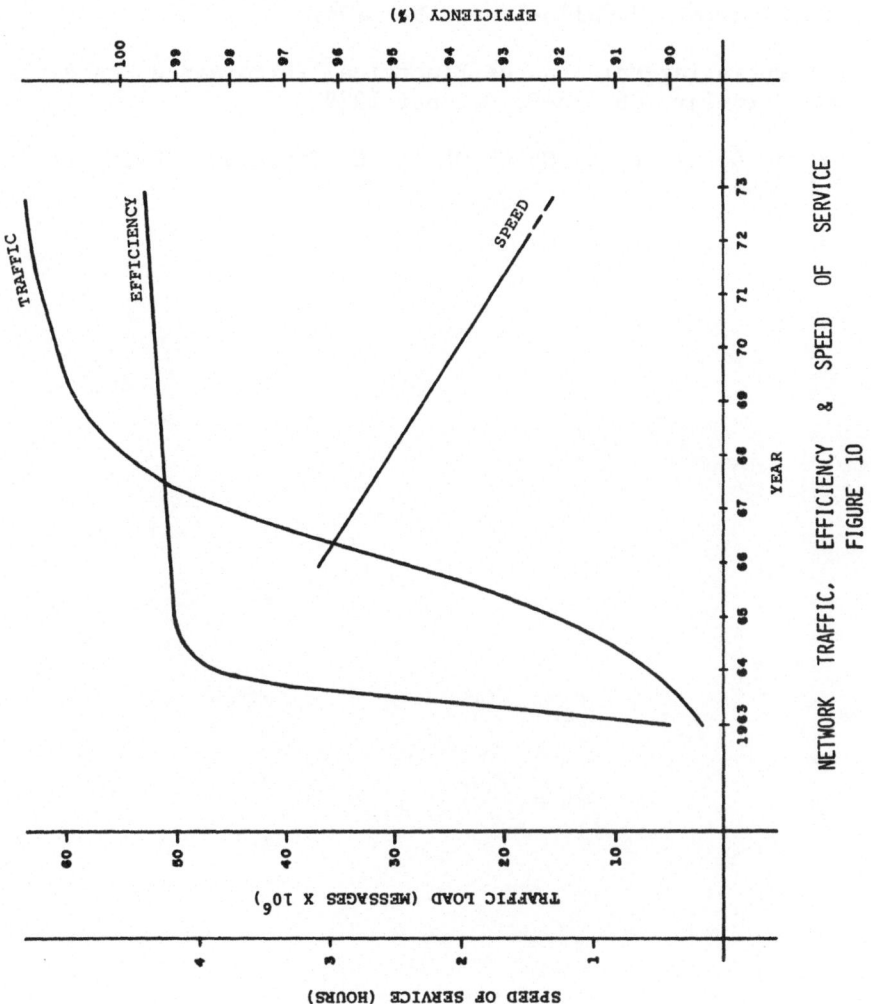

NETWORK TRAFFIC, EFFICIENCY & SPEED OF SERVICE
FIGURE 10

BIBLIOGRAPHY

1. AFDATACOM System; RCA Instruction Book, Appendix III, Volume I; September 1963

2. Automatic Digital Message Switching Centers; Technical Manual, TM 11-5895-391-15; October 1968

3. DCS AUTODIN Interface and Control Criteria; DCA Circular 370-D175-1; October 1967

4. DCS Operating-Maintenance Electrical Performance Standards; DCA Circular 300-175-9; October 1969

5. System Description DCS-AUTODIN; DCA Circular 370-D95-1; July 1967

THE SITA NETWORK

G.J. Chretien   W.M. Konig   J.H. Rech

Société Internationale de Télécommunications
Aéronautiques

(SITA) Neuilly France

INTRODUCTION

1.1.   SITA (Société Internationale de Télécommunications
Aéronautiques), a cooperative company founded in 1949,
embraces the majority of the international air carriers
(more than 160). It provides to its members a worldwide message switching network.

1.2.   Initially the network consisted of manual (torn-tape)
centres, interconnected by low speed circuits (50, 75
Bauds, 60, 30, 15 words per minute, asynchronous).
The Airline terminal equipment (teleprinters, Telex) was
connected to the SITA manual centres, thus enabling
airline messages to be exchanged via nodes of the SITA
network, with consequent reduction in costs to the
airlines by their sharing of communications facilities.

1.3.   With the rapid development of the Air Transport Industry,
the airline communications needs became increasingly
important and thus the SITA network expanded very
quickly, by 1963 covering the world.
Network development was not, however, restricted to
geographic extension; in 1963 a number of the busiest
manual centres were replaced by semi-automatic systems,
and three years later, due to the continuing steady
increase of traffic volumes, SITA equipped the Frankfurt
centre with its first computer system to perform the
message switching functions.
Then, in 1969, SITA began replacing the other most
heavily loaded centres (Western Europe and New York) with

computer systems and established a computer communication data network by interconnecting these centres with voice grade circuits (medium speed). This network, called the High Level Network, performing the task of block switching, was interfaced at that time with the rest of the network composed of manual centres.
This step was soon followed by the automation of other manual centres using what are in SITA terminology called satellite processors. These stand-alone computers act as concentrators of airline teleprinter traffic and controller of airline CRT terminals, each of them connected to one High Level Centre by medium speed circuits.
By mid-1973, the SITA network comprised 150 centres including 8 high level centres and 21 satellite processors. The 29 automated centres will be referred to as the SITA medium speed network (see figure 1).

In the remaining part of the network, referred to as the low speed network, there is one other centre (Hong Kong) equipped with computer systems and connected to the overall network by means of low speed circuits. A number of other European centres are equipped with multiplexers (1200 bits per second: 24 or 12 low speed circuits) and included in the low speed network.

1.4.   The traffic carried at present by the SITA network can be subdivided into two main types, not taking into account special messages necessary to guarantee safe and error-free transmission. These two main types of traffic are telegraphic and conversational.

1.4.1   Telegraphic Traffic (or Type B)

These are messages generated under a given (ATA/IATA) format, using CCITT No. 2 code. They are one-way single or multi-addressed, destined to and generated by airline teleprinters or computers.
Such messages may be sent or received also by the local Telex networks.
The security requirements imposed on these messages are stringent, i.e. the SITA network is fully responsible, (no loss or undetected duplication and capability for message retrieval).
On the other hand, the transmission time constraints are not very severe, i.e. in the order of several minutes. The average length of such messages is around 200 characters.

1.4.2   Conversational Traffic (or Type A)

This is Query/Response traffic. The Query is generated

by an agent set (CRT) in an airline office connected by
medium speed lines to the SITA network, then sent via
the SITA medium speed network to the parent reservations
computer. There the Query is processed, a Response is
generated and sent back to the enquiring CRT. The
response time required on such a transaction is around
three seconds.
At the same time, the degree of security demanded for
these messages is low compared to that for telegraphic
traffic, as, due to the nature of such messages, an
operator at an agent set terminal will re-enter his
Query should there be no reply within a few seconds.
Average message lengths are in the order of 30
characters for a Query and 120 for a Response. Used for
these messages are the CCITT No. 5 and the IBM BCD
codes.

1.4.3   Comparing the time constraints imposed on the two types
of traffic, Type A has priority over Type B.

2.   THE SITA MEDIUM SPEED NETWORK

This comprises the SITA High Level Network and its
satellite processors (see Figure 1).

2.1.   The High Level Centre interfaces

Each High Level Centre (HLC) will interface with the
following systems, exchanging with them messages or
blocks, (see Figure 2):

a)   other high level centres, through medium speed lines;

b)   airline reservation computers, by means of medium
     speed lines (2.4, 4.8 kilobits);

c)   satellite processors (SP) via medium speed lines
     (2.4, 4.8 kilobits);

d)   teleprinters, via low speed lines (50, 75 Bauds);

e)   local Telex networks, through low speed lines (50,
     75 Bauds);

f)   ARQ, 60, 30, 15 w.p.m.

In each HLC there are High Level functions and Low Level
functions. The High level functions allow communication
between any pair of HLCs via the interconnecting links.
By definition, the High Level Network (HLN) consists of
the HLCs with only their High Level functions and the
interconnecting links. The remainder of the SITA network
is referred to as the Low Level Network (LLN).

2.2. The Satellite Processor Interfaces

Each Satellite Processor (SP), (see Figure 2), interfaces with the following systems:

a) its parent HLC by means of medium speed line (2.4, 4.8 kbps);

b) teleprinters, via low speed lines (50, 75 bauds);

c) local TLX network;

d) Agent sets via medium speed lines.

3. THE HIGH LEVEL NETWORK

Physical description

The network is at present composed of eight high level centres interconnected by eleven full duplex medium speed lines. The centres are located in Amsterdam, Brussels, Frankfurt, London, Madrid, New York, Paris and Rome, (see Figure 1). All circuits are operated at 4.8 kilobits, except for those connected to the Brussels Centre, but this is a transitional situation.

3.1 Principles of the High Level Network

The SITA High Level Network (HLN) follows a block switching principle.
Each message which has to be transmitted over the HLN is received first by an HLC called HLC of entry. The message is then subdivided into blocks with an appropriate header. Each of them is now sent independently towards the HLC of exit which will reassemble the message before passing it to the Low Level Network.
An HLC of transit, that is a High Level Centre which receives a block while not being the HLC of exit, will perform only switching functions in accordance with the address in the block header.

3.2 High Level User Requirements

The requirements of the SITA users on the network are two-fold:

i) Low transit time, i.e. the time to transmit a block through the network.

ii) High availability, i.e. the monthly average downtime of the paths between any two high level centres must be as small as possible. For the HLN, the mean transit time is in the order of 700 milliseconds.

As far as the availability is concerned, continuous service on a 24-hour basis is expected and any downtime in a high level centre should not exceed 2 hours monthly. For this reason:

a) each high level centre is equipped with two or three computer systems, one of them being in a standby mode while the other(s) is (are) performing the necessary switching functions. A typical configuration of an HLC is given by figure 3.

b) between any two high level centres there are at least two independent paths (i.e. paths having no links or centre in common). Thus each HLC is connected to at least two other HLCs.

c) The maximum distance between any two centres is 3 links.

3.3 Organisation of the Network

Messages received by an HLC of entry for transmission on the HLN are segmented into blocks of a maximum length of 240 characters (7+ parity bits). The upper limit for the number of blocks per message is 16.
In order to guarantee high transmission performances across the HLN one needs to provide:

a) secure transmission of blocks between two adjacent HLCs by a link control procedure;

b) addressing information for each block;

c) message reassembly for multi-block messages;

d) high security for type B messages.

3.4 Link Control Procedure

A synchronous full duplex link control procedure over one circuit (point-to-point symmetric for each direction) on which the two centres send their blocks continuously is used. Each data block has an envelope which comprises a sequence number and a block check character (longitudinal, transversal parity). A block, to be accepted as valid by the receiving centre has to be in the proper sequence and must have a correct block check. In this case an acknowledgement is sent, otherwise a negative acknowledgement is generated. Furthermore, the sending centre initiates a timer each time it sends a block. This timer is killed when the acknowledgement of the block is received. Otherwise at its expiration, the sending centre repeats all blocks following the first unacknowledged block. Type A blocks have priority over Type B blocks, realised by a priority indication in the envelope. Link Control blocks (e.g. acknowledgement, negative-acknowledgement, etc.). have the highest priority at the output queues in each HLC.

Note: The subdivision of messages into blocks serves a dual purpose:

a) to increase the line efficiency, i.e. to increase the ratio of the total number of data characters to be transmitted over the total number of characters effectively transmitted (data, envelope, link control messages, repetition due to erroneous trans- mission) in the case of a line with a high error rate, e.g. 10^{-4} bit.

b) to avoid long waiting times in an output queue for Type A blocks.

3.5 Addressing

In order to be routed through the HLN, each blocks needs the address of the HLC of Exit. The blocks are switched through core memory in each transit HLC and transmitted in a store and forward mode according to paragraph 3.4.

3.6 Reassembly of messages

Since blocks of any one message are sent independently and possibly via different paths, each message needs to be reassembled in the HLC of exit. To achieve this, each block envelope contains a sequence number per Entry/Exit pair which means that the address of the entry centre is also needed in the envelope. To properly control the sequencing of blocks for reassembly, special "end to end control messages" are used.

3.7 Security Requirements

Type B messages have very high security requirements. Therefore, to avoid any loss in case of HLC CPU failure, these messages will be stored on duplicated mass memory units (drums) in the HLC of Entry and reassembly will be performed on drums in the HLC of Exit. For Type A multi-block messages, the reassembly will also be performed on drums although this is not essential for security reasons (see 1.4.2.)
Single block type A messages, since no reassembly is needed, are not stored on drums.
Each time a certain number of messages has been re- assembled, an End to End acknowledgement (see 3.6) is sent to the HLC of Entry. As a result, this centre no longer has responsibility for these messages and therefore may drop them from drums (see Figure 4).

3.8 Retrieval

Type B messages are stored on magnetic tapes for retrieval purposes in the HLC of Entry.

3.9 Transparency

Messages received by an HLC from the Low Level side in 5-bit per character code, will be padded up in 7+ parity bit characters.

3.10 Routing

The routing scheme adopted for the HLN can be described as follows:

a) for a given configuration of the HLN i.e.(no change in conditions of link or centre), there will be always just one route selected between any two centres.

b) Each centre will inform all others with status messages every time it observes a change in the condition of the links to which it is connected i.e. each centre in the HLN will have a map of the whole network configuration.

c) Each HLC A has listed all possible routes between any centre and itself. Routes corresponding to one particular HLC B are listed in Centre A according to pre-established priorities.
Obviously to each route there corresponds one outgoing link in Centre A.

d) Each time Centre A has to send a block to Centre B, it will, according to paragraph 3.10.c, select the highest priority route available and so determine the corresponding outgoing link.
This routing scheme is, of course, not the optimum with regard to the actual traffic pattern but it is simple. The updating of the routing tables is done three times a year.

3.11 Traffic flow control on the HLN

Should any centre be in overload situation, it will stop accepting blocks from other HLCs and will inform them about its situation. If a centre receives such information, it will

a) drop all received blocks to be transmitted to the overload centre

b) stop transmitting blocks of messages received from outside sources.

4. THE SITA LOW LEVEL NETWORK

On this network there is just Type B traffic.
Each time a message arrives in a centre, it is stored on
paper-tape (or on mass memory units in the Hong-Kong
Centre) before being sent to the next SITA centre or
delivered to its addre-sees. For message protection,
each sending centre (SITA centre or airline office) will
number sequentially all messages it sends and each
receiving centre will make sure that there is no break
in the sequence. Since Type B messages can be multi-
addressed, each SITA centre will have a responsibility
table. For illustration, consider the example in
Figure 5.
Station A has a multi-address message to send to stations
B and C, thus A sends the message to SITA Centre 1, which
then sends to B one copy and another to SITA Centre 2;
Centre 2 in turn relays the message to Station C. Centre
2, not being responsible for Station B when the message
is sent over link 1-2. and having received the message
from Centre 1, will not send it back to Centre 1 for
onward transmission to Station B.
This responsibility table avoids infinite duplication of
multi-address messages.

5. THE HIGH LEVEL CENTRE

In this paragraph only the low level functions of such a
centre are considered (see paragraph 2.1).

5.1. Airline Reservation Computers

An HLC exchanges type A and type B messages with a
connected airline reservations computer. The type A
messages received by the HLC are sent through the SITA
medium speed network (see figure 6) to the enquiring
airline display terminal.
The exchange of messages is effected by using a synchronous
full duplex link control procedure (point to point,
symmetric for each direction) over a multi-circuit link.
This procedure follows the ATA/IATA standard. For each
full duplex circuit, functionally it is comparable to
the procedure briefly outlined in paragraph 3.4. All
blocks of a given message are sent via one single circuit.
In the envelope of each block there is a sequence number
which allows message reassembly.
Type B messages and multiblock type A messages are reassembled and stored on duplicated drums in the HLC.
Single block type A messages are just core switched. Each
time any message is correctly reassembled and stored on
drums the HLC generates a message acknowledgement
comparable to that described in paragraph 3.7.

5.2 Satellite Processor

Message exchange between HLC and SP is described in paragraph 6.1.

5.3 Teleprinters

An HLC exchanges type B messages with low speed tele-printers. Messages, if received correctly by the HLC (e.g. proper format, serial number in sequence etc...), are stored on duplicated drums for security reasons. The HLC will then analyse the address(es) contained in the message before sending it on the appropriate circuit(s).

5.4 Telex

HLCs can also be connected to local telex networks and exchange messages with telex subscribers. As soon as the connection is established messages are processed as teleprinter message.

5.5 HLC computer systems

At present, SITA uses 3 types of computer systems. Philips DS 714 MK II, UNIVAC 418 II, UNIVAC 418 III. The Philips DS 714 MK II and UNIVAC 418 II are briefly described in the following paragraphs. The UNIVAC 418 III machine belongs to the same family as the 418 II but is faster and more efficient.

5.5.1 Philips Centres

Two DS 714 processors equipped with 2 drums, 7 tape units, 1 console, 1 papertape reader, 1 printer.
Each DS 714 processor has: 32 bit words, 2.2 μs memory cycle (memory is byte addressable), 96 K words memory and direct memory access.
Two types of communication multiplexers are used:

a) up to 125 asynchronous lines with speeds from 45 up to 100 bauds;

b) up to 30 synchronous or asynchronous lines with speeds from 200 up to 9600 bps.

At present, for example, the Paris HLC is equipped with 3 multiplexers of type a for 300 lines and one of type b for 12 lines.

5.5.2 Univac 418 II Centres

Each processor has: 18 bit words, 2 μs memory cycle, a 64 K word memory, direct memory access.

The "two 418 II" system has one card reader, one printer, 4 drums of 260 K words each. The line controllers (CTMC) can control up to 32 low speed asynchronous lines or up to 16 synchronous lines. The Rome HLC, for instance, is at present equipped with 2 CTMSs (5 medium speed lines, 50 low speed lines plus 2 remote multiplexer lines).

5.6 Example

As an example this paragraph describes the handling of a type B message received by a UNIVAC 418 II centre.

5.6.1 The UNIVAC 418 II design and program structure

The executive of the 418 II provides 4 levels of priority (1. for real time program and the executive; 2. for time dependent jobs; 3. for batch; 4. for computations).
The main routine called "the switcher" gives control to the programs according to their priority.
When an interrupt occurs the interrupt-answering routine takes control of the processor to toggle the buffers and log the generated status. Then according to the priority of the interrupted program, the control will be returned to the interrupted program or to the main routine.
Within each priority level an application program (the sequencerroutine) defines the order in which the application programs are scheduled.

5.6.2 Processing of Type B messages coming from the Low Level Network (see Figure 7).

Each time 5 characters have been received, the interrupt is processed by the interrupt-answering routine which performs the toggling of two 7-word buffers (5 words are used for the input character and 2 words to chain the buffers).
The pre-edit routine performs:

a) the character packing in an input staging buffer (3 characters per word);

b) the checking of message delimiters and errors which can occur (stuck tape, over length, cancel signal, line open...).

The input staging buffer is taken in a list of free chained buffers. When such a buffer is full or the message completely received (for the last buffer) the input staging routine writes this buffer on drums.

"EDIT" gets control from the "sequencer" routine and is scheduled by the Input staging routine. The main function of EDIT is to process the input messages and to build the output messages.

The "output staging" routine and "the real time interrupt answering service output" perform the following functions:

- reading of message on drum;

- logging on tape unit;

- unpacking of characters in the two alternate buffers used for output.

5.7 HLC system recovery

In each HLC one (or two) processor(s) perform the traffic handling functions while another is in a standby mode. This standby processor may perform off-line functions (e.g. batch processing). Then should the on-line processor fail, the standby system takes over.

5.7.1 For the UNIVAC system

Switchover is effected manually. An alarm warns the system control room when the on-line processor fails. The supervisor then switches manually the drums and line controllers to the standby processor.

5.7.2 For the Philips system

If the on-line system fails the system control is automatically transferred to the standby processor which aborts any off-line operation in progress and immediately starts the traffic handling function.
A failure in the on-line system may be detected:

a) by the hardware or software traps of the on-line system which then ceases to operate.

b) by the alarm and switcher unit which should receive periodically a signal from the on-line processor.

5.7.3 Since the on-line processor records the current status of the dynamic tables on both drums, the standby processor will use this "snap-shot" of the current work to take over the task whenever necessary. A drum failure has no effect on either system as two drums in the system are always maintained as images of each other.

5.8   <u>HLC Saturation</u>

All sources which send traffic to an HLC have free access to that HLC.

5.8.1   In case of memory congestion the on-line processor in the HLC stops receiving traffic from other HLCs in accordance with paragraph 5.3.1.

5.8.2   In case of drum overload, telegrams are automatically sent to stop teleprinters from generating traffic and stored messages are drained on to magnetic tapes.

5.9   <u>Statistics</u>

Each HLC records statistics of the incoming traffic loads, type A and type B, of the High Level circuits, for performance measurements and billing purposes.

6.   <u>SATELLITE PROCESSORS (SP)</u>

These computer systems are stand-alone processors with
simply a communication controller and no peripherals.
They each depend on only one HLC.
S.Ps are built to operate without manual intervention.
As previously mentioned, they act as traffic
concentrators and solicit/send traffic from/to airline
CRT terminals.

6.1   <u>HLC - SP</u>

Data is exchanged between an SP and its parent HLC via a
multi-circuit link using a full duplex synchronous link
control procedure with message control (point to point,
symmetric for each direction of each circuit), almost
identical to that described in paragraph 5.1, Type B
message reassembly is not performed in the SP. Blocks of
one message are always sent via the same circuit unless
the considered circuit is down, in which case the
remaining blocks are transmitted via another circuit. Each
message the SP receives from TTY, TLX or agent set is,
after having been divided into blocks, sent to its
parent HLC. The SP does not perform local switching
functions.
The message, whether Type B or multi-block Type A, is
reassembled on drum in the HLC of entry; if single block
Type A, it is just core switched.
Each data block exchanged between an HLC and an SP carries
an identification number of the TTY/Agent set circuit
over which the message has been received (input) or
over which the message has to be sent (output).
Furthermore, SP and HLC exchange service messages,
allowing the HLC to have a remote control of the
stations connected to the SP.

6.2   <u>Teleprinter Lines</u>

SPs accept messages from teleprinters using the ATA/IATA
format. As soon as one block of TTY data (here maximum
length 240 characters) is received, it is immediately
sent with an envelope to the HLC. To reduce memory
occupancy, the SP does not wait for receipt of the
complete message.
Should an abnormal situation occur, (e.g. incomplete
messages, line open, etc.) the SP informs its HLC by
sending an appropriate service message.
HLCs send messages to SPs block-by-block, using the
above mentioned link control procedure. However, Type B
messages are not transmitted continuously. As soon as
the first block is sent, the HLC does not send the

following block of the same message until it is
informed by the SP via a·service message that the block
(which at the link level had already been acknowledged)
is completely transmitted to the outstation. Here
again, this method of sending Type B messages reduces
memory occupancy in the SP.

6.3   Telex

An SP has capability of carrying out automatic
connection or response in conjunction with the local
telex network. The SP utilises service messages to
inform its HLC of all the steps of connection and dis-
connection. The messages received/sent from/via the
Tlx network are processed according to paragraph 6.2.

6.4   Agent Set Lines

SPs control lines with Agent sets, using three different
polling procedures: IBM 1006; Raytheon DIDs 400;
Uniscope 100. Each Agent set enquiry received by the
SP is sent block-by-block to the parent HLC, where it is
reassembled on drums, if multi-block, and sent via the
HLN towards the parent reservation computer (see
Figure 6). Type A response messages generated by a
reservations computer are sent by the HLC to the SP,
block-by-block, according to the link control procedure.
The message, if multi-block, is reassembled in the SP
before being sent on the Agent Set line.

6.5   Satellite Processor Implementation

Two types of machines are used to perform satellite
processor functions:

a)   Raytheon 706: 16 bit words; $1\mu s$ memory cycle; 32 K
     words memory; the communication controller works with
     one control word group - its limits are 8 full
     duplex synchronous and 72 full duplex asynchronous
     lines; Direct Memory Access; special characters are
     recorded in main memory.

b)   Thomson Houston (GE) 4020: 24 bit words; $1.6\,\mu s$ memory
     cycle; 32 K words memory; the communication
     controller works with two groups of control words -
     its limits are 64 synchronous or asynchronous full
     duplex lines; special characters are wired.

Each system provides a protected memory area for remote
load of the program sent by the parent HLC, an auto
restart against power failure and an interrupt stall.
This is to avoid as far as possible any manual intervention. In each system the communication controller

generates interrupts when buffers are full (receipt) or
empty (sending), or when special characters are
detected and when error conditions occur (data lost,
parity error, carrier lost, etc.). Programs are
arranged in order of priority.

6.6   Example

One of the two systems is described hereunder in more
detail. This example is based on the Thomson Houston
system.

6.6.1   Each program has a priority level and the priority is
re-considered after each unit of the system timer (100 ms).
Each procedure (see 2.2a,b,c,d) involves one program for
input and one for output, associated with their specific
interrupt sub routine (see Figure 8) which performs
special character recognition and buffer switching up to
the complete reception or transmission of a data block.
Input and output programs analyse the validity of the
block according to the procedure rules. Blocks correctly
received are transferred with their identifiers in a
general chained queue and the input program disregards
them completely. A "Message Analyser and Message
Transfer" program scans the above-mentioned queue. In
each block found there, it checks the following points:

a)   is the output circuit operational;

b)   is the code of the characters in the block
     consistent with the receiving end of the output
     circuit;

c)   is the block of the message in sequence with the
     preceding block of the same message;

d)   is the output program ready to process the block
     (output queue).

If all the above mentioned conditions are met, the block
is transferred to the corresponding output program.
Otherwise it may be dropped or remains in the queue. If
it is dropped the SP informs the HLC by a service
message.

6.6.2   The main memory is partitioned in fixed length buffers
which are taken one after the other in a free chained
list. When the buffers again become available they are
returned to the free chained list.
A block correctly received is stored in chained buffers.
After each buffer pickup the SP checks, if memory is still
available. In case of saturation, the SP first informs
teleprinters to stop generating traffic, then, if

necessary, reduces the poll rate on the agent set circuits and finally stops receiving traffic from HLCs. Return to normal working conditions is always done progressively to avoid burst effects. The parameters of each data block received (address of the first buffer, block chaining number, input line, priority etc.) are placed in a special buffer called the "Block Identifier" which is of 3 character length and taken from a pool of chained buffers. All the blocks are then represented by these special buffers.
The number of special buffers is computed so that it corresponds to the maximum number of blocks that can be received in the main memory.

6.6.3 Each time an SP restarts after a failure (power failure, watchdog timer, interrupt stall) it informs its HLC that it is ready for reload by means of a simplified version of the Link Control procedure via the HLC-SP link. The HLC can at will,

a) load the SP

b) reconfigure the SP circuits

c) dump its memory

d) reinitialise it.

7. RESULTS - PERFORMANCES

At present the majority of traffic handled by the SITA network is still type B. However, a rapid increase of the type A is expected within the next few years.

7.1 High Level Centres

As an example consider the High Level Centre in Paris: the traffic switched there from the Low Level Network to the High Level Network or vice versa, is in the order of 1.2 messages per second during peak conditions.
If the messages switched from Low Level to Low Level are also taken into account, 4 messages per second are received and 5.5 are sent. The difference between the last two figures is due to multi-addressing.
Average switching times for type B messages entering or leaving the HLN are around 150 ms.
As far as blocks which are just core switched are concerned, the mean value is in the order of 20 ms.
Downtimes per month of HLCs are around 2 hours, including all scheduled stops for service reasons (configuration changes, new program versions, etc.)

7.2 HLN

The probability that any pair of HLCs is completely
isolated i.e. no route between them is available, is
negligible. The corresponding downtimes are in the order
of minutes a month.
The average number of messages leaving the HLN during
peak conditions is about 7 per second.
Usual line loads during normal peak conditions are
between 0.30 and 0.40 Erlang.

7.3 Response Time

The average response time for Type A messages, i.e. the
time lapse between the instant an operator presses the
transmit key of his terminal to send his query and the
instant the first character of the reply appears on the
screen (see Figure 6) ranges from 1.4 seconds to 3
seconds, depending on the number of links involved in route.
A typical response time distribution is shown in figure 9.

7.4 Satellite Processors

The downtime of SPs is around 16 hours per month including
scheduled and unscheduled stops (e.g. preventive
maintenance, configuration changes, etc.)
Presently, certain SPs switch up to 6 message blocks per
second during peak conditions of traffic.
Switching times are in the order of 5 ms per block for
both systems.

*   *   *

Note:

The Authors have restricted their article to the SITA
operating network in 1973. However, it is clear that
this network is in continuous expansion and that new
automated centres will be operational within a few months.

*   *   *

390

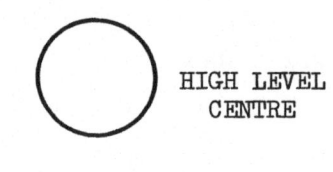

HIGH LEVEL
CENTRE

SATELLITE
PROCESSOR

CPH

AMS

BRU

LON

STO   TLV

BER
DUS

MUC   FRA

NYC

NCE   GVA   ZRH

VIE

PAR   ROM

CAS   TUN

MAD

MIL   ATH

BCN   PMI

FIGURE I   The SITA Medium Speed Network

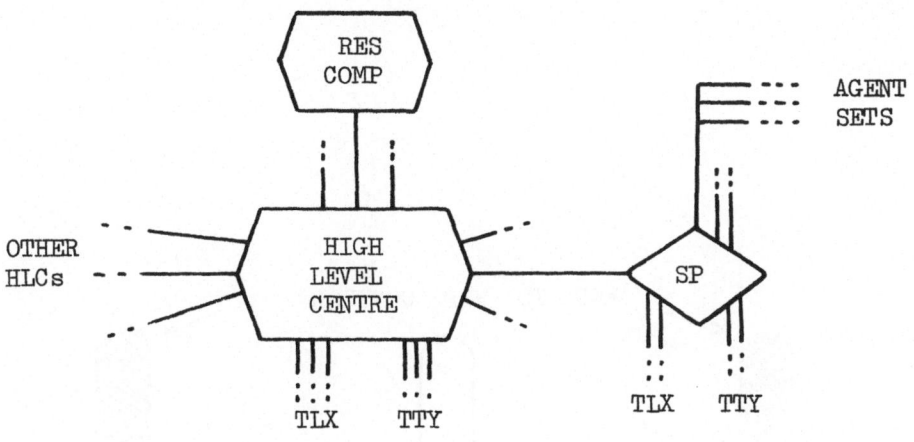

FIGURE II   High Level Centre and Satellite Processor
Interfaces

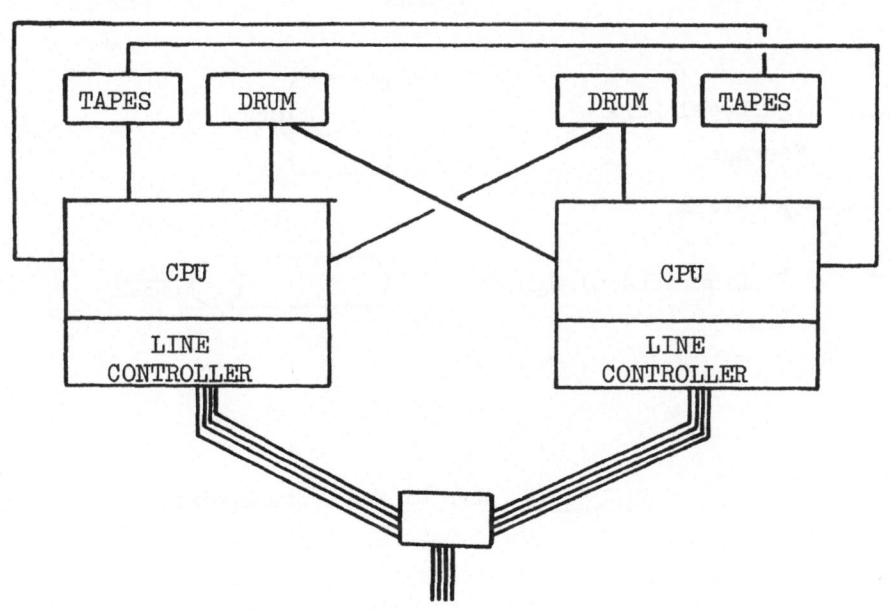

FIGURE III   A Typical High Level Centre Configuration

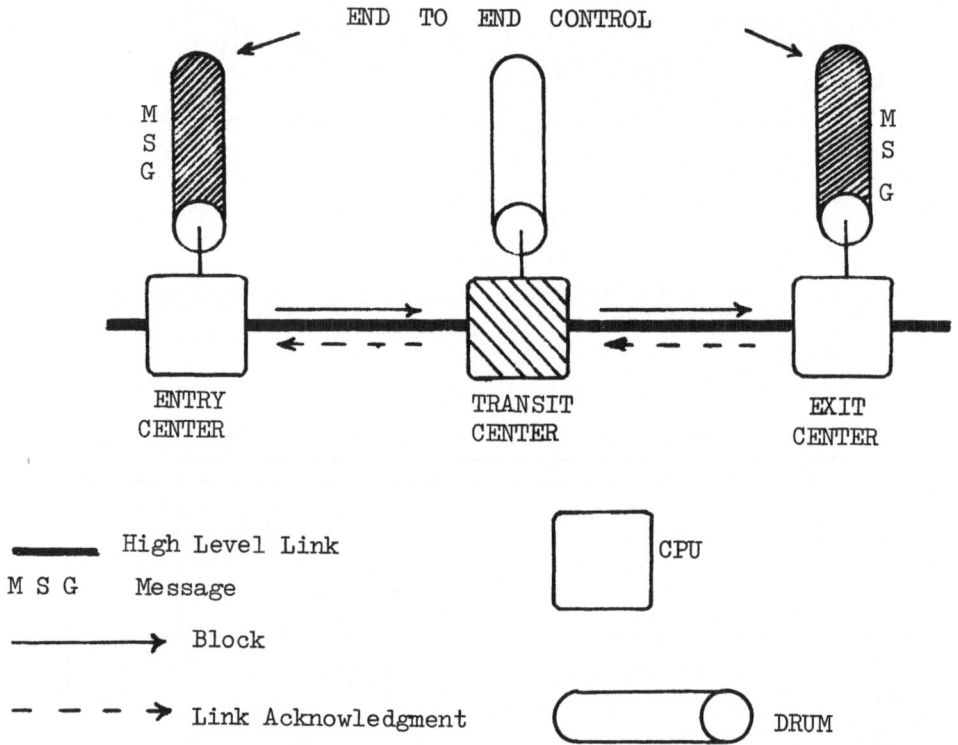

END TO END CONTROL

M S G ... M S G

ENTRY CENTER   TRANSIT CENTER   EXIT CENTER

——— High Level Link

M S G   Message

——————→ Block

— — — → Link Acknowledgment

CPU

DRUM

FIGURE IV   End to End Acknowledgment

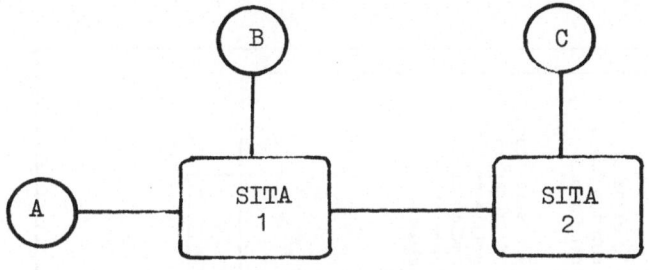

FIGURE V   Message Responsibility

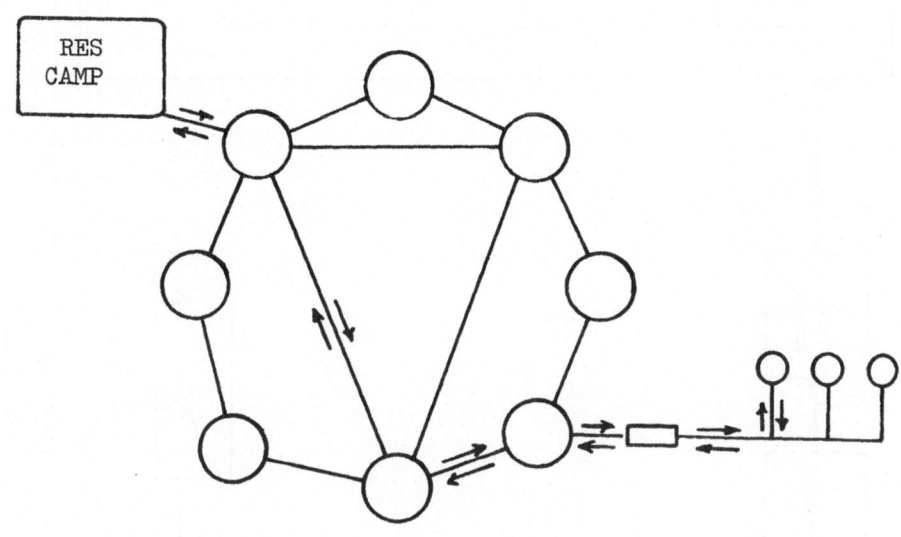

HIGH LEVEL CENTRE

SATELLITE PROCESSOR

CRT

FIGURE VI   Type a Message Path

394

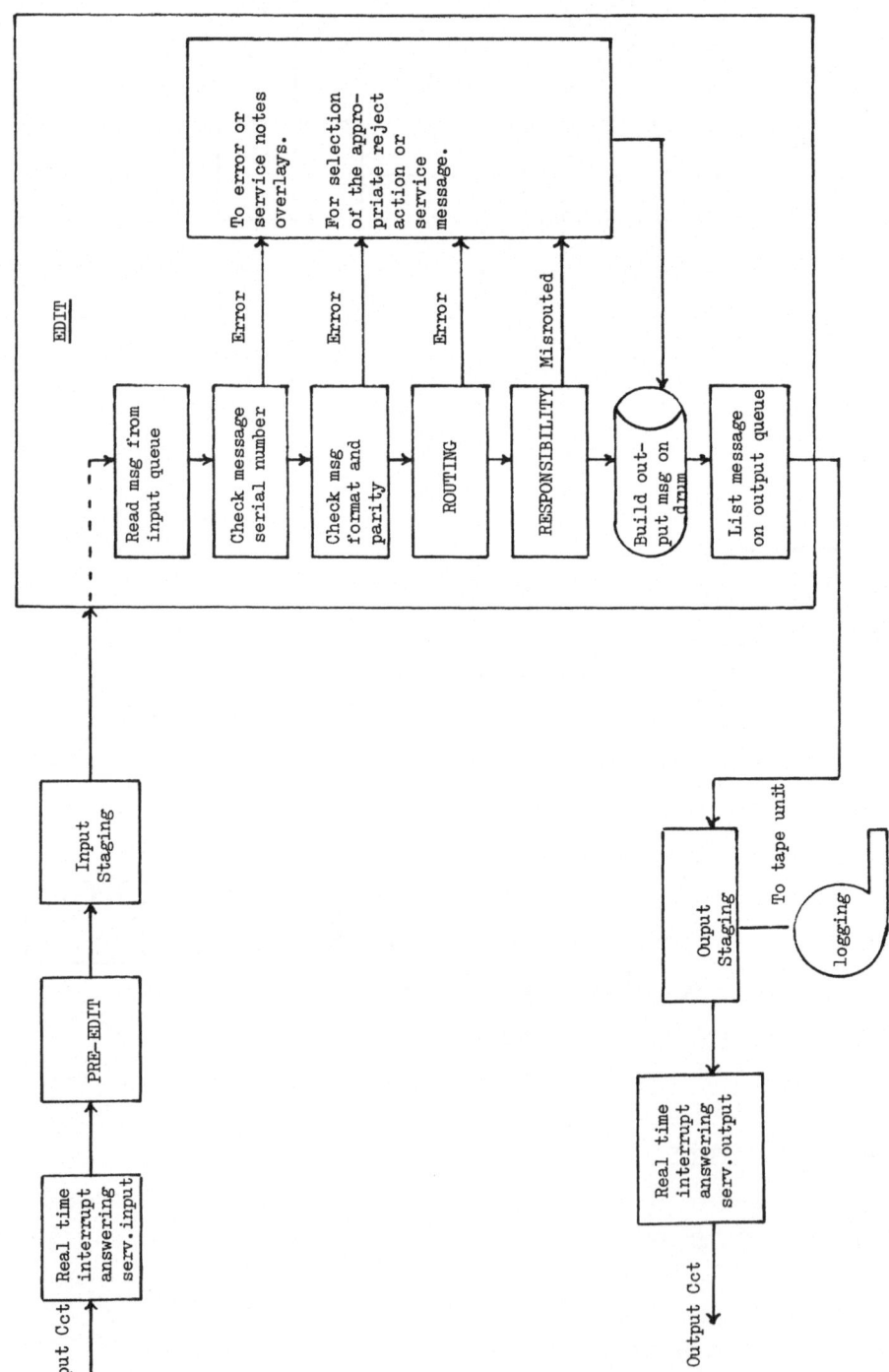

FIGURE VII   Message Switching Programs for Type "B". (Simplified description).

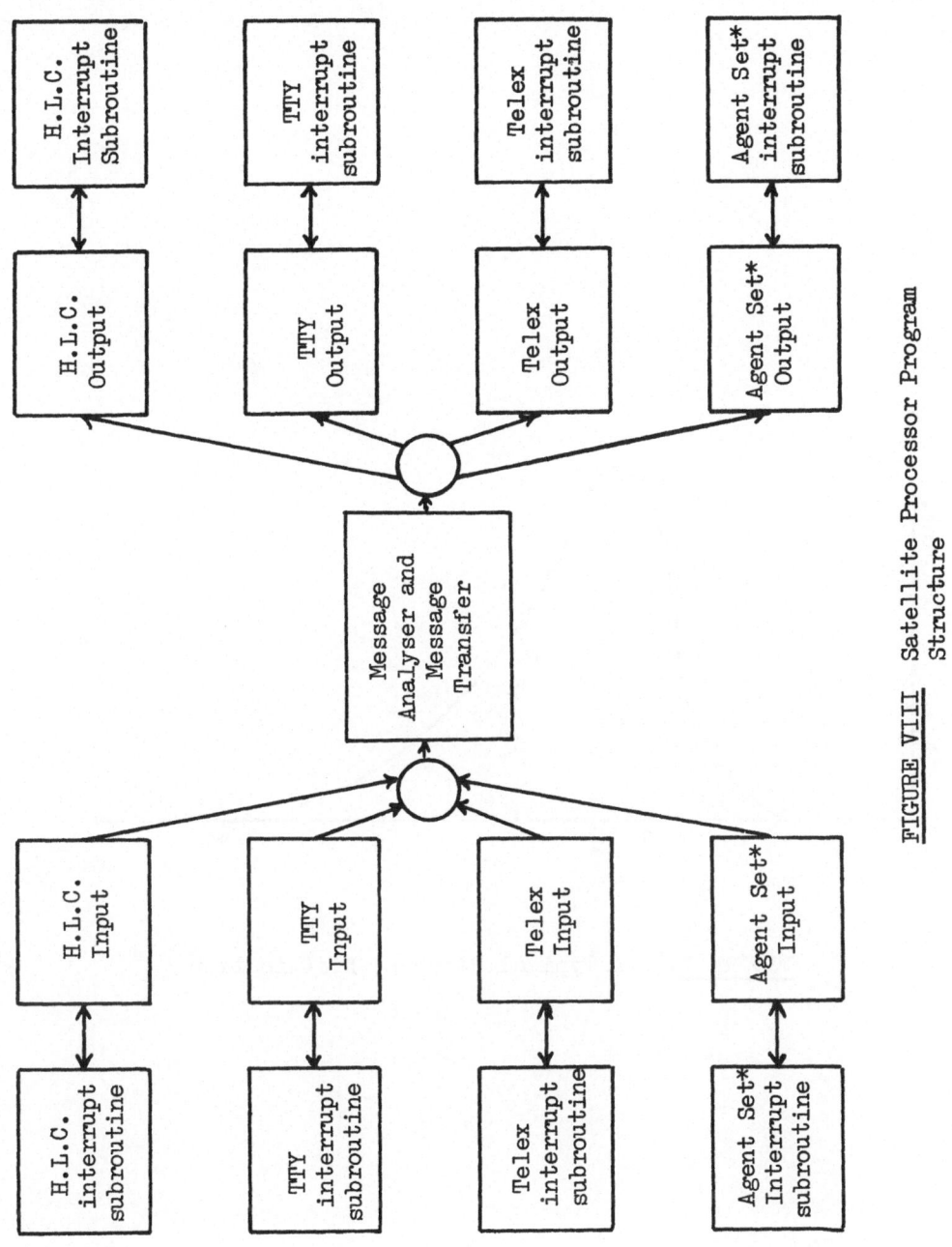

FIGURE VIII   Satellite Processor Program
Structure

* Here just one Type A handler is included.

396

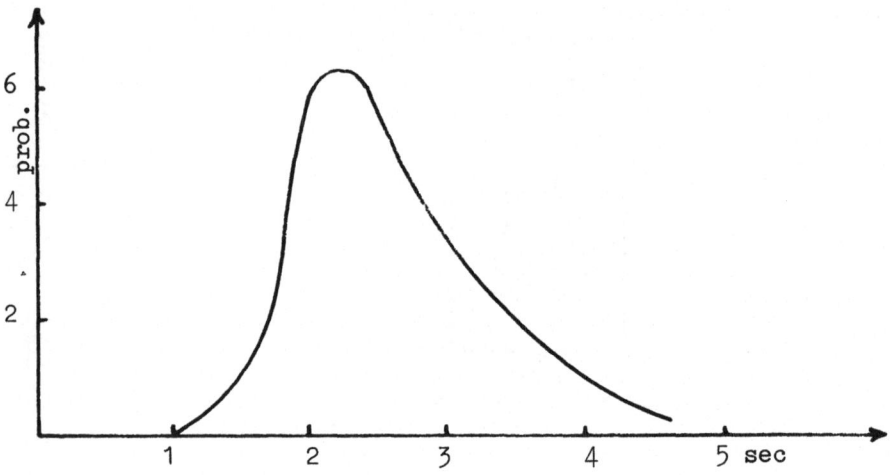

<u>FIGURE IX</u>   A Typical Response Distribution

COMPUTER-COMMUNICATIONS BY RADIO AND SATELLITE: THE ALOHA SYSTEM*

Franklin F. Kuo and Richard D. Binder

THE ALOHA SYSTEM, University of Hawaii

ABSTRACT

In this paper we describe an experimental UHF radio computer communication network - THE ALOHA SYSTEM - under development for the past five years at the University of Hawaii. Presently in operation on an experimental basis, the existing ALOHA SYSTEM computer-communication network uses two 24,000 baud channels at 407.350 MHz and at 413.475 MHz in the upper UHF band. The system uses packet switching techniques similar to that employed by the ARPANET, in conjunction with a novel form of random-access radio channel multiplexing. Recently THE ALOHA SYSTEM has become the first satellite node on the ARPANET in which a TIP (Terminal Interface Processor) located at the University of Hawaii campus communicates through a 50 kilobit data channel using INTELSAT IV with the NASA/AMES TIP and into the ARPANET. The 50 kilobit satellite channel occupies a single PCM voice channel on INTELSAT IV.

Our current activities are concentrated on two major areas--radio and satellite. In the radio area, we are presently developing a Phase II ALOHA SYSTEM with minicomputers used as programmable terminals and repeaters. In the satellite area we are working on a project involving the NASA satellite ATS-1 with small inexpensive

---

*THE ALOHA SYSTEM is a research project at the University of Hawaii, supported by the Advanced Research Projects Agency of the Department of Defense and monitored by NASA Ames Research Center under Contract No. NAS2-6700, the U. S. Air Force Office of Aerospace Research (SRMA) under Air Force Contract No. F44620-69-C-0030 (a Project THEMIS award) and the National Science Foundation under NSF Grant No. GJ-33220.

ground stations. This study is linked to another ALOHA SYSTEM project--that of a feasibility study of a Pacific Educational Computer Network (PACNET) to link computers in developed countries and developing countries in the Pacific.

1. THE ALOHA SYSTEM

THE ALOHA SYSTEM is composed of a related series of contracts and grants from a variety of funding agencies which deal with two main themes: computer communications, and computer structures.

Under computer-communications there is work in (a) Studies on computer-communications using radio and satellites, (b) The development of a prototype radio-linked time-sharing network, (c) System studies and planning for a Pacific area computer communications network linking major universities in the U. S., Japan, Australia and other Pacific countries.

Under computer structures, we are engaged in research, development in multiprocessor computing structures, computer networks, and geographically distributed computing systems. This work is being undertaken in two phases: 1) the establishment of a research facility and 2) the research work itself. The research facility is centered around the BCC 500 computing system which is presently under development. This system, when completed in a few years' time will have the capability of handling a large number of university user terminals and will become a significant university resource.

In this paper we will be mainly concerned with the work in computer-communications.

2. RADIO COMMUNICATIONS

Developments in remote access computing during the latter part of the 1960's have resulted in increasing importance of remote time-sharing, remote job entry and networking for large information processing systems. The present generation of computer-communication systems is based on the use of leased or dial-up common carrier facilities, primarily wire connections. Under many conditions such communication facilities offer the best possible communications option to the overall system designer of a large computer-communication facility. In other circumstances, however, the organization of common carrier data communication systems seriously limits the possibilities of a large information processing system.

Since September 1968, THE ALOHA SYSTEM Project at the University of Hawaii has investigated alternatives to the use of conventional wire communications in a geographically diffuse computer system. When the constraint of data communications by wire is eliminated a number of options for different methods of organizing data communications within a computer-communications net are made available to the system designer. THE ALOHA SYSTEM Project has investigated the use of a new and simple form of random access communications for a statewide university computing system; the first links in this UHF radio-linked computer system, were set up in mid-1971.

In Fig. 1 we show the present configuration of THE ALOHA SYSTEM. The central computer of the University, an IBM 360/65 with 2.5 Mbytes of core memory presently runs under OS MVT and in addition to background batch, runs two timesharing systems, APL and TSO. THE ALOHA SYSTEM is one of the TSO users and is connected to the 360 computer via the HP2100 computer which serves as a data-concentrator and multiplexor. Since the functions of the 2100 machine is much like that of the Interface Message Processor (IMP) [1] used in the ARPANET [2] we have dubbed the 2100 the MENEHUNE, a legendary Hawaiian imp. The modem operates at 24,000 baud and uses differential phase shift keyed modulation. The demodulator has been specially designed for our application so as to optimally operate on the coherent signal by using a phase-locked-loop to recover bit timing and a matched filter to recover the signal in the presence of noise. The transmitter-receivers are primarily standard commercial FM transceivers, modified to accommodate the system specifications. On the terminal (which we call KEIKI) end, the central piece of equipment is the communications module developed by THE ALOHA SYSTEM called the Terminal Control Unit (TCU) (Fig. 2). The TCU consists of a UHF antenna, transceiver, modem and buffer control unit all in a compact chassis. Thus the TCU duplicates on the terminal end, all of the separate pieces of equipment on the HOST side. A TCU can interface a wide variety of terminals operating at speeds up to 24,000 baud. We have connected teletype terminals (TTY), CRT displays (Hazeltine 2000), graphics processors (ARDS and Imlac) and minicomputers (HP2114 and Imlac) to the TCU's with equal ease into the ALOHA channels. In the minicomputer connections the buffer control function of the TCU is handled by a software package in the minicomputer. Because of the efficient use of channel capacity by the ALOHA burst random access communication method the present channel is only lightly loaded. We have calculated that well over 500 active alphanumeric terminals could use the present communication channels of THE ALOHA SYSTEM.

At present we are conducting system studies to investigate properties of the random-access channel used in different modes (unsynchronized, synchronized, contention, file scheduling, multiple frequency, etc.) by both analytical and computer simulation

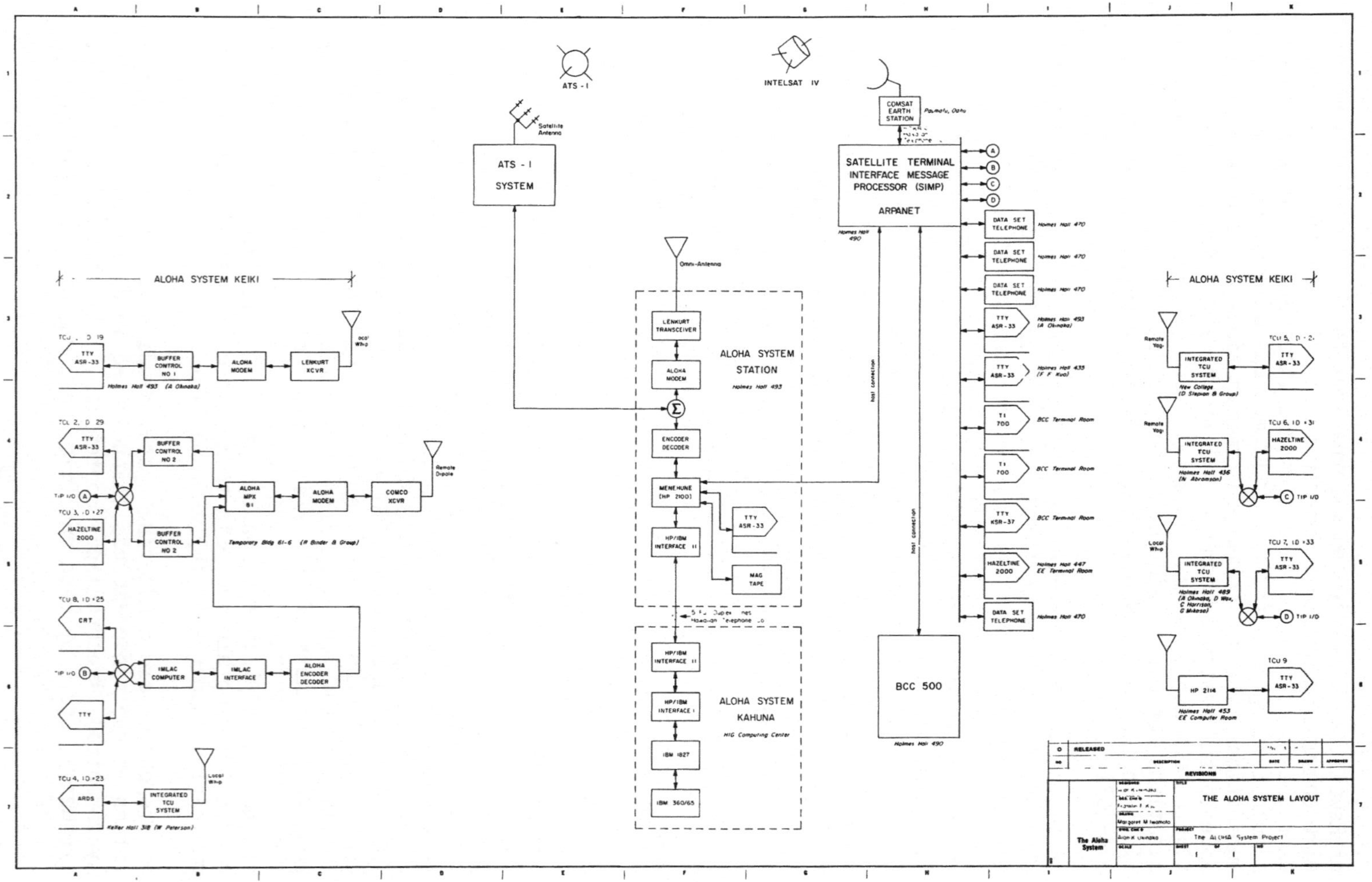

Figure 1. The ALOHA System Layout

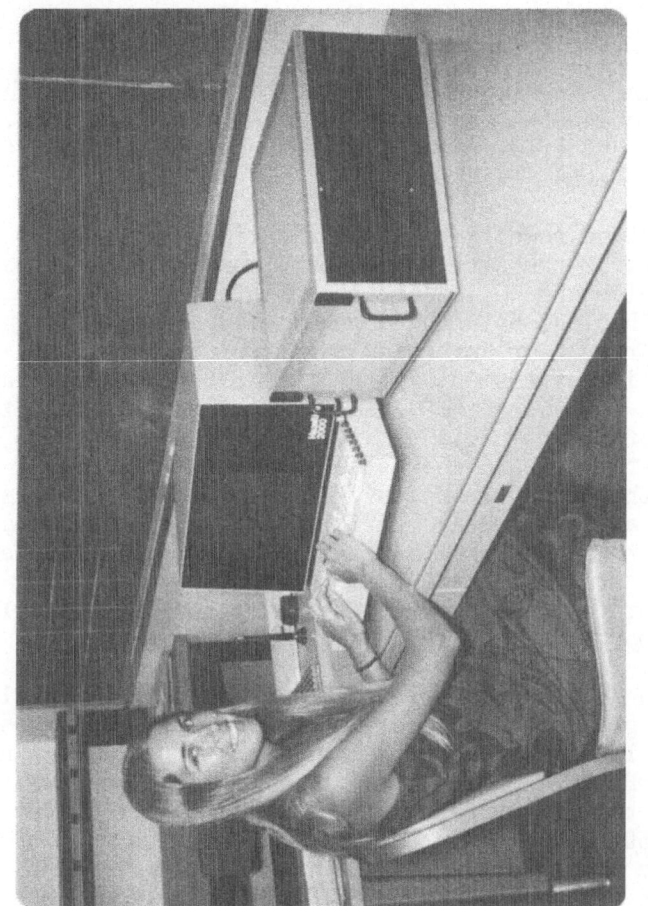

Figure 2   An ALOHA Terminal Control Unit (TCU)

methods. We are also investigating the effects of different
channel protocols upon system performance. We have purchased an
INTEL CPU on a single integrated circuit chip for the purpose of
developing a TCU with considerably more flexibility than the
present hard-wired versions. The TCU-on-a-chip will enable the
system to respond to a variety of different transmission protocols,
including variable length packets and character-by-character
transmission. Various error control procedures can also be
studied and implemented with this new TCU.

3. SATELLITE COMMUNICATIONS

We are now conducting experiments on the effective uses of high
capacity satellite channels for packet switched communications.
The experiments are centered around the geosynchronous satellites
ATS-1 of NASA and INTELSAT IV of COMSAT.

With the development of new digital communications systems by
COMSAT in which data at the rate of 50 Kbaud can be transmitted
through a single voice channel, data transmission by satellite
has become both technologically and economically realizable.
During the past year we have initiated two specific research
projects for satellite extension of THE ALOHA SYSTEM and several
theoretical studies involving the unique properties of satellite
channels. The first of the projects involves the use of large
commercial ground stations and the establishment of an ARPANET
SATELLITE SYSTEM; the second involves the use of small inexpensive
ground stations in a joint research effort with NASA Ames Research
Center. In regard to the ARPANET SATELLITE SYSTEM, we have been
involved in a joint study with ARPA, BBN, UCLA, and Xerox PARC to
design a suitable protocol for packet communications via satellite.
The results are reported in the 1973 NCC Proceedings [3], [4], [5].

In December 1972, a digital communications subsystem was installed
between the COMSAT ground stations at Paumalu, Hawaii and Jamesburg, California. The first subscriber of this service was ARPA
for inclusion of THE ALOHA SYSTEM into the ARPANET. The Hawaiian
TIP [6] has become the first operational satellite node on the
ARPANET. The BCC 500 computer is planned to be the main HOST of
the Hawaii TIP. We are also planning to connect the MENEHUNE
(the communications computer for the ALOHA net) as the second
HOST.

The second satellite project involves the use of the NASA satellite
ATS-1 using small inexpensive ground stations which cost less than
$5,000 each. Thus far we have progressed to the point where an
ALOHA random access burst mode channel is in operation between
the University of Hawaii, NASA/AMES Research Center and the
University of Alaska. During 1974 we plan to interface this

channel into computers near each of these ground stations, extend
the number of ground stations to other sites, including possibly
universities in Japan (Tohoku), Australia (Sydney), and other
Pacific countries and establish a small ground station satellite
network on an experimental basis.

We are also studying the possibility of using a complete trans-
onder on a U. S. domestic satellite for ARPA Network operation.
Such a transponder might provide megabit or higher data rates
using a transponder dedicated to packet switched operation and
terminating in a large number of moderately priced ground stations
at a cost of only a fraction of the expected land line costs by
the end of 1974. In addition to lower costs and higher speeds, a
packet switched transponder on a domestic satellite would provide
for higher network connectivity and enhanced possibilities for new
forms of resource sharing.

4. NETWORK INTERFACING

As mentioned in the previous section, we are presently connecting
the ARPANET to THE ALOHA SYSTEM MENEHUNE. In addition, a Telex
line to Tohoku, Japan and the ATS-1 satellite link to NASA/AMES
and the University of Alaska are being connected to the MENEHUNE.
Thus we have essentially four separate networks being interfaced
at the MENEHUNE (Fig. 3), each with different protocols. Let us
call the resulting interconnection configuration a gateway.

Some of the protocol differences which must be resolved in a gateway are: error control, flow control, and formatting [7], [8].
An example of error control is whether the network requires a
positive acknowledgement for each message sent to or from terminals
In addition to the control of errors, this aspect of protocol has
a direct effect on the amount of buffering required in the system.
Flow control, while influenced by error control, generally requires
separate signaling to indicate when a destination can or is willing
to accept new messages. For example, in THE ALOHA SYSTEM a completion signal is sent to the 360 HOST computer whenever a terminal
has finished displaying the last message sent to it, minimizing
buffer requirements in the communication system. The generation
of this signal requires knowledge of the terminal display rate,
which may not be available when connected to different networks.
Reformatting is essentially not a problem as long as sufficient
computing power exists at the gateway so as not to introduce un-
desired delays.

A consideration not mentioned above, but perhaps the most important for gateway design, is that of growth. Each network should be
able to expand its resources without requiring changes to the gateway (within reasonable constraints). This has a strong effect on

404

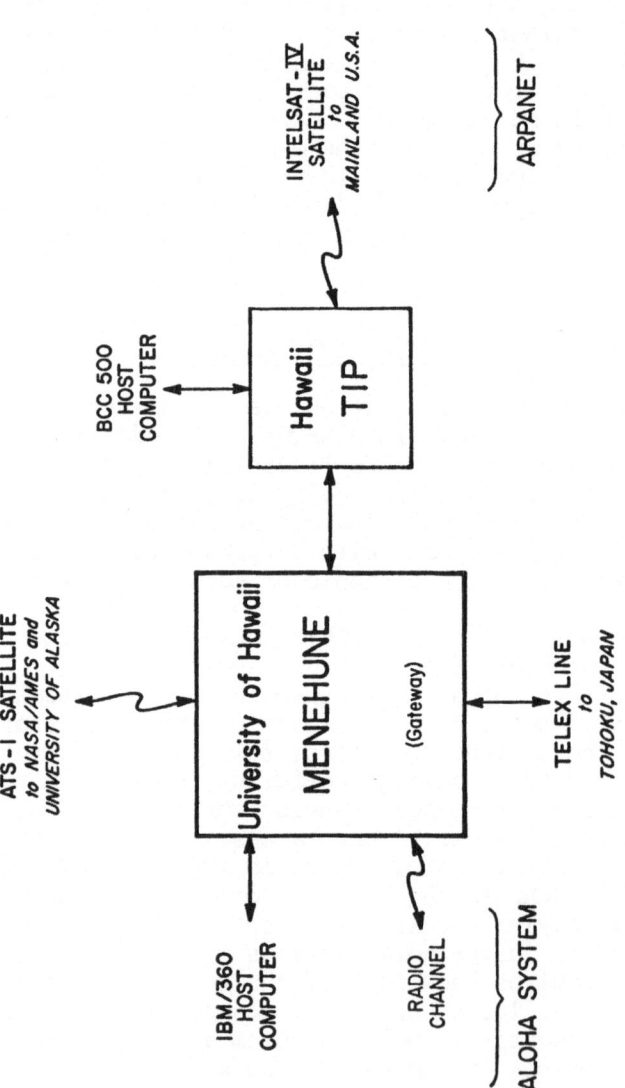

Figure 3 Gateway Configuration

the type of organization which can be used in the gateway, such as the use of permanent tables which reflect the organization and current resources of the individual networks.

The University of Hawaii gateway design approach is to interface each network through a central routing interface. The routing interface will be independent of individual network protocol, and will instead have a standard protocol of its own. This common protocol will have provisions for dynamically establishing different error and flow control procedures between network interfaces. This approach results in network interface "drivers" (analogous to terminal I/O drivers) and a single central routing module (the central interface).

Each network driver must know both the common interface protocol and the idiosyncracies of the network it is directly interfacing. The drivers will contain network-specific tables of required information, and in general, may need to be modified when changes are made to their respective networks. The drivers need not be located in the same machine as the central router; the common interface protocol is designed to allow communication between a driver and the router over phone lines or other media if desired.

The central router, on the other hand, will not contain network-specific information. Each network driver will be assigned an ID for use in its communications with the central router. The Driver ID will in effect form an "area code", and will be prefixed to each individual terminal or HOSE ID passed between the drivers and the router. All messages sent to or from the router will contain both originator and destination ID's; the router will simply pass a received message on to the destination Driver; except for certain special messages to be described in the following paragraphs.

Some functions now provided by individual networks seem more appropriately placed in the central interface, where they may be used by all networks while simplifying (at least some) drivers. Two that will be initially implemented in the University of Hawaii router are (1) establishing a connection between two or more nodes in different networks, and (2) allowing two or more terminals to link together (whether in the same or different networks).

To establish a connection with a node in another network, a user will communicate directly with the router by use of a special "escape" character. If the request is accepted by the destination network, the router will pass information to the originating node's network driver to be used for subsequent messages. When the user is finished, he will again send a special message to the router, which will cause the connection to be erased in the tables of the originator and destination drivers.

Centralized linking requires more sophistication on the part of the router, but no new mechanism in the drivers.

5. CONCLUSIONS

A major new effort now underway is the inclusion of radio repeater nodes in the existing ALOHA SYSTEM, which is being undertaken as part of a larger ARPA project to develop a nationwide packet radio system. The first repeater installation will link the island of Maui with the existing system on Oahu.

The new repeaters are planned to have considerable intelligence in that microcomputers will be incorporated into the design. It is expected that these repeaters, together with the portable TCU's that are being developed will add considerable flexibility in the development of a statewide computing facility for the University.

The ATS-1 satellite computer communications project is the first step in the development of a Pacific Educational Computer Network (PACNET) which is projected to be an international resource-sharing network of computers, terminals, data banks, and software linked by advanced techniques in satellite and data transmission. If PACNET is successful, it will usher in a new age of international cooperation in resource-sharing.

6. REFERENCES

[1] Heart, F. E., Kahn, R. E., Ornstein, S. M., Crowther, W. R., Walden, D. C., The interface message processor for the ARPA computer network, *AFIPS Conference Proceedings*, 36, 551, 1970.

[2] Roberts, L. G., and Wessler, B., The ARPA network, in *Computer-Communication Networks*, Abramson, N., and Kuo, F. F., Eds., Prentice-Hall, New Jersey, 1973, 13.

[3] Abramson, N., Packet switching with satellites, *AFIPS Conference Proceedings*, 42, 695, 1973.

[4] Kleinrock, L. and Lam, S. S., Packet-switching in a slotted satellite channel, *AFIPS Conference Proceedings*, 42, 703, 1973.

[5] Roberts, L. G., Dynamic allocation of satellite capacity through packet reservation, *AFIPS Conference Proceedings*, 42, 711, 1973.

[6] Ornstein, S. M., Heart, F. E., Crowther, W. R., Rising, H. K., Russell, S. B., Michel, A., The terminal IMP for the ARPA computer network, *AFIPS Conference Proceedings*, 40, 243, 1972.

[7] Frank, H., Kahn, R. E., Kleinrock, L., Computer communication network design-experience with theory and practice, *AFIPS Conference Proceedings*, 40, 255, 1972.

[8] Kahn, R. E., and Crowther, W. R., Floor control in a resource-sharing computer network, *Second Symposium on Problems in the Optimization of Data Communications Systems*, 108, 1971.

THE COST PROJECT 11: THE EUROPEAN INFORMATICS NETWORK

D.L.A. Barber B.Sc.(Eng.); C.Eng.; M.I.E.E.

Director - E.I.N. Project

Introduction

In November 1971 the Ministers of eight European nations: France, Yugoslavia, Italy, Norway, Portugal, Switzerland, Sweden, and the United Kingdom, together with the Euratom Centre at Ispra, signed an agreement to start a project aimed at building a European computer network. The location of these centres is shown in Figure 1.

The background to the formation of the project and the description of its early stages is described in a previous paper given at the ICCC meeting in Washington in October 1972. This short paper brings the subject up to date by reporting recent developments.

The unique feature of the Cost Project 11 is its truly international nature, with several countries combining and supporting it financially. This feature makes the project very important in a number of respects; apart from technical aspects a key feature is the management of a distributed project. An apparently inevitable disadvantage is the time it takes to carry out some of the phases of the project, but this seems to be improving as experience is gained.

Some of the early stages of the Cost Project 11 have taken a considerable time to complete, because they were concerned with establishing the project, and several precedents had to be created. However, the way now seems clear for the project to go ahead, and it is to be hoped that most of the remaining difficulties will be technical problems.

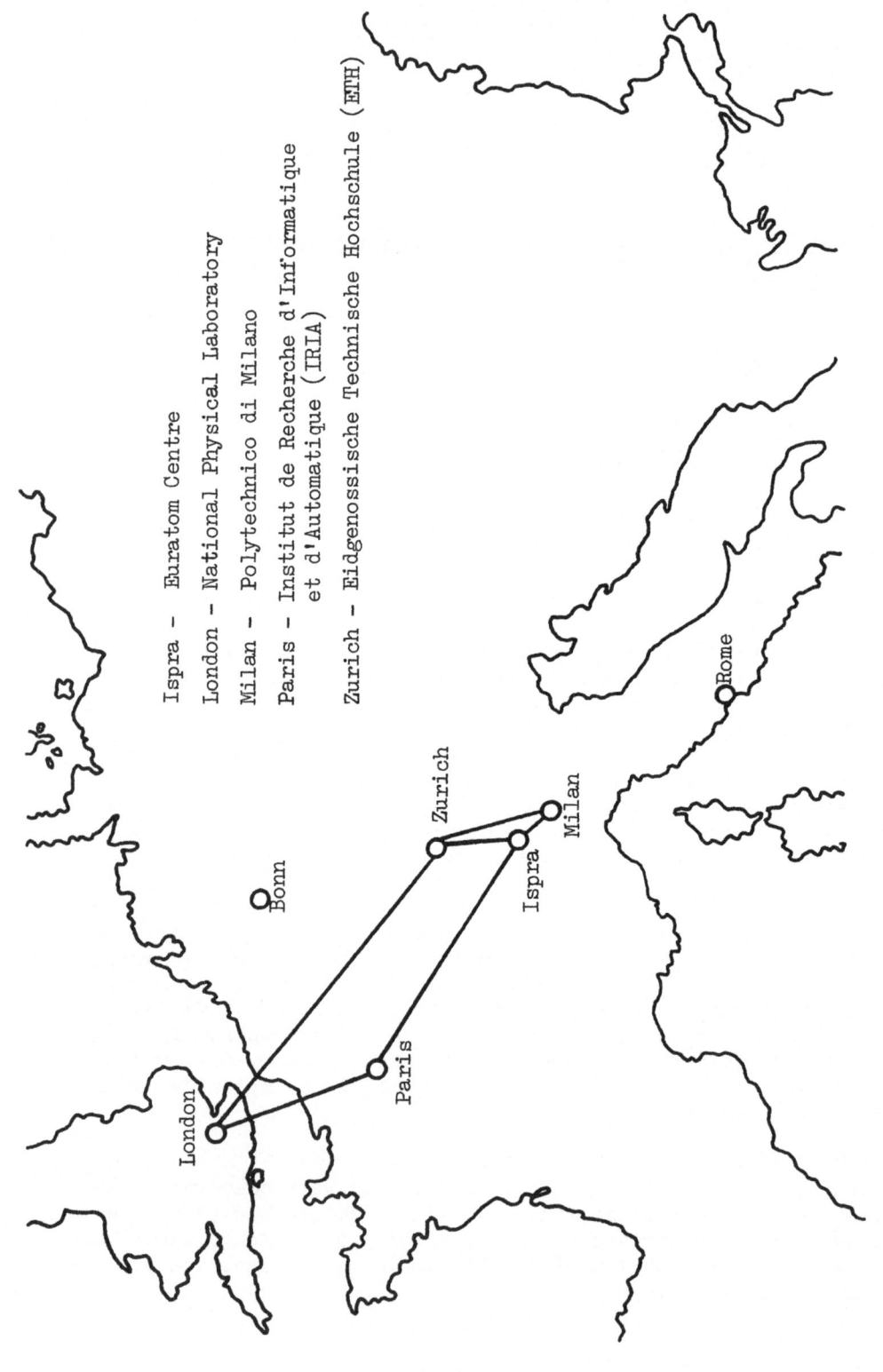

Ispra – Euratom Centre

London – National Physical Laboratory

Milan – Polytechnico di Milano

Paris – Institut de Recherche d'Informatique
et d'Automatique (IRIA)

Zurich – Eidgenossische Technische Hochschule (ETH)

Background to Project

Following the signing of the treaty there was a delay while
the various countries concerned signified their ratification of
the treaty. This took a differing time depending on the internal
procedures adopted by each country. The treaty called for a 2/3
ratification by signatories before work could begin; the necessary
condition was met on the 1st February 1972. Immediately after
this, work began on finalizing the specification for the network.
This was based on a draft previously prepared by a study group
before the signing of the treaty.

In May 1972 the author of this paper was appointed Director of
the Executive Body which was charged with implementing the project
and the negotiations for the appointment of the Technical Assist-
ants to the Executive Body were completed by the end of August.
Meanwhile, the specification had been completed and circulated to
organisations thought to be interested in submitting tenders as
main contractor for the project. A meeting of the interested organisations was held in Brussels at the end of August, so that
the project could be described and questions about the specification answered.

Present Situation

At the meeting with contractors an invitation was extended to
the organisations present to form consortia to submit tenders. A
number of criteria to be met by a consortium were put to the meeting and an invitation was extended to those present to write a
letter expressing interest to the Director of the Executive Body.
At the time of presentation of this paper, the letters are awaited
with keen interest. The invitation to organisations was as follows:

The Management Committee believe that an undertaking of such
complexity, involving international co-operation, can best be done
by a contractor having a head office in Europe, and willing to
undertake responsibility for the whole Project. This responsibility
would include the design of the Network, and possibly, the installation and the subsequent maintenance of the complete Network for
the term of the project.

There is no objection to the sub-contracting of work to other
organisations, but the main contractor must undertake the responsibility for the success of the whole project.

In the interest both of the organisations invited to tender,
and of the Management Committee for the project, it is desirable
to invite tenders only from those organisations that can demonstrate an ability to undertake it successfully. For this reason,

organisations submitting tenders must indicate clearly their competence in the following areas:

1. The design of real-time computer systems.

2. The design and successful implementation of data communications systems.

3. The design of an interrupt-driven operating system and its implementation in a medium-level or a high-level language.

4. The installation and subsequent maintenance of a computer system of comparable scope.

5. The resolution of the problems of communication between computers, particularly those of defining a network control language.

6. The development of high-level protocols for co-operation between mixed computer systems.

7. The use of modern management methods for the control of a development project.

The organisation should also describe briefly its approach to system definition, documentation and production, and indicate the compilers diagnostic aids etc., that will be employed.

The tender must also include evidence that the financial stability of the organisation concerned is guaranteed for the term of the proposed contract.

Because the project is an international one, it will be desirable, but not essential, that the organisation undertaking it is a consortium of companies from two or more of those countries taking part in the Agreement. Such an organisation must be able to give evidence of other international projects successfully undertaken.

The Communication-Sub-network

The specification lays down many of the properties of the communication sub-network, but many detailed features remain to be determined by the contractor appointed to implement the project. One of the key features of the network is the interface that it will present to the computers which are connected to it. The present specification has suggested an interface similar to that for the Experimental Packet Switching Service of the British Post Office, but certain modifications are introduced to cover the

special requirements of the International Network. The early definition of the network interface is of prime importance to allow
the parallel development of systems and the modification of equipment and software at the National Centres.

The Use of the Network

Once the communication sub-network interface is defined it becomes possible to prepare for the use of the network in parallel
with its development. Working parties have been established comprising members of the National Centres to examine a strategy for
the development of equipment, software and other facilities necessary to make use of the network. These activities lie broadly in
two areas; the first of these is the development of machine independent high level protocols and a network control language to
allow users to command the use of the network's resources; the
second activity is the definition of fairly simple projects which
can be carried out in the absence of the network in order to promote early interactions between the centres it will ultimately
join. Examples of these experiments might be the connection of the
information retrieval system at Ispra with the Scrapbook interactive data manipulation system at the National Physical Laboratory.
Scrapbook is being used to hold all the documentation for the Cost
11 Project and there will be very definite advantages in making the
access to Scrapbook one of the early features of the network project.

To promote these kinds of co-operation leased lines will be introduced between centres at an early stage. The first of these
between NPL and IRIA is expected to be available before the end of
this year.

Conclusion

In conclusion, there is no doubt that the Cost Project 11 will
play an important role in Europe in the next few years. It is not
clear at this stage what the future will bring and there are many
problems to be solved. But the extreme goodwill and eagerness for
the project to succeed which has been shown by all those involved
in it from the beginning augers well for its eventual success. Considering the international nature of this project and the consequent
differences between it and most other computer network projects,
progress to date has been surprisingly good. Given that the bene-
volent attitudes remain, some very valuable lessons will be learned
about international communication networks and also about the management of small scale international projects, i.e. about the
problems of communication between people.

PRESENTATION AND MAJOR DESIGN ASPECTS

OF THE CYCLADES COMPUTER NETWORK[1]

by Louis POUZIN

Institut de Recherche d'Informatique et d'Automatique (IRIA)

Rocquencourt, France

[1] This paper has been originally published in the proceedings of the Third Data Communications Symposium, Tampa, Nov. 1973. It is reproduced with kind permission of ACM-IEEE.

SUMMARY

A computer network is being developed in France, under government
sponsorship, to link about twenty heterogeneous computers located
in universities, research and D.P. Centers. Goals are to set up
a prototype network in order to foster experiment in various
areas, such as : data communications, computer interaction, cooperative research, distributed data bases. The network is intended
to be both an object for research, and an operational tool.

In order to speed up the implementation, standard equipment is
used, and modifications to operating systems are minimized.
Rather, the design effort bears on a carefully layered architecture, allowing for a gradual insertion of specialized protocols
and services tailored to specific application and user classes.

A particular objective, for which CYCLADES should be an operation-
nal tool, is to provide various departments of the French
Administration with access to multiple data bases located in
geographically distant areas.

Host-host protocols, as well as error and flow control mechanisms
are based on a simple message exchange procedure, on top of which
various options may be built for the sake of efficiency, error
recovery, or convenience. Depending on available computer resources, these options can be implemented as user software, system
modules, or front end processor package. For each of them, network-
wide interfaces are defined to conserve consistency in human communications.

CYCLADES uses a packet-switching sub-network, which is a transparent message carrier, completely independent of host-host
conventions. While in many ways similar to ARPANET, it presents
some distinctive differences in address and message handling,
intended to facilitate interconnection with other networks. In
particular, addresses can have variable formats, and messages
are not delivered in sequence, so that they can flow out of the
network through several gates toward an outside target.

Terminal concentrators are mini-hosts, and implement whatever
services users or applications require, such as sequencing, error
recovery, code translation, buffering, etc... Some specialized
hosts may be installed to cater for specific services, such as
mail, ressource allocation, information retrieval, mass storage.
A control center is also being installed and will be operated by
the French PTT.

I. INTRODUCTION

CYCLADES is one of the more recent computer network projects, which has been launched in France beginning with 1972. Its conception carries most of the characteristics found in the type of general purpose heterogeneous computer network such as experimented by ARPA, or proposed by NPL.

Our goals are to construct a prototype network in order to foster experiments in various areas, such as : data communications, computer interaction, cooperative research, distributed data bases. This action is two-fold. In order to acquire valid experience, the network must also be used in a realistic environment, which requires a variety of operational services acceptable by customer standards.

In order to speed up the implementation, standard equipment is used, and modifications to operating systems are minimized. Rather the design effort bears on a carefully layered architecture, providing for an extensible structure of protocols and network services, tailored to various classes of traffic and applications.

This concern for built-in evolutionism translates itself in putting as few features as possible at levels buried in the sensitive parts of the network. With experience gradually building up, and depending on trends in international standards, more stable characteristics will eventually emerge. By putting them at some lower system level, it will be possible to obtain higher efficiency and reduce duplication, at the cost of freezing a few more parameters.

The Cyclades design attempts to be both precise and independent from the implementation at the user level, so that heterogeneous sites can have their way, and still communicate with others in a consistent manner.

II. PARTICIPANTS AND EQUIPMENT

Cyclades is sponsored by the Délégation à l'Informatique, a government agency in charge of coordinating all activities related to computing. Participating centers are only partially funded and put their own contribution on a voluntary basis. In a first stage, all network centers are research oriented organizations, universities, or engineering schools. In a second stage some D.P. centers of the French Administration will be connected to phase in real applications.

Participating centers are :

- Institut de Recherche en Informatique et Automatique (IRIA), (2 centers)

- Compagnie Internationale pour l'Informatique (CII), (2 centers)

- Météorologie Nationale (METEO)

- Institut de Recherche des Transports (IRT)

- Université de Grenoble (IMAG)

- Centre Universitaire de Calcul de Lyon (CCILS)

- Ecole des Mines de Saint-Etienne (MINES)

- Université de Toulouse (TOU)

- Centre d'Etudes et de Recherches de Toulouse (CERT)

- Centre Electronique de l'Armement (CELAR)

- Université de Rennes (REN)

- Centre Commun d'Etudes de Télécommunications et Télévision (CCETT)

- Ecole Supérieure d'Electricité (ESE)

- Centre National d'Etudes des Télécommunications (CNET)

Computers are :

9 CII - 10070, 2 CII - IRIS/80, 2 CII - IRIS/50, 1 IBM 360/67, 1 CDC 6600, 1 PHILIPS - 1200. Communications computers are CII-MITRA/15.

The Cyclades topology is shown on Fig. 1. Transmission lines range from 4.8 kb up to 48 kb. The French PTT are providing lines and modems free of charge till end 1975. Also they will run the network control center.

III. PLANNING

The Cyclades project was launched on the beginning of 1972. First host-host communications have been tested in June 1973, without packet switching, which started working in August 1973, on one node. Thereafter the network will come up gradually, until all hosts are connected in April 1974. More centers will be introduced in 1975, along with real applications.

IV. GENERAL OBJECTIVES

1. Incremental implementation :

Systems such as computer networks are still in the mainstream
of research, and it would be inappropriate, if not unrealistic,
to delay implementations until all issues are entirely understood,
evaluated, and all possible functions completely designed. Some
experimentation is necessary to gain insight, acquire know-how,
and test hypotheses that appear initially in a most subjective
context.

Furthermore, building a computer network is by essence a distributed effort, in order to create the motivations and common
understanding so necessary for coordinating tasks and achieving
network standards. Involving users in a proper way is a guarantee
to have productive feedback and imaginative suggestions to cure
the deficiencies of the network and extend its capabilities in a
useful manner.

For all these reasons, Cyclades is being brought up stepwise and
should be capable of providing some services at an early stage
of implementation. Versatility, convenience, efficiency, will be
phased in gradually, with the introduction of new components,
and substitution of old ones.

2. Design approach :

Since Cyclades was not the first of its kind, it was more than
advisable to study other networks before starting out. Most
available documents were originating from ARPA [8] and NPL [10]. A
few ones were centered on other networks, MERIT [2], TYMNET [11],
INTENET [9].

From this preliminary study and various live discussions with
"networkers", one could draw some tentative conclusions :

a - Data communications should be an independent sub-problem.
    Its main virtues are simplicity, reliability, transparency.

b - Packet switching can work.

c - Computer-computer protocols are still toddlers.

d - Homogeneous computers are a lot easier.

e - Ill defined protocols mean distributed headache.

f - Computer communications require human communications.

Bearing these headlines in mind, the Cyclades design concentrated
initially on the communications interface as seen at the basic
user level. A common user interface was felt to be a keystone
for building more elaborate functions. From there on, the design

proceeded inwards down to the packet switching interface, and
outwards up to virtual terminals protocols, (TELNET like) [3].

By basic user level is meant in a broad sense a process executing
a user program in a conventional operating system. Since Cyclades
computers were deliberately heterogeneous, there were to be
unavoidable variations in implementing the user-network interface.

Consequently, it was all the more important to produce specifications such that these local variations would not introduce
ambiguities and misfits between any pair of users.

3. Data transfer :

Access to multiple data bases is a major operational objective
for Cyclades, while time-sharing will take only a modest share.
Even though a sophisticated system of distributed data bases may
require some time to emerge, there will be a rising demand for
file transfer, mainly because users tend to minimize adversity
by splitting their tasks. Thus, basic protocols should provide
for efficiency in using whatever bandwith is available.

4. Standards :

Emphasis is put on using standards wherever possible, so as to
protect present or future investments. A standard may be a set
of recommendations promulgated by an official body. By default,
it can be a widely accepted convention among network users.
Specifically, communications hardware and procedures should
conform to manufacturer or CCITT standards

On the other hand, when standards do not exist , or are ill-suited,
proper interfaces should insulate the domain, in order to allow
for future adjustment, and defer commitment.

5. Private user groups :

In any large conglomerate of persons or associations, some groups
tend to develop special ties and preferred relationship, based
on common interest or necessity. Such a phenomenon should be
expected as a natural ingredient of computer network sociology.
Consequently, basic communications procedures should leave enough
flexibility, at the user level, to allow for private conventions
tailored to specific applications. On the other hand, standard
network communications should be compatible with this customi-
zation.

6. Inter-network communications :

The motivations for computer networks apply as well to networks
of networks, which means that interconnecting with other networks
should be a capability built in Cyclades. Presently, some networks

communicate at terminal level. Although this may suit well some
types of interactions, it is too restrictive for a broad class
of applications. Interconnection at user, or communications
network level should be anticipated.

V. COMMUNICATIONS ENTITIES

1. Network model (Fig. 2) :

All host computers communicate with one another through a host
software called ST (transfer station), and a communications
network [7]. There may be several ST's within a host. Except for
this latter characteristic, ST's correspond to Arpanet NCP's.
They are local network subsidiaries within a host town [5].

Host entities, such as processes, users, devices, etc... communicate by exchanging letters, which are handed over to a local ST,
shipped to the appropriate addressee's ST, and finally delivered
to the destination entity.

Not every host entity may enjoy the privilege of sending letters
using network services. To do so, one has to be formally introduced to the network as a subscriber. Roughly speaking, a
subscription is a badge that allows its bearer to obtain network
services, presumably at a cost some day. It is network business,
viz. ST, to manage subscriptions, but it is host business to
manage their association with local entities, and enforce rules
for proper sharing and privacy. In other words, as seen from
host, a subscription is usually a capability attached to a local
process or user under host operating system protection.

2. Subscribers :

As seen from within the network, they are permanent names known
network-wide. Opening and cancellation of subscriptions are
administrative procedures which require some agreement from the
network Authority. At a future stage of design, subscribers might
be given capabilities and resource credit. For the moment, they
are just global names.

Usual subscribers are attached to a particular ST : <global
subscriber name > : : = <ST name> <local name > . But there can be
general subscribers whose location might change in time.

Typically, a subscriber could be a software processor, a subsystem, a human user, a device, a special answering service, etc...
But this association is immaterial as far as the network is
concerned, provided that basic exchange protocols are adhered to.

For the sake of convenience in network operation, particularly in
human communications, it is expected that associations between
subscribers and host entities will be rather stable, like the
pair : person name - telephone number. It should be worthwhile to
print and disseminate subscriber directories reasonably up to
date. If at all necessary, administrative delays or costs will be
tacked on subscription changes to make them sufficiently unfre-
quent.

Since most subscribers will use network services only occasionally, it would be wasteful to maintain subscription information
at all times within ST's in high speed memory. Therefore, a
subscription can be <u>enabled</u> or <u>disabled</u>, very much like login-
logout for a time-sharing user. This operation is executed
dynamically on subscriber's request.

3. <u>Ports</u> :

Many software systems deal with data exchange in terms of flows,
streams, channels, or similar concepts. One could argue on
whether this is a so called natural way or if it is just bequea-
thed by a persistent addiction to card readers, magnetic tapes,
and other sequential devices. Nevertheless, I/O-like techniques
permeate most forms of inter-process communications. The concept
of port has come to be commonly used to designate an abstract
entity on which data flows may be anchored, and addressed.

To that effect, a subscriber can apply to its ST for port names.
They are created dynamically and are local to the subscriber.
They can also be exchanged between ST's, as part of specific
protocols, to set up links between subscribers.

In other words, subscribers and ports make up a hierarchical name
space, network-wide. The subscriber component is global and
basically stable, while the port component is local and basically
transient.

So far we have not felt the need for further levels. Should it
appear useful, growing sub-ports would not be a technical problem.

4. <u>Letters</u> :

It is a piece of information exchanged between two subscribers.
There may be several varieties of letter mechanisms. Presently,
4 have been designed.

a) <u>Regular letter</u> :

It can be sent at any time to any subscriber, as long as both
subscriptions are enabled. A priority may be specified, and an
acknowledgement may be requested. By acknowledgment is meant

a return message sent back to the sender subscriber, after
the letter has been delivered to the receiver subscriber. A
letter can contain up to 240 octets of text (1920 bits).

b) Liaison :

Letters are sent over a port, and delivered from a port. An
initial set up is necessary to open a liaison, and exchange
port names, which are only paired by order of creation. The
liaison machinery includes error and flow control, and it is
bidirectional. A symmetrical procedure solves all contention
problems.

c) Connection :

It has the same properties as a liaison. But letters are delivered to the receiver subscriber in the same order as they
have been sent. Furthermore, letters can be indefinite strings
of bits. The connection machinery includes error and flow
control, and it is bidirectional. The same symmetrical procedure as for liaisons applies to connections.

d) Events :

They are short letters (16 bits) transmitted with higher
priority. They may be sent separately or over an existing
liaison or connection amidst text flow, as out-of-band
messages.

The previous set of mechanisms is intended to provide basic user
facilities on top of which more sophisticated services may be
built. Each one is aimed at a particular class of traffic which
is expected to be frequently encountered in the network.

Regular letters are intended for conversational traffic between
slow terminals and server processes. They can also be used as
control messages between several processes cooperating within
a distributed activity.

Liaisons are intended for bulk traffic such as file transfer
or data base processing, where letters contain self-identifying
items of information, and are well suited for parallel
processing.

Connections are intended for I/O streams, typically remote
sequential devices or files, as well as conventional inter-
process communications.

Events are intended for control information when it is desirable
to send it asynchronously with data flow. A typical case is
attention or diagnostics messages to be used by a control

424

environment rather than the normal receiver process.

VI. FUNCTIONAL COMPONENTS

1. Component hierarchy (Fig. 3) :

Starting with the communications network, one finds :

a) A host communications interface, implementing a line transmission procedure. Initially, it will be one the bi-synchro-
   nous family, depending on the host at hand. In the future,
   an ISO standard procedure of the HDLC type [12] will be installed, when I-O adapters will be available on the market. One
   may notice that a host can have more than one physical link
   with the communications network, to provide for more reliability in case of node or line failure.

b) A transfer station (ST), implementing the subscriber name
   space, ports, and a basic letter handling at an intermediate
   system interface. There may be several ST's, for testing new
   versions, implementing special services, and communicating
   with foreign host protocols, e.g. Arpanet, or COST-11 [13].
   Monitoring and diagnostic aids are also introduced at this
   level.

c) A set of user oriented letter handling functions implementing
   error and flow control, queue management, and liaison/connec-
   tion management when applicable. This approach results from
   the recognition that there is no ideal way of handling data
   exchange. It depends on user environment. Rather than piling
   layer upon layer of functions, with the associated overhead
   and duplication, it appeared more efficient to leave room for
   expansion not only upwards as usual, but also sideways. Again,
   it becomes a casual matter to try out new options, and to
   develop private network access methods, without loosing the
   benefit of standard interfaces.

2. Transfer station structure :

Our objective was not limited to specify a set of rules for
exchanging messages between hosts. Rather, it was ideally to
write the specifications of a complete ST, including various
letter handling, so that every network user would see a common
interface, regardless of the host type.

It is clear that this is a trivial problem in homogeneous networks.
One possible approach for a heterogeneous network would be to use
a portable programming language. But operating system peculiari-

ties introduce a variety of discrepancies and inefficiencies. Consequently, the design could not be so ideal ; it could only attempt to define functions without referring to specific host facilities. This objective resulted in the following scheme.

An ST is thought of as an abstract machine (Fig. 4), driven by commands, and exchanging information with the external world through a communications area. Some internal states may be observed through a glass window. Communications mechanisms are implementation dependent, but they should not bear any relation-ship with the ST internal logic. On the other hand, they can be implemented using well known engineering techniques.

An ST is then further broken down into individual components given maximum autonomy (Fig. 5). So as to allow for implementation freedom, individual components can be thought of as asynchronous machines cooperating via state variables, or queues. These constituent machines are listed below.

- Command : checks arguments and signals appropriate machine ; 1 mach

- Subscription : enables/disables subscriptions ; 1 mach/subscriber

- Regular letter : send/receive regular letters ; 1 mach/ subscriber

- Port : handles ports ; 1 mach/subscriber

- Liaison : handles liaisons ; 1 mach/subscriber/liaison

- Connection : handles connections ; 1 mach/subscriber/connection

- Communications : send/receive packets ; 1 mach

- Debug : special modes ; 1 mach

- Operator : manual/automatic control ; 1 mach

Readers may not have failed to notice the structured programming approach used as a design methodology [4]. Of course, implementation may deviate somehow in making machines less autonomous, such as sub-routines. But the design structure should be kept highly visible, or else unanticipated interferences may well creep in.

The logic of each machine is specified in natural language algorithms, using a loose form of pseudo-Algol. It was not felt at this point that a genuine programming language would have helped human communications.

3. Subscriber interface :
Although communications between a user process and an ST machine are implementation dependent, it was considered important to specify ST commands in a non-ambiguous way, resembling a sub-

routine or macro-call. Therefore, all commands have been given some sort of formal representation, using mnemonics and argument names, as they should be passed over to the ST. Message formats and states are also specified.

E.g. : OPEN, LI, LOC-SUB, DIS-SUB, LI-X, MIN, MAX

meaning : open a liaison from local subscriber to distant subscriber, liaison number, minimum and maximum characteristics proposed in terms of buffer allocation, letter length, bandwith.

In an actual implementation, OPEN LIAISON could be a system primitive, DIS-SUB and LI-X could be arguments in registers, MIN and MAX packed into a liaison control block, and LOC-SUB supplied by the operating system.

4. Communications network interface :

The ST makes packets out of letters, and vice versa. Letters are stitched with control information, and if at all possible several letters are blocked within a single packet towards the same destination. Infinite letters are fragmented. Thereafter, the packet is passed to a line handler to be delivered to the communication network. The packet format is :

Header : 72 bits (9 octets), Text : 2040 bits (255 octets) max. As usual, additional bits are inserted when output to transmission lines takes place : synchro, CRC, etc...

VII. PACKET SWITCHING

Packet switching technology is just emerging, and building a computer network is an adequate opportunity to experiment and acquire know-how in this domain. So far well defined problems have been solved quite satisfactorily, e.g. fault detection, remote loading, packet ordering, etc... On the other hand, there are ill defined problems, such as congestion, routing , topology, which are only partially understood, and most likely inter-dependent. Our concern in a first stage is not to make break-through in packet switching technology, but to build a reliable communications tool for Cyclades, while preserving the possibility of a major redesign when more experience becomes available.

Consequently we have been very strict in insulating logically, and even physically, functions related to computer network on one hand, and those germane to packet switching on another hand. E.g. terminal concentration will be done by mini-hosts containing a stripped down ST, implementing unsophisticated connections.

Some specific features of our packet switching network, called
CIGALE [7], are presented in the following.

1. Addressing :

The basic purpose of a packet switching network is to deliver
messages to an addressee located outside of the network, and not
to reach its own components. Therefore, there is a need for a
global name space network-wide, to designate source and destination of messages. In Arpanet such a name space maps onto network
components, viz. node and line number. There are two consequences:
a - addressees can only be reached through a unique gateway,
b - topology changes may require address changes.

Let us assume that an addressee is not a single computer, but a
distributed computer, i.e. a network, then it will likely be
required to link them by multiple paths, for reliability, traffic
smoothing, response time, etc... An addressee becomes an outside
target, which may be reached through several possible gateways.
Thus, we need an independent name space.

In Cigale, names are ST's, which can be reached from several nodes.
Furthermore, there may be several ST's on one line. In a large
network, it would be a severe constraint if every node should
know all possible addressees. Therefore, we use a hierarchical
name space : region - ST.

Each node has only to know region names, and ST names within its
own region. Any ST belongs to only one region. But let us note
that this does not prevent from reaching an ST directly from a
node in a different region, as long as this ST name is also
listed in the node name space. But this practice should be
restricted to isolated ST's, as it tends to make address look up
more costly.

International communications will have to deal with a jumble of
address formats, and the only practical way out will be to
introduce variable formats as a way of switching. This will bring
another hierarchical structure, for which every network should
be prepared. In anticipation of that, an address type component
is provided in Cigale.

The general address format would be : type (3 bits), region
(5 bits), ST (8 bits). But Cyclades does not need such a large
name space, and some bits may be set aside for future use,
leaving region (4 bits), ST (4 bits).

2. Internal ST (STI) :

Some special functions are useful within a packet switching
network, e.g. collecting bad messages, echoing, traffic generation,
... Rather than having specially formatted packets along with
the decoding software, it is much easier to reserve a subset of
the ST name space to address those special components. Since the
general addressing mechanism applies, STI's may be either located
within nodes, or be within real hosts considered as extensions of
the network, and supported by the network Authority. Also some
services may be experimented within a real host, and once appro-
ved, integrated within the network functions.

In commercial networks some services should be offered to attract
customers and add more convenience : e.g. data conversion,
mailboxes, broadcasting, file editing, etc... Using STI's is a
handy way to hook those services without disturbing network
operation.

In Cigale, some address variations allow a few STI's to be
located : - at only one node, - at every node, - at some nodes.
Through that facility, STI's may be distributed according to
traffic requirements, and even moved about the network during
operation.

3. Message reassembly :

Cigale does not fragment messages. It only takes in packets.

4. Message ordering :

Cigale delivers packets as soon as they arrive at a destination
gateway. There is no ordering. On the other hand ordering does
not appear compatible with multipaths to a host.

5. Flow control :

Cigale does not apply flow control to any specific flow. On the
other hand, it will attempt to resist congestion, but the techniques to be used are not yet clear. An approach would be to
allocate input traffic according to available buffer space,
using exponential smoothing. Simulation studies are planned.

VIII. INTER-NETWORK COMMUNICATIONS

Inter-network communications have still to demonstrate their
practical feasibility, if one excepts the present situation where
a network mimics a terminal to the other. It seems that key-
points include simplicity and open-endedness.

The more sophisticated a network, the less likely it is going to
interface properly with another. In particular, any function except sending packets is probably just specific enough not to work
in conjunction with a neighbor. The result is an intersection of
properties rather than a union.

In this respect Cigale does not present any excess properties.
All functions are self-contained, none extends across network
boundary. As long as packets are within the maximum size, with
proper format, they will be delivered to a known ST. Some
mismatch may result from error messages sent back to the source
in case of wrong progress. A possible solution would be to use
an STI as middle man, in charge of the necessary format conver-
sions.

Trans-network communications bring up another problem. Assuming
that interface problems are solved, intermediate networks, supposed to carry messages along, do not possess the final destination
in their name space. Thus a new function arises : international
routing. But this is a general problem unrelated to specific
network characteristics.

Cyclades hosts are also well suited to inter-network exchange,
since : - their basic letter protocol is simple, - more ST's or
protocols can be added. In the worst case a special ST must be
built to interface with a foreign host. However there may be some
devious timing problems that can probably be solved on an ad hoc
basis. But this would provide only a straight-forward type of
exchange. The whole set of procedures and practices that make
up a computer network environment is a much larger task.

IX. CONCLUSIONS

Cyclades is one of the largest computer projects in France. Major
universities and research centers are actively working on its
development. It is expected that techniques and insight acquired
during the project will benefit research and industry, specifically at a moment when several communications networks are being
planned by large corporations, and the French Administration. Its
extensible structure at several levels makes it well suited to all
sorts of experiments on a national and international scene.

X. ACKNOWLEDGMENTS

The Cyclades design is largely a teamwork, and it is quite
difficult to trace back the genesis of ideas. Our work stemmed
mainly from earlier research accomplished at NPL and within the
ARPA community. Among individuals who contributed major parts of
the design, are M. ELIE (CII) and J.L. GRANGÉ (Cyclades). A
particular acknowledgment is due to H. ZIMMERMANN (Cyclades) for
an outstanding contribution on host protocols (ST). Stimulating
discussions with D. WALDEN (BBN) brought substantial improvement
and simplification.

XI. <u>REFERENCES</u>

1 - CARR C.S., CROCKER S.D., CERF V.G. - Host-Host communication protocol in the Arpa network. SJCC (1970), 589-597.

2 - COCANOWER A.B. - Functional characteristics of CCOS. Merit computer network, (Jun. 1971), 39 p.

3 - CROCKER S. et al. - Function oriented protocols for the Arpa computer network. SJCC (1972), 271-279.

4 - DIJKSTRA E.W. - Notes on structured programming. (Aug. 1969), 84 p.

5 - ELIE M., ZIMMERMANN H. et al. - Spécifications fonctionnelles des stations de transport du Réseau Cyclades. SCH 502, (Nov. 1972), 105 p.

6 - GIRARDI S. - SOC project, an experimental computer network. Intern. Comp. Symp. Venice, (Apr. 1972), 210-220.

7 - GRANGE J.L., POUZIN L. - Cigale, la machine de commutation de paquets du Réseau Cyclades. Congrès AFCET 1973, 24 p.

8 - ROBERTS L.G., WESSLER B.D. - Computer network development to achieve resource sharing. SJCC (1970), 543-549.

9 - RUTLEDGE R.M., et al. - An interactive network of time-sharing computers. 24th ACM Nat. Conf. (Aug. 1969), 431-441.

10 - SCANTLEBURY R.A. - A model for the local area of a data communication network. Objectives and hardware organization. ACM Symp. on problems in the optimization of data communications systems (1969), 179-201.

11 - TYMES L.R. - Tymnet, a terminal oriented communication network. SJCC (1971), 211-216.

12 - ISO/TC 97/SC 6. Doc. 731 - HDLC procedures. Proposed draft international standard on frame structure (Feb. 1973), 4 p.

13 - BARBER D.L.A. - The European computer network project. ICCC, Washington D.C., (Oct. 1972), 192-200.

432

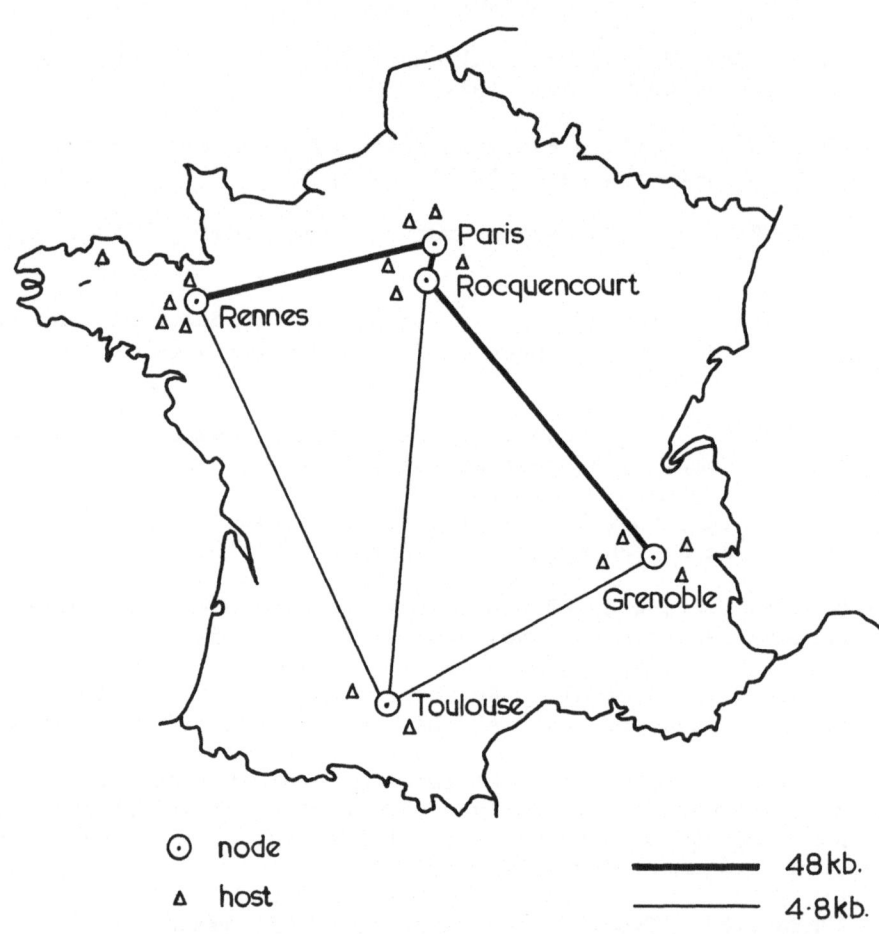

⊙ node

△ host

━━━━ 48 kb.

──── 4·8 kb.

16 Hosts – 6 types of computers – 8 operat. systems

Fig. 1   <u>CYCLADES NETWORK</u>

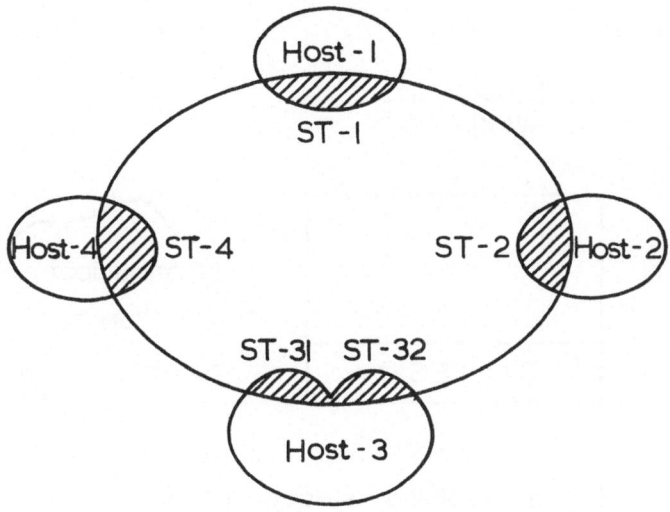

Fig. 2 CYCLADES Model

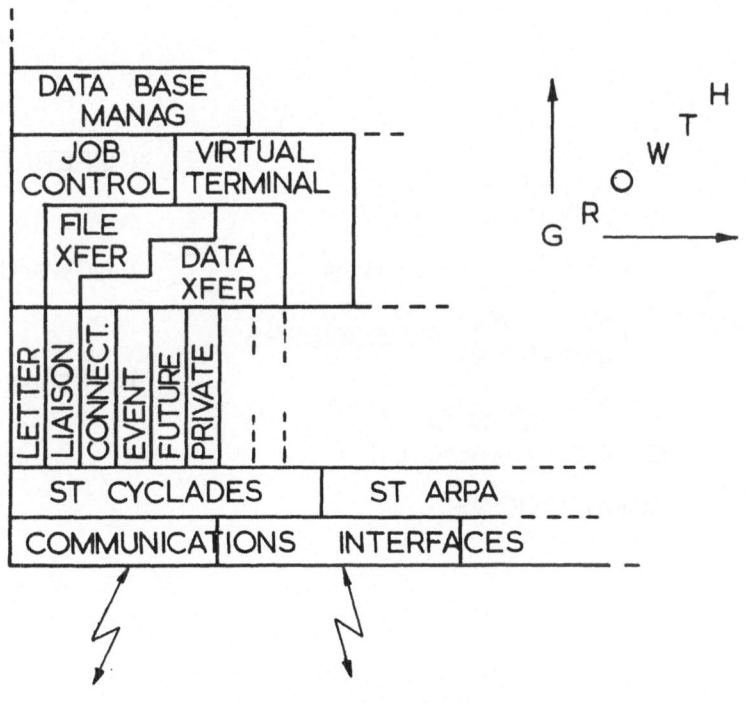

Fig. 3 CYCLADES Architecture

434

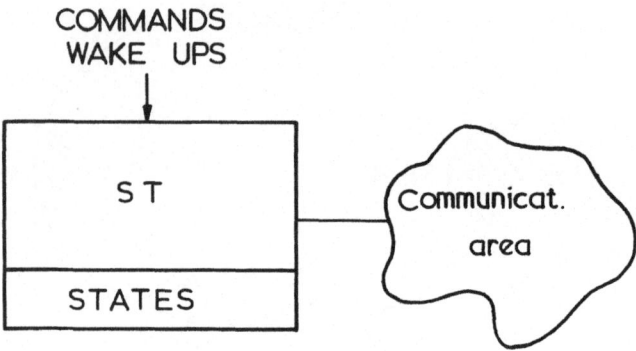

Fig. 4 Transfer station model

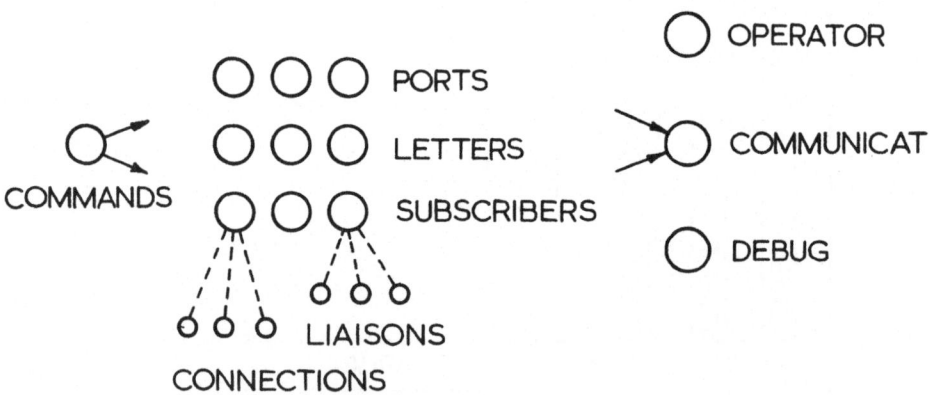

Fig. 5 Transfer station components

EXPERIMENTAL PACKET SWITCHING PROJECT OF THE UK POST OFFICE

Part 1: Facilities and Customer Participation

Roy D. Bright

UK Post Office, Data Communications Division,
Marketing Department.

Network Configuration and Accass Arrangements

For the purposes of this experimental Service, a three node
network has been designed. This consists of three packet switching exchanges (PSEs) located at centres of high data concentration
in the UK including London, Manchester and Glasgow. These, incid-
entally, are approximately 200 miles apart. The three exchanges
will be fully interconnected by 48 kHz lines operating at 48 kbit/s.

Opening in early 1975, the service will be limited to 4 hours
continuously per day, but this will be progressively increased to
24 hours per day, if demand warrants, within two years of opening.

Each PSE will be equipped with two types of interface with
users' equipment; a packet interface and a character interface. The
former will be used for intelligent devices including computers and
will convey formatted packets and acknowledge their delivery. This
mode of access is significantly different from some other packet
switching networks elsewhere, which look to the user for conventional character by character operation with the node taking on
the role of packet assembly/ disassembly. This latter mode of
access is also available in the EPSS for character terminals –
typically keyboard/printer terminals operating at 110 and 300 bit/s
asynchronously. This facility may not, in fact, be required as a
permanent feature but is primarily designed to facilitate user
participation in the experiment. Similarly, each user is expected
to handle packets at one end of their link with EPSS if not all
terminal points. It is the ability of user configurations to interface at a packet level which is of prime importance in the experiment. Thus users operating terminals with packet handling capa-

436

bilities will access PSE at 2.4 kbit/s or 48 kbit/s; in addition provision has been made for 4.8 and 9.6 kbit/s access should this be required by some users. Both telephone switched network and/or direct access will be permitted utilising normal Datel arrangements including 2400 Dial-up.

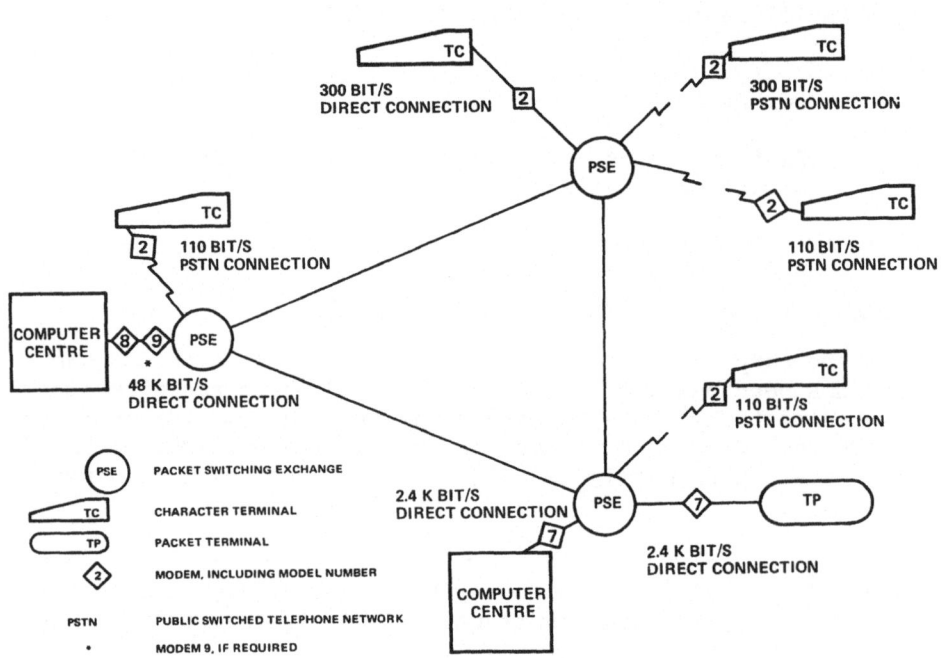

EPSS CONFIGURATION AND ACCESS ARRANGEMENTS

Facilities

In addition to packet assembly/disassembly mentioned earlier
a number of important facilities are also to be tested out in conjunction with the users.

(i)   Interleaved Packets   This is possibly one of the
most significant areas insofar as it will allow the establishment of several simultaneous calls over one link
between the user's computer and a number of distant terminals. The value of this facility is enhanced by its
ability to handle packets in a dynamic fashion rather than
on dedicated time slots as would be the case in a conventional multiplexer.

(ii) Data Rate Conversion will be provided by the service
rather than the user incurring the cost in his terminal
equipment thus the ability to link terminals operating
at different speeds will be an inherent feature of the
service.

(iii) Code Conversion   The potential requirement to
allow communication between character terminals operating in IA2 and IA5 codes will be tested.

(iv) Link by Link Error Control Currently, a good
leased line provides an undetected error rate of $1:10^6$.
Using a 16-bit error-checking code, this should be improved by four or five orders of magnitude. This check
will be applied at each stage of the packet's transmission
between PSEs and for terminals operating in the packet mode
will also apply on the access links.

(v)   Closed User Groups On joining the service, users will
be able to nominate those terminals etc. to which he wishes
to restrict access. The PSE will effect this by the use of
interlock codes designed to bar access from unauthorised
terminals.

Cost/Benefits

A key objective in defining the service was to combine the
advantages of leased and dial-up operation while minimizing their
respective short-comings. Thus an existing leased line user will
no longer pay a rental for a circuit extending tens or hundreds
of miles but will rent only access lines. This will still provide
the wide range of speeds and could also reduce the incremental
cost of changing to a higher speed e.g. from 9.6 kbit/s to 48
kbit/s by several orders of magnitude enabling future growth of
traffic to be accommodated without expensive upgrading of both

lines and equipment. Similarly, the dial-up user while retaining the ability to pay only for usage will gain the benefit of the wide range of speeds (up to 48 kbit/s) previously restricted to leased line users. Other operational benefits can be cited including automatic protection against 'call cut-offs' and automatic re-routing - not previously available to the leased line user. Coupled with the numerous novel facilities identified earlier, there should emerge a significant opportunity for users to reduce their data communications costs, but, as in many cases these represent less than 10 per cent of the total system costs it is the foreseeable impact of the service on this latter cost which could have the most dramatic effects on users' attitudes.

While it would be premature to make positive claims in this area, a number of potential savings seem attainable:

(i)   less buffering required at the users' host computer site with no commensurate increase at the remote terminals.

(ii) a measure of standardisation and some simplification of the communication OS module thereby freeing core for other uses.

(iii) elimination of the wider needs for customer provided concentrators/multiplexers.

(iv) more efficient processing by virtue of the standard formatted messages.

(v)   some reduction in complexity and therefore cost of the front-end processor

(vi) improved diagnostic capabilities.

Participation

Following a gradual build-up of interest since the plans for EPSS were first announced, potential users, encouraged by swinge-ing tariff concessions for the first twelve months, are appearing in growing numbers. To date some twenty organisations have de-clared their intention to participate; the latest commitment being those of a Central Government department and the National Engineer-ing Laboratory at East Kilbride. The range of applications and equipment configurations now represented is extensive; among the commercial users are two joint stock banks - Barclays and Midland; a consortium of Trustee Savings Banks; Joseph Lucas - a large manufacturer of automotive electrical equipment and two commercial service bureaux - SICON and CRC Information with others expected. Many main-frames and front-enders are represented; among others

are a Burroughs 6500/6700, Univac 1108, Sigma 9, IBM 360/40 and
various PDPs, Modular 1s etc. As expected, several non-commercial
organisations such as Universities and research establishments
will also take part including NPL with its in-house packet network
and the Institute of Computer Science of London University with
its ARPA TIP.

A number of interesting developments have already been stimu-
lated by the EPSS proposals. For example, NPL and the Computer
Aided Design Centre, Cambridge, are to collaborate in using EPSS
customer protocols over a leased 48 kbit/s circuit throughout 1974.
This will enable some pre-service experience to be obtained prior
to the opening of the first (London) PSE at which time the link
will be rerouted to incorporate the switch disciplines. Secondly,
a study is being mounted to consider the feasibility of utilising
EPSS as a means of interconnexion between a large number of British
universities and allied centres thereby eliminating the growing
matrix of leased lines. In a similar manner, there are signs of
a potential use for serving a group of nationalised industry needs
where a measure of commonality can be seen to exist.

These and other emergent trends – both national and international underline the potential value of a packet switched service and more than justify the decision to mount the experiment.
Now under active consideration by the UK Post Office is the next
step which, assuming a successful experiment, will be the need to
expand and develop into a national packet switching service.

Part 2: Technical Specification and Development

Michael A. Smith

UK Post Office, Data Network Development Coordination Division
Telecommunications Development Department.

Note: In view of the very brief period available for this description, the main topic covered is the packet interface between
Customers and the Network, which is possibly the most unique and
critical feature of the system.

Network Structure

More than one arrangement of switching nodes could be used to
provide communications paths between customers' equipment, the
two extremes of which may be regarded as a 'mesh' with switching
nodes located only at customers' premises and a 'star' with only
one switching node located centrally. In the first case the
switching costs are high, network maintenance personnel access

to the switches is very difficult to guarantee at all times, and hence reliability may be low. In the second case line costs will be high and the lines will be underutilised, but the reliability of the switching node could be made very high by equipment duplication and with continuous maintenance staffing if necessary. A compromise between these two extremes seems to be desirable and this has led to the arrangement described by Roy Bright.

Customer to PSE Packet Transfer Procedures.

In this area of the system definition the question of standards is very important. The UK Post Office endeavour is to work harmoniously with Industry, Users and through established International bodies like the ISO and CCITT to achieve such standards. Initially, the methods of connecting customers' equipment to the PSEs will depend mainly on modems, but eventually it is intended to utilise elements of the UK DDS (Digital Data Service) for this purpose. To summarise:-

a. Contiguous 8 bit bytes will be transmitted by the customers' equipment and PSE between and during packets

b. The customers' equipment is required to return bytes in a fixed relationship with the received bytes

c. Each line signal (byte) depends on the incoming byte

d. Only one packet may be sent before an acknowledgement is received

e. A packet may only be transmitted after the receipt of three particular line signals

f. A packet is acknowledged by returning 3 identical bytes

g. An acknowledgement is transmitted (i) by the customers' equipment after 40 bits delay (max.) and (ii) by the PSE within 8 bits delay (max.)

h. An acknowledgement will interrupt any packet in transmission but does not pass through the cyclic redundancy check (CRC)

i. The receiving end detects the acknowledgement from a knowledge of the loop delay

j. The acknowledgement bears the following diagnostic aids:-

    (i)   If the packet has any detected errors
    (ii) If the link sequence number is in sequence
    (iii) If the receiver has the resources to handle the packet

k. Packets are only retransmitted after receiving 3 Idle 1 bytes

l. The PSE has a maximum of 3 attempts at transmitting a packet

To amplify some of the detail of the above summary, the following is offered:

Loop delay measurement

The procedure will be carried out

    (i)   After powering up of the line interfacing equipment
    (ii) After loss of byte synchronism (see next heading)
    (iii) After three unsuccessful attempts to transmit a packet

Sequence of bytes transmitted between the customer and the PSE;

```
W   2 2 2 T C B H H H H H H H 1 1 1 1 1 1 1 H H H A₁A₁A₁ 1 1 1 1
X   2 2 2 2 T C B H H H H H H H 1 1 1 1 1 1 1 H H H A₁A₁A₁ 1 1 1
Y   H H H H H H H H A₂A₂A₂H H H H H H H H T C B H H H H H H H 1 1
Z   H H H H H H H H H A₂A₂A₂H H H H H H H H T C B H H H H H H H 1
```

```
            │ PSE sets │               │ Cust. sets │
            ├──────────→│               ├──────────→ │
            │   delay   │               │   delay    │
```

Where   1   Idle 1   H   Packet Hold A_2 Ack 2

           2   Idle 2 A_1 Ack 1 N_2 Nack 2

           T C B Loop delay measurement packet (SOP/Type + check)

and   W is the stream of bytes transmitted by the PSE

         X is the stream of bytes received by the customer

         Y is the stream of bytes transmitted by the customer

         Z is the stream of bytes received by the PSE

Assuming: the delay at the customers' equipment = 8 bits

             The delay at the PSE   = 8 bits

             The physical loop delay   = 16 bits

Note 1: If the correct response is not received after 30 bytes
of Packet Hold being transmitted following the sending
of the loop delay measurement packet, a further loop
delay measurement packet will be sent.

Note 2: If three unsuccessful attempts are made to send a packet
the loop delay measurement packet will be sent after 15
Packet Hold line signals have been transmitted. If a
packet is received during this period, the loop delay
measurement packet will be sent after at least 15 Packet
Hold line signals and the acknowledgement ($A_2A_2A_2$ or
$N_2N_2N_2$) to the received packet.

Note 3: Loop delay measurement packets may be sent whilst Packet
Hold is being received.

Loop Synchronism

Under the previous heading the concept 'Loss of byte synchronism' was introduced, and this is defined as follows:-

'When 3 contiguous identical line signals are received which do
not correspond with the previous byte synchronism counter position,
providing a packet is not being received'.

If this condition is detected by (a) the customers' equipment,
the outgoing byte stream will be realigned with the incoming stream
(if a packet is being transmitted, this is done at the end of the
packet) and the loop delay will be redetermined; or (b) by the PSE,
the received stream byte synchronism counter will be repositioned
and the loop delay will be redetermined.

Line Signals

When no packets or acknowledgements are to be sent (quiescent
state) the conditions for the transmission of line signals are as
follows:-

Line Signal Transmitted	
Idle 1	When Idle 1, Idle 2, Packet Hold, Ack 1, Ack 2 or Ack 3 is being received, and incoming packets can be handled
Packet Hold	When Idle 1, Idle 2, Packet Hold, Ack 1, Ack 2 or Ack 3 is being received and incoming packets cannot be handled, or a packet is being received
Idle 2	When the conditions for the transmission of Idle 1 or Packet Hold do not obtain, and no packet is to be sent

When acknowledgements are to be sent i.e. after the receipt of a packet, they will consist of three identical contiguous line signals which are unique except where shown. The significance of the signals and the action taken following their occurrence are as follows:-

Line Signal (3)	CRC Check OK?	Seq. No.in order?	Can Handle Packet	Action	
				Transmitting End	Receiving End
Ack 1	YES	YES	YES	Send next packet (if any) without delay	Pass packet to next level of protocol
Ack 2	YES	YES	NO	The packet is retransmitted after receiving 3 Idle 1 signals	Packet
Ack 3	YES	NO	–	Send packet with next sequence no. without delay	Packet discarded
Nack 1 (Idle 1)	NO	–	YES	The packet is retransmitted without delay	–
Nack 2 (Packet Hold)	NO	–	NO	The packet is retransmitted after receiving 3 Idle 1 signals	–

The transmission of each line signal or acknowledgement from customers' equipment may be delayed by a fixed number of bits in the range 1 to 40 bits after the byte or packet to which it refers has been received.

Conditions for Transmission of Packets

A packet may only be transmitted if the last three line signals received are Idle 1, Ack 1 or Ack 3. If a packet is being received at the time at which a packet is to be sent, the last three line signals received are defined as the three line signals which immediately preceded the packet. If line signals are being received at the time at which a packet is to be sent, the last three line signals to be received are defined as the three line signals which immediately precede the fixed delay in the customers' equipment.

Sequence Numering of Packets

In order to enable receiving equipment to detect duplicate packets (e.g. arising because an acknowledgement was corrupted by 'noise', and the duplicate results from retransmission) and discard them, each packet transmitted will bear a 'Customer-to-PSE link sequence number i.e. 0, 1, 0, 1, etc. To initialise this sequence (e.g. after powering up equipment) the first packet will bear the sequence number 2, the next 0 and so on.

Conditions for Retransmission of Packets

A packet will be retransmitted within 30 bytes of the time out (i.e. loop delay) expiring providing that three Idle 1 bytes have been received. If the 30 byte period expires and 3 contiguous Idle 1 bytes have not been received, the packet will be retransmitted as soon as three contiguous Idle 1 bytes have been received.

Packet Formats

A packet consists of three main fields: header, containing address, call label and control information; data field, which contains customers' data if the packet is originated by a customer's terminal or computer, or may contain service signals if generated by the network (PSE); and these two fields are followed contiguously by the error check information. Efforts have been made to reduce the overhead represented by the header field by the use of short headers for packets forming part of a call; only the packets used for originating a call are required to contain the full address and control information. The PSE attaches full addressing, routing and interlock code information before transmitting the packet to a distant PSE, which removes this additional information before delivery to the recipient.

Studies of possible uses of packet switching systems have shown a wide variation of numbers of bytes or characters likely to be included within each packet data field. Systems which use fixed length data fields can have quite high overheads as a result of this variability which leads to numbers of packets with most of the data field unused. The EPSS uses a variable length data field packet, with the length of the packet indicated in bytes by an 8 bit sub-field of the header. This method of indicating the length of the packet has been chosen to avoid restricting binary sequences in the data field which would result from the use of a special terminating byte, and to avoid the overheads which result from the use of bit-stuffing coding methods, e.g. HDLC.

The error check polynomial used is $x^{16} + x^{12} + x^5 + 1$, which corresponds to that used in CCITT Recommendation V 41 (Vol. VIII*)

A COMPUTER/COMMUNICATIONS NETWORK DESIGN FOR
A NATIONAL ELECTRONIC FUNDS TRANSFER SYSTEM

Barry D. Wessler
Telenet Communications Corporation

INTRODUCTION

In the middle to late 1960's there was a great deal of
enthusiasm about the concept of a "checkless/cashless" society.
This concept held that most money transactions between individuals,
businesses, and governments would take place electronically
rather than using paper checks or paper money. Bankers and others
who looked in greater detail at the concept, however, had some
sobering second thoughts. By the end of the 60's, the concept
has changed to a "less-check" society where attempts would be made
to effect a substantial reduction in the amount of paper work to
consummate financial transactions but not attempt to get rid of
all checks and cash.

Recent activity in the area of electronic funds transfer
systems (EFTS) seems to indicate that at least part of the enthusiasm in the middle 60's was, in fact, warranted. While we're a
long way from even a "less-check" goal, the foundations for substantial progress in this area do appear to be making headway.
Not only have conceptual designs been developed but, more
importantly, actual experimentation is now taking place. This
is exemplified by the California SCOPE (Subcommittee on Paperless
Entry) activities, the Atlanta COPE (Committee on Paperless Entry)
group, and the point-of-sale experiments in Upper Arlington, Ohio
and Hempstead, New York. There is a growing body of literature
now being accumulated that will provide a clear insight into the
application of the electronic transfer of funds. The California
SCOPE project has provided invaluable standards for establishing
automated clearing houses and it now appears that this effort will
be copied by other SCOPE groups established in a dozen or more

cities in the country. The Atlanta project, performed by Georgia
Institute of Technology and funded by the Federal Reserve System
has provided a wealth of research information, particularly as it
relates to the marketing aspect of an EFTS. Thus, a substantial
amount of work has been done on the local or regional level. With
the notable exception of the Bank Administration Institute (BAI)
research study in 1969,[1] however, there has been relatively little
discussion in the literature concerning the requirements for or
the design of a nationally-oriented EFTS. This paper suggests
such a design and presents a recently developed communications
technology that now appears to make such a nationally-oriented
system both economically viable and technically capable of meeting
all of the requirements of an EFTS network. The paper does not
attempt to justify an EFTS but rather to add to the body of
technical literature so that more informed decisions can be made
by the managers of the financial industry.

THE PAYMENT SYSTEM

     The principal difficulty with checks in the current payment
system is that handling paper tends to be a slow, labor-intensive
operation. A great deal of effort has been spent in the financial
community to minimize the paper handling cost. Estimates of the
cost of processing a check range from $.10 to $.20 per check. A
breakdown of that cost can be found in the Atlanta Study.[2] With
21 billion checks being processed annually this represents at
least $2 billion per year in processing costs.[3] The check pro-
cessing system, therefore, has the potential of tremendous
economic impact if a new, more effective, transfer mechanism is
found.

     Examples of current payment system processes are shown in
figures 1, 3 and 5. Basically, a check is written by someone who
gives it to a creditor, who in turn exchanges it at his bank for
some other form of money. His bank passes the check on to the
writer's bank causing a debit to his account and a credit to the
depositor's account. The check is then held in the bank until it
is returned to the writer in a monthly statement. Figures 1, 3
and 5 show three different uses of this payment system. These
figures show the traditional check processing system familiar to
everyone.

     The mechanism for getting the check from one bank to another
varies widely depending on the relationship (geographic and
otherwise) between the two banks. In the simplest case, the check
is sent directly to or exchanged in a local clearinghouse. In
extreme cases, the check may go to a correspondent bank, then to
the Federal Reserve Bank for interdistrict transportation, then
to another correspondent bank and finally to its destination (see

figure 7). The bulk of the checks written are in the same region, and about 63% are "on us" (bank of debit and credit are the same). Statistics and distribution can be found in the Bank Administration Institute Study.[4]

One of the principal effects of changing the payment system is to change the "float." Float is basically money in transit. Banks generally take advantage of float by being able to use the money that a check has been written for but is not yet debited. On occasion the writer will take advantage of float by not having the money in his account when the check is written, then putting the money in immediately before the expected debit time. In corporate accounts this technique is called "money management" whereas in personal accounts this is called "kiting". The Atlanta Study claimed that 46% of all accounts surveyed were kited (or floated) during the month. The total float is difficult to obtain, but a quick estimate can be made: If average transit for a check is one day and total check volume in the U.S. is $20 Trillion annually (both reasonable assumptions today), then the float is $54 Billion and interest on the float, if it's possible to take advantage of all of it at 6%, is $3.3 Billion per year. The problem with using the reduction of float as an economic argument for a new payments system is that some banks make money on the float, some lose money, and most break even. It is essentially money traded within the Financial Community rather than paid to the outside world, so there is little net gain to the community in removing float.

The argument for the coming Electronic Funds Transfer System—and we are convinced that it is coming—must be based on a reduction in per-transaction cost. Before we rush into an argument of cost let us first see what the EFTS will be like.

There are several applications being considered by the developers of EFTS. In the near term there are Payroll, the Bill Check, and Pre-authorized Payment systems. After that may come Point-of-Sale systems and Business-to-Business transactions. In the long term we may have consumer-oriented locally initiated (home terminal) systems. The prime movers of EFTS at this time are the Paperless Entry groups in San Francisco (SCOPE) and Atlanta (COPE). Most of the ideas and data in this section come from documentation prepared by those groups.[2,5] The EFTS has been designed to work on a regional basis. No visible effort has yet been displayed for connecting these regional systems together. The procedure adopted by SCOPE for inter-district transactions is to prepare a paper document representing each transaction and send it through the normal check clearing system.

Below, some of the new applications are briefly described. This should not be used as a source of information for the serious banking individual. It is, instead, intended to inform the casual reader of the nature of EFTS without forcing him to do an outside literature search.

Payroll

The payroll check and electronic payroll are contrasted in figures 1 and 2. The payroll check is created by the employer, passed to the employee (1)*, given to his bank (2), credited to his account, sent to the employer's bank (if different), debited from his account, then the check is returned to the employer(5). One of the most expensive steps in this process is the cost of labor by the employee's bank at step 2 when he deposits his check. Interestingly he is not usually charged for this service. (This always portends marketing problems for a new service since savings in the service do not directly affect the party served.)

In the electronic payroll system, the employer will electronically prepare the payroll and give it to his bank(1a) and concurrently send the employee a statement(1); the employer's bank will debit the account and transmit the information to the employee's bank for crediting(2)(3), who will in turn inform the employee of the transaction(4). This kind of operation may be why banks are being thought of more and more as Financial Intermediarie Both the cost of Branch deposit and the cost of generation and transportation of the paper check are saved.

Bill Check

A very interesting system was devised by the Atlanta COPE group for capturing bill payments and converting them into electronic form early in their journey. Figure 3 shows the normal route of the payment of a billed account (charge cards, utilities, property taxes, etc.). The bill is sent to the consumer (1), the check and bill (or some identification of it) are returned, the check is deposited crediting the merchant's account (3), it is then sent to the consumer's bank and debited (5), and finally returned to him in his monthly statement (6).

In the proposed Atlanta "Bill Check" system the bill would be sent to and signed by the consumer (1), returned to the merchant (2), who would prepare an electronic entry for his bank (3), the bank would credit the merchant's account and transmit the information to the consumer's bank for debiting (5) with an acknowledgment of the transaction sent to the consumer (6), (probably in his

* Numbers in ( ) refer to numbered steps in the corresponding figure.

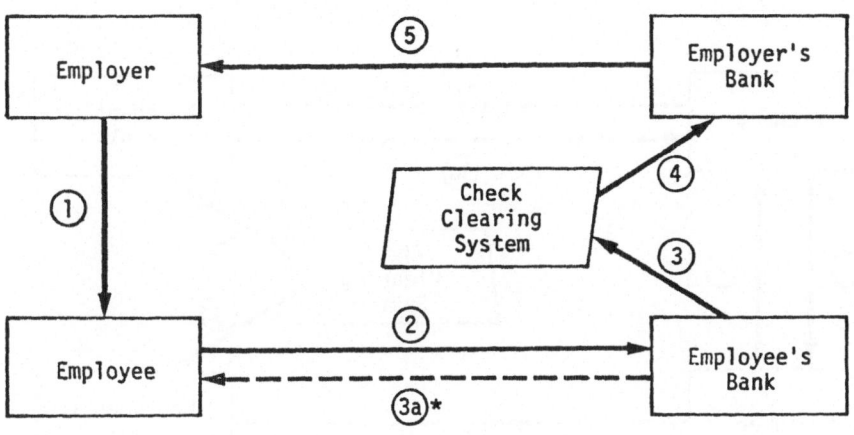

Figure 1   PAYROLL CHECK

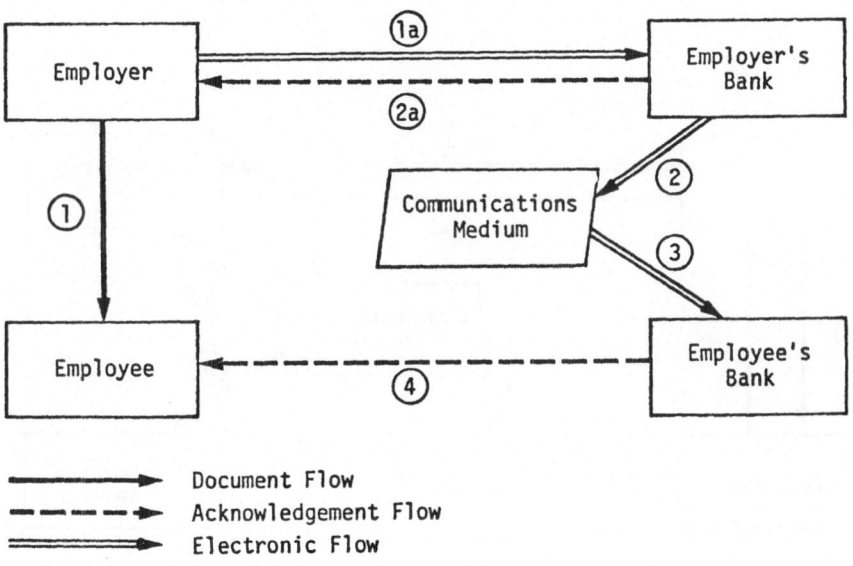

Document Flow
Acknowledgement Flow
Electronic Flow

* Lettered operations are concurrent with all operations
  of the same numerical value.

Figure 2   ELECTRONIC PAYROLL

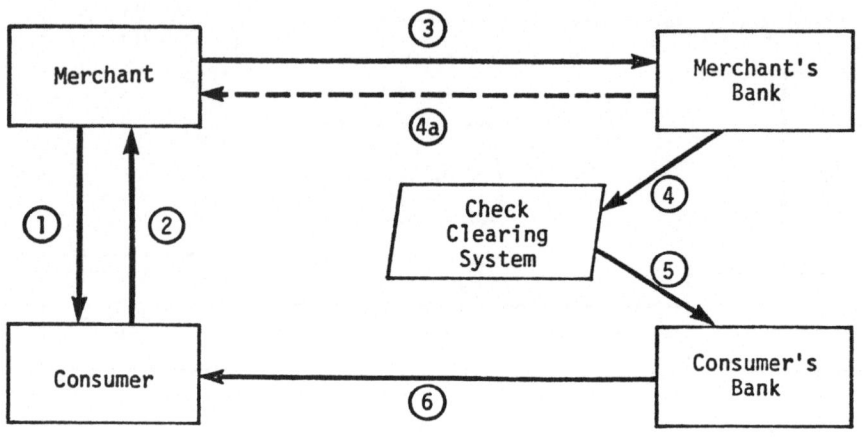

Figure 3   BILLS AND CHECKS

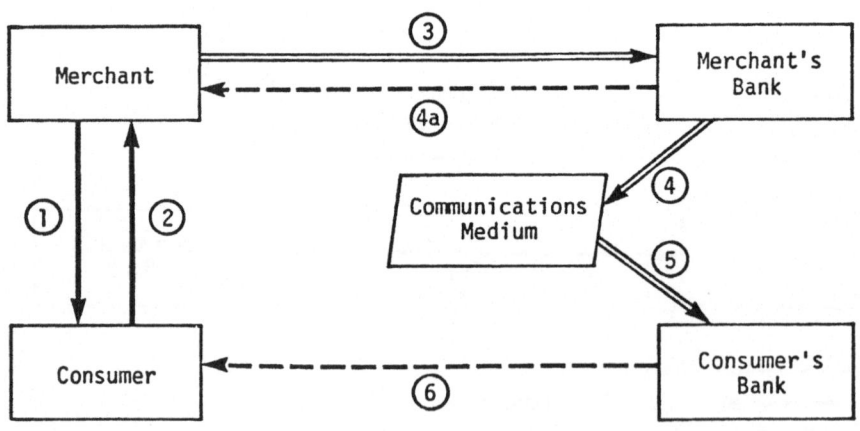

Figure 4   BILL CHECK

monthly statement). The advantages of the Bill Check to the Consumer, Merchant, and Bank are described in the Atlanta Study.

Point of Sale

The consumer transaction at the store (rather than the billed transaction) is much harder to capture electronically than the systems described above. Moreover, the greatest value of the Electronic Point of Sale system will stem from the reduction of bad debt and fraud. The data flow for the Electronic POS system, as pictured in Figure 6, consists of: Consumer initiation of the transaction (1), transfer request from merchant to the consumer's bank (2)(3), message sent to the merchant's bank crediting his account for the sum of the purchase (4), and acknowledgment of transfer returned to the merchant (4a)(5a). In order for the system to be a useful deterrent against bad debt and fraud the acknowledgment (5a) must be received within a reasonable time after the transaction request (2). A "reasonable" time is probably less than 2 minutes, but this needs to be studied by marketing and behavioral experts. If merchants' losses are 1% on checks, then in order to make this system viable for $10 checks, the total cost of the purchase validation must be less than $.10.

The same communications medium would be required for credit card purchases. Rather than transmitting debit information to the Bank, the merchant would transmit the information to the credit card company for verification and account updating.

CURRENT IMPLEMENTATION OF EFTS

The previous section attempted to describe the EFTS on a functional basis without referring to implementation-dependent questions. The computer and communications technologies are changing so rapidly that it is important to recognize "what you want to do" rather than "how you want to do it." This allows one to postpone the implementation question as long as possible in order to choose the best technology for the functional characteristics desired.

Automated Clearing House

An implementation of the electronic payroll, preauthorized payment, and bill check systems has been proposed and implemented by the California SCOPE project. The technique chosen for implementation is the "Automated Clearing House" (ACH), designed and built by Touche Ross & Company. The ACH uses magnetic tape as its communications medium. The ACH accepts tapes containing electronic transactions from multiple banks, sorts the transactions on the tape according to the destination bank, merges all transactions for a given bank onto a single tape, and then sends each prepared

452

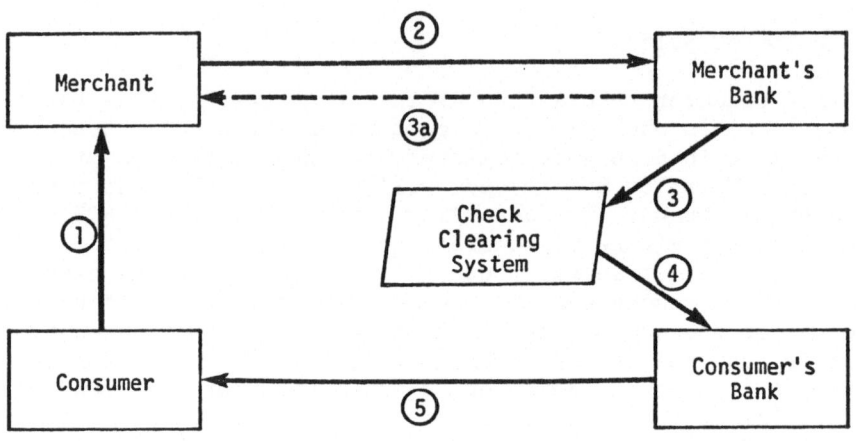

Figure 5   POINT-OF-SALE CHECK

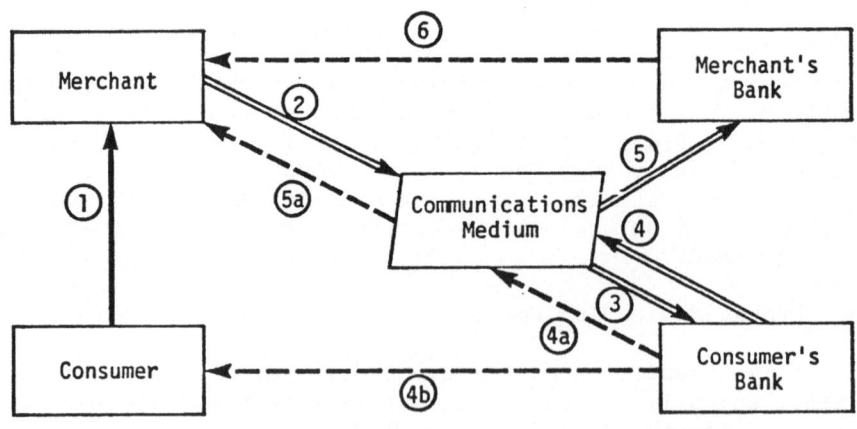

Figure 6   ELECTRONIC POINT-OF-SALE

tape to the appropriate destination bank. The ACH can be thought of functionally as a form of message switch. It takes "batches" of incoming messages and sends the messages to the appropriate output channel (tape). The ACH therefore "interconnects" many, potentially dissimilar, computing machines together. The vehicle for exchange is compatible magnetic tape in a prescribed format.

The input tapes are physically delivered to the ACH and the output tapes are picked up after preparation in the current implementations of the ACH. But this needn't be so. The tapes could be sent by mail or transmitted via a tape-to-tape transmission unit; and the transmitted tape could go directly into the ACH, the information could flow directly from the bank to the ACH, or it could go from one bank directly to another. The choice between these alternatives is almost purely economic.

The basic characteristic of the "Communications Medium" shown in figures 2 and 4 is that it must pass the transaction messages from the sending bank to the receiving bank. For local systems, like the two Paperless Entry systems under development today, the chosen mode of transmission is probably the one having the lowest cost. (A courier carrying a full magnetic tape has very high bandwidth.) The requirement of processing all transactions overnight makes implementation of local magnetic-tape-oriented ACH systems traightforward, but would tax a national system because of transportation delays in getting tapes from one ACH to another. It is likely, then, that a national system of ACH's would require electronic transmission between ACH's in order to satisfy the overnight requirement. During the evening's processing the ACH would prepare a tape containing interregional transactions; the tape would then be forwarded to the national ACH for sorting and redistribution to the destination ACH. The destination ACH must receive the transaction information in time to make the final sort run before sending the tapes to the commercial banks.

The national ACH is, in fact, a further implementation of the "Communications Medium" shown in figures 2 and 4. It is only one possible implementation; another will be suggested below. The number of ACH sites is expected to be between 12 (Federal Reserve Bank cities) and 44 (planned Regional Check Processing Center cities).

Summary of Communications Requirements for ACH Operation

A. Large traffic volume;

B. Overnight operation;

C. 86% local traffic, remainder for other regions;

454

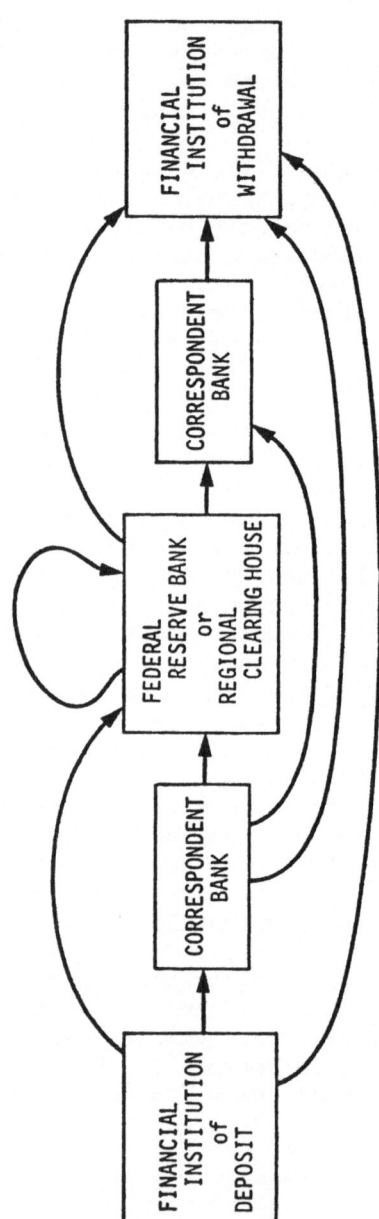

Figure 7   THE CHECK CLEARING SYSTEM

D. Extremely low undetected transmission error probability;

E. System uptime must be sufficient to guarantee overnight service;

F. Very large number of nodes in national system (100-2,000 participating banks); and

G. Nodes are not homogenous in either hardware or software.

Point-of-Sale Switch

A far more demanding application, both from the banks' computer system and the communications systems' point of view, is the Point-of-Sale system. The principal attribute of POS causing the difficulty is the rapid response required to satisfy the merchant and his customer. The transaction data must be entered, transmitted to the customer's bank, posted to his account, then an acknowledgment returned to the merchant and customer within the 1-2 minutes it currently takes to complete a credit card or cash transaction. Other applications planned for the POS system which also require rapid response are credit card and check validation service.

In the POS system the data traffic flows from the merchant's terminal to the customer's bank. The terminal must therefore speak to a number of different banks, not just the merchant's bank. Rather than having each terminal call many banks and having a bank talk to many potentially different terminals, the Atlanta Study suggests that a message switch called the Switching and Processing Center (SPC) be installed as the go-between from the terminals to the banks and back. It also serves as a transaction logging station for preparation of tapes and paper for the automated and nonautomated banks, respectively, that are not able to handle the on-line traffic during the day. In addition, there is a separate system proposed for negatively acknowledging known bad accounts called the Negative Authorization System (NAS). The NAS will have messages automatically routed to it for validation of a transaction in the event that the customer's bank's computer is inoperative-- either because it is not yet able to handle the communications from the SPC or because it is temporarily out of service. In the first case, the NAS serves as a full time authorization system for the bank, whereas in the latter case, it is used as a backup facility. In either case, the NAS system does not take financial responsibility for the transaction, it merely gives the merchant a higher expectation of payment.

The Atlanta Study POS system is designed to be a local system. Its generalization to a national system is not discussed in detail in the Atlanta report. The difficulty with local-based systems is that all fraud attempts would soon be made with non-local cards making merchants much more suspicious of the honest traveler. A National System could be created to perform the NAS function, but it is not likely that on-line debit would be feasible with the current design.

The Upper Arlington (Project POST) and Hempstead experiments were conducted by a single bank in each area. Problems of multiple banks, heterogenous terminals and servicing nonautomated banks were not considered.

Summary of Communication Requirements for Point-of-Sale System:

A.   Large traffic volumes;

B.   Immediate inquiry-response;

C.   Most traffic local but with eventual demand for national capability system;

D.   Extremely low undetected transmission error probability;

E.   Extremely high uptime;

F.   Mixture of terminal-to-bank, bank-to-terminal, and bank-to-bank traffic; and

G.   Must service 5,000 potentially dissimilar terminals.

DISTRIBUTED COMMUNICATIONS

In the past five years a new type of communications network has been developed for providing rapid, dependable, and economical data transmission service. The system was designed to permit responsive communications between terminals and a computer and between two computers. The technology used in these systems is called "packet switching"; this technology is briefly described below; a thorough description may be found in the literature.[6,7] This technology appears to offer the only practical answer to the communications requirements of the future EFTS.

The principal attributes of Distributed Communications are: 1) Responsiveness, rapid delivery of messages through high speed communication lines (.2 to 2 seconds per message); 2) Reliability, internal error detection and retransmission to obtain delivery error rates of 1 message in 10^{12}; 3) Low downtime, automatic routing of messages and inherent alternate path capability permit continued service through all single and some multi-line failures; and 4) Economy, as the system approaches capacity the cost of transmitting a message is less than $.01. Packet switching networks are in operational use in the computer science research community (under the sponsorship of the Advanced Research Projects Agency [ARPA] of the U.S. Department of Defense); under test at the National Physical Laboratory, Great Britain; in design by the French Government (Cyclides), British Post Office (Experimental Packet Switching System [EPSS]), and Canadian Government Research community (CANUNET); and under consideration and study by the Defense Communications Agency in the U.S. and by several corporations. In the U.S., also, several applications have been filed with the Federal Communications Commission for common carrier authority to provide packet switched service to the public.

The basic approach in a Distributed Packet Switched Communications System is to use very small, fast, reliable minicomputers as routing centers between nodes. The minicomputers, or Interface Message Processors (IMPs, in the ARPA terminology), are inexpensive enough so that messages can flow through several IMPs without affecting the cost of message transmission and fast enough so that processing by several enroute IMPs will not seriously affect the time required to deliver a message. Thus many IMPs can be sparsely connected to one another with high speed communication lines and achieve system performance comparable to a system where each pair of nodes is connected together with a physical communication line.

The IMP makes the communication system look to the node computer which it serves (called a Host) like a high performance Input-Output device. Its performance is virtually error free; a message is received in error once in a trillion (10^{12}) times. It accepts and delivers messages at computer compatible speeds (100 to 200 kilobits per second) although the average bandwidth is considerably less. It acknowledges receipt of the message back to the sender, generally within 0.5 seconds (when wideband transmission lines are used), or informs the sender of the reason for non-delivery, such as receiving site is not in service or would not accept the message, etc. The IMP is easily interfaced to a variety of computers, as already proven in the ARPA Network. It can handle multiple computers (up to three) at any site. It is highly reliable, having no moving parts except fans, and can easily be duplexed for even greater reliability. And it is inexpensive, costing only $40,000 for the purchase of each (simplex) IMP.

The IMP separates the Host computer from the communication lines used for the actual transmission of information. The Host is not aware of the topology of the communication lines or any of their characteristics, such as speed, error performance, current operational status, etc. These details are the responsibility of the IMP. Without any change in the Host, any network communication line can be varied from 9.6 kilobits per second to 230.4 kilobits per second. If a line is removed entirely, the IMP will route the message along a different path making the communication system impervious to single line failures. If the network is properly organized, it can be made impervious to multiple line failure to any level of reliability required.

Messages may be routed through several IMPs until they reach their destination Host. The IMP is clever enough to choose a route on the basis of prevailing traffic conditions in the network at the time of transmission. This maximizes the amount of traffic that can be handled by the network and allows transmission of bursts of information at higher than the average rated capacity for short periods of time without degrading the service.

The ARPANET uses 50 kilobit per second transmission facilities throughout and has achieved the following performance levels:

Capacity:	16 kilobits per second per node or 40 messages (of 50 characters each) per second per node or 1.44 million (50 character) messages per day per node.
Burst Rate:	60 kilobits per second.
Service Outages:	Less than 1% average.
Delivery Time:	0.2 seconds for 125-character message.
Cost:	$40 per hour per node for 10-hour day, 5 days per week, or about $.28 per 1,000 messages at capacity.

APPLICATION OF DISTRIBUTED COMMUNICATIONS TO
AN ELECTRONIC FUNDS TRANSFER SYSTEM

The approach taken in this section is to design an evolutionary plan showing the growth of a distributed communications system to encompass the known requirements of the EFTS. The design is a top-down analysis with the backbone or spine network being implemented first, and regional distribution systems developing later. Alternative evolutionary plans can be constructed. The purpose of this section is to indicate to the financial community that a viable, economical solution exists for the transmission of funds transfer requests in electronic form on a national (and international) basis. The financial community should therefore begin resolving the important issues of: 1) Form and format of the transactions; 2) Public acceptance of the concept; and 3) The

security features required to protect the corporations and
individuals who use the system.

The plan proposed has five levels of development: 1) The
interconnection of automated clearing houses; 2) The connection
of financial institutions to their local clearing house; 3) The
interconnection of financial institutions directly; 4) The connection of commercial corporations to their finaicial institutions;
and 5) The introduction of point-of-sale terminals.

System 1:   National Automated Clearing House

California has an operational Automated Clearing House
(ACH), Atlanta is getting one, and several other cities are expected to follow suit. Once these centers have been established
there will remain the problem of sending interregional data
between them. It will clearly be unreasonable to expect the
practice to continue of printing interregional transactions on
paper and mailing them to their destination. Several alternatives
exist for attaining national ACH service. They are: 1) Mail sorted
tapes to appropriate ACH; 2) Transmit sorted tapes electronically
on tape-to-tape transmission units; 3) Send unsorted tapes of all
outgoing traffic to a central ACH for sorting and transmission;
or 4) Connect the local ACHs together into a network permitting
the transmission of transactions as they are received by the ACH.

The final alternative is both more general than the
others and more difficult to achieve. It is more general in the
sense that it provides an extensible environment in which to
functionally grow. It is more difficult to achieve in that it
requires a communications network to transmit the transactions
from one ACH to another and it requires reprogramming the ACH
system to use the network for sending and receiving interregional
transactions. This paper will hopefully show, through the following design examples, that the extra effort is worthwhile.

A distributed, packet switched network for a national
ACH could be implemented by placing a simplex or duplex (depending
on the level of reliability required) IMP at each ACH site. The
IMPs would then be connected together by communications lines
whose size and number would depend on the estimated or actual
traffic volume. Lines could be added or upgraded individually as
traffic demand grew.

It is this flexible growth potential of the distributed
communications concept that provides the main advantage to this
design. The number of nodes may vary from 2 to 40 (the current
size of the operational ARPANET) to more than 500 (the maximum
number of nodes simulated in a design study)[8] without any change
in the system--using, in fact, the current ARPA implementation of

the technology. The network traffic capacity can also grow by upgrading the existing transmission services or adding more lines.

The network can also grow functionally, adding more services, because the communications system has no knowledge of the data portion of the message. Different services, changing the content of the messages, can be offered without change to the communications system. The messages contain a simple header with little more than the address for delivery. The changing of the message format or content would therefore have no effect on the communications portion of the National ACH.

The primary design problem yet unresolved is the software modification to the existing ACH system needed to permit the sending and receiving of interregional transactions via the communications network. The principal alternatives for receiving are: 1) Allowing transactions to come in anytime the system is operational and either processing them as they enter the system or "spooling" them out on intermediate storage for later servicing in batch mode; and 2) Polling the other systems one at a time, collecting all cumulative traffic. The sending policy must reflect the receiving policy chosen. The trade-offs in the alternatives are very complex, but basically the more interactive the choice, the more difficult it is to program. The more interactive the communications network, however, the closer it will resemble the system of immediate posting, check verification and Point-of-Sale Systems (to be described further in System 5).

The cost per node in a National ACH communications system has been estimated and is given below. Only the major identifiable items are listed; no attempt has been made at completeness.

	Description	Per Node Purchase	Yearly Cost
1.	Duplex IMP with Host interface	$50-150K	$12- 37K
2.	Equipment and System Maintenance		$10K
3.	Transmission facilities		$20- 50K
4.	ACH Reprogramming	$50K	$12K
5.	TOTAL	$100-200K	$54-109K

The Atlanta Payments Study projected a traffic volume through the Atlanta ACH in the 5th year, of 2.2 million transactions per month or 26.4 million transactions per year. If 14% of those transactions are inter-district, the transmission cost per transaction would be 1.5 to 3¢. This traffic level would absorb less than 5% of the total network capability. Even the current technology used in implementing the ARPA Network has enough growing room to handle a reasonable fraction of the total 21 billion checks per year now being written. An analysis of cost vs. traffic for the National ACH system was performed for the Federal Reserve System[9] which shows the cost per transaction falls rapidly with increasing traffic to less than one mill for a full EFTS.

System 2: Connecting Financial Institutions to
          Automated Clearing Houses

The communications path between the ACH and Financial Institutions* (FI) is currently a courier carrying magnetic tape. For short distances this path can be modeled as a high bandwidth (a full tape traveling for one hour has a bandwidth of approximately 30K bits per second), low cost (a full tape at $20 total transportation cost is approximately 20¢ per million bits) communications channel. The bandwidth and cost estimates are very difficult to improve upon electronically. The one thing the channel lacks, however, is response (delivery) time.

The response time may be improved in a number of ways and at an expected increase in cost. The reasons for improving response time may include: 1) Same-day handling of return (rejected) transactions, 2) Immediate posting of the transaction desired, or 3) Acknowledgment of transaction or verification of funds available. The extent to which the response time need be improved is indeterminant until the Financial Community determines what services it wishes to provide. If, for example, the Community intends to provide immediate posting service from point of sale terminals it is clear that a more responsive communications system is required.

If the fast response requirement does exist there are several ways to meet it. Three alternatives are shown in figure 8; these designs assume that a National ACH communications system exists. All three are considered good designs that may co-exist simultaneously in the network. The choice of design will depend on such factors as: traffic level, reliability desired, response time, and services offered by local ACH.

*The term Financial Institution is used as a generic description of today's Commercial Bank; changes in the payments system may in fact be accompanied by some restructuring in the Financial Community.

462

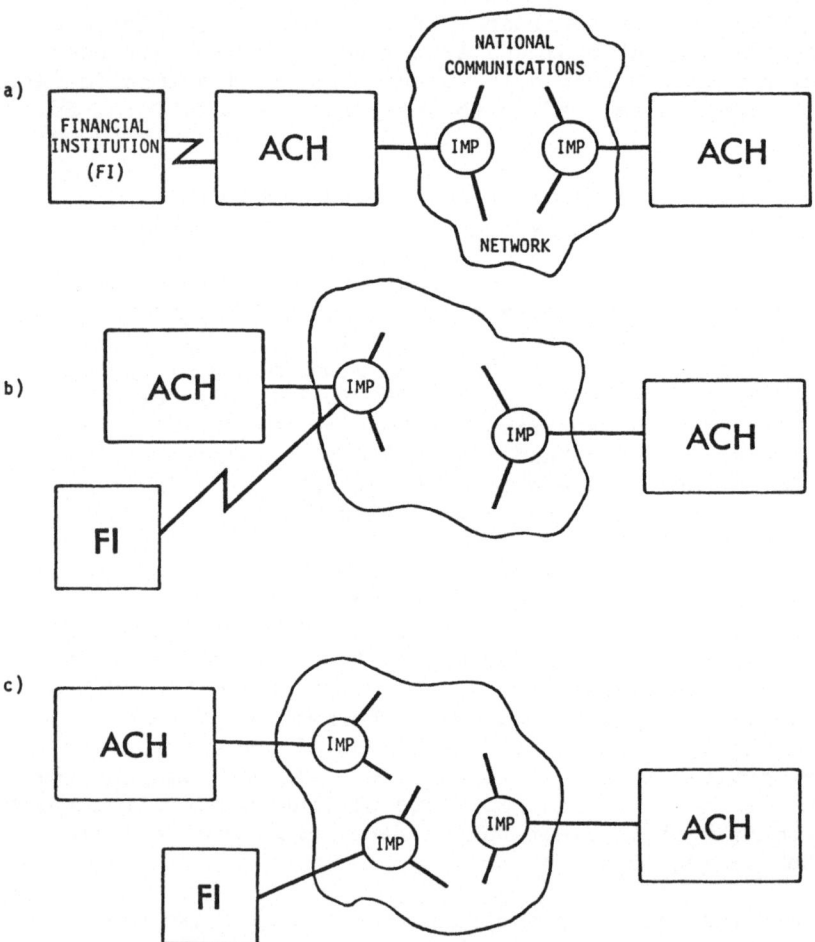

Figure 8   POSSIBLE INTER-CONNECTION OF FINANCIAL INŞTITUTION
            AND AUTOMATED CLEARING HOUSE

Figure 8a shows the FI computer connected directly to the local ACH via communications line. This configuration requires that a communications protocol be established between the ACH and FI. The ACH must be designed to handle several such connections if this form of connection is permitted. The primary advantage of this design is low cost, with the major cost categories being data sets, line charges, communications interfaces for FI and ACH reprogramming.

The second design has the FI communicating directly with the local IMP rather than the ACH. The advantage of this organization is that the FI can receive traffic from other ACHs without going through the local ACH. The communications protocol is also well defined and tested by the ARPANET.[10] A slight re-design of the IMP is required to permit a large number of these interfaces to be connected to one IMP. Reliability may be a problem in this design unless multiple lines are used between the FI and IMP. The major cost items are: data sets, line charges, IMP reprogramming and interface charges, and FI reprogramming and interface.

The third alternative (figure 8c) connects the FI into the network in precisely the same way as the ACH. The primary advantage of this design is homogeneity. All of the advantages of having a distributed network as described in System 1 for the ACHs are now granted to the FI. Due to traffic considerations the FIs may be physically connected together with local lines between their IMPs. The system may then look like a backgone or spine connecting the ACHs and local subnetworks connecting the FIs to the local ACH. Logically, however, every node is identical, with every FI capable of sending messages to any other FI without having the messages pass through an intermediary. The local sub-networks may have comparable bandwidth lines to the backbone network since most of the data in the Financial Community (96%) remains local. The costs and major items for this alternative remain about the same as in System 1, or about $54K to 109K per year per FI.

System 3:   Financial Institution to Financial Institution

In the current payment system, FIs in the same geo-graphic area may set up a separate clearing arrangement. This special arrangement may reduce clearance time, may reduce the cost of the transaction, or may accrue some other positive benefit to both banks. In an EFTS, the benefits may change but there still may be a need for direct FI-to-FI transactions without an intermediary.

Having FIs communicate directly with one another is a natural outgrowth of design 2 or 3 in System 2. Since everyone is an equal partner in the network it is just as natural for two FIs to communicate as it is to have two ACHs communicate.

The FIs may establish services outside of that provided by the NACH. Special protocols may be developed, and exchanges take place not under control of the NACH. The systems developed would only be subject to regulation and control by some overseeing body rather than being limited by communications system design constraints.

There is no additional cost in allowing FI-to-FI communication other than the reprogramming cost in the FI computer for handling any new protocols developed.

System 4:   Commercial Corporations to Financial Institutions

The basis for establishing an ACH was to be able to transmit a financial transaction from one FI to another. The financial transaction is to be created in digital form by one of three methods: 1) Electronic Payroll, 2) Preauthorized Payment, or 3) the Bill-Check. Although some payroll and most of the pre-authorized payment transactions are generated within the FI, the other transactions will be created elsewhere. The payroll will be created on a corporation's computer or at some service organi-zation. The bill check will be keyed in, at the utility company or wherever bill check service is offered. The current plan is to have these organizations prepare magnetic tape for physical delivery to the FI.

For many organizations this may remain the most cost-effective way to provide this service. For others the traffic and service may demand direct connection to the Financial Community Network. The interconnection designs for connecting commercial corporations into the network are identical to those in System 2. In this case, however, the connection point would be to a FI.

One of the primary advantages to a corporation joining the network using design 2 or 3 is that the corporation can choose one or more FIs for service no matter where they are located. The corporation could choose the FI based on the services it provides, such as payroll, collection services, planning and management services, immediate short term notes, etc. Some FIs may offer immediate inquiry service on account information for better money management. The FIs may therefore use the network to provide the corporation with services beyond the EFTS.

A number of corporations would be likely near-term candidates for this service. These are organizations which currently use some form of automated billing system. At present, such systems prepare customer bills on paper for mailing. The system would be modified to prepare an electronic transaction to be passed on to the corporation's FI for collection. Corporations which seem natural for this activity include: airlines, stock brokers, car rental agencies, credit card companies, central billing systems, etc.

Since the designs for connecting corporations into the network are identical to those for connecting the FIs, the cost and major cost elements would be the same. The number of nodes in the network may now be large enough to affect the IMP production cost, the maintenance cost and service, and the transmission line cost. Larger networks exhibit more reliable and more responsive service because there are more alternative paths for the traffic and greater transmission line bandwidths. The distributed communications system is interesting and perhaps unique in that as the traffic and the number of nodes increase the reliability increases and the response time decreases.

System 5: Point of Sale Systems

The capture of transactions at the point of origin is both the most interesting and the most demanding application. The point-of-sale (POS) terminal must generate a message, the message must go to the customer's FI, (perhaps through an intermediary computer system to put the message into standard form), the FI must check the balance of the account, subtract the value of the purchase, and return a positive or negative acknowledgment to the terminal (again perhaps through an intermediary). This entire transaction should take place within the normal transaction time of today's credit card, check, or cash transaction. Decisions must be made concerning: 1) What security should be afforded the customer; 2) What should the terminal look like (this undoubtedly does not have a unique answer); 3) What should be the message formats; 4) What procedure should be followed if the FI's computer is down or if the terminal intermediary is down. Some work has been done to answer these questions (Upper Arlington, Hempstead, and Atlanta Payments Project) but much remains unresolved.

The Financial Community Network designer/supplier has two major alternatives vis-a-vis POS: 1) Supply all needed service, including terminals, terminal intermediary (if needed), alternate processor as backup for the FI's computer center, etc.; or 2) Provide a standard message transmission service from any terminal intermediary site to any FI. Although the first alternative might lead to quicker and more uniform service and greater standardization, this service does not appear to have the characteristics of a natural monopoly. For the latter alternative, on the other hand, a case could be made that it is in the public interest to provide a single source of message transmission service.

If the second alternative is followed, the implementation of a national POS network is a natural extension of the system designs presented above. The terminal intermediary (a computer system designed to accept the keystrokes or block input from the POS terminals and create a standard financial transaction message addressed to the customer's bank) would be connected to an IMP in the same manner proposed for ACHs, FIs, and large corporations. The terminal intermediary may be provided by: 1) a FI, 2) the terminal manufacturer, 3) the local shopping center, 4) a large department store or chain store, or 5) a private company.

The key to the success of this implementation of POS would be the responsiveness and low cost characteristics of the packet-switching system. The POS would also benefit from the natural wide coverage (national) of packet-switching. Since one of the cost justifications of POS is reduced fraud and bad debt losses it would be ludicrous to create a local verification system for nationally valid cash or credit cards. A local system would cause all card misuse to gravitate out of the area of coverage. (This is due to the strong natural selection process which would occur; individuals who don't go outside the local area would get caught.) In a national system a lost or stolen card would presumably be valueless. If the cards become internationally valid the scope of coverage of the POS verification must follow.

In order to minimize the complexity of the terminal intermediaries and reduce the redundant backup required by FIs, the Financial Community Network might demand a prespecified alternate site for traffic in the event of node outage. The alternate site may be another machine in the same FI, another FI, or a "Ghost Bank." The "Ghost Bank" would be a special site set up to do standardized message processing services for FIs that are temporarily out of service or that are not of sufficient size to warrant entry into the network. The Ghost Bank, in addition to recording the message, may provide negative acknowledgement service for accounts whose cards have been lost or stolen or which have been previously overdrawn. The Negative Acknowledgment System is described in the Atlanta Payments Study. The "Ghost Bank" service may be provided by: 1) The communications system, 2) A consortium of FIs, 3) A private company, or 4) A government agency. One prime candidate may be the existing Automated Clearing Houses.

The cost of the POS system would be largely dependent upon the cleverness of the terminal intermediary since most of the cost of POS is in local distribution. Communication of transactions from the terminal intermediary to a FI anywhere in the country would cost less than 1¢ per transaction.

CONCLUSION

The Electronic Funds Transfer System with its expected high volume, reliability and responsiveness requirements seem to be well matched with the capabilities of packet-switching technology. The economics of a national EFTS are not well developed, making it difficult to analyze the overall cost. The following summary is included to show that packet switching technology provides a viable communication system for the EFTS. The cost per year per node for such a system would be approximately $100K, including duplexed IMP, transmission facilities, hardware and software interfaces, and maintenance. For a site with more than 10 million transactions per year the communications cost of sending the transaction anywhere in the country would therefore be less than 1¢. For a Financial Community Network of a thousand nodes (e.g. 50 clearing houses, 200 banks, Fortune 500 corporations, and 250 POS terminal intermediaries) the total communications cost would be approximately $100 million, which is a small fraction of the $3 billion spent annually for check clearing and settlement. The national communications system would therefore be a small part of overall EFTS cost.

The network could begin with a modest investment by connecting existing and planned Automated Clearing Houses together using packet-switching. Capability to add Financial Institutions, Large Corporations and Point-of-Sale subnetworks must be allowed to permit the Financial Community Network to grow into its full potential.

1. Bank Administration Institute, <u>An Electronic Network for Interbank Payment Communications: A Design Study</u>, April 1969.

2. Committee on Paperless Entry, <u>Atlanta Payments Project</u>, Federal Reserve Station, Atlanta, Georgia, 1972.

3. Richardson, Dennis W., <u>Electronic Money: Evolution of an Electronic Funds Transfer System</u>, MIT Press, 1970.

4. Bank Administration Institute, <u>The Check Collection System: A Quantitative Description</u>, 1970.

5. San Francisco Clearing House Association, <u>SCOPE Procedural Guide</u>, August 1970.

6. Roberts, L.G., and Wessler, B.D., <u>Computer Network Development to Achieve Resource Sharing</u>, SJCC, 1970.

7. Heart, F., et al, <u>The Interface Message Processor for the ARPA Computer Network</u>, SJCC, 1970.

8. Network Analysis Corporation, <u>Fifth Semi-annual Technical Report for the Project, "Analysis and Optimization of Store-and-Forward Computer Networks"</u>, Defense Documentation Center, Alexandria, Virginia, June 1972.

9. Network Analysis Corporation, <u>Packet-Switched Communications Networks for Electronic Funds Transfer Systems: A Feasibility Study</u>, performed for the Federal Reserve, January 1973.

10. Bolt Beranek and Newman Inc., <u>Specification for the Interconnection of a Host and an IMP</u>, Report No. 1822, revised December 1972.

COST TRADEOFFS BETWEEN LOCAL AND REMOTE COMPUTING

Bennet P. Lientz

University of Southern California*

ABSTRACT

A major problem in communication networks analysis is to determine the degree of centralization of computer power that is desirable from both an operational and cost/benefit point of view. An example of this problem occurs in a manufacturing complex wherein decisions must be made on the distribution of data, process power, and redundancy.

Because of the many parameters involving hardware, system software, and communications, a purely analytical approach is often impractical. The method here is to employ an analytical simulation model to obtain measures of cost, throughput, and response time. After the model itself is examined, focus is placed on several experiments which reveal the superiority of semi-centralized configurations. Application to logistic and manufacturing systems are explored along with the development of a network link construction method.

The above mentioned experiments reveal the dependence of the analysis on the characteristics of the actual or anticipated message traffic. For a manufacturing system, a method is developed for isolating parts of a computer network as a specific degree of importance to the network functioning and failing. This is examined in the context of the message traffic rather than graph theoretic methods. More specifically, in a manufacturing environment we wish to consider the importance of hardware,

*This work was partially supported by the U. S. Office of Naval Research under contract N00014-67-A-0269-0027.

management information systems, and data bases to the functioning of a computer network system. Viewed mathematically, the importance of functioning of a subsystem is the differential between the conditional probability of the system working given that the subsystem is functioning and the probability of the system working. To minimize downtime the objective is to level the importance of certain centers so that overall system reliability is maintained and yet reaches high level by spreading the risk of failure. Using the network model described above, we can construct estimates of importance of selected subsystems. This method allows for the measurement of the network in terms of overall performance rather than in terms of specific single performance measures.

1. INTRODUCTION

There is increasing attention being directed toward evaluating the feasibility and optimal design of computer networks for specific government and private organizations. The question as to whether to construct a network then becomes one of cost effectiveness and tradeoffs between cost and performance. Further consideration must be given to existing facilities, hardware, data bases, and personnel staffing. Such questions are important because they affect the degree and success of implementation of a network.

This paper is directed at several questions involving the degree of centralization. We first consider some of the factors affecting implementability. In Section 2 a summary of some centralization experiments appear along with a discussion of their impact. These experiments reveal that traffic in the network is a prime factor in considering tradeoffs. Section 3 presents some preliminary results on design with sensitivity to message traffic. In Section 4, some applications of the work is examined along with the criteria of measurement in cost.

Determining the proper degree of centralization requires detailed knowledge of parameters involving the location of centers, hardware characteristics, the nature of the jobs and messages in the network, and the communications arrangement in a proposed network. For a short or intermediate term analysis, it is possible to obtain statistics on hardware associated with both computation and communication. However, the sensitivity of the results to the message traffic, job type, and job mixture requires that some analysis must be done to predict future traffic requirements. Without a network, this can be done statistically using past data and information provided by users of the facilities. However, a network can have a profound effect on both the nature and type of work done. For example, a job presently heavily I/O oriented for a small machine may be modified so that it is cpu oriented and bound on a large computer. Thus, elements of transferability need to be considered. Having additional capabilities in the network may spur the creation of large data bases as well as acquiring new software systems. These systems may not have been cost effective prior to the construction of the network, but become much more effective with the larger number of users provided by the network. The impact of the network deserves further future study. Of interest here is the importance that its impact may have on the message traffic itself.

Having proper parameter values in considering the network structure is of interest in implementation. Certainly it is highly unlikely that all values can be predicted accurately. However, enough realism is necessary to insure that a cost effective transition can be made from present configurations to future systems. Here we need to further consider both cost effectiveness and physical transfer. The results of sample network run are summarized in Figure 1. At point 1 we have the system with

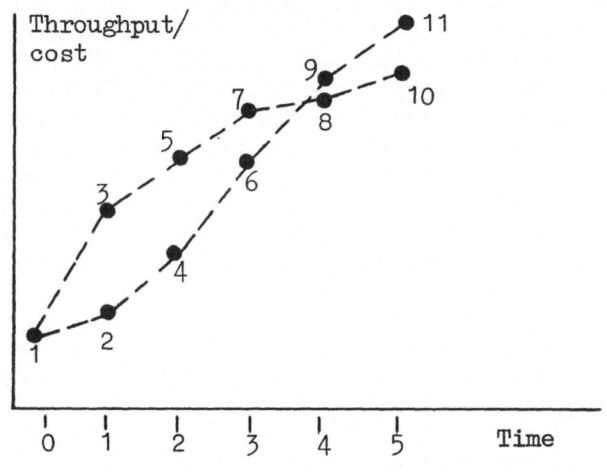

Figure 1

Graph of Implementation of a Sample Network

its cost effectiveness at an initial time. At point 11 we have
the optimal end design results. Cost effectiveness is measured
here in throughput per unit cost. Intermediate points are
attained by sequentially altering the computation or communication hardware. There are two paths shown from point 1. The
first is less cost effective in intermediate time ranges, but
reaches point 11. The second path strays into hardware configurations that cannot reach point 11 without major changes. The
second path is also locally cost effective at certain times.
This example points out that non-local planning must be done
before embarking on an upgrading of system components.

Having briefly discussed some implementation considerations,
let us turn to the analysis task itself. To perform the necessary experimentation two levels of models are required. First, a
general, analytic model is necessary to determine overall degrees
of centralization and to assist in selecting the steps in
accomplishing a phasing in of the network. Secondly, we require
a detailed, discrete model to evaluate behavior at specific sites.

The analytic model is discussed in Cady, Lientz, and Willmorth.[1] Input includes characteristics of message traffic,
hardware, jobs to be processed, priority arrangements, and communications topology. This model does not consider individual
jobs and messages. Instead it analyzes the input in terms of
averages using queueing results for communication with a similarly based model for computation. On the other hand the discrete model considers individual jobs and messages. The discrete analysis tools have considerable appeal in application to
more than local environments. However, the computer time and
effort needed to collect data prohibit wide usage. A number of
discrete models have been constructed. In particular a simulation language, ECSS, oriented toward computers has been developed
at the Rand Corporation. ECSS is written through SIMSCRIPT and
has shown to be useful in expressing parameters for computer
simulation.

Validation of the models is discussed in [1]. Specific
application to several military networks are considered in Lientz
and Willmorth.[6] In applications and validation, attention must
be paid to each area of the system. For example, validation
must be done separately for hardware and for the modeling of I/O
and cpu balance and overlap. Further experiments using these
models are discussed in the next section.

2. EXPERIMENTATION

This section summarizes briefly some of the experiments that
have been conducted with regard to centralization of computation.

To provide a background for the experiment results, we first consider the setting of the network. A 40 center network was
hypothesized in 26 distinct American cities with eight cities
having multiple centers. The network topology was based on a
link removal process discussed in [1]. At a given iteration the
least cost effective link was removed in terms of throughput per
unit cost. The process was constrained by requiring an articula-
tion level 2 being maintained. Line size was selected at 50 kb
with standard line costs. Message traffic was based on a function of population and distance. For hardware, the IBM 360 line
was selected for consistency in cost as well as hardware characteristics. Characteristics were obtained from Keydata and Auer-
bach references. Standard configurations were selected for each
machine. A fixed cost ceiling was assumed with approximately
10-12% of the fiscal resources devoted to communications, the
balance in computation. Three job types were hypothesized. The
first type was a scientific nature which is characterized as
being 90% cpu and 10% I/O. Mixed jobs were 50% cpu and 50% I/O.
The third type, commercial jobs, were 10% cpu and 90% I/O.

The centralized configuration placed 360/85 or larger computers in one city (New York) with 360/20 at remote sites. The
semi-centralized configuration located these larger computers
across the nation. The distributed case provided each site with
a 360/30 or a more powerful machine. Jobs sent from one site
were sent to the nearest machine capable of processing the job.

With all inputs collected, the analytic model was used to
construct the network configuration. In parallel, ECSS was
employed to analyze each of the individual hardware configurations.
Following this stage, a response time threshold was specified
(e.g., -- x% of jobs processed in y time units). Repeated experimentation was done to determine the throughput possible for
each job type and degree of centralization. Cost effectiveness
was measured in terms of throughput per unit cost.

The results of the experiments are summarized in Figure 2.
In this figure a relative scale appears on the horizontal scale.
Although three basic job types were considered scientific jobs
were considered in terms of sizes. In all but the large scientific jobs, the semi-centralized configuration was shown to be
more cost effective, following by the centralized configuration.

Some remarks should be made at this point. The exact input
values are given in [1]. Furthermore, it is possible to construct a set of parameters which could favor almost any configuration. Thus, the results should not be taken as theorems to be
applied in general. Rather, similar methodology can be employed
to evaluate and perform these trade-offs. The extent to which
trade-offs can be constrained will also affect results. For an

474

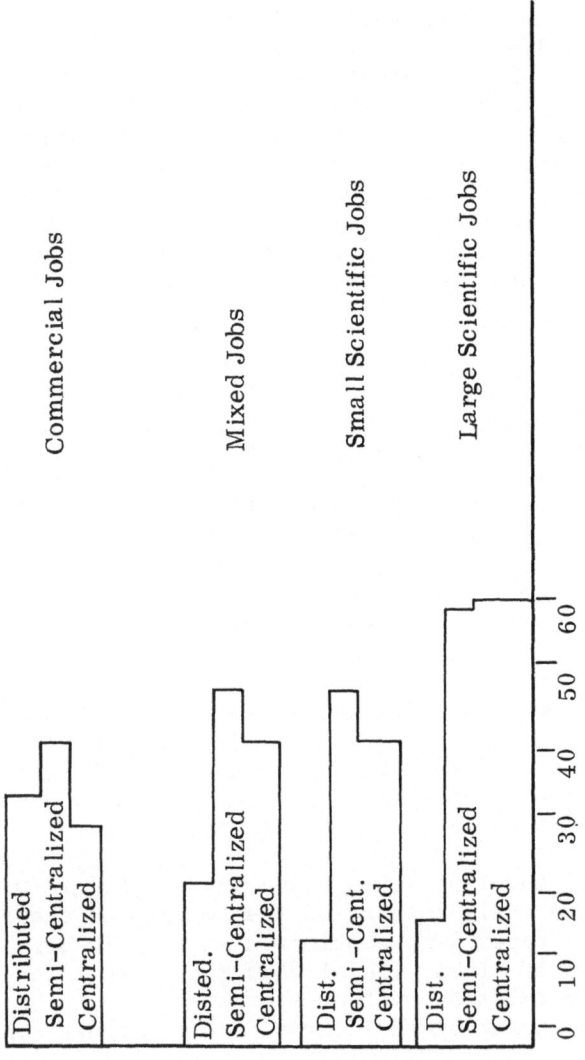

Figure 2: Relative Cost-Effectiveness of Job Types and Configuration

existing system of disjoint computers, a fixed budget, and very specific requirements as to the job types, message size, response time, and similar properties, several experiments were conducted. As an example, a Request for Proposal from General Services Administration[7] was considered. The network involves 15 regional center cities with each center having one center except Washington, D. C. which had two centers. Response time was such that 90% of the messages had to have a mean total response time for computation and communication of 10 seconds or less. In planning such a network, we first developed the configuration. The optimal percentage of communications with respect to total cost was shown to be 9.9%. The next phase consisted of determining the percentage of computation resources devoted to cpu. Here for percentages of cpu to I/O of 10, 25, and 50%, the best policy was to spend as high a per cent as possible (62%). Theoretical experiments revealed that were configurations available giving higher percentage in cpu. The highest throughput would be attained at slightly more than 65%, the exact point dependent on the fraction of cpu to I/O.

The above discussion has summarized a series of experiments conducted to determine the most desirable degree of centralization. A main result of the analysis was the degree to which the results are dependent on message traffic. This leads us to the problem not being mathematically well behaved, but combining many inter-related characteristics. This is explored further in Section 3.

3. DESIGN CONSIDERATIONS

Using the model and results obtained in the preceding sections, we can proceed to consider network design with sensitivity to message traffic. In theory it should be a condition that any two centers have at least two paths for message transmission to provide adequate reliability and redundancy. In practice with a large network, this is not economically possible. Instead we seek out the most "important" centers for the functioning and/or failing of the network and devote primary focus to these. Let N represent the set of centers along with known parameters concerning traffic, hardware, and communications. Let S be a subset of N so that S could be a sub-network or even consist of disjoint components of S.

With this notation, we can proceed to examine the functioning and failing of the network. As in reliability, there are several possible approaches. First, degrees of failure can be defined. The system can then be measured against these. However, in many military and commercial situations, the system either satisfies conditions on throughput and response time or

it does not. In the former (latter) case, we say the system has
functioned (failed). Let the event $\{N=0\}$ ($\{N=1\}$) denote the
event that the system fails (functions). Of the spectrum of
parameters, some are fixed throughout the analysis. Others are
either variable with respect to time or have statistical distributions. Examples are the mixture of high priority traffic over
time, error rate, and frequency of repair. By specifying a level
for each parameter, we can employ the analytic model to determine
whether the resulting system satisfied conditions on throughput,
response time, and overall system reliability. By successive
runs of the model (which can be done in a few batch processing
runs) the distribution of the functioning and failing of the
system can be estimated. Because of the number of parameters,
an analytical approach is difficult. For example, some centers
could fail completely and yet the overall system functions at an
acceptable level. Some remarks on the distribution of the system
are necessary. For a fixed set of inputs, there are only two
states possible. The distribution of functioning enters in that
functioning occurs over only certain combinations of ranges of
parameters. Mathematically we have an indicator function over a
multi-dimensional topological space. Because of the number and
interrelation of the variables, the individual ranges over which
a system works have little meaning for even moderately sized
networks. The situation, in general, is much more complex than
the common reliability situation. For example, in reliability,
we can delete components as inessential if their performance has
no effect on that of the system. For a network, a component
is only inessential with respect to certain values of the other
parameters. In view of the above remarks, it is understood that
the probability of a system working ($P(N=1)$) is really the probability that the values of the input variables produce, in the
aggregate, acceptable levels of performance.

We can now define the importance of a subsystem S of a network N for the functioning and failing of the network. Formally,
we have:

Definition 3.1. The importance of functioning and failing are
given respectively by:

$$IM_1(S,N) = P[N=1|S=1] - P[N=1] \qquad (3.1)$$

and

$$IM_0(S,N) = P[N=0|S=0] - P[N=0] \qquad (3.2)$$

Adding these we define:

Definition 3.2. The general importance of S with respect to N is:

$$IM(S,N) = P[N=1|S=1] + P[N=0|S=0] - 1 \qquad (3.3)$$

Implicit to this concept of importance is the equal weight given to failure and success. In some applications such as command and control, failure may be of more concern.

Definition 3.3. The α-importance of S with respect to N is defined by:

$$IM(S,N,\alpha) = \alpha P[N=1|S=1] + (1-\alpha) P[N=0|S=0] - 1 \qquad (3.4)$$

From these definitions we have:

$$IM(S,N,\alpha) < IM(S,N)$$

and

$$2IM(S,N,1/2) = IM(S,N)$$

The following proposition relates to subsets of N.

Proposition 3.1. If S_1 and S_2 are two subsets of N with $S_1 \subset S_2$, then:

$$IM_i(S_1,N) \leq IM_i(S_2,N) \quad i = 0,1$$

and

$$IM(S_1,N,\alpha) \leq IM(S_2,N,\alpha)$$

for $0 \leq \alpha \leq 1$.

Importance is used here in a mathematical context. The distribution is tied to the network parameters. However, it is possible to relate the results to traditional network analysis. We will make the following definition for a cut set.

Definition 3.4.   S is a cut set for N if

$$IM_0(S,N) = P[N=1]$$

Thus, all cut sets have the same importance for failing. Furthermore, we have the following proposition.

Proposition 3.2. If S_1 and S_2 are subsets of N and S_2 is a cut set of N then:

$$IM_0(S_1,N) \leq IM_0(S_2,N)$$

with equality if and only if S_1 is a cut set of N.

This proposition shows that cut sets are the most important subsets of N.

Having given some initial results for importance, we can consider its application in upgrading an existing network. By determining the most $\mathscr{L}$-importance components, we can now consider these as the first candidates for being upgraded to enhance the performance of the network. In applications, the problem of determining the values to use to estimate importance are of interest. Here we can employ the concept of modal intervals as given in Lientz.[4,5] For f in continuous density, β a point in [0,1], and x a real number, we define $S(x;\beta,f)$ as the smallest non-negative quantity satisfying

$$\int_{[x-S(x;\beta,f),\ x+S(x;\beta,f)]} f(y)dy = \beta$$

(3.5)

Then we can select the point x_0 at which the infimum of $S(.)$ is attained for values of x. The endpoints and midpoint of the modal interval $[x_0-S(x_0;\ .),\ x_0 + S(x_0;.)]$ can then be used as inputs for the parameters. This provides an estimate of the mass location for the particular parameter. For some cases where conservative estimates are necessary, lower (or upper) percentage points can be employed.

4. APPLICATIONS AND REMARKS

Several applications to computer networks have already been discussed. With the spread of network concepts, there is an increasing need for considering the impact of networks on production facilities and firms. Networks can influence not only the profitability of the firm, and productivity, but also, in the aggregate, balance of payments. Let us first consider the economic analysis aspects of networks. A network should be considered as possible acquisition of any new capital asset. Using concepts of engineering economy (see for example Fleischer[2] and Grant, Bell and Ireson[3]),we can compute the present worth and rate of return of the network. It will be necessary to demonstrate the utility of the network in this context since the network is competing with other projects for the same limited funds.

To apply capital budgeting or engineering economy, it is necessary to be able to estimate the effect of network technology on the productivity of the facility. To model this effect, a network model must be used in conjunction with production simulation and inventory models to arrive at effects on productivity. An analysis is needed to determine the effects of networks on project management.

In conclusion we have seen how analysis of centralization can be accomplished along with some aspects of a new focus needed to transfer the technology of computer networks to military and commercial users. Needed now is analysis of the impact and implementation of network concepts.

REFERENCES

1. Cady, G., Lientz, B. P., and Willmorth, N. E., Experiments in communication networks, Naval Res. Logist. Quart., (to appear).

2. Fleischer, G. A., Engineering Economy, Appleton-Century-Crofts, New York, 1969.

3. Grant, E. L., Bell, L. F., and Ireson, G., Principles of Engineering Economy, Ronald Press, New York, 1965.

4. Lientz, B. P., Properties of modal intervals, SIAM Journal of Applied Math., September 1971.

5. Lientz, B. P., A stochastic method of allocation of components, IEEE Transactions on Reliability, (to appear).

6. Lientz, B. P., and Willmorth, N. E., Systems analysis in communication networks, (submitted for publication).

7. General Services Administration, Request for Proposal for the PBS Information System, Public Building Services, Washington, 1 July 1971.

LIST OF PARTICIPANTS

Aarvold, Mr. Arne W.
Norwegian Telecommunications
Administration Research Establishment
Kjeller, Norway.

Abramson, Prof. N.
The ALOHA SYSTEM, University of Hawaii,
Honolulu, U.S.A.

Adam, Mr. T.W.
Post Office Corp., London, U.K.

Anderson, Mr. D.
Computer Centre, University of Birmingham,
Birmingham, U.K.

Andrews, Dr. Clayton,
IBM Research Laboratory, Ruschlikon, Switzerland.

Aufenkamp, Dr. Don,
National Science Foundation,
Office of Computing Activities, Washinton, U.S.A.

Bache, Mr. Alain,
C.N.E.T., Issy les Moulineaux, France.

Bacon, Mr. M.
Computer Science Dept., Hatfield Polytechnic,
Hatfield, U.K.

Banks, Mr. W.
Electrical Eng. Dept., University of Waterloo,
Waterloo, Canada.

Barber, Mr. D.L.A.
National Physical Laboratory, Teddington, U.K.

Bayliss, Dr. D.J.,
P.A. International Management Consultants,
Knightsbridge, U.K.

Barry, Mr. P.
RAF Medmenham, Marlow, U.K.

Beeforth, Mr. T.H.
School of Applied Sciences, University of Sussex,
Brighton, U.K.

Beizer, Dr. B.
Data Systems Analysts, Pennsauken, U.S.A.

Belsnes, Prof. Dag.
EDB-SENTERET, Blinder-Oslo, Norway.

Belton, Mr. Rex,
PO/THQ/TDD14.3, London, U.K.

Bengi, Dr. Halil,
Electrical Engineering Dept.,
Middle East Technical University, Ankara, Turkey.

Berg, Mr. D.N.
Stanford Research Institute, Stanford, U.S.A.

Berjak, Mr. M.
Dept. Of Computing & Cybernetics,
Brighton Polytechnic, Brighton, U.K.

Bianchi, Dr. A.
IBM Italy, Milano, Italy.

Bolognani, Mr. M.
Commission of the European Communities,
Joint Research Centre, Ispra, Italy.

Booker, Mr. J.
Computer Analysts and Programmers Ltd., London, U.K.

Borocin, Mr. L.
Eurosystem, S.A., Paris, France.

Bradley, Mr. T.
Electronic Associates Ltd., Sussex, U.K.

Braekhus, Mr. J.
A.S. Computas, Oslo, Norway.

Bright, Mr. R.D.
Post Office, London, U.K.

Broadbent, Mr. K.
ICL GmbH, Düsseldorf, W. Germany.

Brown, Mr. D.A.H.,
R.R.E., Malvern, U.K.

Bruins, Mr. T.
CERN, Geñeve, Switzerland.

Brunet, J-M, Mr.
Honeywell Bull, Paris, France.

Bryan, Mr. R.F.
Computer Systems Laboratory, University of
California, Santa Barbara, U.S.A.

Cabrini, Ing. T.
IBM Italy, Milano, Italy.

Cacciamani, Dr. E.R.
Earth Station Engineering, America Satellite
Corporation, Germantown, U.S.A.

Cain, Dr. G.
Polytechnic of Central London, London, U.K.

Can, Mrs. A. and Can, Mr. S.
Elektrik Boulmu, Istanbul, Turkey.

Casaca, Dr. A.D.
Electrical Engineering Dept.,
Instituto Superior Technico,
Lisbon, Portugal.

Cerf. Prof. V.
Stanford University, Stanford, U.S.A.

Cetincelik, Dr-Eng. M.
Ass. of Engineers and Architects in Turkey,
Ankara, Turkey.

Chambon, Mr. J-F.,
Ecôle des Mines, St. Etienne, France.

Chrétien, Mr. G.
S.I.T.A., Neuilly, France.

Chupin, Mr. J-C,
Enserg, Grenoble, France.

Clark, Mr. A.
GTE Information Systems Ltd., Feltham, U.K.

Clowes, Dr. G.
Bell-Northern Research, OTTAWA, Canada.

Cohen, Prof. D.
Harvard University, Center for Research in
Computing Technology, Cambridge, U.S.A.

Crick, Mr. P.
CDC Data Services, Barnet, U.K.

Curran, Mr. A.
Bell Northern Research Ltd., Ottawa, Canada.

Dahle, Mr. O.J.
Norwegian Defense Research Establishment,
Kjeller, Norway.

Danthine, Prof. A.
University de Liège, Liège, Belgium.

Davies, Mr. D.W.
National Physical Laboratory, Teddington, U.K.

D'Eath, Mr. J.
Data Communications, London, U.K.

Dervisoglu, Dr. A.
Technical University of Istanbul,
Istanbul, Turkey.

Dewis, Dr. I.G.
National Physical Laboratory, Teddington, U.K.

Dickins, Dr. Grahame J.
Dept. of Trade & Industry, London, U.K.

Dunn, Prof. D.A.
School of Engineering, Stanford University,
Stanford, U.S.A.

Eckardt, Mr. M.
Institut für Software Technologie, St. Augustin,
W. Germany.

Elie, Mr. M.
Cyclades Network, Louveciennes, France.

Engelbart, Mr. D.
Stanford Research Institute, Stanford, U.S.A.

Enslow, Dr. P.
U.S. European Research Office, London, U.K.

Ernst, Mr. H.
Naval Ship R & D Center, Bethesda, U.S.A.

Fedida, Mr. S.
P.O. Research Centre, London, U.K.

Figueiredo, Mario Joao,
Instituto de Investigacao Cientifica de Mozambique,
Laurenco Marques, Mozambique.

Flood, Prof. J.
Elec. Eng. Dept., University of Aston, Birmingham, U.K.

Foxley, Dr. E.
Dept. of Mathematics, University of Nottingham, U.K.

484

Frank, Mr. H.
Network Analysis Corporation, New York, U.S.A.

Fraser, Dr. A.G.
Bell Laboratories, Murray Hill, U.S.A.

Fratta, Dr. L.
Politecnico di Milano, Instituto di Elettrotechnica ed
Elettronica, Milano, Italy.

Gardner, Mr. A.
The Post Office, London, U.K.

Georges, Mr. J.
MBLE Research Lab., Brussels, Belgium.

Gibby, Mr. D.
Shape Technical Centre, The Hague, Holland.

Gill, Dr. S.
AP International Management Consultants Ltd.,
London, U.K.

Gitman, Dr. I.
Network Analysis Corporation, New York, U.S.A.

Gjertsen, Mr. T.
Norwegian Defence Research Establishment,
Kjeller, Norway.

Goddard, Mr. F.
H.Q. 90 Group, RAF Medmenham, U.K.

Greene, Mr. J.
IBM France, La Gaude, France.

Professor R.L. Grimsdale,
School of Applied Sciences, University of Sussex,
Brighton, U.K.

Halatsis, Mr. C.
NRC Democritus, Comp. Centre, Athens, Greece.

Hall, Miss J.
University of Bristol, School of Mathematics,
Bristol, U.K.

Handler, Prof. Dr. W.
Universität Erlangen-Nurnberg, Erlangen, W.Germany.

Hardman, Mr. V.
International Computers Ltd., London, U.K.

Heap, Mr. J.
CDC Data Services, Barnt, U.K.

Heart, Mr. F.E.
Bolt Beranek & Newman Inc., Cambridge, U.S.A.

Higgins, Mr.
Institute of Computer Science, London, U.K.

Holt, Mr. F.
IBM A/S, Lyngby, Denmark.

Hughes, Mr. P.
Logica Ltd., London, U.K.

Joachim, Dipl-Ing. Klaus,
NATO-NICSMA, Brussels, Belgium.

Johnson, Mr. P.
ICL, London, U.K.

Kahn, Dr. R.
Advanced Research Projects Agency, Arlington, U.S.A.

Kalra, Dr.
University of Waterloo, Waterloo, Canada.

Keen, Mr. D.G.
ICL, E & PS, Manchester, U.K.

Kennington, Mr. C.
U.C.L. Comp. Centre, London, U.K.

Kirstein, Prof. P.
Institute of Computer Science, London, U.K.

Kleinrock, Prof. L.
University of California, Los Angeles, U.S.A.

Knightson, Mr. K.G.
THQ/NPD/NP 4.2.2., London, U.K.

Konig, Mr.
SITA, Neuilly, France.

Kuo, Prof. F.F.
The Aloha System, University of Hawaii,
Honolulu, U.S.A.

Lalla, Mr. D.
University of London Comp. Centre, London, U.K.

Langguth, Mr. P.O.,
US Army Material Command, Alexandria, U.S.A.

Le Moli, Prof. G.
Politechnico di Milano, Instituto di Elettrotechnica
ed Elettronica, Milano, Italy.

Levilion, Mr. M.
IBM France, La Gaude, France.

Lientz, Dr. B.
University of Southern California, Los Angeles, U.S.A.

Linders, Dr. J.
University of Waterloo, Waterloo, Canada.

Lockwood, Mr. L.A.
Data Communications Marketing Dept., London, U.K.

Long, Mr. P.
Ohio College Library Centre, Columbus, U.S.A.

Lugaro, Dr. C.
IBM Italia, Milano, Italy.

Lundh, Mr. Y.
Norwegian Defence Research Establishment,
Kjeller, Norway.

McKenzie, Mr. A.
Bolt Beranek & Newman Inc., Cambridge, U.S.A.

Maffioli, Prof. F.
Politechnico di Milano, Milano, Italy.

Mahl, Dr. R.
Ecôles des Mines, St. Etienne, France.

Majithia, Prof. J.C.
University of Waterloo, Waterloo, Canada.

Malik, Mr. R.
London, U.K.

Mann, Mr. David,
Logica Ltd., London, U.K.

Manning, Prof.,
University of Waterloo, Canada.

Maritsas, Dr. D.
NRC Democritos, Athens, Greece.

Mauro, Dr. G.
IBM Italia, Milano, Italy.

Metaxaki- Kossionides, Mrs. C.
University of Athens, Athens, Greece.

Metcalfe, Mr. R.
Rank Xerox Inc., Palo Alto, U.S.A.

Miller, Mr. A.H.
Data Communications, London, U.K.

Mitchell, Mr. G.
P.O. Corporation, London, U.K.

Moreau, Mr. A.
CTN-EIA, Liège, Belgium.

Morgan, Prof. D.
University of Waterloo, Waterloo, Canada.

Nasr, Ir. S.
Kath. Univ. Leuven, Heverlee, Belgium.

Newell, Mr. R.
South West London College, London, U.K.

Newhall, Prof. E.E.
University of Toronto, Toronto, Canada.

Noirel, Mr. Y.
CCETT, Rennes, France.

Obakan, Mr. Y.
ITU Mim. Muh. Fakultesi Elektrik Bolumnu,
Istanbul, Turkey.

Odeyemi, Dr. I.A.
University of Ife, Ile-Ife, Nigeria.

Oizumi, Dr. J.
Tokyo University, Sendai, Japan.

O'Neill, Mr. J.
Burroughs Corporation, Paoli, U.S.A.

Oskasson, Prof. S.
University of Iceland, Reyjavik, Iceland.

Ozker, Prof. Dr. T.
Technical University of Istanbul, Istanbul, Turkey.

Paesler, Mr. M.R.A.
Plessey Telecom. Res. Ltd.
Taplow, U.K.

Palandri, Dr. E.
Division of Computing Research, Canberra, Australia.

Palmer, Mr. T.
Computer Weekly, London, U.K.

Paoletti, Mr. L.
DCA/DCEO H520, Reston, U.S.A.

Parish, Mr. M.
CERL, Leatherhead, U.K.

Parkes,
HQ90 Group, RAF Medmenham, U.K.

Peebles, Dr.,
University of Waterloo, Waterloo, Canada.

Philykyprou, Dr. G.
NRC Democritus, Athens, Greece.

Pouzin, Dr. L.
IRIA, Rocquencourt, France.

488

Powers, Mr. I.
Plessy Co. Ltd., Liverpool, U.K.

Prior, Dr. J.
R.R.E., Malvern, U.K.

Pyke, Mr. T.
National Bureau of Standards, Washington, U.S.A.

Randall, Mr. S.J.
British Steel Corporation, Birmingham, U.K.

Repichini, Mr. A.
SIP, Roma, Italy.

Riley, Miss J.
Post Office, London, U.K.

Roberts, Dr. L.
Bolt Beranek & Newman, Arlington, U.S.A.

Roeros, Mr. H.
Norwegian Defence Research Establishment,
Kjeller, Norway.

Roderer, Mr. G.
Rechenzentrum DTU, Munchen, W. Germany.

Rudin, Mr. H.
IBM Research Laboratory, Ruschlikon, Switzerland.

Samuelson, Dr. K.
Stockholm University, Stockholm, Sweden.

Santos, Mr. Manuel,
Instituto Investigacao Cientifica de Mocambique,
Lourenco Marques, Mozambique.

Saydam, Prof. Dr. T.
Marmara Scientific and Industrial Research Inst.,
Izmir, Turkey.

Scherer- Goossens, Mrs. Dr. P.
Centre Nationale de Documentation Scientifique et
Technique, Bruxelles, Belgium.

Schmalfeld, Mr. H.
Universität Munchen, Munchen, W. Germany.

Sennett, Dr. C.
R.R.E., Malvern, U.K.

Sewell, Mr. I.
International Computers Ltd., London, U.K.

Shepard, Dr. C.D.
Communications Research Centre, Ottowa, Canada.

Smith, Mr. B.T.
Central Computer Agency, London, U.K.

Smith, Miss E.
International Computers Ltd., Manchester, U.K.

Smith, Mr. J.M.
Plessey Radar, West Drayton, U.K.

Smith, Mr. M.B.
Post Office, London, U.K.

Smith, Mr. P.
Directorate of Telecommunications, London, U.K.

Smith, Mr. S.
Bureau Berenschot-Diebold, Utrecht, Netherlands.

Spence, Dr. R.
Imperial College, London, U.K.

Stackpole, Mr. D.
Digital Equipment Corp. Maynard, U.S.A.

Stagner, Mr. H.
Singer Business Machines, Bruxelles, Belgium.

Stokes, Dr. A.
Institute of Computer Science, London, U.K.

Stopford, Mr. A.
Government Communications, Cheltenham, U.K.

Storey, Mr. M.
P.O. Telecommunications, London, U.K.

Sucksmith, Mr. K.
Plessey Co. Ltd., Liverpool, U.K.

Svela, Mr. K.
Norwegian Telecommunications Administration,
Oslo, Norway.

Swahn, Mr. L.G.
Stockholms Universitet, Stockholm, Sweden.

Szentivanyi, Mr. T.
Systems Engineering Institute, Budapest, Hunary.

Tibbals, Dr. E.
University of Glasgow, Glasgow, Scotland.

Tomlinson, Mr. P.N.
THQ/TD15.2.2., London, U.K.

Torkildsen, Mr. A.
BBK, Kjeller, Norway.

Turner, Dr. L.
Imperial College, London, U.K.

Van der Veer, Mr. G.
South African Railways, Johannesburg, South-Africa.

Vanooteteghem, Mr. H.
State University Gent, Gent, Belgium.

Vassort, Mr. P.
EDF Etudes et Recherches, Clamart, France.

Verdon, Mr. F.P.
Computer Board for Universities and Research
Councils, London, U.K.

Watson, Miss P.
Data Communications, London, U.K.

Wessler, Dr. B.
Talenet Communications Corp., Arlington, U.S.A.

Wetherall, Mr. P.
R.R.E. Min. of Defence, Malvern, U.K.

Wilkinson, Mr. P.T.
National Physical Laboratory, Teddington, U.K.

Williams, Dr. L.H.
Triangle Universities Computation Centre, U.S.A.

Wong, Dr. K.K.
National Computing Centre, Manchester, U.K.

Wood, Mr. B.
Computer Analysts & Programmers Ltd., London, U.K.

Woodward, Dr. M.E.
University of Technology, Loughborough, U.K.

Woollons, Dr. D.J.
University of Sussex, Brighton, U.K.

Yon, Dr. G.
Honeywell Bull, Paris, France.

Yucel, Dr. N.
Technical University, Istanbul, Turkey.